Cryptocurrency

ALL-IN-ONE

by Kiana Danial, Tiana Laurence, Peter Kent, Tyler Bain, Michael G. Solomon

A Wiley Brand

Cryptocurrency All-in-One For Dummies®

Published by: **John Wiley & Sons, Inc.**, 111 River Street, Hoboken, NJ 07030-5774, www.wiley.com

Copyright © 2022 by John Wiley & Sons, Inc., Hoboken, New Jersey

Published simultaneously in Canada

For general information on our other products and services, please contact our Customer Care Department within the U.S. at 877-762-2974, outside the U.S. at 317-572-3993, or fax 317-572-4002. For technical support, please visit https://hub.wiley.com/community/support/dummies.

Wiley publishes in a variety of print and electronic formats and by print-on-demand. Some material included with standard print versions of this book may not be included in e-books or in print-on-demand. If this book refers to media such as a CD or DVD that is not included in the version you purchased, you may download this material at http://booksupport.wiley.com. For more information about Wiley products, visit www.wiley.com.

Library of Congress Control Number: 2021950430

ISBN 978-1-119-85580-4 (pbk); ISBN 978-1-119-85581-1 (ebk); ISBN 978-1-119-85582-8 (ebk)

Contents at a Glance

Table of Contents

Introduction

The foundation of cryptocurrencies such as Bitcoin lies in a new technology called the *blockchain*; it's the infrastructure that cryptocurrencies are built on. Blockchain is a disruptive technology that many argue is bigger than the advent of the Internet. The applications of blockchain don't end with cryptocurrencies, though, just like the applications of the Internet don't end with email. If you want to find out what blockchains are, the basics of how to use them, which cryptocurrencies are lucrative investments, and what hardware is needed for cryptocurrency mining, this is the book for you.

About This Book

In this book, you find helpful advice for navigating the blockchain world and cryptocurrencies that run them — from the ins and outs of wallets, exchanges, Bitcoin, and Ethereum to investing in cryptocurrencies and even mining your own.

You don't have to read the book cover to cover. Just flip to the subject that you're interested in.

As you dip into and out of this book, feel free to skip the sidebars (shaded boxes) and the paragraphs marked with the Technical Stuff icon. They contain interesting but nonessential information.

Within this book, you may note that some web addresses break across two lines of text. If you're reading this book in print and want to visit one of these web pages, simply key in the web address exactly as it's noted in the text, pretending as though the line break doesn't exist. If you're reading this as an e-book, you've got it easy — just click the web address to be taken directly to the webpage.

Some of the web addresses are affiliate links, meaning that if you click them and start using a company's services through that specific web address, the author may earn an affiliate payment for making the introduction.

Foolish Assumptions

We didn't want to make too many assumptions about you and your experience with cryptocurrency, blockchains, mining, and legal matters, but we do assume the following:

>> You have a computer, a smartphone, and access to the Internet.

>> You know the basics of using your computer and the Internet, and how to download and install programs.

>> You know how to navigate through menus within programs, how to find files on your computer, and how to create folders.

>> You're new to blockchain and you aren't a skilled programmer. (Of course, if you are a skilled programmer, you can still get a lot out of this book — you just may be able to breeze past some of the step-by-step guidelines.)

>> You may have heard of, or even purchased, some cryptocurrencies (like Bitcoin or Ether, for example), but you don't really know how they work.

>> Although you may have invested in other markets like the stock market before, you aren't necessarily familiar with the terminology and the technical aspects of trading and investing in cryptocurrencies.

>> You are unfamiliar with cryptocurrency mining but are interested to know more and determine whether it's something you want to undertake.

Note: If you don't have high-speed access to the Internet, you may want to get it before diving into this book. You need high-speed access to be able to work with many of the valuable online tools that we recommend.

Icons Used in This Book

Throughout the margins of this book are icons drawing your attention to certain bits of information. Here's what those icons mean.

The Tip icon marks tips and shortcuts that you can use to make your life with cryptocurrency easier.

The Remember icon marks the information that's especially important to know — the stuff you'll want to commit to memory.

TECHNICAL STUFF

When you see this icon, you know the information is of a highly technical nature. You can skip over these icons without missing the main point of the topic at hand.

WARNING

Watch out when you see this icon! It marks critical information that may save you headaches — or tokens.

Beyond the Book

In addition to the material in the print or e-book you're reading right now, this product also comes with some access-anywhere content on the web. Check out the free Cheat Sheet for more on the topics covered in the book. To get this Cheat Sheet, simply go to www.dummies.com and type **Cryptocurrency All-in-One For Dummies Cheat Sheet** in the Search box.

Where to Go From Here

The *Dummies* series tells you what you need to know and how to do the things you need to do to get the results you want. Readers don't have to read the entire book to learn about a topic. Like all good reference tools, this book is designed to be read when needed and it's divided into several parts.

If you're interested in investing, for example, you can head to Book 5 to learn about risk management, strategy development, and the whole industry in general. Book 1 provides an overview of the world of cryptocurrencies, and Book 2 is your gateway to the blockchain technology.

Book 3 takes a deep dive into Bitcoin, which is the oldest cryptocurrency and probably the most well-known. Book 4 lays the foundation of Ethereum and teaches you, in clear language, how to design and write your own software for the Ethereum blockchain environment.

If you want to delve into cryptocurrency mining, check out Book 6, which can help you decide if and how you're going to begin mining, including which is the right cryptocurrency for you to mine.

1

Cryptocurrency Basics

Contents at a Glance

» Getting an overview of your first steps before starting your crypto journey

Chapter **1**

What Is a Cryptocurrency?

So you've picked up this book, and your first question is probably this: "What the heck is a cryptocurrency, anyway?" Simply stated, a *cryptocurrency* is a new form of digital money. You can transfer your traditional, non-cryptocurrency money like the U.S. dollar digitally, but that's not quite the same as how cryptocurrencies work. When cryptocurrencies become mainstream, you may be able to use them to pay for stuff electronically, just like you do with traditional currencies.

However, what sets cryptocurrencies apart is the technology behind them. You may say, "Who cares about the technology behind my money? I only care about how much of it there is in my wallet!" The issue is that the world's current money systems have a bunch of problems. Here are some examples:

» Payment systems such as credit cards and wire transfers are outdated.

» In most cases, a bunch of middlemen like banks and brokers take a cut in the process, making transactions expensive and slow.

» Financial inequality is growing around the globe.

» Around three billion unbanked or underbanked people can't access financial services. That's approximately half the population on the planet!

Cryptocurrencies aim to solve some of these problems, if not more. This chapter introduces you to crypto fundamentals.

Beginning with the Basics of Cryptocurrencies

You know how your everyday, government-based currency is reserved in banks? And that you need an ATM or a connection to a bank to get more of it or transfer it to other people? Well, with cryptocurrencies, you may be able to get rid of banks and other centralized middlemen altogether. That's because cryptocurrencies rely on a technology called *blockchain*, which is *decentralized* (meaning no single entity is in charge of it). Instead, every computer in the network confirms the transactions. Flip to Book 2 to find out more about the blockchain technology that enables cool things like cryptocurrencies.

The following sections cover the basics of cryptocurrencies: their background, benefits, and more.

The definition of money

Before getting into the nitty-gritty of cryptocurrencies, you need to understand the definition of money itself. The philosophy behind money is a bit like the whole "which came first: the chicken or the egg?" thing. In order for money to be valuable, it must have a number of characteristics, such as the following:

>> Enough people must have it.

>> Merchants must accept it as a form of payment.

>> Society must trust that it's valuable and that it will remain valuable in the future.

Of course, in the old days, when you traded your chicken for shoes, the values of the exchanged materials were inherent to their nature. But when coins, cash, and credit cards came into play, the definition of money and, more importantly, the trust model of money changed.

Another key change in money has been its ease of transaction. The hassle of carrying a ton of gold bars from one country to another was one of the main reasons cash was invented. Then, when people got even lazier, credit cards were invented. But credit cards carry the money that your government controls. As the world becomes more interconnected and more concerned about authorities who may or may not have people's best interests in mind, cryptocurrencies may offer a valuable alternative.

Here's a fun fact: Your normal, government-backed currency, such as the U.S. dollar, must go by its fancy name, *fiat currency,* now that cryptocurrencies are around. Fiat is described as a legal tender like coins and banknotes that have value only because the government says so. Get the scoop on fiat currencies in Book 5, Chapter 9.

Some cryptocurrency history

The first ever cryptocurrency was (drumroll please) Bitcoin! You probably have heard of Bitcoin more than any other thing in the crypto industry. Bitcoin was the first product of the first blockchain developed by some anonymous entity who went by the name Satoshi Nakamoto. Satoshi released the idea of Bitcoin in 2008 and described it as a "purely peer-to-peer version" of electronic money.

TECHNICAL STUFF

Bitcoin was the first established cryptocurrency, but many attempts at creating digital currencies occurred years before Bitcoin was formally introduced.

Cryptocurrencies like Bitcoin are created through a process called *mining.* Very different than mining ore, mining cryptocurrencies involves powerful computers solving complicated problems. Book 6 covers mining, but flip to Book 6, Chapter 1 for an introduction to cryptocurrency mining.

Bitcoin remained the only cryptocurrency until 2011. Then Bitcoin enthusiasts started noticing flaws in it, so they decided to create alternative coins, also known as *altcoins,* to improve Bitcoin's design for things like speed, security, anonymity, and more. Among the first altcoins was Litecoin, which aimed to become the silver to Bitcoin's gold. But at the time of this writing, over 5,000 cryptocurrencies are available, and the number is expected to increase in the future. Check out Chapter 4 of this minibook for just a sampling of cryptocurrencies that are available now.

Key crypto benefits

Still not convinced that cryptocurrencies (or any other sort of decentralized money) are a better solution than traditional government-based money? Here are a number of solutions that cryptocurrencies may be able to provide through their decentralized nature:

>> **Reducing corruption:** With great power comes great responsibility. But when you give a ton of power to only one person or entity, the chances of their abusing that power increase. The 19th-century British politician Lord Acton said it best: "Power tends to corrupt, and absolute power corrupts absolutely." Cryptocurrencies aim to resolve the issue of absolute power by distributing power among many people or, better yet, among all the members of the network. That's the key idea behind blockchain technology, anyway (see Book 2).

>> **Eliminating extreme money printing:** Governments have central banks, and central banks have the ability to simply print money when they're faced with a

serious economic problem. This process is also called *quantitative easing.* By printing more money, a government may be able to bail out debt or devalue its currency. However, this approach is like putting a bandage on a broken leg. Not only does it rarely solve the problem, but the negative side effects can also sometimes surpass the original issue.

For example, when a country like Iran or Venezuela prints too much money, the value of its currency drops so much that inflation skyrockets and people can't even afford to buy everyday goods and services. Their cash becomes barely as valuable as rolls of toilet paper. Most cryptocurrencies have a limited, set amount of coins available. When all those coins are in circulation, a central entity or the company behind the blockchain has no easy way to simply create more coins or add on to its supply.

>> **Giving people charge of their own money:** With traditional cash, you're basically giving away all your control to central banks and the government. If you trust your government, that's great, but keep in mind that at any point, your government is able to simply freeze your bank account and deny you access to your funds. For example, in the United States, if you don't have a legal will and own a business, the government has the right to all your assets if you pass away. Some governments can even simply abolish bank notes the way India did in 2016. With cryptocurrencies, you and only you can access your funds. (Unless someone steals them from you, that is. To find out how to secure your crypto assets, flip to Chapter 3 of this minibook.)

>> **Cutting out the middleman:** With traditional money, every time you make a transfer, a middleman like your bank or a digital payment service takes a cut. With cryptocurrencies, all the network members in the blockchain are that middleman; their compensation is formulated differently from that of fiat money middlemen and therefore is minimal in comparison. Check out Chapter 2 of this minibook for more on how cryptocurrencies work.

>> **Serving the unbanked:** A vast portion of the world's citizens has no access or limited access to payment systems like banks. Cryptocurrencies aim to resolve this issue by spreading digital commerce around the globe so that anyone with a mobile phone can start making payments. And yes, more people have access to mobile phones than to banks. In fact, more people have mobile phones than have toilets, but at this point the blockchain technology may not be able to resolve the latter issue. (Flip to Book 5, Chapter 1 for more on the social good that can come from cryptocurrencies and blockchain technology.)

Common crypto and blockchain myths

During the 2017 Bitcoin hype, a lot of misconceptions about the whole industry started to circulate. These myths may have played a role in the cryptocurrency crash that followed the surge. The important thing to remember is that both the blockchain technology and its byproduct, the cryptocurrency market, are still in their infancy, and things are rapidly changing. So let's get some of the most common misunderstandings out of the way:

>> **Cryptocurrencies are good only for criminals.** Some cryptocurrencies boast anonymity as one of their key features. That means your identity isn't revealed when you're making transactions. Other cryptocurrencies are based on a decentralized blockchain, meaning a central government isn't the sole power behind them. These features do make such cryptocurrencies attractive for criminals; however, law-abiding citizens in corrupt countries can also benefit from them. For example, if you don't trust your local bank or country because of corruption and political instability, the best way to store your money may be through blockchain and cryptocurrency assets.

>> **You can make anonymous transactions using all cryptocurrencies.** For some reason, many people equate Bitcoin with anonymity. But Bitcoin, along with many other cryptocurrencies, doesn't incorporate anonymity at all. All transactions made using such cryptocurrencies are made on public blockchain. Some cryptocurrencies, such as Monero, do prioritize privacy, meaning no outsider can find the source, amount, or destination of transactions. However, most other cryptocurrencies, including Bitcoin, don't operate that way.

>> **The only application of blockchain is Bitcoin.** This idea couldn't be further from the truth. Bitcoin and other cryptocurrencies are a tiny byproduct of the blockchain revolution. Many believe Satoshi created Bitcoin simply to provide an example of how the blockchain technology can work. Almost every industry and business in the world can use the blockchain technology in its specific field.

>> **All blockchain activity is private.** Many people falsely believe that the blockchain technology isn't open to the public and is accessible only to its network of common users. Although some companies create their own private blockchains to be used only among employees and business partners, the majority of the blockchains behind famous cryptocurrencies such as Bitcoin are accessible by the public. Literally anyone with a computer can access the transactions in real time. For example, you can view the real-time Bitcoin transactions at www.blockchain.com.

Risks

Just like anything else in life, cryptocurrencies come with their own risks. Whether you trade cryptos, invest in them, or simply hold on to them for the future, you must assess and understand the risks beforehand. Some of the most talked-about cryptocurrency risks include their volatility and lack of regulation. Volatility got especially out of hand in 2017, when the price of most major cryptocurrencies, including Bitcoin, skyrocketed above 1,000 percent and then came crashing down.

However, as the cryptocurrency hype has calmed down, the price fluctuations have become more predictable and followed similar patterns to stocks and other financial assets.

Regulations are another major topic in the industry. The funny thing is that both lack of regulation and exposure to regulations can turn into risk events for cryptocurrency investors. See Book 5, Chapter 2 to explore these and other types of risks, as well as methods of managing them.

Gearing Up to Make Transactions

Cryptocurrencies are here to make transactions easier and faster. But before you take advantage of these benefits, you must gear up with crypto gadgets, discover where you can get your hands on different cryptocurrencies, and get to know the cryptocurrency community. Some of the essentials include cryptocurrency wallets and exchanges.

Wallets

Some *cryptocurrency wallets*, which hold your purchased cryptos, are similar to digital payment services like Apple Pay and PayPal. But generally, they're different from traditional wallets and come in different formats and levels of security.

REMEMBER

You can't get involved in the cryptocurrency market without a crypto wallet. Get the most secure type of wallet, such as hardware or paper wallets, instead of using the convenient online ones. Flip to Chapter 3 of this minibook to explore how these wallets work and how you can get them.

Exchanges

After you get yourself a crypto wallet (see the preceding section), you're ready to go crypto shopping, and one of the best destinations is a cryptocurrency exchange. These online web services are where you can transfer your traditional money to buy cryptocurrencies, exchange different types of cryptocurrencies, or even store your cryptocurrencies.

WARNING

Storing your cryptocurrencies on an exchange is considered high risk because many such exchanges have been exposed to hacking attacks and scams in the past. When you're done with your transactions, your best bet is to move your new digital assets to your personal, secure wallet.

Exchanges come in different shapes and forms. Some are like traditional stock exchanges and act as a middleman — something crypto enthusiasts believe is a slap in the face of the cryptocurrency market, which is trying to remove a centralized middleman. Others are decentralized and provide a service where buyers and sellers come together and transact in a peer-to-peer manner, but these exchanges come with their own sets of problems, like the risk of locking yourself out. A third type of crypto exchange is called *hybrid*, and it merges the benefits of the other two types to create a better, more secure experience for users. Flip to Book 5, Chapter 3 to review the pros and cons of all these types of exchanges and get to know other places where you can go cryptocurrency shopping.

Communities

TIP

Getting to know the crypto community can be the next step as you're finding your way in the market. The web has plenty of chat rooms and support groups to give you a sense of the market and what people are talking about. Here are some ways to get involved:

>> **Crypto-specific Telegram groups.** Many cryptocurrencies have their very own channels on the Telegram app. To join them, you first need to download the Telegram app on your smartphone or computer; it's available for iOS and Android.

>> **Crypto chat rooms on BitcoinTalk or Reddit:** BitcoinTalk (https://bitcointalk.org/) and Reddit (www.reddit.com/) have some of the oldest crypto chat rooms around. You can view some topics without signing up, but if you want to get involved, you need to log in. (Of course, Reddit isn't exclusive to cryptos, but you can search for a variety of cryptocurrency topics.)

>> **TradingView chat room:** One of the best trading platforms out there, TradingView (www.tradingview.com/) also has a social service where traders and investors of all sorts come together and share their thoughts, questions, and ideas.

>> **Invest Diva's Premium Investing Group:** If you're looking for a less crowded and more investment/trading-focused place to get support, you can join Kiana's investment group (and chat directly with her as a perk) at https://learn.investdiva.com/join-group.

REMEMBER

On the flip side, many scammers also target these kinds of platforms to advertise and lure members into trouble. Keep your wits about you.

Making a Plan Before You Jump In

If you're interested in cryptocurrency investing, you may just want to buy some cryptocurrencies and save them for their potential growth in the future. Or you may want to become more of an active investor and buy or sell cryptocurrencies more regularly to maximize profit and revenue. As discussed in Book 5, Chapter 4, you can select cryptocurrencies based on factors like category, popularity, ideology, the management behind the blockchain, and its economic model.

Even if your transaction is a one-time event and you don't want to hear anything about your crypto assets for the next ten years, you still must gain the knowledge necessary to make the following decisions:

>> What to buy

>> When to buy

>> How much to buy

>> When to sell

TIP

If you're not fully ready to buy cryptocurrencies, no worries. You can try some of the alternatives to cryptos: initial coin offerings and stocks (see Book 5) or mining (see Book 6). To learn more about two well-known cryptocurrencies — Bitcoin and Ether — before investing in either one, head to Books 3 and 4, respectively.

Over 5,000 cryptocurrencies are out there at the time of writing, and the number is growing. Some of these cryptos may vanish in five years. Others may explode to over 1,000 percent of their present value and may even replace traditional cash. Chapter 4 of this minibook covers all different types of cryptocurrencies, including Ethereum, Ripple, Litecoin, Bitcoin Cash, and Stellar Lumens.

TIP

Because the crypto industry is pretty new, it's still very hard to identify the best-performing cryptos for long-term investments. That's why you may benefit from diversifying among various types and categories of cryptocurrencies in order to manage your risk. By diversifying across 15 or more cryptos, you can stack up the odds of having winners in your portfolio. On the flip side, overdiversification can become problematic as well, so you need to take calculated measures. Flip to Book 5, Chapter 5 for more on diversification.

WARNING

When you've narrowed down the cryptocurrencies you like, you must then identify the best time to buy them. In 2017, many people started to believe in the idea of Bitcoin and wanted to get involved. Unfortunately, many of those people mismanaged the timing and bought when the price had peaked. They had to settle for buying fewer bits of Bitcoin (pun intended) and also had to sit on their losses and wait for the next price surge.

Chapter **2**

How Cryptocurrencies Work

C ryptocurrencies, and more specifically Bitcoin, have been one of the first use cases for blockchain technology (covered in detail in Book 2). That's why most people may have heard about Bitcoin more than they have about the underlying blockchain technology.

This chapter gets into more detail about how cryptocurrencies use blockchain technology, how they operate, and how they're generated, as well as some crypto geek terms you can impress your dates with.

Explaining Basic Terms in the Cryptocurrency Process

Cryptocurrencies are also known as digital coins, but they're quite different from the coins in your piggy bank. For one thing, they aren't attached to a central bank, a country, or a regulatory body.

Here's an example. Say you want to buy the latest version of *Cryptocurrency All-in-One For Dummies* from your local bookstore. Using your normal debit card, this is what happens:

1. You give your card details to the cashier or the store's point-of-sale system.

2. The store runs the information through, essentially asking your bank whether you have enough money in your bank account to buy the book.

3. The bank checks its records to confirm whether you do.

4. If you do have enough, the bank gives a thumbs-up to the bookstore.

5. The bank then updates its records to show the movement of the money from your account to the bookstore's account.

6. The bank gets a little cut for the trouble of being the middleman.

Now if you wanted to remove the bank from this entire process, who else would you trust to keep all these records without altering them or cheating in any way? Your best friend? Your dog walker? In fact, you may not trust any single person. But how about trusting *everyone* in the network?

REMEMBER

Blockchain technology works to remove the middleman. When applied to cryptocurrencies, blockchain eliminates a central record of transactions. Instead, you distribute many copies of your transaction ledger around the world. Each owner of each copy records your transaction of buying the book.

Here's what happens if you want to buy this book using a cryptocurrency:

1. You give your crypto details to the cashier.

2. The shop asks everyone in the network to see whether you have enough coins to buy the book.

3. All the record holders in the network check their records to see whether you do. (These record holders are called *nodes*, and are explained later in this chapter.)

4. If you do have enough, each node gives the thumbs-up to the cashier.

5. The nodes all update their records to show the transfer.

6. At random, a node gets a reward for the work.

That means no organization is keeping track of where your coins are or investigating fraud. In fact, cryptocurrencies such as Bitcoin wouldn't exist without a whole network of bookkeepers (nodes) and a little thing known as *cryptography*.

The following sections explain that and some other important terms related to the workings of cryptocurrencies.

Cryptography

Shhh. Don't tell anyone. That's the *crypto* in *cryptography* and *cryptocurrency.* It means "secret." In the cryptocurrency world, it mainly refers to being "anonymous."

Historically, cryptography was an ancient art for sending hidden messages. (The term comes from the Greek word *krypto logos*, which means *secret writing.*) The sender *encrypted* the message by using some sort of key. The receiver then had to *decrypt* it. For example, 19th-century scholars decrypted ancient Egyptian hieroglyphics when Napoleon's soldiers found the Rosetta Stone in 1799 near Rosetta, Egypt. In the 21st-century era of information networks, the sender can digitally encrypt messages, and the receiver can use cryptographic services and algorithms to decrypt them.

What does Napoleon have to do with cryptocurrencies? Cryptocurrencies use cryptography to maintain security and anonymity. That's how digital coins, even though they're not monetized by any central authority or regulatory body, can help with security and protection from double-spending, which is the risk of your digital cash being used more than once.

Cryptography uses three main encryption methods.

>> **Hashing:** Hashing is something like a fingerprint or signature. A *hash function* first takes your input data (which can be of any size). The function then performs an operation on the original data and returns an output that represents the original data but has a fixed (and generally smaller) size. In cryptocurrencies such as Bitcoin, it's used to guess the combination of the lock of a block. Hashing maintains the structure of blockchain data, encodes people's account addresses, and makes block mining possible. You can find more on mining later in this chapter, and in much more detail in Book 6.

>> **Symmetric encryption cryptography:** *Symmetric encryption* is the simplest method used in cryptography. It involves only one secret key for both the sender and the receiver. The main disadvantage of symmetric encryption is that all parties involved have to exchange the key used to encrypt the data before they can decrypt it.

>> **Asymmetric encryption cryptography:** *Asymmetric encryption* uses two keys — a public key and a private key. You can encrypt a message by using the receiver's public key, but the receiver can decrypt it only with their private key.

Nodes

A *node* is an electronic device that does the bookkeeping job in the blockchain network, making the whole decentralized thing possible. The device can be a computer, a cellphone, or even a printer, as long as it's connected to the Internet and has access to the blockchain network.

Mining

As the owners of nodes (see the preceding section) willingly contribute their computing resources to store and validate transactions, they have the chance to collect the transaction fees and earn a reward in the underlying cryptocurrency for doing so. This process is known as *mining,* and the owners who do it are *miners.*

REMEMBER

Let me make something clear: Not all cryptocurrencies can be mined. Bitcoin and some other famous ones can. Others, such as Ripple (XRP), avoid mining altogether because they want a platform that doesn't consume a huge amount of electricity in the process of mining; power usage is one of the issues with blockchain that are discussed in Book 6, Chapters 7 and 8. Regardless, for the most part, mining remains a huge part of many cryptocurrencies to date.

Here's how mining works: Cryptocurrency miners solve cryptographic puzzles (via software) to add transactions to the ledger (the blockchain) in the hope of getting coins as a reward. It's called mining because of the fact that this process helps extract new cryptocurrencies from the system. Anyone, including you, can join this group. Your computer needs to "guess" a random number that solves an equation that the blockchain system generates. In fact, your computer has to calculate many 64-character strings or 256-bit hashes and check with the challenge equation to see whether the answer is right. That's why it's so important that you have a powerful computer. The more powerful your computer is, the more guesses it can make in a second, increasing your chances of winning this game. If you manage to guess right, you earn Bitcoins and you get to write the "next page" of Bitcoin transactions on the blockchain. Head to Book 6 if you're interested to learn more.

Because mining is based on a form of guessing, for each block, a different miner guesses the number and is granted the right to update the blockchain. Whoever has the biggest computing power combined, controlling 51 percent of the votes, controls the chain and wins every time. Thanks to the law of statistical probability, the same miner is unlikely to succeed every time. On the other hand, this game can sometimes be unfair because the biggest computer power will be the first to solve the challenge equation and "win" more often.

Proof of work

If you're a miner and want to actually enter your block and transactions into the blockchain, you have to provide an answer (proof) to a specific challenge. This proof is difficult to produce (hence all the gigantic computers, time, and money needed for it), but others can very easily verify it. This process is known as *proof of work,* or PoW.

For example, guessing a combination to a lock is a proof to a challenge. Going through all the different possible combinations to come up with the right answer may be pretty hard, but after you get it, it's easy to validate — just enter the combination and see whether the lock opens! The first miner who solves the problem for each block on the blockchain gets a reward. The reward is basically the incentive to keep on mining, and it motivates the miners to compete to be the first one to find a solution for mathematical problems. Bitcoin and some other mineable cryptocurrencies mainly use the PoW concept to make sure that the network isn't easily manipulated.

REMEMBER

This whole proof-of-work concept has some downsides for blockchain technology. One of the main challenges is that it wastes a lot of computing power and electricity just for the sake of producing random guesses. That's why new cryptocurrencies have jumped on an alternative wagon called *proof of stake* (PoS), covered in the next section.

Proof of stake

Unlike PoW, a *proof-of-stake* (PoS) system requires you to show ownership of a certain amount of money (or *stake*). That means the more crypto you own, the more mining power you have. This approach eliminates the need for the expensive mining extravaganza. And because the calculations are pretty simple to prove, you own a certain percentage of the total amount of the cryptos available.

Another difference is that the PoS system offers no block rewards, so the miners get transaction fees. That's how PoS cryptos can be several thousand times more cost-effective than PoW ones. (Don't let the PoS abbreviation give you the wrong idea.)

REMEMBER

But of course, PoS also has its own problems. For starters, you can argue that PoS rewards coin hoarders. Under the proof-of-stake model, nodes can mine only a percentage of transactions that corresponds to their stake in a cryptocurrency. For example, a proof-of-stake miner who owns 10 percent of a cryptocurrency would be able to mine 10 percent of blocks on the network. The limitation with this consensus model is that it gives nodes on the network a reason to save their coins instead of spending them. It also produces a scenario in which the rich get richer because large coin holders are able to mine a larger percentage of blocks on the network.

Proof of importance

Proof of importance (PoI) was first introduced by a blockchain platform called NEM to support its XEM cryptocurrency. In some ways, PoI is similar to PoS because participants (nodes) are marked as "eligible" if they have a certain amount of crypto "vested." Then the network gives a "score" to the eligible nodes, and they can create a block that is roughly the same proportion to that "score." But the difference is that the nodes won't get a higher score only by holding onto more cryptocurrencies. Other variables are considered in the score, too, in order to resolve the primary problem with PoS, which is hoarding. The NEM community, in particular, uses a method called "harvesting" to solve the PoS "hoarding" problem.

Here's how Investopedia defines harvesting: "Instead of each miner contributing its mining power in a cumulative manner to a computing node, a harvesting participant simply links his account to an existing supernode and uses that account's computing power to complete blocks on his behalf." (See the section, "Harvesting," later in this chapter.)

Transactions: Putting it all together

REMEMBER

Here's a summary of how cryptocurrencies work (check out the preceding sections for details on some of the terminology):

1. When you want to use cryptos to purchase something, first your crypto network and your crypto wallet automatically check your previous transactions to make sure that you have enough cryptocurrencies to make that transaction. For this, you need your private and public keys (explained in Chapter 3 of this minibook).

2. The transaction is then encrypted, broadcast to the cryptocurrency's network, and queued up to be added to the public ledger.

3. Transactions are then recorded on the public ledger through mining. The sending and receiving addresses are wallet IDs or hash values that aren't tied to the user's identification, so they are anonymous.

4. For PoW cryptos, the miners have to solve a math puzzle to verify the transaction. PoS cryptos attribute the mining power to the proportion of the coins held by the miners, instead of utilizing energy to solve math problems, in order to resolve the "wasted energy" problem of PoW. The PoI cryptos add a number of variables when attributing the mining power to nodes in order to resolve the "hoarding" problem that's associated with PoS.

Cruising through Other Important Crypto Concepts

Earlier sections of this chapter talk about the basics of cryptocurrencies and how they're related to blockchain technology. This section digs into other factors that make cryptocurrencies so special and different from government-backed legal tender, also known as fiat currency, such as the U.S. dollar.

Adaptive scaling

Adaptive scaling is one of the advantages of investing in cryptocurrencies. It means that it gets harder to mine a specific cryptocurrency over time. It allows cryptocurrencies to work well on both small and large scales. That's why cryptocurrencies take measures such as limiting the supply over time (to create scarcity) and reducing the reward for mining as more total coins are mined. Thanks to adaptive scaling, mining difficulty goes up and down depending on the popularity of the coin and the blockchain. This can give cryptocurrencies a real longevity within the market.

Decentralization

The whole idea behind blockchain technology is that it's *decentralized.* This concept means no single entity can affect the cryptocurrencies.

TECHNICAL STUFF

Some people claim cryptocurrencies such as Ripple aren't truly decentralized because they don't follow Bitcoin's mining protocol exactly. Ripple has no miners. Instead, transactions are powered through a "centralized" blockchain to make it more reliable and faster. Ripple in particular has gone this route because it wants to work with big banks and therefore wants to combine the best elements of fiat money and blockchain cryptocurrency. Whether non-mineable currencies such as Ripple can be considered true cryptocurrencies is up for discussion, but that fact doesn't mean you can't invest in them, which is the whole purpose of this book anyway!

Harvesting

Harvesting is an alternative to the traditional mining used to maintain the integrity of a blockchain network. It was designed by a blockchain platform called NEM to generate its own currency called XEM. According to finder.com, this is how harvesting works: "Every time someone carries out a transaction, the first computer to see and verify the transaction will notify nearby users of that transaction, creating a cascade of information. This process is called 'generating a block.' Whenever someone with more than 10,000 vested XEM generates a block in NEM, they receive the transaction fees on that block as payment." Also, as explained earlier in this chapter, harvesting uses a PoI system rather than PoS and PoW.

Open source

Cryptocurrencies are typically *open source*. That means that miners, nodes, and harvesters alike can join and use the network without paying a fee.

Public ledger

A ledger is the age-old record-keeping system for recording information and data. Cryptocurrencies use a *public ledger* to record all transactional data. Everyone in the world can access public blockchains and see entire transactions happening with cryptocurrencies.

Note that not all blockchains use a public ledger. Some businesses and financial institutions use private ledgers so that the transactions aren't visible to the world. However, by doing so, they may contradict the original idea behind blockchain technology.

Smart contracts

Smart contracts are also called *self-executing contracts, blockchain contracts,* or *digital contracts.* They're just like traditional contracts except that they're completely digital. Smart contracts remove the middleman between the buyer and the seller so that you can implement features like automatic payments and investment products without the need for a central authority like a bank.

A smart contract is actually a tiny computer program that's stored and runs on a blockchain platform. Because of that, all the transactions are completely distributed, and no centralized authority is in control of the money. Also, because it's stored on a blockchain, a smart contract is *immutable.* Being immutable means that after a smart contract is created, it can never be changed again; it can't be tampered with, which is an inherited feature from blockchain technology.

However, being immutable comes with its own disadvantages. Because you can't change anything in the smart contract, that means that if the code has any bugs, you can't fix them either. This makes smart contract security more difficult. Some companies aim to combat this problem by auditing their smart contracts, which can be very costly.

As time goes by, users can expect better coding practices and development life cycles to combat smart contract security problems. After all, smart contracts are still a pretty young practice, with their whole life of trial and error ahead of them.

Stick a Fork in It: Digging into Cryptocurrency Forks

What you get from a cryptocurrency fork won't fill your tummy, but it may fill your crypto wallet with some money! Many popular cryptocurrencies were born as a result of a split (fork) in another cryptocurrency like Bitcoin. The following sections explain the basics of these cryptocurrency splits and how you may be able to profit from them.

What is a fork, and why do forks happen?

Sometimes when a group of developers disagrees with the direction a specific cryptocurrency is going, the members decide to go their own way and initiate a *fork*. Imagine an actual physical fork. It has one long handle, and then it divides into a bunch of branches. That's exactly what happens in a cryptocurrency fork.

Some cryptocurrencies are implemented within open-source software. Each of these cryptocurrencies has its own protocol that everyone in the network should follow. Examples of such rule topics include the following:

>> Block size

>> Rewards that miners, harvesters, or other network participants get

>> How fees are calculated

REMEMBER

But because cryptocurrencies are essentially software projects, their development will never be fully finished. There's always room for improvement. Crypto developers regularly push out updates to fix issues or to increase performance. Some of these improvements are small, but others fundamentally change the way the original cryptocurrency (which the developers fell in love with) works. Just as in any type of relationship, you either grow together or grow apart. When the disagreements among a group of developers or network participants intensify, they can choose to break up, create their own version of the protocol, and cause a potential heartbreak that requires years of therapy to get over. Okay, the last part doesn't really happen.

Hard forks and soft forks

Two types of forks can happen in a cryptocurrency: a hard fork and a soft fork.

Most cryptocurrencies consist of two big pieces: the protocol (set of rules) and the blockchain (which stores all the transactions that have ever happened). If a segment of the crypto community decides to create its own new rules, it starts by copying the original protocol code and then goes about making changes to it (assuming the cryptocurrency is completely open source). After the developers have implemented their desired changes, they define a point at which their fork will become active. More specifically, they choose a block number to start the forking. For example, as you can see in Figure 2-1, the community can say that the new protocol will go live when block 999 is published to the cryptocurrency blockchain.

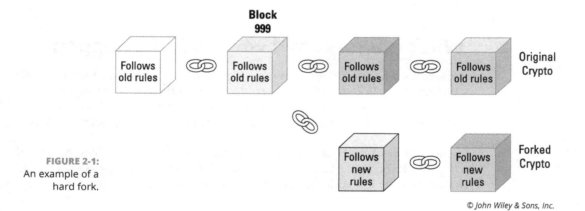

FIGURE 2-1:
An example of a
hard fork.

When the currency reaches that block number, the community splits in two. Some people decide to support the original set of rules, while others support the new fork. Each group then starts adding new blocks to the fork it supports. At this point, both blockchains are incompatible with each other, and a *hard fork* has occurred. In a hard fork, the nodes essentially go through a contentious divorce and don't ever interact with each other again. They don't even acknowledge the nodes or transactions on the old blockchain. See Book 2, Chapter 5 for more about correcting actions with a hard fork on a blockchain like Ethereum. (And if you're curious about forking in the context of cryptocurrency mining, flip to Book 6, Chapter 8.)

On the other hand, a soft fork is the type of breakup where you remain friends with your ex. If the developers decide to fork the cryptocurrency and make the changes compatible with the old one, then the situation is called a *soft fork*. You can see the subtle difference in the example shown in Figure 2-2.

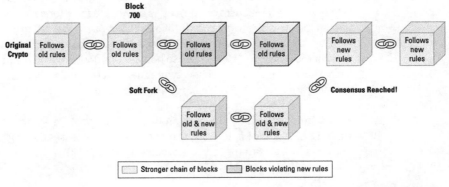

© John Wiley & Sons, Inc.

FIGURE 2-2: An example of a soft fork.

Say the soft fork is set to happen at block 700. The majority of the community may support the stronger chain of blocks following both the new and old rules. If the two sides reach a consensus after a while, the new rules are upgraded across the network. Any non-upgraded nodes (that is, stubborn geeks) who are still mining are essentially wasting their time. The community comes back together softly, and everyone lives happily ever after — until the next major argument, of course.

Free money on forks

Because a new fork is based on the original blockchain, all transactions that previously happened on the blockchain also happen on the fork. The developers of the new chain take a "snapshot" of the ledger at a specific block number where the fork happened (like 999 in Figure 2-1) and therefore create a duplicate copy of the chain. That means if you had a certain amount of cryptocurrencies before the fork, you also get the same amount of the new coin.

REMEMBER

To get free coins from a fork, you need to have the cryptocurrency on a platform that supports the fork before the block number at which the fork occurs. You can call this free money. But how valuable the coins are all depends on how well the new fork performs and how popular it gets within the community.

A FORKING EXAMPLE: BITCOIN VERSUS BITCOIN CASH

Even the celebrity of cryptocurrencies, Bitcoin (BTC), has seen forks. One of the well-known Bitcoin forks happened on August 1, 2017. That's the birthday of Bitcoin Cash. In this case, the developers couldn't agree on what the size for a block should be. Some wanted the block size to go from 1MB to 2MB, but others wanted to increase it even more, to 32MB. Some people in the community loved the new big idea, while others thought the other group was crazy. So both groups decided to go their own ways. Bitcoin Cash adapted a brand-new symbol (BCH), too. People who already had BTC got the same amount of BCH added to their crypto wallets.

As of August 2018, BCH is valued at around $750, while BTC is worth ten times more, around $7,500. Only time will tell whether BCH ever surpasses the original protocol's value. But hey, at least the forkers got some value out of it!

Chapter **3**

Introducing Cryptocurrency Wallets

A traditional wallet is where you keep your valuable personal items such as cash, credit cards, and identification cards. But now that you're using the most advanced, futuristic form of money (cryptos, baby!), you're gonna need a brand-new type of wallet to go with it: a cryptocurrency wallet.

With a cryptocurrency wallet, you not only can store the value of your digital money but also send and receive currencies. Additionally, you can monitor your balance the way you'd do with your bank account. This chapter walks you step by step through understanding types of cryptocurrency wallets and choosing which is best for you.

Defining Cryptocurrency Wallets

A *cryptocurrency wallet* is a software program that helps you manage your digital money. Although you may be the type of person who doesn't like to carry around traditional wallets and would rather put your cash and credit cards right in your back pocket, you must have a digital cryptocurrency wallet if you want to use any type of cryptocurrency. There's no way around it. Cryptocurrencies aren't stored in a bank reserve like other types of traditional assets such as gold and cash. Without crypto wallets, the whole idea of cryptocurrencies dies! Cryptocurrency wallets are the air that keeps the system alive.

TECHNICAL STUFF

While, in theory, Bitcoin is decentralized and nobody controls anything, it's actually run by a network that's controlled and maintained by someone (whoever is hiding behind the name Satoshi Nakamoto). In other words, Bitcoin is distributed and miners are somewhat anonymous, but the actual blockchain is stored in its entirety by the network. It's so large that miners have maybe 30 days' worth of transactions and blocks stored on their devices; the full blockchain is actually stored in a somewhat centralized form by the network.

A few important terms

Before you get started, here are some terms to know as you explore the world of crypto wallets:

>> **Hot wallet:** A wallet that stores your keys online. You can easily access your keys, and your cryptocurrency assets, from anywhere in the world. All you need is an Internet connection and access credentials.

WARNING

Although hot wallets are convenient, that convenience comes at a cost. If someone steals your access credentials, they can steal your Ethereum assets. Also, you have to trust the wallet organization that stores your keys. If your wallet organization is hacked, or goes out of business, you could lose everything. If that organization is a target of an investigation, your information could be divulged or your assets frozen.

>> **Cold wallet:** A wallet in which you store your keys offline. You need to provide your keys only when you want to access your assets. You can store keys offline in multiple ways, but this approach requires a few extra steps when you want to buy or sell crypto-assets (or interact with smart contracts, which we introduce in Book 2, Chapter 5).

Although cold wallets are a little less convenient, they can be more secure. You have control over your keys with a cold wallet and can take whatever precautions you feel are necessary to protect your keys. Using a cold wallet gives you an alternative and mitigates the threat of an attacker hacking into your online wallet and harvesting lots of keys.

WARNING

With a cold wallet, you're responsible for protecting your keys. You have to make sure that every place you store your keys is as secure as possible.

>> **Wallet address:** A number that functions in a similar way to a traditional bank account number.

>> **Public key:** A code that allows you to receive cryptocurrencies into your account or wallet. It's mathematically linked to your wallet address, but it isn't identical.

>> **Private key:** A code that's coupled with the public key to ensure your security. It's something like your own private password that you use to enter your bank account in the real world.

The following section explains how some of these items work together so you can complete crypto transactions.

How a wallet works

Crypto wallets don't actually store the cryptocurrency itself; rather, they store the cryptocurrency's private and public keys. These keys are something like the PIN code you use to access your bank account.

REMEMBER

No two wallet addresses are ever the same. They're something like fingerprints. This distinction means that there is a very low chance that somebody else can get your funds by mistake. Also, you have no limit to the number of wallet addresses you can create.

To give you an example of what a cryptocurrency address looks like, here is the wallet address believed to belong to the creator of Bitcoin, Satoshi Nakamoto!

1A1zP1eP5QGefi2DMPTfTL5SLmv7DivfNa

As you can see, it uses a combination of numbers and letters, both uppercase and lowercase. Don't worry; as long as you have a safe and secure wallet, you don't have to memorize your crypto wallet address. You can also consider printing your keys and storing them somewhere safe that you won't forget about.

A private key is a unique individual password to your individual crypto wallet address. A public key then adds an extra layer of security and ensures that your wallet can't be hacked. Here is a quick example of what the keys look like:

Private key:
03bf350d2821375158a608b51e3e898e507fe47f2d2e8c774de4a9a7edecf74eda

Public key: 99b1ebcfc11a13df5161aba8160460fe1601d541

These addresses look completely different to the eye, but the software technology knows that the two keys are specifically linked to each other. That proves that you're the owner of the coins and allows you to transfer funds whenever you want.

TECHNICAL STUFF

Addresses in Ethereum (see Book 4 for more about Ethereum) take up the last (rightmost) 20 bytes of the hash of the owner's public key. To calculate an address, just calculate the Keccak-256 hash of a public key, and then copy the rightmost 20 bytes. The resulting value is the address for that account's public key. The code to calculate an address from a public key looks like this:

```
addr = right(keccak256(pubkey),20)
```

REMEMBER

When someone sends you any type of cryptocurrency, they are essentially signing off ownership of those cryptos to your wallet's address. For you to be able to spend those cryptos and unlock the funds, the private key stored in your wallet must match the public address the currency is assigned to. If the public and private keys match, the balance in your wallet increases, and the sender's balance decreases accordingly. No exchange of real coins actually occurs. The transaction is signified merely by a transaction record on the blockchain and a change in balance in your cryptocurrency wallet. Cryptocurrencies rely on blockchain technology, which you can learn about in Book 2.

Looking at Different Types of Wallets

First, you need to understand the difference between a traditional digital wallet and a cryptocurrency wallet. You may already be using digital wallets, also known as e-wallets, through your mobile phone. Cryptocurrency wallets are a whole different animal and come in several different types of wallet client software that each caters to different needs. The following sections cover the five most popular types of cryptocurrency wallet client software, in order of their security level (from least to most secure).

In Figure 3-1, you can see a summary of the most common crypto wallets and their examples that Kiana shared with Invest Diva students in 2018. *Note:* According to Bitcoin Wiki, a "seed phrase, seed recovery phrase, or backup seed phrase is a list of words which store all the information needed to recover a Bitcoin wallet. Wallet software will typically generate a seed phrase and instruct the user to write it down on paper. If the user's computer breaks or their hard drive becomes corrupted, they can download the same wallet software again and use the paper backup to get their bitcoins back." A PoS stands for proof of stake, a mining concept explained in Book 6, Chapter 2.

REMEMBER

Specific wallet brands mentioned here aren't the only options available, and you shouldn't take their inclusion as a recommendation. You must do your own research to find the best options available in your area as well as for your needs and chosen cryptocurrencies and activities.

SUMMARY OF CRYPTOCURRENCY WALLETS

	SOFTWARE	ONLINE	HARDWARE	PAPER
PROS	User-controlled Security For POS coins, allows minting	High convenience, Accessible from any browser without needing to download the Blockchain	Protects user's private keys, which are stored on the device Can be recovered with PIN and seed	Extremely secure. Can't be hacked using digital means Great for long term storage
CONS	Must download entire Blockchain for each type of coin/token	Susceptible to key logging hacks Can't stake POS coins Unknown level of security	Doesn't support all coins/tokens Can't stake POS coins	Inconvenient to use for transactions
EXAMPLES	Electrum Armory	Blockchain MyEtherWallet	Ledger Trezor	

FIGURE 3-1: Popular cryptocurrency wallet types.

© John Wiley & Sons, Inc.

Online wallet

Online wallets may be less secure, but they do have a bunch of advantages for small amounts of cryptocurrencies. An *online* (or *web*) *wallet* allows you access to your cryptos via the Internet. Therefore, as long as you're connected to the Internet (the cloud), you can reach and store your coins and make crypto payments. The online wallet provider stores your wallet's private key on its server. The provider may send you the crypto code but store your keys and give you the ability to access your keys. Different services offer various features, with some of them linking to multiple devices such as your mobile phone, tablet, and computer.

Advantages of online wallets include the following:

>> They enable fast transactions.

>> They may be able to manage multiple cryptocurrencies.

>> They're convenient for use on the go and for active trading.

Disadvantages include the following:

>> They risk your online security because of potential vulnerability to hacks and scams.

>> They risk your personal security because of potential exposure to computer viruses.

>> You aren't storing your cryptos; a third party is.

Introducing Cryptocurrency Wallets

CHAPTER 3 Introducing Cryptocurrency Wallets **31**

Table 3-1 shows some popular online wallets.

TABLE 3-1   **Popular Web Wallets**

Name	Description	Pros	Cons
MyEtherWallet, `www.myetherwallet.com`	Open-source, decentralized cold wallet. You locally control your keys.	Most popular Ethereum web wallet. Works well with hardware wallets.	Has been hacked and may be vulnerable to phishing attacks.
Coinbase, `www.coinbase.com`	Popular cryptocurrency exchange that also provides a hot wallet.	Provides more than just wallet services. Long history handling cryptocurrency.	Limited tokens and coins supported. Keys stored online.
Guarda, `https://guarda.co`	Cold wallet that supports multiple cryptocurrencies and makes it easy to transfer funds between cryptocurrencies. Also offers a desktop wallet.	One of the first to support multiple types of coins and tokens. Doesn't store personal information.	User must manage local key storage.

Mobile wallet

Mobile wallets are available on your cellphone through an app. You can use mobile wallets when shopping in physical stores as cryptocurrencies become more acceptable. *Note:* Other types of wallets, such as online wallets (see the preceding section), offer mobile versions as well. But some wallets are specifically and only used for mobile phones.

Mobile wallets (see Table 3-2 for some popular ones) fall into the category of software wallets and have these advantages:

>> They can be safer than online wallets.

>> They're convenient for use on the go.

>> They offer additional features such as QR code scanning.

Some disadvantages of mobile wallets include the following:

>> You risk losing your crypto assets if your phone is lost or damaged.

>> They run the risk of getting mobile viruses and malware.

TABLE 3-2   **Popular Mobile Wallets**

Name	Description	Pros	Cons
Jaxx, https://jaxx.io/	Cold wallet available on mobile devices and desktops (Windows, macOS, Linux).	Multi-platform support. Stores keys on specified device.	Code is not open source. Limited number of coins and tokens supported.
Coinomi, www.coinomi.com	Cold wallet for multiple cryptocurrencies that runs on iOS and Android mobile devices.	Runs on Android, iOS, and desktops. Extensive list of supported coins and tokens. Focus on privacy.	Code is not open source.
Bread (BRD), https://brd.com/	Cold wallet for multiple cryptocurrencies that runs on iOS and Android mobile devices.	No central server. Easy to use and fast. Code is open source.	Limited number of supported coins and tokens. No two-factor authentication.

Desktop wallet

You can download a *desktop wallet* and install it on your computer. Some argue that desktop wallets are safer if your computer isn't (or even better, has never been) connected to the Internet. If a desktop computer has never been connected to the Internet, it essentially becomes a cold wallet. On the other hand, a computer that has never been connected to the Internet may expose you to malware that may automatically move from the wallet drive that you connect to the computer and infect the desktop because it's never been patched with software updates that require an Internet connection. Talk about a catch-22!

TIP

To set up your wallet on a computer that has never been connected to the Internet, you must first download the latest version of the wallet on a computer that *is* connected to the Internet. You then move the file to a USB drive or something similar in order to move it to your offline computer.

See Table 3-3 for examples of popular desktop wallets. Some advantages of desktop wallets (which fall into the category of software wallets) include the following:

>> They're a convenient choice if you trade cryptos from your computer.

>> You aren't storing your private keys on a third-party server.

>> If your computer has never been connected to the Internet, a desktop wallet can be safer than an online wallet.

TABLE 3-3   **Popular Desktop Wallets**

Name	Description	Pros	Cons
Exodus, `www.exodus.io`	First to offer multiple cryptocurrencies in a single wallet. Cold wallet with easy key backup-and-restore operations.	Visually appealing and informative, easy-to-use interface.	Source code is not open source.
Mist, `https://sourceforge.net/projects/ethereum-wallet.mirror`	Cold wallet and the official Ethereum wallet, developed by those who created Ethereum.	Created by the Ethereum Foundation, and an officially endorsed wallet.	Less user-friendly than other wallets.
MetaMask, `https://metamask.io/`	Cold wallet running as a Firefox or Chrome extension. Supports easy switching between test and live Ethereum networks.	Partially funded by the Ethereum Foundation, easy to use in Chrome. Easy to switch between test and live networks.	Released only as a Chrome extension, making it possible for other websites to see that you have a wallet installed.

But desktop wallets do come with some disadvantages:

>> Using your crypto assets on the go is more difficult.

>> If you connected the wallet to the Internet, it turns into a less secure hot wallet.

>> If you don't back up your computer and it dies, you lose your cryptos.

Hardware wallet

A *hardware wallet* can arguably be one of the safest types of crypto wallets out there. These wallets store your private keys on a device like a USB drive. You're still able to make online transactions, but the wallets are offline most of the time, so you can consider them cold wallets. Check out Table 3-4 for a short list of popular hardware e-wallets.

TIP

For security purposes, a hardware wallet is an absolute must (and a bare minimum) for large crypto amounts. Keeping a ton of your assets on other, less secure types of wallets increases your risk of unrecoverable hacking attacks. Even safer than hardware wallets are paper wallets (see the next section).

TABLE 3-4   **Popular Hardware Wallets**

Name	Description	Pros	Cons
Ledger Nano S, www.ledger.com/products/ledger-nano-s	Most popular hardware wallet. Secure physical device that supports multiple cryptocurrencies and uses two-factor authentication.	Small. Hardware designed for security. Supports over 700 types of coins and tokens.	Cost ($59). Requires client software to control crypto-assets.
Trezor, https://trezor.io/	Secure physical device that supports multiple cryptocurrencies and uses two-factor authentication.	Established reputation. Physical buttons or touchscreen. Supports nearly 700 types of coins and tokens.	Cost ($59 for Model One). Requires a web wallet to control some stored crypto-assets.
KeepKey, www.keepkey.com	Similar to the Ledger Nano S and Trezor features, but with a slightly larger screen.	Firmware is open source. Designed to meet current blockchain requirements.	Cost ($49). Relative newcomer. Limited number of supported coins and token types.

Here are some advantages of hardware wallets:

» They're one of the safest crypto wallet options.

» They're great for storing large amounts of cryptocurrencies that you don't want to use on a day-to-day basis.

Some disadvantages of hardware wallets include the following:

» They're the most expensive type of wallet.

» They aren't as user-friendly as other wallets, especially for beginners.

Paper wallet

A *paper wallet* is a super-cold crypto wallet; see Table 3-5 for examples. To use it, you print out your private and public keys. You can send funds by transferring the money to the wallet's public address, and you can withdraw or send your currencies by entering your private keys or by scanning the QR code on the paper wallet.

Some of the advantages of paper wallets include the following:

» They're ultra hacker-proof.

» You don't store them on a computer, mobile phone, or third-party server.

TABLE 3-5   **Popular Paper Wallets**

Name	Description	Pros	Cons
ETHAddress, `https://github.com/ryepdx/ethaddress.org`	Open-source project with source code you can compile and run on your own computer to generate private and public keys.	Open-source code. Useful for creating multiple accounts and keys.	No easy-to-use interface. Must download and run code or use Chrome add-in.
MyEtherWallet, `www.myetherwallet.com`	Provides the option to print your keys instead of storing them. The easiest way to create your own paper wallet.	Easy-to-use web interface for creating accounts and keys.	You must protect generated keys.

Paper wallets do have some disadvantages, though:

>> They aren't user-friendly for non-geeks.

>> They're harder to use for day-to-day transactions than other wallet types are.

>> They can catch fire.

TIP

Some paper wallet generators include WalletGenerator (`https://WalletGenerator.net`), Bitcoinpaperwallet (`Bitcoinpaperwallet.org`), and Mycelium (`https://mycelium.com/mycelium-entropy.html`). Book 2, Chapter 4 has steps for setting up a paper wallet through `http://www.bitaddress.org/`. Mycelium offers an original and even more secure way to generate paper wallets, with a USB device that you plug directly into your printer. The device generates a paper wallet that automatically gets printed out without ever having touched your computer.

Choosing a Crypto Wallet

Depending on your cryptocurrency needs and goals, you may need more than one type of cryptocurrency wallet. For example, Kiana uses cold wallets to store larger crypto reserves and hot wallets for active trading. Regardless, you can choose your cryptocurrency wallet (or wallets) based on different characteristics, some of which are discussed in the following sections.

REMEMBER

Make sure you've gathered everything you need to know about a given wallet before committing to getting one.

Based on security

REMEMBER

Even if you're an active crypto trader, we recommend that you have a super-secure cold wallet where you store your larger amounts of crypto assets. Online wallets aren't the most secure option, however convenient they may be. You can always transfer your assets to an online wallet if you need immediate access to your cryptocurrencies for an investment or shopping opportunity.

Also remember that the most secure hardware wallets are normally the most expensive ones. So you should calculate whether spending that much money for a particular wallet makes sense for the amount of crypto you're going to store in it.

Some questions you must ask before choosing the most secure wallet include the following:

>> What sort of authentication does the wallet use?

>> Is the website secure?

>> What do online reviews say?

TIP

CoinCentral.com, 99Bitcoins.com, and CryptoCompare.com are websites that provide an annual crypto wallet review. We recommend checking with two or more websites before making a decision.

TIP

At the time of writing, the Ledger Nano S hardware wallet is one of the most popular and highly rated secure wallets out there. You can find out about other Ledger products at www.ledger.com. The Trezor Bitcoin hardware wallet (created by SatoshiLabs) is another example. One catch about these wallets is that if the USB drive dies, all your cryptos go with it. That's why you should always have a backup and keep your security codes elsewhere so that you can recover your assets.

Based on your crypto ownership

Not all crypto wallets can handle your different types of cryptocurrency assets. In fact, some wallets are purpose-built for just one cryptocurrency; many cryptocurrencies have their own official wallets, which can handle only that one crypto.

For example, Bitcoin-specific wallets include Bitcoin Core Wallet (https://bitcoin.org/en/choose-your-wallet), Mycelium (https://wallet.mycelium.com/), and Electrum (https://electrum.org/#home). See Book 3, Chapter 3 for more about Bitcoin and wallets. For Ethereum, you have options such as Ethereum Wallet (www.ethereum.org/) and MyEtherWallet (which is a paper wallet; see www.myetherwallet.com/). Book 2, Chapter 5 has steps on setting up a wallet through www.ethereum.org/. And Book 4, Chapter 5 has more specific information about choosing an Ethereum wallet.

TIP

If you're not planning to diversify among other types of cryptocurrencies, a singular official cryptocurrency wallet may be right for you. Most of the time, you can find the official wallet of a cryptocurrency on the company's website.

Multicurrency wallets are an option for people who want to hold more than one cryptocurrency. The majority of online wallets provided on the exchanges (introduced in Book 5, Chapter 3) give you the opportunity to store and transact among multiple cryptos. However, if you're using these wallets to store your crypto assets, know that your wallet security may be compromised.

WARNING

We do *not* recommend leaving your coins in an online exchange wallet.

TIP

Coinomi (www.coinomi.com/) is a popular multicoin mobile wallet. It supports more than 200 different digital tokens and a number of blockchains. It's a great multi-asset cryptocurrency wallet. Exodus (https://www.exodus.io/) is another multicoin wallet. Your private keys remain secure on your device and never leave it. Exodus can even encrypt the private keys for you.

Based on transaction fees

If you're planning to do a lot of crypto shopping and use digital coins on the go, you may need to be mindful of the transaction fees you're paying along the way. This point is especially true for active traders. If you're a day trader and you're paying more on transaction fees than what you're making in the market, doesn't that defeat the purpose of trading?

Based on anonymity

Anonymity is an extra layer of security you can take into consideration when choosing a crypto wallet. If you use an anonymous wallet, you can separate your personal information from your funds, therefore making it harder for anyone to track down your cryptos and potentially steal them. This factor is something that can be very personal. Some wallets offer full anonymity, while others don't. If anonymity is something that's really important to you, choose among more-private wallets. Note that prioritizing anonymity may affect transaction fees and the price of the wallet.

To find the latest, most popular anonymous wallets, you can simply search the term "anonymous cryptocurrency wallets" on your favorite search engine. Anonymous wallets come in the forms of mobile, hardware, software, and so on. You can have one or more anonymous wallets based on your needs. Some of the popular anonymous wallets at the time of writing include the following.

>> **BitLox:** This hardware Bitcoin wallet ensures both security and anonymity. It's capable of holding over 100 wallets with the ability to create millions of addresses for each wallet. Check it out here: `http://www.bitlox.com?ref=196`.

>> **Electrum:** This desktop Bitcoin wallet appears to be one of the most trusted software wallets by the cryptocurrency community. Check it out here: `https://electrum.org/#home`.

>> **Samourai:** This wallet is a mobile Bitcoin wallet. According to the Samourai website, their aim is "to keep your transactions private, your identity masked, and your funds secure." You can check out the company here: `https://samouraiwallet.com/index.html`.

Keeping Your Wallet Secure

After you've selected the cryptocurrency wallet (or wallets) aligned with your goals, you want to actively keep your investment safe. No matter how secure a wallet is, you still need to take personal steps to enhance that security, just like you'd do with your traditional personal wallet. Because you may be storing a higher value in your cryptocurrency wallets, keeping them safe becomes that much more important. This effort is basically the price you pay for wanting to manage your own money without having to rely on third parties, governments, and big banks. Here are some tips on keeping your wallet safe.

Back up your wallet

REMEMBER

Back up your cryptocurrency wallets like you back up your photos, work files, and computer data. A backup of your wallet can protect you against computer failures and many human mistakes. It can also allow you to recover your wallet if your mobile phone or computer is stolen. Of course, you need to keep your backup wallet in a safe place, away from your original wallet. And make sure you back up regularly to ensure that all recent crypto addresses are included in your original wallet.

Additionally, you should also consider keeping a backup of PIN codes, usernames, and passwords if your wallet provides these features. This measure is a backup in case you forget these things. A hidden file with these items on a secure local cloud for your personal use is a good choice as it's almost impossible to hack.

Have multiple wallets

It's diversification time, baby! If you're having a hard time choosing among the many secure wallets, don't worry. Keeping your assets across multiple wallets is actually a great practice anyway. That way, if any of your wallets are somehow compromised, you don't go bankrupt of cryptocurrencies.

TIP

A good combination is using two or more hardware wallets for larger crypto amounts, with the rest of your smaller amounts spread across mobile, desktop, or online wallets, depending on your everyday use of cryptocurrencies. Of course, all these need to have their own specific backups (as explained in the preceding section).

Add more security levels

You can add to the security level of your wallets in a number of ways. Here are some suggestions:

>> **Use two-factor authentication (2FA).** If your wallet allows it, *two-factor authentication* is a great way to take the security of your wallet to the next level. It's simply a double authentication of who you are, though it can be done in different ways. The Google Authenticator app, which provides a six-digit code that changes every minute and is unique to you, is one option.

>> **Encrypt your wallet.** Encrypting your wallet or your smartphone allows you to set a password for anyone trying to withdraw any funds. This act helps protect against thieves, though it can't protect against keylogging hardware or software (which tracks your keystrokes). You should also consider encrypting your backups. ***Note:*** Some methods to encrypt may need a bit more technical familiarity. The best way to encrypt your wallet is to contact your wallet provider for more information.

>> **Use a strong password.** A strong password must contain letters, numbers, and punctuation marks and must be at least 16 characters long. Avoid passwords that contain only letters, only numbers, or only symbols. Recognizable English words are also a no-go because they're easy to break.

TIP

You can make a very long, strong password by memorizing a pattern on your keyboard instead of selecting a word. For example, start from the left side of the keyboard and type, top to bottom, the keys along the lines of this pattern (using the shift key after the last lowercase letter): 1qaz2wsx!QAZ@WSX. It's an extremely strong password, and you don't have to memorize it! Of course, if you try to log in to your software from a mobile phone, things can get complicated.

Update your software

REMEMBER

If you're using a mobile or desktop wallet, make sure you're using the latest version of the wallet's software. Reputable companies constantly send stability and security fixes. By updating your software regularly, you can make sure that you're using the newest safety features that can prevent problems from minor to severe. (Updating your wallet's software isn't the same as backing it up; see the earlier section, "Back up your wallet.")

Remember where you hide it!

This suggestion may sound a bit silly, but if you're one of those people who hides things so well that even you can't remember where they are, make sure that you choose a location you won't forget. If you lose your cryptocurrency wallets, you may also lose your shirt in the long run.

» Navigating cryptocurrencies in different categories

Chapter **4**

Different Types of Cryptocurrencies

By now, you probably have heard of the cryptocurrency that started it all: Bitcoin. But Bitcoin is hardly the only famous or even investment-worthy cryptocurrency out there anymore. Heck, some people even think that Bitcoin may be the worst cryptocurrency to own or to invest in. This is because so many other digital coins are available that have made massive improvements to the Bitcoin model to avoid its disadvantages.

This chapter covers some of the most famous cryptos as of 2021. But because the cryptocurrency market is ever-changing, you also find out how to navigate your way through all the up-and-coming cryptos for years to come.

Celebrating Celebrity Cryptocurrencies by Market Cap

One of the fastest ways to navigate through popular cryptocurrencies is to check out their ranking based on their *market capitalization,* or *market cap.* Traditionally, market cap is the value of a company that's traded on the stock market. You can calculate it by multiplying the total number of shares by the present share price.

In the cryptoworld, market capitalization shows the value of all units of a specific cryptocurrency that are for sale right now. To calculate a cryptocurrency's market cap, simply multiply the cryptocurrency's current price by its *circulating supply*. Circulating supply is the best approximate number of coins that are circulating in the market and in the general public's hands.

Market cap = Price × Circulating supply

REMEMBER

Knowing about a crypto's market cap and its ranking versus other coins is important because that information can quickly show you how popular the coin is and how much money you may be able to make from it. You can find out about all cryptocurrencies' market caps by visiting websites such as `http://coinmarketcap.com`, `www.cryptocompare.com/`, `https://coincodex.com/`, and `www.coingecko.com/`.

WARNING

Market cap can't tell you everything about a cryptocurrency's investment potential. Lots of other factors, such as forks, regulation, rumor, and so on, can affect a cryptocurrency's value. See Book 5, Chapter 4 to find out more about analyzing a cryptocurrency's performance.

TIP

A higher market cap isn't necessarily a good thing. Investors who can take higher risks may prefer cryptocurrencies with a lower market cap because those may offer more room for the market cap to increase. However, if you want to play it safe and avoid volatility or vanishing risk, you may prefer going with cryptocurrencies with a higher market cap. See Book 5, Chapter 2 for more.

With a knowledge of what role a coin's market cap plays in the industry, you can start to evaluate cryptocurrencies based on that metric.

MINEABLE VERSUS NONMINEABLE CRYPTOCURRENCIES

Where does cryptocurrency come from? Cryptocurrency can be mined — the least common form, actually — or it can be pre-mined.

To say that a cryptocurrency has been pre-mined, or is nonmineable, simply means that the cryptocurrency already exists. The blockchain is a ledger containing information about transactions. When the blockchain was first created, the ledger already contained a record of all the cryptocurrency that the founders planned for. No more will be added; it's all there in the blockchain already.

Bitcoin

Ranking number one on the list, Bitcoin was developed in 2008. As of September 2021, Bitcoin's market cap is around $951 billion.

A bit of Bitcoin background

TECHNICAL STUFF

An entity called Satoshi Nakamoto invented Bitcoin. Satoshi claimed to be a man living in Japan, born on April 5, 1975. Kiana was actually living in Japan, completing her studies in electrical engineering in Tokyo, when Bitcoin hit the scene. Bitcoin wasn't really a big thing in Japan at that time. That's why most speculation about the true identity of Satoshi points to a number of cryptography and computer science experts of non-Japanese descent living in the United States and various European countries.

But Satoshi's anonymity isn't really a big deal, because Bitcoin (and other cryptocurrencies, for that matter) is supposed to be open source and decentralized, as we explain in Chapter 2 of this minibook. In fact, according to Bitcoin.org, no single person or entity "owns the Bitcoin network much like no one owns the technology behind email." Bitcoin users around the world control Bitcoin, with the developer improving the software and the forkers making some radical changes. However, the main idea behind Bitcoin and Bitcoin's protocol can't be changed.

In mid-April 2011, Bitcoin's market cap was about $6 million. In April 2021, the market cap was over a trillion dollars. If you had bought 1 Bitcoin for $2 in November 2011 (something Kiana's investor friends told her to do that she ignored), your single Bitcoin would have been worth $64,000 in April 2021. Of course, many initial investors bought more than one Bitcoin at the time, which is exactly how all those Bitcoin millionaires were made. If you had bought 100 Bitcoins in November 2011 for a paltry sum of $200, by April 2021 they would have been worth $12.8 billion!

But by the time everyone started talking about Bitcoin, it went crashing down to around $120 billion and stayed there for most of 2018. It maintained its number one ranking among all other cryptocurrencies, though. The main reason behind this position may have been that most people had heard a lot (relatively speaking) about Bitcoin but not so much about other cryptocurrencies. So even though they had several hundred other altcoins to choose from, even some that may have been better long-term alternatives to Bitcoin, most newbies who wanted to get involved in the market started out with Bitcoin.

Another reason for Bitcoin's huge market cap is its accessibility. It's pretty safe to say that all cryptocurrency exchanges (see Book 5, Chapter 3) carry Bitcoin. But not all exchanges list all altcoins, at least for now.

Bitcoin characteristics

Here are some main features of Bitcoin:

>> Bitcoin's trading symbol is BTC.

>> Bitcoin is mineable.

>> Coin creation occurs through proof of work (PoW; see Chapter 2 of this minibook).

>> Transaction time is between 10 minutes and 24 hours.

>> Transactions aren't fully anonymous.

>> Bitcoin is decentralized.

>> Mining Bitcoin requires a lot of (wasted) energy.

TIP

Because Bitcoin has been the superstar of all cryptocurrencies, it tends to pull the entire market along. Generally speaking, the whole market sentiment follows the volatility of Bitcoin in longer-term time frames (with many past exceptions). You can use this piece of information in technical analysis for investing, as covered in Book 5, Chapter 10. Head to Book 3 to find out more about Bitcoin.

Ethereum

Ranked number two based on coin market cap as of 2021, Ethereum is another major cryptocurrency. As of September 2021, its market cap is around $465 billion.

Brief Ethereum background

Compared to Bitcoin, Ethereum is a pretty young currency; Russian-American Vitalik Buterin proposed it in 2013. It's almost five years younger than Bitcoin, which in the cryptoworld is still a big deal.

TECHNICAL
STUFF

Buterin was born in 1994. That's the year the Cranberries sang their hit song "Zombie" and two years before the Backstreet Boys and Spice Girls became famous. If this math makes you feel old, imagine how Bitcoin's Satoshi must feel.

Ethereum uses the old Bitcoin's wisdom and philosophy, but it has a different purpose and capability. According to its website, www.ethereum.org, "Ethereum is a decentralized platform that runs smart contracts." Chapter 2 of this minibook explains that *smart contracts* allow people to create agreements without a middleman. Ethereum creates these smart contracts by employing the same blockchain technology as Bitcoin. Just as Bitcoin's blockchain and network validate Bitcoin ownership, Ethereum's blockchain validates smart contracts, which the encoded rules execute.

Ethereum versus Bitcoin

The main difference between Ethereum and Bitcoin is that Ethereum wants to be the place users go to execute their decentralized applications. In fact, its goal is to be a sort of massive, decentralized computer that executes smart contracts. That's why many other cryptocurrencies can run on the Ethereum platform. The Ethereum blockchain forms a decentralized network where these programs can be executed.

Bitcoin is different in this sense. Its platform gets the miners to compete and solve complicated blockchain math problems. The first one who solves the problem is the winner and gets rewarded. But miners can use Ethereum's platform as a co-working space to create their own products. They get compensated for providing the infrastructure so that inventors can cook their own new types of products. Book 6 covers cryptocurrency mining.

TIP

In fact, even major technology players like Intel and Microsoft and financial behemoths like JPMorgan and Credit Suisse are using the Ethereum platform to create new stuff of their own. Along with other giant founding members, various blockchain start-ups, research groups, and Fortune 500 companies have created a group called the Enterprise Ethereum Alliance (EEA). By October 2018, the alliance had more than 500 members, including Accenture, AMD, Credit Suisse, Dash, Pfizer, Samsung, and Toyota, to name a few. You can find out more about the EEA and their current memberships list at https://entethalliance.org/.

Ethereum characteristics

Here are some main attributes of Ethereum:

>> Ethereum's token symbol for investors is ETH.

>> Ethereum is mineable.

>> Coin creation occurs through proof of work (PoW).

>> Transaction time can be as little as 14 seconds, although it can go higher based on confirmation requirements.

>> Transactions aren't fully anonymous.

>> Ethereum is more decentralized than Bitcoin.

>> Mining Ethereum requires less wasted energy than Bitcoin mining does.

TIP

You can find out about different cryptocurrencies' mining profitability at any given time by visiting www.cryptocompare.com/mining/calculator/eth?HashingPower=20&HashingUnit=MH%2Fs&PowerConsumption=140&CostPerkWh=0.12&MiningPoolFee=1.

Ripple

For most of 2018, Ripple was the third-largest cryptocurrency by market cap, at around $19 billion. However, during the first half of 2021, Ripple's market cap hovered at around $30 billion but dropped to sixth place in the ever-changing market cap listings. As of this writing, Cardano, Tether, Ethereum, and Bitcoin have larger market caps, but these rating orders can change overnight!

Some Ripple background

The idea of Ripple actually goes all the way back to 2004. That's way before Satoshi and Bitcoin. In 2004, Ryan Fugger founded a company called RipplePay. According to https://blog.bitmex.com/the-ripple-story/, the idea behind the protocol was a "peer-to-peer trust network of financial relations that would replace banks."

By 2011, Ripple's target demographic started paying attention to Bitcoin, which was just becoming popular and was doing a better job as a peer-to-peer payment network than Ripple. Ripple's architecture started to shift when an early Bitcoin pioneer, Jed McCaleb, joined the Ripple network in May 2011. Others joined the Ripple bandwagon as time went by.

Finally, Ripple's XRP, a cryptocurrency that also acts as a digital payment network for financial institutions, was released in 2012, according to their website, https://ripple.com/xrp/. Like many other cryptocurrencies, XRP is based on a public chain of cryptographic signatures. That being said, Ripple is very different from traditional cryptos like Bitcoin and even Ethereum.

REMEMBER

Some people don't consider Ripple a true cryptocurrency. Also, Ripple as a company and Ripple the cryptocurrency are two different things, although they're connected. Ripple the coin, which trades as XRP, is the cryptocurrency used with some of the company's payment systems. Ripple the company does business as Ripple Labs, Inc., and provides global payment solutions for big banks and such using blockchain technology.

Ripple versus Bitcoin

Here are some of the key differences between these two cryptocurrencies.

>> **Ownership and decentralization:** Bitcoin is not owned by any particular person or entity, and Bitcoin the cryptocurrency is pretty much the same as Bitcoin the open-source platform. That's why Bitcoin is highly decentralized and open source, and owned by a community that agrees on changes. This setup can make upgrades tough and is why Bitcoin has had a ton of forks (hard and soft; see Chapter 2 of this minibook) in its history.

By contrast, Ripple is a private company called Ripple Labs, with offices all over the world. Ripple's digital asset (cryptocurrency) is called XRP and is also owned by Ripple Labs. The company constantly looks to please everyone (especially its partners) and come up with consensus, which can allow for faster upgrades. It has an amendment system with which the developers seek consensus before making changes to the network. In most cases, if an amendment receives 80 percent support for two weeks, it comes into effect, and all future ledgers must support it. Basically, Ripple is a democracy that tries to avoid hard forks and nasty splits!

TIP

You can find out more about Ripple and its most recent updates at `https://ripple.com/`.

>> **Transaction speed and fees:** This area is where Ripple really starts to shine. Bitcoin's transaction speed can sometimes go up to an hour depending on fees. And the fees can reach $40 depending on demand.

Ripple's transactions, on the other hand, can settle in as little as four seconds. Fee-wise, even when the demand was high in mid-2021, Ripple's transaction fees averaged $0.003 — a fraction of that of Bitcoin.

TIP

You can compare different cryptocurrencies' historical transaction fees at `https://bitinfocharts.com/comparison/transactionfees-btc-xrp.html`.

>> **Number of transactions per second:** At any given second, you can make around four Bitcoin transactions. Enter Ripple and recent wonder-coin Solana, and raise the number to 1,500 and 29,000 respectively. Although some Bitcoin forks aim to resolve this issue, at the time of this writing, Ripple and Solana are well ahead of the game.

>> **Coin amount limits:** Bitcoin and other mineable cryptocurrencies have finite numbers of coins, which come into the market only through mining. But XRP is limited to the 100 billion coins in circulation now, largely to appeal to Ripple's (the company's) biggest clients, which are large financial institutions.

Ripple characteristics

The following list gives you a summary of Ripple's main features:

>> Ripple's token symbol for investors is XRP.

>> Ripple's XRP isn't mineable. There are no miners whatsoever.

>> Coin creation and algorithm processing happen through consensus, *not* PoW.

>> Transaction time can be as little as four seconds.

>> Transactions can be made anonymously.

>> Ripple isn't fully decentralized.

>> Energy cost per transaction is minor.

REMEMBER

Because these unique features are so different from Bitcoin's, some people believe Ripple's XRP isn't truly a cryptocurrency. Ripple is actually a strange hybrid of a *fiat currency* (the traditional form of currency backed by a local government, such as the U.S. dollar) and a traditional cryptocurrency. This is because generally speaking, Ripple specializes in serving financial institutions like American Express more than focusing on the spread of Ripple's XRP among everyday users.

Cardano

Cardano has been hovering around the top five-largest cryptocurrencies by market cap in 2021. As of September 2021, its market cap is around $67 billion, making it the fourth-largest cryptocurrency after Bitcoin, Ethereum, and Tether.

A little Cardano background

Ethereum co-founder Charles Hoskinson established Cardano in 2015, and successfully launched it in 2017. Hailed as a greener, environmentally friendly alternative to other computational-heavy coins, Cardano's ADA coin has skyrocketed in popularity. Since its launch, an investment in Cardano has returned over 7,000 percent to its investors.

Fun fact: ADA, Cardano's coin, is named after Countess Augusta "Ada" King, daughter of the poet Lord Byron. She worked on a theoretical computation engine in the 1840s, and is regarded by many to be the first computer programmer.

TECHNICAL STUFF

If you had invested $1,000 in Bitcoin on January 1, 2019, it would've grown 1,004 percent by the end of September 2021. But if you had invested $1,000 in Cardano, then it would've grown about 4,930 percent. Not too shabby.

Cardano versus Bitcoin

Cardano and Bitcoin are both decentralized, they both act as a medium of exchange, and they both have bright futures as absolute trust in fiat currencies is on the decline. Cardano is very different than Bitcoin in a few notable ways, however. Cardano is built from the ground up to serve as a smart contract platform. It also doesn't have the extreme computer processing requirements that Bitcoin miners face every day. Here's a basic list of how Cardano and Bitcoin compare to each other:

>> **Mining:** One of the major differences between Cardano and Bitcoin has to do with mining. Mining Bitcoin is becoming more difficult and expensive as time goes by. To really make money mining Bitcoin, you need very powerful computers. Cardano, on the other hand, doesn't require mining, and so there is no need for ultra-expensive, dedicated computer equipment and air-conditioned facilities.

TECHNICAL STUFF

Bitcoin mining uses a proof-of-work protocol, meaning that your specialized computer hardware churns through a mind-boggling number of computations per second. Cardano's system requires a fraction of the computing power, as you swap, in a manner of speaking, the heavy computational load of Bitcoin mining for the staking of your own Cardano ADA coins. *Staking* means that you make a certain amount of your ADA coins temporarily un-spendable until a Cardano transaction has been verified as complete. This somewhat over-generalized explanation is called proof of stake (PoS).

>> **Total number of coins:** Bitcoin has a finite number of 21 million coins. Cardano also has a finite, maximum supply of coins, totaling 45 billion.

>> **Transaction speed and fees:** On Bitcoin's network, transaction confirmation time averages around ten minutes and sometimes much longer. For Cardano, the speed can be as short as the generation of one block in 20 seconds. Cardano's transaction fee is also considerably lower than Bitcoin's, averaging less than $0.30 in mid-2021.

Cardano characteristics

Cardano's main traits include the following:

>> Cardano's token symbol for investors is ADA.

>> Cardano is not mineable.

>> It uses a proof-of-stake (PoS) protocol rather than proof of work (PoW).

>> Transaction time for a new block is around 20 seconds.

>> Transactions can sometimes be made anonymously using certain exchanges.

>> Cardano is decentralized.

>> Cardano's energy cost per transaction is a fraction of Bitcoin's.

TIP

Although team Bitcoin and team Cardano argue their respective cryptocurrencies are the best, each cryptocurrency has their own unique advantages and drawbacks. The best way to go about your investment strategy may be to diversify your assets not only between these options but also among the other categories of cryptocurrencies in this chapter. Find out more about diversification in Book 5, Chapter 5.

Other top ten major cryptos

The preceding sections introduce some of the most well-known cryptocurrencies that also have some of the largest market capitalization on average. But being famous doesn't necessarily mean they're better. In fact, many analysts and investors believe some of these celebrity cryptocurrencies may vanish within ten years (see Book 5, Chapter 2 for more). Also, having a bigger market cap doesn't necessarily mean having a brighter future. Their current popularity may just be the proverbial 15 minutes of fame, and they may therefore have lower growth opportunity compared to those that are less known.

REMEMBER

Chances are that if anything should happen to a core cryptocurrency, a hard fork may come along that saves it. As explained in Chapter 2 of this minibook, if you've already invested in a cryptocurrency when it forks, you get the same number of new coins anyway. That's why I've recommended to my Premium Investing Group members to start their cryptocurrency portfolio by first diversifying among the top ten largest ones by market cap and then get into other, different categories. You can stay up to date with my most recent cryptocurrency investing strategies at https://learn.investdiva.com/join-group.

The remaining cryptocurrencies in the top ten keep bouncing on and off the list, but Table 4-1 shows some that were on the list more consistently in 2021.

TABLE 4-1   Some Top Ten Cryptos As of 2021

Crypto	Symbol	Description
Tether (www.tether.to)	USDT	A stablecoin that mirrors the price of the U.S. dollar.
Binance Coin (www.binance.com)	BNB	Binance is a crypto exchange with their own coin.
Solana (www.solana.com)	SOL	Created for dApp (decentralized app) and DeFi (decentralized finance) projects.
USD Coin (www.circle.com)	USDC	A stablecoin that mirrors the price of the U.S. dollar.
Polkadot (www.polkadot.network)	DOT	Helps different chains communicate with each other.
Dogecoin (www.dogecoin.com)	DOGE	A meme coin with a Shibu Inu dog as its mascot.
Terra (www.terra.money)	LUNA	A token used to stabilize the price of Terra's various stablecoins.
Avalanche (www.avax.network)	AVAX	A smart contract platform using three individual chains.
Uniswap (www.uniswap.org)	UNI	A decentralized trading protocol facilitating automated trading of DeFi tokens.
Chainlink (www.chain.link)	LINK	Allows integration of off-chain data into smart contracts.

Top 100 major cryptos

You can dive into the top 100 major cryptocurrencies and still not find *the one* you want to have a long-term relationship with. At this point, selecting cryptocurrencies that match your portfolio really becomes like online dating. You've got to make some decisions based on first impressions and then go on dates (start making small investments and do more research) to discover whether a currency is worthy of a bigger chunk of your crypto portfolio. Table 4-2 lists some options.

TABLE 4-2   **Some Top 100 Cryptos as of 2021**

Crypto	Symbol	Description
Litecoin (www.litecoin.org)	LTC	Created to offer faster block transaction times and cheaper transaction fees than Bitcoin.
Algorand (www.algorand.com)	ALGO	Using a PoS protocol, ALGO was created for fast transaction times, efficiency, and low transaction fees.
Bitcoin Cash (www.bitcoincash.org)	BCH	A peer-to-peer cash transfer platform with no middlemen such as banks.
Wrapped Bitcoin (www.wbtc.network)	WBTC	A tokenized version of Bitcoin that runs on the Ethereum blockchain.
Cosmos (www.cosmos.network)	ATOM	Offers an ecosystem of connected blockchains using the less energy-dependent PoS protocol.
Polygon (www.polygon.technology)	MATIC	Can transform Ethereum into a multi-chain system and specializes in scalability.
Internet Computer (www.dfinity.org)	ICP	An infinitely scalable and revolutionary network that can operate at web-speed.
Stellar (www.stellar.org)	XLM	Helps financial firms connect with each other, and allows money to be transferred and stored.
Filecoin (www.filecoin.io)	FIL	A decentralized version of cloud storage for digital files.
VeChain (www.vechain.org)	VET	A decentralized supply-chain management platform.

Cryptocurrencies by Category

As an alternative to selecting cryptocurrencies by market cap, the best way to truly diversify your portfolio, for both value and growth purposes, may be to go about selecting cryptocurrencies by category. After you've flipped through the categories and selected the finalists that best fit your risk tolerance (see Book 5,

Chapter 2), you can then move on to advanced investing techniques throughout the later chapters of Book 5.

Based on their popularity and total market cap as of 2021, here are some of the most popular cryptocurrency categories and the leading cryptos in each space. The following sections describe just a few examples of many categories in the exciting cryptocurrency world; you may recognize some of the currencies from their coverage earlier in this chapter. Other people may categorize these cryptos differently. Some popular cryptocurrency categories include the following:

>> Gaming/gambling

>> Supply chain

>> Transportation

>> Medical

>> Internet of Things (IoT)

REMEMBER

Keep in mind that some categories are hotter as of this writing, but others may have become more popular by the time you get this book in your hands. Also know that some cryptos are hybrids of multiple categories and are hard to fit in only one box. You can find different crypto categories on websites such as www.upfolio. com/collections#Go and www.investitin.com/altcoin-list/.

Payment cryptos

Payment cryptos are by far the biggest category in terms of total market cap. In this group, you find cryptocurrencies that mainly aim to be used as a store of value, transaction, and payments, just like fiat currencies such as the U.S. dollar. Examples of cryptocurrencies that fall into this category include the following:

>> Bitcoin (BTC)

>> Litecoin (LTC)

>> Bitcoin Cash (BCH)

>> OMG Network (OMG)

>> Dash (DASH)

>> Ripple (XRP)

>> Tether (USDT)

TIP

With Bitcoin as the pioneer, it is no wonder that this category started out being so popular. Blockchain technology can be applied to so much more than just payment systems. Check out Book 2, Chapter 1 for more current blockchain uses and potential future applications.

Privacy cryptos

Privacy cryptos are heavily focused toward transaction security and anonymity, a lot more than those in the payment category are. In fact, the idea that Bitcoin and other cryptocurrencies in the payment category are fully anonymous and untraceable is a common misconception. Many blockchains only disguise users' identities while leaving behind a public record of all transactions that have occurred on the blockchain. The data in the ledger often includes how many tokens a user has received or sent in historical transactions, as well as the balance of any cryptocurrency in the user's wallet.

Privacy cryptos can be a bit controversial because authorities see them as an illicit tool that makes it possible for criminals to engage in illegal activities, such as money laundering. Nonetheless, some of them have gained popularity. Here are some examples:

>> **Monero (XMR):** Monero is the most famous privacy crypto as of 2018.

>> **Zcash (ZEC):** Zcash is similar to Monero but has a different protocol (set of rules). Check it out at https://z.cash/.

>> **CloakCoin (CLOAK):** A lesser-known privacy crypto, CloakCoin has a number of added layers of security. See www.cloakcoin.com/en.

>> **Dash (DASH):** Also mentioned in the payment category, Dash is a bit of a hybrid. In addition to Bitcoin's core features, Dash also includes the option for instant and private transactions.

Platform cryptos

Platform cryptos are also referred to as *decentralized application protocol cryptos, smart contract cryptos,* or a hybrid of all three. In this category, you can find cryptocurrencies that are built on a centralized blockchain platform; developers use them to build decentralized applications. In other words, such cryptocurrencies act as platforms where people build upon blockchain applications (and thus other cryptocurrencies).

TIP

In fact, some analysts suggest that you may want to forget about payment cryptocurrencies and invest in crypto platforms instead. They're generally considered good long-term investments because they rise in value as more applications are created on their blockchain. As blockchain technology becomes more mainstream, the number of applications and their usage will increase, along with the price of such coins. The most famous example in this category is Ethereum (ETH). Others include the following:

>> **NEO (NEO):** A smart contracts ecosystem similar to Ethereum, NEO wants to be a platform for a new smart economy. NEO is China's largest cryptocurrency.

>> **Lisk (LSK):** Lisk is a smart contracts platform similar to Ethereum but based on JavaScript. See https://lisk.io/.

>> **EOS (EOS):** Another smart contracts platform similar to Ethereum, EOS has performance and scalability benefits.

>> **Icon (ICX):** Icon wants to "Hyperconnect the World" by building one of the largest decentralized global networks. See https://m.icon.foundation/?lang=en.

>> **Qtum (QTUM):** Qtum is a Singapore-based Ethereum and Bitcoin hybrid. See https://qtum.org/.

>> **VeChain (VEN):** VeChain is a blockchain-based platform that gives retailers and consumers the ability to determine the quality and authenticity of products they buy.

>> **Ark (ARK):** Ark wants to provide an all-in-one blockchain solution for developers and start-ups. See https://ark.io/.

>> **Substratum (SUB):** Substratum wants to create a new generation of Internet. See https://substratum.net/.

These are just a few of the hundreds of cryptocurrencies that are emerging in this category.

Exchange-specific cryptos

Exchange-specific cryptos are mainly introduced and used by the cryptocurrency exchanges. You can think of these cryptos as incentives that bring people to the exchanges' platforms. For tips on selecting the best exchange-specific cryptocurrency and choosing the best cryptocurrency exchange, see Book 5, Chapter 3. Here are a few examples of these currencies.

- >> **Binance Coin (BNB):** Issued by Binance exchange, Binance Coin runs on the Ethereum platform and has a strict maximum limit of 200 million BNB tokens. See www.binance.com/.

- >> **KuCoin Shares (KCS):** KuCoin Shares is just like Binance Coin but for the KuCoin exchange. See www.kucoin.com/.

- >> **Bibox Token (BIX):** Bibox Token is one of the smaller exchanges that has successfully launched its own token. See www.bibox.com/.

Finance/fintech cryptos

This section groups pure financial cryptos with financial technology (fintech) cryptocurrencies. These cryptos facilitate the creation of a financial system for the blockchain and for people around the world:

- >> **Ripple (XRP):** Ripple is a blockchain payment system for banks, payment providers, digital asset exchanges, and other companies. It's designed to move large amounts of money quickly and reliably.

- >> **Stellar Lumens (XLM):** Stellar Lumens aims to develop the world's new financial system. It's building an open system where people of all income levels can access financial services.

- >> **Populous (PPT):** Populous is a global invoice trading platform designed to help businesses. Smart contracts automatically perform funding and release payment without a third party.

- >> **OMG Network (OMG):** OMG is designed to enable financial services for people without bank accounts. It works worldwide and with both traditional money (fiat currency) and cryptocurrencies.

- >> **Bancor (BNT):** Bancor lets you convert between two cryptocurrencies of your choice without another party. See www.bancor.network/.

- >> **Crypto.com:** This cryptocurrency-funded Visa debit card allows you to spend your coins on everyday purchases. See https://crypto.com/.

Legal and property cryptos

More cryptocurrencies are emerging in the two categories of legal and property cryptos. But because they're related, I've grouped them together here for now. Here are a couple of examples:

» **Polymath (POLY):** Polymath helps provide legal advice for token investors and smart contract developers. See https://polymath.network/.

» **Propy (PRO):** Propy solves problems that arise from purchasing properties across borders when using fiat currencies or cryptocurrencies. It's the first company to ever sell a property on the blockchain and using Bitcoin. See https://propy.com/.

Other up-and-coming property cryptocurrencies include Meridio, Republic, SafeWire, and Vairt.

2

Blockchain Basics

Contents at a Glance

Chapter **1**

Introducing Blockchain

Originally, *blockchain* was just the computer science term for how to structure and share data. Today, blockchains are hailed as the "fifth evolution" of computing.

Blockchains are a novel approach to the distributed database. The innovation comes from incorporating old technology in new ways. You can think of blockchains as distributed databases that a group of individuals control and that store and share information.

Many different types of blockchains and blockchain applications exist. Blockchain is an all-encompassing technology that is integrating across platforms and hardware all over the world.

Beginning at the Beginning: What Blockchains Are

A *blockchain* is a data structure that makes it possible to create a digital ledger of data and share it among a network of independent parties. Many different types of blockchains exist:

- » **Public blockchains:** Public blockchains, such as Bitcoin, are large, distributed networks that are run through a native cryptocurrency. A *cryptocurrency* (introduced in Book 1) is a unique bit of data that can be traded between two parties. Public blockchains are open for anyone to participate at any level and have open-source code that their community maintains.

- » **Permissioned blockchains:** Permissioned blockchains, such as Ripple, control roles that individuals can play within the network. They're still large and distributed systems that use a native token. Their core code may or may not be open source.

- » **Private blockchains:** Private blockchains, also known as distributed ledger technology (DLT), tend to be smaller and do not utilize a token or cryptocurrency. Their membership is closely controlled. These types of blockchains are favored by consortiums that have trusted members and trade confidential information.

All three types of blockchains use cryptography to allow each participant on any given network to manage the ledger in a secure way without the need for a central authority to enforce the rules. The removal of central authority from the database structure is one of the most important and powerful aspects of blockchains.

REMEMBER

Blockchains create permanent records and histories of transactions, but nothing is really permanent. The permanence of the record is based on the dependability and health of the network. In the context of blockchains, this means that if a large portion of the blockchain community wanted to change information written to their blockchain, they could. Cryptocurrency is used as a reward to incentivize lots of users to facilitate the healthy function of the network through competition. If the records are changed inappropriately, this is known as a *51 percent attack.* Small networks with few independent minors are vulnerable because it doesn't take much effort to change their information, and powerful miners could do so and gain extra cryptocurrency. Ethereum Classic experienced just this type of attack.

When data is recorded in a blockchain, it's extremely difficult to change or remove it. When someone wants to add a record to a blockchain, also called making a *transaction* or *entry,* users in the network who have validation control verify the proposed transaction. This is where things get tricky because every blockchain has a slightly different spin on how this works and who can validate a transaction.

What blockchains do

A blockchain is a peer-to-peer system with no central authority managing data flow. One of the key ways to remove central control while maintaining data integrity is to have a large, distributed network of independent users. This means that the computers that make up the network are in more than one location. These computers are often referred to as *full nodes.*

Figure 1-1 shows a visualization of the structure of the Bitcoin blockchain network. You can see it in action at http://dailyblockchain.github.io.

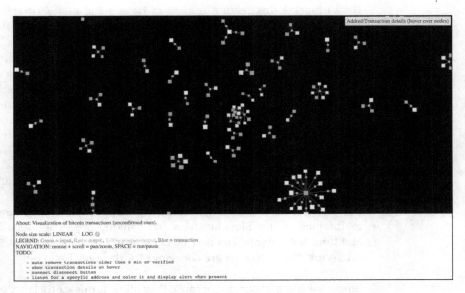

FIGURE 1-1:
The structure
of the Bitcoin
blockchain
network.

To prevent the network from being corrupted, not only are blockchains decentralized, but they often also utilize a cryptocurrency. Blockchain networks produce cryptocurrencies as an incentive to maintain the integrity of the network. Many cryptocurrencies are traded on exchanges like stocks.

Cryptocurrencies work a little differently on each blockchain. Basically, the software pays the hardware to operate. The software is the blockchain protocol. Well-known blockchain protocols include Bitcoin, Ethereum, Ripple, Bitcoin Cash, Stellar, and EOS. The hardware consists of the full nodes that are securing the data in the network. Book 3 covers Bitcoin, and Book 4 covers Ethereum.

Why blockchains matter

Blockchains are recognized as the "fifth evolution" of computing because they're a new trust layer for the Internet. Before blockchains, trust was established by central authorities that would issue certificates. One you may be familiar with is Secure Sockets Layer (SSL) client certificates. An SSL certificate is the "green lock" that appears next to a web domain. It lets you know you're on a secure website.

SSL certificates have proven not to be foolproof. Certificates have been stolen from the domains of the Central Intelligence Agency (CIA), the U.K.'s Secret Intelligence Service (commonly known as MI6), Microsoft, Yahoo!, Skype, Facebook, and Twitter. Relying on a third party allows for a single point of failure.

Blockchains, on the other hand, establish trust in novel ways. Proof-of-work (PoW) blockchains require miners to have a full and accurate history of their transactions to participate on the network. Proof-of-stake (PoS) blockchains create trust by requiring nodes that are processing transactions to "stake" some cryptocurrency that may be forfeited if they're caught defrauding the network. Private blockchains build confidence by distributing data across a network of connected but independent participants that are known by each other and can be held accountable. Each type of blockchain uses different incentive systems to establish trust that each participant in the network will cooperate in keeping a full and unaltered history of each transaction or entry that is made within the database they share.

When data is permanent and reliable in a digital format, you can transact business online in ways that, in the past, were only possible offline. Everything that has stayed analog, including property rights and identity, can now be created and maintained online. Slow business and banking processes, such as money wires and fund settlements, can now be done nearly instantaneously. The implications for secure digital records are enormous for the global economy.

Blockchains are important because they allow for new efficiency and reliability in the exchange of valuable and private information that once required a third party to facilitate, such as the movement of money and the authenticity of identity. This is a big deal because much of our society and economy has been structured around establishing trust, enforcing trust when it's broken, and third parties that facilitate trust. You can imagine how this simple software can be utilized to fix areas that have proven not to be foolproof, such as voting, supply chain management, money movement, and the exchange of property.

The Structure of Blockchains

Each blockchain is structured slightly differently. However, Bitcoin is a great blockchain to study because it was used as a template for most subsequent blockchains. The data on Bitcoin is structured so that each full *node* (the computers running the network) contains all the data in the network. This model is compelling from a data persistence point of view. It ensures that the data will stay intact even if a few of the nodes become compromised. However, because every node has a full copy of the history of transactions since the very beginning, and every transaction in the future, it requires that the entries be as small as possible from a storage capacity point of view.

Comparatively, other distributed networks you may have heard of, like Napster and Pirate Bay, are online indexes of data. Individual files are shared from specific nodes in the network. This allows sharing of large files. However, because the data you may be interested in is not available on all the participants in the network, obtaining the data you're interested in is problematic. It's also difficult to know if the data that you're pulling down is intact and has not be corrupted or contains information you don't want, such as a virus.

The way that Bitcoin coordinates the organization and input of new data consists of three core elements:

>> **Block:** A list of transactions recorded into a ledger over a given period. The size, period, and triggering event for blocks is different for every blockchain.

Not all blockchains are recording and securing a record of the movement of their cryptocurrency as their primary objective. But all blockchains do record the movement of their cryptocurrency or token. Think of the *transaction* as simply being the recording of data. A value is assigned to it (as happens in a financial transaction) in order to interpret what that data means.

>> **Chain:** A hash that links one block to another, mathematically "chaining" them together. This is one of the most difficult concepts in blockchain to comprehend. It's also the magic that glues blockchains together and allows them to create mathematical trust.

The hash in blockchain is created from the data that was in the previous block. The hash is a fingerprint of this data and locks blocks in order and time.

TECHNICAL STUFF

Although blockchains are a relatively new innovation, hashing is not. Hashing was invented over 30 years ago. This old innovation is being used because it creates a one-way function that cannot be decrypted. A hashing function creates a mathematical algorithm that maps data of any size to a bit string of a fixed size. A bit string is usually 32 characters long, which then represents the data that was hashed. The Secure Hash Algorithm (SHA) is one of the cryptographic hash functions used in blockchains. SHA-256 is a common algorithm that generates an almost-unique, fixed-size 256-bit (32-byte) hash. For practical purposes, think of a hash as a digital fingerprint of data that is used to lock it in place within the blockchain.

>> **Network:** The network is composed of "full nodes." Think of nodes as the computers that are running an algorithm that is securing the network. Each node contains a complete record of all the transactions that were ever recorded in that blockchain.

The nodes are located all over the world and can be operated by anyone. It's difficult, expensive, and time-consuming to operate a full node, so people don't do it for free. They're incentivized to operate a node because they want to earn cryptocurrency. The underlying blockchain algorithm rewards them for their service. The reward is usually a token or cryptocurrency, like Bitcoin.

TIP

The terms *Bitcoin* and *blockchain* are often used interchangeably, but they're not the same. Bitcoin has a blockchain. The Bitcoin blockchain is the underlying protocol that enables the secure transfer of Bitcoin. The term *Bitcoin* is the name of the cryptocurrency that powers the Bitcoin network. The blockchain is a class of software, and Bitcoin is a specific cryptocurrency. See Book 3 for more about Bitcoin.

Blockchain Applications

Blockchain applications are built around the idea that the network is the arbitrator. This type of system is an unforgiving and blind environment. Computer code becomes law, and rules are executed as they were written and interpreted by the network. Computers don't have the same social biases and behaviors as humans do.

The network can't interpret intent (at least not yet). Insurance contracts arbitrated on a blockchain have been heavily investigated as a use case built around this idea.

Another interesting function that blockchains enable is impeccable record keeping. They can be used to create a clear timeline of who did what and when. Many industries and regulatory bodies spend countless hours trying to assess this problem. Blockchain-enabled record keeping will relieve some of the burdens that are created when someone tries to interpret the past.

The Blockchain Life Cycle

Blockchains originated with the creation of Bitcoin. It demonstrated that a group of individuals who had never met could operate online within a system that was desensitized to cheat others that were cooperating on the network.

The original Bitcoin network was built to secure the Bitcoin cryptocurrency. It has around 5,000 full nodes and is globally distributed. It's primarily used to trade Bitcoin and exchange value, but the community saw the potential of doing a lot more with the network. Because of its size and time-tested security, it's also being used to secure other smaller blockchains and blockchain applications.

The Ethereum network is a second evolution of the blockchain concept. It takes the traditional blockchain structure and adds several new programming languages that are built inside of it. Like Bitcoin, it has over 10,000 full nodes and is globally distributed. Ethereum is primarily used to trade Ether and create smart contracts. The most popular Ethereum smart contract is the ERC-20. It allows for the generation of interchangeable tokens, which can be used for fundraising purposes. We introduce smart contracts in Chapter 5 of this minibook. In Book 4, Chapters 6 and 7, you can read more about how smart contracts work, and learn how to start writing them.

A third evolution in blockchain technology, which is under active development, is addressing speed and data size constraints. Fixing these issues will enable blockchain technology to be used more realistically with mainstream applications. It will take several years before it is clear which structure will win out.

Popular new developments include *sharding,* a type of database partitioning that separates large databases into smaller parts called *data shards.* An Ethereum development effort called *fork choice rule* splits the Ethereum blockchain into several parallel networks. This may allow Ethereum to scale more efficiently and reduce the congestion on the network, increasing transaction speeds and lowering transaction costs.

A second popular scaling theory is called PoS (proof of stake). Broadly, PoS is the concept of putting up tokens or cryptocurrency as a bond for processing transactions. If the node is corrupted and does not process the transactions accurately, the node may forfeit their tokens or cryptocurrency.

A third effort to scale blockchain technology utilizes trusted nodes. For example, the Factom network operates with federated nodes and an unlimited number of auditing nodes. These nodes are trusted with ensuring the system. Factom's elected network is small, with just over 60 nodes. To hedge for security risks, Factom anchors itself into other distributed networks to piggyback on the security of more extensive systems. Factom also partitions its network into smaller, faster, more easily managed parts called *chains.* Factom has faster transaction speeds and lower transaction costs than PoW blockchains.

Consensus: The Driving Force of Blockchains

Blockchains are powerful tools because they create honest systems that self-correct without the need of a third party to enforce the rules. They accomplish the enforcement of rules through their consensus algorithm.

In the blockchain world, *consensus* is the process of developing an agreement among a group of commonly mistrusting shareholders. These are the full nodes on the network. The full nodes are validating transactions that are entered into the network to be recorded as part of the ledger.

Figure 1-2 shows the concept of how blockchains come to agreement.

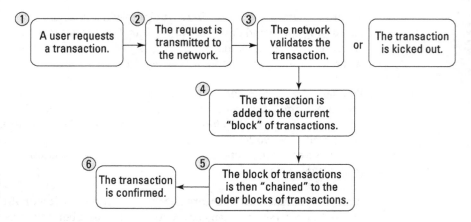

FIGURE 1-2:
How blockchains work.

① A user requests a transaction. → ② The request is transmitted to the network. → ③ The network validates the transaction. or The transaction is kicked out.

④ The transaction is added to the current "block" of transactions.

⑤ The block of transactions is then "chained" to the older blocks of transactions. → ⑥ The transaction is confirmed.

Each blockchain has its own algorithms for creating agreement within its network on the entries being added. There are many different models for creating consensus because each blockchain is creating different kinds of entries. Some blockchains are trading value, others are storing data, and others are securing systems and contracts.

Bitcoin, for example, is trading the value of its token between members on its network. The tokens have a market value, so the requirements related to performance, scalability, consistency, threat model, and failure model will be higher. Bitcoin operates under the assumption that a malicious attacker may want to corrupt the history of trades in order to steal tokens. Bitcoin prevents this from happening by using a consensus model called "proof of work" that solves the Byzantine general's problem (which we discuss further in Book 6, Chapter 1): "How do you know that the information you are looking at has not been changed internally or externally?" Because changing or manipulating data is almost always possible, the reliability of data is a big problem for computer science.

Most blockchains operate under the premise that they will be attacked by outside forces or by users of the system. The expected threat and the degree of trust that the network has in the nodes that operate the blockchain will determine the type of consensus algorithm that they use to settle their ledger. For example, Bitcoin and Ethereum expect a very high degree of threat and use a strong consensus algorithm called *proof of work*. There is no trust in the network.

On the other end of the spectrum, blockchains that are used to record financial transactions between known parties can use a lighter and faster consensus. Their need for high-speed transactions is more important. Proof of work is too slow and costly for them to operate because of the comparatively few participants within the network and the immediate finality needed for each transaction. They also do not need a token or cryptocurrency to incentivize transaction processing. So, they eliminate these components from their system, which enables them to run faster and cheaper than PoW systems. You can learn more about PoW and PoS algorithms in Book 6, Chapter 2.

Blockchains in Use

Thousands of blockchains and blockchain applications exist today. The whole world has become obsessed with the ideas of moving money faster, incorporating and governing in a distributed network, and building secure applications and hardware.

You can see many of these public blockchains by going to a cryptocurrency exchange, which we explore further in Book 5, Chapter 3.

Figure 1-3 shows the altcoin exchange for Poloniex (https://poloniex.com), a cryptocurrency trading platform.

Blockchains are moving beyond the trading value market and are being incorporated into all sorts of industries. Blockchains add a new trust layer that now makes working online secure in a way that was not possible beforehand.

FIGURE 1-3:
The altcoin
exchange
platform.

Current blockchain uses

Most up-and-running blockchain applications revolve around moving money or other forms of value quickly and cheaply. This includes trading public company stock, paying employees in other countries, and exchanging one currency for another.

Blockchains are also now being used as part of a software security stack. The U.S. Department of Homeland Security has been investigating blockchain software that secures Internet of Things (IoT) devices. The IoT world has the most to gain from this innovation, because it's especially vulnerable to spoofing and other forms of hacking. IoT devices have also become more pervasive, and security has become more reliant on them. Hospital systems, self-driving cars, and safety systems are prime examples.

Initial Coin Offerings (ICOs) are another exciting blockchain innovation. They're a type of smart contract that allows the issuer to offer a token in exchange for investment funds. Often used as a non-dilutive fundraising option, entrepreneurs globally have raised billions of dollars. Governments and regulators have been quick to crack down on ICOs. The tokens may be unlicensed securities, and the offering may be defrauding investors. Nonetheless, the technology is impressive even if compliance issues are still being addressed.

One of the fantastic innovations inherent in ICO tokens is that they're a self-clearing and self-settling instrument. In the current system for trading securities, two types of clearing agencies exist: clearing corporations and depositories.

Clearing corporations audit transactions and act as intermediaries in making settlements. *Depositories* hold securities certificates and maintain ownership records of the securities. Blockchains perform both of these functions for tokens without needing third parties to audit and retain possession of the assets. You can learn more about ICO tokens in Book 4, Chapter 2, and about investing in ICOs in Book 5, Chapter 6.

Future blockchain applications

Larger and longer-run blockchain projects that are being explored now include government-backed land record systems, identity, and international travel security applications.

The possibilities of a blockchain-infused future have excited the imaginations of business people, governments, political groups, and humanitarians across the world. Countries such as the U.K., Singapore, and the United Arab Emirates see it as a way to cut costs, create new financial instruments, and keep clean records. They have active investments and initiatives exploring blockchain. For information about how blockchain is fueling the economy of the future and why that may influence your decision to consider investing in cryptocurrencies, see Book 5, Chapter 1.

Blockchains have laid a foundation where the need for trust has been taken out of the equation. Where before asking for "trust" was a big deal, with blockchains it's small. Also, the infrastructure that enforces the rule if that trust is broken can be lighter. Much of society is built on trust and enforcement of rules. The social and economic implications of blockchain applications can be emotionally and politically polarizing because blockchain will change how people structure value-based and socially based transactions.

Chapter **2**

Picking a Blockchain

The blockchain industry is complex and growing in size and capabilities every day. When you understand the three core types of blockchains and their limitations, you'll know what's possible with this new technology.

This chapter is all about assessing blockchain technology and developing a project plan. It puts the later chapters about the Bitcoin and Ethereum blockchain platforms and applications into context.

Here, you see how to assess the three different types of blockchain platforms (public, permissioned, and private, which we introduce in Chapter 1 of this minibook), what's being built on each type, and why. This chapter shows you a few tools that can help you outline your project, predict obstacles, and overcome challenges.

Where Blockchains Add Substance

There's a lot of buzz surrounding blockchains and the cryptocurrencies that run them. Some of this buzz just stems from the fluctuation in the value of cryptocurrencies and the fear that blockchain technology will disrupt many industry and government functions. A lot of money has poured into research and development because stakeholders don't want to be made obsolete and entrepreneurs want to explore new business models.

When it comes to finding an opportunity for blockchain technology to add value to an organization, often the question arises, "Where do blockchains add value, and how are they different from existing technologies?"

Blockchains are a special type of database. They can be utilized anywhere you would use a normal database — but it may not make sense to go through the trouble and expense of using a blockchain when a normal database can do the job.

You really see value in using some form of a blockchain when you want to share information with parties you don't fully trust, your data needs to be audited, or your data is at risk of being compromised internally or externally. None of these questions are simple, and the correct solutions can be difficult to ascertain.

This section helps you to narrow down your options.

Determining your needs

Blockchains come in a lot of flavors. Although you will find one that matches your needs, the trick is in finding it! Mapping your needs to the right blockchain can be overwhelming. Whenever you have lots of options and often conflicting needs, consider using a weighted decision matrix.

A *weighted decision matrix* is an excellent tool for evaluating the needs of a project and then mapping those needs to possible solutions. The key advantage of the matrix is to help you quantify and prioritize individual needs for your project and simplify decision making. Weighted decision matrixes also prevent you from becoming overwhelmed by individual criteria. If used properly, this tool allows you to converge on a single idea that is compatible with all your goals.

To create a weighted decision matrix, follow these steps:

1. **Brainstorm the key criteria or goals that your team needs to meet.**

    TIP

    If you aren't sure of the criteria you need to consider when evaluating your blockchain project, here are a few things to keep in mind:

    - Scale and volume

    - Speed and latency

    - Security and immutability

    - Storage capacity and structural needs

    Your team will have its own list of objects and priorities. These are just a few to consider while evaluating the correct platform to use to meet your needs.

2. **Reduce the list of criteria to no more than ten items.**

TIP

If you're having a hard time refining your list of needs, consider using a comparison matrix tool.

3. **Create a table in Microsoft Excel or a similar program.**

4. **Enter the design criteria in the first column.**

5. **Assign a relative weight to each criterion based on how important that objective is to the success of the project.**

Limit the number of points to 10 and distribute them between all your criteria — for example, 1 = low, 2 = medium, and 3 = high priority.

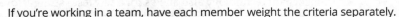

TIP

If you're working in a team, have each member weight the criteria separately.

6. **Add up the numbers for each objective and divide by the number of team members for a composite team weight.**

7. **Make any needed adjustment to weights to make sure each criterion is weighted correctly.**

Congratulations! You now have a ranked list of criteria you need to meet to be successful with your blockchain project.

Defining your goal

You can easily get lost building a blockchain project that doesn't have a clear goal or purpose. Take the time to understand where you and your team would like to go and what the final objective is. For example, a goal might be to trade an asset with a partner company with no intermediary. This is a big goal with many stakeholders.

Build back to a small project that is a minimal viable use case for the technology that clearly articulates added value or savings for your company. Along the same lines as the earlier example, a smaller goal would be to build a private network that can exchange value between trusted parties.

Then build on that value. The next win might be building an instrument that is tradable on your new platform. Each step should demonstrate a small win and value created.

Choosing a Solution

Three core types of blockchains exist: public networks like Bitcoin, permissioned networks such as Ripple, and private networks like Hijro.

Blockchains perform a couple of straightforward functions:

>> They move value and trade value quickly and at a very low cost.

>> They create nearly permanent data histories.

Blockchain technology also allows for a few less-straightforward solutions, such as the ability to prove that you have a "thing" without revealing it to the other party. It is also possible to "prove the negative," or prove what is missing within a dataset or system. This feature is particularly useful for auditing and proving compliance.

Table 2-1 lists common use cases that are suited for each type of blockchain.

TABLE 2-1   **Common Uses for Different Types of Blockchains**

Primary Purpose	Type of Blockchain
Move value between untrusted parties	Public
Move value between trusted parties	Private
Trade value between unlike things	Permissioned
Trade value of the same thing	Public
Create decentralized organization	Public or permissioned
Create decentralized contract	Public or permissioned
Trade securitized assets	Public or permissioned
Build identity for people or things	Public
Publish for public recordkeeping	Public
Publish for private recordkeeping	Public or permissioned
Perform auditing of records or systems	Public or permissioned
Publish land title data	Public
Trade digital money or assets	Public or permissioned
Create systems for Internet of Things (IoT) security	Public
Build systems security	Public

There may be exceptions depending on your project, and it is possible to use a different type of blockchain to reach your goal. But in general, here's how to break down different types of networks and understand their strengths and weaknesses:

>> **Public networks** are large and decentralized, and anyone can participate within them at any level — this includes performing tasks like running a full node, mining cryptocurrency, trading tokens, or publishing entries. These networks tend to be more secure and immutable than private or permissioned networks. They're also often slower and more expensive to use. They are secured with a cryptocurrency and have limited storage capacity.

>> **Permissioned networks** are viewable to the public, but participation is controlled. Many of them utilize a cryptocurrency, but they can have a lower cost for applications that are built on top of them. This feature makes it easier to scale projects and increase transaction volume. Permissioned networks can be very fast with low latency and have higher storage capacity than public networks.

>> **Private networks** are shared between trusted parties and may not be viewable to the public. They're very fast and may have no latency. They also have a low cost to run and can be built in an industrious weekend. Most private networks do not utilize a cryptocurrency and do not have the same immutability and security as decentralized networks. Storage capacity may be unlimited.

Hybrids between these three core types of blockchains seek to find the right balance of security, auditability, scalability, and data storage for applications built on top of them.

Drawing a blockchain decision tree

Some of the decisions you face while working on a blockchain project within your organization can be difficult and challenging. It pays to take time while making decisions that involve the following:

>> **Uncertainty:** Many of the facts around blockchain technology may be unknown and untested.

>> **Complexity:** Blockchains have many interrelated factors to consider.

>> **High-risk consequences:** The impact of the decision may be significant to your organization.

>> **Alternatives:** There may be alternative technologies and types of blockchains, each with its own set of uncertainties and consequences.

>> **Interpersonal issues:** You need to understand how blockchain technology could affect different people within your organization.

A decision tree is a useful support tool that can help you uncover consequences, event outcomes, resource costs, and utility of developing a blockchain project.

You can draw decision trees on paper or use a computer application. Here are the steps to create one for uncovering other challenges around your project:

TIP

1. **Get a large sheet of paper.**

   The more choices you have, and the more complicated the decision, the bigger the sheet of paper you'll need.

2. **Draw a square on the left side of the paper.**

3. **Write a description of the core goal and criteria for your project in that square.**

4. **Draw lines to the right of the square for each issue.**

5. **Write a description of each issue along each line.**

   Assign a probability value to encounter each issue.

6. **Brainstorm solutions for each issue.**

7. **Write a description of each solution along each line.**

8. **Continue this process until you've explored each issue and discovered a possible solution for each one.**

Have teammates challenge and review all your issues and solutions before finalizing your decision tree.

Making a plan

At this point, you should have a clear understanding of your goals, obstacles, and what blockchain options you have available.

Here's a simple road map for building your project:

1. **Explain the project to key stakeholders and discuss its key components and foreseen outcomes.**

2. **Write a project plan.**

   This is a living set of documents that will change over the life of your project.

3. **Develop the performance measurements, scope statement, schedule, and cost baselines.**

4. **Consider creating a risk management plan and a staffing plan.**

5. **Get buy-in and define roles and responsibilities.**

6. **Hold a kickoff meeting to begin the project.**

   The meeting should cover the following:

   - Vision for the project
   - Project strategy
   - Project timeline
   - Roles and responsibilities
   - Team-building activities
   - Team commitments
   - How your team will make decisions
   - Key metrics the project will be measured against

REMEMBER

After you complete your project, you aren't done! Go back and analyze your successes and failures. Here are some questions to ask yourself:

>> Are my key stakeholders happy?

>> Did the project stay on schedule?

>> If not, what caused it to be delayed?

>> What did I learn from this project?

>> What do I wish I had done differently?

>> Did I actually create new value for my company or save money?

TIP

You may want to return to this chapter when you have a deeper knowledge of blockchain technology and you're developing a plan to build a project.

Chapter **3**

Getting Your Hands on Blockchain

B
lockchains are very powerful tools and are positioned to change how the world moves money, secures systems, and builds digital identities. If you aren't a core developer, you probably won't be doing any in-depth blockchain development in the near future. That said, you still need to understand how blockchains work and what their core limitations are because they'll be integrated into many everyday online interactions in the near future — from how businesses pay people to how governments know that their systems and data are intact and secure.

In this chapter, you dive right into blockchain technology. You purchase your first cryptocurrency and find out how to exchange it for other currencies. You set up special applications that will give you access to a whole ecosystem of decentralized applications (known as dApps). You also set up a secure environment to use your cryptocurrency, and create and lease out digital blockchain assets through a blockchain game.

This chapter provides you with an understanding of many of the basic functionalities that blockchain technology offers. You also develop a basic understanding of some of the additional security you need to have while working with cryptocurrency. And you begin to establish the basic crypto accounts that you need in later chapters.

Diving into Blockchain Technology

The Ethereum blockchain is one of the largest and most powerful blockchains in the world. It was designed to build dApps, which are applications that are built within a trustless, decentralized network. Within the Ethereum network, developers utilize smart contracts to build these applications. Ethereum also utilizes a cryptocurrency called Ether to reward users for providing computing power and creating the trustless system that these smart contracts need in order to execute.

Smart contracts are not really like a typical business contract. Instead, smart contracts are code deployed across a decentralized network. Like a business contract, they have predefined terms. A key difference is that smart contracts are enforced by their blockchain network. They're an important computing innovation because they allow individuals who don't know or trust one another to collaborate without fear that the other party won't perform as outlined by the terms that the two parties have agreed on.

TIP

Blockchains that utilize a cryptocurrency can sometimes be called "trustless" systems because the code is enforced by the network (as opposed to a business contract, which is enforced by a court system).

In the following sections, you set up accounts to purchase your first Bitcoin. You also exchange some of the Bitcoin you buy for Ether so you can utilize Ethereum dApps in the following sections.

Creating a secure environment

You first need to create a secure environment to work online. A growing number of reasons exist for you to think about using a secure browser and a virtual private network (VPN); they prevent your data from being collected without your consent and help to avoid hackers. The average user can be targeted by hackers when using cryptocurrency and an unsecured Internet connection.

In this section, you download the Brave web browser, ProtonVPN, and a MetaMask browser extension. You can use all three of these services without paying. However, they also offer improved service for a fee.

TIP

Get a piece of paper and a pen ready to write down important information. Never take a screenshot or photo of things like passwords or seed phrases.

Downloading and installing the Brave browser

Brave is a new Google Chromium–based secure web browser that is fast, open source, and privacy focused. It blocks advertisements and trackers, and has a feature that lets you reward publishers that you like with tokens. Internet pioneer Brendan Eich created Brave; he also invented JavaScript and co-founded Mozilla.

To download the Brave web browser, follow these steps:

1. Go to https://brave.com.

2. Click Download Brave.

3. Go to your downloads folder.

4. Double-click the Brave browser file.

5. Drag and drop the new Brave browser icon to your applications folder.

Now that you have a more secure web browser, you can add the blockchain extension to it that allows you to explore decentralized applications.

Downloading and installing ProtonVPN

ProtonVPN is a VPN run by a Swiss company. When you use ProtonVPN to browse the web, your Internet connection is encrypted so any would-be attackers can't eavesdrop on your activity. It also allows you to access websites that may be blocked.

To download ProtonVPN, follow these steps:

1. Go to https://protonvpn.com.

2. Click Get ProtonVPN Now.

3. Click Get Free.

4. Enter your email address when prompted.

To install ProtonVPN, follow these steps:

1. Go to the download folder on your Mac or PC.

2. Double-click the ProtonVPN file.

3. Drag and drop the new ProtonVPN icon to your applications folder.

A VPN is a good second layer of security to help make sure that your connection is secure. To find out more about how you can protect yourself and your devices, check out *Cybersecurity For Dummies* by Joseph Steinberg (John Wiley & Sons, Inc.).

Downloading, installing, and securing MetaMask

MetaMask is a browser extension that allows you to run Ethereum dApps right in your browser without running a full Ethereum node. (Ethereum is one of the largest blockchains in the world; see Chapter 5 of this minibook and also Book 4 for more information.) MetaMask includes a secure identity vault. It allows you to log into websites, manage your identities on the web, and sign blockchain transactions. You can also keep some Ether cryptocurrency in your MetaMask wallet to make payments online.

To download and install MetaMask, follow these steps:

1. **Open the Brave web browser.**

   See the section, "Downloading and installing the Brave browser," earlier in this chapter if you haven't installed it already.

2. **Go to** `https://metamask.io`.

3. **Click Download.**

4. **Click Install MetaMask for Brave.**

5. **Click Add to Brave.**

   You now see a small puzzle-piece icon in the upper-right corner of your Brave browser. When you click that puzzle piece, click the pin icon, which will make accessing MetaMask quick and easy. You now see a little fox icon at the top right of your Brave browser screen.

Because MetaMask is a wallet, you need to secure and back up your wallet with a strong password and secure your backup seed. A *backup seed* allows you to recover your wallet if you lose your password.

Grab a pen and notebook or a piece of paper that you can keep private. Then follow these steps:

1. **At the top of your piece of paper, write "MetaMask," "Brave browser," the date, and the device you've downloaded it to.**

2. **Open the Brave web browser.**

3. **Click the fox icon in the upper-right corner.**

4. **Click Get Started.**

5. **Click Create a Wallet when asked if you are new to MetaMask.**

6. **Create a password of your choice.**

7. **Review the instructional video titled Secure your Wallet.**

8. **Click the box labeled CLICK HERE TO REVEAL SECRET WORDS.**

Get another notebook or a separate piece of paper for this next series of steps. (Don't use the same notebook or piece of paper on which you've just written down your username and password.)

1. **At the top of your piece of paper, write "MetaMask," "Brave browser," the date, the device you downloaded Brave to, and "Seed phrase."**

2. **Write down and number the 12 secret words that you see onscreen.**

3. **Click Next.**

4. **Confirm your secret backup phrase by clicking all 12 secret words in proper order, and then click Confirm.**

5. **Read through the tips listed on the Congratulations page.**

6. **Click All Done.**

TIP

Consider laminating the pieces of paper with your username and password and your backup seed. Also remember not to store these two pieces of paper in the same location.

Buying your first Bitcoin

There are several places where you can purchase your first Bitcoin. If you're within the United States, there will be some friction in setting up an account and linking it to your credit card or bank account. It may take a day or two for you to be authenticated and allowed to purchase your first cryptocurrency. Book 5, Chapter 3 dives deeper into cryptocurrency exchanges and brokers, but we recommend using one of the following websites if you're within the United States.

>> **Coinbase:** www.coinbase.com

>> **Cash App:** https://cash.app

>> **Gemini:** https://gemini.com/

>> **Robinhood:** https://robinhood.com

Go to one of these sites, or another of your choosing, and set up an account. You'll want to purchase $20 to $30 worth of cryptocurrency. We suggest purchasing

Bitcoin because it's universally accepted and traded for all other cryptocurrencies. You may also have the option to purchase Ether, the Ethereum cryptocurrency used for running dApps. If so, go ahead and purchase $10 to $20 worth.

REMEMBER

Cryptocurrency can be in the regulatory gray zone in certain countries, and illegal in other countries. For example, in September 2021, China banned all cryptocurrency mining and transactions. On the flip side, El Salvador installed Bitcoin as an official currency! Buying and withdrawing cryptocurrency may not be available in the future or within your country or region. If that's the case, you may want to move on to Chapter 5 of this minibook. There, you'll be able to mine on the test net and receive test Ether.

Building a Private Blockchain with Docker and Ethereum

Private blockchains hold the promise of having both the benefits of a private database and the security of blockchains. The idea is most appealing for two reasons:

>> **Private blockchains are great for developers because they allow them to test ideas without using cryptocurrency.** The developers' ideas can remain a secret as well, because the data has not been published publicly.

>> **Large institutions can capitalize on the security and permanence of blockchain technology without their transactions being public the way they are in traditional blockchains.**

TIP

Most of this minibook assumes you're just finding out about blockchain for the first time and have little to no programming skills, but this section requires some knowledge of GitHub, Docker, and how to use your computer's terminal. If you need a quick recap on coding before you dive in, *Coding For Dummies* by Nikhil Abraham (John Wiley & Sons, Inc.) provides a great overview on coding for non-technical people. If you don't plan to ever be hands-on with blockchain technology, you might want to skip the rest of this chapter.

In this section, you dive into building your first blockchain. You build it in two steps. The first step is to prepare your computer to create your private blockchain. Don't worry — it's made easier with tools from Docker and work that has been done by talented developers on GitHub. The second step is building your blockchain inside your Docker terminal.

Preparing your computer

You need to download some software on to your computer in order to try this blockchain project. Start by downloading Docker Desktop. Go to `https://www.docker.com/get-started` to download the correct version for your operating system.

Next, download GitHub Desktop from `http://desktop.github.com`. After you've installed GitHub Desktop, a pop-up screen asks you if you want to sign in to GitHub.com (if you already have an account). If you're new to GitHub, click Create Your Free Account.

Now you need to create a place to store your blockchain data. Create a folder on your computer's desktop called `ethereum`. You'll use this folder to hold your future repository and other files. After you sign in or create a new GitHub account, GitHub Desktop presents you with a Let's Get Started welcome screen. Click Create a New Repository on your Hard Drive, and then follow these steps to complete the process:

1. **Name your repository `ethereum`, and give it a description of your choosing.**

2. **Point the Local Path to your desktop's `ethereum` folder.**

3. **Click the Create Repository button.**

4. **Return to your web browser and go to `www.github.com/Capgemini-AIE/ethereum-docker`.**

   You see the page shown in Figure 3-1.

5. **Click the Code button.**

   You're given three choices: Clone, Open with GitHub Desktop, or Download Zip (see Figure 3-2).

6. **Select the Open with GitHub Desktop option.**

   The GitHub Desktop application reopens.

   In the GitHub Desktop application pop-up window, make sure the Local Path points to the project folder `ethereum` that you created on your desktop, and then click Clone.

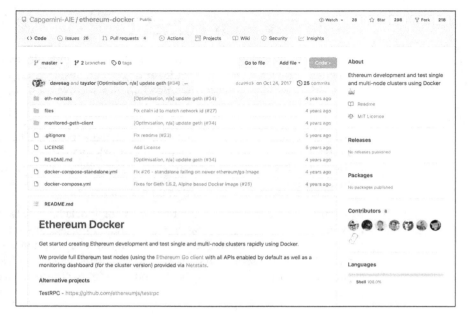

FIGURE 3-1:
Navigate to this
page at GitHub.

FIGURE 3-2:
Open with GitHub
Desktop.

Cloning from GitHub copies the information you need to build your new blockchain. Follow the steps in the next section to get started building your private blockchain.

Building your blockchain

You're going to use the free Docker Desktop tool to build your blockchain. This tool gives you access to a virtual machine, cutting down the time required to set up and debug your system. Because of these features, it lets you create a stable environment for your blockchain, so you don't have to worry about the settings on your machine, and you can get up and running faster.

Follow these steps:

1. **Launch Docker Desktop on your computer.**

   The Docker Desktop application launches a terminal you will use to build your blockchain.

TIP

2. **Change directories in the terminal to** `ethereum`.

   The files you create making the new blockchain will go into the desktop file you made in the preceding section. You need to give a command to your computer's terminal in order to change directories. If you're on a Mac or running Linux, enter the following command:

   ```
   cd ~/Desktop/ethereum/ethereum-docker/
   ```

   If you're on a PC, enter the following command:

   ```
   cd ~\Desktop\ethereum\ethereum-docker\
   ```

TIP

   If these commands don't work for some reason, search the web for tutorials that explain how to change directories for your type of system.

   Now you can utilize the Ethereum–Docker files.

3. **Create one stand-alone Ethereum node by entering the following command into your terminal:**

   ```
   docker-compose -f docker-compose-standalone.yml up -d
   ```

   This one line of code creates the following:

   - One Ethereum bootstrapped container
   - One Ethereum container that connects to the bootstrapped container
   - One Netstats container with a web UI to view activity in the cluster

4. **Take a look at your new blockchain by opening a web browser and going to** `http://$(docker-machine ip default):3000`.

Congratulations! You've built your own private blockchain. If you're so inclined, say a word of thanks to Graham Taylor and Andrew Dong, who put a lot of time into creating the Ethereum–Docker integration.

Chapter **4**

Beholding the Bitcoin Blockchain

W arning! After reading this chapter, you may become hooked on this cool emerging technology. Read at your own peril.

Bitcoin demonstrates the purest aspects of blockchain technology. It's the baseline that all other blockchains are compared to and the framework that nearly all have drawn upon. Knowing the basics of how the Bitcoin blockchain operates will allow you to better understand all the other technology you encounter in this ecosystem.

This chapter covers the fundamentals of how the Bitcoin blockchain operates. It offers safety tips to make your Bitcoin experience smoother and more successful and shows you practical things you can start doing now with Bitcoin. In these pages, you find out how to mine Bitcoin tokens, which gives you a new way to get your hands on Bitcoins without buying them. Finally, you discover how to transfer your tokens to paper wallets, and other practical ways to keep your tokens safe online. You can consider this chapter your quick and dirty introduction to Bitcoin. To dive deeper into Bitcoin, check out Book 3.

Getting a Brief History
of the Bitcoin Blockchain

Bitcoin and the concept of its blockchain were first introduced in the fall of 2008 as a whitepaper and later released as open-source software in 2009. (You can read the Bitcoin whitepaper at www.bitcoin.org/bitcoin.pdf.)

The author who first introduced Bitcoin in that 2008 whitepaper was an anonymous programmer or cohort working under the name of Satoshi Nakamoto. Nakamoto collaborated with many other open-source developers on Bitcoin until 2010. This individual or group has since stopped their involvement in the project and transferred control to prominent Bitcoin core developers. Many claims and theories exist concerning the identity of Nakamoto, but none of them have been confirmed as of this writing.

Regardless, what Nakamoto created is an extraordinary peer-to-peer payment system that enables users to send Bitcoin, the value transfer token, directly and without an intermediary to hold the two parties accountable. The network itself acts as the intermediary by verifying the transactions and assuring that no one tries to cheat the system by spending Bitcoins twice.

Nakamoto's goal was to close the large hole in digital trust, and the concept of the blockchain was his answer. It solves the Byzantine general's problem (a problem we explore further in Book 6, Chapter 1), which is the ultimate human problem, especially online: How do you trust the information you are given and the people who are giving you that information, when self-interest, malicious third parties, and the like, can deceive you? Many Bitcoin enthusiasts feel that blockchain technology is the missing piece that will allow societies to operate entirely online because it reframes trust by recording relevant information in a public space that cannot be removed and can always be referenced, making deception more difficult.

Blockchains mix many old technologies that society has been using for thousands of years in new ways. For example, cryptography and payment are merged to create cryptocurrency. *Cryptography* is the art of secure communication under the eye of third parties. Payment through a token that represents values is also something humans have been doing for a very long time, but when merged, it creates cryptocurrencies and becomes something entirely new. Cryptocurrency lets you take the concept of money and move it online with the ability to trade value securely through a token.

Blockchains incorporate *hashing* (transforming data of any size into short, fixed-length values). Hashing also incorporates another old technology called Merkle trees, which take many hashes and squeeze them down to one hash, while still being able to verify each piece of data that was individually hashed (see Figure 4-1).

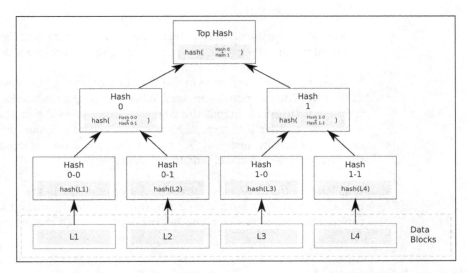

FIGURE 4-1:
A Merkle tree.

Ultimately, blockchains are ledgers, which society has been using for thousands of years to keep financial accounts. When all these old models are merged and facilitated online in a distributed database, they become revolutionary.

Bitcoin was designed primarily to send the Bitcoin cryptocurrency. But very quickly, the creators realized that it had a much greater potential. With that in mind, they architected the blockchain of Bitcoin to be able to record more than the data concerning the movement of the token. The Bitcoin blockchain is the oldest, and one of the largest, blockchains in the world. It's composed of thousands of nodes that are running the Bitcoin protocol. The protocol is creating and securing the blockchain.

REMEMBER

In very simple terms, the *blockchain* is a public ledger of all transactions in the Bitcoin network, and the *nodes* are computers that are recording entries into that ledger. The *Bitcoin protocol* is the rules that govern this system.

Nodes safeguard the network by mining for the cryptocurrency Bitcoin. New Bitcoins are created as a reward for processing transactions and recording them inside the blockchain. Nodes also earn a small fee for confirming transactions.

Anyone can run the Bitcoin protocol and mine for tokens. (Read more about cryptocurrency mining in Book 6.) It's an open-source project that thrives as more individuals participate in the network. The fewer people who participate, the more centralized it becomes — and centralization weakens the system. The primary thing that makes Bitcoin a secure system is the large number of independent nodes that are globally distributed.

The most successful miners have robust systems that can outperform slower miners. Early in its history, you could run the Bitcoin protocol and earn Bitcoins on a desktop computer. Now, in order to have any hope of ever receiving Bitcoins, you need to purchase expensive specialized equipment or use a cloud service.

In order to create a message in the Bitcoin blockchain, you have to send some Bitcoin from one account to another. When you send a transaction in Bitcoin, the message is broadcast across the whole network. After the message is sent, it's impossible to alter it because the message is recorded inside the Bitcoin blockchain. This feature makes it imperative that you always choose your message wisely and never broadcast sensitive information.

Broadcasting the same message to thousands of nodes and then saving it forever in the token's ledger can add up in a hurry. So, Bitcoin requires that you keep your communications very short. The current limit is just 40 characters.

The New Bitcoin: Bitcoin Cash

There is significant conflict around the core development of Bitcoin. Dubbed the "Bitcoin Civil War" or the "block size limit debate," the general conflict is between keeping Bitcoin core as it is and enlarging the functionality of the software. This conflict appears simple, but the repercussions are enormous. Bitcoin's permanent nature and the billions of dollars' worth of assets that Bitcoin software secures mean that every code change is rigorously reviewed and debated.

Bitcoin hard-forked and split into two separate blockchains in 2017. The community of developers and Bitcoin miners couldn't agree on how to address growth. Bitcoin had become increasingly unreliable and expensive to use. It had once been a nearly instant and almost free system; now transactions were costing more than $50 and taking hours to days to clear. The high cost and slow speed drove away users.

A primary issue was that Bitcoin's transaction speeds were too slow, at seven transactions per second, to meet the demand on the network. Transaction fees climbed as users competed to have their transactions processed faster. One of the limiting factors was that Bitcoin's block size limit was 1MB in 2017.

Bitcoin Cash used the same codebase as Bitcoin but adjusted the block size limit. They increased the block size to 32MB. At the time of the fork, anyone holding Bitcoin was also given the same amount of Bitcoin Cash. The increase was controversial because it disenfranchised smaller miners who had slower equipment.

Many miners feared that they couldn't be competitive mining larger blocks. There was also concern that the larger block size would lead to centralization of the Bitcoin blockchain network.

THE LIMITATIONS OF BITCOIN

Blocks that make up the Bitcoin blockchain are limited to 1MB in size. This limits the number of transactions that the Bitcoin blockchain can handle to seven transactions per second. New blocks occur on average about every ten minutes, but they aren't guaranteed.

These limitations are hard-coded into the Bitcoin protocol and help ensure that the network stays decentralized. And decentralization is key to Bitcoin's robustness. Larger blocks would impose hardships on the miners and might push out small operations.

Bitcoin has built-in limitations that prevent it from handling the global volume of monetary transactions. It is also being used to secure other types of data and systems. The demand to use the secure Bitcoin ledger is high. This difficulty is referred to as *Bitcoin bloat,* and it has slowed down the network and increased the cost of transactions.

At this point, most blockchain developers are only experimenting with expanding the utility of the Bitcoin blockchain. Most are not at a point where they need to scale up their prototypes and concepts so that the Bitcoin blockchain can handle their requests. Other new blockchain technologies have also helped bring down the pressure on Bitcoin and have given developers cheaper options to secure data.

Bitcoin is a living and ever-changing system. The Bitcoin core development community is actively seeking ways to improve the system by making it stronger and faster. Anyone can contribute to the Bitcoin protocol by engaging on its GitHub page (www.github.com/bitcoin). However, there is a small community of dominant core developers of Bitcoin. The most prolific contributors are Wladimir Van Der Laan, Pieter Wuille, and Gavin Andresen.

AS THE WORLD TURNS: THE DRAMA OF BITCOIN

Bitcoin is under intense scrutiny from the outside. The decentralized nature of Bitcoin that may displace central authorities made it a target for regulators. Bitcoin is also favored by people who want to purchase illicit items anonymously or move money from a controlled economy to a noncontrolled economy, bypassing governmental controls. All these factors have given Bitcoin a bad rap and drawn the judgment of society. Entrepreneurs who wanted to capitalize on the technology of Bitcoin rebranded it. The change in terminology was used to differentiate the software structure of Bitcoin and other cryptocurrencies. Software that used the structure of cryptocurrencies began to be called *blockchain.* The shift to deemphasize the controversial tokens and highlight the structure of cryptocurrencies changed both government and commercial views of Bitcoin from fear to excitement.

Debunking Some Common Bitcoin Misconceptions

People are often suspicious of anything new, especially new things that aren't easy to understand. So, it's only natural that Bitcoin — a totally new currency unlike anything the world had ever seen before — would confound people, and a few misconceptions would result.

Here are some of the misconceptions you might have heard about Bitcoin:

>> **Bitcoin was hacked.** There was one known instance in 2011 where someone double-spent their Bitcoin, but it was resolved within an hour. Since this issue, there have been no known successful attacks on the Bitcoin blockchain that resulted in stolen Bitcoins. However, many central systems that use Bitcoin have been hacked. And wallets and Bitcoin exchanges are often hacked due to inadequate security. The Bitcoin community has fought back by developing elegant solutions to keep their coins safe, including wallet encryption, multiple signatures, offline wallets, paper wallets, and hardware wallets, just to name a few.

>> **Bitcoin is used to extort people.** Because of the semi-anonymous nature of Bitcoin, it's used in ransomware attacks. Hackers breach networks and hold them hostage until payment is made to them. Hospitals and schools have been victims of these types of attacks. However, unlike cash, which was favored by thieves in the past, Bitcoin always leaves a trail in the blockchain that investigators can follow.

>> **Bitcoin is a pyramid scheme.** Actually, Bitcoin is the opposite of a pyramid scheme from the point of view of Bitcoin miners. The Bitcoin protocol is designed like a cannibalistic arms race. Every additional miner prompts the protocol to increase the difficulty of mining. From a social point of view, Bitcoin is a pure market. The price of Bitcoins fluctuates based on market supply, demand, and perceived value. Bitcoin is not a pyramid scheme, but many scams exist surrounding Bitcoin, so be careful.

>> **Bitcoin will collapse after 21 million coins are mined.** Bitcoin has a limit to the number of tokens it will release. That number is hard-coded at 21 million. The estimated date of Bitcoin issuing its last coin is believed to be in the year 2140. No one can predict what will happen at that point, but miners will always earn some profit from transaction fees. Plus, users of the blockchain and the Bitcoins themselves will be incentivized to protect the network, because if mining stops, Bitcoins become vulnerable and so does the data that has been locked into the blockchain.

- » **Enough computing power could take over the Bitcoin network.** This is true, but it would be extremely difficult, with little to no reward. The more nodes that enter the Bitcoin network, the harder this type of attack becomes. In order to pull this off, an attacker would need the equivalent of all the energy production of Ireland. The payoff of this sort of attack is also extremely limited. It would only allow the attacker to roll back their own transaction. They couldn't take anybody else's Bitcoins, or fake transactions or coins.

- » **Bitcoin is a good investment.** Bitcoin is a new and interesting evolution in how people trade value. It isn't backed by any single government or organization, and it's only worth something because people are willing to trade it for goods and services. People's willingness and ability to utilize Bitcoin fluctuates a lot. It's an unstable investment that should be approached cautiously. Learn more about investing in cryptocurrencies in Book 5.

Bitcoin: The New Wild West

The Bitcoin world is much like the early days of the Wild West. It's best to approach cautiously until you figure out who the good guys and bad guys are and which saloon serves the coldest beer. If you fall victim to a scam, you'll have little to no protection.

WARNING

Bitcoins and other decentralized cryptocurrencies are considered currency in many countries, but little to no oversight or protection is in place for consumers.

This section covers three common scams that are prevalent in the cryptocurrency world. They all revolve around stealing your coins and look a lot like traditional cons you might already be familiar with. This list isn't exhaustive, and crooks are nothing if not creative, so be very cautious when using Bitcoins. You never know what's around the next corner.

Fake sites

Websites that look like exchanges or web wallets but are fakes have plagued some of the top Bitcoin websites. This type of scam is common in the Bitcoin world and on the web in general. Scammers hope to make money by stealing login information from users or misleading them into sending Bitcoins.

TIP

Always double-check the URL and only use secure websites (those that start with `https://`) to avoid this problem. If a website or claim seems doubtful, check to see if it's listed on Badbitcoin.org (`www.badbitcoin.org`). This is not an exhaustive list, but it includes many of the bad players.

Beholding the Bitcoin Blockchain

No, you first!

"Send me your Bitcoins, and then I'll ship you the goods." Smells fishy, right? Scams like this are similar to money wire fraud. In this type of fraud, an individual pretends to sell you something but never delivers.

The semi-anonymous nature of Bitcoins — combined with the inability to do a charge back — make it tough to get your money back. Plus, governments do not currently offer protection for Bitcoin transactions, so you're up that proverbial creek without a paddle.

Fraudsters will try to win your trust by sending fake IDs or even impersonating other people you may know. Always double-check the information they send you.

TIP

The best way to dodge this sort of scam is to listen to your instincts and never put more Bitcoins at risk than you're willing to lose. If there is a way to verify the identity of the person offline, do so.

Get-rich-quick schemes

Crazy get-rich-quick schemes have proliferated in the cryptocurrency world. The good news is: It's easy to recognize them if you know what to look for.

Often, you are promised massive returns, and there is some kind of recruitment and indoctrination process. This process could include things like sales training, asking you to recruit your friends and family, and promising that this is a risk-free investment and that you'll never lose your money. In this situation, never give anyone access to your private keys.

The bottom line: If a scheme looks too good to be true, it probably is. No matter what, take a hard look at how the investment is generating value outside of what you'll receive from your investment. If there is no clear and rational reason that a significant amount of value is generated, it's a scam.

TIP

Run all investments by a lawyer and a CPA. They can help you understand your risks and tax implications.

Mining for Bitcoins

You can get started earning Bitcoins in a variety of ways. Mining for Bitcoin is how you earn Bitcoins by participating in the network. It's usually handled by special mining hardware that is expensive and specialized. The equipment also needs

Bitcoin mining software to connect to the blockchain and your *mining pool* (a collaboration of many miners jointly working together and then splitting the rewards of their efforts; see Book 6, Chapter 3 for more about pool mining).

Here are three standard ways to explore mining Bitcoin:

>> **Bitcoin-QT:** The Bitcoin-QT client is the original software written by Satoshi Nakamoto. You can download it at https://bitcoin.org/en/download.

>> **CGMiner:** CGMiner is one of the most popular mining software applications. It is open source and available for Windows, Linux, and iOS at www.github.com/ckolivas/cgminer.

>> **Multiminerapp:** The MultiMiner app is an easy Bitcoin client to run. You can download it at www.multiminerapp.com.

REMEMBER

Bitcoin is a very competitive environment, and unless you buy specialized mining equipment, you may never earn any Bitcoins. The industry is constantly changing and equipment can become quickly out of date. Expect to pay between $500 and $5,000 per machine on average. For more information, head to Book 6, which goes into much more detail about cryptocurrency mining, including what equipment you need and other cost and risk factors.

Making Your First Paper Wallet

A *paper wallet* is a paper copy of your public and private key for your Bitcoins. Because they're completely offline, paper wallets are one of the most secure ways to hold Bitcoins when created correctly. The advantage is that your private key is not stored digitally, so it isn't subject to hacking. Making a paper wallet is fairly easy. Just follow these steps:

1. Go to www.bitaddress.org.

2. Move your mouse around the screen until the amount of randomness shows 100%.

3. Click the Paper Wallet button.

   This gives you the option to create a paper wallet that you can print.

4. In the Addresses to Generate field, enter 1.

   You can make several wallets at once, if you need to, but you might as well just start with one to get the hang of it.

5. **Click the Generate button.**

Figure 4-2 shows a paper wallet.

6. **Click the Print button.**

WARNING

Do not let anyone watch you create your paper wallet. This isn't something you want to do at a public computer. Make sure to use a printer that is private and not connected to the Internet so you're not at risk of your private keys being hacked.

TIP

Laminate your paper wallet to make it a little more durable.

FIGURE 4-2:
A paper wallet.

Chapter **5**

Encountering the Ethereum Blockchain

The Ethereum project is one of the most developed and accessible blockchains in the ecosystem. It is also an industry leader in blockchain innovation and use cases. Understanding this technology is essential because it's leading the charge in smart contracts, decentralized organizations, and token offerings.

This chapter covers the makeup of Ethereum and explains the new way to build organizations and companies on the Ethereum blockchain. It also goes into safety and practical business applications of the Ethereum blockchain, including how the project started and where it plans to go.

This chapter sets you up to create your own decentralized organization and explains how to mine the cryptocurrency on the test net to fuel your projects. After reading this chapter, you'll be able to set up your own Ethereum wallet and trade the token. You'll also be able to generate your own custom token that can be traded globally. Consider this chapter your introduction to Ethereum. To dive deeper into Ethereum, check out Book 4.

Exploring the Brief History of Ethereum

Ethereum was first described in 2013 in a white paper written by Vitalik Buterin, who was very active in the Bitcoin community as a writer and programmer. Buterin saw that there was significantly more potential in Bitcoin than the ability to move value without a central authority. He had been contributing to the colored coin effort within Bitcoin to expand the utility of Bitcoin beyond the trade of its native token. Buterin believed that other business and government use cases that require a central authority to control them could also be built with blockchain structures.

At that time, there was a fierce debate about the Bitcoin network being "bloated" by lots of low-value transactions from applications securing themselves against Bitcoin. The main concerns were that additional applications, built on the Bitcoin protocol, would have problems scaling in volume. Also, at that time there was not the ability to do scripting to allow for things like smart contracts. Bitcoin was not built to handle the number of transactions needed by the applications. Vitalik and many others saw that in order for people to build decentralized applications in the Bitcoin blockchain, either the blockchain would need a massive code overhaul or they would need to build a new blockchain altogether.

Bitcoin had already been well established at that point. It was clear that the kinds of upgrades to core code that were needed were well beyond what was realistically possible. The politics of Bitcoin would stall any changes to the network. Vitalik and his team established the Ethereum foundation in early 2014 to raise funds to build a blockchain network with a programming language built within it. Vitalik hoped to create a network that would allow him to build blockchain-secured applications.

The initial development was funded by an online public crowd sale during July and August of 2014. The foundation initially raised a record $18 million through the sale of its cryptocurrency token called *Ether*. People have passionately debated whether this sort of crowd sale is illegal because it may constitute an unlicensed security offering.

The regulatory gray zone has not hindered the project. If anything, the cutting-edge nature of the project has attracted more attention and talent to the foundation. Discontented and disenfranchised developers and entrepreneurs from around the world have flocked to the project. Decentralization is seen as the perfect solution to corrupt and oppressive central authorities.

The $18 million raised in the token sale gave the foundation the funds it needed to hire a large development team to build Ethereum. Ethereum Frontier, the first release of the Ethereum network, went live to the public in July 2015. It was a bare-bones software release that only the more technically savvy could use to build their applications.

Homestead, the current Ethereum software release, was made available in 2016. It's much more user-friendly. Almost anyone can utilize the application template available on it. It has intuitive and easy-to-use interfaces and a large, devoted development community.

Metropolis is the next planned Ethereum release. The main difference will be that applications will be fully developed and well tested. It will also feature even easier-to-use applications and have a larger market appeal where even nontechnical people will feel comfortable using it.

Serenity is the last planned phase of Ethereum development. It's where Ethereum will move from a *proof of work (PoW) consensus* (in which miners compete to create the next block) to a *proof of stake (PoS) model,* in which nodes are chosen pseudo-randomly with the possibility of being selected increasing based on their stake in the network. Their stake is measured by the amount of cryptocurrency in their possession. The main benefit of the change will be the reduction in the cost of energy associated with proof of work. This may make it more attractive for individuals to run nodes in the network, which would increase decentralization and increase security. Book 6, Chapter 2 further explains the PoW and PoS models.

Ethereum: The Open-Source World Wide Computer

Ethereum may be one of the most complex blockchains ever built. It has several of its own *Turing-complete programming languages* (full-functioning programming languages that allow developers to create any application). These new programming languages closely resemble popular programming languages such as JavaScript and Python. The Ethereum protocol can do just about anything that your regular programming languages can do. The exception is that the code is written to the Ethereum blockchain and has the added benefits and security that come with that. If you can imagine a software project, it can be built on Ethereum.

The Ethereum ecosystem is currently the best place to build decentralized applications. It has lovely documentation and user-friendly interfaces that get you up and running quickly. Rapid development time, security for small applications, and the ability for applications to easily interact with one another are key characteristics of this system.

The Turing-complete programming languages are the main feature that makes the Ethereum blockchain vastly more potent than the Bitcoin blockchain for building new programs. Ethereum's scripting language makes programs like Twitter applications possible in a few lines of code, as well as extremely secure.

Smart contracts, like the one you create in Chapter 3 of this minibook, can also be built on Ethereum. (You can find out even more about smart contracts in Book 4, Chapters 7 and 8.) The Ethereum protocol has opened up a whole new genre of applications. You can take just about any business, government, or organization's processes and build a digital representation of it inside of Ethereum. Currently, Ethereum's platform is being used to manage *digital assets* (a new class of asset that lives online and may represent a whole digital asset such as a Bitcoin token or a digital representation of a real-world asset such as corn commodities), financial instruments (like mortgage-backed securities), records of ownership of assets such as land, and decentralized autonomous organizations (DAOs).

Ethereum has also sparked a major global fundraising effort by start-ups that used the ERC token standard to raise capital to build their innovations. Ethereum has opened a new way of organizing business, nonprofit, and government. It has made it possible to hold, share, and trade value without ever meeting the other party or using a third party to facilitate. The code does the work.

Decentralized applications: Welcome to the future

The most revolutionary and controversial manifestation of Ethereum is the self-governing and decentralized application (dApp). dApps can manage things like digital assets and DAOs.

dApps were created to replace centralized management of assets and organizations. This structure has a lot of appeal because many people believe that absolute power corrupts absolutely. For those who are fearful of losing control, this type of structure has massive implications.

New dApps are popping up every day. You can explore and discover new dApps built on Ethereum by going to `https://dappradar.com`. DappRadar updates a list of all the latest Ethereum dApps and gives you a preview of what they do. One of the first ever created was Etheria (see Figure 5-1).

FIGURE 5-1:
The world's first immortal digital game, Etheria.

The power of decentralized autonomous organizations

DAOs are a type of Ethereum application that represents a virtual entity within Ethereum. When you create a DAO, you can invite others to participate in the governance of the organization. The participants can remain anonymous and never meet, which could trigger Know Your Customer (KYC) rules (the process a business must go through to verify the identity of its clients) and anti-money-laundering (AML; the laws and regulations designed to stop the practice of generating income through illegal means) compliance issues.

DAOs have been created for raising funds for investing, but they could also be designed for civic or nonprofit purposes. Ethereum gives you a basic framework for governance. It's up to the organizers to determine what's being governed. Ethereum has created templates for you to help in the creation of DAOs.

Figure 5-2 shows a depiction of the organization of an Ethereum application.

Here's how DAOs basically work:

1. A group of people write a smart contract to govern the organization.

2. People add funds to the DAO and are given tokens that represent ownership.

   This structure works kind of like stock in a company, but the members have control of the funds from day one.

3. When the funds have been raised, the DAO begins to operate by having members propose how to spend the money. Voting may be affected by how much Ether the member risks or stakes in the DAO.

4. The members vote on these proposals.

5. When the predetermined time has passed and the predetermined number of votes has accrued, the proposal passes or fails.

6. Individuals act as contractors to service the DAO.

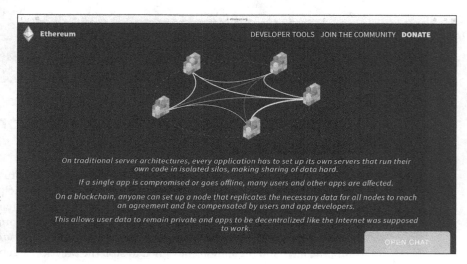

FIGURE 5-2:
Ethereum.
org blockchain
application
depiction.

Unlike most traditional investment vehicles, where a central party makes decisions about investments, the members of a DAO control 100 percent of the assets. They vote on new investments and other decisions. This type of structure threatens to displace traditional financial managers.

DAOs are built with code that can't be changed on the fly. The appeal of this is that malicious hackers can't monkey with the funds in a traditional sense. However, hackers can still find ways to execute the code in unexpected ways and withdraw funds. Also, the immutable nature of a DAO's code makes it nearly impossible to fix any bugs once the DAO is live in Ethereum.

WITH GREAT POWER COMES . . . GREAT POWER

The first Ethereum DAO ever built is called, confusingly enough, "The DAO." It's an example of some of the dangers that come with decentralized and autonomous entities. It is the largest crowdfunded project in the world — its founders raised approximately $162 million in 26 days with more than 11,000 members. What people had thought was the greatest strength of The DAO became its greatest weakness. The immutable code within The DAO locked into place how the organization would be governed and how funds would be distributed. This allowed the members to feel secure in their investment. Although the code was well reviewed, not all the bugs had been worked out.

The first significant threat to Ethereum came from the hack of The DAO. An unexpected code path in The DAO's contract allowed any sophisticated user to withdraw funds. An unknown user managed to remove about $50 million before he could be stopped.

The Ethereum community debated bitterly about whether it could or should reclaim the Ether. The DAO hacker had not technically done anything wrong or even hacked the system. Fundamentalists within the Ethereum community felt that code was law and, therefore, nothing should be done to recover the funds.

The very thing that made Ethereum strong was also its greatest weakness. Decentralization, immutability, and autonomy meant no central authority could quickly decide what to do. There was also no one to punish for the misuse of the system. It really did not have any consumer protection measures. It was a new frontier, like the software name suggested.

After spending several weeks discussing the problem, the Ethereum community decided to shut down The DAO and create a new Ethereum. This process is called *hard forking*. When the Ethereum community hard-forked the network, it reversed the transaction the hacker had committed. It also created two Ethereums: Ethereum and Ethereum Classic.

Not everyone was in agreement with this decision. The community continues to use Ethereum Classic. The tokens for Ethereum Classic are still traded but have lost significant market value. The new Ethereum token still hasn't regained its old high from before the hack.

The decision to fork rocked the blockchain world. It was the first time a majority blockchain project had hard-forked to make whole an investor. It called into question many of the principles that make blockchain technology so attractive in the first place.

Hacking a Blockchain

Ethereum has never been hacked. The hard fork in 2016 due to the DAO hack mentioned in the sidebar, "With great power comes . . . great power," was not an actual hack of the system, but confusingly it is often referred to as a hack. Ethereum worked perfectly. The problem was it was too perfect. It became necessary to restart the system when a large amount of money and a majority of its users were threatened.

The only way to correct an action on a blockchain like Ethereum is to do a *hard fork*, which allows for a fundamental change to the protocol. (You can read more about forking in the context of cryptocurrency mining in Book 6, Chapter 8.) A hard fork makes previously valid blocks and transactions invalid. Ethereum did this to protect the funds that were being pulled out of the first DAO by a user. The DAO hack was, conceptually, one of the largest bug bounties ever.

That said, many scams and hacking attempts occur in the cryptocurrency space. Most of these attacks target centralized exchanges and applications. Many hackers want to steal cryptocurrency. It has real value and isn't protected in the same ways that regular money is protected by governments. The anonymous nature of cryptocurrency also makes it appealing to crooks. Catching and prosecuting these individuals is difficult. However, the cryptocurrency community is fighting back and creating new measures to protect themselves.

REMEMBER

Hacking one place is significantly easier and cheaper than trying to overcome a decentralized network. When you read about hacking in the blockchain world, it's likely just a website or a cryptocurrency wallet that has been hacked, not the whole network.

Understanding smart contracts

Ethereum smart contracts are like contractual agreements, except there is no central party to enforce the contract. The Ethereum protocol "enforces" smart contracts by attaching economic pressure. They can also enforce implementation of a requirement if it lives within Ethereum, because Ethereum can prove certain conditions were or were not met. If it doesn't live within Ethereum, it's much harder to enforce.

WARNING

Ethereum smart contracts are not yet legally enforceable and may never be because the perception is that you don't need outside authorities enforcing agreements. Legal systems are controlled by governments. As they stand now, governments are central authorities — some with more or less consent and democratic principles. Within an Ethereum smart contract, each participant has an inalienable vote.

Ethereum smart contracts do not include artificial intelligence. This is a cool possibility in the near future. But for now, Ethereum is just software code that runs on a blockchain.

Ethereum smart contracts are not safe. The DAO hack is a great example of the type of dangers that can occur. It is still early days, and putting a lot of money into an unproven system isn't smart. Instead, experiment with small amounts until all the bugs have been worked out of new contracts.

Discovering the cryptocurrency Ether

Ether is the name of the cryptocurrency for the Ethereum blockchain. It was named after the substance that was believed to permeate all space and make the universe possible. In that sense, Ether is the substance that makes Ethereum possible. Ether incentivizes the network to secure itself through proof-of-work mining, like how the token Bitcoin incentivizes the Bitcoin network. Ether is needed to execute any code within the Ethereum network. When utilized to execute a contract in Ethereum, Ether is referred to as *gas*.

Executing the code within a smart contract also costs some amount of Ether. This feature gives the token added utility. As long as individuals want to use Ethereum for applications and contracts, Ether will hold a value beyond speculation.

The wild growth in the value of Ether has made it a popular token to speculate on. It's widely traded on exchanges around the world. Some new hedge funds are looking at it as an investment vehicle. However, the volatile nature and low market depth make Ether a risky investment. Find out more about Ether, including how to buy, spend, and trade it, in Book 4, Chapter 1.

Getting Up and Running on Ethereum

This section walks you through how to get started in the Ethereum blockchain ecosystem. Before you can build anything on Ethereum, you need a wallet containing some Ethereum (ETH). Book 2, Chapter 3 explains the process of downloading and installing MetaMask for the Brave browser, which you can use for the instructions found in the remainder of this chapter.

Mining for Ether

Ethereum is kept running by a network of computers all over the world that are processing the contracts and securing the network. These computers are sometimes referred to as *nodes*, and they're mining crypto Ether.

In order to reward individuals for the time and cost involved in mining, there is a prize of five Ethers about every 12 seconds. The prize is given to the node that was able to create the latest block in the Ethereum blockchain.

All new blocks have a list of the latest transactions. The proof-of-work consensus algorithm guarantees that prizes are won most often by nodes with the most computational power. Computers that aren't as powerful can win, too — it just takes longer. If you want to try your hand at mining Ether, you can do it with your home computer, but it will take a very long time to successfully mine a block and win Ether.

Building your first decentralized autonomous organization

DAOs will change how the world does business in the future. They allow anyone in the world to create a new type of company online that is governed by pre-agreed-upon rules that are then enforced through the blockchain network. Creating a DAO is easier than you might think. In this section, you build your first DAO.

REMEMBER

To successfully complete your DAO, you need to have set up a wallet such as MetaMask and have loaded it with some Ethereum ETH.

Open the browser (such as Brave or Chrome) that you use to access your MetaMask wallet, and follow these steps to create your first DAO:

1. Go to https://alchemy.daostack.io/.

2. Click the blue Connect Wallet button at the top right of your screen.

3. Click the Create a DAO button at the top right of your screen.

4. Within the Set Description box, name your organization.

5. Under Symbol, type in your ticker name, such as WXYZ, and click Set Description.

   The name of your ticker symbol should be related to your organization's actual name. For example, Tesla's Nasdaq symbol is TSLA, and Apple's is AAPL.

6. **Within Configure, keep all options as they are by default and click Set Configuration.**

   Feel free to manually alter the Configure options if you know what you are doing.

7. **Add members to your DAO by adding their ETH addresses.**

   Figure 5-3 shows what the Add Members section looks like.

8. **Click the Launch button.**

   Your MetaMask wallet opens as a pop-up window.

9. **Confirm the Gas Fee cost, and click Confirm.**

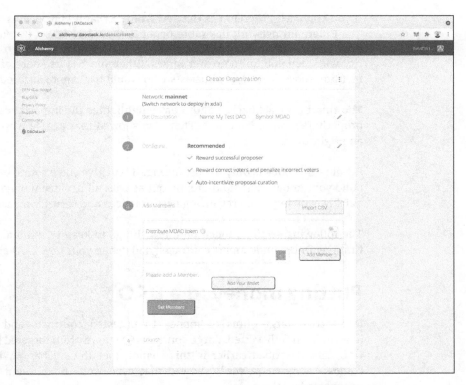

FIGURE 5-3:
The Add
Members box.

REMEMBER

Important! If you don't have enough ETH in your wallet to cover the gas fee to create your DAO, just stop at this point. You can always quit this DAO setup and return to these instructions at a later date when your wallet has more ETH. If you have enough ETH to cover the transaction, it takes a few minutes to create your DAO. You are asked to Confirm one more time, and then your DAO is created. Congrats!

Afterwards, you will have many options to fine-tune your organization within the dashboard. For example, you will be able to establish funding and voting protocols, manage members, and so much more.

Uncovering the Future of DAOs

Smart contracts and decentralized organizations hold a lot of promise. Their pure democratic and hyper-rational nature is very appealing. However, at this point, more possibilities exist than knowns, and each contract that's created could be groundbreaking or a massive flop.

If you approach Ethereum as the new frontier that it is, you'll have more success. The Ethereum network has more benefits than drawbacks if you're careful. But expecting everything to work flawlessly and all the participants to act with integrity will open you up to greater losses. Ethereum has its share of bandits, not to mention those friendly enthusiasts who would like you to succeed.

The smart contract hacks of 2016 have highlighted the importance of security and properly reviewing contracts. They also showed that people with integrity exist, and fight to fix issues.

Reading this book is only the beginning. It will give you a sound basis on which to build your knowledge of Ethereum, but as with all new technologies, Ethereum is quickly evolving. Keep reviewing best practices and security measures.

The following sections touch on a few things to keep in mind as you build your first few DAOs, build smart contracts, and debug your new blockchain systems.

Putting money in a DAO

Don't trust large sums of money to untested contracts and contracts that haven't been fully vetted. Large contracts are more often targeted by hackers. The DAO hack described earlier in this chapter (see the sidebar, "With great power comes . . . great power") showed that even well-thought-out contracts have unexpected weaknesses.

REMEMBER

Although smart contracts and blockchains let you conduct business with anyone around the world, it's still early days. You can mitigate your risk by working only with known and trusted parties.

TIP

The security landscape will constantly be evolving with new bugs. Reviewing all new best practices is imperative. Manage the amount of money you're putting at risk and roll out contracts slowly and in phases. Ethereum is a fairly new technology, and mature solutions are not yet built.

Building smarter smart contracts

Smart contract programming requires a different mindset than standard contract writing. There is no third party to make things right if the contract executes in a way that you didn't expect or intend. The immutable and distributed nature of blockchains makes it tough to change an unwanted outcome.

REMEMBER

Your contract will have flaws and may fail. Build safety valves into your contracts so you can respond to bugs and vulnerabilities as they come up. Smart contracts also need an off switch that lets you pull the plug and pause your contract when things are going wrong.

TIP

If your contract is big enough, offer bug-hunting bounties that incentivize the community to find vulnerabilities and flaws in your contract.

As with many things, the complexity of your contract also increases the likelihood of errors and attack vectors. Keep your contract logic simple. Build out small modules that hold each section of the contract. Creating a contract in this manner will help you compartmentalize any issues.

Finding bugs in the system

Don't reinvent the wheel by building your own tools such as random number generators. Instead, leverage the work that the community has already done and that has been well tested.

WARNING

You can only control for things within your own contract. Be cautious of external contract calls. They can execute malicious code and take away your control.

The Ethereum community has an excellent known bug list and even more helpful tips on how to build secure smart contracts. You can find it at `eth.wiki/en/howto/smart-contract-safety`.

Creating Your Own ERC-20 Token

This section shows you how to create your own token on the Ethereum network. Before you read through this section, make sure that you've set up MetaMask. If you haven't, refer to Chapter 3 of this minibook, where you find detailed instructions for setting up your computer and downloading MetaMask.

To create your token, follow these steps:

1. **Go to** `https://www.createmytoken.com`.

2. **Click Ethereum Network.**

3. **Click Create ERC-20 Token for free!.**

4. **Connect your MetaMask wallet by clicking Connect.**

5. **Name your token and give it a Token (ticker) Symbol.**

6. **Make sure that All Functionality is set to the On position.**

7. **Type in your initial supply of tokens, such as 100,000,000.**

   Under the Ready to Deploy? box, make sure you have enough ETH in your MetaMask wallet to cover the gas fees. For example, at the time of this writing, the estimated cost was 0.05 ETH. If this amount is acceptable to you, click Deploy Token!.

Congratulations! You've created your own token. With tools like `https://www.createmytoken.com`, it's easy and fast to create a token on various platforms. If you're curious to find out more about Ethereum, head to Book 4.

Chapter **6**

Getting Your Hands on Hyperledger

H yperledger is a foundation that supports a community of software developers and technology enthusiasts who are building industry standards for blockchain frameworks and platforms. Hyperledger's work is crucial because they're creating blockchain technology that fits the needs of businesses. Cryptocurrencies on public blockchains have regulatory implications and liabilities that prevent many companies from utilizing these networks. Hyperledger has many of the same benefits of public blockchain technology but operates without a cryptocurrency. With big supporters such as Intel and IBM, Hyperledger is the "trusted" deployment platform for enterprise teams.

Hyperledger and its unique project are growing every day. As of this writing, it has 190 member companies and several blockchain applications. Hyperledger's first few projects include Fabric, Iroha, and Sawtooth. These are frameworks that developers can use to build private blockchains, create smart contracts, and build distributed identity for people and things.

This chapter shows you how to create an asset tracking and a smart auction application using Hyperledger's Composer tool and introduces you to the Fabric, Iroha, and Sawtooth projects. You'll gain a deep understanding of what the future of commercialized blockchain will hold for your company and industry. This knowledge can help you as you explore which technologies to utilize and which to avoid, saving you development time and resources.

Getting to Know Hyperledger

At the end of 2015, the Linux Foundation formed the Hyperledger project to develop an enterprise-grade and open-source distributed ledger framework. They hoped to focus the blockchain community on building robust, industry-specific applications, platforms, and hardware systems to support businesses.

The Linux Foundation saw that many different groups were building blockchain technology without a cohesive direction. The industry was duplicating effort, and the tribalism was leading teams to solve the same problem twice. The foundation members saw similarities between the birth of the Internet and the emergence of blockchain technology: If blockchain was going to realize its fullest potential, an open-source and collaborative development strategy was desperately needed.

The Hyperledger project is led by Executive Director Brian Behlendorf, who has decades of experience dating back to the original Linux Foundation and Apache Foundation, as well as being a chief technology officer (CTO) of the World Economic Forum. So, it's not surprising that Hyperledger has been well received. Many of the top business and industry leaders have joined the project, including Accenture, Visa, Fujitsu Limited, IBM, FedEx, JPMorgan Chase, and Microsoft. It has also attracted many of the top blockchain organizations.

Hyperledger's technical steering committees ensure robustness and interoperability between these different technologies. The hope is that the cross-industry, open-source collaboration will advance blockchain technology and deliver billions of dollars in economic value by sharing the costs of research and development across many organizations.

Hyperledger is identifying and addressing the critical features and requirements missing from the blockchain technology ecosystem. It's also fostering a cross-industry open standard for distributed ledgers and holding open space for developers to contribute to building better blockchain systems.

Hyperledger has a project life cycle similar to that of the Linux Foundation. A proposal is submitted, and then the accepted proposal is brought into incubation. When a project has reached a stable state, it graduates and is moved into an active state. Each of the projects were initially led by a large corporation or start-up, and since then, many of them have created strategic partnerships to share in the project's development. For example, Fabric was led by IBM, Sawtooth by Intel, and Iroha by Soramitsu, but now many additional partnerships have helped advance each project.

TIP

Hyperledger, like many open-source projects, uses GitHub (www.github.com/hyperledger) and a chat service (https://chat.hyperledger.org) to connect with teams working on each of the projects. These are great places to get the latest updates and to check on the progress that these projects are making in development.

Identifying Key Hyperledger Projects

Hyperledger has several revolutionary projects either with Active or Incubation status. This section covers three prominent and well-developed projects. These blockchain technologies include distributed ledger frameworks, smart contract engines, client libraries, graphical interfaces, utility libraries, and sample applications.

Focusing on Fabric

Fabric was the first blockchain implementation on Hyperledger. It has become the foundation for developing most blockchain applications. Fabric is unique within the blockchain ecosystem because it allows developers to use pieces of Fabric without committing to all the functionality — a truly tailored plug-and-play experience. Fabric also can create smart contracts called *chaincode*.

Fabric is a permissioned blockchain and does not utilize a cryptocurrency. This means that all the participants are known (as opposed to on a typical public blockchain where all the participants are anonymous by default). Fabric works like most blockchains in that it keeps a ledger of digital events. These events are structured as transactions and shared among the different participants. The transactions are executed without a cryptocurrency. (In contrast, a public blockchain uses its native cryptocurrency to pay the network to operate and to allow all the participants to remain anonymous.) To dive deeper into the subject of Fabric, go to https://trustindigitallife.eu/wp-content/uploads/2016/07/marko_vukolic.pdf.

All transactions are secured, private, and confidential. Fabric preserves its integrity by only allowing updates by consensus of the participants. When records have been inputted, they can never be altered.

Fabric is an enterprise solution interested in scalability and complying with regulations. All participants must register proof of identity to membership services to gain access to the system. Fabric issues transactions with derived certificates that are unlinkable to the owning participant, thereby offering anonymity on the network. Also, the content of each transaction is encrypted to ensure that only the intended participants can see the content.

Fabric has a modular architecture. You can add or take away components by implementing its protocol specification. Its container technology can handle most of the mainstream languages for smart contract development.

Investigating the Iroha project

Hyperledger's Iroha project is built on the work completed in the Fabric project. It's meant to complement Fabric, Sawtooth, and the other projects under

Hyperledger. Hyperledger added the Iroha project because the other projects didn't have any infrastructure projects written in C++. Not having a C++ project severely limited how many people could benefit from the work on Hyperledger and the number of developers who could contribute to the project.

Besides, most blockchain development at this point has been at the lowest infrastructure level, and there has been little to no development work on user interaction or mobile applications. Hyperledger believes that Iroha is necessary for the popularization of blockchain technology. This project fills the gap in the market by bringing in more developers and providing libraries for mobile user interface development.

Iroha's iOS, Android, and JavaScript libraries provide supportive functions like digitally signing transactions. It's handy for commercial app development, and it adds new layers of security and business models that are only possible with blockchain technology.

Sumeragi's consensus algorithm

Blockchains have systems that allow them to first agree on a single version of the truth and then record that agreed-upon truth in their ledger. An agreement system is called a *consensus*. A consensus is complicated, and grasping the nuances of how and why a consensus acts in the way it does is far more than a business professional needs to know. (If you're curious, though, or interested in getting into cryptocurrency mining, check out Book 6.) What *does* matter for you are the consequences of different consensus mechanisms and how they affect what you're doing on that particular blockchain. Iroha's consensus, Sumeragi, is worthy of note because it's very different from traditional blockchains.

Here are a few key things that make Sumeragi different:

>> **Sumeragi does not have a cryptocurrency.**

>> **Nodes that start consensus are added into the system by the Fabric member services.** Nodes build a reputation over time based on how they've interacted with the ledger. This is a permission blockchain run by known entities.

>> **New entries are added to the ledger in a unique way.** The first node that starts consensus, called the *leader,* broadcasts the entry to a group of other nodes; those nodes then validate. If they don't validate, the first node will rebroadcast after a predetermined duration of time.

Depending on your use case for blockchain, Iroha may be positive or negative. If you're worried about censorship, Iroha may not be right for you. In this case, you'll be better off looking at a blockchain that is censorship resistant. If you're worried about other players on the network committing arbitrage, Iroha may also not be right — further investigation is needed. If you want to know all the players in your blockchain, Iroha may be exactly what you're looking for.

Developing mobile apps

TIP

Skip this section if you aren't part of the app development space.

Iroha is built for web and mobile app developers so they can access the strengths of the Hyperledger systems. The Iroha team saw that having a distributed ledger wasn't useful if there were no applications utilizing it.

Iroha was developed for the following encapsulated C++ components:

>> Sumeragi consensus library

>> Ed25519 digital signature library

>> SHA-3 hashing library

>> Iroha transaction serialization library

>> P2P broadcast library

>> API server library

>> iOS library

>> Android library

>> JavaScript library

>> Blockchain explorer/data visualization suite

One of the major hurdles of the blockchain industry has been in making systems user-friendly. Iroha has created open-source software libraries for iOS, Android, and JavaScript and made common application programming interface (API) functions convenient to all.

Diving into Sawtooth

Sawtooth by Intel is another distributed ledger project in Hyperledger. It's focused on being a highly modular platform for building new distributed ledgers for companies.

Sawtooth does not operate with a cryptocurrency. It maintains the security of the platform by allowing businesses to create private blockchains. These businesses running private blockchains then share the burden of computational requirements with the network. In its documentation, Sawtooth states that this type of setup will ensure universal agreement on the state of the shared ledger.

Sawtooth has taken the basic model of blockchains and turned it on its head. Most blockchains have three elements:

>> A shared record of the current state of the blockchain

>> A way of inputting new data

>> A way of agreeing on that data

Sawtooth merges the first two into a signal process it calls a *transaction family*. This model is best in use cases where all the participating parties have a mutual benefit to having a correct record.

Intel has allowed its software to be flexible enough to accommodate custom transaction families that reflect the unique requirements of each business. It also built three templates for building digital assets.

>> **EndPointRegistry:** A place to record items in a blockchain

>> **IntegerKey:** A shared ledger that is used for supply chain management

>> **MarketPlace:** A blockchain trading platform for buying, selling, and trading digital assets

Exploring the consensus algorithm: Proof of Elapsed Time

The consensus algorithm for Sawtooth is called proof of elapsed time (PoET). It was built to run in a secure area of the main processor of your computer, called a *trusted execution environment* (TEE). PoET leverages the security of the TEE to prove that time has passed by time-stamping transactions.

Other consensus algorithms have some kind of time-stamping element as well. The way they ensure that the records have not been changed is through publicly publishing their blockchains as proof that they have not been altered. The published ledger acts as a public witness that anyone can roll back and check. It's sort of like publishing an ad in a newspaper to prove something happened.

PoET also has a lottery system that works a bit differently from other blockchains using proof of work. It randomly selects a node from the pool of validating nodes. The probability of a node being selected increases proportionally to how much processing resources that node contributed to the shared ledger. Measures may be put in place to prevent nodes from gaming the system and corrupting the ledger.

Check out Book 6, Chapter 2 for information about other consensus algorithms.

Deploying Sawtooth

The Hyperledger website has some fantastic documentation and tutorials at `https://www.hyperledger.org/use/tutorials`. When you are within the tutorials page, navigate to Hyperledger Sawtooth to go through their collection of helpful tutorials.

TIP

You may also want to review *Coding For Dummies,* by Nikhil Abraham (John Wiley & Sons, Inc.), prior to trying these tutorials.

Building Your System in Fabric

A lot of work has gone into making Fabric accessible. The Hyperledger Composer is an easy-to-use tool that allows you to create blockchain application proof of concepts (PoCs). The best part is that it will enable you to define your business network with JavaScript, one of the most popular development languages in the world. This feature alone will significantly cut down on your need for specialized blockchain developers.

The Hyperledger Composer will decrease the development time and cost and enable you to get to the production-ready stage sooner. Another benefit of the Composer is that it utilizes LoopBacks. *LoopBacks* communicate digital data streams back to your existing business system, keeping your operations in sync. You still need a good development team to do this, but you can easily mock up your business logic.

TECHNICAL STUFF

A *LoopBack* is a bit of code that sits in your software and communicates a digital data stream back to a source without intentional processing or modification.

Building Asset Tracking with Hyperledger Composer

You can try the Hyperledger Composer in your browser without needing to download any special software. The Composer also has a download option that works great if you need to work offline or need to use the Composer's full application development capabilities.

For this quick tutorial, you need a web browser and an Internet connection. In the following sections, we show you how to deploy your own network, set up a tracking demo, and move assets from one location to another. It's mostly a point-and-click demo, but you also need to copy and paste a few snippets of code.

You'll use the Animal Tracking Business Network framework. It was built as a use case for the U.K. government and farmers. In this demo, a farmer can move animals between fields, and the U.K. regulator can track the locations of the cows. The assets in this demo happen to be animals, but they could represent any type of object that needs to have its location tracked by a third party, such as a regulator or insurance provider.

Working with Smart Contracts on Hyperledger

A *smart contract* is computer code that is written inside a blockchain protocol. Smart contracts are created to facilitate, verify, or enforce the prenegotiated terms between two or more parties. The blockchain protocol takes the place of enforcement of contracts. Smart contracts, in effect, allow two or more parties to work together without trust or the need to have authoritative judgment or settlement if things go wrong. At least that's how they work in theory. Many different platforms enable smart contracts. On Hyperledger, they're called chaincode.

Chaincode is conveniently written in Go, node.js, and Java and runs in a secured Docker container. Unlike other smart contract platforms that must expose your contract to a public network to enforce them, chaincode is isolated from the endorsing peer process of public blockchains. This allows you to keep your business logic private.

Another feature that distinguishes chaincode from many other platforms is that each chaincode contract is isolated. Other organizations using Hyperledger can't access your chaincode directly unless permissioned. This feature may reduce attack vectors on your contracts by keeping third parties from accessing them.

A *smart auction* is a type of smart contract. Its function is to transfer ownership of an item after predetermined parameters of the agreement are met.

» Uncovering new investment vehicles

» Exposing risk in the banking blockchain

» Developing new financing strategies

Chapter **7**

Financial Technology

The first institutions to adopt blockchain technology were banks, governments, and other financial organizations — and they're the fastest-growing blockchain users, too. The powerful tools that are being built to manage and move money will reshape our world in new and unexpected ways, so it makes sense that financial technology (fintech) would jump onboard.

This chapter gives you the inside scoop on what governments are currently doing with blockchain technology and how it will affect you. Fintech touches your life every day, whether you're aware of it or not.

This chapter introduces you to future banking trends, new regulations, and the new tools that can help you move money faster and more cheaply. You discover new types of investment vehicles and other blockchain innovations. And finally, we warn you about potential risks of investments involving virtual currency and new blockchain-technology-enabled financial products. To read more about how blockchain technology may affect the economy of the future, head to Book 5, Chapter 1, and check out the rest of Book 5 to learn about cryptocurrency investing.

Hauling Out Your Crystal Ball: Future Banking Trends

Banking was the first industry to recognize the threat of Bitcoin and then the potential of blockchain to transform the industry. The banking sector is highly regulated, and the fees to organize and operate as a bank are expensive. These heavy regulations have been an insulating and protective shield for the whole industry, as well as a burden. The application of fast, efficient, digital money that doesn't carry the cost of handling cash and that is traceable as it moves through the financial system was an intoxicating and threatening proposal. The idea that value can be held outside the control of central authorities also piqued the interest of financial institutions and governments that back currencies.

Initially, these financial institutions and governments tried to squelch blockchain with regulation. Today, they're embracing blockchain through investment across the board.

In 2013 and 2014, the U.S. Securities and Exchange Commission (SEC) issued a warning to investors about the potential risks of investments involving virtual currency. The warning was that investors might be enticed with the promise of high returns and would not be skeptical enough of the new investment space that was so novel and cutting edge. According to the SEC, digital currency was one of the top ten threats to investors. Today, the SEC stands ready to engage with companies and investors as cryptocurrency gains traction within all industries.

Not even two years later, countries around the world — including the U.K., Canada, Australia, Japan, and China — began investigating into how they could create their own digital currencies, seize cryptocurrency for themselves, and put money on the blockchain. History was made in 2021 by Purpose Investments, a Canadian asset management company that launched the world's first Bitcoin ETF (exchange-traded fund). The Purpose Bitcoin ETF further shocked the investment world by crossing the $1 billion-in-assets mark within 30 days!

Blockchain's promise of an uncompromisable ledger has made it an appealing system for governments that are seeking to reduce fraud and improve trust. Innovations in blockchain technology promise to increase its ability to handle the billions of transactions needed to support economies, making a cryptocurrency feasible at scale.

Blockchains are in themselves permanent and unalterable records of every transaction that is inputted. Putting a country's money supply on a blockchain controlled by a central bank would be utterly transformative because there would be a permanent record of every financial transaction, existing at some level within their blockchain records, even if the records weren't viewable by the public. Blockchain technology and digital currencies would reduce risk and fraud and give central banks ultimate control in executing monetary policy and taxation. It would not be anonymous in the way that Bitcoin initially was. In fact, it would be quite the opposite, giving central banks a full and auditable trail of every digital transaction made by individuals and companies. This system might even allow central banks to replace commercial banks' role in circulating money.

The question of what the future for banking will look like can be both scary and exciting. Consumers can now pay friends through their phones almost instantly in almost any type of currency or cryptocurrency. More and more retail stores have begun utilizing cryptocurrency as a way to pay for goods and accept payment from customers. In Kenya, using cryptocurrency is now the norm. But this is still not the mainstream option for most of the world. Western markets are still in the early adoption phase.

Given that most individuals have their wealth locked into legal tender issued by governments or locked into assets that are within existing government systems, fintech innovations must merge with these existing systems before the public sees the mainstream utility of blockchain or digital currencies. If regulators find ways to tax and register accounts, then mass adoption of customer-facing wallets with digitized tokens is only two or three years down the road.

The business-to-business market will start utilizing blockchain much more quickly. In fact, a production-hardened system with the associated policies and operations is now being tested. Ripple and R3, among others, have been hard at work making this possible. These systems will first focus on the institutional creation of digitized representations of deposits. These are IOUs between internal organizational departments and between trusted partners, like vendors. Regulators, central banks, and monetary authorities are all investing heavily in making this possible. Canada and Singapore are two countries that have been moving very quickly in this direction.

Know your customer (KYC) and anti-money-laundering (AML) regulations require banks to know who they're doing business with and to ensure that they're not participating in money laundering or terrorism. Banks issuing cryptocurrencies still have significant challenges to overcome. In order to stay compliant with KYC and AML regulations, they need to know the identity of all the individuals utilizing their currency. In many cases, people's bank accounts are already offering debit and credit service transactions, like distributed ledgers in blockchains. The first candidates in this area are going to be regions where regulators, banks, and central banks work together. Singapore and Dubai are good candidates that already have blockchain initiatives: Singapore used blockchain technology to verify COVID-19 test results, and the UAE government launched the Emirates Blockchain Strategy in 2021, aiming to transform 50 percent of government transactions into the blockchain.

Moving money faster: Across borders and more

It is difficult to assess the transaction volume that needs to be met by a blockchain handling the currency of an economy like that of the U.K. or U.S. The U.S. alone is processing billions of transactions a day and over $17 trillion in value a year. That's a lot of responsibility for a new technology! The nation would be crippled if its monetary supply were compromised.

The International Monetary Fund, the World Bank, the Bank for International Settlements, and central bankers from all over the world have met to discuss blockchain technology. The first step toward faster and cheaper money would be adopting a blockchain as the protocol to facilitate bank transfers and interbank settlement. Official digital currencies that ordinary citizens use on a daily basis would come much later.

Individual consumers wouldn't directly feel the cost reduction from utilizing a blockchain for interbank settlement. The savings would be seen in the bank's bottom line as cost reductions for fees charged by intermediaries.

Consumers will still want retail locations and commercial banks for the foreseeable future. But millennials have already adopted app-activated payments through PayPal, Venmo, Cash, and more. A new way of paying through their phones won't faze them.

The great challenge is that if all money is digital, compromising it could be catastrophic. It's possible that the architecture of blockchain systems could be strong enough. Instead, the issue might be that the code within the system is executed in an unexpected manner, as happened in the decentralized autonomous organization (DAO) hack on Ethereum (see Chapter 5 of this minibook). If the cryptocurrency were operating on a traditional public blockchain, then 51 percent of the nodes in the network would have to agree to fix the issue. Getting an agreement in place might take a lot of time, and it wouldn't be practical for businesses and people who need stable and secure money at all times.

Many blockchains operate as democracies. A majority (51 percent) of a blockchain's nodes network is needed to make a change.

Creating permanent history

Data sovereignty and digital privacy are going to be huge topics in the future. Fraud prevention will be easier because if the entire economy is utilizing a cryptocurrency, then there will always be an auditable trail inside the blockchain that secures it. This is enticing for law enforcement but a nightmare for consumer privacy.

From a customer perspective, there's already an audit trail for everything you purchase with a credit or debit card. From an institutional perspective, it's beneficial to have audit trails because it increases transparency of documentation and life cycles of the movements of these assets between different regions. It adds legitimacy to the trading of assets and allows them to bake compliance into their day-to-day transactions.

The "right to be forgotten" rules in Europe, which allow citizens the right to not have their data forever propagated on the Internet, are a difficult challenge for blockchains, because blockchains can never forget. Governments and corporations would have permanent historical records of every transaction, which could be devastating to national security if they were exposed to the public. In a company's case, it may allow their competitors to have an inside scoop on how that company is investing.

The biggest challenge to using a permissionless blockchain such as Ethereum or Bitcoin would be in guaranteeing that you haven't sent money to an OFAC (Office of Foreign Assets Control) country to support terrorism. The answer is that you can't, because they are somewhat anonymous and anyone can open a wallet. It is possible to create algorithms to trace transaction movement — the U.S. government has been doing this for years — but anyone can move value in a permissionless world.

TECHNICAL STUFF

The OFAC maintains sanctions on specific organizations or individuals in what are considered high-threat countries. The government is unable to track the history of transactions when people and organizations use permissionless platforms anonymously.

The need for KYC and AML makes a case for the permissioned blockchain in the shared ledger space. The software company R3 developed Corda, a private and permissioned blockchain-like platform, to meet many of these challenges directly. They specifically do not globally broadcast the data from their participants. This keeps the data within the Corda blockchain private, and it was the primary nonfunctional requirement requested by the more than 75 banks that worked with R3 to adopt blockchain technology. They need to maintain their privacy and meet strong regulatory demands.

Going International: Global Financial Products

Blockchains will usher in many new types of securities and investment products. New markets will be opening with more efficient ways of calculating risk because collateral will be a lot more transparent and fungible across institutions when they account for it within a blockchain back system.

Blockchain technology also has applications in helping reduce scams within the global warehouse market for fraudulent double-sold goods. Blockchain entries enable manufacturers and regulators to document the provenance of products and, in turn, allow buyers to check the authenticity of what they're buying. Several solutions exist in the market, including Everledger and Provenance.

TIP

Hernando de Soto, the famous Peruvian economist, estimates that providing the world's poor with titles for their land, homes, and unregistered businesses would unlock $9.3 trillion in assets. This is what is meant by the term *dead capital*: unfinanceable real property owned by people and organizations.

It is imaginable that countries that can free their dead capital will be able to bundle and sell the interests in these assets across a global marketplace. This would include assets like transparent mortgage-backed securities for new real estate developments in Colombia or Peru.

In the future, countries will be able to free up their dead capital. Owners of undeveloped land and un-financeable properties will then have the opportunity to sell the interests in these assets across a global marketplace.

These assets will be appealing because asset managers will be able to actively parse underperforming assets given the transparency and capability of one being substituted in place of another through blockchain-based technology. The use of blockchains to manage these assets will give managers the power always to own top-performing securities, removing the rotten apples, reclassifying them, and selling them as new securities.

For non-institutional customers, micro-investments will be an attractive outlet that is enabled globally and locally through blockchain trading platforms. Using blockchain technology will also give them the means of investing in companies and their specific activities without having minimums or going through intermediaries that take a percentage of the investment.

Decentralized autonomous organizations (DAOs) are already out there and making DAO investment pools happen for a few risk-tolerant and more technically savvy investors. It may be some time before an institutional investor utilizes one of these vehicles, or a portfolio manager recommends putting money into a DAO-based vehicle for their clients.

DAOs remove a lot of the necessary paperwork and bureaucracy involved in investing by creating a blockchain-based voting system and giving shares to those who invest in their product. To any blockchain, the "code as law" concept makes it unforgiving. The risks are many, particularly when poorly written code executes in unintended ways. The consequences are that hacks to this system can be severe. The transparent nature of the system and the poor code give hackers a wider attack vector and allow them to attack multiple times as they gain more and more information with each attack.

In the following section, we discuss the effects and benefits of blockchain technology on the world economy.

Border-free payroll

Our world is global, and companies don't have borders. Instant and nearly free payroll is enticing and would save a lot of headaches for organizations. But there are drawbacks, too.

The largest risks will be with the loss of funds through hacking. If you're compensated in cryptocurrency, and you are hacked, it will be impossible to retrieve your funds. There's no dispute resolution center. There's no customer service to complain to for the loss of these funds. Thieves of digital currency have global access while being somewhat anonymous. The hacker could be anywhere.

With the current structure of blockchains, consumers are responsible for their own security. Currently, customers don't have the main burden of protecting and insuring themselves from a loss. Larger companies and governments offer protection and insurance, and they have for as long as anyone can remember. Regular individuals haven't had to protect themselves in this manner since they stopped holding their own gold during medieval times (more or less).

These challenges haven't stopped companies from processing payroll using cryptocurrency. Bitwage and BitPay are both competing in the market for payroll processing via Bitcoin. Bitwage allows employees and independent contractors to receive part of their paychecks in cryptocurrency, even if their employers don't offer the option. BitPay, on the other hand, has payroll service providers Zuman and Incoin integrated into its payment and payroll APIs. Again, early adoption is happening in areas that had nonexistent or inadequate solutions before.

Faster and better trade

Blockchains will facilitate faster and possibly more inclusive trade. Global trade finance has become restricted in recent years, and some banks, like Barclays, have even pulled out of growing African markets. They have left behind a vacuum for the finance trade, as companies still need capital to ship their goods.

DAOs and micro investments could meet that need and give investors more profitable returns than are currently available on the market. Transparency of all the goods being sold, secure identity, and seamless global tracking that is all connected to a blockchain would open up this opportunity for small investors.

The interoperability between currencies, which companies like Ripple facilitate, will also allow for more trade because they offer flexible ways of calculating foreign exchange rates than through the transfer mechanisms. The introduction of more popular digital currencies into foreign currency exchanges will add to the adaptability and integration of underserved markets.

BitPesa is a company that converts M-pesa phone minutes from Kenya into Bitcoin. With this technology, it offers businesses a faster and cheaper way to send or receive payments between Africa and China. The trade between Africa and China is a market of over $170 billion. It takes days to settle payments across borders, and the fees are high. When you use BitPesa's digital platform, payments are instantaneous and cheap.

Guaranteed payments

Guaranteed payments that are permitted through blockchain-backed transactions will increase trade in places where trust is low. Poorer countries can compete on the same playing field as wealthier nations within these types of systems. As this happens over the next ten years, the global economies will shift. The cost of commodities and labor may increase.

Global companies pay their employees based on competitive pricing, as well as on employees' previous salaries. If blockchains allow for equality across economic divides, it won't happen overnight. Developers and other knowledge workers would be the exception because it'll be easier for them to support themselves based on anonymous work.

Financial inclusion and equal global trade are very important topics for governments. Adoption of digital currencies will more likely take place nationwide in small and developing countries. Most large countries have decentralized power structures that prevent quick changes to vital systems like money.

The central power structures of small countries will allow them to leapfrog over legacy infrastructure and bureaucracy. For example, most African and South American countries don't have landlines or addresses, but they all have smartphones and the ability to create cryptocurrency wallets. The missing piece is overall trade liquidity and capacity to pay for basic needs such as utilities, rent, and food through a cryptocurrency.

Micropayments: The new nature of transactions

Micropayments are the new form of transactions. Credit card companies may use blockchain technology to settle the transaction, reduce fraud, and lower their own costs.

Global institutions like Visa and MasterCard, which provide the benefit of delayed payments, will always be needed by consumers in capitalistic societies. Even if the backend changes, you still have the same access points for customers. But physical cards will go away. In fact, that's happening now, even without blockchain technology. With blockchain technology, the customer identities behind payments will be more hardened against theft.

People still need credit to operate a business and get by personally. Credit card companies will keep making money through transaction fees. Credit runs the world, and capital markets will always exist in our current social structure. The cost of sending money between groups will decrease, but that's a good thing for financial institutions. They want to focus on the service of providing their customers with the best choices in their investment or banking markets.

Squeezing Out Fraud

Bitcoin was created as an answer to the financial crisis, where fraud and other unethical actions caused the world economy to collapse. It shifts from a "trust or doesn't trust" view of the world to a trustless system. This subtle difference is lost to most. A *trustless system* is one in which you equally trust and mistrust every person within the network. More important, the blockchain provides a framework that allows transactions to occur without trust.

These same types of frameworks can be used for more than just exchanging value over the network. Here's an example to help illustrate their potential.

If you go to a bar, a man at the door stops you and asks to see your ID. You reach into your wallet and hand him your driver's license. Your license has a lot of information on it that the bouncer doesn't need, nor should he have access to (like your address). All he needs from the ID is that you're over the age of 21. He doesn't even need to know how old you are, just that you meet the regulation requirements.

In the future, blockchain ID systems will let you choose what information you expose to what person and at what level. The more anonymous data it has, the safer it will be. Blockchain systems will help curb the theft of identity and data by not sharing information with those who don't need it or have permission to see it.

Another aspect of blockchain technology is that it will shift fraud from where it happened (past tense) to where it is currently happening in real time. Within our current system, audits are fractional postmortems of what has happened. A group of outside auditors comes in, pulls a few random files, and sees if everything is in place. Doing anything beyond this is too costly and time-consuming.

Record systems that have blockchain technology integrated within them will be able to audit a file as it's created, and flag incomplete or unusual files as they're created. This will give managers the tools they need to proactively correct files before they become a problem.

Another feature of blockchain systems will be their ability to share data with third parties transparently. In the future, sharing data will be as easy as emailing a Zip file, except the receiver will then have access to the original copy, not a copy of the file sent via email. When someone sends a file, they now have a version on their computer and the receiver has a version. With blockchain technology, the two people will be sharing only one version.

Blockchains act as a third party that witnesses the age and creation of files. They can tell at a granular level each person who interacted with a file across systems, internally and externally. They can show what is missing from a file, not just the data that is contained in it now. Blockchain files can also be shared in a redacted fashion that does not compromise the validity of documents.

What this means is that you'll be able to see the age of a file, the complete history of a file, and what it looked like over time as it evolved. More interestingly, you'll also be able to see if anything is missing from a file. This concept is called *proving the negative*. Most file systems at this point can only tell you what they have within them. But you'll be able to tell what a file *doesn't* have.

Auditing will be less expensive and more complete. Audit rules could be updated in a more centralized way. When regulatory nodes within a blockchain network have a shared and transparent view into asset transactions, the reporting of these transactions can be done through the regulator's location, without mandating 100 or more other institutions to adhere to the same rule set.

Blockchain-based systems that are fully integrated across an organization will be able to know where every penny was spent. The last mile of how money is spent is the most difficult to account for across organizations and governments. Because it's so difficult to account for, those wishing to steal funds have the opening they need.

The last mile could become a company's greatest opportunity to save wasted resources and identify corrupt individuals. Nonprofits that have strict guidelines on accounting for how they spend their money could benefit from this type of system the most. They could meet their needs for auditing and accountability to their donors without being impeded in their greater missions for good.

One system that has been explored would integrate directly into the workflow of aid workers. This system was originally designed to track medical records but could also track back all the supplies that are used with each medical patient. The benefits of this system would be monumental, given that so much fraud and theft occur within the NGO world.

Bitcoin

Contents at a Glance

» Finding out about public-key cryptography

» Sending messages to the Bitcoin ledger

» Understanding how cryptography proves you own your Bitcoin

Chapter **1**

Bitcoin Tech Explained

How Bitcoin works is a mystery to most of the world. *Don't let it be so to you!* If you're going to get involved with Bitcoin — perhaps invest in it — then you really should know what you're working with.

Although we give you an intro to Bitcoin in Book 2, Chapter 4, here we dive a little deeper because understanding the specifics of how Bitcoin functions as "money" — as well as other aspects of this cryptocurrency — is important. First, it's always nice to sound intelligent when someone asks you, "*So what is Bitcoin, anyway?*" (It's *so* embarrassing to admit that you've just invested in something and have no idea what it is!) But more importantly, if you don't understand how Bitcoin works, it's hard to keep it safe. Thousands of people have had their Bitcoin stolen from them, or have simply lost access to it, primarily because they really don't understand how it works. (It's *so* sad to know exactly where your Bitcoin is but to never be able to touch it!)

So in this chapter, we explain just that: how Bitcoin really works at a high level. We explain the specifics of securing your Bitcoin in Chapter 4 of this minibook. But for now, let's start with a high-level, Bitcoin-101 explanation of what's actually going on when you buy, sell, and store Bitcoin.

Before we get started, though, be prepared. This is complicated stuff that you don't need to remember in order to buy and sell Bitcoin. We've tried to simplify it as much as we can, and we believe that grasping this information is necessary to your understanding of a few important points, which are themselves valuable in helping you keep your Bitcoin safe. We want you to understand, at the very least, the background information that explains these critical issues:

>> Bitcoin is stored in the blockchain, *not* in your Bitcoin wallet.

>> The Bitcoin wallet stores information about your addresses in the blockchain.

>> The wallet stores the private and public keys that allow you to control your address (and thus control your Bitcoin).

Understanding That There Is No Bitcoin!

The first thing to understand is that *there is no Bitcoin*! Bitcoin as a "physical thing" doesn't exist, of course. There is no tangible object, no "thing"; no coins, no bills or notes. But more than that, if you were to dig into the programming source code that makes Bitcoin work, you wouldn't even see a "digital representation" of Bitcoins. That's because Bitcoin is, plain and simple, information about transactions.

That's okay, though. There is no physical or digital representation of most of your everyday money, either, whether you use dollars, pounds, euros, yen, or whatever. As historian Yuval Harari has said, "90 percent of all money is nothing more than entries in a computer server." You can confirm this for yourself; do an Internet search for information about different money supply numbers — M0, M1, M2, and so on — and you'll find that only around 10 percent of a major currency's value is represented by actual, physical money (M0) by bills and coins. Instead, the great majority of money is nothing more than entries in a computer server — entries in what we may term a *ledger*.

Discovering the Bitcoin Ledger

Spend some time around Bitcoin folk, and you'll start to hear talk of the *Bitcoin ledger*. So let's back up a moment. What is a ledger? The Merriam-Webster online dictionary defines a ledger as "a book containing accounts to which debits and credits are posted from books of original entry." Wikipedia defines a ledger as "a book or collection of accounts in which account transactions are recorded."

So a ledger is a record of transactions. You've seen ledgers. Your bank statement, on paper or on your computer screen, is a form of ledger. Your checkbook register is a form of ledger (does anyone still use a checkbook register?). If you use Quicken or Mint or some other form of accounting program, you've seen ledgers.

Well, there's also a Bitcoin ledger, and inside that ledger is a record of Bitcoin transactions. There is no actual Bitcoin, but there is a record of Bitcoin coming into your account and leaving the account. Which is pretty much what you see when you look at your bank statement, which is a record of currency transactions, too, payments to and from your account. It's generally not, however, a record of actual, *physical* money transactions. In fact, in the U.S., only one-quarter of transactions are cash (mostly under $25), and more than one-half of transactions are plastic (credit and debit cards). The rest are various electronic payment methods (and a few checks).

Here's a quick question for you: What's the difference between U.S. dollars and Bitcoin? With U.S. dollars, 90 percent of all the money is nothing more than entries in a computer server. With Bitcoin, it's 100 percent!

Now, the Bitcoin ledger is often described as being *immutable*. The word *immutable* means "not capable of or susceptible to change," and of course the Bitcoin ledger *can* change; hundreds of thousands of transactions are added to the ledger every day. But what *immutable* means in this context is that once a transaction has been committed to the ledger, that's it; it can't be changed. The ledger can't be "hacked" and modified, for instance. (You'll find out why in a few moments.)

So, because the ledger is immutable, it means that whatever is recorded in the ledger is the truth. If the ledger says that you own, say, half a Bitcoin, then the fact is *you own half a Bitcoin!*

So where is this "Bitcoin ledger"?

Well, there is another very important difference between everyday money and Bitcoin. The transactions are not mere entries in a computer server. Rather, they are entries in a duplicated, distributed ledger spread across a network of thousands of servers.

Bitcoin is sometimes known as a "trustless" system; not because it can't be trusted, but because trust in a single person or company isn't required. In a sense, trust is already *baked into* the system. It's "trustless" because you don't have to trust any particular individual, or any particular organization. This is because of the way the mathematics behind Bitcoin functions (keeping participants honest, in effect): It ensures that many servers are involved, and that the *system itself* can be trusted.

So we have Bitcoin transactions stored in the Bitcoin ledger. Where and how is that ledger stored? To understand that, we have to take another step back, and understand a little about blockchains.

Bitcoin uses a blockchain ledger

The Bitcoin ledger — the record of Bitcoin transactions — is saved in the Bitcoin blockchain. What's a blockchain, you ask? A *blockchain* is a very special type of database. So once again, we need to step back — very quickly this time — to ask, what's a database?

Quite simply, a *database* is an electronic store of information that is being stored in a structured format on a computer. If you open a word-processing file and type a bunch of names and addresses into a document and save it, that's not really a database; it's just a jumble of information. But if you open a spreadsheet document and save the names and addresses — first name in the first column, last name in the second column, street address in the third, and so on — then you are creating a form of simple database where the information is stored in an organized, structured format.

Blockchains are a form of database; more specifically, they are specialized, sophisticated databases with special features that make them immutable, unchangeable, and unhackable.

The first significant characteristic is (and perhaps once we've said this, it may not be a surprise) that the blockchain uses blocks of data that are, um, chained together in a manner that makes it impossible to change any piece of data — a particular transaction, for instance — without changing the entire chain of blocks (we'll explain how that works in a moment).

The other important characteristic is that the blockchain database is duplicated and distributed. Let's look at these two issues one by one, starting with the duplication and distribution.

Looking at the Bitcoin Distributed, Peer-to-Peer Network

Without the Internet, there's no Bitcoin. Bitcoin is an Internet technology, just as email and the World Wide Web are Internet technologies. And all three of these technologies require *networks*. (You might think of the Internet as the road system, and the different networks as different types of traffic — cars, trucks, buses — running over those roads.)

The Bitcoin ledger is stored on Bitcoin "nodes" on what is known as a *peer-to-peer* network: thousands of computers spread across the world. Each of these nodes contains a full copy or a portion of the blockchain, and so in effect thousands of copies of the ledger exist. Because of this, if you wanted to hack into the ledger and change a transaction, you'd have to convince all these computers to agree. By *peer-to-peer*, we mean that every one of these nodes is "equal"; there is no central server (or central group of servers) that manages the process, as there is with, say, a bank's or credit card network's transactions. Rather, the process is managed according to a set of rules by which the entire community abides (again, the rules are baked into the mathematics that runs the system).

The nodes make the entire Bitcoin system function; they add transactions — including your transactions when you buy and sell Bitcoin — to the blockchain. Some of these nodes are also *mining* nodes, by the way, the nodes that are part of the process that brings new Bitcoin into existence (in the form of what is known as a *coinbase* transaction in the blockchain, a transaction in which new Bitcoin is added to the ledger). Check out Book 6 for more about mining.

However, having said that the Bitcoin network is a *peer-to-peer* network, it also works in some ways like a *client-server* network. Consider, for instance, the email system. Computers throughout the world exist that can manage email (we call them *email servers*). And what we call *email clients (servers* provide services to *clients)* also exist. An email client is a program such as Microsoft Outlook that sends email to a server — or the web program you see when you log into Gmail or Yahoo! Mail; that's a client, too. These programs communicate with the *servers*. So, for instance, when you send email from, say, your Gmail account to, perhaps, grandma, that message first goes from your Gmail account to one of the Gmail system's email servers, which then sends the email across the Internet to the server that manages gran's email. Gran then uses her client program — Outlook, Gmail, Yahoo! Mail, or whatever — to get the email from that server.

The Bitcoin network is very similar. For example, it's a *peer-to-peer* system of *nodes* that communicate with each other, each storing a copy of part (or all) of the blockchain ledger. But most Bitcoin owners don't run one of these nodes. Instead, they have *wallets*. Now, different types of wallets exist, including what are known as *cold wallets*, wallets that are not connected to the Internet, which we introduce in Book 1, Chapter 3 and dive deeper into in Chapter 3 of this minibook. And while some of these wallets are offline most of the time, but online when needed, other wallets are never connected to the Internet at all (such as paper wallets, brain wallets, and metal wallets).

However, *hot wallets* also exist, which are essentially wallet software programs connected to the Internet (and the program might be running on a personal computer, a tablet, a smartphone, or even a dedicated computer, known as a *hardware wallet*). These hot wallets can be regarded as client programs, and the Bitcoin nodes as servers.

You, the Bitcoin owner or buyer or seller, communicate with the servers that validate transactions using your Bitcoin client program (your wallet). (Wallets, by the way, are also a form of node — a device connected to the network — but typically when someone is talking about a Bitcoin node, they are talking about more than a simple wallet.) Let's say you want to sell some Bitcoin, or buy something with Bitcoin (which is essentially the same thing, right? You give some Bitcoin to someone and in return get something back). You use your wallet to send a message to the Bitcoin network, asking the nodes to add your transaction to the blockchain, showing a transfer from your address in the blockchain to someone else's address (don't worry, we'll get to addresses in a moment!).

With us so far? There's a network of computers — the Bitcoin network — all talking to each other to manage the processing of Bitcoin transactions. Nodes exist that add transactions to the blockchain ledger, some of which are also mining, and wallets are used by individuals to manage their Bitcoin, acting as clients sending messages to the server nodes to move Bitcoin around in the ledger.

How many servers are there? It's hard to tell. Servers come, servers go, and in fact, one can run a server privately, so it can't be seen on the network. The number of active nodes fluctuates greatly, in particular based on the price of Bitcoin; as the price rises, more nodes come online, because mining becomes more profitable (remember, some nodes, but not all, are also mining Bitcoin).

Thus, estimates for the number of active nodes vary greatly; and the number you end up with also depends on what exactly you are trying to measure. Some surveys are looking for all nodes, both *full nodes* and *listening* nodes, while others are looking for only full nodes or only listening nodes.

TECHNICAL STUFF

Full nodes — or more properly, *fully validating nodes* — are those that are involved in the process of validating and adding transactions to the ledger (some of them are mining, too). A subset of these fully validating nodes are also *listening nodes* (also known as *super nodes*), which are full nodes that are publicly connectable, not behind a firewall or locked port.

When we did a quick Google search on the subject, we found sources claiming anywhere from 13,000 to 47,000 to 76,000 to 83,000 to 100,000 nodes but it doesn't really matter. Just be aware that thousands of Bitcoin servers exist that contain a partial or full copy of the ledger. And, by the way, those nodes are in scores of different countries — certainly more than 100. As a result, no single government can stop Bitcoin, should it decide to do so.

Using the Bitcoin Blockchain's Blocks of Business

So now you know about the Bitcoin network — thousands of nodes holding a copy of the ledger, along with wallets owned by ordinary Bitcoin owners (like you) which send transactions to the network. Now let's look at the actual ledger.

You found out earlier why a blockchain is known as a *blockchain*: because it chains blocks of data together. What does that mean, though? *How* are blocks chained together? Let us explain. (By the way, we're focusing here on the Bitcoin blockchain; blockchains can be used for many different purposes, and may have different characteristics, but they generally follow the same overall structure.)

First, we start with blocks of data. In the case of the Bitcoin blockchain, each block of data contains information about transactions. We'll explain *addresses* in a moment, but suffice it to say that a transaction is a record of a transfer from one address in the blockchain to another address.

Wallets send transactions to the network, and the nodes add them to a list of transactions that need to be added to the blockchain. Every ten minutes, more or less, these transactions are gathered together into a block of data, and added to the blockchain. But remember, these blocks are not merely connected to one another; they are *chained together*. In a sense, they are *locked together*, and this is done using a complicated piece of mathematics called *hashing*.

Hashing the blocks

All these blocks of data containing a record of transactions are, as you've discovered, stored on multiple computers — thousands of them, in scores of countries. That's a powerful thing in itself; how can you hack all those computers? But there's more; the chaining of the blocks from which blockchains get their name further complicates any attempt at hacking. Here's how it works.

The Bitcoin network uses a *hash* to identify each block of transactions. The block is passed through a special hashing algorithm, a bit of complex mathematics that has very useful characteristics:

>> When you hash a block of information, you end up with a very large string of characters.

>> This string of characters is unique, and only matches that particular piece of hashed data. It acts like a fingerprint, uniquely identifying a particular block of data.

>> Every time you hash the data, you will always end up with the same unique hash number.

>> If you were to change a single character in the list of transactions, the hash would no longer match. That is, should you hash the modified data *again*, you would end up with a completely different hash.

How does this hashing mathematics do all this? *You don't need to know!* We don't know, after all, so why should you? Just accept that the mathematics does all this (it does), and don't worry about *how* (you accept the way your smartphone works, but do you really know how it does?)"?.

So here's how the overall process works:

1. **A node puts together a block of transactions.**

2. **The hash — the long string of characters acting as a "fingerprint" — copied from the *previous block* is also added to the block of transactions.**

3. **The node then *hashes* the block, previous-block's hash and all. That is, it passes the combination to the hashing algorithm, which reads it and then creates the "fingerprint" the hash.**

   Here's a real example, taken from the Bitcoin blockchain:

   ```
   0000000000000000012b707bf6d172f0de94cfb311113c5d26dfe
   92764acc95
   ```

4. **The hash is added to the block of transactions.**

5. **The block of transactions is added to the blockchain.**

So, as the process moves along, and more transactions are added, we have a series of blocks of data, each containing two hashes: the hash identifying the previous block, and the new hash identifying the current block (including the current transactions *and* the previous block's hash).

That's how blocks are chained together into the blockchain (see Figure 1-1). Each block contains the previous block's hash — in effect, a copy of the previous block's unique fingerprint. Each block is also, in effect, identifying its position in the blockchain; the hash from the previous block identifies the order in which the current block sits.

The Bitcoin blockchain is "immutable"

Remember when we said earlier that the Bitcoin blockchain is *immutable*, that once created, it can't be changed? It's the hashes that make it immutable. If the

Bitcoin blockchain says you own *x* Bitcoin, then you do own *x* Bitcoin, and there can be no disagreement . . . and nobody can go into the blockchain and hack it or somehow change or alter it.

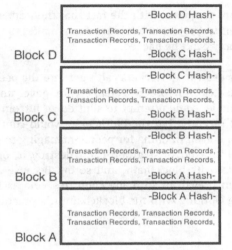

FIGURE 1-1: Each block's hash is stored in the next block of data. The hashes chain the blocks together in an orderly fashion.

Block D
-Block D Hash-
Transaction Records, Transaction Records, Transaction Records, Transaction Records,
-Block C Hash-

Block C
-Block C Hash-
Transaction Records, Transaction Records, Transaction Records, Transaction Records,
-Block B Hash-

Block B
-Block B Hash-
Transaction Records, Transaction Records, Transaction Records, Transaction Records,
-Block A Hash-

Block A
-Block A Hash-
Transaction Records, Transaction Records, Transaction Records, Transaction Records,

Imagine what would happen if someone went into a block (we'll call it Block A) and changed a little bit of data — for example, they went in and showed that instead of sending someone one Bitcoin, you sent nine.

Well, the hash in Block A would no longer match its data. Remember, a hash is a fingerprint that identifies the data, so if you change the data, the hash no longer matches.

Okay, so the hacker could rehash Block A's data and then save the "corrected" hash. But wait, now the next block (Block B) would not match because Block B is carrying Block A's original hash, and they just changed that. So now, the hacker needs to change the Block A hash stored in Block B.

But now Block B's hash doesn't match Block B's data, because that hash was created from a combination of Block B's transaction data and Block A's hash!

So, Block B would have to be rehashed, and the hash updated. But wait! That means Block B's hash stored in Block C now doesn't match!

See where we're going? This would ripple through the entire blockchain. The entire blockchain would now be broken above the "hacked" block, by modifying just one single character in that block. In order to fix the problem, the entire blockchain

Bitcoin Tech Explained

would have to be recalculated. From the hacked block onwards, it would need to be "re-mined," as they say in the Bitcoin world. What may look like a simple hack and database edit has now turned into a major computational headache that cannot be easily completed.

So, this hashing function, combined with the fact that thousands of other nodes must be in sync with identical copies of the blockchain, makes the blockchain virtually immutable; it simply can't be hacked.

Nobody can change it or destroy it. Hackers can't get into the peer-to-peer node network and create transactions in order to steal crypto, governments can't close it down (China, for example, could attempt to shut down Bitcoin within its borders, as they have tried recently, but the blockchain would continue to exist in many other countries, and even in China for people managing to get through the Chinese "Great Firewall"), a terrorist group can't destroy it, one nation can't attack another and destroy its blockchain, and so on. Because so many copies of the Bitcoin blockchain prevail in so many countries, and as long as enough people want to continue working with the blockchain, it's practically immutable and indestructible.

Finding Out How the Ledger Functions

So what do we have so far? You found out that Bitcoin is stored as a history of Bitcoin transactions in a ledger and that ledger is stored in a distributed, "immutable" blockchain, with blocks of transactions chained together, spread across scores of countries and tens of thousands of nodes. Now it's time to look into the ledger and see how it works. The first thing to know about is the *address*.

Your address: where your money is stored in the ledger

Every Bitcoin or fraction of a Bitcoin is "stored" in the ledger associated with a particular "address." An address is a unique string of letters and numbers. Here's an example of a real one I just grabbed from the Bitcoin blockchain using the blockchain explorer at www.blockchain.com:

```
1L7hHWfJL1dd7ZhQFgRv8ke1PTKAHoc9Tq
```

Trillions of different address combinations are possible, so this address is fundamentally unique. All your Bitcoin is associated with one or more addresses. There's nothing in the blockchain identifying you specifically, which is why Bitcoin is called *pseudonymous*; it's partly anonymous. Nothing in the blockchain says who owns what. However, the blockchain is also open and public. Anyone can look into the blockchain and see, within the ledger, how Bitcoin is being transferred from one address to another. So if you know who owns a particular address (as Bitcoin exchanges do, for instance; you'll find out more about those in Chapter 2 of this minibook), you can see what that person did with their Bitcoin. That's why it's not completely anonymous.

Now, where do addresses come from? They come from *wallets,* which are software programs that generate addresses mathematically from a public key, which in turn was generated from a private key. In fact, wallets contain at least one private key, one associated public key, and one associated blockchain address. Which brings us to another subject you're going to have to discover (just a little) about.

What's the crypto in cryptocurrency?

The *crypto* in cryptocurrency refers to *cryptography.* So, what exactly is cryptography?

According to The Oxford English online dictionary, cryptography is "the art of writing or solving codes." Wikipedia's explanation is more complicated and more digital: "The practice and study of techniques for secure communication . . . cryptography is about constructing and analyzing protocols that prevent third parties or the public from reading private messages."

The history of cryptography goes back at least 4,000 years. People have always needed to send secret messages now and then, and that's what cryptography is all about.

Today's cryptography, with the help of computers, is far more complicated than the ancient ciphers of the classical world, and it's used more extensively. In fact, cryptography is an integral part of the Internet; without it, the Internet just wouldn't work in the way we need it to work.

Almost every time you use your web browser, you're employing cryptography. Remember the little lock icon, shown in Figure 1-2, in your browser's Location bar?

The lock icon means the page is secured. When you send information from your browser to the web server (and receive information back), that information is *encrypted* — scrambled — so that if it's intercepted on the hundreds or thousands of miles of Internet transmission between the two, it can't be read. When your credit card number is transmitted to an e-commerce site, for example, it's scrambled by your browser, sent to the web server, and then unscrambled by the receiving server.

Ah, so, the blockchain is encrypted, right? Well, no. Cryptocurrency uses cryptography, but not to scramble the data in the blockchain. The Bitcoin blockchain is plain text which is open, public, and auditable. Figure 1-3 shows you an example of a blockchain explorer designed for Bitcoin. Using a blockchain explorer, anyone can investigate the blockchain and see every transaction that has occurred since the genesis block (the first block of Bitcoin created).

No, the cryptography in cryptocurrency isn't used to encrypt the data in the blockchain, it's used to sign messages that you send to the blockchain. These messages are the ones that trigger transactions and updates to the blockchain ledger. We'll explain this signing process in a moment, but to understand that, you have to understand a little about the magical keys.

ENCRYPTED BLOCKCHAINS

It is possible to build encrypted blockchains and encrypt data within a blockchain. For example, it is possible to create encrypted blockchains that obscure the transaction data, such as the Zcash blockchain, and some blockchains used for purposes other than cryptocurrencies may be encrypted. In general, though, cryptocurrency blockchains are not encrypted — the Bitcoin blockchain is not — so anyone can read the transactions stored within them.

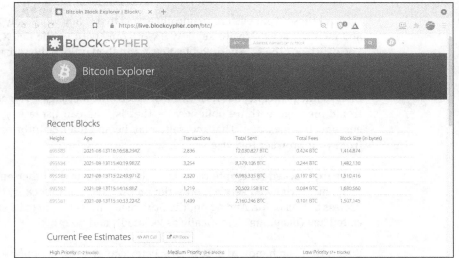

FIGURE 1-3:
An example of
a blockchain
explorer tool,
found at
`https://live.`
`blockcypher.`
`com/btc/.`

Public key encryption magic

Public key encryption is a clever little trick created using digital cryptography. This type of encryption is all accomplished using hugely complicated mathematics — the sort of mathematics that even most people with advanced degrees in mathematics don't understand, the sort of mathematics that has names like *Carmichael numbers* and *Goppa codes*, the sort of mathematics that we certainly don't understand, and you don't either (well, most of you, dear readers, don't). But that's fine; gravity isn't well understood either, but we all use it every day. So, forget *how* this amazing stuff works, and consider instead what it is actually accomplishing. Peter likes to call this *mathemagics*; sure, it's mathematics, but it's amazing and almost nobody understands it, so it might as well be magic! Here's how it works.

First, imagine a safe, with two keyholes and two associated keys. We'll call one the public key, and one the private key. Now imagine that you put something into the safe and lock it using the public key. Once the door is closed and locked, the public key no longer has access to the safe; it can't be used to unlock the safe and extract the item. The private key, however, will work. In fact, once the safe is locked, the only way to open it is to use the private key.

That's weird enough, but it gets even stranger. This magical mathematical safe actually works both ways. You can also lock it with the *private* key, but after you lock it, you can't use the private key to open the safe. Only the public key will open a safe locked with a private key.

Bitcoin Tech Explained

Oh, and these two keys are magically associated. They work only with each other and no other keys. Private Key X will work only with Public Key X, and vice versa. You can't lock the safe with Public Key X and then unlock the safe with Private Key W or Private Key K, for example.

Okay, same principle, but now think of electronic messages. You can lock an electronic message with a public key — that is, you can use a key to scramble, or encrypt, the message. That message may be an email or information being sent from your browser to a web server.

After that locked (encrypted) message is received at the other end (by the email recipient or the web server), only the private key can unlock it; the public key is useless at this point. And again, the private key must be the mathemagically associated key (okay, mathematically associated), and no other.

Encryption is a handy tool. It means Peter can give you a public key, and you can write him a message and encrypt it using the public key; once it is encrypted, nobody in the world can read it unless they have the private key. So, if Peter carefully protects his keys, he's the only person in the world who can read it.

The names of these keys aren't arbitrary. The private key should be truly private — only you, and nobody else in the world, should have access to it. The public key can be truly public. You can give it away. For example, if you want to have people email encrypted messages to you, you could publish your public key — on your website, in the footer of your emails, on your business card, or whatever — so that anybody who wants to send a message to you can encrypt it with your public key, knowing that you are the only person in the world who can read it (because you keep the private key secret).

This process is essentially what your web browser uses when you send your credit card information online; the web browser uses the web server's public key to scramble the data so that only the web browser, with the associated private key, can decrypt and read the credit card information. (Okay, that's a simplification. Browser-to-server communication is more complicated than this description, involving temporary session keys and so on; but the basic principle still applies.)

HOW DO YOU ENCRYPT EMAILS?

Email encryption has been around for decades, but it simply never caught on with the public at large. Still, you can encrypt email from most email systems, such as Outlook, Gmail, and Yahoo! Mail, and systems, such as ProtonMail, can encrypt it by default. If you're interested, you can dig deep into the Help pages.

Messages to the blockchain

That's public key encryption, then. But if the blockchain is not encrypted, what does it have to do with Bitcoin? Well, you use public-key encryption when you send transactions to the blockchain. When you want to send Bitcoin to someone else, you send an encrypted message to the blockchain saying, "Send x.xx of my Bitcoin to this address."

But wait. We just told you the blockchain isn't encrypted, and now we're telling you a message to the blockchain is encrypted! So why do you care if the message going to the blockchain is encrypted if you're just going to decrypt it anyway?

Well, remember that we told you this lock-and-unlock mechanism works both ways. You can lock with the public key and unlock with the private key or lock with the private key and unlock with the public key. Either way, the data is scrambled. The difference is in who has the ability to unscramble it. If you scramble something with the public key, the only person in the world who can unscramble it is the person with the private key. But if you scramble it with the private key, the only person in the world who can open it is . . . everybody! Anybody and everybody can get to the public key. It's public, remember!

So, what's the purpose of encrypting a message with the private key? Not to secure it, obviously, because anybody can decrypt it. No, the purpose is to *sign* the message (transaction) and prove ownership of the associated public key.

Signing messages with the private key

Let's go back to the concept of encrypted email for a moment, to help you understand. Let's say that Peter publishes his public key on his website, in his emails, and on his business cards. Now, one day you get a message that seems to come from Peter. But how can you be sure it's from him? Well, he encrypted the message using his private key. So, you take his public key (which is publicly available) and use it to decrypt the message. If the message really is from Peter, his public key will decrypt it, and you'll be able to read it. If it isn't, the decryption won't work, because it came from someone else.

So, by encrypting the message with the private key, Peter has in effect *signed the message,* proving that it came from him. The recipient knows that the message was created by the person holding the private key that is associated with the public key that opened the message up and made it readable.

Okay, back to Bitcoin. Remember that these three things are mathemagically associated with each other. Your address in the blockchain was created by your wallet software, which has a private key that was used to create a public key, and which then used the public key to create an address. All done with the magic of mathematics.

Thus, the private key is associated, through the public key, with the address. Remember also that these elements are all unique and operate with each other. The address is associated with just one private key and one public key, each of which are uniquely associated with each other.

Sending a transaction message to the Bitcoin ledger

So, here's how cryptography is used when you want to send a transaction to the blockchain, to transfer a Bitcoin balance within the ledger to another person. Let's say you own the address 1L7hHWfJL1dd7ZhQFgRv8ke1PTKAHoc9Tq. This is a real Bitcoin ledger address, by the way; when we checked, it had a balance of 0.10701382 Bitcoin.

TIP

You can see this address for yourself in a blockchain explorer. (Use this link to get to it: https://blockstream.info/address/1L7hHWfJL1dd7ZhQFgRv8ke1PTKAHoc9Tq.) By the time you see it, of course, the balance associated with the address may be different.

Now, let's say this is your Bitcoin, and you want to send, perhaps, 0.05 Bitcoin to a friend, an exchange, or a merchant from whom you are buying goods or services.

You send a message to the blockchain saying, essentially, "I own address 1L7hHWfJL1dd7ZhQFgRv8ke1PTKAHoc9Tq, and I want to send 0.05 Bitcoin to address 1NdaT7URGyG67L9nkP2TuBZjYV6yL7XepS."

If you just sent a plain text (unencrypted) message to the blockchain, there would be a huge problem of verification and validity. How would the Bitcoin node receiving this message know that you do indeed own this address and the money associated with it? You could just be spoofing this information and making it up, right?

What we do is use the wallet to sign the message using the private key associated with the address. In other words, we use the private key to encrypt the message. Then we take the public key, add it to the encrypted message, and send it all out across the Bitcoin network.

MESSAGE TO THE BLOCKCHAIN

How do you send a message to the blockchain? That's what your wallet software does. In fact, wallet software is less like a wallet — your wallet contains no Bitcoin — and more like an email program. Your email program sends messages across the email network. Your wallet sends messages (about transactions) across the Bitcoin network. More on wallets soon.

Unraveling the message

So, the node — a computer containing a copy of the Bitcoin blockchain — receives the message. It takes the public key that has been attached to the encrypted message and decrypts the message. The node "learns" something: "This message must have been encrypted — signed — by the private key associated with the public key." Of course, that's not really saying much. It's virtually a tautology! By definition, if the public key can decrypt a message, the message must have been encrypted with the matching private key. Whoop-de-doo.

But remember, the public key must be mathematically associated with the address 1L7hHWfJL1dd7ZhQFgRv8ke1PTKAHoc9Tq. So now the node can examine the address specified in the message, along with the public key sent with the message, asking, in effect, "Is the public key associated with the address?" If the answer is yes, then the node also knows that the private key held by the person sending the message is associated with the address (all three are uniquely associated with each other).

So, what does the node tell itself? It says, in effect: "This message, sending money from the address 1L7hHWfJL1dd7ZhQFgRv8ke1PTKAHoc9Tq, was sent by the private key that was used to create this same address so the address must have been sent by the person who owns the address and therefore owns the money associated with the address."

TIP

We know this concept can be confusing and hard to get your head around. So here's another way to think about it: The only person who could have sent an encrypted message with transaction instructions for this address, along with the public key that originally created the address, is the person controlling the associated private key — that is, the owner of the address and the money associated with it. Thus they are verifying ownership and validating the transaction.

So that's the crypto in cryptocurrency! You can control money in the Bitcoin blockchain ledger anonymously through the use of cryptography, using public and private key pairs and associated addresses, by cryptographically signing messages.

REMEMBER

The public key is associated with the private key; in fact, it's created from the private key. The address is associated with the public key; in fact, it's created from the public key. So, all three are mathematically, and uniquely, associated with each other.

But you'll need a wallet

TECHNICAL STUFF

As we mention earlier, it's the wallet that sends messages to the blockchain. But it's more than that. The *wallet* is where everything begins as far as your Bitcoin is concerned. When you create a wallet file, the wallet software creates a private key. That private key is used to create a public key, and the public key is used to create an address. The address has never before existed in the blockchain and still doesn't exist in the blockchain yet.

After you have an address, you have a way to store Bitcoin. You can give the address to someone from whom you're buying Bitcoin or to an exchange, for example, and they can send the Bitcoin to that address — in other words, they send a message to the blockchain saying, "Send *x* amount of Bitcoin from address *x* to address *y*." Now the address exists in the blockchain, and it has Bitcoin associated with it.

A *wallet program* is a messaging program that stores your keys and addresses in a wallet file. The wallet program does these primary things:

>> It retrieves data from the blockchain about your transactions and balance.

>> It stores your private and public keys.

>> It sends messages to the blockchain transferring your crypto from your addresses to other addresses, such as when you make a purchase using your Bitcoin.

>> It uses your public keys to create addresses you can give to other people when they need to send Bitcoin to you.

There's lots more to find out about wallets; you can discover more about them in Chapter 3 of this minibook.

REMEMBER

Here's a quick summary and an image (see Figure 1-4) to reiterate the wallet's role and to help you put it all together:

1. Bitcoin is stored in the blockchain.

2. Your Bitcoin is associated with an address in the blockchain.

3. That address is mathematically associated with a public key.

4. The public key is mathematically associated with a private key.

5. Those keys are stored in your wallet.

FIGURE 1-4:
The bitcoin is associated with an address in the blockchain; the address is derived from the public key, which is associated with a private key . . . which is kept safe in a wallet.

Chapter **2**

Buying, Using, and Selling Bitcoin

hapter 1 of this minibook shows you how this Bitcoin thing works; hopefully by now you have a good idea of how Bitcoin, merely a record in a ledger of transactions, can hold value. That chapter also shows how advanced mathematics and cryptography identify you as the owner of your Bitcoin, and how important private keys are. In this chapter, you begin to understand how to buy and sell Bitcoin.

WARNING

We suggest that you not buy a lot of Bitcoin until you really understand what you're doing because of the risks involved: the risk of having your Bitcoin stolen, of "losing" your Bitcoin, or even of being sold fake Bitcoin. We explain these risks as we go, so our recommendation is that for the moment, you do nothing more than small "test" transactions until you have a better understanding of what's going on. In particular, make that sure you read through Chapter 4 of this minibook to find out how to keep your Bitcoin safe, before going beyond small transactions.

Finding the Price of Bitcoin

Before we start, a quick note about pricing per coin — that is, the *exchange rate* between Bitcoin and dollars (or whatever local currency you're using). *Where* you buy your Bitcoin affects the price you'll pay; and in fact, pricing can range dramatically, as you find out in this chapter. So how do you know how much you *should* pay? Of course, you'll want to pay as little as possible, although if the price is too low, something fishy is going on; you may be in the middle of getting scammed in some way, and scams abound in the cryptocurrency markets. We talk a little later in this chapter about how to compare pricing and find the best rates. But a few benchmark sites can give you an idea of the ballpark you should be playing in.

First, there's Google. Go to Google and type **1btc** into the search bar; Google shows you the current price, which it gets from Coinbase, in dollars, *unless* it recognizes your computer as being in a different location. If you are in Germany, for instance, you see the price in euros. (We cover Coinbase later in this chapter, in the section, "Bitcoin exchanges.")

TIP

You can pick a different currency conversion from the drop-down list box and even specify in your search query what you want. For instance, *1btc in pounds sterling* gets you the price in British pounds.

These search strings work on Bing.com, too, but Bing gets its pricing from a company called Refinitiv, a financial news service. The Refinitiv price of Bitcoin is lower than Google's Coinbase-derived price because it's closer to the "wholesale price" than Google/Coinbase; thus, Bing.com may be a better place to check pricing. Coinbase is an exchange, so it feeds Google the price at which it is currently selling Bitcoin. And as we show you in this chapter, it does not have the best price.

Of course the bitcoin exchanges, where you can buy bitcoin, also have their own published exchange rates. So, here's the pricing for one Bitcoin at four different pricing sources (all at the same moment), from lowest price to most expensive. (You need to set up an account at BlockFi.com to see their pricing.)

Bing.com/Refinitiv	$46,422.19
BlockFi.com	$46,435.73
CoinMarketCap.com	$46,488.10
Google.com/Coinbase	$46,529.20

The reason we include BlockFi.com in this list is because, as we touch on in the section, "How to find the best exchange rate," later in this chapter, it has a pretty good price compared to other exchanges. The Bing.com price from Refinitiv is still better (slightly). This is perhaps closer to the wholesale than the retail price. That doesn't mean you can buy at this price, but at least it gives you a solid benchmark.

REMEMBER

The differences in these prices are minimal; the Google price is only 0.23 percent higher than the Bing price. Oh, and one more thing: you may be charged fees to purchase Bitcoin (you usually are), so you have to consider that when comparing sources; it's not all about the exchange rate.

Your Options for Acquiring Bitcoin

You have numerous ways to get your metaphorical hands on Bitcoin. We begin by giving you a quick list of a few options, and then show you the quickest and easiest ways for a Bitcoin newbie to get started.

TIP

You may actually be able to run out and buy a little Bitcoin at your local super-market, liquor store, or drugstore. These are not locations where you should make significant investments, but they are pretty good ways to "get your feet wet" while you follow through the instructions in this chapter.

Here are a few options for obtaining Bitcoin:

>> Buy at an ATM

>> Buy at a retail store

>> Buy from another individual (person-to-person trading)

>> Buy at an exchange

>> Earn it from credit or debit card transactions

>> Work for it

>> Mine it

>> Find it all over the place

In the sections that follow, we cover each of the first three options in the pre-ceding list in more depth, starting with the method that many people in North America can use very quickly and easily: buying from a Bitcoin ATM.

Bitcoin ATMs

The fastest and easiest way to grab a little Bitcoin is through a Bitcoin ATM. If you live in a major city in the United States, there is likely a Bitcoin ATM somewhere close by; the same is true in many other countries.

We want to say up front that buying from Bitcoin ATMs is most certainly *not* the best — or most economical — way to buy Bitcoin. But as a fast-learning experience, we think it can be worthwhile. And once you have a wallet set up by an ATM company, you can move on to other forms of purchase — such as through an exchange — and then send funds to and fro between the wallets to get familiar with using Bitcoin.

Buying Bitcoin from Coinme

To help you get a feel for how you can buy, here's a quick look at one Bitcoin ATM network. In this example, we use the Coinme network, which is the largest Bitcoin ATM network in North America, thanks to their partnership with Coinstar. In fact, they claim to be the "largest cash to Bitcoin network in the world." You may have seen the Coinstar kiosks in grocery stores, at which you can convert large quantities of loose change into cash or gift cards. (Not into Bitcoin, ironically! You can only use bills for Bitcoin.) They have 60,000 kiosks around the world, though at the time of this writing, they are only selling Bitcoin at their kiosks in the United States (at many, though not at all of them, so check the website before you rush off to buy).

We are going to use this network because it's big and, well, there's a kiosk less than a mile from co-author Peter Kent's house. We're willing to bet that you're more likely to find a Coinme ATM near *you*, too, than one from another network.

Peter bought 20 bucks' worth of Bitcoin — wait, no, $19.20 worth after they took out a 4 percent commission — at a Coinme/Coinstar kiosk. After the purchase (we'll show how this works in a moment), he checked pricing against CoinMarketCap.com, Google/Coinbase, and ATM Coiners, an ATM competitor, and discovered the following:

Coinme/Coinstar	1 BTC = $54,182.50
CoinMarketCap.com	1 BTC = $50,592.81
Google/Coinbase	1 BTC = $50,592.60
ATM Coiners	1 BTC = $50,552.77

So that means it would take $54,182.50 to buy a full Bitcoin at Coinme (before their 4 percent fee), but only $50,573.99 through Coinbase (without considering the fee). Or $50,552.77 from ATM Coiners, a smaller Bitcoin ATM network, though we don't know what fees they charge. (Bitcoin pricing fluctuates quickly, of course, but all four of these prices are from the same point in time, almost to the second.)

Interestingly, once you own Bitcoin and it's controlled by a Coinme wallet, all of a sudden Coinme shows you the *real* Bitcoin price. Peter installed a Coinme wallet on his phone, and the wallet had a price "ticker," showing a price remarkably close to that shown by Google. It also showed the day's high price: $50,997.43, apparently despite the fact that they sold the Bitcoin at the $54,182.50 price less than three hours earlier!

But wait, we're not finished. How about that fee? Coinme also takes a 4 percent transaction fee. That is, it's going to take 4 cents out of every dollar you put into the machine, before that money is used to buy Bitcoin. Buying a full Bitcoin wouldn't just cost $54,182.50; it would cost $56,440.10 — that is, almost 12 percent more than the Coinbase price! (Hidden deep within the small print on the Coinme.com website is a note that they have both the 4 percent "transaction fee" and an additional "cash convenience fee," which they build into the Bitcoin price, for a total of what they say is 11 percent. It's more like 12 percent compared to Coinbase.)

WARNING

Buying from Coinme is not the cheapest way to get Bitcoin. But hey, with the way Bitcoin fluctuates so wildly in price, you stand to make a lot of money or potentially lose it all, so what does it matter!?

PARTIAL BITCOIN?

Yes, you can buy a fraction of a Bitcoin. As we explain in Chapter 1 of this minibook, just as dollars are made up of cents, and pounds are made up of pence, Bitcoin are made up of Satoshi. The major difference is that there's a whole lot more Satoshis in a Bitcoin than cents in a dollar. One hundred million, in fact.

So, when Peter purchased $19.20 worth of Bitcoin from Coinme, at a price of $54,182.50 per BTC, he got 0.0035424 BTC um, $19.20 divided by $54,182.50 is actually 0.0003543579569, not 0.0035424, but that's what Coinme gave him. Anyway, he got 0.0035424, which is 354,240 Satoshi, or *sats*, as they say in the Bitcoin world.

Quite frankly, as we've already told you, Bitcoin ATMs are not a great way to buy Bitcoin due to the higher fees and worse exchange rate compared to other sellers. You may still want to use them just to get your feet wet. Get your hands on some Bitcoin, see a wallet in action, and you can always transfer your coin to another wallet later (we show you how). We actually think Bitcoin ATMs are a really good way to start: buy 20 bucks' worth — or ten, or less — and consider the small amount you'll lose in fees as the price of education.

So, if you don't mind the overpriced Bitcoin with a "cash convenience fee," the 4 percent commission, and the weird math apparently programmed into Coinme's machines, and you just want to get your hands on some Bitcoin, we show you how in the following steps.

You can use a different Bitcoin ATM network if you want, which may or may not be cheaper. We've seen fees of 10 percent, and they reportedly go as high as 25 percent with some networks, so be careful!

In any case, read this Coinme walk-through to get an idea of the process, and then read the note at the end of the steps about the other Bitcoin ATM networks:

1. **Find an ATM!**

   You can check using a locator page at `https://www.coinstar.com/findakiosk` or `https://CoinMe.com/locations`.

2. **Go to the ATM (okay, obviously).**

   Here's the process Peter used at the local Coinme/Coinstar kiosk.

3. **Read a bunch of small print and agree to various conditions.**

   Understand that once your cash is in the machine, you're not getting it back, it's not an anonymous transaction (that's a big misunderstanding among Bitcoin newbies), the transfer is permanent, and so on.

4. **Provide a phone number.**

   This needs to be a phone that can receive text messages. (You won't get one right now, but later in the process you'll have to enter your phone number again, and you will get a text message in response.)

   The next screen shows the exchange rate; in Peter's case, it told him that a dollar would get 0.00001845 BTC; as we're sure you quickly figured out, that's 1,845 sats.

5. **Put in as much cash as you want to change (bills only, at least $1).**

   Peter chose $20, mainly because he only had $20 bills in his wallet.

6. **Click the Buy button.**

A few moments later, out pops a "voucher." Apart from background information, the voucher contains a few really important pieces of information.

- **A redemption code:** The process isn't finished yet, as you still have to set up an account with Coinme. You'll need that redemption code to transfer the record of the purchased Bitcoin to the new wallet Coinme gives you.

- **A PIN number:** For some obscure reason.

- **A URL for the account setup webpage:** https://coinme/redeem (Note that the Coinme service — and thus these Coinme URLs — may not function outside the US; perhaps you can experiment with a bitcoin ATM service that functions in your country.)

At this point, you can complete the process in front of the kiosk, using a smartphone, or return home to use a laptop, which is what Peter opted to do.

7. **Go to http://coinme/redeem to create an account.**

It's the usual thing, you've done it a thousand times before: Enter an email address and a password, click a couple of approval buttons, and then click the Create Account button.

Save the login information into a password-management program! You have one, don't you? You really should! Find out more about protecting your information in Chapter 4 of this minibook.

REMEMBER

8. **Enter a phone number.**

Coinme confirms the number by sending it a text code; enter the code into the Coinme page.

9. **Follow the instructions to log into** https://account.coinme.com/login **on the mobile phone.**

Coinme provides a QR code that you can photograph on your phone to take you to the login page, or you can type the link into your smartphone's browser, or have Coinme text you the link. (There is an alternative process if you don't have a smartphone.)

10. **Log into the page on the smartphone.**

11. **Go through the process to identify yourself.**

Any reputable company in the United States buying and selling Bitcoin has KYC (know your customer) and AML (anti-money-laundering) regulations they have to comply with. For Coinme, this process involves copying the front and back of your driver's license, taking a selfie, and confirming the information scanned from the license. (See Figure 2-1. And you thought Bitcoin was anonymous, eh?)

QR WHAT?

By the way, a quick note for those of you who have never used a QR code (we know there are many of you). The cameras in smartphones are often set up to read these codes automatically. You can often simply point the camera at the square — what's known as a "matrix barcode" — and within a split second the camera recognizes the barcode, reads the URL (the web address) embedded into the code, and asks if you want to load the URL into your phone's web browser. As we discuss later in this chapter, most Bitcoin wallets also have QR codes and QR code readers, which you use when sending Bitcoin to the wallet. In this case, when the camera on the sending device sees the QR code, it grabs the blockchain address provided by the recipient wallet and drops it straight into the sending wallet's To Address box.

However, sometimes smartphone cameras do not automatically recognize QR codes. There should be a setting somewhere to turn this feature on. This has been a problem with many iPhones; QR scanning may require that you turn it on in the camera settings.

Finally, a little trivia for you, something your friends don't know: QR means *quick response*.

Get used to this process if you're going to play in the Bitcoin pond a while. Every company in the U.S. selling Bitcoin, that's trying to stay on the right side of the law, has these processes. You'll provide a picture of your driver's license, front and back — through your smartphone camera, through your laptop's webcam, or by scanning and uploading the images — and often take a selfie, too. You may even have to provide "proof of life," by taking a video of your head and face and moving it around a little!

At this stage, you have your new Coinme wallet (as shown in Figure 2-2). This is a *custodial wallet,* which is in the custody of Coinme. In other words, they manage the wallet for you, and all you need to remember is your login information.

This wallet has not seen any Bitcoin transactions yet. But Peter purchased $19.20 worth (well, $19.20 in Coinme/Coinstar valuation, which is more like $17 worth in real-world Bitcoin valuation).

12. **Locate the voucher from the kiosk, enter the redemption code and the PIN number, and click the big green Redeem button.**

Why both a redemption code *and* a PIN number? Hmmm, we'll think about that and get back to you

FIGURE 2-1: You're going to have to prove who you are.

FIGURE 2-2: The Coinme wallet.

Coinme sets aside in its ledger some of the Bitcoin it owns, 0.0035424 BTC (354,240 Satoshi), assigning it to you. The Bitcoin purist would say you don't really own the Bitcoin, and indeed you don't, at least not directly. Essentially, you now have an IOU from Coinme for that amount of Bitcoin.

13. **Click HOME to go back to the wallet.**

The kiosk purchase has been assigned to this wallet.

The Coinme wallet is pretty basic; obviously, it's designed to be very simple for nonexpert users. (As we've explained, ATMs are not an ideal way to buy Bitcoin.) What the wallet doesn't show is the *status* of the transaction; this is relevant because Bitcoin transactions don't happen immediately.

Understanding your custodial Coinme wallet

The Bitcoin purist will tell you that you should never allow anyone else to control your wallets, but A: hey, it's only 20 bucks, B: realistically, large quantities of Bitcoin are stored in custodial wallets, so you're by no means alone, and C: unless custodial wallets become safe and easy to use, there's really no glowing future for Bitcoin. Not everybody can be a Bitcoin expert, but not everyone has to be.

REMEMBER

Wallets *do not contain Bitcoin!* Wallets contain your address in the blockchain, and the private and public keys that control that address. The Bitcoin itself — at least, the record of the transaction — is in the blockchain associated with your address. At least, this is how wallets usually work: Each wallet controls one or more addresses, your addresses. In this case, however, your Bitcoin is being held by Coinme, in combination — commingled — with all its other clients' Bitcoin holdings. So you don't own the Bitcoin *directly*; rather, Coinme owns the Bitcoin and you are, in effect, holding an IOU from Coinme to you for the amount of Bitcoin you bought. (We show you later how to "collect on the IOU" by sending Bitcoin from Coinme to another wallet that's in your direct control.)

Notice the long, strange string of letters and numbers in the bottom-left corner of the Coinme wallet window (under the words *Bitcoin Receive Address* in Figure 2-2); that's an address to which you can send Bitcoin from another wallet, an address in the blockchain that's managed by this Coinme wallet. Click COPY, and the address is copied to your computer's clipboard. You may be wondering where this address came from, and how it got to be yours. Wallet software can create addresses as needed. When a new address is required, the software simply creates it based upon the private key.

That may sound dangerous — there are millions of wallets, so if wallets make up addresses randomly, duplicates happen, right? Well, if Bitcoin addresses were just numbers from, say, zero to a million, then yes, duplicates would occur now and then. But in fact, there are 1,461,501,637,330,902,918,203,684,832,716,283,01 9,655,932,542,976 possible combinations of Bitcoin addresses! That's enough for everybody on earth to have 196,385,600,286,334,710,857,791,565,804,391,698,4 21 addresses each!

There are so many possible combinations of these 34-character addresses that even *millions* of wallets, creating new addresses at random, are quite simply not going to create the same address twice. Okay, yes, it is *theoretically possible* (such an event is known as a *collision*). But with so many possible combinations, and the chance being so low, it is more or less impossible for it to happen — perhaps once or twice in the lifetime of the universe. (Google this subject if you don't believe us!)

So that's your new address in the blockchain. In fact, let's peek into the blockchain and take a look. Figure 2-3 shows this address, in the Blockchain.com *blockchain explorer* (https://www.blockchain.com/explorer). Blockchain explorers let you look into the blockchain and see what's going on. In this case, you can see that address 3BgtadMBFAQBqwNJoVqWwsSHzCX5uEvVck has a balance of 0 Bitcoin. In fact, it's never received any Bitcoin; remember, this is not where the Bitcoin you bought at the ATM is held. That's assigned to a Coinme addresses, and this is simply an address belonging to Peter to which he — or anyone else — can send Bitcoin.

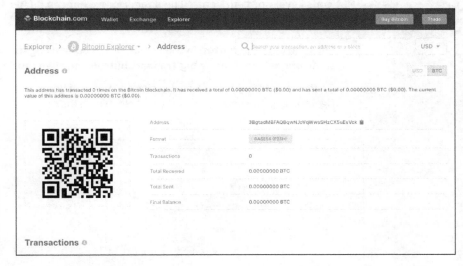

FIGURE 2-3:
The new address shown in the Blockchain. com blockchain explorer.

Notice that QR code? That is the address encoded into the QR format; someone wanting to send Peter money could scan the code from their smartphone wallet and do so. Remember that addresses are *not* private, *not* secret. Peter can send the address to someone, and they can send him money. Or *you* could type it straight from the page here and send money! Go ahead, give it a try! (Make sure that you get every character correct, please.)

3BgtadMBFAQBqwNJoVqWwsSHzCX5uEvVck

TIP

We're not suggesting that you send Bitcoin to your Coinme wallet, at least not beyond just playing around while learning. This is a super-simple wallet, managed by a third-party service that is not the optimal place to buy Bitcoin (and likely not the best place to store it, either).

If you do send Bitcoin to your Coinme account from another wallet, don't freak out if the sending wallet says it's gone but the Coinme wallet doesn't show the transaction right away. Until there are six "confirmations" that the transaction has been accepted into the blockchain, it's not regarded as completed, and so the Coinme wallet won't show it. That could take an hour or more.

Sending Bitcoin from your Coinme wallet

Later, once you have another wallet set up, you'll probably want to transfer control over your Bitcoin from your Coinme wallet to that other wallet. (See the section, "Not your keys, not your coins: The danger of exchanges," later in this chapter.) Here's how that's done:

1. **Click the big Send button in the wallet, or, if you're using the Coinme smartphone app, tap the big Transact button and then tap Send.**

   On the computer, you see a screen similar to what's shown on the left in Figure 2-4; on the phone, you see what's shown on the right.

FIGURE 2-4:
Sending Bitcoin from the Coinme web console and smartphone app.

The web app asks for a Bitcoin Address; the smartphone app asks for a Wallet Address, same thing. They are both asking for the blockchain address to which you want to send your Bitcoin.

2. **Provide this information by scanning a QR code from the wallet that controls the address you're sending to.**

Most wallets provide one. In fact, if you've been following along and have set up a Coinme account, you can see the Coinme receipt QR code by clicking the little square to the left of the *Bitcoin Receive Address*. The QR code pops up.

In this case we're sending money *from* the Coinme wallet, so it's the address from the *other* wallet we need, the wallet that manages the address to which we're sending the Bitcoin.

If you're using the smartphone app, tap the little QR icon in the top right and scan the other wallet's QR code from another phone or from your computer monitor.

If you're using the web console on your laptop or desktop and you have a webcam, click the big camera icon to scan through the webcam.

If you have both programs open on the same device — the Coinme wallet and the wallet that controls the address to which you are sending — the QR code isn't helpful. Instead, copy the address from the destination wallet and paste it into the Bitcoin Address/Wallet Address field.

3. **Enter the amount of Bitcoin (measured in dollars' worth) that you want to send to the other address.**

You can't send all the Bitcoin, because there are fees to be paid (these are paid to the miners; see Book 6). If you want to clear out the Bitcoin and send it all, you have to allow for those fees (the web console shows how much the fees are, while the smartphone app tells you what your "available balance" is after the fee). You can see the filled-out form in both the web console and smartphone app in Figure 2-4.

4. **Click the Send button and away it goes; you then see a confirmation message.**

The wallet software sends a message to the Bitcoin network. The first node picks it up, and sends it further into the network so that it also gets picked up by other nodes. This is a complicated process involving the mining of Bitcoin, but essentially, the transaction is bundled into a block of data containing a bunch of other transactions — how soon this happens depends on how much of a fee you paid — and added to the blockchain.

A few notes to keep in mind as you send Bitcoin:

>> **Most wallet software allows you to pick the fees you want to pay.** The more you pay, the faster the transaction is added to the blockchain. The Coinme wallet is very basic, so they pick the fee for you. (See Book 1, Chapter 3 for an introduction to cryptocurrency wallets; Chapter 3 of this minibook has more details about wallets in the context of Bitcoin.)

>> **Make sure you get the address to which you are sending absolutely correct!** Either copy and paste the address, or use the QR code; if you really have to type it, check, check, and check again!

If you get one character wrong, the Bitcoin will be sent to a different address and will be totally unrecoverable. In fact, what will happen is that a new address will be created in the blockchain, an address with no matching private key. This is like dropping a gold bar over the side of a ship; it will disappear into the depths. The only difference is that there's a chance that a scuba diver may one day find the gold bar; with Bitcoin, it's gone until the end of time.

>> **Most wallets provide a different address each time you request the address or QR code, so wallets can end up controlling many different addresses in the blockchain.** This isn't totally necessary, but many people believe you should use a different address for every transaction for privacy reasons.

As Satoshi Nakamoto said in his Bitcoin white paper, "a new [address] should be used for each transaction to keep [it] from being linked to a common owner. The risk is that if the owner of a key is revealed, linking could reveal other transactions that belonged to the same owner."

More Bitcoin ATM networks

There are other Bitcoin ATM networks, some of which may have better pricing. Some also allow the purchase of Bitcoin using debit cards (Coinme doesn't), though we don't believe any networks allow the use of credit cards. But, before buying — in fact, preferably before turning up at the ATM — you should ask these three questions:

>> **What's the pricing?** Some networks actually display the Bitcoin price on their websites, so you at least check the price against Google, Bing, and CoinMarketCap.com.

>> **Do you need a wallet?** The process described earlier for Coinme provides a *custodial* wallet. Some ATMs want you to set up a wallet of your own first, and then, when you buy Bitcoin from the ATM, the Bitcoin is sent to the address in the blockchain managed by your wallet. In fact, Bitcoin purists would say it's

far better for you to manage your own wallet, so they would regard these ATM networks as better than Coinme. (On the other hand, Bitcoin purists are almost certainly not buying Bitcoin from Bitcoin ATMs!)

>> **What are the transaction fees?** Figuring these out isn't always easy because some fees are hidden. Before you make a very large purchase through an ATM, do your homework (figure out the wallet issue, the pricing, and the fees), and then make a small purchase and run the math to see what the actual costs are. You shouldn't be making large purchases through a Bitcoin ATM, because you can get more BTC for your money elsewhere.

Still, perhaps you like spending more than you need to. Here are a few other Bitcoin ATM networks you can check.

>> ATM Coiners: `https://atmcoiners.com/`

>> Bitcoin Depot: `https://Bitcoindepot.com/`

>> Coinflip: `https://coinflip.tech/`

>> DigitalMint: `https://www.digitalmint.io/`

>> LibertyX: `https://libertyx.com/`

>> XBTeller: `https://www.xbteller.com/`

You can find more ATMs at a Bitcoin ATM directory such as Coin ATM Radar (`https://coinatmradar.com/`) or by Googling. These things are proliferating like proverbial rabbits. You'll find them at gas stations, liquor stores, supermarkets, and even convenience stores. Not exactly hotbeds of finance, in other words.

Retail Bitcoin

Okay, now onto the number two easy (and not advisable) way to buy Bitcoin: over the counter at a Bitcoin "retail" location. There are plenty of places in which you can purchase Bitcoin from a real live person, but some of these are simply using the retail location as a place for you to deliver cash. That is, you set up an account online, then take your requisite cash to one of the retail locations and hand it over.

LibertyX, for instance, claims to have 20,000 "trusted stores" at which you can pay cash for Bitcoin. (The company has ATMs, too.) These guys have a partnership with CVS Pharmacy and Rite Aid. You can go to `www.LibertyX.com`, find locations on a map near you, filter to remove the Debit purchases (those are through their ATMs), and select the Cash locations. Once you pick a location, you have to set up an account with LibertyX, install the LibertyX app on your smartphone, scan your driver's license front and back, and take a selfie. (It may take up to two business days, in theory — more in practice — for the information to be approved before you can buy Bitcoin.)

Also, before you can buy from LibertyX, you need a wallet set up. Unlike with the Coinme ATM transaction described in the previous section, LibertyX does not provide a wallet for these cash transactions, and so you have to provide one yourself.

Coinme has a similar system (not requiring your own wallet; as with the ATMs, Coinme provides a custodial wallet). You create an account online, use your smartphone to set up a transaction, and then take your cash to a MoneyGram location. (MoneyGram is a money transfer service, with hundreds of thousands of offices in 200 countries and territories.) You give the clerk at the counter your cash and the transaction ID, and the Bitcoin is transferred to your wallet.

Azteco is another such company (www.Azte.co). Azteco sells "vouchers" you can take to a store along with your cash, and get Bitcoin in return, which is sent directly to your own wallet. It's very popular in Europe, less so in North America, though they do have a few locations in some major cities.

There are many other places, local stores such as pawn shops and coin dealers, that buy and sell Bitcoin. Just be very careful. These sorts of transactions are not for the newbie. You really must understand how the whole Bitcoin process works, and how to use a wallet (make sure you read and understand Chapters 3 and 4 of this minibook) before you risk such purchases.

Person-to-person trading

You can, of course, buy from, and sell to, individuals. But you need to understand two things:

>> You have to have a wallet.

>> Personal transactions are very risky!

Scams abound, so be careful. Here's one common trick. The seller gives you a wallet in some form — perhaps a hardware wallet — with Bitcoin already in the wallet. If the seller had control over the wallet when handing it over to you, the seller probably still has control after. Remember, the wallet contains the private keys that control the address in the blockchain. Just because you now have the private keys, doesn't mean the seller no longer has them — they may have kept a copy of the wallet, or even of the private keys themselves (or the "seed" used to create the keys; see Chapter 3 of this minibook). By the time you get home, the Bitcoin may have been moved from the wallet and your Bitcoin is gone!

You can also find sellers in the Craigslist classifieds site; some of these sellers are store owners, such as pawn shops. Some are individuals. Again, such transactions can be very risky, especially as the seller will likely want you to turn up in person with cash to fund the transaction. We would recommend that, if a physical exchange of goods or currency for Bitcoin is required, you select a safe, neutral public place, ideally in daylight. Better still, some police stations even provide safe spaces for the exchange of goods, for Craigslist transactions, for instance. See `http://www.safetradestations.com/safetrade-station-list.html` for a list of police stations in the U.S. that provide safe trade spaces. If you can't find something on this list, call your local police station and ask.

But again, there are lots of scams, and you should not do these kinds of transactions until you really understand Bitcoin well.

LocalBitcoins.com

LocalBitcoins.com is a long-established Finnish company that puts buyers and sellers together. Sellers accept a wide range of payment methods: Apple Pay, Zelle, Walmart2Walmart transfers, PayPal, cash deposits to bank accounts, and so on. The company holds the Bitcoin in escrow. That is, the seller sends the Bitcoin to LocalBitcoins.com, you pay, and then once payment is shown to have been received, LocalBitcoins.com transfers the Bitcoin to you.

However, while until recently LocalBitcoins.com operated throughout the U.S. (and many other countries; it's one of the biggest Bitcoin marketplaces in some African countries), in the spring of 2021 it stopped trading in all U.S. locations except Florida, Connecticut, Utah, Arkansas, Nevada, Nebraska, Mississippi, Iowa, the District of Columbia, North Dakota, Minnesota, Kentucky, and Vermont.

A number of businesses in the Bitcoin arena are only semilegal, operating in a "gray area." Some LocalBitcoins.com sellers have been prosecuted for operating unlicensed MSBs (money service businesses) — one had sold $25 million worth of Bitcoin through the website.

One study (by a company called CipherTrace) showed that a huge proportion of illicit Bitcoin was being sold through LocalBitcoins.com. About 12% of all the Bitcoin flowing through the site, CipherTrace believed, was coming from criminal activity.

Bisq

Bisq (`https://bisq.network/`) is a unique decentralized person-to-person Bitcoin exchange. Bisq provides an app that facilitates the trading of Bitcoin for local (fiat) currency directly between individuals without them meeting in person, verifying identity, or needing a trusted third party to hold their Bitcoin in escrow. The Bisq network is a Bitcoin trading platform that removes the trusted third party from the equation, and is designed and operated a lot like the Bitcoin network itself.

WARNING

Bisq is an advanced system, and so perhaps only users comfortable with operating a Bitcoin node should attempt to use it.

Trusted sellers

Perhaps one of the best ways to buy Bitcoin is from a trusted friend or relative, someone who you know isn't out to rip you off. You'll need to understand how to use a wallet, of course, because you'll need a Bitcoin blockchain address to which your friend can send the Bitcoin.

Bitcoin exchanges

This section covers the places most investors are likely to use: the major Bitcoin exchanges. There are numerous exchanges, but we'll start by looking at Coinbase. We're not saying that everyone should use Coinbase, but it's a good place to start because it's the most popular exchange in the U.S. Since early 2021, it's been a public company, traded on Nasdaq (the ticker symbol is COIN). In an arena of more than 1,000 exchanges, some of which are less than reputable, the idea that Coinbase gets the kind of oversight that public companies in the U.S. are subjected to may be comforting.

They have been in business around a decade, and have literally millions of accounts, from over one hundred countries. Coinbase's holdings are also at least partially insured (rare in the cryptocurrency space!); however, their policy does not cover unauthorized access into your account. (So protect your password! See Chapter 4 of this minibook.) One more reason to go with Coinbase: At the time of this writing, when you sign up, you get $5 worth of Bitcoin to experiment with. So let's play with Coinbase, and then we'll reconvene and talk a little more about the different types of exchanges.

Buying from Coinbase

This section shows you how to set up a Coinbase account and buy a little Bitcoin.

TIP

When you visit cryptocurrency sites, make sure that you type domain names carefully and check them after typing. Large companies such as Coinbase police their domain names, registering alternative versions that are close to their primary domain name — spelling mistakes, for instance — and suing "cybersquatters," people who have registered domain names using spelling mistakes and similar terms. For instance, in 2018 Coinbase filed a complaint against a company in Hong Kong that had registered the coinbae.com domain name, and was forwarding people accidentally using this domain name to Bitcoin.com and binance.com. So you're unlikely to end up at the wrong place when trying to get to Coinbase.com, but be careful. Scams abound in the cryptocurrency space.

1. **Go to Coinbase.com, and when the home page loads, click the signup button.**

   If you're in the United States, you may see a promotional message such as "Get $5 in free Bitcoin for signing up."

2. **Do the usual KYC (know your customer) exercise: Enter your name, email address, state, and a password, click a checkbox, and click Create Account.**

3. **In the confirmation email, click the link in the email; another webpage loads.**

4. **Enter your phone number and click Submit; you're sent a text message with a verification code.**

5. **Enter the code into the text box that appears in your web browser, and click Submit.**

6. **On the next page, select your nationality from the Citizenship drop-down box.**

7. **Fill out the Verify Your Identity box: your date of birth, address, social security number, and so on.**

   You then see a box in which you have to answer a couple of questions: the amount of crypto you expect to trade each year, and the industry in which you work.

8. **Fill in your answers and click Submit.**

   And you're in, but you're not finished. Before you get your free $5 worth of Bitcoin (assuming they are still running that promotion), you need to finish verifying your ID.

9. **Click the Verify Your ID or equivalent button or link.**

   A screen appears asking you to verify your identity.

10. **Click to choose your driver's license or another form of state-issued ID card.**

    Depending on the type of device you're using, you can use your laptop's webcam or your phone's camera, or you can scan documents and upload them.

11. **Load your account with money by clicking Add Payment, choosing how to transfer funds, and following the directions.**

    You can choose a direct transfer from your bank account (surprisingly easy to set up for most banks), PayPal, debit cards (only for small amounts), and wire transfers (for large amounts).

After you are verified and have money in your account, you can buy a little Bitcoin by following these steps:

1. **Click the Buy Crypto button.**

    Up pops the transaction box, as shown in Figure 2-5.

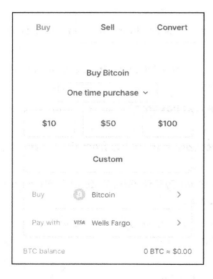

FIGURE 2-5:
Let's buy!

2. **Click the $10, $50, or $100 button, or click Custom to enter a specific sum (a minimum of $1.99 for some reason).**

3. **Click the One Time Purchase drop-down menu if you want to set up timed purchases.**

    The choices are every day, once a week, twice a month, or once a month (you can always cancel these scheduled purchases later). The little button to the right of value field, with the two up and down arrows, is for toggling the value between dollars and Bitcoin (on the right in Figure 2-5).

    The two boxes at the bottom show what you're going to buy (Bitcoin) and where the funding is coming from.

4. **Click the Bitcoin box to see a list of cryptocurrencies bought and sold by Coinbase.**

5. **When everything's set the way you want it, click Preview Buy, and Coinbase shows you a confirmation box outlining your choices (Figure 2-6).**

   Notice that the fee is coming out of the sum entered in Step 2 — in this example, $5. Coinbase subtracts a 99-cent fee, and Peter gets to buy $4.01 worth of Bitcoin. (Larger transactions have much lower fees proportional to the purchase.)

   You see a box confirming the transaction, and you're done.

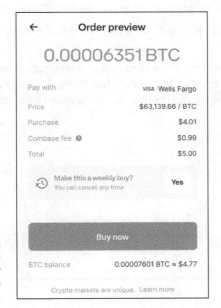

FIGURE 2-6: You're ready to buy; click Buy Now when you're sure.

What has just happened? Well, you purchased Bitcoin from Coinbase; that is, you have a custodial wallet within your Coinbase account, and Coinbase has set aside, in its own ledger, the purchased Bitcoin. You don't have an address on the Bitcoin blockchain, as all of this is internal to Coinbase; you just own legal claim to a small part of Coinbase's hundreds of millions of dollars' worth of Bitcoin.

You can find your transaction on the Assets page (sometimes called Portfolio) of the web app; on the smartphone app, you tap Assets, then tap Bitcoin in the list of currencies, and then tap the BTC Wallet.

Sending Bitcoin to another wallet

At some point you may prefer to manage your Bitcoin yourself, rather than leave it up to a third party (in this case, Coinbase) to look after it for you. You may want to send your Bitcoin to another wallet. Or you may want to use some of it to buy something. In this section, we show you how to send Bitcoin from Coinbase to somewhere or someone else. In fact, if you set up a Coinme account earlier in this chapter, you may want to play with sending a small sum to the Coinme wallet.

Go to the Coinbase web app, and follow these steps:

1. **Click the big Send/Receive button at the top. (In the smartphone app, tap the big button with two horizontal arrows at the bottom of the app, select Send, and in the screen that appears, tap the Bitcoin wallet.)**

    If you have other wallets from purchasing other cryptocurrencies, they are listed here.

    Figure 2-7 shows the Send box in the web app. (The smartphone app breaks some of these inputs into steps: the amount being sent first, then where the money is being sent, and so on.) These steps follow the web app process.

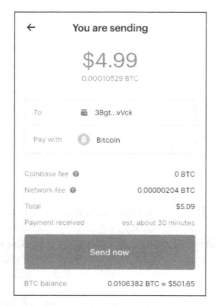

FIGURE 2-7:
Sending money from Coinbase to somewhere else.

2. **In the To box, enter a mobile number, an email address, or a wallet address.**

    Coinbase has tens of millions of accounts, and someone you know may have an account there. If you need to send Bitcoin to another Coinbase account holder, instead of sending the transaction to the blockchain, you can enter the phone number or email address the recipient used for their Coinbase account, and Coinbase will transfer Bitcoin directly to that person's Coinbase wallet. If you know the recipient has a Coinbase wallet, use this method — it's faster than sending a transaction to the blockchain, and it's free. (Sending a transaction to the blockchain is not.)

Peter is sending to an address in the blockchain controlled by another wallet using the address from his Coinme wallet (refer to Figure 2-2).

3. **Ignore the Note box unless you're sending to another Coinbase account holder and you want to add a message. The Pay With box should be set to Bitcoin.**

4. **Click Continue, and a summary box appears.**

   Notice that Coinbase isn't charging a fee for this withdrawal transaction, but a network fee does apply (which goes to the miners adding your transaction to the blockchain; Book 6 covers cryptocurrency mining in some detail, so be sure to check out that minibook.) This transaction is going to cost 0.00000204 BTC (204 Satoshi), a little over 9 cents at the time of the transaction (notice the rounding going on; we're getting charged $5.09, and sending $4.99 worth of Bitcoin). Notice also that Coinbase is estimating 30 minutes for the transaction to complete.

5. **Click Send Now.**

   You may see a warning about the dangers of sending people Bitcoin, and you get a verification code from Coinbase on your cellphone.

6. **Enter the code, and the Bitcoin is on its way.**

To see the transaction in the web app, go into the Portfolio screen (you may have to click on Assets in the left navigation column, or it may say Portfolio), and scroll down until you see Recent Transactions. Click on the most recent transaction, and you see the screen in Figure 2-8. In the smartphone app, tap Assets, scroll down and tap Bitcoin, then BTC Wallet, and finally tap your pending transaction to see information similar to what's shown in Figure 2-8:

» The amount sent, in Bitcoin and dollars, including the network fee.

» The blockchain address to which you are sending Bitcoin.

» The number of confirmations. We discussed this earlier; your transaction has to be added to all the nodes eventually, but once it's been confirmed as added by six nodes, it's regarded as irreversible. It may take a while to see all these confirmations.

» The portion of the sum you sent that is going to be paid as a fee.

>> A View Transaction link. (We'll come back to that, but here's a clue: on the smartphone app, there's a button labeled View on Blockchain Explorer instead.)

>> A line showing the date and time of the transaction, and a status; in this case, the status is Pending, because we haven't yet got our six confirmations.

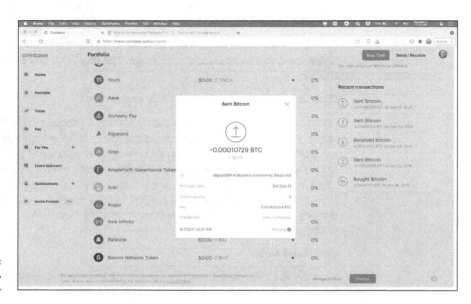

FIGURE 2-8:
Your transaction,
still pending.

Click the View Transaction link (or tap the smartphone's View on Blockchain Explorer button). A webpage opens, showing the transaction in the Blockchain. com blockchain explorer (see Figure 2-9).

And now, we're betting that you're saying, "Woah, what the &^%!! is that? Surely we're sending five bucks from one blockchain address to another, aren't we?" Well, not quite.

On the left, you see the block's hash:

```
a4ff5b80776bfd41b1574cc727652bcf0619240472c514c8e0e70a865dfc7ea2
```

We introduce the hash in Chapter 1 of this minibook; it's a kind of fingerprint that uniquely identifies the block of transactions. Below that is an address:

```
35ULAM4KDUdGX6XEiwRt3KSTU5nK1zFKNA
```

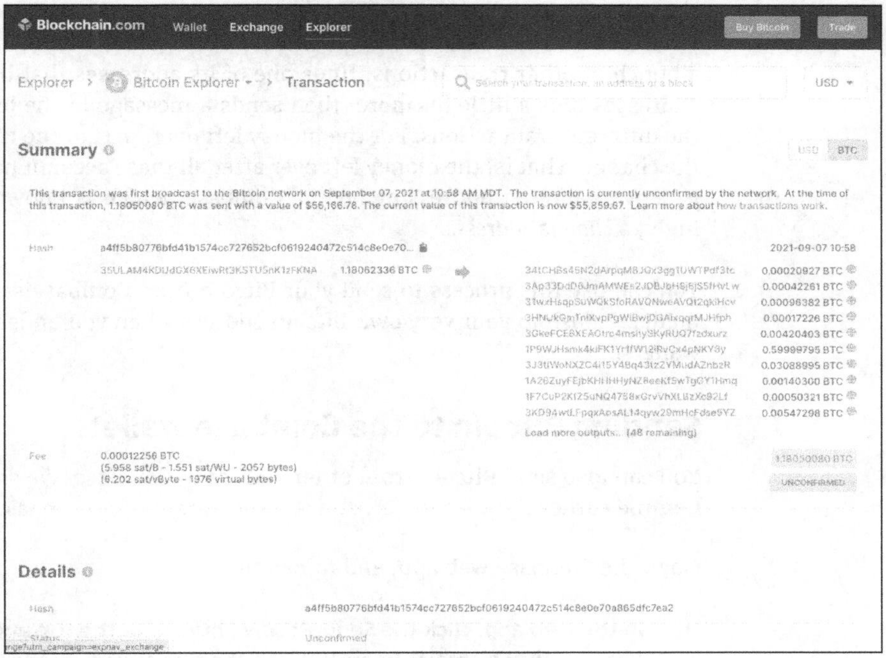

FIGURE 2-9:
Your transaction,
in the blockchain
explorer.

This is where the Bitcoin is coming from; it's one of Coinbase's blockchain addresses. It can be interesting to dig around in blockchain explorers and see what you can find. Click on that address to see a page that shows the history of the address; it is used to hold 1.18062336 BTC ($55,865.47), and in fact that's the exact sum "spent" in the current transaction, as shown on the right of the address in Figure 2-9.

On the left in Figure 2-9 is the input to the transactions. On the right are the outputs, the various addresses to which the Bitcoin is being sent. This is obviously more than a paltry five-dollar transaction (it's more than 11,000 times that).

In fact, if you look closely at the addresses on the right, you won't even see the address from Step 2 of the previous steps (3BgtadMBFAQBqwNJoVqWwsSHzCX-5uEvVck). To see that, click the "Load more outputs" link several times until the list expands to include that transaction. (Click on the address to see information about that address.)

So, here's what's going on: When you set up a Coinbase wallet and buy Bitcoin, your Bitcoin is not associated with your own address in the blockchain. Rather, you own a small part of Coinbase's huge stash of Bitcoin, and Coinbase keeps track of how much of it is yours.

When you do a Send transaction, Coinbase bundles together your transaction with a bunch of other transactions, finds one of its addresses that has the sum of the addresses plus a little bit more, then sends a message to the blockchain with all the different transactions. For the money left over, part of the transaction returns the change. That is, the money left over after all those account holder transactions is sent to another address owned by Coinbase, which is known as, not surprisingly, a *change address.*

You can use this process to send your Bitcoin from Coinbase's combined account holders' stash to your very own Bitcoin address when you understand more about wallets.

Sending Bitcoin to the Coinbase wallet

You can also send Bitcoin from other wallets to Coinbase. We show you how with Coinme earlier in this chapter, and it's very similar for Coinbase.

Go to the Coinbase web app, and follow these steps:

1. **In the web app, click the Send/Receive button at the top and then click Receive. In the smartphone app, tap the two arrows at the bottom and then tap Receive.**

   The person sending you Bitcoin can scan the QR code directly into their wallet software. Clicking the Copy button in the smartphone app (in the web app, it's a small icon showing two overlapping rectangles) lets you copy the address and then email it or text it, or copy it directly into another program. The smartphone app also has a Share Address button that lets you drop the address into another app so you can send it directly through email, or text, or whatever.

   Don't type the address! One mistyped character and the Bitcoin is gone forever.

2. **Click Share Address and wait for your Bitcoin to come in.**

Now you own an address on the Bitcoin blockchain, right? Well, not so fast. Um, no this is an address under the control of Coinbase. It's Coinbase's private keys; whoever has the keys, owns the money! Legally, you own that Bitcoin — or at least a share of the Bitcoin that Coinbase owns, equal to the amount just sent to the address — but it's in the custody of Coinbase.

If you go to a blockchain explorer later in the day, you'll probably find "your" address is already empty. Coinbase bundles up Bitcoin from numerous individual account holders' addresses — hundreds at a time — and combines them into a larger bundle on a single address. Within minutes of his five-dollar receipt,

Peter's address was empty and the five bucks ended up being combined with more than 400 other transactions, on an address holding a third of a million dollars' worth of Bitcoin.

How to find the best exchange rate

When you get started with Bitcoin, ease of use is really important. As you learn more, however, you may naturally want to focus on getting the very best deal when you buy your Bitcoin. After all, where you buy can have a huge effect on how much Bitcoin you get for your money. You've seen how expensive buying from an ATM can be, for instance, but even among the top, reputable exchanges, you'll get more Bitcoin for your buck at some than at others, though the difference is often not huge. Some of the smaller, less reputable exchanges, are expensive but some may offer a good deal.

Co-author Tyler Bain likes River.com, SwanBitcoin.com, Kraken.com, Coinbase.com, Strike.me, and Cash.app. How do you know which exchange provides the best deal? We haven't yet found a service that ranks exchanges by value for money. You can easily find lists of exchanges, perhaps even ranking them, showing how much they charge in fees. And BitcoinAverage has a handy list (`https://Bitcoinaverage.com/en/currency-markets/btc-to-usd`) comparing exchange rates between numerous exchanges. But you can't find the best deal by looking just at fees or just at exchange rates. How much Bitcoin you get for your buck is a function of two things:

>> How much is charged as fees

>> What the dollar/Bitcoin exchange rate is

Coinme "only" charges a 4% fee (you'll find that the exchanges have much lower fees), but they also adjust their exchange rate to take another seven or eight percent. That is, they sell Bitcoin at an inflated price. The Bitcoin exchanges also have varying exchange rates, with some exchanges being more favorable to you than others.

As mentioned, you can't just look at fees and ignore the exchange rate (after all, *most* of Coinme's earnings come from the exchange rate, not the fees). The only way to be sure about which exchange has the best price is to compare carefully. Look at the exchange rate, and all the fees, based on the size of transaction you're going to make. Fees may vary depending on the value of the trade, with smaller trades being charged a higher percentage. For instance, a $100 trade may be charged $2.50 — 2.5%, of course — while a $500 trade may be charged $7.50 (1.5%). In some cases, *how* you pay the fees also affects how much you pay. For example, the Binance exchange has its own cryptocurrency, Binance Coin (BNB); if you pay your fees in BNB, you get a lower rate.

We checked trades at four major exchanges that are available to U.S. customers: Coinbase, Gemini, BlockFi, and Binance. We checked pricing at the exact same time, and then figured out fees for a $500 trade. (We assumed that we would have $500 to spend, and so subtracted the fees from the $500 and then converted the remainder into Bitcoin.) We then figured out how many Satoshi we'd get for our $500, sorted Table 2-1 from best to worst, and calculated the different percentages so that you can see how they compare against the best price.

TABLE 2-1

$500 Trades Compared

Exchange	1 BTC=Dollars	Fees	Satoshi	Percent of Best
BlockFi	$52,467.78	$0	952,966	100%
Binance.US	$52,470.51	$3.75	945,769	99.25%
Gemini	$52,477.51	$7.45	938,593	98.49%
Coinbase	$52,509.28	$7.34	938,234	98.45%

The difference isn't huge, about one-and-a-half percent from the top to the bottom. In other words, Coinbase, on a $500 trade, would provide you with 1.55% *less* Bitcoin than BlockFi. (At least at that particular time and day; things change.) One way to look at this is to consider that if we assume BlockFi, the best in the table, sold us $500 worth of Bitcoin, then Coinbase sold us only $492.25 worth of Bitcoin for $500.

Still, price isn't everything. Ease of use is important, and Coinbase has a special, unusual advantage: The Bitcoin is, at least partially, insured. (Note that if someone steals your Coinbase password from you, your Bitcoin is not covered! In other words, the insurance partially covers Coinbase getting hacked, but not *you* getting hacked.)

REMEMBER

When comparing exchange rates showing how many dollars it costs to buy a Bitcoin, you are, of course, looking for the lower numbers. Smaller dollar numbers mean more Bitcoin (or Satoshi) per dollar. An exchange rate of $52,267.78 to the dollar means each dollar is worth 1,913 sats; an exchange rate of $52,509.28 is 1,904 sats.

Different types of exchanges

We describe Coinbase and Coinme (which, in effect, is a form of exchange) in the previous sections. Exchanges come in essentially two categories (with lots of permutations):

>> **Brokers:** At these exchanges, the exchange itself owns the Bitcoin, and sells it
to you or buys it back from you. The exchange often holds the Bitcoin, and
you own a portion of the holdings. Coinbase is a broker exchange.

>> **Trading platforms:** These exchanges connect buyers with sellers. They
facilitate the transaction, generally holding the funds in escrow while the
transaction completes. Binance, Bitstamp, and ShapeShift are trading
platforms.

Most of the brokers provide you with a wallet; some of the trading platforms
expect you to have your own wallet (ShapeShift, for instance), while others (such
as Bitstamp) provide a wallet, though, of course, they also allow you to transfer
to your own wallet.

Exchange brokers make money through a combination of fees and the "spread"
between the buy and sell prices. Just like the foreign-exchange desks at international airports, the price to buy Bitcoin from them is higher than the price to sell
to them. For instance, we just checked Coinbase, and if we buy one Bitcoin from
them, it will cost us $46,594.61. But if we sell a Bitcoin back to Coinbase, we'll
earn $46,072.93. So, if they buy from us, and sell to you, they make about 1.1%,
before their fees. (They charge fees for both buying and selling.)

As for the trading platforms, the price is set by you and the other party, and the
platform makes money by taking a cut of the transaction: a fee.

You can find far more advanced exchanges and trading platforms than Coinbase,
platforms designed for serious and professional traders. Here are a few well-
known and reputable systems:

>> Kraken: www.kraken.com

>> Poloniex: www.poloniex.com

>> Gemini: www.gemini.com

>> BitMEX: www.bitmex.com

>> Bitstamp: www.bitstamp.net

>> Binance: www.binance.com

>> FTX: www.ftx.us

>> ShapeShift: www.shapeshift.com

Coinbase also offers one of these more complex trading platforms, which
allows users to place market, spot, or limit orders: Coinbase Pro (https://pro.
coinbase.com/).

Not your keys, not your coins: The danger of exchanges

Before we move on, a quick word about why Bitcoin purists believe you *should not* leave your Bitcoin to be controlled by an exchange, and why you should manage your own wallet.

In February 2014, the world's leading exchange, a Japanese company named Mt. Gox, filed for bankruptcy, claiming that it had somehow lost 850,000 Bitcoins — today worth somewhere around $42 *billion* (back then, about $450 million, still nothing to sneeze at)! Over time, it was revealed that someone had been siphoning Bitcoin out of the exchange for a couple of years. Almost a quarter of the Bitcoin was eventually retrieved, but seven years later, more than three quarters have not.

Mt. Gox is not alone. Bitfinex (120,000 BTC stolen), Zaif (5,966 BTC), Altsbit (6,929 BTC, as well as a bunch of other cryptocurrencies), and *dozens* of other exchanges have been hacked, some losing Bitcoin, some losing other cryptocurrencies, some losing both.

QuadrigaCX is a Canadian exchange that lost 26,500 BTC, but wasn't hacked. When the owner died under strange circumstances, however (taking the exchange's private keys with him), account holders lost access to their Bitcoin, and discovered that in any case, much of the Bitcoin had been transferred out of the exchange a few months before his death. (Now the big question is *is he really dead*?) ShapeShift lost hundreds of thousands of dollars' worth of Bitcoin to an "inside job."

"How can this happen?" we hear you asking. "If cryptocurrency is so darn crypto, how can it possibly be hacked? Isn't the blockchain unhackable?"

Yes, it is. But these exchanges aren't. As long as the private keys that control the addresses are safe, the addresses — and the Bitcoin assigned to those addresses — are safe, too.

But the private keys have to be kept somewhere, they have to be managed by software, and the software has to be under the control of someone. So if you hack into the systems that control the private keys, then that gives you control over the addresses and the Bitcoin, too. *Not your keys, not your coins!*

Now, exchanges are certainly getting better (though a dozen were hacked in 2019, and at least one in 2020). And some, of course, are better than others. It's likely that Coinbase, for instance, invests a lot in protection. Some exchanges save large amounts of their Bitcoin in "cold wallets," which cannot be hacked into because they are "offline." Coinbase claims that 98 to 99 percent of all its crypto is stored in such wallets. And a portion of the rest is insured.

But still, this is why, according to the Bitcoin purists, you need to have your own wallets and manage your own private keys. Managing your own keys may reduce the risk of hacking and theft — but it doesn't eliminate it. And it does dramatically increase the risk of *loss* — of losing your keys, and thus losing access to the blockchain address and your Bitcoin.

Coinbase states that "In case of a covered security event, we will endeavor to make you whole. However, total losses may exceed insurance recoveries so your funds may still be lost." This is an interesting situation. While you don't directly own Bitcoin at Coinbase — you own a portion of the overall Coinbase holdings — in the event of a big hack, you would lose "your" Bitcoin.

Chapter 4 of this minibook can help you take total control and manage your own blockchain addresses, by managing your own wallet. We're not saying you *have* to do this; it's a choice you have to make. In some cases, leaving your Bitcoin on a well-managed, insured exchange may actually be safer than managing your own wallet, and the inherent problems with doing so.

"Bitcoin Back" on Credit and Debit Cards

You've seen credit cards that pay you bonuses in airline miles, or cash back. Well, how about Bitcoin? Every time you buy gas or go out for dinner, you can earn a few Satoshis. In fact, this is becoming popular with exchanges, some of which have their own credit cards. Consider the four big exchanges that we mention in the preceding sections. Gemini has a credit card coming soon, giving up to 3% Bitcoin back on purchases; BlockFi already has a Visa credit card, giving 1.5% back; Binance has a Visa card that supposedly gives up to 8% back on certain transactions; and Coinbase has a debit card paying up to 4% back when used through Apple Pay and Google Pay.

Some of these cards also allow you to *spend* your Bitcoin, too. When you buy something in dollars, the money is taken from your Bitcoin account and converted. Numerous other companies provide spending rewards. See, for instance, CoinCorner.com, FoldApp.com, Lolli.com, and Stekking.com.

Earning Your Bitcoin

One of the more recent trends in the Bitcoin market is folks demanding to be compensated for their work in Bitcoin instead of their local currency. From everyday workers, skilled laborers, and tradespeople to celebrities and professional athletes, everyone's getting in on the game. It was widely reported, late in 2020, that Russell Okung, an offensive lineman for the Carolina Panthers, was taking part of his salary — half of his $13 million! — in Bitcoin. Search Google or Twitter for *#paymeinBitcoin* and you'll find plenty of activity in this area.

In fact, a number of companies are offering the service of managing the Bitcoin payment of employees. If you want to get paid in Bitcoin, check with one of these companies:

>> **Bitwage:** https://www.bitwage.com/

>> **Strike:** https://strike.me/

You would have your employer submit your payments to the company you work with, which then converts to Bitcoin and sends the Bitcoin on to you. There are also companies that claim to help people work on freelance projects for Bitcoin, such as these:

>> **FreelanceForCoins:** https://freelanceforcoins.com/

>> **WorkingForBitcoins:** https://workingforBitcoins.com/

These freelance-directory companies are unlikely to last, though; it's a case of the tail wagging the dog. Other sites have a far greater inventory of freelance jobs listed, and if enough demand builds for payment in Bitcoin, those companies — the Upworks of the world — will do it, putting these two out of business.

WARNING

We must mention one teensy problem with this whole pay-for-Bitcoin thing: Paying employees in Bitcoin may not be legal. Certainly, demanding that employees accept Bitcoin as payment is not legal. But even if employees *want* to be paid in Bitcoin, it may still not be legal under the Fair Labor Standards Act, which specifies that wages must be paid "in cash or negotiable instrument payable at par." (And no, Bitcoin doesn't fit the definition of a "negotiable instrument" and obviously isn't cash.) Also, some states demand that wages be paid in "U.S. currency," though they often have exemptions. In Georgia, for instance, you don't have to pay your turpentine-industry employees with U.S. currency! (Turpentine is evidently a big thing in Georgia.) More usefully, Texas allows employees to opt out in writing and accept payment in another form.

Employers should only pay employees in Bitcoin if employees agree in writing (acknowledging awareness of the risks), and it's probably a good idea for employers to pay minimum base pay in U.S. currency. Having your pay submitted to an intermediary company, such as Bitwage or Strike, likely gets around these legal issues.

Mining Bitcoin

You've probably heard of the Bitcoin mines. Yep, Bitcoin is *mined*, not underground, but within computers. Bitcoin mining is very complicated, and most definitely not for the newbie. You really need to understand what you're doing and to be pretty computer literate. To mine, you need advanced computer skills and the willingness to invest significant sums in equipment and electricity. If you want to become a mining master, check out Book 6.

Finding Bitcoin Everywhere

We went into depth with a couple of mechanisms through which you can buy Bitcoin: the ATMs and the major exchanges. But there's more. Bitcoin, it seems, is popping up everywhere. You can buy it through the Robinhood investment app. You can buy it through the PayPal app. You can buy it through the Venmo app. (These apps sell Bitcoin in the U.S. and not necessarily in your country.)

Your brokerage account may let you buy into Bitcoin funds (you're buying a share in a fund that invests in Bitcoin, not Bitcoin itself) or purchase Bitcoin futures. Very soon, you'll probably be able to buy it from your bank. Bitcoin is being picked up widely in the financial industry, which is why many people are confident that it will survive, thrive, and go up in value.

REMEMBER

With most of these mechanisms, and with most of the "wallets" provided by such sources, you don't directly own any Bitcoin. Rather, you own a claim to a portion of that company's Bitcoin holdings. You don't have your own address in the blockchain. The wallet addresses belong to the company.

If you trust the organization you're working with to look after your concerns, and if the price of Bitcoin goes up, you will benefit. Bitcoin exchanges are doing their best to protect your Bitcoin, and the large companies are likely to "make customers whole" in the case of smallish hacks (as ShapeShift did in 2016). Still, hacks continue, in particular with the smaller, less-well-protected exchanges.

Selling Your Bitcoin

Selling your Bitcoin through an exchange where you bought it is generally easy. It's basically a matter of clicking the SELL button or tab and following the instructions.

But Bitcoin is money, and, of course, money can be used to buy stuff. We've shown you how to buy Bitcoin and also how to buy with it. For both Coinme and Coinbase, we'll now show you how to *send* Bitcoin to another party. That's essentially what you do when you buy something with Bitcoin. Generally, the process goes like this:

1. During the checkout process, the seller's software generates an address; this address "belongs" to your transaction, and none other.

2. You send Bitcoin to that address.

3. When the seller's software sees Bitcoin arrive at that address, it knows the payment has arrived and can complete the transaction.

There really aren't that many places you can buy things with Bitcoin. Not Amazon, not Starbucks, not Walmart. You could once buy Tesla cars with Bitcoin, but no longer. Many stores that jumped on the "buy with Bitcoin" bandwagon jumped off not long after. There's even the lovely story of the North American Bitcoin Conference in Miami, during January of 2018. With tickets at $1,000 each, the conference accepted cryptocurrency payments . . . until they didn't. They had to stop "Due to network congestion and manual processing." When it's too much hassle for a Bitcoin conference to take payments in Bitcoin, you know the problems are real!

The following list highlights three major problems with accepting Bitcoin for everyday transactions:

>> **Volatility:** The value of Bitcoin can rise and fall very quickly, sometimes within minutes. Sellers don't like seeing payments suddenly drop in value during or soon after a sale.

>> **Fees:** The buyer has to pay fees to the miners to have the transaction completed. While these fees are minimal for large transactions, they are a significant percentage of small transactions.

>> **Time:** It can take time to process Bitcoin transactions, making it completely unworkable in many retail situations. If you can buy your coffee at Starbucks with a credit or debit card within about three seconds, you're not going to stand around while your coffee gets cold waiting for six Bitcoin confirmations! (However, see Chapter 3 of this minibook for a discussion of the Lightning network, which speeds up Bitcoin transactions and is growing dramatically.)

The Bitcoin cryptocurrency is not a real currency, at least not yet. A *currency*, according to Google and the *Oxford English Dictionary*, is "a system of money in general use in a particular country." We would argue that Bitcoin is a system of money ("the assets, property, and resources owned by someone or something; wealth"), but it's by no means "in general use" in any country, let alone the United States.

Buying things with your Bitcoin doesn't make a lot of sense at the moment, any more than buying things with your gold makes sense. Currently, Bitcoin is a speculative asset, and there seem to be only two options: Either Bitcoin survives and flourishes, in which case its price will rise as it gains acceptance by a wider swath of the public, or it won't. And thus:

1. If you believe Bitcoin will rise in value in the near future, then it makes sense to own some.

2. If it makes sense to own it — because you think it will rise in value — then why on earth would you use it to buy stuff?

3. If you don't believe Bitcoin will rise in value in the near future, it doesn't make sense to own it.

4. If you don't believe Bitcoin will rise in value in the near future, then why would you own it just so you can buy things with it, when other options for purchasing abound?

Most people who own Bitcoin see it as a way to make money. Buy it, hold it (*hodl* it, as they say in the Bitcoin world; see Chapter 3 of this minibook), and the price will go up. For this reason, most people who own Bitcoin don't want to use it to buy things. They already have plenty of ways to do that (cash, credit and debit cards, ACH, checks, PayPal, Zelle, Venmo, and so on).

We're reminded of the world's most expensive pizza. In 2010, when Bitcoin was worth next to nothing, Laszlo Hanyecz found a pizzeria willing to be paid in Bitcoin. He bought two pizzas from Papa John's — the particular style is lost to history, it appears — and paid *gulp* (if you excuse the pun!) 10,000 Bitcoin! As we write this, according to Google, those pizzas cost, in today's value, $468,368,000! At its peak price so far (and many believe it will go far higher), that pizza purchase was worth $640,000,000. (We'd love to know what happened to those 10,000 coins, and how much Mr. Hanyecz enjoyed his pizza!)

Certainly, there are Bitcoin enthusiasts who look forward to the day when Bitcoin takes over and everyone's using it for everything. But even most of these people still buy their beer and groceries with cash or credit cards. True believers are stockpiling Bitcoin, not using it for everyday purchases.

Chapter **3**

Taking Control of Your Wallet (and Hodling Your Bitcoin)

We show you how to buy and sell Bitcoin using other peoples' wallets — the *custodial wallets* of the exchanges — in Chapter 2 of this minibook. Here we show you how to manage your own wallet. Before we jump in, though, we start by talking about what a wallet actually *is* (because it's not entirely clear even to most Bitcoin owners).

Bitcoin purists believe that unless you manage your own wallet, you don't truly own your Bitcoin. *Legally* you do own Bitcoin that you buy from an exchange, for instance, even if it's held by the exchange and you use a custodial wallet provided by the exchange. That hasn't helped all the people who have had their Bitcoin stolen from exchanges! To really understand Bitcoin, and have total control over your Bitcoin, you need to understand wallets. You need to *hodl* (that is, hold) your own Bitcoin for yourself. (For more about hodl, see the sidebar, "Hodl?")

HODL?

Okay, so it's a bit of Bitcoin jargon, a cryptocurrency joke. Instead of "holding" your Bitcoin, you — in Bitcoin parlance — *hodl* it. It all comes from a message posted in the Bitcoin talk forums (https://bitcointalk.org/) in 2013, from a forum member named GameKyuubi, explaining (reportedly while drunk) that he couldn't figure out the ups and downs of Bitcoin, and thus intended to simply hold (mistyped hodl) his Bitcoin for the long term. The long term has been good to GameKyuubi, if indeed he did hold long term. He created a widely used term in the Bitcoin community, and his Bitcoin went from an exchange rate of $716 per Bitcoin down to $438 and then, over the years, up to a peak (so far, at the time of this writing) of almost $64,000.

What Is a Wallet?

Physically, a wallet can be a number of things. It may be a piece of software running on a Windows PC, a Mac, or Linux machine, or any number of other computer types. It may be a piece of software running on a web server or on a smartphone or tablet. But it may also be a small device similar to a USB thumb drive. It could even be a piece of paper, a piece of metal, or even a brain! What, then, defines a wallet?

Wallets store private keys

So here's the very basic thing about wallets (without this, they're not wallets): At the very least, a wallet holds one or more *private keys*. (Or at least a way to get to your keys. A wallet may hold a wallet *seed*, which allows you to rebuild a wallet and get to the private keys, as we'll explain in this chapter.)

Your Bitcoin is associated with an address (maybe multiple addresses) in the Bitcoin blockchain ledger. That address is mathemagically associated with a public key (see Chapter 4 of this minibook). And that public key is mathemagically associated with a private key.

The address is totally public, of course; anyone can see it. Remember the blockchain explorer from Chapter 2 in this minibook? You can dig around in the blockchain and see anybody's addresses. (You can't tell who each address belongs to, but you can see how much Bitcoin is associated with each address.)

But the associated public key is also totally public. It doesn't matter who has it or who sees it. In fact, as explained in Chapter 4 in this minibook, the public key is used to sign the messages that go to the blockchain, to prove ownership of the address.

So the single most important thing that a wallet does to store your private keys (or seed). As you'll learn reading this chapter, that's *all* some wallets do: store private keys. That's essential — lose the private key, and you've lost your Bitcoin. Lose your public key or address, and that's okay; you can always re-create them if you have the private key.

TIP

Although wallets store private keys, you may never see them. Some wallets, like the BlueWallet (which we look at later in this chapter), hide them from you. Others, such as Electrum, provide a way for you to find them.

Wallets create and store keys and addresses

Some wallets can be used to *create* private keys, public keys, and addresses, and to store these things. We're talking now about software wallets, of course.

Wallet software uses complex math to create your private keys — you'll see this in action later in this chapter — and from the private keys, it creates public keys, and then it creates addresses from the public keys; again, all three are mathematically associated.

Even if you have other forms of wallet, you need a software wallet to get started; that's where you'll get your private key to begin with.

Wallets communicate with the Bitcoin network

Software wallets are designed to help you communicate with the Bitcoin network, so you can adjust the Bitcoin ledger held in the blockchain. You do this by using your wallet software to send messages to the blockchain asking the network to transfer Bitcoin from your address to someone else's. If you sell some of your Bitcoin, for instance, you'll send a message to the network, saying, "Send a bit of my Bitcoin from my address to this other person's address."

Wallets provide a way for you to remember your address so someone else can send Bitcoin to your address, such as when you are buying Bitcoin. You don't really need a wallet to *receive* Bitcoin, of course; it's your address that receives the Bitcoin, not the wallet. So you can just store your address, or the QR code, outside the wallet, and tell people where to send money.

Wallets often create new addresses so that each time you receive Bitcoin, it goes to a different address. (Although not essential, this can be a good privacy practice; see Chapter 4 of this minibook, where we discuss security issues.)

Wallets can be hot or cold

There are two important classifications of wallets: hot and cold. The distinction is simple. A *hot wallet* is a software wallet of some kind operating on a computing device — a laptop, smartphone, or whatever — that is connected to the Internet.

A *cold wallet* is any kind of wallet — software, paper, metal, anything holding private keys — that is *not* connected to the Internet. If you have a smartphone with wallet software running on it, and your device is connected to a Wi-Fi hotspot, which in turn is connected to the Internet, that's a hot wallet.

A *paper wallet* is a piece of paper with a seed or private key written on it. It's a cold wallet because (obviously) it isn't connected to the Internet (and never will be).

Some people even use old computers to do nothing but run Bitcoin wallet software. Or they have dedicated hardware wallets that operate in conjunction with wallet software running on a computing device that is connected to the Internet. The hardware wallet itself stores the private keys but is never connected to the Internet itself.

Why this distinction? It's all about the degree of security you want. A hot wallet can be hacked. For the moment, understand that cold wallets can't be hacked, because nobody can get to them across the Internet. (If you use weak passwords, perhaps a cold hardware wallet can still be "hacked" by someone who gets hold of the device, but at least it can't be hacked from afar.)

Companies with large amounts of Bitcoin often keep the bulk of it offline, in cold storage wallets. Coinbase, for instance, has something it calls the *vault*: cold wallets storing most of its Bitcoin (and probably in some kind of actual vault, too).

Exploring Wallet Hardware

So, any kind of wallet can be a cold wallet, and some can on occasion be hot wallets. But there's another type of categorization of wallets: the "hardware" the wallet is on. These are the different types of wallets you may hear about (and which we cover in this section): brain, paper, metal, hardware, web, dedicated full nodes, and software.

Brain wallets

The *brain wallet* is more theoretical than real or even practical. A brain wallet is a brain (your actual human brain) that stores (memorizes) a private key or a seed or mnemonic phrase. (*Seeds* — a unique list of a dozen or a couple of dozen short words — are used to *create* private keys, so if you save the seed, you can always re-create the private key. This concept becomes clearer when you see it in action; see the section, "Creating and securing your first wallet," later in this chapter, for more information.)

Brain wallets are, quite frankly, a terrible idea. If you have the world's best memory — if you can lock this kind of thing into your "brain vault" and are able to retrieve it months or years later — then perhaps it's practical. But what happens if you're hit by the proverbial bus? If you're the only person who knows the private key or seed, the Bitcoin dies with you! So much for passing on an inheritance.

This is also a problem if you, and only you, have the passwords to your software wallets. In Chapter 4 of this minibook, we talk about how to get around the problem of lost passwords, seeds, and private keys after one's death. You want to be able to pass on the necessary info when you get hit by that bus but keep it safe until you shuffle off this mortal coil.

Paper wallets

A *paper wallet* is, you guessed it, a piece of paper with the private key — or maybe just the *seed* — written down.

Here's the problem with paper wallets. Paper is vulnerable. It can be lost, it can burn, it can be ruined by water, it can be easily stolen. You can eliminate the physical vulnerability problems by using multiple paper wallets, of course, but then you increase the risk of theft. They are, quite frankly, not a great idea.

Metal wallets

One way around the physical vulnerability of a paper wallet is to replace the paper with metal! It won't burn, nor will it be destroyed when the pipes burst and your home floods. But it still has the problem that you need duplicates, which increases the likelihood of theft.

There are companies selling metal-wallet kits, generally designed to save the seed (see Figure 3-1) that come with a selection of characters that you can use to string together the mnemonic words. Still these are not a great idea. They are often expensive — some not so much, perhaps — and one is not enough, of course.

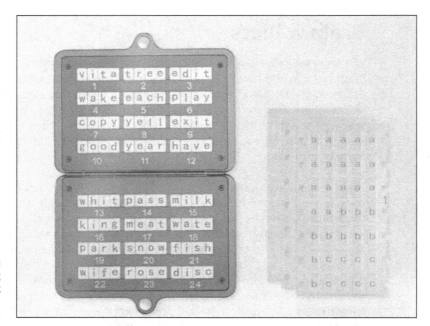

FIGURE 3-1:
The Cryptotag
metal wallet
kit (www.
cryptotag.io).

Here are a few options:

>> Billfodl: https://billfodl.com/products/the-billfodl

>> Blockplate: https://www.blockplate.com

>> Coldbit Steel: https://coldbit.com/product/coldbit-steel

>> Cryptotag: https://www.cryptotag.io

>> Cryptsteel Capsule: https://cryptosteel.com/

>> CypherWheel: https://cyphersafe.io/product/cypherwheel/

>> Key Stack: https://cryptokeystack.com

>> Seedplate: https://bitcoinseedbackup.com

Hardware wallets

A *hardware wallet* is a small, dedicated computing device that runs wallet software. You can create your own hardware wallet by getting a dedicated device — a laptop or desktop computer, a smartphone, or a tablet — installing wallet software on it, and using that device solely as a wallet. Keep it turned off most of the time and it's a cold wallet, too. (You'll often hear the term *air-gapped* to describe these things, because there's a gap — nothing but air — between the device and the Internet.)

A number of companies make dedicated hardware wallets, too. Some more recent hardware wallets are designed with two parts: One part connects to the Internet to send a transaction message to the Bitcoin network, and the other part stores the private key. The part storing the private key is never connected to the Internet, and thus cannot be easily hacked. The Ellipal device, shown in Figure 3-2, functions in this manner.

ONLY
$119.00

ELLIPAL Gold Titan

FIGURE 3-2:
An Ellipal
hardware
wallet.

We don't describe these devices in this book, but we provide enough information for you to get a good understanding of what wallets are and how they work. So, if you do decide you want one of these hardware wallets, the vendor's instructions will be enough to get you started.

WARNING

Be careful where you buy your wallet. Scammers have bought hardware wallets, opened them up, replaced the instructions with their own, repackaged them, and then sold them on eBay and Craigslist. Unsuspecting and not-so-knowledgeable buyers have then followed the instructions, which direct the user to enter a particular "seed" that creates the seller's private key on the device. Then, when the buyer of the device sends Bitcoin to the address associated with the key, the seller quickly sweeps the Bitcoin away from the address! (This will all make sense when you understand what the seed is, which you will soon.)

Here are a few popular hardware wallets:

>> BitBox02: `https://shiftcrypto.ch/bitbox02`

>> Coldcard: `https://coldcardwallet.com`

>> CoolWallet: `https://coolwallet.io`

- Ellipal: https://www.ellipal.com
- KeepKey: https://shapeshift.io/keepkey
- Ledger: https://shop.ledger.com/products/ledger-nano-s
- Trezor: https://shop.trezor.io/product/trezor-model-t

Web wallets

We show you how to set up a form of web wallet in Chapter 2 of this minibook, but that's a custodial wallet provided by an exchange, in this case Coinbase. What we're talking about here are websites where you can create an account and get a wallet that is accessible through your web browser.

WARNING

This is a pretty terrible idea. You *really* have to trust the website. Not only do the site owners need to be legitimate — and web-wallet sites have been set up to scam Bitcoin owners — but they also have to be extremely capable, providing wallet software that protects you against dishonest employees of the site and external hackers. An additional danger is that the site could go out of business, taking your private keys with it. We recommend you stay away from these.

Dedicated full nodes

Dedicated full nodes are full peers on the Bitcoin network running your own Bitcoin nodes. A node can be anything from a laptop running the Bitcoin core software (https://bitcoin.org), or as cheap and simple as a mini-computer Raspberry Pi running Raspiblitz (https://raspiblitz.com/).

This is not beginner's stuff, though, so it definitely shouldn't be your first step into the world of Bitcoin wallets. Just in case you want to learn more, though, we provide a few resources.

Dedicated hardware full nodes

Some companies sell dedicated hardware specifically designed to run Bitcoin node software right out of the box; here are a few options:

- Lightning in a Box: https://lightninginabox.co/shop
- myNode One: http://mynodebtc.com/products/one
- Nodl: https://www.nodl.it

> The Bitcoin Machine: https://thebitcoinmachines.com

> Embassy: https://start9labs.com

Full-node software

And here are a few software resources you may want to check out:

> Bcoin: https://github.com/bcoin-org/bcoin/releases

> BitcoinCore: https://bitcoin.org/en/download

> Blockcore: https://github.com/block-core/blockcore/releases

> Libbitcoin: https://github.com/libbitcoin/libbitcoin-node/releases

> RaspiBolt: https://stadicus.github.io/RaspiBolt

> Samourai Dojo: https://samouraiwallet.com/dojo

> Umbrel: https://getumbrel.com

Software wallets

A *software wallet* is simply a computer program — usually running on a Windows PC, Mac computer, Linux computer, iOS device, or Android device — that saves your keys and addresses, and enables you to communicate with the Bitcoin network. Even if you have a hardware wallet, there's a software wallet running on it.

Finding a Wallet

For the rest of this chapter, we focus on software wallets. If you like the idea of the other wallet types, you can do a little research to learn more about them. But, regardless of which wallet type you use, remember the following:

> **At some point, you must have a hot software wallet.** That's the device you're going to use to communicate your transactions to the Bitcoin network.

> **You must have a way to save the important information — private key or seed — in multiple locations.** If you save this critical information in one location, it can be destroyed, by fire, flood, computer failure, and so on. Many Bitcoin owners have lost their Bitcoin because they stored this essential information in only a single location and lost access to it. If they had just one more location, they could have recovered their Bitcoin. (Two more locations would be better.)

>> **You must have a way to save the important information so that other people cannot steal it.** Many Bitcoin owners have lost their Bitcoin because they stored this essential information insecurely — on paper wallets, for instance — and had the information stolen by someone who stumbled upon it.

REMEMBER

Another quick technical issue. We're looking at two things: first, wallet *software*; and second, the actual wallet, which is a file opened and managed by the software program. People (even us) often use the term *wallet* to mean the software, but the actual wallet is the file holding your information — private keys, public keys, addresses, and so on. The wallet software we're going to use allows you to create multiple individual wallets, and the data in each wallet is stored in a separate file.

So where do you get a wallet? As with everything else Bitcoin, it's not a simple answer. We're recommending the BlueWallet—and using it here as an example—which is very well known, popular, and widely used. So you might start there. But many wallet programs are available, with different features and usability. You may have a friend who recommends something else, for instance.

TIP

Be careful that the software you use is safe and widely reviewed and audited by the Bitcoin community. There have been many scams, such as Bitcoin-wallet software with "backdoors" that allow the software publisher to access your private keys. We recommend that you pick software that has been recommended by a reputable source. Not by your friend Joe, because he's just an individual who may himself have been tricked into picking something unsafe. Only use software that is, well, well known, popular, and widely used.

One good source is Bitcoin.org; this is the original Bitcoin website set up by Satashi Nakamoto, and it recommends a variety of wallet programs. It even provides a wizard that asks you various questions and lists the wallet programs that match your answers (`https://bitcoin.org/en/choose-your-wallet`). You might also check `https://bitcoin-only.com/wallets` and `https://www.lopp.net/bitcoin-information/recommended-wallets.html`.

Here are a few things you need to be concerned with, and some features you may find useful:

>> **Operating system:** Wallet software is mostly available for Android devices, iOS devices, Windows, macOS, and Linux. Not all programs are available for all the operating systems, so decide which operating system you're going to use first.

>> **Multiple operating systems:** You may want to run the wallet software on both a mobile device and your laptop or desktop, so it would be best to have a

program that runs on both your systems. (You can use different wallet software on different devices, but for simplicity's sake, you'll most likely want to use the same software.)

» **HD wallets:** Make sure you get an HD — hierarchical deterministic — wallet program. HD wallet programs use "seeds." Most wallet programs these days create HD wallets.

A *hierarchical deterministic wallet* is the type of wallet that you really should use, because it adds a layer of security. If it has a *seed* — a list of words — then it's an HD wallet. And this seed can help you rebuild your wallet if you run into problems. You can even enter the seed into different wallet software on a different device and recover your transactions and access to your Bitcoin. If the device on which you installed your wallet is destroyed, or lost or stolen, as long as you have your seed saved somewhere, all is not lost! You can recover everything. (Try doing that with the money under your mattress when your house burns down! We said this cryptocurrency thing was magic, eh?)

» **Multi-sig wallets:** Some programs have a function that allows you to create *multi-sig wallets,* wallets that cannot be used to send transactions to the Bitcoin network unless two or more people, using two or more wallet programs, agree. That is, there must be multiple signatures to complete the transaction. Check out the section, "Understanding multi-sig wallets," later in this chapter to learn more about them.

» **2FA:** A 2-factor authentication wallet program requires that you provide a code the software sends you (via text, or that you get from an authentication program) after logging in. Not all wallet programs have this, as it requires a 2FA server, and the programs that do have it — such as Electrum — may charge a fee to use the server.

» **Core wallets:** These are wallets that are full nodes on the blockchain; they contain much or all of the blockchain — a huge amount of data — but have a direct connection to the Bitcoin network and validate transactions. We don't recommend these for beginners and don't cover them in this book.

Setting Up a Bitcoin Wallet

In this section, we show you how to set up and work with a very popular wallet, the BlueWallet, which is available in various flavors. You can run it on your Android smartphone or tablet, your iPhone or other iOS device, or on a Mac, Windows, or Linux PC. So you can take your pick.

We're using the Mac app as an example, but the various versions work much the same way; the screen layout for each is slightly different, but your options are similar.

Creating and securing your first wallet

You can have multiple wallets; you may start with one wallet for testing and later create another wallet for your personal Bitcoin investments, another for Bitcoin you've invested for your children, and so on.

To create a wallet using BlueWallet, follow these steps:

1. **Go to** `https://bluewallet.io/` **and download and install the version you want to work with.**

    You can run it on multiple devices if you like; we show you how to duplicate your wallets on two or more devices, such as your laptop and your smartphone.

2. **Start the software; you see a screen like that shown in Figure 3-3 (in the Mac version).**

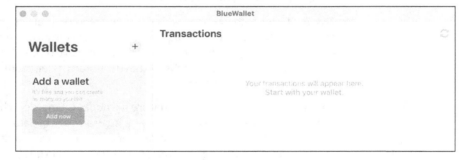

FIGURE 3-3:
The Blue home
screen.

3. **Click the + button (top right) or press the blue Add Now button.**

    The screen shown on left in Figure 3-4 appears, giving you three choices:

    - **Bitcoin wallets:** You know what these are, and this is the type we're going to work with right now.

    - **Lightning wallets:** These are for use on the Lightning Network, which interfaces with the Bitcoin network to help speed up transactions and reduce transaction fees. See the section, "Using the Lightning Network," later in this chapter, for more information.

- **Vault wallets:** This option is used to create a multi-sig wallet, a wallet that works in combination with one or more other wallets. See the section, "Creating a multiple-sig wallet," later in this chapter, to learn more.

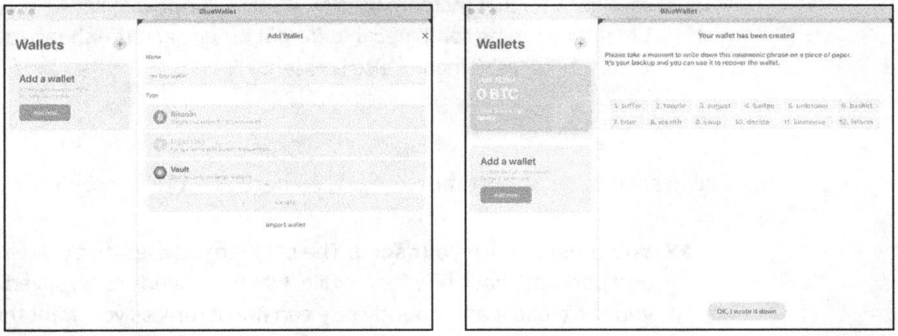

FIGURE 3-4: Picking your wallet type and saving your seed.

4. **Type a wallet name, click Bitcoin, and click Create at the bottom.**

   The screen shown on the right in Figure 3-4 appears. This screen contains your *seed:* a series of 12 words. The seed is as important to you as the private key, maybe *more* important. (Although this is generally called a seed in the Bitcoin world, Blue calls it both a *mnemonic phrase* and a *backup phrase*.)

   There are two critical things you must do with this seed:

   - *Do not forget or lose it!*
   - *Do not let it fall into the wrong hands.*

5. **Write down your seed and store it in a safe place; then click the OK I Wrote it Down button at the bottom.**

   You've created your wallet. An empty transaction screen appears (see Figure 3-5), and your wallet is ready to be used.

6. **Go to Settings or Preferences, click Security, click Encrypted and Password Protected, and enter the password twice.**

   You need to save that password carefully, too, along with your seed, in a password-management program (which you can read about in Chapter 4 in this minibook).

DIGGING INTO SEED ORIGINS

The seed is simply a list of words randomly taken from a particular dictionary of 2,048 terms. The program creates this list of terms and then runs the list through a mathematical algorithm that mathemagically creates your private key. Enough words are in the list that they can be combined in different orders, and the chance of you getting the same combination as someone else is essentially zero.

The seed is an important element, so here are a few more notes about it:

>> **You must secure your seed.** The program advises that you write it down, and perhaps that's fine for a while. Ideally, it needs to be saved securely so you can't lose it and nobody else can find it (unless you want them to have it).

There are a couple of theories about this. Co-author Tyler suggests storing the seed in a metal wallet that you keep in a safe place. Co-author Peter likes the idea of using a password-management program. No solution is perfect, and both have problems. Metal wallets can't be hacked across the Internet, of course, but you'll need at least two, each stored in a different location. Password-management programs are necessarily connected to the Internet, which bitcoin purists don't like.

THE GEEKY STUFF

By default, your wallet is going to be what is known as a SegWit HD (BIP84 Bech32 Native) wallet. It's a hierarchical deterministic (HD) wallet, so it creates multiple addresses for incoming transactions and uses the latest format of blockchain address, which can actually save you money on transaction fees. You can actually pick a couple of other formats. In the BlueWallet Preferences or Settings, select General and then Advanced Mode. Now, when you create a wallet, you can choose a type. But there's no need to do this unless you have a good reason and know what you're doing.

HD wallets have a single master private key, from which *child keys* can be created. Many wallet programs create a new address each time you want to receive Bitcoin. To do this, the wallet has to create a child private key, from which it then creates a public key, from which it creates the address. So, HD wallets have a single master private key, and numerous child private keys with associated public keys and addresses.

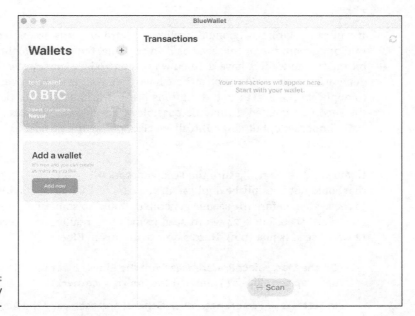

FIGURE 3-5:
Your wallet, ready
for work.

>> **You need to decide how to pass these wallets to family members in the event of your incapacitation or death.** Password-management programs provide an easy way to pass on the information (we explain how in Chapter 4 of this minibook), and duplication is easy, too. But if someone figures out your master password, you could be in trouble.

>> **Some wallet software hides the private key because the seed can be used to re-create the private key.** The theory is that you don't *need* to see it, so showing it to you simply raises an unnecessary security risk. BlueWallet does not provide a way for you to see the raw private key.

Creating a 24-word seed

In the previous section, we show you how Blue automatically generates a seed for you, and in fact all HD wallets do this — using complex mathematics and cryptographic techniques that have names like elliptic curve multiplication and hashing. They do a very good job at randomly picking a seed. The words are selected randomly from a dictionary of 2,048 words, and the order in which they appear in the seed is also random, which means there are 2^{132} possible combinations. (What's that? Well, it's 5,444,517,870,735,020,000,000,000,000,000,000,000,000 combinations. Enough for you?)

If you're working with popular wallet software or hardware, you can rely on the random generation of this seed as being unique, but some Bitcoin purists want a bit more. The wallets have defined ways to introduce randomness into the seed-generation process. In the past there have been concerns that if someone was able to duplicate the exact same conditions present in the device at the very moment the seed was created, it may be possible to regenerate the seed. This is essentially impossible, but some Bitcoin purists prefer the possibility to be *absolutely* impossible.

If you want to be *really* sure the seed generation is completely random, in a way that could not possibly be duplicated, you can, on many wallets, introduce *entropy* to the system before the seed is generated. Doing so sometimes results in not just a 12-word seed, but a 24-word seed (which you really don't need because your 12-word seed is just fine). Here's how to do this in Blue:

1. **On the Mac, select Preferences from the BlueWallet menu (in the Android app, tap the ellipsis ( ) menu in the top-right corner).**

2. **In Settings or Preferences, click General and then click the Advanced Mode switch to turn it on.**

    Now, when you create a new Bitcoin wallet, you see the additional options shown on the left in Figure 3-6.

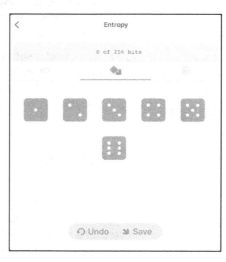

FIGURE 3-6: Advanced options enable you to add more randomness.

3. **Click the "provide entropy via dice rolls" link.**

    The screen shown on the right in Figure 3-6 appears.

4. **Click on these dice randomly, and you see the measure at the top (0 of 256 bits) increment each time you click.**

   You can also click on the little coin icon to the left of the dice icon under the count line, to see two coins, a head and a tail, on which you can randomly click as well. And there's also an icon to the right of the dice icon; click this, and you see 20 numbered boxes that you can click on.

5. **When you get to 256 of 256 bits, click Save.**

6. **In the Add Wallet box, click Create.**

   This time, a 24-word seed appears.

Increasing security with a fake account

One of the problems with Bitcoin is that it is very liquid, far more liquid than bank deposits. Suppose you have a few million dollars' worth of Bitcoin, managed by your BlueWallet program. And you also have a few million dollars in a bank account. Which can you move faster? Right, your Bitcoin.

Of course, the primary concern is hacking, and that's how most Bitcoin has been stolen over the years. But some folks have been concerned with what has been termed a *$5 wrench attack:* What happens if a mugger finds you alone at night and beats you with a wrench — regardless of the price — until you hand over your private keys?

Blue can help you in this situation with a *Plausible Deniability* option, which appears in Blue's Settings/Preferences area after you set up password protection. Click Plausible Deniability, then click the Create Encrypted Storage button that appears. The password box appears again, where you enter a *different* password, twice. You want this password to be easily remembered; you don't want to open up your password-management program to get to it.

Now, suppose one day you're forced to open BlueWallet. You enter your Plausible Deniability password, and the wallet opens, but it opens into the fake account. If you want to use this feature, you have to create a fake wallet with a little Bitcoin in it, so your deniability looks plausible!

Receiving Bitcoin

Until you have Bitcoin associated with one of your wallet addresses, it's actually not much of a wallet. So here we give you a quick look at how to send Bitcoin from another source to the wallet address. If you created a Coinme or Coinbase account while reading Chapter 2 of this minibook — or both — you might send a little Bitcoin across just to experiment. Follow these steps:

1. **If the wallet you've created isn't already open, open it by clicking on the big Wallet icon.**

   The Transactions screen appears, as shown in Figure 3-7.

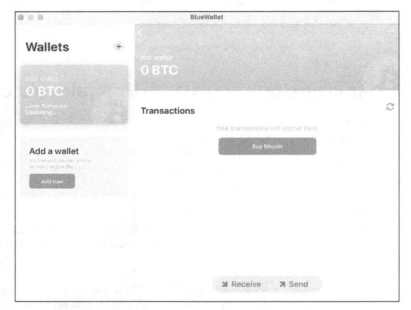

FIGURE 3-7:
The BlueWallet, ready for a transaction.

2. **Click the Receive button.**

   A QR code and notification question box appears, as shown in Figure 3-8.

3. **Choose OK to have Blue check the blockchain now and then to see when the Bitcoin has arrived, and notify you.**

   Find out more about this issue in the next section, "Getting those notifications."

4. **Take a snap of the QR code with the wallet software from which you're going to transmit your Send message.**

   Alternatively, you can click on the address shown below the QR code to copy the address to your device's clipboard, and paste it into the other wallet.

Notifications

Would you like to receive notifications when you get incoming payments?

No, and don't ask me again

OK

Ask me later

FIGURE 3-8:
Tell Blue if you want to receive a notification when your Bitcoin arrives.

5. **Click the big wallet button in Blue (on the left of the screen in Figure 3-7) to go back to the transaction screen.**

   Once you've sent the transaction from the other wallet, you can sit back and wait. It can take a little while for the transaction to process, depending on how much of a transaction fee you're paying, how busy the network is, and so on.

TIP

On the Transactions screen (refer to Figure 3-7), you can click the big blue Buy Bitcoin button to see if you can sign up for an account with a partner exchange; you may see a message saying the feature isn't available in your region. For instance, Blue may allow you to work with MoonPay (https://www.moonpay.com/). At the time of this writing, MoonPay won't sell within the United States. Perhaps a U.S. option will be available by the time you read this. In any case, this would simply be an exchange purchase, and MoonPay's exchange rate and fees may not be the best.

REMEMBER

As we caution you in Chapter 2 of this minibook, you need to check exchanges to find a good deal.

Getting those notifications

To get notifications, the wallet needs to be connected to an "Electrum server." That's your connection to the Bitcoin network, and through that network to the blockchain. Your BlueWallet talks to the Electrum server, and sends and receives information through that server.

You can set up your own Electrum server if you want — but we're not going to get into that here — or you can simply use Blue's own, default Electrum server. However, you may want to check the settings, because sometimes Blue has an intermittent problem with the connection.

Go to the wallet's Settings or Preferences, and click Network. Then click Electrum Server; the screen shown in Figure 3-9 appears. Under status, it shows the server is Connected. If it's not, try clicking the Offline Mode button to turn off the connection, then click it again to turn it back on, and the connection should reestablish. If that doesn't work, check your Internet connection.

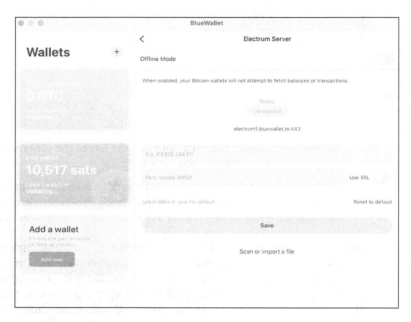

FIGURE 3-9:
The Electrum connections.

You can ignore the text boxes. Those are for people who want to run their own Electrum server, which some Bitcoin fanatics do. Again, that's an advanced subject we don't cover in this book.

TIP

If you don't have notifications turned on, click the refresh button to the right of the Transactions heading in the wallet's main screen (the little circle created by two curved arrows). Clicking this button updates the transaction to show the number of confirmations received so far.

Checking your addresses

You can look at your wallet's addresses to see where in the blockchain your Bitcoin is stored. While viewing the wallet's main screen, click the little ellipsis ( ) menu in the top right to display the wallet's information screen. Click the "Show addresses" link just above the Export/Backup button, and you see the screen in Figure 3-10. You may enjoy checking the addresses page after sending Bitcoin to your wallet the first time. You'll see exactly where it is stored.

FIGURE 3-10:
Your wallet's
addresses.

This screen shows you the addresses that have been created — more will be created as needed — and how much Bitcoin has been associated with each.

Sending Bitcoin

Once you have Bitcoin in your wallet, you can experiment with the flip side: sending Bitcoin from the BlueWallet address to another wallet's address. Here are the steps:

1. **With the wallet open, click the Send button (refer to Figure 3-7) to see the Send screen (see Figure 3-11).**

   By now, you're probably getting comfortable with this.

2. **Enter a value into the number field at the top.**

3. **(Optional) Click the little vertical arrows button on the right side to change between Bitcoin, Satoshi, and dollars.**

4. **Paste a wallet address into the Address box, or click the little Scan button to use your smartphone's camera or laptop's webcam to scan it.**

5. **(Optional) Add a note to yourself — a reminder of the purpose of the transaction — that will appear in your transactions list.**

FIGURE 3-11:
The BlueWallet
Send screen.

6. **Click the little green button on the right side of the Fee line.**

A box like that shown in Figure 3-12 appears (this time, shown in the Android app). You can determine the network or miner's fee you want to pay and choose how quickly the transaction should process: Fast, Medium, or Slow, from around 10 minutes to as much as a day.

FIGURE 3-12:
Choose your
miner's fee.

**TECHNICAL
STUFF**

The system shows you the cost in sats (Satoshis) per byte, which isn't terribly helpful. However, had we already entered a transaction value, in the left side of this box, you would see the fee translated into dollars. Fees can vary dramatically from moment to moment. You may pay 10 cents for fast processing now and a couple of dollars in a few hours.

7. **Back in the Send screen, click Next.**

You'll see a confirmation screen showing the amount you're sending, the address to which it's going, and the fee amount.

8. **Click Send Now in the confirmation screen and the bitcoin is on its way.**

TIP

The wallet is set to work with U.S. dollars by default, but you can pick whatever currency you want. Go into the Settings/Preferences for the wallet software (your selection will affect all wallets managed by the software), click Currency, and click on your currency choice in the list box that appears. The exchange rate used by the software is currently provided by CoinDesk (`https://www.coindesk.com/`).

Regarding the network's or miner's fee, by default, *fee bumping* is turned on. If network conditions change, and the fee required for your selected speed of trans-action goes up, the system can automatically bump up the fee you're willing to pay to get the same service. If you don't like this, you can turn Allow Fee Bump off in the menu that appears if you click the little menu icon in the top right of the Send screen (see Figure 3-11).

A variety of other options are available to you in this menu:

>> **Use Full Balance:** Send all the Bitcoin managed by this wallet.

>> **Sign a Transaction:** This is used for signing multi-sig transactions, a subject we discuss in the later section, "Exploring multiple signature wallets."

>> **Add/Remove a Recipient:** You can send multiple transactions in the same outgoing transaction message; doing so saves fees, because you are charged for the amount of data in your message, not the actual transaction value.

>> **Coin Control:** You will eventually have Bitcoin assigned to different addresses managed by your wallet. Coin Control gives you some control over which address will be used for the transaction; you can *freeze* an address, so the Bitcoin associated with that address is not used, or select the Use Coin option to specify that a particular address should be used.

WARNING

Be careful, though. If you find you can no longer send transactions, you may discover that you've frozen an address (coins are not frozen merely for the transaction you're working on, but for all transactions until you unfreeze the address).

TIP

If you have multiple wallets in the smartphone app, swipe right and left to switch between them. In the Mac app, it's a little more difficult. On the MacBook, a two-finger swipe on the trackpad with the mouse pointer above the Address box seems to do it.

Taking Control of Your Wallet (and Hodling Your Bitcoin)

Following the money

Don't be shocked, after sending Bitcoin somewhere, that all your Bitcoin seems to have disappeared when you check the Addresses screen (see Figure 3-12). Let's say you had an address with $100 worth of Bitcoin associated with it, you sent $5 worth to someone, and now the address has nothing! What gives?

Well, let's find out a little bit more about the idiosyncrasies of the Bitcoin blockchain. You need to understand UTXOs: *unspent transaction outputs,* which represent the amount of Bitcoin (or any cryptocurrency) that's left over after a transaction has fully completed.

When you send the transaction to the blockchain, the network takes *all* the Bitcoin from the output address, the address from which the Bitcoin is coming. It then sends the transaction amount to the recipient's address, takes out the miner's fee, and sends the rest of the Bitcoin — the unspent Bitcoin — back to an associated address, what is known as the *change address.* Refer to Figure 3-10, which is showing the Receive addresses for this transaction. Click on the Change button to see the change addresses. Figure 3-13 shows two change addresses. The first one has already been used; $1.34 is assigned to this address. The second one has not yet been used; it's been set up and is ready for the next send transaction.

FIGURE 3-13:
Your change
addresses.

Backing up your wallet

Keeping a backup of your wallet (or your wallets, if you have multiple wallets managed by Blue) helps you protect your Bitcoin (a subject we discuss further in Chapter 4 of this minibook). You may have already backed up your wallet; we suggest you do so when you first create the wallet. Similarly, Peter suggests that you save your seed (or mnemonic phrase or backup phrase, as Blue calls it) in a password-management program; Tyler recommends a metal wallet. One way or another, you should save this information, even if you write it on a piece of paper. That's not a great idea, but it's better than nothing.

If you didn't save the seed when you created the wallet, Blue provides a menu option so you can get back to it:

1. **Open the wallet, then click the ellipsis ( ) menu in the top right of the screen, which opens the screen shown on the left in Figure 3-14.**

    This screen shows you basic information about the wallet: the name and type of wallet, and so on.

FIGURE 3-14:
Checking out basic wallet info and the export info with a seed.

2. **Click the Export/Backup button to see the box on right in Figure 3-14.**

    The seed is at the bottom of the box (you may have to scroll down), with the words appearing in a tiny row.

3. **If you haven't done so already, save this in a password program or write it down.**

    You can't copy it to the clipboard, so whether you write it on paper or type it into a password program, *do it very carefully and check then check again*. One small typo — type *kit* instead of *kite*, for instance — and the seed is useless. How can the seed be a "backup" of the wallet? Don't worry about that; we'll explain in a moment.

TIP

You could also take a screenshot of the screen shown on right in Figure 3-14 and print it or save it. (Note that this is a bad long-term security practice, although perhaps okay temporarily.) Of course, Figure 3-14 also shows a QR code; this encodes the seed, allowing you to import the wallet on another device, which we discuss in the next section. You'll be able to snap the QR code during the Import process.

Importing (or recovering) a wallet

Blue also provides a way to import a wallet from another program, which is the same process you can use to recover a lost wallet (which you can do because you saved your seed, right?).

For instance, perhaps you want to manage your Bitcoin on both your smartphone *and* your MacBook. You could create the wallet on one device, and import it into Blue on the other device. At that point, you would have two wallet programs, each capable of sending transactions to the network and each tracking transactions on the same addresses.

If your BlueWallet is on your iPhone, and it's stolen, you can recover the wallet on your *new* iPhone, or any other device on which Blue runs: Mac, Windows, Android, or Linux. You can even recover your wallet on some other wallet programs, too, such as the Electrum wallet. Here's how:

1. **In the main BlueWallet screen, click the Add Now button (refer to Figure 3-3).**

2. **Click the Import Wallet link, at the bottom of the screen in Figure 3-4.**

   An Import screen appears, as shown in Figure 3-15.

FIGURE 3-15:
The wallet
import box.

3. **Type the seed into this box.**

You have a few alternative ways of completing this step:

a. Click the Scan or Import a File link to open up your camera or webcam, and scan the QR code (from Figure 3-11) directly from the other wallet.

b. Upload a picture of the QR code if you saved that. (Which we recommend not doing.)

c. Paste a private key into the box, if you have that.

4. **Click the Import button.**

Blue passes the seed words through its mathemagical functions and creates the private key and addresses. It also connects to the Bitcoin network, finds your transactions, and loads them into the wallet. Depending on where the wallet comes from, you may be prompted for a passphrase, with which some wallets may be protected.

That's it; you now have the wallet imported on the new device—or recovered if you're importing from a backup of a wallet that you lost or was destroyed.

TECHNICAL STUFF

What's a WIF, in the list of import options in Figure 3-15? WIF means *Wallet Import Format,* a way to encode a private key to make it easier to transfer — in theory, anyway. It really doesn't make much difference, and you're not likely to run into it.

TIP

You could try this for yourself. Create a wallet on one device — your laptop or desktop PC, for instance — then load BlueWallet onto another device, such as your smartphone. Then import the seed into your second device and watch BlueWallet set up the wallet and grab the existing transactions from the blockchain.

Creating a watch-only wallet

You can also use the Import function to create a *watch-only wallet,* a wallet that cannot send transactions to the blockchain, but that can keep an eye on an address in the blockchain so you can always check the balance. Instead of providing a seed or private key, you enter a public key or an address, and the wallet watches the associated address.

For instance, you could use the watch-only wallet to receive incoming Bitcoin transactions — the wallet will provide you with the address and QR code you can give to the sender — and the most recent balance. However, to *spend* the Bitcoin, you would have to use another wallet, presumably a *cold wallet* that is usually disconnected from the Internet.

You can play with this setup if you like, to see how it all works. Assuming you have a wallet already set up but want to create a watch-only wallet on your mobile device, based on a wallet on your laptop, here's what you would do:

1. **Find the address that contains Bitcoin by opening the wallet and clicking the small menu icon in the top-right corner.**

   The Wallet information screen appears (refer to Figure 3-10).

2. **Click the little "Show Addresses" link immediately above the Export/Backup button.**

   The screen shown on the left in Figure 3-16 appears.

   Your wallet can create multiple addresses, one for each transaction. You can see which of your addresses contain balances in this list.

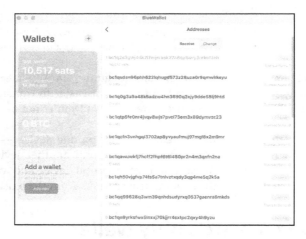

FIGURE 3-16:
Choose an address to access its QR code.

3. **Click the address you want to track to open the box shown on the right in Figure 3-16.**

4. **Scan the QR code from the BlueWallet software on the other device.**

   Alternatively, click on the address under the QR code and email or text it to the other device. (Remember, this is an address, not a private key, so it's perfectly safe to send it "insecurely.")

5. **On the device on which you want to create the watch-only wallet, go through the import process: click the Add Now button and then select Import Wallet.**

6. **In the screen, scan or paste the address from the *other device's* wallet.**

   Your new wallet is created. Even if you gave the wallet a name, it will likely be named *Imported Watch-only* (though this seems like a bug, so maybe it won't by the time you read this).

REMEMBER

Notice that in the wallet's main screen, there's a Receive button but no Send button. The wallet will monitor the address, and also can be used to send the address to someone who needs to send Bitcoin to you. But you can't use it to send Bitcoin to someone.

Exploring multiple-signature wallets

This section dives into the multi-sig feature, the ability to create wallets that require two or more wallets to work together to sign a transaction that will be sent to the Bitcoin network.

Originally multi-sig wallets were a way for joint owners of Bitcoin to work together to manage their joint ownership. For instance, a married couple or a group of business partners may use multi-sig transactions, or a business may use multiple employees to provide signatures for corporate transactions. Transactions cannot be completed by one person; two or more are needed to sign transactions.

Multi-sig wallets also provide an individual with more security. Even if someone manages to gain access to one wallet — they find your password to the program, for instance — they still can't send a transaction without the other wallet (or several other wallets). Ideally, each wallet is stored on a different device in a different location. Some owners of sizeable Bitcoin holdings (hodlings?) use this method to make it harder to send transactions. One wallet may be stored in a bank safe-deposit box and another at home, for instance. Thus, Blue calls this type of wallet a *vault* rather than a multi-sig wallet.

Understanding multi-sig wallets

In the next section, we show you how to set up a very simple multi-sig wallet. If you want to do a more complex wallet, with three or more wallet holders and, perhaps, a smaller number required for signing, you need to read the documentation and review some videos to see how it's done, and then experiment with it to figure out how it all works. We recommend that you don't save large sums using a multi-sig wallet until you're absolutely sure you understand how it works and have tested a few small transactions.

Be careful with multi-sig wallets. Everyone managing one of the group's wallets must follow good security processes. Hacking or unauthorized access is perhaps less of an issue in a group, of course. If you need, say, three signatures out of a five-wallet group, an attacker has to hack three of the five wallets to be able to process a transaction. Thus, if one wallet holder is a little sloppy in the security arena, it's not a total disaster.

However, what happens if you don't have backups? If, for instance, you have a group of three and you require all three wallets to process a transaction, it only takes one wallet holder to lose their password, and the Bitcoin associated with the multi-sig wallets' address is now useless!

It's tempting for one person to save the seeds for all the group's wallets, especially if some of the group's wallet holders are likely to lose access to their wallets. That defeats the purpose of the multi-sig wallet. Multi-sig wallets require that all members save their wallet passwords and backup seeds carefully, so that they cannot be lost or stolen.

Creating multi-sig wallets

You can set up multi-sig wallets (or vaults) in BlueWallet in various configurations, from "2 of 2" (meaning a group of two wallets of which both are required to sign a transaction) to "7 of 7" (a group of seven wallets, all of which must sign). You could, for instance, have a group of five wallets of which three must sign ("3 of 5").

You can do this with BlueWallet on several different devices. But you can also do it using various wallet types on different kinds of devices: BlueWallet on a smartphone, for instance, along with some kind of hardware wallet.

To demonstrate how this works, we assume you're using BlueWallet on two different devices. For more complex configurations, we recommend you do more research and experiment.

By default, Blue creates "2 of 3" wallets, with no option to change the settings, *unless* you have Advanced Mode selected in the General area of the program Settings or Preferences. If you want to follow along, make sure you have Advanced Mode selected, and follow these steps:

1. **Click the Add Now button or + button on the BlueWallet main screen.**

2. **In the Add Wallet box (refer to Figure 3-4), click Vault, then click the Create button.**

   The box shown on the left in Figure 3-17 appears. The box says, "A vault is a 2-of-3 multisig wallet. It needs 2 vault keys to spend and a third one you can use as a backup." In other words, you need to set up two other wallets, on other devices, and in order to process a transaction, you need at least two of the devices to sign.

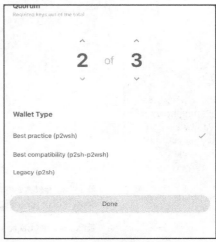

FIGURE 3-17: Create a multi-sig wallet; you choose how many wallets in a group.

3. **Change these settings by clicking on Vault Settings, above the Let's Start button; you see the box on the right in Figure 3-17.**

4. **Use the little up and down arrows to choose how many wallets you want in your group.**

   For instance, 4 of 6 means the entire group is six separate wallets, of which only four are required to process a transaction. (The maximum is 7 of 7.) For this demonstration, we're using 2 of 2.

5. **Click the Done button and then click Let's Start.**

   The box in which you set up your wallets appears (on the right in Figure 3-18).

6. **To create the first wallet in the group of two on this device, click the Create New button on the first line.**

7. **Save the new seed carefully (see on the left in Figure 3-18).**

   You've created a wallet, and that wallet is the Vault Key 1 in your group of two keys.

8. **On the second device, you'll do the same thing; you'll create a new 2 of 2 Vault (multi-sig) wallet (Figure 3-17). However, this time, don't click the Create New button in Figure 3-18. We have work to do on the other device first.**

FIGURE 3-18:
Setting up your
vault wallet and
getting your first
wallet seed.

9. **On the first device, click the Share link on the Vault Key 1 line to open the Share box (see Figure 3-19).**

   This allows you to transfer the wallet you have just created to another device.

10. **Use the QR code or click the Share button under the QR code to save a file that can be transferred to the other device.**

    This is actually transferring what is known as an XPUB, an extended public key.

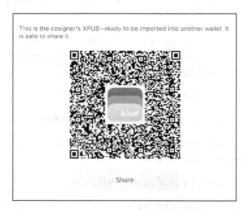

FIGURE 3-19:
Your XPUB
QR code.

11. **On the second device, click the Import button (located below Create New, on the Vault Key 1 line) to see a screen like that shown in Figure 3-20 (shown on a smartphone).**

12. **Click the "Scan or import a file" link and point the device's camera at the first device's XPUB QR code; your device scans in the code and creates your Vault Key 1.**

Insert a seed to import your existing Vault key.

Import

Scan or import a file

||| ◯ ‹

FIGURE 3-20:
The Import screen (on an Android device).

If you can't scan a QR code, you can use the file-save function and transfer the file, which can then be opened via the Import box.)

You are now ready to set up Vault Key 2.

13. **Now we'll set up Vault Key 2.** We're essentially going to repeat what we just did, for Vault Key 2, starting on the second device. On the second device, on the Vault Key 2 line, click the Create New button to create a wallet and see the seed.

14. **Save the seed, then click the Share link to open the XPUB QR code.**

15. **On the first device, click the Import button to see the Import box, the "Scan or import a file" link, and scan the QR code into the first device.**

16. **On both devices, click the Create button on the Vault Key lines.**

On both devices, Blue creates a wallet called Multisig Vault. (You can rename it if you want in the Wallet information screen; click the ellipsis ( ) menu at the top right of the main wallet screen.)

Sending Bitcoin from a multi-sig wallet

Here we show you how to send money from a multi-sig wallet. First, of course, you need to load some Bitcoin into it; that's done in the same way as with a regular wallet, using the Receive button. Sending starts off the same, too:

1. **In the multi-sig wallet, click the Send button, and then enter the amount you're sending and the address to which you're sending.**

2. **Click the Next button, and the screen shown in Figure 3-21 appears.**

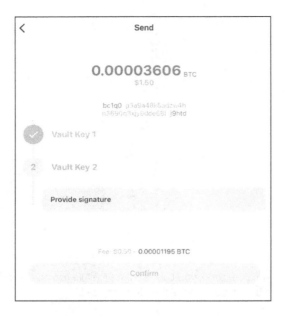

FIGURE 3-21:
The Import
screen.

3. **Click the Provide Signature button, and a QR code appears.**

4. **On the other device, click the Send button; then click the ellipsis ( ) menu in the top right of the Send screen and select Sign a Transaction.**

   You see the device's camera screen.

5. **Scan the QR code from the other device.**

6. **After the camera has grabbed the QR code, a message box appears, asking you to co-sign the transaction. Click YES.**

   You see a screen like that shown in Figure 3-22. As you can see, you now have two vault keys that have signed.

7. **Click the Confirm button.**

   A summary screen appears, showing the amount of the transaction, the address it's going to, and the fee being paid.

8. **Click the Send Now button, and the transaction is on its way!**

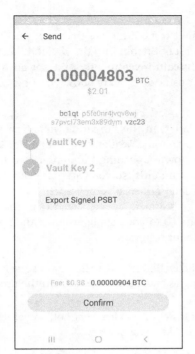

FIGURE 3-22:
The Import
screen (on an
Android device).

Using the Lightning Network

Bitcoin transactions have two significant problems: They're slow and expensive. This doesn't matter too much for purely investing purposes, but it's a real nuisance for making purchases.

An ancillary network known as the Lightning Network is an attempt to fix these problems. This network is a payment protocol that sits "on top" of the Bitcoin network; when you use Lightning, your transactions are sent to the Lightning Network, bundled together, and sent on to the Bitcoin network. The transactions occur very quickly and with very low transaction fees, a fraction of what you would pay for a direct-to-blockchain transaction. The Lightning Network makes "microtransactions" possible, something that content publishers have long been hoping for. A publisher can charge just a few cents for an article or a podcast, for instance. (With credit cards and regular Bitcoin payments, this simply isn't possible, as the fees exceed the transaction.)

You can create a Lightning wallet to hold money that you can then use to make purchases, but you won't put a lot of Bitcoin into the wallet. Lightning wallets are not suitable for hodling your Bitcoin investments. And not all wallets can work with Lightning, but BlueWallet can. We quickly show you how to work with the network using the BlueWallet.

In the steps to set up a BlueWallet, in the "Creating your first wallet" section, rather than selecting Bitcoin in the Add Wallet box, you select Lightning (refer to Figure 3-4). If you have your own Lightning hub, enter that into the text box labelled LNDHub — of course, you don't, so you can just keep the default Blue-Wallet Lightning hub. Click Create, and you're prompted to back up the wallet. A QR code appears, which can be scanned, as well as a Lightning wallet ID (refer to Figure 3-19); click to copy the ID to your clipboard, and then paste it into, for instance, a password-management program.

You now have to add funds to the wallet. In the wallet main screen, click the Manage Funds button near the top, and choose an option from the drop-down menu:

>> **Refill:** This choice lets you transfer Bitcoin from your other wallets, within the BlueWallet program, into your Lightning wallet.

>> **Refill from External Wallet:** This lets you send Bitcoin from another wallet to your BlueWallet Lightning wallet.

>> **Refill with Bank Card:** This lets you buy Bitcoin from an exchange.

>> **Exchange:** This lets you use ZigZag.io to exchange other cryptocurrencies into Bitcoin and deposit into the Lightning wallet.

After you fund your wallet, you can send and receive Bitcoin via the network in a similar way to how you would with regular Bitcoin wallets, though with one significant difference. To receive money, you create an invoice rather than a Bitcoin address, and send the invoice to the person sending you Bitcoin; when you send Bitcoin to someone else, they send you an invoice that you pay.

Chapter **4**

Keeping Your Bitcoin Safe

You've probably heard stories of people "losing" their Bitcoin; thousands of people have done so. In fact, in 2017 researchers estimated that somewhere between 2.8 million and 3.8 million Bitcoin had been lost for good. . .perhaps more than 150 billion dollars' worth at current value. But many millions of dollars' worth have also been *stolen* from owners.

This chapter helps you to understand how these losses can happen and what to do so they don't happen to you!

Understanding How You Can Lose Control of Your Bitcoin

Bitcoin actually can't be literally "lost." In Chapter 1 of this minibook, we explain that there really isn't any actual Bitcoin; instead, there's a record of Bitcoin transactions in the blockchain ledger. So Bitcoin can't be lost; it's still where it's always been, sitting in the blockchain ledger.

What can happen, though, is that you can *lose control* of your Bitcoin. Sure, the Bitcoin is still recorded as a series of transactions in the blockchain, but you can no longer get to it, and you can no longer control it. And that can happen in a couple of ways:

1. You *lose* your private key, and thus the ability to control your Bitcoin.

2. Someone else *steals* your private key — thus gaining the ability to control your Bitcoin — and transfers it away from the address controlled by that private key.

REMEMBER

Your Bitcoin is associated with a particular address in the Bitcoin blockchain. That address is under the control of the associated private key, which you are, hopefully, keeping safe. The private key allows you to control that address. The only person who can send a message to the blockchain to transfer some or all of the Bitcoin associated with the address is the person who controls the private key; that's the *mathemagics* we talk about in Chapter 1 of this minibook.

Let's look at the first way you could lose your Bitcoin. Imagine what would happen if you lost your private key. You'd lose the ability to send transaction messages to the blockchain. You'd lose control of the Bitcoin associated with the address associated with the lost private key! No private key, no Bitcoin.

Now consider the second way you could lose control. What happens if someone else gains access to the private key? They now have control over your Bitcoin. Of course, if you still also have the private key, you both have control, and it becomes a game of who gets to it first. If you ever suspect that someone else may have found your private key — or the seed used to create it (see Chapter 3 of this minibook) — you should *immediately* transfer your Bitcoin to an address controlled by *another* private key. Create a new wallet if necessary. And then never use the old wallet again.

If someone who knows what they're doing steals your private key (or, again, the seed used to create the private key), then you probably won't have a chance. The Bitcoin will be gone before you ever discover the key has been lost — in fact, that's probably how you'll discover the key has gone; your wallet will have no Bitcoin left.

There's a popular phrase in the Bitcoin community: *not your keys, not your coins*. In other words, if someone else has access to your private key, they have control over your Bitcoin; it's as if you don't really own the Bitcoin, because someone else can take it from you at any moment. Sure, legally, you own it. But laws haven't helped the thousands of people who have had their Bitcoin stolen.

HOW 7,500 BITCOINS WERE LOST

A bigger risk these days than having your Bitcoin stolen from a custodial wallet in an exchange hack is the risk of simply losing the hardware where your wallet lives. We're always reminded of the famous case of James Howells, in the United Kingdom. In 2013, he owned 7,500 Bitcoins, at that point worth around $975,000. But that year, he lost a hard drive containing his wallet file; he's not even sure how he lost it, but he thinks it was thrown out during a house cleaning, and that it ended up in the local landfill.

If Mr. Howells had read and understood this chapter, and put into action what we teach here, his Bitcoin would be worth — as we write these very words — $361,893,000, more or less. Actually, even though he hasn't read this chapter, the Bitcoin *is still* worth that sum; it's just that he'll never be able to touch it. Unless, that is, he can convince the local council to allow him to dig up the landfill (he offered them $70 million early in 2021), is lucky enough to find the drive, and can retrieve his seed or private key from a piece of hardware that has been rotting away in the dampness of a Welsh trash heap for eight years (and counting).

But it's not just theft you have to worry about. It's the proverbial screw-up, a mistake you make that leads to the loss. This happens a lot. It's easy to find horror stories of people who lost their wallets, and thus their keys and thus control over their Bitcoin. Co-author Peter Kent has a friend who owns millions of dollars' worth of Bitcoin — sitting somewhere in the blockchain — which he'll never be able to access because he sold a computer that had the wallet holding the associated keys.

Well, no, that's not really why he's millions of dollars poorer than he could be; he's millions of dollars poorer *because he didn't have a backup of the seed used to create the wallet on the sold computer!* It's as simple as that. With a little knowledge and a few minutes' work, you can protect your Bitcoin so that you can't just lose it. With a little foresight, Peter's friend would still have access to his Bitcoin, *even though* he sold the computer on which the wallet sat.

Grasping the Goal: Private Key and Seed Protection

To sum it up in a nutshell, your two risks to losing control of your Bitcoin are as follows:

1. You can lose your private keys.

2. Your private keys can be stolen.

Thus, your two goals in keeping your Bitcoin safe and accessible only by you are as follows:

1. Safeguard your keys, so they can't be stolen.

2. Back up your keys so that you cannot lose them.

Here's the problem, though: These two requirements are at odds with each other. The harder you make it to *steal* your keys, the easier you may make it to *lose* your keys. And the harder you make it to *lose* your keys, the easier it becomes to *steal* them.

For instance, you can easily ensure that you don't lose your private key by writing down your seed on Post-it notes and giving them to, say, half a dozen friends and family. (Recall from Chapter 3 of this minibook that if you have your seed, you can re-create your private key, and in any case, some wallet software hides the private key from you and only provides you with the seed.) You'd better really trust them, though! And not simply trust that they won't rip you off, but trust that they will keep the notes safe from theft by others. The more people who have the keys, the easier it is to steal them.

Or you can make it really hard for someone to steal your private key or seed by keeping a single copy, in a location known only to you. But the fewer backups you have of your seed or private key, the easier it is to lose it, through flood or fire, for instance. (We recall the Bitcoin owner who had his seed backed up on a piece of paper *and* a thumb drive; his computer burned up in a freak malfunction. As the paper and the thumb drive were right next to the computer, the small fire burned them, too, and with them, any hope of getting to his Bitcoin.)

TIP

Here are a couple more goals you may consider:

>> **Ensure that you have access to your Bitcoin wherever you happen to be in the world, whenever you need it.** If you have a wallet on your home computer, with a seed saved in a local bank's safe deposit box, well, the only way you can get to your Bitcoin is by being in your hometown. This is an *electronic* currency, so surely it should be available anywhere in the world with Internet access, no? The methods in this chapter teach you how to have access to your Bitcoin anywhere, anytime.

>> **How to pass Bitcoin on to your heirs.** Many Bitcoin owners have shuffled off this mortal coil (as Hamlet put it), *and taken their Bitcoin with them!* (Well, not literally; we did mention the Bitcoin never leaves the blockchain, right?) In this chapter, you find out how to leave it with your family once you're pushing up daisies, even if they don't have access to it while you're alive.

REMEMBER

Chapter 3 of this minibook covers wallets, both hot and cold. A hot wallet is connected to the Internet and, at least in theory, is at a potential risk for being accessed by a nefarious third party. A cold wallet, on the other hand, is not connected to the Internet, and cannot be hacked. It may still be at risk of theft, though. Here are a couple points to keep in mind as you read the rest of this chapter:

>> **Combine the techniques in this chapter with your wallet strategy for maximum effect:** Whether your wallet is a hot wallet, a cold wallet, or one that's cold most of the time and hot just when you need to send transactions, you still need backups. If you have a single cold wallet, totally immune from being hacked across the Internet but still vulnerable to a fire, you're still taking a huge risk!

>> **Backups — such as storing a wallet seed in a password-management program — are a form of wallet themselves:** So this chapter is about keeping your wallets, hot or cold, safe from theft, and duplicated so you can't lose control over your Bitcoin.

Making a Choice: Custodial or Private Wallet?

The first choice you have to make is who is going to manage your Bitcoin wallet (or wallets). Are you going to manage it yourself (a private wallet), or will you allow someone else to manage it (a custodial wallet, which we introduce in Chapter 3 of this minibook)?

Bitcoin purists hate the idea of letting someone else manage their wallets; remember the phrase *not your keys, not your coins?* Whoever controls the private keys has access to your Bitcoin.

The problem has been, historically, that a number of exchanges have been hacked over the years, with the hackers accessing the clients' private keys and stealing their Bitcoin. Some exchanges have been run by scammers, who stole their customers' Bitcoin and disappeared (known in the Bitcoin field as an "exit scam").

WARNING

As we caution you throughout this book, managing Bitcoin can be complicated. Today, the bigger risk for the Bitcoin neophyte is losing access to their Bitcoin rather than having it stolen from them. There are benefits to doing it yourself, but there are dangers, too. If you screw up managing your own Bitcoin, you can lose it, after all. The risks notwithstanding, you may find it easier to allow a large, reputable exchange to manage it for you.

This is a choice you have to make, and many people will choose the option of allowing professionals to look after their Bitcoin. As the market develops, this option will probably become less and less of a danger. As these large companies become better insured, for instance, and their defenses against theft become better, the risk will decline. (Many would say that it's already pretty low for some of the big institutions, at least.)

Still, in the following sections, we discuss how to protect your Bitcoin for yourself. And people who own very large amounts of Bitcoin almost always manage this process themselves, and develop a sophisticated system to do so.

TIP

If you decide to keep your Bitcoin in a custodial wallet, you still need to protect the login information for the account. So the rest of this chapter can still be useful to you; after all, whether you are protecting a login password or a wallet seed, the goal is to ensure that a piece of text is not stolen or lost.

Devising Your Cryptocurrency Safety Plan

Understanding how to protect all your Bitcoin-related information (and other important information, too, such as bank-account logins) begins with the basics: a plan to create strong, safe passwords.

Producing powerful passwords

Whatever you do — whether you use an exchange's custodial wallet, or one or more wallet apps on your various devices — you'll have passwords you need to protect. These should be passwords that can't be guessed, and also that you never lose or forget. Again, we're back at that situation in which the harder it is to forget a password, the easier it is to steal (or guess), and conversely, the harder it is to steal (or guess), the easier it is to forget. For instance, here's a bad password (let's assume that the password owner has a daughter and a son; see if you can guess their names):

JaneAndJoe

Okay, here's a pretty good password; see if you can memorize it:

iu$kG7pNnbs3z^RYe$yiBh

And here, according to a study, is the world's most commonly used password:

123456

That's closely followed by 123456789, by the way; and let's not forget the word *password* itself, which millions of people use as a password! Incidentally, these last three passwords can be guessed by a password-cracking program in less than a second.

TIP

This list highlights a few good (and common) rules for passwords:

>> **Use unique passwords for every login you have; *do not reuse passwords*.** Yes, you'll end up with hundreds, but we're going to explain how to deal with that problem.

>> **Don't use simple passwords such as the ones suggested here.** When hackers attack systems, they often use programs with dictionaries of common passwords; they already know the passwords used by many people!

>> **Don't use easily guessed passwords.** These include your spouse's date of birth, the names of your pets, your kids' names, and so on. These passwords make it easy for someone who knows you, and has time to experiment, to get into your system.

>> **Create passwords using multiple unrelated words connected with special characters and digits.** dog!!sure13%blurt, for instance. This is strong, but relatively easy to remember.

>> **Use long, random strings of characters**. RkTWGQd9Xy%4#hbcY4t!6J or iW28LQKnJm%Aw8i9Ku4wHYFofZ^vho, for instance.

This last type of password is essentially impossible to guess, for either a password-cracking program or someone who knows you. Of course, they are also impossible for a normal human being to remember, which is why you need a password-management program. In the next section, we show you how to create and use passwords such as iu$kG7pNnbs3z^RYe$yiBh, without having to remember them.

REMEMBER

We're not talking about using strong passwords only for your Bitcoin-related logins, but for *all* your logins, in particular your email login. Hacking into an email system is often the first step a thief uses to access your other systems, such as bank and Bitcoin accounts.

Protecting passwords with password programs

Everybody these days should be using password-management software. It's just not possible, in the modern world, to remember all the passwords you need, unless you re-use passwords between systems and use simple passwords, both of which you should not be doing!

We know what a lot of you are doing, of course. You're writing your passwords down on paper, sometimes leaving the paper right next to your computer as an invitation to anyone who breaks in, or to a tech-savvy house cleaner — an invitation to, um, take you to the cleaners!

The more sophisticated among you are typing the passwords into a word-processing document or spreadsheet — probably named something like *passwords.docx* — and saving the file on your computer's hard drive, very thoughtfully providing the guy who steals your computer with the software preinstalled and the appropriate access passwords all in one place!

When your house burns down, you lose the passwords you wrote on paper. Or when your computer hard drive dies, you lose the passwords in the Word file. There's a better way! Use a *password-management program,* which stores your passwords — along with login URLs and IDs, various notes, and perhaps things like credit-card numbers and PINs, passport and drivers-license numbers, and so on — in encrypted files. You can log into the program to access your passwords, but without the master password, the data is not accessible. It's stored in a scrambled format that cannot be cracked, even by the FBI, CIA, or KGB (okay, *FSB* now, but that doesn't trip off the tongue like *KGB*). Sure, you can encrypt word-processing and spreadsheet files, too, but don't think that's safe; in most cases, these systems' form of encryption is very weak and easily cracked.

Password-management programs allow you to store hundreds — thousands even — of complex passwords, without you needing to remember any of them. All you need to remember is the *master password* that lets you get into the program.

Lots of these programs are available: Dashlane, Roboform, LastPass, TrueKey, NordPass, and many others. Pick something that is well known and widely recommended. Check a few comparative reviews. You'll find these programs have a lot of nifty features that make life so much easier for the password-laden citizens of the modern world. One of the most important is *centralized backup:* You can get to your passwords on your smartphone or laptop, but also through a web browser. The data is synchronized across devices and also stored — in an encrypted format — on the program publisher's servers. So if your house burns down and you lose all your devices, you haven't lost your passwords.

And those complicated passwords? They look this one:

    woVib%8fQa67#EL8jQ5YgVq4n^9$rk

You don't even have to create them; the program creates them — and saves them — for you.

Of course, you can use the password-management program to store all sorts of things: login information, seeds, actual private keys if your software provides access to those, and notes explaining where all your assets are (bank accounts, types of cryptocurrency, brokerage accounts, the name of this book, and so on).

You should also consider using a program that has a *digital inheritance* or *digital legacy* feature, something we explain in the aptly named section, "Using a digital inheritance feature," later in this chapter. This feature helps you pass on your passwords to your family if you suddenly find yourself in a pine box.

You need a good password to get into your password program, the *master* password. This has to be something you can remember, so those long, complicated passwords are out (forget the master password and you won't be able to get into the system, and no, the program publisher won't be able to help you get in either). But it can't be something easily guessed. So, string a few words together with special characters and digits. You may take a line from a book, poem, or song (as long as it's not a short poem that you recite to people every day!), and replace the spaces with those special characters. You may end up with, for instance, something like this:

shuffle@OFF&this*mortal

If you're still concerned about forgetting it, combine this with the digital legacy feature, so if your memory *does* fail you, you still have a way back into your passwords, with the help of a friend or family member.

WARNING

This master password is the password program's Achilles heel. Lose that, and you can't get in. Have it stolen or guessed, and someone else can. So protect it carefully!

Protecting your computer

Protecting your computer is also important because, if your computer becomes "infected" in some way, it can compromise everything you do on the computer. You want to keep your master password safe, but there are programs that can spy on your computer and see what you're up to, such as programs that can see every character you type when you log into your password-management program.

A program called Cryptoshuffler, for instance, tracks computer clipboards, in particular, looking for strings of text that look like Bitcoin addresses. It then replaces the address — likely copied out of the Receive box of a Bitcoin wallet (see Chapter 3 of this minibook) — with an address belonging to the Cryptoshuffler programmer. When the address is then pasted into another program — likely the Send box of a Bitcoin wallet — the computer user then unknowingly sends Bitcoin to the publisher. Hundreds of thousands of dollars (millions?) of Bitcoin have been stolen by this program.

Then there's *keyloggers* or *keystroke loggers,* programs that watch everything that's being typed on the infected computer, and report back across the Internet to the attacker. Such programs can steal seeds and passwords. They can be installed on your computer by viruses that infect your computer, or by someone with access to your computer. (Parents sometimes install keystroke loggers on their kids' computers, jealous people on their spouses' computers.)

Even without these threats, lots of bad things (viruses, Trojan Horses, malware, adware, and so on) can happen to your computer if you don't protect it from infection, so you need to do this anyway. *Ransomware* has been in the news a lot recently; it's malicious software that encrypts all your computer's data, locking you out of the data and only unlocking it once you've paid a ransom.

REMEMBER

Keep your computer clean and do these two things:

>> **Protect your computer with anti-virus software.** Search for terms such as *best windows antivirus software* or *best mac virus protection*. Find something well-known, reputable, and highly rated. Understand it and run it.

>> **Set up your computer to require a password to access it — and never leave it in a public place unlocked.** Don't even leave it unlocked in a *private* space if you have reason to believe someone close to you may be interested in spying on your computer activities (that definitely includes your employer's office). Before you walk away to get that coffee, lock it!

TIP

Requiring a password to access all your devices, including smartphones, is smart. If you have a password program or wallet on your smartphone, you must also protect that device with a secure login — a password, PIN, or fingerprint, for instance. The wallet software itself should have its own password, too. (All password programs require a password to log in.)

Watching out for sophisticated phishing

Take a look at the text message in Figure 4-1, something coauthor Peter received not too long ago. It seems pretty clear; it's a message from Coinbase saying someone had logged into Peter's account. Peter knew he hadn't done so recently, so his initial reaction was one of concern. Someone had logged into his account! How?

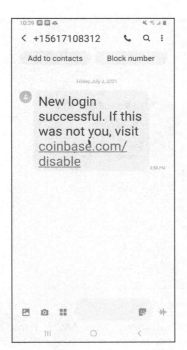

FIGURE 4-1:
A warning from
Coinbase.com?

Peter's second reaction was, "This doesn't sound real. I've never had a login noti-fication before." His third reaction: "But wait, there's a URL here, pointing to Coinbase.com" He felt this must be a faked message from Coinbase, but how can you fake a URL in an SMS message? That can't be done, can it? SMS messages are plain text; unlike links in an email message, for instance, the link is what it says it is! (In an email message, you may see link text, but the real, underlying link could be different.)

Peter didn't click the link. Instead, he went to his browser on his laptop and typed the URL, coinbase.com/disable into his browser, which loaded a 404 (page not found) message. Hmmm. He went back to his SMS message, positive that it was a fake (*phishing*) message, still wondering how it was possible to type a link into an SMS message, but have the link go to a different URL. Then he noticed something. Take a look at Figure 4-2, where we've enlarged the message to show more detail.

That's not the letter a! That's the letter a *with a diacritic*, a small symbol — the dot — underneath. What Peter had originally thought was a bit of dust on his smartphone screen, was part of the letter (specifically, a dot under the letter), half-covered by the link's underline. This wasn't Coinbase.com at all, it was actu-ally Coinbaạse.com!

FIGURE 4-2:
What's going on
with the letter a?

The Internet's domain name system only accepts ASCII characters, which don't include these symbols with diacritics. However, it's still possible to register domain names using these symbols. When you use a URL that includes a diacritic in the domain name, the *Punycode* system converts the letter with the diacritic to an ASCII representation; Coinba̧se.com, for instance, is really the domain xn--coinbse-en4c.com.

When Peter went to the referenced page (we do not recommend you click on links in phishing emails), he went to a login page that *looked* like it was on Coinbase.com, but was on a completely different website (at xn--coinbse-en4c.com). Had he logged in, the "phisher" would have received Peter's login ID and password and, most likely within minutes — or even seconds — would have attempted to log into Peter's Coinbase account and transfer all his Bitcoin! (This is an example of why you should use two-factor authentication, which we discuss in the next section.)

Phishing is a form of *social engineering,* in which scammers try to convince you to provide them with information they can then use to get into your online accounts. It's getting pretty sophisticated these days. In Peter's case, the message masqueraded as a message from Coinbase. It really did look like a Coinbase URL.

Watch out for these kinds of phishing scams. If you get an email or text that you find suspicious, or that you don't expect, don't blindly click the link. One way to identify such a scam in an email is to point your mouse pointer over the link; the actual underlying URL should pop up so you can see where the link actually goes. And in text messages, carefully read the URL! If you're still unsure, contact the service, not through the text or email, but by going to the website directly and checking with customer service.

PHISHING?

The word *phishing* is a form of "leetspeak," a system in which familiar words are intentionally misspelled. *Leet* itself comes from the word *elite*, and refers to the "elite" membership status in some electronic bulletin board systems in the 1980s. Leetspeak may have been a way to get around the use of text filters these systems used to block discussions of unauthorized subjects, such as hacking and cracking (*cracking* is actually the more correct word for what most of society calls hacking these days). But leetspeak is almost certainly a form of community language used to exclude those outside the community. Anyway the term *phishing,* perhaps not surprisingly, is leetspeak for *fishing*. The scammers are fishing for your login information.

Employing two-factor authentication

You've almost certainly run into two-factor authentication by now (often known as 2FA). You're familiar with basic logins, of course; you provide an ID (often an email address) and a password. With 2FA, you have to provide something more. The three most common additional authentication factors are as follows:

>> A code sent to you via text message by the system you are logging into (some systems can deliver the code by speech to a voice-only phone number)

>> A code sent to you via email

>> A code created by an authenticator app

For those of you who have just emerged from the proverbial cave into this new online world, here's how it typically works:

1. You go to the website you want to log into.

2. You enter your ID and password and press Enter or click Login.

3. The system sends a 2FA code to your email address or in a text message to your phone, or it requests a code from your authenticator app.

4. You enter the code you've received, or taken from the authenticator, and the system lets you in.

And what, you may be asking, is this about some kind of *authenticator*? Well, these are apps — typically running on smartphones but also available for Windows and the Mac — that provide a code you can use to log in. Figure 4-3 shows an example of one — the Google Authenticator, which runs on the iPhone and iPad, as well as Android phones. These tools don't need to be connected to the Internet. Even if your phone's service is down, they still provide you with a usable code.

FIGURE 4-3:
The Google
Authenticator
app.

When you set up an account that offers the 2FA feature, you're given the option of setting it up — or you may be told you *must* set it up. Just follow the instructions.

TIP

You may want to set up two or more 2FA methods. For instance, if you lose your smartphone, you can't get SMS texts or use your authenticator, and you are therefore locked out of your systems (such as your Bitcoin exchange accounts). Thus, many systems provide backup codes, half a dozen or so one-time 2FA codes that you can save for future use. These should be stored safely somewhere, such as in your password-management program.

There are various 2FA mechanisms, such as codes provided via voice calls, and even hardware devices that you plug into your computer. You may have come across *push notifications,* too. Each time you try to log into your account, a message (the push notification) is sent to your phone, alerting you that someone is trying to log in. You're not provided with a code; you simply respond Yes or No to show whether or not that current login attempt is coming from you.

With these 2FA methods, though, always ask yourself the question, "What happens if I can't get to my 2FA code?" Figure out a fallback position.

HOW'S THAT AUTHENTICATOR THING WORK?

Have you ever wondered how those authenticator apps magically work? How can an app on your smartphone possibly know what code a web server thousands of miles away wants to see? Well, it's magic. Mathemagic!

When you first set up your account for 2FA using an authenticator, you are given a special code to enter into the authenticator. This is a secret key that the app saves for future use. Later, when you need a login code, both systems use this secret key, in combination with the time and date, to both mathemagically calculate the same code; because both the server and the authenticator have the same secret key, and both know the time, they both come up with the same code.

The dangers of 2FA

We believe you should use 2FA, which provides an additional, significant layer of protection. However, as with everything else, 2FA has weaknesses. If someone has access to the 2FA code, they have access to your account. For instance, they know your email address, which means they likely know your login to various systems, such as your Bitcoin-exchange accounts. Now, even without knowing your password, they can gain access to your account by doing a password reset, *if* they have access to the system that will receive or create your 2FA code.

In some cases, it could be that they have access to your email account (if you're receiving the code via email); perhaps they have hacked into your Gmail account, for instance. Or perhaps they have gained access to your smartphone. In many cases, if they have access to your smartphone, they likely have access to all three of the normal 2FA code systems: your text messages, your emails, and your authenticator app. So, how do you protect yourself?

>> **You *must* have smartphone login protection,** with a secure login that can't easily be guessed.

>> **Never leave your smartphone unattended and unlocked.** In fact, you should always know where your smartphone is. Keep it on your person or close by.

>> **Protect your email account.** Use a good password that can't be guessed or easily cracked, don't leave your computer unlocked when unattended, and so on.

>> **Protect yourself from SIM swaps!** SIM stands for *subscriber identity module*. The SIM card is a chip that holds information about the user and the mobile network — unique information that nefarious people can use to get control of your stuff.

The danger of SIM swaps

This really isn't a huge risk for most people, but it is a risk for people who are known to have large Bitcoin holdings, and who then become a juicy target for thieves. The idea is that the thief directs your phone line to their phone, using a process known as a *port-out scam*, *SIM swapping*, *simjacking*, and so on. Here's how it works:

1. The thief — let's call him Jesse James — discovers that Ritchie Rich owns a huge amount of Bitcoin. (**Bonus security tip:** Don't boast about owning a huge amount of Bitcoin!)

2. Jesse discovers that Ritchie has stored much of his Bitcoin with a large exchange. Jesse also finds out Ritchie's email address and phone number, something that's pretty easy to discover.

   Jesse has spent days, weeks maybe, investigating Ritchie, and now knows everything about Mr. Rich, from his social security number to the names of his family members. He may have even tricked Ritchie Rich into giving him some of the information directly, but plenty is available online anyway.

3. Jesse hacks into Ritchie's email account. Now, if Jesse can just get hold of Ritchie's phone line, he can go to the exchange, use Ritchie's email address to do a password reset, get the 2FA code sent to the phone, use the code to authenticate, get a password-reset link, and get his filthy hands on Ritchie's riches.

4. Jesse calls the mobile-phone service Ritchie uses, and tells them that he has a new phone, and needs to switch SIMs — that is, point the phone number to the SIM card on the new phone.

5. Jesse provides them with enough information to convince them that he's Ritchie, and they switch the phone line to Jesse's phone!

6. And away Jesse goes, into Ritchie's account and, with Ritchie's Bitcoin in hand, off to a tropical paradise.

WARNING

Yes, this has actually happened. The phone companies can be pretty bad with security at times. You may want to call your mobile-phone company and ask how to protect against SIM swaps. Some companies, for instance, issue a PIN number without which your SIM cannot be swapped (you would save the PIN in your password-management program, of course).

In the U.S., the Federal Communications Commission has gotten involved in this issue, and is in the process of issuing new rules that the phone companies will have to follow to reduce the risk of SIM swaps.

Exploring More Ways to Protect Your Bitcoin (and Everything Else)

Security really is a big subject. There's plenty you can do to protect yourself, and the more you have at risk, the more time and energy you'll want to spend doing so. But remember, we're not just talking about your Bitcoin. We're also talking about your bank accounts, investment accounts, retirement accounts, and so on. Sensible security measures are important for everyone, Bitcoin owner or not.

So, here are a few more things to consider:

>> **Use a separate email for your Bitcoin.** Some people use special email accounts to access their various Bitcoin accounts, email accounts that they use for nothing else. This makes it hard for a potential hacker to figure out their login IDs.

TIP

You can simply set up another freebie email account — Yahoo! Mail, Gmail, or whatever — or perhaps set up an account with a secure email provider such as ProtonMail.com. This particular service is set up in Switzerland, making it hard for even law enforcement in other countries to access information about your email. You can use a system such as Tor to access your Proton emails through a web browser in a totally untraceable way.

>> **Be very careful about using public Wi-Fi.** Whenever you connect to Wi-Fi, you should use VPN software to protect the connection between your computer and the websites you access. (Search for VPN; you'll find plenty of information.)

>> **Be extremely careful with public computers, such as those in libraries and Internet cafes.** It's not unheard of for such computers to have keylogging software installed, watching every keystroke made on the computer; if you log in to a site, the text you type into the ID and password fields is recorded.

>> **Install wallets only on your own devices, not a device owned by an employer.** You never know how much control over the device the employer has, or when you may lose it at a moment's notice.

TIP

There's a simple trick to confuse (some) keyloggers. You type a character of your password, then click outside the password box and type a jumble of random characters. Then click back in the password box and type the next character . . . then outside the box and hammer away at the keyboard again. This protects your password as the keylogger records all the text and doesn't know which characters are part of the password and which are not — *unless* the keyword logger is also recording mouse clicks!

Yet another problem is that some browser plugins can actually read text as it is being typed into a password field. So, keylogger software or not, mouse-click tracking or not, your password can be stolen that way.

How can you use a public computer if you really need to? Well, it's possible, if you plan ahead. You can use an "OS on a stick," a simple operating system on a USB stick. You plug the USB stick (thumb drive) into a USB port, then reboot the computer and have it boot from the thumb drive, which has a clean, simple operating system installed. Now you have a computer running *your* operating system, not the Internet cafe's, so no keylogger software or password-reading browser plugin. Here are a few sites to check out if you're interested in an OS on a stick:

>> https://www.makeuseof.com/tag/5-best-linux-distros-installation-usb-stick/

>> https://tails.boum.org/install/mac/usb-overview/

>> https://elementary.io/

There's still one problem: It's possible to install keyloggers on keyboards! So even though the computer is not recording what's going on, the keyboard itself may be recording what you type, such as the domain name of a bitcoin exchange followed by login information.

How do you get around that? As much as possible, use the operating system; use the mouse to select bookmarks to load Web sites; use a password-management program to automatically log in, or use an on-screen keyboard. Or you can also use the trick we explain earlier, typing a character of the password, clicking outside the password box, typing a jumble of characters, and so on.

This is not the end. People with very large holdings create very complex and sophisticated protection methods. Consider the Winklevoss twins, for instance, Tyler and Cameron. They sued Facebook for breach of contract, and won a settlement variously reported as between $65 million and $120 million. They took most of this money and put it into Bitcoin. That makes them billionaires now!

How do they protect their billions of bucks of Bitcoin? Well, you can believe they're not managing it all from an old Android phone. One system they use is a combination of paper wallets, in which they printed just part of a private key on each piece of paper, then deposited these papers in various safe-deposit boxes stored around the country. This makes it very hard for someone to put a gun to one of the twin's heads and say, "Send someone to the safe deposit box to bring back the private key."

Knowing What Happens When You Kick the Bucket

So you've invested in Bitcoin. You made some money, perhaps a lot, and your family's future is assured. Then you get hit by a bus. What's next? Maybe you're in a coma: perhaps your family is making funeral plans what happens to your Bitcoin?

Well, it's still where it has always been: in the blockchain. The question now is, if you've hidden your information — the seed and the private key — will they be able to find the information and thus access the Bitcoin?

You actually need to pass two things on to your heirs:

>> Your wallet seed phrase

>> Information about how to use it

As for the latter, maybe a copy of this book would be helpful. Or the name and phone number of someone you trust to guide them through the process of rebuilding a wallet and gaining access to your Bitcoin. Or maybe teach your family about Bitcoin *before* you move on from this planet. As for saving the seed in a manner in which it can be passed on when you've gone, well, read on.

The challenge is to keep your Bitcoin's seed, and thus the private key, safe while at the same time providing a way for your family to get it when you're no longer here.

WARNING

What you definitely shouldn't do is to simply give everyone in your family a printout of your seed. That's asking for trouble. Five years from now, how many of the printouts will be lost? And there's always the risk of careless talk among friends leading to a theft.

A better option is to simply put the information into a safe deposit box (or better still, two), and make sure your family knows where the box is and where the key is. In most cases, this scenario is fine, but it still carries risks. Sad to say, sometimes couples divorce, and sometimes children are "out of control," so your safe deposit box can become not so safe.

Choosing the multi-sig solution

We're mentioning the multi-sig option because it's often cited as a way to solve the inheritance problem (not because we believe it's a great solution). We cover multi-sig wallets in Chapter 3 of this minibook. Let's say you have a spouse and three children. You could set up a multi-sig wallet group with five wallets, and three required to sign (five, because you need to have one of the wallets, right?). If you pop your clogs, your family can get to the Bitcoin as long as three of them still have access to their wallets.

However, this really isn't a great option. First, to access your Bitcoin when you're alive, you need the assistance of two of your family members. There's a way around that problem, though. You set up a *four*-wallet group for your spouse and kids, with an address that has no Bitcoin. Then you manage your Bitcoin using wallet software that allows you to schedule transactions in the future. You schedule a transaction that moves all your Bitcoin from your address to the family wallet group six months in the future. Then, you cancel the transaction a few days before the event, and reschedule *another* six months in the future. If you ever become incapacitated — or die — when the time comes around, the Bitcoin automatically transfers.

However, there are other problems with the multi-sig solution. What happens if multiple family members are hit by the same bus at the same time, or if some family members lose access to their wallets? You could end up in a situation in which the Bitcoin is inaccessible.

Scheduling future transactions

The scheduled transaction system could also be used in another way. You set up a single wallet with an empty address, then set up a scheduled (periodically canceled) transaction from your wallet to that address, and then provide the seed for that wallet to each family member. In this case, you still have the problem of the seed being found by someone else or lost by someone, or of a family race to see who can get a wallet set up first after you've gone.

There's another problem, though; you'll need a wallet app that can schedule transactions, and few can right now, even though there are functions built into the Bitcoin code that can accomplish this. This may become a more viable option in the future. (Some wallet software will help you set up transactions prior to sending them, but the software needs to be online to actually send the transaction when the scheduled date comes around. If you're in line at the Pearly Gates, you may find it hard to accomplish this.)

Using a digital inheritance feature

But here's a nifty way to do what you need to do, to ensure that you, and only you, have access to your essential Bitcoin information while you're alive and *compos mentis* and yet ensure that your loved ones have access when you're counting worms.

You can use a password-management program's *digital inheritance* or *digital legacy* feature. We talk about password-management programs earlier in this chapter. Here we quickly describe how this particular feature works. Not all such programs have this feature, but most of the more popular, sophisticated ones do.

Here's essentially how they work:

1. You decide who you want to pass on the information to in the event of your death or incapacity; that person installs a copy of this software.

   Most of these programs duplicate and distribute the data, so there is a copy online, on the user's smartphone, and on the user's laptop, for instance, which helps assure a hardware error on one device (or even both) won't lead to a loss. In some cases, a free version of the software may be enough for this feature to function.

2. On your version of the software, you designate that person as your heir, or emergency contact, and you also enter a *timeout period,* an amount of time that must pass before your heir gets access.

3. You become incapacitated or die. Using their version of the software, your heir requests access to your passwords.

   They don't get access right away because you set a timeout period, and they won't get in until it's over. For instance, perhaps you set it to three weeks.

4. The company that publishes the password-management software emails you a message, saying your heir has requested access. You can't respond because you're in hospital in a coma, or you're taking the proverbial carriage ride.

5. After three weeks, your heir is granted access. However, if, by some miracle, you revive and read your email *before* the timeout ends, you can deny access to your heir.

Keeping Your
Bitcoin Safe

To be really safe, you'll probably want to provide emergency access to two or more people. Redundancy is always a good thing in computing. If two of you are hit by the same bus, the third can still get to the information. If one of your heirs forgets the password, the other heir can still get in. You could even set up accounts for all of your heirs, along with *cascading timeouts,* in order of who you want to have access to the information first. Your spouse gets the shortest timeout, for instance, your oldest child (or perhaps a sibling if your children are young) gets the next shortest, and so on.

Ethereum

4

Contents at a Glance

Chapter **1**

Getting to Know Ethereum

B lockchain technology is the most disruptive technology introduced in our generation, and Ethereum is by far the most popular blockchain implementation in use today. You can't read many technology articles or blogs without seeing something about how blockchain changes everything. Although some claims seem to be a little far-fetched, blockchain technology really is a game-changer.

Blockchain, which first burst onto the scene in 2008, has gained global notoriety for what it has already changed and what is coming. At first, blockchain was all about a new type of electronic currency. But now, partially thanks to Ethereum, blockchain is so much more than a new way to pay for things. It's a new way to think about things. It enables people and organizations to conduct business without many of the obstacles that have existed in trade relations for centuries. Head to Book 2, Chapter 1 for a full introduction to blockchain technology.

Ethereum is a comprehensive, decentralized application platform that expands the range of capabilities beyond what was possible before blockchain technology. Whereas legacy solutions to data and process sharing required third-party authorities to enforce integrity, Ethereum provides process and data integrity, along with disintermediation. Book 2, Chapter 5 provides an overview of the Ethereum blockchain. This chapter introduces you to Ether (Ethereum's main cryptocurrency), consensus, mining, smart contracts, and ICOs. You also dive into the Ethereum environment and development tools.

Exploring Ethereum's Consensus, Mining, and Smart Contracts

Ethereum provides integrity in the way it implements immutability and smart contracts. Immutability isn't actually a blockchain guarantee. You can change data in any block — even after other blocks are added to the blockchain. However, as soon as you change a block, that block and all subsequent blocks fail integrity checks, and your node is out of sync. Instead of saying that the blockchain is immutable, it is more accurate to say that any changes (mutations) to the blockchain are easily and immediately detected.

Ethereum is based on democracy. Each node gets an equal vote. Every time nodes get a new block to add to the blockchain, they validate the block and its transactions, and then vote whether to accept or reject the block. If several different blocks are submitted by different nodes, only one of the blocks can receive votes from a majority. The block that gets more than half of the network node's votes gets to join the blockchain as its newest block.

One of the first problems is to determine when a new block is ready for the blockchain. When too many conflicting blocks are submitted, the voting process slows down. Ethereum makes it hard to add new blocks to keep the number of new block collisions low and to make voting faster. This is because Ethereum uses a consensus protocol called *proof of work (PoW)*, which sets the rules for validating and adding new blocks. PoW makes adding blocks to the blockchain difficult but profitable.

Ethereum defines Ether as its cryptocurrency. You can transfer Ether between accounts or earn it by doing the hard work of adding blocks to the Ethereum blockchain. The Ethereum PoW mechanism requires that nodes find a number that, when combined with the block's header data, produces a cryptographic hash value that matches the current target, which is a value that is adjusted to keep new block production at a steady rate. Finding a hash value that matches the current target is hard. You have to try, on average, more than a quadrillion values to find the right one. That's the point. Using a PoW mechanism makes it so hard to submit a block that fewer blocks are submitted, which reduces the number of collisions. The node that finds the right value gets a small Ether payment for the effort. This process is called *mining,* and the node that wins the prize is that block's *miner.* You can read more about PoW (and other consensus mechanisms) in Book 6, Chapter 2, which covers different types of cryptocurrency mining.

Mining regulates the speed at which new blocks get submitted as candidate blocks and results in a number that is easy to validate. Finding the right number to solve the puzzle is difficult, but verifying the number is fast and easy. Another interesting aspect of mining is that each block's header contains a hash from the previous block. Ethereum nodes use the hash to easily detect unauthorized block changes. If a block changes, the hash result doesn't match and the block becomes invalid.

Mining is also a way to make money using blockchain technology. Mining has become competitive, and most of today's miners invest in high-performance hardware with multiple GPUs to carry out the complex operations. To keep the mining process fair, Ethereum uses a complexity value that makes the mining process even harder as miners get faster. Adjusting the complexity allows Ethereum to regulate the new block frequency to an average of one new block every 14 seconds.

The glue that holds the Ethereum environment together is the smart contract, which is introduced in Book 2, Chapter 5. Ethereum is much more than just a financial ledger, and smart contracts provide much of its rich functionality. Each Ethereum node runs a copy of the *Ethereum virtual machine (EVM).* The EVM runs smart contract code in a way that guarantees that smart contracts execute the same way on all nodes and produce the same output. Running smart contract code is not optional. Smart contracts execute based on specific rules and cannot be subverted or halted. The EVM smart contract guarantees provide a stable platform for automated transaction processing that you can trust. Smart contracts provide the primary power of the Ethereum environment. Check out Chapters 6 and 7 of this minibook to learn more about and create your own smart contracts.

REMEMBER

One of the known weaknesses with software is that attackers can sometimes bypass its controls and carry out unintended actions. That type of attack is more difficult in Ethereum, primarily due to its smart contract implementation. Attackers can't directly attack the blockchain and make unauthorized changes because any such changes will be immediately detected.

The next most likely attack vector is the smart contract interface to the blockchain data. Ethereum guarantees that smart contract code, which is translated into *byte-code* before it is written to the blockchain, executes on every EVM instance in the same way. Also, the EVM determines when code executes and what code executes. Attackers have few opportunities to leverage smart contract code, which makes Ethereum an even more secure environment.

Buying, Spending, and Trading Ether

Ethereum runs on Ether (ETH), its main cryptocurrency. The majority of all existing Ether was pre-mined when Ethereum first went live on July 30, 2015. Miners continually create Ether, but the amount of mined Ether is less than 30 percent of all Ether in existence. The life cycle of Ethereum transactions requires that you first acquire Ether to participate in Ethereum. Many exchanges support exchanging legal tender, also called *fiat currency,* for cryptocurrency, including Ether. Check out Book 5, Chapter 3 to learn more about cryptocurrency exchanges.

Before you can interact with the Ethereum blockchain, you need to create at least one account. Book 2, Chapter 3 introduces you to various accounts you need in order to interact with blockchain technology and cryptocurrencies, but creating an Ethereum account essentially involves just creating a cryptographic private and public key pair, and generating the associated address, which is based on your public key. The software that handles this process is called an Ethereum *wallet.* You learn about different options for wallets in Book 1, Chapter 3.

You can use a wallet provided by an exchange or a stand-alone wallet. After you create your Ethereum account, you need to select an exchange to purchase Ether. After you select an exchange, you set up an exchange account and provide a funding source. Your main funding source is generally a bank account. The most common way to buy Ether is to withdraw funds from your bank account and use that money to exchange for Ether. Figure 1-1 shows the web page for purchasing Ether through the coinbase.com exchange. Note that the funding source for this account is a Bank of America account.

You can also purchase Ether using cash. A growing number of cryptocurrency ATMs allow you to exchange cash for different types of cryptocurrency. All you need is the private key you generated using your Ethereum wallet and cash. However, you will pay for this convenience. Cryptocurrency ATMs often use exchange rates that are less favorable than more traditional exchanges. One current service, Localcoin ATM, works just like a regular ATM. Navigate to `https://localcoinatm.com` to see where you can find ATMs and how to use them. Figure 1-2 shows several steps in the process of purchasing Ether with cash from an ATM.

After you own Ether, you can interact with other Ethereum accounts and send them some of your Ether in exchange for good or services. Or you can simply hold on to your Ether in hopes that it goes up in price. Ether, along with other cryptocurrencies, fluctuates in price continuously. Many investors buy and sell cryptocurrencies as investments, just like trading fiat currencies or commodities. Figure 1-3 shows the main coinbase.com dashboard with popular cryptocurrency prices.

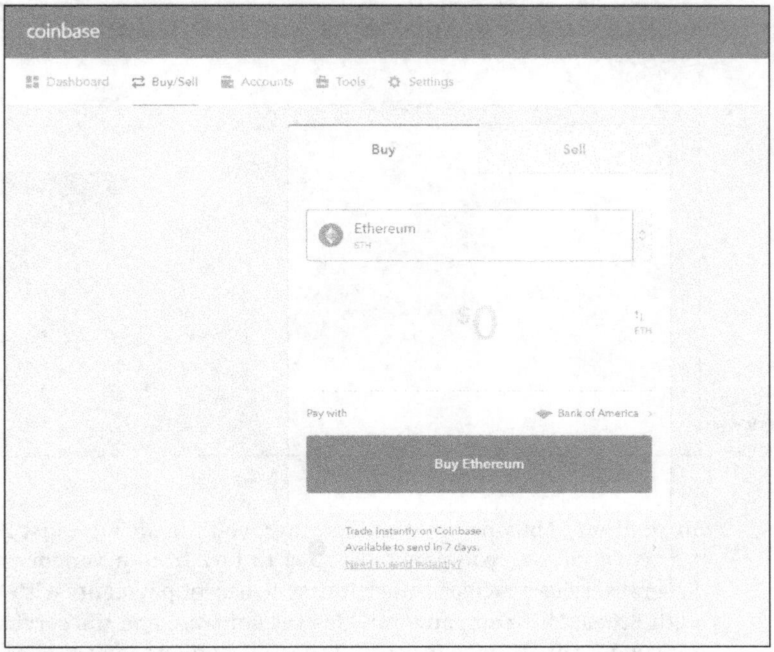

FIGURE 1-1:
Purchasing
Ether using
coinbase.com.

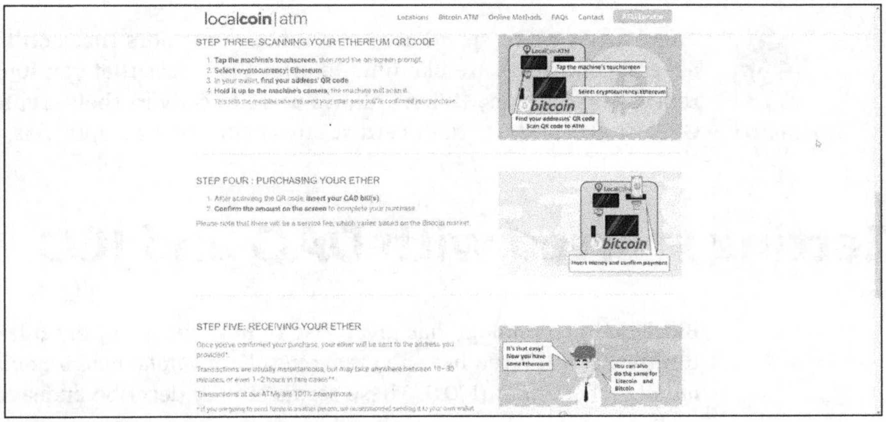

FIGURE 1-2:
Purchasing Ether
with cash.

At its highest price, Ether sold for around $4,362. At the time of this writing, it was down by about $400. Whether cryptocurrency is a good investment depends on your appetite for risk and belief in its long-term value. Head to Book 5 to learn more about cryptocurrency investing.

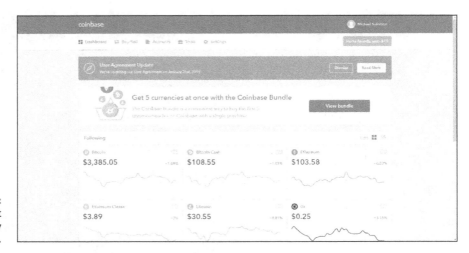

FIGURE 1-3:
Current
cryptocurrency
prices.

In addition to buying and trading Ether, you can spend it just like any other currency. Of course, you generally have to buy from a vendor that accepts Ether. Several service providers make it easy to accept payments with Ether, such as Pay with Ether. This company provides the software and the services to make it easy for vendors of any size to accept Ether as payment. Visit www.paywithether.com/ to find out more about this payment option.

TECHNICAL STUFF

There are ways to spend cryptocurrency at vendors that don't directly accept it. Several companies are planning to offer Visa cards that you fund with cryptocurrency. One company, Wirex, allows users to convert their cryptocurrency to USD, GPB, or EUR and use their card at any vendor that accepts Visa.

Getting Started with DAO and ICO

Blockchain technology has given rise to new classes of organizations and opportunities. You'll often hear about *decentralized autonomous organizations (DAOs)* and *initial coin offerings (ICOs).* These terms simply describe endeavors that Ethereum makes possible.

A *DAO* is an organization that operates only on the rules set forth in its smart contracts. In reality, most DAOs require some human interaction, but the majority of the functionality is automated. A DAO conducts business and engages in transactions without requiring human interaction. Today's DAOs are relatively simple, but it is expected that they will grow in complexity and eventually replace (or at least compete with) some existing human-based businesses. For a more detailed introduction to DAOs, see Book 2, Chapter 5.

Like all businesses, Ethereum-based or Ethereum-related businesses need funding to operate. Many traditional methods for raising funds exist, including soliciting private investors, securing loans, or selling shares in the company. In addition, Ethereum opens new options for funding businesses. Businesses that use Ethereum often create their own tokens, also called coins, that represent value associated with the business ventures. Businesses sell these tokens to raise funds to launch the business. These *ICOs* essentially exchange one type of currency for a digital item of equivalent value.

Tokens may represent an expected future value as ownership in a new venture or current value that entitles the holder to some benefit. Either way, tokens are similar in some ways to stock shares. An ICO is a popular method to fund a new blockchain-based business. Read more about ICOs in Book 5, Chapter 6.

The *Ethereum environment*, or ecosystem, is made up of several different parts. You've already learned about most of these pieces, but it helps to put them together in one place. Starting from the lowest level of the blockchain, Ethereum is made up of the following components:

>> **Blockchain:** The collection of data blocks that comprise the core of Ethereum. Each block contains data and smart contract code, and is cryptographically linked to its predecessor, creating a chain of blocks.

>> **EVM:** The Ethereum virtual machine, which runs smart contract bytecode. Each Ethereum node runs an instance of the EVM.

>> **Wallet:** Software, hardware, or physical paper that stores the public and private keys that correspond to an Ethereum account. The wallet stores the capability to access crypto-assets on the Ethereum blockchain.

>> **Exchange:** A service that allows its users to exchange fiat currency for cryptocurrency.

>> **Development environment:** The set of tools used to write, compile, and perform unit tests on smart contract software.

>> **Testing environment:** A simulated Ethereum blockchain used to perform integration testing on smart contracts and to complete decentralized applications (dApps).

>> **Client interface:** The client user interface's software and libraries that are used to interact with Ethereum smart contracts.

You learn much more about the details of each of these components in Chapter 3 of this minibook.

Delving into Development Tools

Developing decentralized applications for Ethereum requires several types of tools. Each of these tools provides support for various phases of software development and is necessary to create dApps for the Ethereum blockchain environment. In Chapter 3 of this minibook, you find out the different categories of development tools and learn about several alternatives for each type of tool.

Tools needed to develop Ethereum dApps fall into the following categories:

>> **Blockchain client:** When developing Ethereum dApps, you'll need to implement a local EVM. A blockchain client launches a local EVM and executes your smart contract code. It also interacts with your Ethereum blockchain.

>> **Development and testing blockchain:** Deploying to the live Ethereum blockchain, also called *mainnet,* is the last step in the development process. Before deployment, you want to interact with a local version of an Ethereum blockchain. Because live blockchain access costs Ether, you should carry out development and testing on a local blockchain to avoid costs and errors.

>> **Compiler and testing framework:** After you have a local EVM and local blockchain, you'll need a way to interact with your smart contract code and place it on your test blockchain for test execution. A development and testing framework provides the tools you need to carry out development and testing tasks.

>> **Source code editor/IDE:** Although you can use any text editor to write smart contract source code, an editor or integrated development environment (IDE) that is designed or extended to support Ethereum smart contract source code development will be very helpful. IDEs can increase developer efficiency and make it easier to create good smart contract code.

Chapter **2**

Exploring Use Cases for Ethereum

E thereum is a great implementation of blockchain technology, but unlike the current marketing hype, it doesn't solve all of the world's problems. However, it does solve some problems that have proved to be hard nuts to crack! The trick is in knowing where Ethereum shines and where it may not be the best choice. Examining successful use cases can help you gain an understanding of when to use Ethereum. In general, blockchain is a good fit when you need to exchange something in an environment in which the players don't trust one another.

First, you need to look at what *exchange something* means. The traditional definition is to trade things of value. But in some cases, the exchange implies simply answering a question. For example, "Who are you?" is a valid question. Today, most answers to that question involve an audible answer that's accompanied by additional proof, such as a picture ID. Blockchain technology in general, and Ethereum in particular, can handle many types of exchanges well.

In this chapter, you discover some of the ways in which Ethereum solves problems elegantly and provides a solution that just can't be addressed as cleanly using non-blockchain approaches. After reading this chapter, you should have a clearer picture of how Ethereum works as an effective tool in your problem-solving toolbox.

Diving into Ethereum Applications

The first thing that comes to mind when you think of blockchain is probably cryptocurrency. Yes, blockchain does that, but it also does far more. Many personal and business interactions involve exchanging funds, products, and services. Entire industries exist to act as brokers that manage the exchanges and provide a level of mutual trust (that is, both parties of an exchange trust the broker). The Ethereum implementation of blockchain can solve many types of problems with exchanges that involve some type of transfer or exchange among untrusting parties. And the beauty of Ethereum is that it removes the need for the broker, or middleman.

For example, suppose you want to buy a used car. You have several options that come with different costs. If you break down all the different options, most of the cost differences are based on trust. You probably have the highest level of trust for a dealer who primarily sells new cars and also offers certified pre-owned vehicles. (The term *used car* has an air of questionable trust.) This trust and assurance make these types of car the most expensive. You pay a higher price to a dealer who has invested lots of time and money into building a reputation you can trust.

On the other hand, you could see a car with a "For Sale" sign parked at the grocery store. Although the car may look good, you have no idea about its owner, condition, or history. You would be taking on risk because of a lack of trust in the seller, which is why this kind of transaction is generally cheaper than buying the same used car from a dealer.

The used car example is one that could benefit from Ethereum. Suppose all car manufacturers, mechanics, and body shop workers were required to submit information to a public Ethereum blockchain whenever a car was serviced or repaired. Anyone could get the complete history of a car at any time. You wouldn't have to trust the seller. If you decide to buy the car, another Ethereum app could allow you to transfer the agreed-upon purchase price to the seller in exchange for the legal title. The app would ensure that the transaction was legal and safe and adhered to all appropriate laws and regulations. And you wouldn't have to pay a middleman to handle your transaction. You would have to pay a small fee to record your transaction on the blockchain, but it would be a tiny fraction of a dealer upcharge.

The used car example highlights a small number of ways in which Ethereum can help solve problems. In general, blockchain provides core features that solve four main problems with exchanges of any type:

>> **Transparent transactions:** No entity "owns" transactions. Anyone with access to the blockchain can view all transactions. You may not be able to see the contents of each encrypted transaction, but you can see the address and the fact that a transaction exists.

This chapter covers public blockchains, to which anyone can add a transaction if they have the right software or pay the right fee. Private blockchains are not generally visible to the public, and only certain parties may add transactions to them. We show you how to set up a private blockchain in Book 2, Chapter 3.

>> **Traceable history of all data:** Because you can see all transactions, you can create a trace of every asset, from its introduction to the blockchain through to the current time. This feature makes it easy to trace the history of anything recorded on the blockchain.

>> **Reduced overhead:** By eliminating middlemen and brokers, producers and consumers can interact directly. This direct interaction can greatly increase efficiency and speed up transaction processing times.

>> **Lower cost:** In addition to making transaction processing more efficient, Ethereum can lower transaction costs by removing extra processing steps and handlers. Instead of paying a broker or other middleman to process a transaction, you only have to pay a small transaction fee to the blockchain.

Ethereum really shines when applications benefit from its core features. In the following sections, you find out about some of the types of applications that are good fits for Ethereum. You see how problems that are hard to solve with other technologies are easy to solve in Ethereum. As you read through these use cases, think of how Ethereum can solve problems for your organization.

The rest of this chapter focuses on four groups of Ethereum use cases:

>> **Financial services:** Applications that manage financial transactions

>> **Digital identity management:** Applications that associate an identity with a person or device

>> **Specific industry vertical applications:** Applications that provide or support services that apply to specific industry vertical markets

>> **Governance services:** Applications that provide services related to government agencies

Exploring Financial Services

Financial services are interactions that involve some exchange of currency. The currency can be legal tender, also called *fiat currency*, or it can be cryptocurrency, such as Bitcoin or Ethereum's default currency, *Ether (ETH)*. Ethereum apps do a great job of handling *pure currency exchanges,* or exchanging some currency for a product or service. Financial services may center on handling payments, but more nuances exist to the many transactions that involve money.

Banking

Historically, banks or other financial institutions were necessary to conduct trade. Although physical currency can change hands between individuals, the process gets more complex when the number of participants grows. For example, if you want to buy food at the grocery store, you have several options to pay at the register: cash, check, and card. All three options involve a bank.

TIP

One of the primary services banks provide is serving as an uninterested, trusted third party to broker transactions. If you trust the person or organization with whom you're doing business, you probably don't need a bank.

Although you don't have to get cash at a bank, there's a good chance that at least some of your cash came from cashing a check someone gave you or withdrawing money from one of your own accounts. Although banks make getting cash easy with ATMs and satellite branches, you still have to interact with bank employees or banking devices at some point.

If you pay with a check or card, you are asking the vendor to trust that your bank or card-issuing institution will provide money to pay what you owe. No money changes hands at that point — just a promise. The entire transaction is based on trust. Only a handful of cards are generally accepted because those are the ones vendors trust. They believe that the bank or payment card company will follow through and provide the payment to complete the transaction.

Financial transactions, except those that simply consist of one person handing cash to another person, involve some middleman to broker the transaction. Vendors generally pay a transaction fee to have the middleman move the money around. For example, paying with a credit card can add a 2 percent to 5 percent service charge to the vendor's cost. Even though you may not see the transaction fees, rest assured, they are built into the price of goods and services!

Cryptocurrency

Blockchain was initially proposed as a vehicle to implement a cryptocurrency, Bitcoin. Ethereum also implements cryptocurrencies. The default currency for Ethereum is Ether, but Ethereum supports many other types of tokens. *Cryptocurrency* is currency that is stored exclusively on a blockchain. Users can access their currency through their blockchain accounts and can transfer units of cryptocurrency to and from other accounts.

Although this sounds a lot like depositing and withdrawing money from an account at a bank, there is a huge difference: There is no bank! That's the beauty of Ethereum. You establish an Ethereum account and then add funds in the form of ETH or any supported token. To do this, you generally have to send fiat currency to an exchange that allows you to buy cryptocurrency and then transfer it to your account.

TIP

Exchanges aren't banks, but linking a traditional bank account to an exchange account is a common practice. You have to transfer money from the "outside world" to your Ethereum account at some point. Linking to a bank isn't technically required — some exchanges operate like ATMs. You can deposit cash to purchase ETH or other tokens directly.

After you have cryptocurrency in your account, you can use it to buy goods and services from any vendor that accepts it. Let's say your local grocery store decides to accept ETH. When you check out, all you have to do is transfer an amount of ETH from your account to the grocery store's Ethereum address. You don't have to involve a bank at all. The ETH goes directly from your account to the grocery store's account. And because you have conducted the transfer using Ethereum, you don't have to trust the grocer and the grocer doesn't have to trust you.

This model cuts out processing middlemen such as the bank or payment card companies. The cryptocurrency is transferred in real time and you pay a small transaction fee, currently less than US$0.01 for a standard transfer, which is far less than the fees traditional processors charge. The transaction works like a person-to-person cash transfer, but you don't have to carry a wad of cash around with you all the time.

Real estate

Another rich field for Ethereum in the financial services domain is real estate transactions. As with banking transactions, Ethereum makes it possible to conduct these transactions without a broker. Buyers and sellers can exchange currency for a legal title directly.

Ethereum's smart contracts can validate all aspects of the transaction as it occurs. The steps that normally require an attorney or a loan processor can happen automatically. A buyer can transfer funds to purchase a property after legal requirements are met, such as validating the title's availability and filing required government documents. The seller receives payment for the property at the same time the title transfers to the buyer.

Ethereum can also go far beyond real estate purchases. Maintaining property commonly requires many documents and records. Property history is required for many decisions and can be a prerequisite for satisfying insurance claims.

Ethereum provides a framework for storing the complete history of a property's title as well as its physical history. Ethereum real estate management apps can keep a transparent log of all property maintenance and ownership details. Ethereum makes it easy to search through a property's history to see if it has ever had a fire, flooding, or a termite infestation. It can also be used to predict upcoming maintenance needs.

Rental property owners often have to expend substantial effort in order to keep track of upcoming reservations, past renter information, maintenance needs and history, and profitability assessments over time. Ethereum can help meet all these needs by storing rental information in a blockchain that is immutable and available to anyone.

Creating Ethereum escrow applications

Many transactions aren't as immediate as shopping at the grocery store. In that situation, you have the groceries with you, you pay for them, and then you leave with them. Other transactions take some time to resolve. Suppose you order a hardcopy of this book from your favorite online bookseller. When you complete your transaction, you've paid for the book, but you won't have a physical copy of the book for at least a day.

Paying for a book up front and then waiting for the delivery isn't a big deal, but what about buying something more expensive, such as a diamond ring? You might be less willing to pay a lot of money up front and then wait for the product. *Escrow accounts* provide a way of holding money while a transaction completes. The buyer places money in an escrow account, and after the seller validates that the money is in the account, the seller ships the product. When the buyer receives the product, the money is released to the seller.

Ethereum's smart contracts can automate escrow accounts and remove the need for an account manager. The seller and the buyer each interact with the Ethereum escrow account directly to provide a trusted way of processing payment for transactions that aren't immediate.

Examining ICOs

Bitcoin provided the first workable alternative currency in the digital realm. It has been wildly popular and has become more than just an alternative to fiat currency. Instead of having to constantly exchange fiat currency for cryptocurrency and vice versa, cryptocurrencies have matured to a point that conversion to another currency isn't always necessary.

Many new business ventures have been created that are entirely funded by cryptocurrency. Such initiatives are commonly funded through an *initial coin offering (ICO)*, which allows investors to purchase tokens specific to a project (the ICO). ICOs aren't specific to Ethereum, but many new Ethereum-based ventures start funding drives through ICOs. The most common Ethereum token standard, and the one most ICOs use, is *ERC-20,* which supports core functions that govern how tokens are created, exchanged, and valued.

The ICO process is similar to an IPO (initial public offering) in more traditional financial environments. An ICO is a way to state a business venture intention and invite investors to invest in the new organization through crowdfunding. In turn, investors own tokens that represent an ownership stake in the new venture. ICOs are largely unregulated and can be risky. But they can also make it possible to get in on the ground floor of new and exciting opportunities. See Book 5, Chapter 6 for more info.

Establishing Digital Identity Management

Asserting one's identity has always been challenging, but doing so in the digital world has proved to be extremely difficult. The process of asserting an identity is fairly simple, but executing it well is the problem. Some entity, normally a person, submits a claim to be the owner of an identity by providing a unique identifier for the identity. In simple applications, you type your user name to claim to be a certain user. This is called the *identification* step.

But you can't just provide any identity. You have to prove that you own that identity by providing additional information. In other words, you have to make additional claims against the identity. The most common way to do this in many applications is to provide a password. This is the *authentication* step. You are asking the application to authenticate that you are who you claim to be.

The application then compares the information you provided (password) with stored information to see whether you provided the correct password. If you enter the password that matches, the authentication system accepts your claim that you own the identity and authorizes you to access the application. More secure applications use techniques other than, or in addition to, passwords, such as smart cards, tokens, or biometrics. Regardless of the techniques used, a trusted authority has to intervene to determine whether an identity claim is valid.

Ethereum apps provide a unique opportunity to help manage identities. Each Ethereum user account has a unique address and is associated with a unique pair of keys. These keys allow the owner to access any blockchain resources associated with the account. A unique identity can be one of the resources associated with an account and is identified by the account's address.

Establishing an identity would require some interaction with a governing authority to verify that you are, in the physical world, who you claim to be. This step is similar to providing a picture ID and is necessary to keep people from creating multiple false IDs. After you establish an identity, you can make additional claims against that identity and provide additional information, such as your name, address, and biometric information. These claims are stored as part of your identity and provide authentication in a similar way that passwords do. But using Ethereum is far safer. You don't have to trust any entity to protect your private information, and only you can access your blockchain data because you control the keys.

Managing individual and device identities

Identities don't have to be limited to people. Each Ethereum account can represent an identity, and that identity can refer to a device. If you're wondering why your toaster needs an identity, think of all the smart devices on the market today. If you have the budget, it isn't hard to have your house lights, refrigerator, stove, heating, air conditioner, entertainment center, and many other electronic devices on your home network. Getting all these devices to talk to one another and play nice can be challenging.

Giving each device a unique identity is a great first step. Just like people, devices have descriptive attributes that describe their state. Devices have names, functional categories, locations, and permissions. As a simple example, your printer could detect that it needs more ink and automatically order more. The printer's identity would be robust enough to tell the vendor where to send the ink and how the order will be paid for. A real person would have to install the ink cartridges, but that might be changing as well.

The explosion of Internet-connected devices, called the *Internet of Things (IoT)*, has raised many questions about securing and managing these devices. Although no comprehensive solution exists, proposing a straightforward way to manage these devices as individuals is a good start. And as more and more IoT devices become more autonomous, having a verifiable identity allows them to operate with minimal oversight or human interaction.

Reducing fraud and identity theft

Ethereum solutions for managing digital identity can help dramatically reduce fraud and identity theft. The offline world has a few globally accepted identifications standards. Most people have a driver's license and many have a passport. These two forms of ID are issued by government agencies and are accepted as proof of identity in most situations.

However, these forms of ID do not have a digital counterpart. If an Ethereum standard for identity management were to be globally accepted, you would be able to present your digital identity upon demand. Having your identification information stored in a blockchain is much more secure. You would be the only one who had access to your identification attributes because you would control your own keys. You wouldn't have to re-enter identification information and a separate user account for every website and remote system you accessed.

In addition to the reduction in data duplication, any changes to your identity claims would be stored in an immutable block. That makes it virtually impossible to use someone else's identity without leaving a clear audit trail leading right to the attacker.

Examining the ERC-725 standard and beyond

Fabian Vogelsteller, the creator of the ERC-20 Ethereum token standard, has proposed *ERC-725*, an Ethereum identity standard. ERC-725 is a smart contract interface that defines how to define, configure, and use identities in Ethereum. Developers can implement the interface in their own smart contracts to manage digital identities in Ethereum. Defining the standard as a smart contract interface allows competing implementations to share the same core functionality and ultimately be compatible with one another. Therefore, an ERC-725 identity should be usable in a wide range of applications.

Examining Industry Applications

Ethereum use cases don't have to be generic and apply to multiple domains. Many vertical markets have specific needs that Ethereum applications can address. In this section, you find out about three vertical markets that benefit from Ethereum solutions.

Healthcare

Healthcare has become one of the most popular topics of conversation, ranging from politics to research to spending. It seems that everyone is interested in increasing the quality of healthcare while reducing its cost. The availability of large amounts of digital data has made advances in healthcare possible.

Researchers can analyze large amounts of data to explore new treatment plans, increase the overall effectiveness of existing drugs and procedures, and identify cost-saving opportunities. This type of analysis is possible only with access to vast amounts of patient medical histories. The main problem for researchers is that a patient's *electronic health record (EHR)* is likely stored as fragments across multiple practices and databases. Although efforts to combine these records are ongoing, privacy is a growing concern (we're back to the trust problem) and progress is slow.

EHR management is a good fit for an Ethereum app. Storing a patient's EHR in an Ethereum blockchain can remove the silos of fragmented data without having to trust each entity that provides or modifies parts of the EHR. Storing the EHR in this way also helps clarify billing and payment for medical services. With comprehensive medical procedure history all in one place, medical service providers and insurance companies can see the same view of a patient's treatment. A full history makes it easier to figure out what should be billed.

Another advantage that Ethereum apps can provide in the healthcare domain is in managing pharmaceuticals. Blockchain EHRs provide the information for medical practitioners to see a full history and a current snapshot of a patient's prescription medications. It also allows researchers, auditors, and even pharmaceutical manufacturers to examine the effect and possible side effects of their products. Having EHRs available but protected can provide valuable information to increase the quality of healthcare services.

Energy

Another vertical market with interesting blockchain opportunities is in energy management. Smart city planners realize that energy management is a core requirement for using technology to enhance inhabitants' quality of life. Just collecting data isn't enough. Smart meters provide real-time information on energy use and allow energy providers to restrict energy distribution at peak times. For instance, summertime demands for electricity in hot climates can push the limits of electricity providers. Smart meters can limit the energy used in single homes to cumulatively lower the overall energy demand.

Ethereum apps make it easy to give each smart meter an identity and allow it to autonomously manage the energy it requires to power devices in its home. When the electricity provider needs to limit overall output, it can contact smart meters identified in the blockchain and request that each one reduce its electricity use. The blockchain provides an up-to-date list of participating smart meters and automatically keeps an audit trail of how well each one manages its energy use. Storing energy usage data by using a blockchain makes it possible for energy suppliers, manufacturers, and service providers to access the data to identify new business opportunities. Using a blockchain takes the data out of the silo.

Smart meters aren't only consumers. As home solar panel installations increase and the panels become more efficient, the likelihood increases that a home will produce more electricity than it uses. In addition to autonomously monitoring energy use, a smart meter with a blockchain identity can also manage energy produced and delivered to the energy grid. The blockchain history of energy production would keep a detailed list of billing offsets that may substantially reduce a homeowner's energy bill.

Supply chain

One of the earliest large-scale Ethereum use cases is the management of supply chains. The process of managing products from the original producer to the consumer is expensive and time-consuming. With today's tracking of goods, consumers have difficulty knowing much about the products they consume. Some products, such as electronics and appliances, might have descriptive tags that identify places and times of manufacture, but most of the products we consume don't provide that type of information.

Suppose you buy Alaskan salmon at your grocery store. Aside from the trust you place in your grocer, there isn't any way to know that the fish really came from Alaska. Ethereum supply-chain apps can provide consumers with complete information that lets them trace their product all the way back to its origin. In the case of the salmon, the fisherman who caught the fish would create the first entry in the blockchain. Every transfer of ownership from that point until the salmon ends up in the grocery store display would be tracked and recorded. A user-friendly Ethereum app could provide a trace all the way back to the day your fish was caught. Or, if you become ill after eating a Caesar salad, you could use blockchain data to find out what farm provided the romaine lettuce.

Implementing supply chain management provides multiple benefits. The first is transparency. Producers, consumers, and anyone in between can see how each fish traveled from the place it was caught to where it was finally purchased. Anyone can trace its path and the time it took to get there. Inspectors and regulatory auditors can ensure that each participant in the supply chain met required standards. This increased transparency occurs while eliminating unnecessary middlemen. Each transfer in the process occurs between active participants, not brokers. With Ethereum supply-chain apps, you can track a product all the way back to its origin and verify the product's authenticity claims.

TIP

Proper tracking of physical products in the blockchain depends on accurately associating the physical product with the digital identifier. For example, Michael recently checked a bag when he flew on a commercial airline. The agent was busily engaged in a conversation with another agent and swapped tags with another traveler. When Michael arrived, his bag was nowhere to be found. After investigating, it was discovered that his tag arrived on the same flight as him, but it was attached to the wrong bag; in other words, Michael's bag had flown to Mexico with the other gentleman's tag attached. It was four days before Michael got his bag back. Always remember that the blockchain only *represents* the physical world — it isn't really the physical world.

Enabling Effective Governance

The last category of potential good use cases for Ethereum apps is in governance. Governing bodies should be responsible and accountable to the people they govern. Although this is not always the case, it is the ideal. Equitability, transparency, and auditability are three characteristics that should describe all government functions. Ethereum apps can help approach these goals by using foundational blockchain features to manage governance functions.

Tax payment

Governments fund their operation through taxes. Taxes are crucial to every governmental function and of vital interest to every taxpayer. Blockchain technology allows governments and taxpayers to interact in a way that provides both parties the transparency and auditability to assess taxes fairly. Taxpayers can record income and expenses in the blockchain ledger, and governing agencies can use that information to assess taxes. Taxpayers can also submit payment, or even accept refunds, through an Ethereum cryptocurrency transfer.

Ethereum-based tax payment maintenance could effectively eliminate the need to keep detailed records and receipts. Audits would take less time and effort because all supporting information would already be recorded in the blockchain. Although the outcome of the audit might not be any more desirable, at least Ethereum might make the process proceed more smoothly. And because audits would be simpler and faster, auditing agencies could carry out more audits using blockchain data.

Government spending

Currently, only some details about how governments spend money is made public. If all government spending were funded by cryptocurrency and recorded on a blockchain, all transactions would be available for review and audit. Any person with blockchain access could track payments. Transaction sources and recipients would either be divulged by the agency creating the payment or noticeably "secret." You may not be able to find out who owns a blockchain account that receives government funds, but you could still see how much cryptocurrency is transferred to the address. This new level of transparency would encourage politicians to reduce or (one hopes) eliminate secret payments.

Voting

A vote is a classic transfer of choice or approval from one person to another. Blockchain technology has the potential to greatly simplify the voting process. You've seen how Ethereum apps and standards can help manage digital identities. In much the same way, Ethereum could support identities in casting votes during an election. Because casting a vote is a transaction, each vote would be associated with a unique Ethereum address. The only piece of the puzzle left to address would be to validate the registration of each account as an authorized voter.

Each voter's identification claims would contain descriptive attributes that identify the voter's eligibility and voting district. Any vote cast would be recorded on the blockchain and become part of the voting record. Calculating election results would be greatly simplified, and the complete immutable record would reduce the many criticisms encountered in today's elections.

Policy development

Public policy development is in many ways an extension of the voting issue. The policy development process generally includes identifying a problem, collecting input from the community, developing a policy to address the problem, and then implementing the policy. Ethereum apps to manage interaction with the public can have multiple beneficial effects. Using blockchain to interact with the public would make governance functions more transparent and auditable by providing members of the public with a full record of the input and actions leading up to a policy change. It should also provide a mechanism for feedback to monitor the results of a new or modified policy.

Notary

The last governance function that represents a good Ethereum use case is the notary function. In the real world, a notary provides assurance that a signature on a document is authentic. In the digital world, an Ethereum account can sign a document in a way that associates the digital identity with that document. If an Ethereum account appends a hash of the document with the author's private key, anyone can verify the signature by decrypting the hash with the account's public key and then comparing the decrypted value with the hash of the document. If the two match, that means the account really did sign the document *and* it has not been altered. In this way, an Ethereum app can provide notary services.

Chapter **3**

Examining the Ethereum Ecosystem and Development Life cycle

The Ethereum blockchain implementation provides a rich environment for developing decentralized blockchain applications. These decentralized applications, or *dApps*, are unique in that the code and data are stored in the blockchain. Each node executes the code in the same way and guarantees that the results are the same.

The capability to deploy application code and data across an entire network ensures that the shared ledger remains the same for all nodes and that changes are allowed only in specific circumstances. The blockchain doesn't need an external authority to determine whether data is valid — the rules that govern the blockchain itself determine whether new data is valid and can be added to the blockchain.

In this chapter, you discover the components of an Ethereum dApp. You also find out how code modifies the blockchain, and how to pay for the ability to add data. And finally, you find out about the Ethereum dApp development process, what tools you need to develop dApps, and how the pieces fit together.

Exploring the Ethereum Blockchain Block Structure

Ethereum dApps primarily populate blocks, add them to the blockchain, and query existing blocks. That sounds pretty simple, but lots and lots of details are hidden in those simple goals. Before you can start to build blocks and add them to the blockchain, you need to know a little bit more about the contents of an Ethereum block and how the chain is built. This section focuses specifically on the Ethereum blockchain. To find out more about blockchain technology in general, see Book 2, Chapter 1.

TECHNICAL STUFF

This section describes only basic block and chain details. The authoritative reference for Ethereum internals is the Ethereum yellow paper, at https://ethereum.github.io/yellowpaper/paper.pdf. You can also find a pretty good third-party detailed discussion of Ethereum block structure internals at https://ethereum.stackexchange.com/questions/268/ethereum-block-architecture.

A *block* is a data structure that contains two main sections: a header and a body. Transactions are added to the body and then submitted to the blockchain network. *Miners* take the blocks and try to solve a mathematical puzzle to win a prize. Miners are just nodes, or pools of nodes, with enough computational power to calculate block hashes many times to solve the puzzle. In Ethereum, the mining process uses the submitted block header and an arbitrary number called a *nonce (number used once)*. The miner picks a value for the nonce, which is part of the block header, and calculates a Keccak-256 hash on the block header. The result has to match an agreed-upon pattern, which gets more difficult over time as miners get faster at mining blocks. If the first mining result doesn't match the pattern, the miner picks another nonce and calculates a hash on the new block header. This process continues until a miner finds a nonce that results in a hash that matches the pattern.

The miner that finds the solution broadcasts that solution to the rest of the network. That miner collects a reward, in ETH, for doing the hard work to validate the block. Because many miners work on blocks at the same time, it's common for several miners to solve the hash puzzle simultaneously. In other blockchains, these blocks are discarded as orphans. In Ethereum, these blocks are called uncles. An *uncle block* is any successfully mined block that arrives after that block has already been accepted. Ethereum accepts uncle blocks and even provides a reward to the miner, but the reward is smaller than the one for the accepted block.

TECHNICAL STUFF

Ethereum rewards miners of uncle blocks to reduce mining centralization and to increase the security of the blockchain. Uncle rewards provide an incentive for smaller miners to participate. Otherwise, mining would be profitable for only large pools, which could eventually take over all mining. Encouraging more miners to participate also increases security by increasing the overall work carried out on the entire blockchain.

The *header* of a block contains data that describes the block, and the *body* contains all the transactions stored in the block. Figure 3-1 shows the contents of an Ethereum block header.

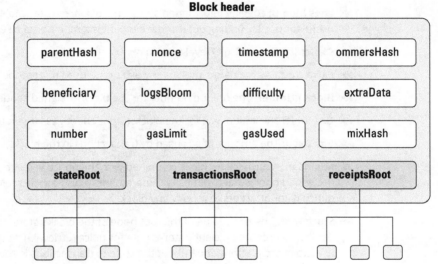

Block header

FIGURE 3-1:
Ethereum block header.

Each Ethereum block header contains information that defines and describes the block, and records its place in the blockchain. The block header contains the following fields:

>> **Previous hash:** The hash value of the previous block's header, where the previous block is the last block on the blockchain to which the current block gets added.

TECHNICAL STUFF

Ethereum uses the Keccak-256 algorithm to produce all hash values. The National Institute of Standards and Technology (NIST) Secure Hashing Algorithm 3 (SHA-3) is a subset of the Keccak algorithm. Ethereum was introduced before the SHA-3 standard was finalized, and Keccak-256 does not follow the SHA-3 official standard.

- **Nonce:** A selected number that causes the hash value of the current block's header to adhere to a specific pattern. If you change this value (or any header value), the hash of the header changes. You find out more about how Ethereum uses the nonce value shortly.

- **Timestamp:** The date and time the current block was created.

- **Uncle hash:** The hash value of the current block's list of uncle blocks, which are stale blocks that were successfully mined but arrived just after the accepted block was added to the blockchain.

- **Beneficiary:** The miner's account that receives the reward for mining the block.

- **Logs bloom:** Logging information stored in a *Bloom filter* (a data structure useful for quickly finding out if some element is a member of a set).

- **Difficulty:** The difficulty level used in mining the block.

- **Extra data:** As the name implies, any extra data used to describe the block.

- **Block number:** The unique number for the block (assigned sequentially).

- **Gas limit:** The limit of gas for the block. (More about gas later in this chapter.)

- **Gas used:** The amount of gas used by transactions in the block.

- **Mix hash:** A hash value that is combined with the nonce value to show that the mined nonce meets difficulty requirements. This hash increases the difficulty for attackers to modify any block.

- **State root:** The hash value of the root node of the block's state trie. A *trie* is a data structure that efficiently stores data for quick retrieval. The *state trie* is used to express information about the state of transactions in the block without having to look at the transactions.

- **Transaction root:** The hash value of the root node of the trie that stores all transactions for the block.

- **Receipt root:** The hash of the root node of the trie that stores all transaction receipts for the block.

The body of an Ethereum block is just a list of transactions. Unlike other blockchain implementations, the number of transactions — and as a result, the size of blocks — isn't fixed. Every transaction has a processing cost associated with it, and each block has a limited budget. Ethereum blocks can contain lots of inexpensive transactions or just a few expensive ones or anything in between. Ethereum designed a lot of flexibility into what blocks can contain. Figure 3-2 shows the content of an Ethereum transaction.

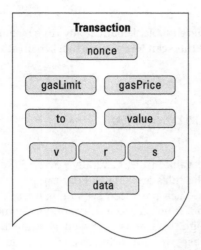

FIGURE 3-2:
Contents of
an Ethereum
transaction.

Ethereum transactions contain the following fields:

>> **Nonce:** Each Ethereum account keeps track of the number of transactions it executes. This field is the latest transaction, based on the account's counter. The network uses the transaction nonce to ensure that transactions for that particular account are executed in the proper order.

>> **Signature:** The digital signature of the account owner, proving the identity of the account requesting this transaction.

>> **Gas limit:** The maximum total amount you are willing to pay to execute this transaction.

>> **Gas price:** The unit price that the account is willing to pay to execute this transaction.

>> **To:** The address that is the recipient of this transaction. For transfers, the address is the account that will receive the transfer. For calling functions, the address is the address of the smart contract.

>> **Value:** The total amount of Ether you want to send to the recipient.

>> **Data:** The actual data submitted as the transaction body. Each type of transaction may have different data based on its functionality. For calling functions, the data may contain parameters.

As users submit transaction requests to nodes, the nodes create transactions and submit them to the transaction pool. Miners then pick transactions from the pool and build new blocks. After an Ethereum mining node constructs a block, it starts the mining process. The first miner to complete the mining process adds the block to the blockchain and broadcasts the new block to the rest of the network.

You can look at the public Ethereum blockchain at any time by going to Etherscan at https://etherscan.io/. Etherscan lets you see blockchain statistics as well as block and transaction details.

Describing Smart Contracts

When you exchange items of value, rules generally govern how the transaction takes place. In many cases, the rules are simple. For example, you give us $1.89, and we give you a soft drink. Each party can see and validate the other party's contribution to the transaction. If you try to give us Monopoly money, you won't get your soft drink. Even though this transaction seems simple, there's more to it than meets the eye. In most cases, if a soft drink costs $1.89, you'll have to tender more than that for it. You'll have to pay taxes as well. So there's another participant in the transaction: the government. Instead of keeping all the money, we have to send some of it to the government for taxes.

Moving even simple transactions like the soft drink example into the digital world takes some careful thought. You can't just send money to people and trust that they'll do their part. You need some way to enforce rules and compliance to make sure that all parties are treated fairly.

Smart contracts help you enforce rules when you exchange anything of value in Ethereum. The simplest way to describe smart contracts is that they are programs that execute when certain transactions occur. For example, if you create a soft-drink-purchase smart contract, that software code will run every time someone buys a soft drink. The smart contract code is stored in the blockchain, so all nodes have a copy of it. Also, it doesn't matter where the software runs: All nodes are guaranteed to run it the same and get the same results as every other node.

Ethereum smart contracts are *Turing complete*, which means they can compute anything that is computable with enough resources. Turing completeness is important because Ethereum smart contracts aren't limited in the types of actions they can carry out. They can carry out any complex algorithms you can design.

The soft-drink smart contract starts with the buyer. Here's how the exchange might happen:

>> The buyer creates a transaction that sends money to the seller in exchange for the soft drink.

>> The buyer sends the seller's address as input to the smart contract's address.

>> The smart contract runs to carry out the transaction. It verifies that you have enough money in your account to pay for the soft drink.

>> The smart contract verifies that the seller has the soft drink you want in stock.

>> The smart contract deducts funds from the buyer, sends the funds to the seller, and tells the seller to send the soft drink to the buyer. In the same step, the smart contract sends the required tax to the tax authority account and sends the remaining amount to the seller's account.

The process may seem tedious, but it is straightforward and makes that sure each transaction occurs in the same way. This example is too simple for real-life exchanges and leaves out some important details. For starters, you assume that the seller will supply the soft drink to the buyer. Real-life exchanges require an extra layer of protection for both sides. Smart contracts use escrow accounts (see Chapter 2 of this minibook) all the time to hold a buyer's money until the seller delivers the goods or services.

Smart contracts provide the governance and predictability of Ethereum. Without them, Ethereum would just be a cool distributed storage technique. But with them, Ethereum is a stable, decentralized platform that supports interactions and exchanges between untrusting users, including extremely complex transactions. It is easy to see the steps necessary to buy a soft drink. Other transactions, such as real estate transactions, are far more complex, have many dependencies and requirements, and generally involve several people and organizations. Ethereum smart contracts can help developers create software that eliminates middlemen, streamlines complex processes, and reduces the overall cost and time required to complete even the most complex exchanges.

Introducing Solidity, the Language of Smart Contracts

Smart contracts are software programs. With enough resources, smart contracts can do anything any other software can do. You can write Ethereum smart contracts in several languages.

>> **Mutan:** An older smart contract language that was deprecated in 2015.

>> **LLL:** A Lisp-like language, obviously developed to look like the language Lisp. Although LLL is still supported, it's not used for many current smart contract projects.

>> **Serpent:** A language that looks like the Python language. As of September 2017, Serpent is not recommended for current development.

>> **Viper:** Another relatively new language that focuses on security and simplicity.

>> **Solidity:** Currently the most popular smart contract development language. Solidity looks like the JavaScript language and provides a full-featured language for developing general-purpose smart contracts.

TIP

Solidity is the most popular language for smart contracts and the one you're most likely to encounter. For that reason, we chose to focus on Solidity in this book.

If you're comfortable with JavaScript, picking up Solidity will be a little easier. If you don't know much JavaScript, that's okay. You're going to gain an understanding of the basics of Solidity from the ground floor, starting with a program that may look familiar: the ubiquitous "Hello world" program.

You'll see this code again in Chapter 6 of this minibook, where you dig deeper into each part of this simple program. For now, take a look at this very simple smart contract code:

```
pragma solidity ^0.4.25;
contract helloWorld {
function printHelloWorld () public constant returns (string) {
return 'Hello world!';
}
}
```

That's what a Solidity smart contract looks like! After the heading, you define your contract, and then any functions that make up the inner workings of the program. After you write and test a smart contract, you can deploy it to a blockchain (more about this in Chapter 6 of this minibook), and then execute it. When you get everything right, your smart contract will show you the iconic "Hello world!" message.

As you find out more about Solidity, you'll see that it does look a lot like JavaScript but also feels a bit like C++ and Python. The developers of Solidity based it on all three languages. Solidity supports inheritance, libraries, and user-defined types that can be quite complex. It is also a statically typed language, which means you have to provide explicit datatypes for the variables you create and use.

Above all, Solidity is a smart contract development language. Even though it looks like other languages, it includes primitives and an orientation designed to interact with the Ethereum blockchain. In Chapters 6 and 7 of this minibook, you find out a lot more about how to write to and read from the Ethereum blockchain by using Solidity.

Working with the Ethereum Virtual Machine

You write smart contract code in Solidity, but it won't run in its source form. Almost all programs written in any language have to be translated into a runnable format. Some languages, such as C++, are compiled languages. When you write a C++ program, you have to use a compiler to compile the program into an executable that an operating system can run. Other languages, such as Python, are interpreted. You run a program that provides a runtime environment, which interprets your code and executes the commands.

Other languages, such as Java and Solidity, exist in between compiled and interpreted languages. You compile the programs you write in both of these languages, but you compile your source code to opcode, also called bytecode. *Opcode* is an optimized sequence of operations that your language's runtime environment can understand. The runtime environment is often referred to as the language's *virtual machine*. In Java, programs run in the Java virtual machine (JVM). All Solidity smart contracts run in the *Ethereum virtual machine (EVM)*.

The EVM is present on all nodes. When you install Ethereum, you get the EVM, and it runs whenever you run Ethereum. That means any time a smart contract runs, it runs on all EVMs across the Ethereum network. Ethereum ensures that smart contracts run the same way on all nodes and get the same results. That's how the blockchain remains consistent across all nodes.

The EVM uses a stack-based architecture, and has its own area in memory for the code it runs and the data it stores in addition to each smart contract's local storage. Although the EVM is a Turing complete virtual machine, its execution is limited by the amount of gas allowed by each smart contract run. That limitation avoids using excessive computing power for nodes across the Ethereum network (or bankrupting an account with a programming error or malicious code that tries to run forever).

As you can see, running every smart contract on every node in the Ethereum network is a lot of work. Every additional instruction in a smart contract causes thousands of nodes to do more work. To reduce the computation waste on so many machines, Ethereum includes incentives for using computation resources conservatively and sets upper limits on just how much work a smart contract can carry out. In the next section, you find out how Ethereum sets these limits.

Fueling Your Code with Gas

A couple of the fields in the block header include the word *gas*. Those fields refer to the cryptocurrency cost of accessing the blockchain and executing code. Because Ethereum storage and processing is distributed across many nodes, individuals and organizations need an incentive to commit their computing resources to blockchain operation. Gas is that incentive.

Gas refers to the fee that transaction initiators pay to process their operations. Ethereum users use Ether to pay miners. To keep costs manageable, each transaction has a maximum amount of gas you're willing to pay. If you set this limit too low, many miners may pass up your transaction and you may have to wait to get your transaction into a block. After your transaction is selected by a miner, you have to pay a small amount of gas for every computational step required to complete the transaction. The good news is that you don't have to pay the maximum each time you start a transaction, and you get a refund for any gas that isn't used in the transaction.

Gas serves several purposes in the Ethereum ecosystem. First, it encourages developers to create efficient smart contracts, which require less computational resources than sloppy or unoptimized smart contracts. Any savings of computational resources are magnified by the thousands of nodes on the Ethereum network. Being conservative lowers costs all around.

Second, gas limits make it harder for malicious users to write code to consume available network resources. Denial of service (DoS) attacks on Ethereum networks could tie up all nodes if unrestrained smart contracts were allowed to run. Gas allows upper limits to be established that stop DoS attacks in their tracks.

Finally, charging gas for accessing data stored on the blockchain discourages blockchain growth because it makes developers think through the justification for putting data on the blockchain. This approach also encourages developers to be creative when determining how to store context data. Although in many cases it would be easier to store data in a block, the cost of gas often leads to other designs that leverage local storage.

Two main variables are used to calculate the total cost of a transaction:

>> **Gas used:** The total amount of gas that a transaction uses. Each computation in a smart contract has an associated computation price.

>> **Gas price:** The price, in Ether, of one unit of gas used in the transaction.

The formula for calculating the cost of gas for a transaction is

Total gas cost = Gas used * Gas price

TECHNICAL STUFF

If you're interested in calculating your own gas usage, every Ethereum operation and its associated cost (in gas) is listed in the spreadsheet at http://ethereum. stackexchange.com/q/52/42.

Gas price is expressed in wei units. *Wei* is a denomination of Ether cryptocurrency. One Ether (ETH) equals 1e18 wei (that's 1,000,000,000,000,000,000 wei). The current gas price fluctuates, but at the time of this writing, it's somewhere around 117.15 Gwei.

Ethereum gives both miners and transaction requesters substantial flexibility. If you request a transaction, you get to set a maximum gas price and total amount of gas you're willing to pay. That gives you the ability to limit your cost. Of course, if your limits are too low, your transaction may never make it to the blockchain. From the miner perspective, you can cherry-pick the transactions you want to put into blocks. When cash flow is high, you can choose only the best-paying transactions. On the other hand, when things are slower, you have the option to take lower-paying transactions. Regardless, Ethereum lets you choose.

Surveying Tools for Developing, Testing, and Deploying Ethereum Apps

You use different tools for every phase of the process of developing and deploying Ethereum dApps. Many tools are available; this section covers a few of the more popular ones.

You need multiple tools to address the requirements of the multiple levels involved in developing Ethereum dApps: source code development, testing, compiling, and deploying your smart contract code. This section briefly describes some of the more popular development tools in each of the following categories:

>> **Ethereum blockchain client:** This software runs the Ethereum blockchain and EVM, making a computer a blockchain node.

>> **Development and testing blockchain:** This tool sets up a local, or non-live, blockchain to use before deploying code to the live blockchain.

>> **Compiler and testing framework:** A compiler translates source code into bytecode for the EVM, and testing tools help to identify and fix bugs.

>> **Source code editor and integrated development environment (IDE):** These tools include editors and suites of tools designed to help developers write code.

Ethereum blockchain client

The Ethereum blockchain client establishes an Ethereum node, downloads part, or all, of an Ethereum blockchain, and launches the EVM. Ethereum client software makes a computer or device an Ethereum node in the blockchain network.

Ethereum client nodes can be full nodes or light nodes. *Full nodes* store the entire Ethereum blockchain, which at the time of this writing is 345GB. You can go to `https://bitinfocharts.com/` to see the current Ethereum blockchain size, along with lots of other stats for popular blockchains. That's a lot of storage to dedicate just to keeping a copy of a blockchain. An alternative to using full nodes is to connect to the blockchain network as a light node. *Light nodes* store only a portion of the blockchain. Either way, you need to install Ethereum client software to connect to the network.

REMEMBER

Remember the root hash fields in the Ethereum block header layout shown earlier in the chapter? Light nodes download and store block headers but don't fetch all of the block contents. That reduces the blockchain storage requirement to a point where small devices, even a Raspberry Pi, can become light nodes. The light node fetches block contents only when a user needs it to complete some task, such as checking a balance or submitting a new transaction.

All Ethereum clients support the Ethereum standard and implement the EVM. The main difference between clients is the programming language in which each one is written. Because all clients provide the same core functionality, the choice is largely based on your language preference. Table 3-1 lists several Ethereum blockchain clients.

Development and testing blockchain

One of the strongest features of blockchain technology is that the blockchain is immutable. Although that's great for integrity, it makes developing smart contract code more difficult. Software rarely works correctly the first time it's written. The development process is made up of multiple snapshots of software as it matures to become the final product.

TABLE 3-1   **Ethereum Clients**

Name	Language	Where to Get It
Cpp-ethereum	C++	`http://ethdocs.org/en/latest/ethereum-clients/cpp-ethereum`
Ethereumjs-lib	JavaScript	`http://ethdocs.org/en/latest/ethereum-clients/ethereumjs-lib`
Geth (go-ethereum)	Go	`https://geth.ethereum.org`
Parity	Rust	`https://www.parity.io/`
Pyethapp	Python	`http://ethdocs.org/en/latest/ethereum-clients/pyethapp`

Putting your code on the live Ethereum public blockchain is the last step in the development process. Before you're ready to do that, you need a local or non-live blockchain environment to use while developing and testing. That way, you put only the final, bug-free (you hope) version of your code on the live blockchain.

Tools in this category provide a development and testing blockchain that you can use while you add features to your code. Table 3-2 lists the four main Ethereum development and testing blockchains.

TABLE 3-2   **Ethereum Development and Testing Blockchains**

Name	Description	Where to Get It
Ganache	Most popular tool with developers for easily creating a private network	truffleframework.com/ganache
Truffle	Suite of development tools that includes its own private network	truffleframework.com
Cliquebait	Uses docker instances to simulate a real blockchain network	`https://github.com/f-o-a-m/cliquebait`
Local Ethereum Network	Easy-to-use scripts to set up private blockchain networks	`https://github.com/ConsenSys/local_ethereum_network`

Compiler and testing framework

The EVM runs bytecode, so you'll need a compiler to translate your source code into bytecode. Tools in this category also provide the functionality for monitoring how your smart contracts execute and identify bugs. Table 3-3 lists several Ethereum compilers and testing frameworks.

TABLE 3-3   **Ethereum Compilers and Testing Frameworks**

Name	Description	Where to Get It
Truffle	Popular suite of tools to manage smart contract development, testing, and deployment	truffleframework.com
Solidity compiler (solc)	Solidity software includes a command-line compiler that can be called from IDEs.	https://github.com/ethereum/solidity
Solidity compiler (solcjs)	Solidity compiler written in JavaScript	https://github.com/ethereum/solc-js
Remix	Web-based suite of Ethereum development tools that includes a Solidity compiler	https://remix.ethereum.org
Embark	Framework for developing dApps for multiple blockchains	https://github.com/embark-framework/embark

Source code editor/IDE

You can use any text editor to write smart contract source code, but several editor environments are designed to help developers write and manage code. These tools help you to develop code efficiently. Table 3-4 lists several source code editors and IDEs that help you develop Ethereum smart contracts in Solidity.

TABLE 3-4   **Source Code Editors/IDEs**

Name	Language	Where to Get It
Atom	Popular IDE with Solidity extensions	https://atom.io
Visual Studio Code	The Microsoft IDE with Solidity extensions	https://marketplace.visualstudio.com/items?itemName=JuanBlanco.solidity
Vim Solidity	Solidity extensions for Vim (a vi-like editor)	https://github.com/tomlion/vim-solidity
Remix	Web-based IDE popular with new Solidity developers	https://remix.ethereum.org
EthFiddle	Web-based IDE focused on simplicity	https://ethfiddle.com

Describing the Ethereum Development Life cycle

Smart contract development generally follows the same process as the traditional software development life cycle, but with a few nuances. The basic steps in the software development life cycle are as follows:

>> **Planning:** This phase includes gathering specifications and designing the solution.

>> **Coding/development:** After planning is complete, developers start writing code to implement the planned solution.

>> **Testing:** Unit testing should occur throughout the coding phase, but after all coding is complete, the entire software product undergoes testing to ensure that all the pieces work together as designed. If testers find flaws, you have to go back at least to the coding phase, and perhaps even to the planning phase, to make changes to fix the flaws.

>> **Deployment:** After fixing any remaining flaws, the properly functioning software is released to the production environment. This phase also includes maintenance activities, which monitor the software and respond to newly identified flaws or requests for enhancements.

Although the main phases of the software development life cycle are the same for smart contract development, the design of blockchain technology raises a few issues. First, remember that the blockchain data is immutable. Also, smart contracts are deployed to blocks in the blockchain. After you deploy a smart contract, it can never change. That's good if you want it to stick around forever, but it can be bad if you find out later that you deployed a smart contract with a bug. Figure 3-3 shows the smart contract software development life cycle.

Examining the Ethereum Ecosystem and Development Lifecycle

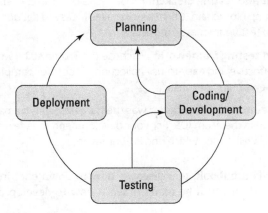

FIGURE 3-3:
Smart contract software development life cycle.

Testing is more important when dealing with blockchain technology because updating smart contracts is awkward and can be difficult. Each new smart contract deployment gets a new address, so you have to ensure that all references to the old smart contract are updated to refer to the new smart contract. Also, you have to be careful about how the updated smart contract handles data. If the changes you made in the smart contract change how it handles data, you'll have to figure out how to deal with the data already in the blockchain. Another issue is that until you deploy a smart contract, you'll be testing it on a local, or private, blockchain. Your test environment may not reflect how the real blockchain operates.

These are just a few issues you'll encounter when developing for a blockchain. Pay attention to the quality of your testing activities. Thorough testing takes time, but it can save a lot more.

Introducing Smart Contract Development Tools

In the following chapters of this minibook, you find out how to set up a development environment and develop smart contracts by using the Solidity language. As you see in this chapter, multiple tools are available for each stage of development. Instead of covering all the tools, we're choosing one from each category so you can focus on finding out more about Solidity. You can use a different tool if you want — all of those listed are good choices.

Here's what you'll use:

>> **Ethereum blockchain client:** You'll use Geth, which is easy to install. Many tutorials use Geth as their client.

>> **Development and testing blockchain:** Ganache-cli is the chosen development and testing blockchain. Ganache-cli makes it easy to set up new blockchains to test your smart contracts.

>> **Compiler and testing framework:** We chose the Truffle suite, which provides an effective and easy-to-use collection of tools for compiling and testing your new smart contracts.

>> **Source code editor/IDE:** This choice was the hardest. From so many good options, we chose the Atom IDE. For your development, try a few alternative editors/IDEs as well, to see which one is your favorite.

In Chapter 4 of this minibook, you discover how to download, install, and configure these tools. Then you'll be ready to learn how to develop your own smart contracts.

Chapter **4**

Getting and Configuring Ethereum Development Tools

The most popular language for developing decentralized applications (dApps) for the Ethereum blockchain is Solidity. Before you can find out how to develop dApps in Solidity, however, you need to have all the tools installed and available. Depending on your needs, you can designate a computer to be your development workstation, or you can use web-based tools to develop code from any web browser.

The examples in this book use software that installs locally on a PC. Installing all these tools will give you the ability to write smart contract software, compile it, deploy it to a test environment, test it, and finally deploy it to the real blockchain.

In this chapter you build your own Ethereum development environment. By the end of the chapter, you'll be ready to start developing your own smart contracts and dApps.

Examining Why Multiple Ethereum Development Tools Are Available

The first thing you might notice when building an Ethereum development environment is that you have a lot of choices. Overall, many choices are a good thing, but they make getting started a little more confusing. Remember that Ethereum is a complete blockchain environment. Running the blockchain is one thing — developing code for the blockchain is a bigger endeavor and requires more tools.

The Ethereum Foundation is the Swiss nonprofit organization that introduced, and now promotes and supports, the Ethereum platform. Their website, `https://ethereum.org/`, is a treasure trove of great information about all facets of Ethereum. Ethereum is an open-source project, which means that the source code for the Ethereum blockchain environment is available to anyone who wants it. Ethereum can theoretically run on any computing device.

The runtime environment for Ethereum smart contracts, EVM (Ethereum virtual machine), is implemented in many different languages. Each implementation allows Ethereum to run on different platforms, giving anyone setting up a new node choices in how to run the EVM. For example, if performance is the highest priority, a C++ implementation might be the best choice. But if the capability to integrate additional functionality with the EVM is a goal, a JavaScript or Python implementation might be a better choice.

The open-source community is a worldwide group of users and developers who contribute to projects in which they have a stake. Ethereum users and developers often engage in rigorous debates about how to best advance the product. These debates commonly result in different opinions about the best way to meet goals. One of the more common debates is over which user interface is better. One school of thought is that a *command-line interface (CLI)* is the most flexible and the easiest to script. This type of user interface tends to work best for lower-level utility-type tools. On the other hand, an integrated *graphical user interface (GUI)* is more user-friendly and makes tasks such as software development easier. That's just one example of why you may see both CLI and GUI versions of tools.

As a result of diverse people contributing to the community, you'll find multiple software products that address the needs of each step in the development process. Several different test network implementations exist because a group in the Ethereum community felt that making it easier to set up a test network would draw more developers to the Ethereum platform. Others focus on integrated testing tools. And still others decided to extend their favorite editors and IDEs with extensions that support Solidity.

As you look at the available options in each tool category, remember that each one is there because a group of Ethereum enthusiasts saw an opportunity to fill a feature gap. Although it may take some time, it can be interesting to read through the features and benefits of some competing products to see how they differ.

TIP

If you want to get involved in the Ethereum community, check out the Ethereum website at https://ethereum.org/. At the bottom of the home page, you'll see an Ethereum Community link under the Ecosystem section with links to various ways to participate.

The tools you'll install and configure in this chapter are the ones you'll frequently see used by other Ethereum developers. You'll find lots of online tips, tricks, and tutorials for Ethereum development using these tools. The environment you build in this chapter will allow you to work through the examples in this book and to use other online resources — without having to start over installing new tools.

Downloading, Installing, and Configuring All the Pieces

Now that you're ready to build your Ethereum development environment, let's dive right in. You'll find out how to set up a PC running Microsoft Windows to be an Ethereum development platform. Windows isn't the only operating system that supports Ethereum. You can just as easily set up a macOS or Linux computer to support Ethereum. If you're running macOS or Linux, each tool in this chapter will work on your computer, too, although the installation steps might be a little different. Each tool's website will provide detailed instructions for each operating system.

Installing the blockchain client

Start by installing an Ethereum client. We're using Go Ethereum (Geth) as the Ethereum client for the examples in this minibook. Geth is written in the Go language and allows you to run a full Ethereum node. Running a full Ethereum node means you'll have access to the complete Ethereum blockchain and also run a local EVM. Geth gives you the capability to mine ETH, create transactions and smart contracts, and examine any blocks that already exist on the blockchain. All remaining tools you'll install in this chapter will depend on Geth to provide the local EVM and allow access to the blocks on the blockchain.

TECHNICAL STUFF

The Geth website provides prepackaged installers for Microsoft Windows, macOS, and Linux operating systems. You can also download the Geth source code and build it for your own custom environment. If you're interested in playing around with devices other than just computers, you can conduct an Internet search and easily find instructions on setting up Geth on smartphones or a Raspberry Pi. That's the beauty of using open-source tools.

Start by downloading and installing Geth, as follows:

1. **Launch your browser and navigate to** https://geth.ethereum.org; **then click or tap the Downloads link at the top of the page.**

   Your web browser will look like Figure 4-1.

2. **Click or tap the Geth button for your operating system.**

   Because we're setting up a Microsoft Windows computer in this tutorial, we selected Geth 1.10.9 for Windows. (When you set up your computer, a newer version of Geth might be available. You should download and install the latest version of each tool.)

3. **Launch the executable file you just downloaded.**

4. **Click or tap I Agree to the GNU General Public License.**

   Always read any license agreement before agreeing to its contents.

REMEMBER

5. **Select the Development Tools check box, and then click or tap the Next button.**

   Make sure that you choose to install the development tools in this window before continuing. Figure 4-2 shows what the Installation Options window looks like.

6. **If you want to install Geth to a different folder than the one that's displayed, change it to your desired destination folder.**

7. **Click or tap the Install button to start the installation process.**

8. **When the installation finishes, click or tap the Close button.**

After you've installed Geth, you can launch it to start the EVM and synchronize with the public Ethereum blockchain.

FIGURE 4-1:
The Go Ethereum
(Geth) download
webpage.

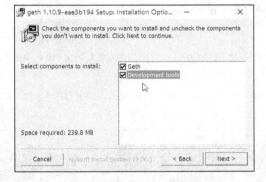

FIGURE 4-2:
The Geth
Setup —
Installation
Options window.

You find out about some other Geth start-up options in Chapter 5 of this mini-book, but the only option you need for now is *syncmode*, which tells Geth how much of the blockchain to download. The syncmode option has the following three values. Note that you'll be using the light value for the syncmode option:

>> **full:** Download and validate the entire blockchain. This option requires the most time and disk space but can provide the fastest response because a full node doesn't ever have to request missing blocks from other nodes.

>> **fast:** Download and validate the block headers and data for the most recent 1,000 transactions. This option is a good choice when you want to conserve some disk space but also want to store the most recent blocks locally.

>> **light:** Download only the blockchain current state and request any missing blocks from other nodes as needed. This option allows you to operate Ethereum with minimal disk space requirements.

For the exercise in this book, you'll use the light syncmode option for Geth. To start Geth in light mode, follow these steps:

1. **Launch a command prompt or PowerShell prompt.**

   To launch a command prompt, type **cmd** in the search bar at the lower-left corner of your desktop and then click or tap the Command Prompt option. To launch a PowerShell prompt, type **PowerShell** in the search bar and click or tap the PowerShell option.

2. **Change the current working directory to the Geth install directory.**

   If you installed Geth to the default location, type the following and then press Enter:

   ```
   cd 'C:\Program Files\Geth\'
   ```

3. **Type the following, and then press Enter:**

   ```
   .\geth --syncmode "light"
   ```

4. **This command launches Geth in light mode. Make sure that you type two dashes before *syncmode*.**

   Figure 4-3 shows the Geth command to start a light Ethereum node.

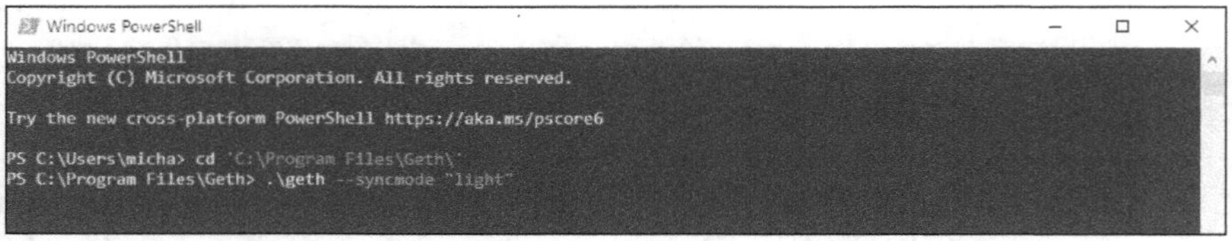

FIGURE 4-3: Geth light node start-up command.

As Geth starts, it establishes a connection with the Ethereum network and begins synchronizing the current blockchain. Geth provides messages at each stage of its start-up process to let you see what is happening. Figure 4-4 shows what the Geth messages look like.

After Geth synchronizes the blockchain, you're ready to use the Geth blockchain client to develop and deploy your own dApps.

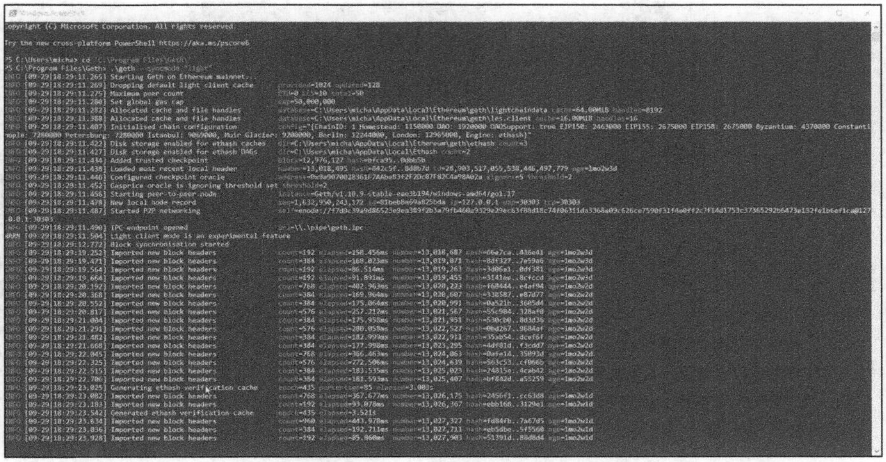

FIGURE 4-4:
Geth runtime
messages.

Installing the test blockchain

When you develop smart contracts and dApps, you don't want to deploy your code or data to the live blockchain until you're sure that everything works correctly. This means that you have to test your code in some non-live environment. To do this, you need a blockchain to use during the development and testing process. Ethereum clients, Geth included, connect to the main public Ethereum blockchain by default, but you can connect to other blockchains as well. You can change the connection settings easily for development and testing.

Several tools make it easy to create and manage test blockchains. Ganache is the test blockchain environment used here. According to the Ganache website (https://truffleframework.com/ganache), "Ganache is a personal blockchain for Ethereum development that you can use to deploy contracts, develop your applications, and run tests."

TECHNICAL STUFF

You aren't limited to the prebuilt Ganache images. Because Ganache is an open-source product, you can also download the Ganache source code and build it for your own custom environment.

To download and install Ganache, follow these steps:

1. **Launch your browser and navigate to** https://truffleframework.com/ganache.

   Your web browser should look like Figure 4-5.

2. **Click or tap the Download (Windows) button to download the Windows installer.**

FIGURE 4-5:
The Ganache
Download
webpage.

3. **Launch the executable file you just downloaded. Then click or tap the Install button to start the installation process.**

   By default, Ganache launches when the installation finishes.

4. **Accept the default, as shown in Figure 4-6, or click or tap the Analytics Enabled toggle box to disable Analytics, and then click or tap the Continue button.**

   Because this is the first time you're launching Ganache, you are asked to allow Google Analytics tracking. You don't have to do this, but allowing analytics helps the Ganache development team understand how different people use Ganache.

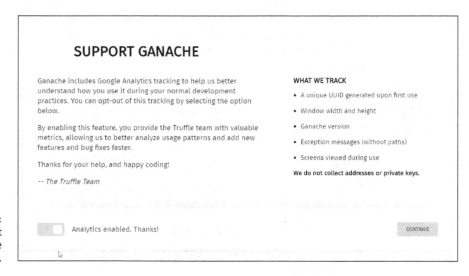

SUPPORT GANACHE

Ganache includes Google Analytics tracking to help us better understand how you use it during your normal development practices. You can opt-out of this tracking by selecting the option below.

By enabling this feature, you provide the Truffle team with valuable metrics, allowing us to better analyze usage patterns and add new features and bug fixes faster.

Thanks for your help, and happy coding!

-- *The Truffle Team*

WHAT WE TRACK

- A unique UUID generated upon first use
- Window width and height
- Ganache version
- Exception messages (without paths)
- Screens viewed during use

We do not collect **addresses** or **private keys**.

Analytics enabled. Thanks!

CONTINUE

FIGURE 4-6:
The Support
Ganache
Analytics window.

5. **Click or tap the Quickstart button to launch Ganache.**

Ganache provides the option to start with an empty test blockchain each time you launch Ganache, or to create a workspace that will save changes to a test blockchain when Ganache shuts down. Ganache workspaces are helpful when developers need to save changes to a test blockchain for later use. Choosing the Quickstart option tells Ganache to create a new, empty test blockchain.

When Ganache launches, you see the main Ganache Accounts window with basic server information and a list of accounts, as shown in Figure 4-7. Because the reason to install Ganache is to create your own blockchain, you need at least one account to access the blockchain. Ganache creates 10 accounts for you, each with a balance of 100.0 ETH. You can create more accounts and give them all the ETH they need to test your smart contracts and dApps.

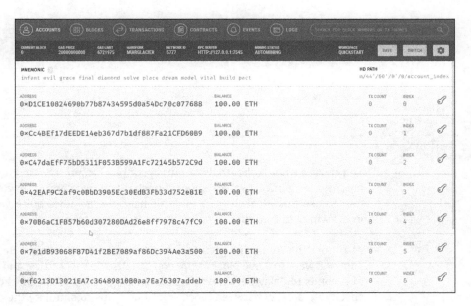

Getting and Configuring
Ethereum Development Tools

FIGURE 4-7:
The Ganache
Accounts window.

That's all it takes to create your own Ethereum blockchain in Ganache. Of course, this blockchain is local to your own computer and isn't distributed to any other nodes. Because no other nodes are on this network, there aren't any miners. This blockchain is set to *automining*, which means that any new transactions are processed immediately. That setting makes it easy to test your smart contracts and dApps without having to pay miners to process your transactions.

When you're ready to start developing software for Ethereum, you need to tell your client and other tools which blockchain to use. Let's see where your new Ganache blockchain is located. In Ganache, click or tap the settings (gear) icon in the upper-right corner to launch the Ganache Settings window. Then click or tap the Server tab to open the Ganache Server Settings window. Figure 4-8 displays the Server tab of the Ganache Settings window.

FIGURE 4-8:
The Ganache Settings window's Server tab.

You can see where other tools can find your blockchain. The Hostname, Port Number, and Network ID values show you what you need any time you want another tool to use this blockchain. You don't need these values quite yet, but now you know where to find them.

Also note the Automine setting, which is enabled by default. Before you deploy your software to a live blockchain, you can disable this setting and enter a number of seconds to delay between new blocks being added to the blockchain. Manually specifying a delay between block creations helps to simulate the effect of miners that you'll encounter in a live blockchain. Testing will be more complex but also more realistic. In Chapter 8 of this minibook, you can find out more about carrying out comprehensive testing.

TIP

Before you leave the Settings window, look at the settings on the other tabs (Workspace, Accounts & Keys, Chain, Advanced, and About). The Ganache Quickstart guide has details on these settings at https://truffleframework.com/docs/ganache/quickstart.

Installing the testing environment

The software development process is made up of multiple steps. In Chapter 3 of this minibook, you can find out about the four main phases of the Ethereum software development life cycle. Although the life cycle has only four phases, many different tasks need to be accomplished. In addition to just writing source code, you have to compile your code, deploy it to a test environment, test the code, and measure how well the code performs against your specifications. Then you need to fix any flaws and repeat the testing process until you're satisfied with the code's operation.

After you complete testing, you need to transition your software from a test environment to a live environment. For this transition, you need to submit your smart contracts to a live blockchain and place any other code where your clients can access it. All tasks related to testing and deployment should be repeatable and as automated as possible. A comprehensive testing framework helps to standardize these tasks and make the entire development process more manageable.

Truffle is the testing environment we're using for the examples in this minibook. You may have noticed that the test Ethereum network, Ganache, is part of the Truffle Suite. One of the reasons we chose both Truffle and Ganache is due to the easy integration of these tools. In the rest of this section, you find out how to install Truffle.

Getting ready to install Truffle

Before you can install Truffle, you have to ensure that your computer meets the prerequisites. Open your browser and navigate to `https://truffleframework.com/docs/truffle/getting-started/installation` to see the Truffle installation requirements, which are shown in Figure 4-9.

The main requirement for Truffle is to have NodeJS version 8.9.4 or later installed. NodeJS is an open-source project that provides a runtime environment for code written in JavaScript. JavaScript was originally designed to run in web browsers, but NodeJS makes it easy to run JavaScript code outside a browser.

It's easy to find out whether NodeJS is installed. Open a command shell or Power-Shell window, type the `node` command, and press Enter. You get either a simple ">" prompt or an error message telling you that NodeJS is not installed. Figure 4-10 shows the error message you see in Windows PowerShell if you don't have NodeJS installed.

FIGURE 4-9:
Truffle installation
requirements.

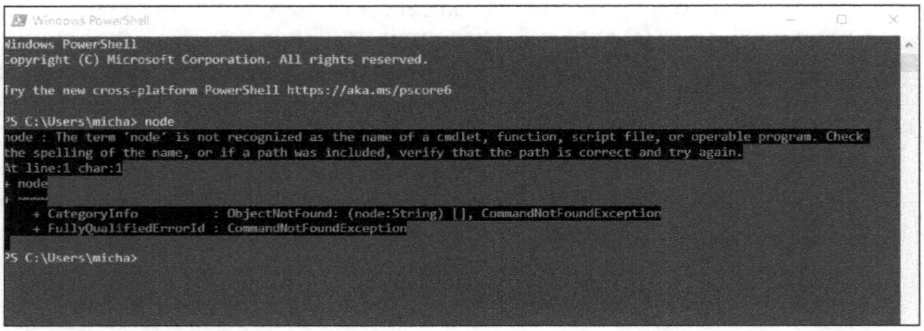

FIGURE 4-10:
Error message
in PowerShell
when NodeJS isn't
installed.

If you do have NodeJS installed, skip to the next section, "Downloading and installing Truffle." If you don't have NodeJS installed, follow these steps to download and install it:

1. **Launch your browser and navigate to** https://nodejs.org/en/.

   Your web browser should look like Figure 4-11. The NodeJS website detects your operating system and suggests the versions for that operating system. If you're using Microsoft Windows, you see download links for Windows.

2. **Click or tap the button for the version you want to install to download the Windows installer.**

   You can download the latest version or the latest stable (long-term support, or LTS) version. We're using the LTS version for the examples in this minibook. (When you set up your computer, a newer version of NodeJS might be available. You should download and install the latest version of each available tool.)

REMEMBER

If you want to install NodeJS on a computer that isn't running Microsoft Windows, or you want to build your own version of NodeJS, click or tap the Other Downloads link. This link takes you to a page with options to download source code or installer packages for multiple operating systems.

3. **Launch the executable file you just downloaded.**

   Click or tap the Next button to start the installation process.

4. **Read the End-User License Agreement, accept it, and then click or tap Next.**

5. **Select NodeJS installation options in the next three windows.**

   Enter the install destination (or accept the default), and then click or tap Next. In the Custom Setup window that appears, click or tap Next to accept the defaults. In the next window, click or tap the Automatically Install the Necessary Tools option and then click or tap Next.

6. **To install NodeJS, click or tap Install.**

7. **To complete the NodeJS part of the installation process, click or tap Finish.**

8. **Install the NodeJS tools.**

   Press any key in the next two windows to run the scripts to install the supplemental NodeJS tools.

FIGURE 4-11:
The NodeJS Download webpage.

You can verify that NodeJS is installed with a simple command. Open a command shell or PowerShell window, type the following command, and press Enter:

```
node --version
```

This time, when you enter the node command, you should see a message showing you the installed NodeJS version. Figure 4-12 shows the version message in Windows PowerShell.

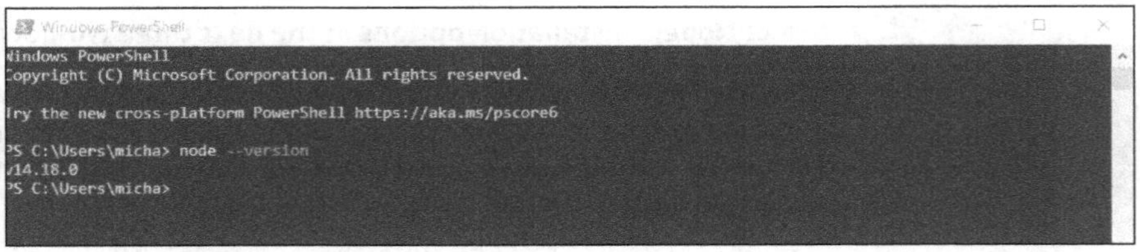

FIGURE 4-12: NodeJS version message.

After you have NodeJS installed, you're ready to install Truffle.

Downloading and installing Truffle

The NodeJS environment makes it easy to find and download new packages, including Truffle. The Truffle installation process requires you to enter just a single command.

To install Truffle, open a command shell or PowerShell window, type the following command, and press Enter:

```
npm install -g truffle
```

You may see some warnings during the installation, but don't worry about them. Figure 4-13 shows what this command and the results look like. Truffle is installed and almost ready to be used.

Truffle organizes development activities into projects. That way, you can work on multiple projects with different configuration requirements. For example, you could set up a different testing blockchain for each of several projects. In Chapter 5 of this minibook, you can find out more about configuring projects. Here, let's look at the basics of setting up a project in Truffle.

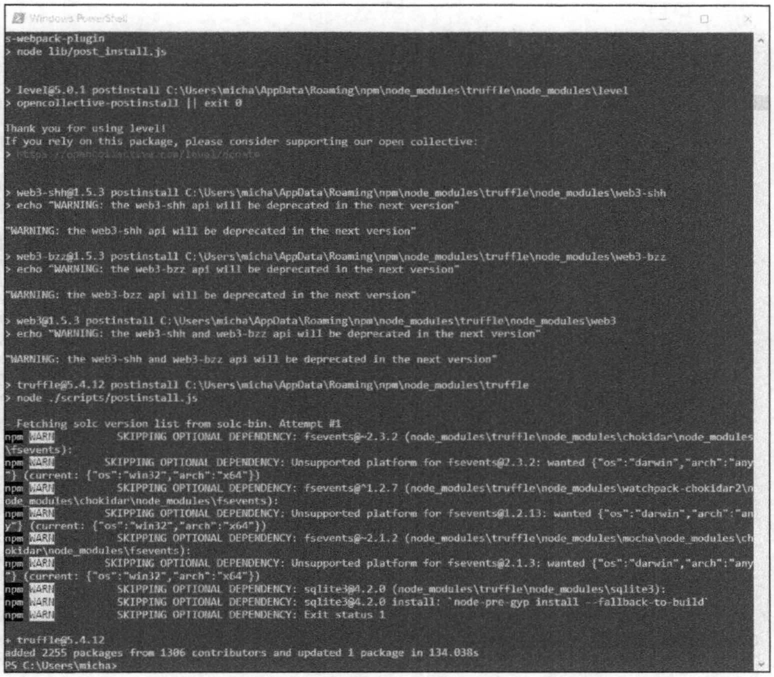

FIGURE 4-13:
Installing Truffle.

Each Truffle project needs its own folder. The first thing you need to do to set up a Truffle project is to create a project folder. To create a new empty project named myProject, for example, open a command shell or PowerShell window, type the following command, and press Enter:

```
mkdir myProject
```

Make the new project folder your current directory by typing the following command and pressing Enter:

```
cd myProject
```

Then, to initialize your new Truffle project, enter this command and press Enter:

```
truffle init
```

Figure 4-14 shows these commands initializing a new Truffle project.

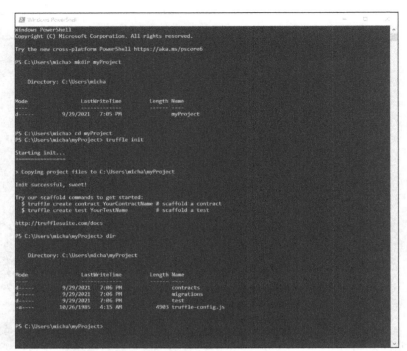

That's it! You now have a new Truffle project named myProject. That's all you do at this point. You can use File Explorer or the `dir` command to look at the myProject folder to see the files and new folders that Truffle created. You can find out more about how Truffle uses these files and folders to define projects when you start writing your own smart contracts. But for now, you're ready to install the last tool to complete your Ethereum development environment.

Installing the IDE

Now that all of the foundational pieces are in place, you're just about ready to start writing code. The most visible part of software development is writing the source code. Many developers consider writing code to be the first "productive" step in the software development process, but that is far from the truth. Before you start writing any code, you should carefully and completely plan and design your application.

You save yourself far more time in the development process by taking the time up front to plan. Planning reduces the number of times you have to rework your code when what you write the first time doesn't do everything that you need it to.

After you have a thorough plan and you know what code you need to write to meet all your application's goals, you're ready to start writing the source code that will become your final application. Although you can use any text editor to write code in Solidity, many tools are available to make your development activities easier. An integrated development environment (IDE) is like a super editor. IDEs enable you to create and edit code as well as provide many supporting features, such as automatic code completion and syntax help, as you type. A good IDE can save you lots of time and help you write better code.

TIP

Use an editor or IDE that you find comfortable. Try out several options before you settle on the tool you'll use.

For the exercise in this book, you use Microsoft Visual Studio Code IDE to write source code. To download and install Visual Studio Code, follow these steps:

1. **Launch your browser and navigate to** https://code.visualstudio.com/.

   Your web browser should look like Figure 4-15.

2. **Click or tap the Windows download button.**

   If you want to install Visual Studio Code on a computer that isn't running Microsoft Windows, click or tap one of the other download buttons that corresponds to the operating system of your choice.

3. **Launch the executable file you just downloaded by clicking the Next button on the Setup — Visual Studio Code window.**

4. **Read and accept the License Agreement, and then click or tap Next.**

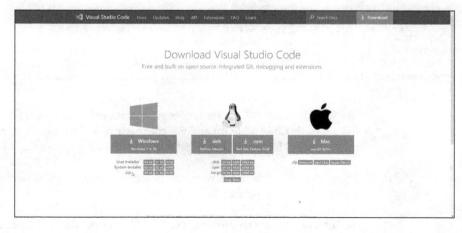

FIGURE 4-15:
The Microsoft Visual Studio Code download webpage.

5. **Select Visual Studio Code installation options in the next three windows.**

Enter the install destination (or accept the default), and then click or tap Next. In the Select Start Menu Folder window, click or tap Next to accept the defaults. In the next window, if you want to place a shortcut to Visual Studio Code on your desktop, click or tap the Create a Desktop Icon option. Then click or tap Next.

6. **To install Visual Studio code, review your install options (see Figure 4-16) and then click or tap Install.**

Your settings should look similar to the ones in Figure 4-16, with the exception of the destination location.

7. **When Visual Studio Code finishes installing, click or tap Finish to complete the installation process and launch the Visual Studio Code IDE.**

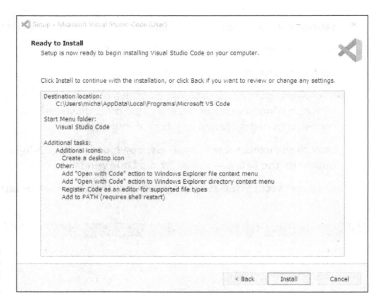

FIGURE 4-16:
The Visual Studio
Code install
options window.

The Visual Studio (VS) Code IDE is now installed. Figure 4-17 shows the default Visual Studio Code tabletop and Welcome window. The Welcome window contains lots of helpful information for getting started using the VS Code IDE.

TIP

If you close the Welcome window, you can always open it again from the Help menu. It's the top option in the Help menu.

You have one more step to complete the installation of your Ethereum development environment. To get the benefit of VS Code's syntax highlighting, code completion, and other features, you need to add an extension so that VS Code understands Solidity. The easiest way to add any extension to VS Code is right from the IDE.

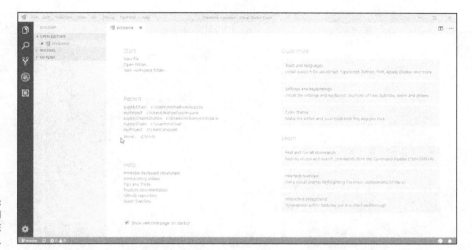

Click or tap the Extensions (square image) icon on the left border of the VS Code tabletop. In the Search Extensions in Marketplace text box, type **Solidity**. A list of extensions that match your search term appears. Find the extension with the title "Ethereum Solidity Language for Visual Studio Code by Juan Blanco" and click or tap the green Install button for that extension. When you successfully install the Solidity extension, your VS Code window should look like Figure 4-18.

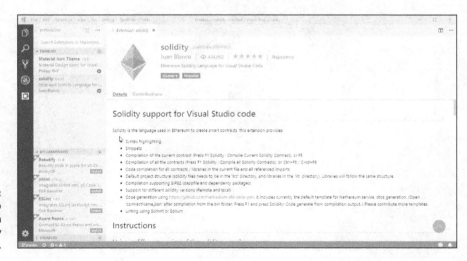

Congratulations! You've successfully built an Ethereum Solidity application development environment.

Chapter **5**

Building Your First Ethereum Apps

The best way to understand how to write apps for the Ethereum blockchain is to start writing them. You can *read* about all the components and language syntax, but until you write some code, it won't sink in. You've already gone through the steps to set up your development environment, so why not start using it?

Don't worry about writing code before you know what you're doing — here, you'll start with small, simple Solidity apps. (Remember that Solidity is the most popular language for developing dApps for the Ethereum blockchain.) And you'll find out about syntax and process as you need to. The typos you enter and other issues you encounter will help you get the hang of it more quickly.

The code we show you in this chapter is really simple. That's okay. You're going to find out how to write code in Solidity, and you're going to start from the very beginning. Whether you're new to programming or you already know several other programming languages, the exercises in this chapter will help ensure that you have a working development environment and know how to write basic Solidity code.

Validating Your Ethereum Development Environment

When you installed the development environment components in Chapter 4 of this minibook, you installed each piece to operate separately. The Geth Ethereum client connects to the live Ethereum network by default. However, we don't want to use the live Ethereum network for app development and testing. For now, you won't need to launch Geth. Instead, you'll use Ganache to provide the blockchain for development and testing. You looked at the settings page when you installed Ganache to view your blockchain's host name, port number, and network ID. But you didn't do anything with that information — until now.

Truffle is the framework you'll use to develop and test your Solidity code. Before you can start writing code, you need to configure Truffle to use the Ganache blockchain. You do that by editing the Truffle configuration file.

Creating a Truffle project

Truffle organizes software activities into projects, and stores project files in directories. If you did not create a project in Chapter 4 of this minibook, follow the instructions in the section on installing and downloading Truffle. After initializing the new project, type **dir** to see a list of files and directories that Truffle created. Figure 5-1 shows a newly initiated Truffle project.

Depending on the version of Truffle you're running, you may have two files in the project directory: truffle.js and truffle-config.js. If you open these two files, you'll see that their contents are the same. You should always use the configuration file named truffle-config.js. To keep things simple, if your version of Truffle created the file truffle.js, just delete it.

You'll be editing the file named truffle-config.js to configure Truffle to use the Ganache blockchain.

TECHNICAL STUFF

Because Truffle runs in Windows, macOS, and Linux, it has to handle subtle differences between the environments. The Windows operating system looks at a file with the js extension as an executable file. That means when you type the `truffle` command, Windows finds the local truffle.js file and tries to execute it. That's why Truffle started including the truffle-config.js file as its default configuration file. Older versions of Truffle still use truffle.js as a default configuration filename, but we recommend that you not use it. Always use truffle-config.js or your own custom filename to avoid conflicts when you try to run Truffle in Windows.

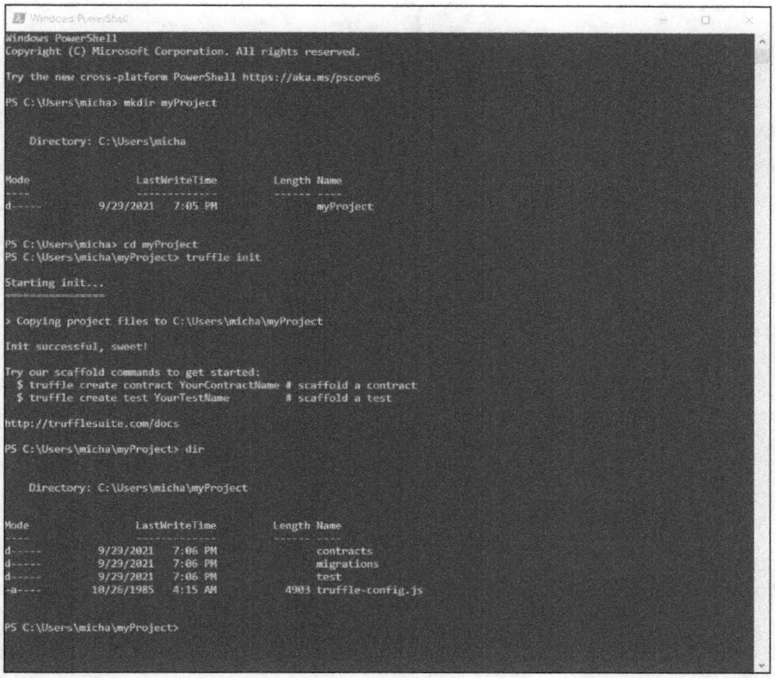

FIGURE 5-1:
Initiating a Truffle
project.

Editing the Truffle config file

You have to edit the Truffle config file to tell Truffle to use the Ganache block-chain. Follow these steps to hook up Truffle and Ganache:

1. **Get the blockchain address from the Ganache settings window.**

   Launch Ganache, and then click or tap the Settings (gear) icon in the upper-right corner of the Ganache window; then click or tap the Server tab. Note the host name, port number, and network ID values. Figure 5-2 shows the Ganache settings window with default values. (You can also get the host name and port number from the main window.) The RPC Server value shows the host name and port number separated by a colon.

2. **Launch Visual Studio Code (VS Code) for your project.**

   Open a Windows Command prompt or PowerShell (our favorite), and navigate to your project directory (myProject.) From here, type the following and then press Enter:

   ```
   code .
   ```

   The code command launches VS Code, and the period tells VS Code to use the current directory as the current project. Figure 5-3 shows what your VS Code window will look like when you launch it in your myProject directory.

FIGURE 5-2:
The Ganache
Settings window.

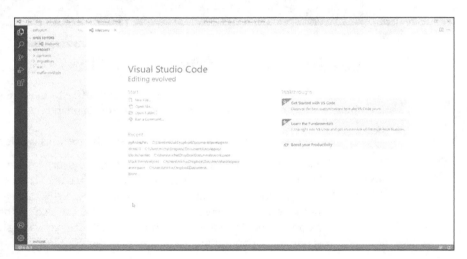

FIGURE 5-3:
Visual Studio
Code in
myProject.

3. **Modify your Truffle project configuration file to reference the Ganache blockchain.**

Click or tap truffle-config.js on the left side of your VS Code window to open the file. Add the sections shown in Figure 5-4. Then save the file (choose File ➪ Save or press Ctrl+S).

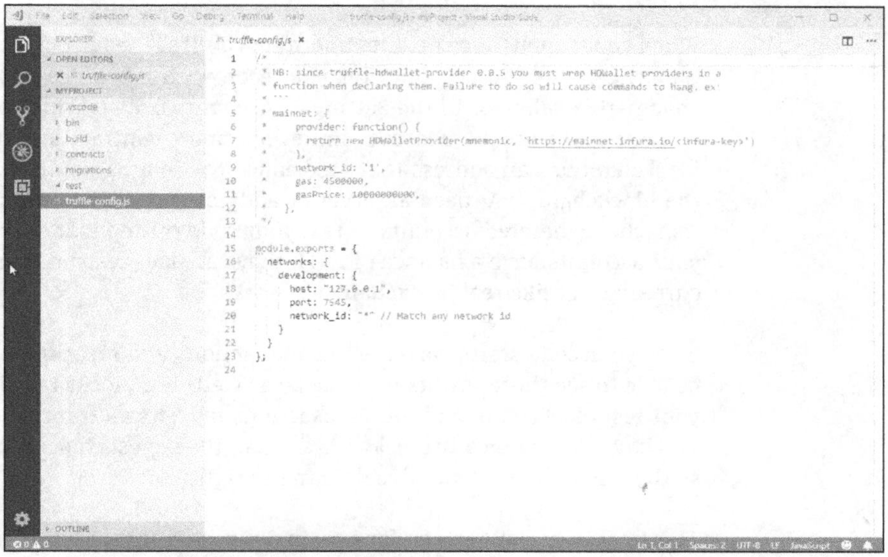

FIGURE 5-4:
The modified
Truffle project
configuration file.

When you finish editing the truffle.js file, the uncommented lines (lines that don't start with /*, *, or */) should look like this:

```
module.exports = {
networks: {
development: {
host: "127.0.0.1",
port: 7545,
network_id: "*" // Match any network id
}
}
};
```

Exploring the Ganache Test Environment

Before you write any code in Solidity, you should take a look around Ganache. You'll come back to this component in your development environment from time to time, so it makes sense to take a few minutes to survey what Ganache offers. Remember that Ganache is your test blockchain. You'll need to simulate real blockchain interactions as you develop and test your code, and Ganache provides you with an environment that looks real.

When you launch Ganache, the first thing you'll see is a list of accounts. By default, Ganache creates 10 accounts for you, each with a balance of 100 ETH. You can change this behavior in the Settings⇨ Accounts & Keys window. Every Ethereum account has a unique address, and every smart contract and transaction on the blockchain has an address that associates it with an account. So, to interact with the blockchain, you need an account address (or maybe several). You'll use the Ganache-generated accounts to test your code throughout development. Because your accounts have a balance of ETH, they can pay fees and even transfer cryptocurrency just like real blockchain accounts.

After your code starts carrying out real actions and creating transactions, you'll be able to see those results in Ganache as well. The Blocks tab shows all blocks on your test blockchain, and the Transactions tab lists all transactions in each block. You haven't created any blocks (other than the genesis block) or transactions yet, so there isn't any substantive data to see right now.

The most important screen for now in Ganache is the Accounts tab, which lists the accounts you'll use as you interact with the blockchain, as shown in Figure 5-5. You'll see these accounts again later in this chapter.

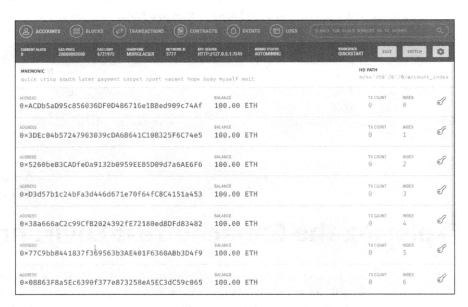

FIGURE 5-5:
Ganache accounts list.

Designing Simple Smart Contracts

Designing smart contracts is different than many other types of software development. You have to consider many blockchain nuances during all aspects of software design and development. For example, any time you access the blockchain or carry out operations, you have to pay a fee. You'll find out about paying for blockchain access later in this chapter, but for now, just be aware that a cost is associated with storage and work, so storing too much data or doing too much work could cost a lot.

Another thing to consider is that after you deploy code to the blockchain, that code can't be changed. If you need to fix a bug or add functionality, you have to tell everyone to ignore the old code and use new code. (Well, you do if your new code works on old data. If not, you'll have to figure out how to bind the code version to the data version.) Plus, the entire process of getting your code from your editor out to the blockchain is a little different than in most development workflows.

Those are just some of the issues you need to keep in mind as you design and develop blockchain apps. For now, to keep things simple, we don't throw too much at you at once because the steps might seem confusing if you're new to blockchain development.

Your first smart contract is the familiar Hello World program. If you've ever written software in any language, chances are that you wrote a simple program that displayed the message *Hello World*. The Hello World program is a tradition that has been around since the early days of computing. Writing this simple program will give you the concrete steps you have to follow for all your development activities.

You'll write a smart contract that displays the message *Hello World*. You might be surprised at the number of steps needed to display that simple message, but as your apps become more complex, you'll essentially follow the same process.

As you design your own smart contacts, consider what each one must do. Smart contracts are objects, so you can think about them as a combination of data and functionality. Each smart contract can store some data and always has actions it can perform. You can think of data as nouns and actions as verbs. Your HelloWorld smart contact has one data item, `helloMessage`, and can do one thing, `getHelloMessage()`. In Solidity, simple data items are variables and actions are functions.

That's all that your HelloWorld smart contract needs to do, so you're ready to start coding.

Coding Your First Smart Contract

Your HelloWorld smart contract has only five lines of code. To get started writing your first smart contract, right-click the Contracts folder in VS Code Explorer, and then click New File to create a new file in the Contracts folder.

Type **HelloWorld.sol** in the filename text box and press Enter. VS Code opens your new file in a new Editor tab. Type the following text in the VS Code editor:

```
// SPDX-License-Identifier: MIT
pragma solidity ^0.8.9;
contract HelloWorld {
string private helloMessage = "Hello world";
function getHelloMessage() public view returns (string) {
return helloMessage;
}
}
```

The semicolons and curly braces may appear to be in random places, but they each have a purpose. Don't worry too much about punctuation right now. Just type the code as shown.

Let's look at each line of code. The first line is:

```
// SPDX-License-Identifier: MIT
```

This line is a special comment. In Solidity, lines that start with two slashes are comments. This special comment tells Solidity the type of license that a smart contract uses. In this example, the HelloWorld smart contract uses the MIT license. You can explore different types of software licenses at https://spdx. org/licenses/.

The next line is:

```
pragma solidity ^0.8.9;
```

The first non-comment line of every smart contract is (or should be) the version pragma. It tells Solidity what version of the compiler is expected to be used to compile this smart contract. Solidity is still a new language, and it changes a little with each version. In fact, major version updates of the compiler often will not compile all Solidity written using earlier versions. The version pragma helps to avoid compilation failures just because you're using a newer Solidity compiler.

To use the version pragma, you provide the lowest version of the compiler that should compile this code. This example provides the specific Solidity version, 0.8.9. We could have used 0.8.0, which means "the latest minor version within the 0.8 major version." Also note that we added the caret (^) to the beginning of the version. The caret tells Solidity to allow only minor versions of the compiler in the 0.8 major version range. In other words, don't use a 0.9.0 compiler.

TECHNICAL STUFF

If you want to see the version of the Solidity compiler that Truffle is using, open a terminal (in VS Code, click or tap Terminal ⇨ New Terminal from the top menu bar). Type the command `truffle version`. You see the Truffle and Solidity compiler versions.

The next line of code defines the smart contract:

```
contract HelloWorld {
```

At this point, all you need to provide is the keyword `contract` and the contract's name, `HelloWorld`.

After defining the smart contract and giving it a name, you define a data item:

```
string private helloMessage = "Hello world";
```

You want to store a string in memory, so you define a Solidity variable. You define the `helloMessage` variable as a `string` datatype. You can find out about more datatypes in Chapter 6 of this minibook; for now, use `string`. Before finishing this line of code, you store the value `"Hello world"` in the `helloMessage` variable. You need to use this variable only in the `helloMessage` function, so you tell Solidity that it is a `private` variable.

In the next line, you define the only action, or function, in your smart contract:

```
function getHelloMessage() public view returns (string memory) {
```

The `function` keyword tells Solidity that you're going to write some code that you'll execute by calling the function's name, `getHelloMessage()`. To declare a function, you provide the function keyword, the function name, who can see it and use it, the mutability modifier, and what type of data it returns to the caller. Your function is named `getHelloMessage`. You want anyone to be able to call it, so you tell Solidity that it is a `public` function. The `view` modifier tells Solidity that this function will be allowed to only read and return state variables. It cannot modify the blockchain. And finally, your function will return, or send back, a string to whatever calls it (`returns`).

The last line of code does all the real work:

```
return helloMessage;
```

This line of code tells the function to `return` control to the caller and pass the contents of the `helloMessage` variable back in the process. The two lines following the `return` statement are just closing curly braces to tell Solidity that the function and contract have ended. The closing braces are like closing parentheses when you write. They finish up whatever you're wrapping in curly braces.

You can save the file at any time by clicking or tapping File ⇨ Save on the top menu bar, or by pressing Ctrl+S. Go ahead and save your first smart contract.

Running Your First Smart Contract

The only thing left is to make your smart contract display *Hello World*. To do that, you have to run your smart contract. Here are the high-level steps for running code in the Ethereum environment:

1. **Write the smart contract source code.**

   This includes the smart contract and any supporting code.

2. **Compile the smart contract.**

   This step creates the bytecode that the EVM executes.

3. **Deploy the compiled smart contract to the Ethereum blockchain.**

   This step writes your smart contract code to a block on the blockchain.

4. **Call (invoke) a function in the smart contract.**

   This step finds your smart contract code and carries out the actions you request.

Writing your code

You've already written the source code for your HelloWorld smart contract, but that isn't all you need to do. You also need a way get your code onto the blockchain. That process is called *deploying code* (as noted in Step 3 in the preceding steps). The deploy step runs *deployment code* (also called *migration code*).

You should go ahead and write it now while you're still in code editing mode:

1. **In VS Code, right-click the Migrations folder in Explorer, and then click New File to create a new file in the Migrations folder.**

2. **Type** 2_contracts_migration.js **in the filename text box and press Enter.**

   VS Code opens your new file in a new Editor tab.

3. **Type the following text in the VS Code editor:**

```
var HelloWorld = artifacts.require("HelloWorld");
module.exports = function(deployer) {
deployer.deploy(HelloWorld);
};
```

We won't go into the details of this JavaScript code. Basically, this file finds the HelloWorld compiled bytecode and calls a deploy function to place the code in a block on the blockchain. You'll understand more about deploying smart contracts when you write more complex smart contracts. For now, just enter the preceding code to set up your project to deploy your new smart contract.

Compiling your code

You can compile your smart contract code at any time in VS Code by pressing the F5 key. When the compile starts, VS Code opens a new view at the bottom of your window with four tabs: Problems, Output, Debug Console, and Terminal. Cross your fingers and hope the compile completes without errors. If you do see errors, go back and make sure that your code looks exactly like the example HelloWorld smart contract in the preceding section.

Sometimes you get errors because of a mismatch between compiler versions. The safest option when grasping Solidity is to ensure that your VS Code extension and Truffle use the same Solidity compiler version. You already know how to find the Truffle compiler version (type **truffle version** at a PowerShell prompt). Click or tap the Output tab in the new view that opened when you started the compile. It should display the compiler version it uses for compiling code in VS Code. If the version doesn't match your Truffle Solidity version, you should change it in VS Code to match the Solidity version that Truffle uses.

If you need to change the Solidity compiler version that VS Code uses, you can do that from within VS Code:

1. **Open the truffle-config.js file.**

2. **Scroll down until you find the comment,** // Configure your compilers.

3. **Replace the value in quotes after** Version: **with 0.8.9.**

The modified line should look like this:

```
Version: "0.8.9",
//Fetch exact version from solc-bin (default: truffle's version)
```

4. **Save the file.**

Your VS Code compiler now matches the version Truffle uses.

After your smart contract compiles in VS Code, you can proceed to the next step.

Deploying your code

After you have finished writing your smart contract code, it's time to test it and eventually place it into production. As mentioned, the process of copying smart contracts to the blockchain is called *deployment.* When you deploy smart contracts, you copy the code into a new block. The new smart contract gets an address and can be run on the EVM.

Because you're using the Truffle framework, the process to deploy your smart contracts is simple. Open the Terminal window (click or tap Terminal in the menu bar), and type the following:

```
truffle deploy --reset
```

WARNING

Make sure that Ganache is running before you type the deploy command. If you use Microsoft Windows and Ganache isn't running, click or tap the Windows button and then type **Ganache**. The Windows Search function finds Ganache and highlights its shortcut. Click or tap the Ganache shortcut to launch the Ganache program. Because the purpose of building dApps is to send smart contracts to the blockchain, a blockchain has to be available.

Truffle compiles your smart contracts and then uses the JavaScript files in the Migrations folder of your project to migrate, or deploy, your smart contracts to the blockchain. Figure 5-6 shows the output of the deploy command. Note that Truffle places each smart contract into a block and returns the address of the smart contract. You'll use this address to find the smart contract again and invoke its functions.

This is the first time you've interacted with the blockchain. The deployment process created a new block and placed your smart contract code into it. To see this activity, click or tap the Blocks tab in Ganache to see the blocks on your blockchain.

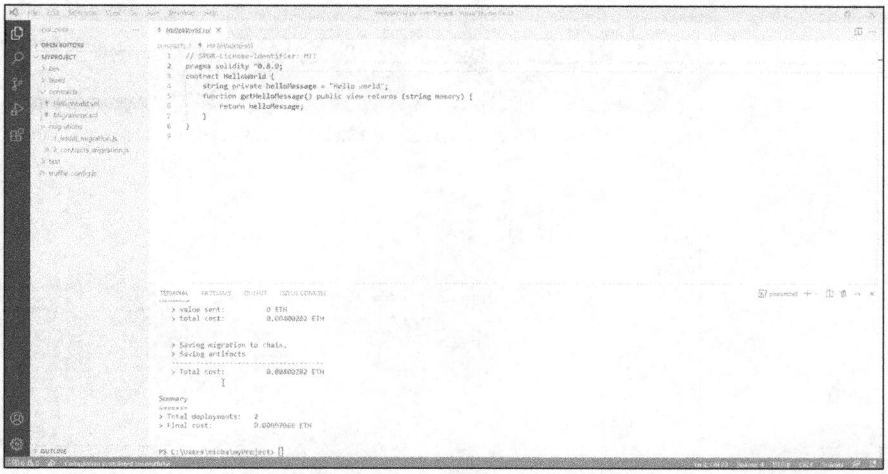

FIGURE 5-6:
Truffle deploy-
ment results.

Each action in the deployment process created a new block with a single transaction. At least four blocks should now be on the blockchain. Figure 5-7 shows the
blocks view in Ganache.

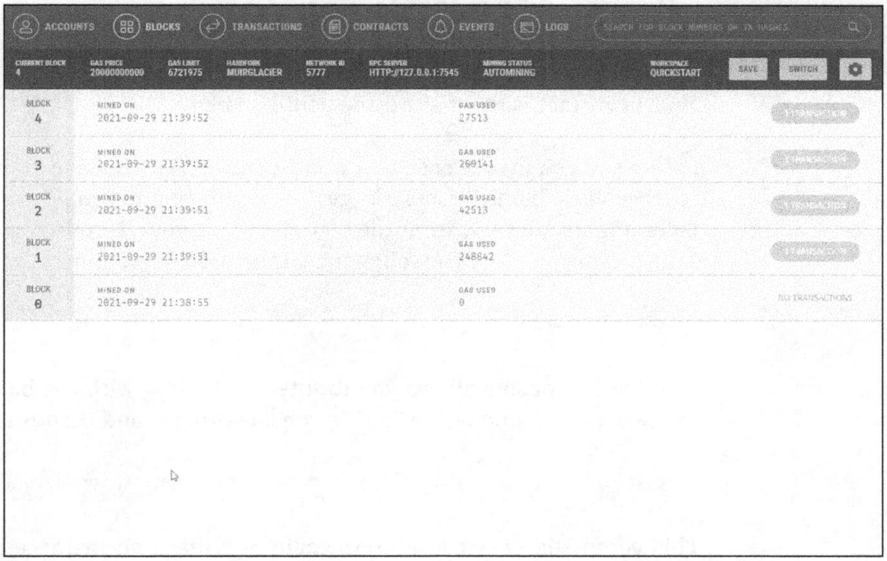

FIGURE 5-7:
Ganache blocks
after deploying
smart contracts.

You can see the bytecode for smart contracts, too. Click or tap the Transactions tab
to list the transactions in your blockchain. Click or tap a Contract Creation button
to view the contents of a smart contract. Figure 5-8 shows the contents of a smart
contract in the Ethereum blockchain. TX Data contains the bytecode for the smart
contract.

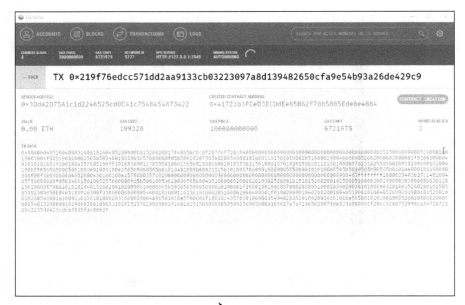

TX 0x219f76edcc571dd2aa9133cb03223097a8d139482650cfa9e54b93a26de429c9

FIGURE 5-8:
Contents of a smart contract block.

Invoking your code's functions

The final step in running smart contract code is to invoke one or more functions in your smart contract. You have only one function, getHelloMessage(), in your smart contract, so that's the one you'll invoke.

Before you can invoke code in a smart contract, you have to know where it resides on the blockchain. First, let's get some information about the smart contract, including its address, from the blockchain. In your Terminal window, launch the Truffle console. Type the following command and then press Enter:

```
truffle console
```

The Truffle console allows you to interact directly with the blockchain. Type the following command at the Truffle console prompt and then press Enter:

```
HelloWorld.deployed().then(function(instance) {return instance });
```

This command goes to the blockchain and reads an instance of the HelloWorld deployed smart contract. It creates a lot of output, including the bytecode and the original source code of your smart contract.

Figure 5-9 shows the Terminal window with the results of the preceding command. Note the deployedBytecode and source values.

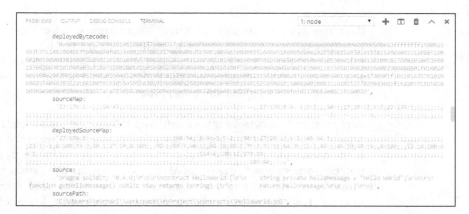

PROBLEMS   OUTPUT   DEBUG CONSOLE   TERMINAL   1: node   ▾ + □ 🗑 ∧ ✕

deployedBytecode:
    '0x608060405260043610601c5760003572c01900000000000000000000003503c02e000000000000000000000000045fffffffff1580633
491b37c1461004657b60e280efd50340015610052576000200f3b50610056610060d654644e510000a20 a1820103025028381815815200280191506065108
6020019000339350002b0802110150100965700002215181840152602003010905963000956b50650505050050960105301e10f140801560200c05700202002e5100
13308620036501000a003185150250026001915e5b5b255b5050450040618090200r35b5e060000a0345a01050011615e1018002293160002030046904f16002a
00910402040200160405198818156401200592091981815200180200182200460181600115155610050220020049001561610e5706001f100510143576101u6
0803356004020352915e200191610156b5b5b2010100000205202600000202d005b81540152035000101a000200101b0610a151015782002b6001F163200915b5a50
5059bae0e50e05000a016037a7a72160002a00e5a1505cr066n0364a0032b0005b45cad33fe4c5e5b73409fe3d31700920e0615fcc00029',
sourceMap:
    ':27:170:1-;;;54:43;;;;;;;;;;;;;;;;;;;;;;;;;;;;;;;;;1-:1;::-1;27:178;8-9--1;5:2;;;30:1;27:28:12;5:2;27:176:1;;;;;;;;
;;;;;;;;;;;;;;;;;;10;;;:;;;:;;;,',
deployedSourceMap:
    ':27:170:11-;;;;;;;;;;;;;;;;;;;;;;;;;106:94;;8-00-1;5:2;;;30:1;27;20:12;5:2;106:94:1;;;;;;;;;;;;;;;;;;;;;;;;;;;
;23:1;-1;8:100;33-3;30:1;27:10;8:100;;;99:1;94:3;40:11;04-18;80:1;75:3;71:11;64:39;52:2,40--1;45:10;40:15;;8:100;;;12-14;106:9
4:1;;;;;;;;;;;;;;;;;;;154:6;130;12:173:19;;;;;;;;;;;;;;;;;;;;;;;;;;;;;;;;;;;106:94;;;;0',
source:
    'pragma solidity ^0.4.0;\r\n \r\ncontract HelloWorld {\r\n   string private helloMessage = "Hello world";\r\n\r\n
function getHelloMessage() public view returns (string) {\r\n   return helloMessage;\r\n\r\n   }\r\n}',
sourcePath:
    'C:\\Users\\michael\\workspace\\MyProject\\contracts\\HelloWorld.sol',

FIGURE 5-9:
Smart contract
instance
information.

Now that you have an instance of your smart contract (that is, a pointer to where your smart contract is running in memory), you can use it to invoke any of its functions. Type the following command at the Truffle console prompt, and then press Enter:

```
HelloWorld.deployed().then(function(instance) {return instance.
    getHelloWorld() });
```

This command invokes the getHelloMessage() function in the HelloWorld smart contract and displays the results. You should see the *"Hello world"* message in the Terminal window. That may seem like a lot of work just to display a message, and it is. But the process you just went through is one that you'll use over and over to develop, test, and deploy smart contracts, regardless of how complex they may be.

Paying as You Go

You may have noticed in Ganache that blocks and transactions each have a Gas Used value. The Ganache main window also shows the Gas Price and Gas Limit for the blockchain. You find out a lot more about gas in Chapter 6 of this minibook, but you need to know a little about transaction costs now, before you start writing bigger and more functional smart contracts.

Gas is a unit of value in Ethereum. Every operation that a smart contract carries out costs some number of gas units. For example, you have to pay 30 gas to calculate a Keccak256 hash, plus another 6 gas for every 256 bits (not bytes) of data you want to hash. The amount you pay for operations is called the *gas cost*.

Charging gas for computation forces smart contract developers to think about how they write code. You can write inefficient code, but it will cost you. Also, gas provides a great way to keep malicious code from taking over EVMs. Every transaction has a gas limit, and when the EVM reaches that limit, it stops the contract. Gas limits protect EVMs from many types of denial of service (DoS) attacks.

Every transaction sets a *gas price*, which is the highest amount of ETH that transaction is willing to pay for each gas unit. Transactions also set a *gas limit*, which is the maximum amount of gas the transaction is willing to pay. If the execution consumes enough gas to equal the gas limit, the EVM stops execution of the transaction. That is one reason a transaction may not succeed. Alternatively, if the gas price is set too low, a transaction may never be added to a block because miners did not want to waste their processing time on a transaction with too small of a reward. Miners generally try to mine blocks with transactions that have a high enough gas price to make the mining process profitable.

The takeaway is that creating transactions in the Ethereum blockchain requires a fee. That fee is charged in gas units and can be limited to a range with which you are comfortable. Paying more gas often means getting your transaction processed more quickly, but paying too much wastes money. As you write smart contract code, pay attention to the operations that incur a gas cost. As you find out more about Solidity in Chapter 6 of this minibook, you'll discover ways to write code that conserves operations that require gas.

Chapter **6**

Discovering Smart Contracts

mart contracts are the functional part of any blockchain solution. Just like the objects described in Chapter 5 of this minibook, a blockchain solution is a combination of data and actions on that data. The data is the content of the blocks on the blockchain. You already know that after data is added, it stays there forever. (Although you could technically change blockchain data, doing so without any other node detecting your change is next to impossible.) Because blockchain data is immutable, it is important to carefully control how that data is added.

The actions that operate on the blockchain data are the smart contracts. Smart contracts, like the data, are stored in blocks on the blockchain. But smart contracts execute on all Ethereum virtual machines (EVMs) and have to work the same way and produce the same results on all EVMs. Smart contracts govern the way that data is added to the blockchain and how that data can be used.

Chapter 5 of this minibook shows you how to write a simple smart contract, but that contract doesn't do anything useful. The only way to create a smart contract to do anything useful is to identify a real-world problem and then create a blockchain solution that solves the problem. One use case that's a good fit for a blockchain solution is supply chain management. In this chapter, you discover some supply chain challenges and how blockchain can address some of them. You also find out more about Solidity smart contracts by developing a solution to a current supply chain problem.

Introducing Supply Chain and Common Challenges

In today's economy, nearly every product you use or service you consume comes from some other source. Although you may grow your own vegetables and herbs, you likely don't raise livestock as a meat source as well. Everything that you buy comes from an original producer. In the case of food products, the original producer could be a grower, a rancher, a fisherman, or a producer of any other type of food.

As society has moved from being self-sufficient to relying on others to supply products and services, consumers have become detached from producers. Geographic distances, regulations, and the suppliers' desires for greater reach and higher profits have given rise to aggregators and middlemen to handle goods. These middlemen provide benefits to producers and consumers but also require fees for their services. These fees increase the consumer price, and the processing may increase the time it takes for goods to arrive to the market or consumer.

Describing supply chain

Consider what happens when you buy fish. If you live near the coast, you may go to the docks and purchase fish directly from a fishing boat. However, it is more likely that you bought the last fish you ate from a market or a restaurant. That means one or more parties were between the fishermen (the producer) and you (the consumer). The framework that connects consumers to producers, along with the system that manages it, is called a *supply chain*. A supply chain may have only a single participant between the producer and consumer, or it may contain many participants along the way. A supply chain manages all assets, along with handling the payments tendered in exchange for products or services.

In a simple supply chain, fishermen may sell their fish directly to markets near the docks where their boats bring a fresh catch each day. Consumers shop at the markets and purchase fish from a single middleman. If you don't live near a market like that, the fish may go to a processor, then to a shipper, then on to a warehouse, and finally to a retail store, where you purchase the fish. That is an example of a common supply chain. As consumers demand more options, supply chains exist to help producers provide the products and services that meet these demands.

Supply chain participants provide value to small and large producers. For the small producers, an aggregator can collect product from multiple producers and provide larger shipments to processors or warehouses. Large producers benefit from having local points of entry into the supply chain, without having to handle point-to-point shipments to all outlets for their products.

Consumers benefit as well because the supply chain makes available a wide variety of products from many producers.

Identifying difficulties when implementing a supply chain

So far, a supply chain sounds like a great way to get products and services to a wide variety of consumers. And it does do all that. But the current supply chain approach has obstacles, or limitations. In general, five types of obstacles are encountered in today's supply chain implementations, as listed in Table 6-1.

TABLE 6-1   Supply Chain Obstacles

Obstacle	Description
Lack of transparency	Today's supply chain participants often manage their own data systems and don't publish their internal data. Separately managed data systems make it difficult to see how items are processed at each step in the chain.
Lack of traceability	With limited transparency at each step, the data required for tracing products to their origin is often not available, making authenticity claims and recall notices for points of origin difficult or impossible.
Transfer time lags	Transferring products from one participant to another requires synchronization between organizations and may not occur in real time. Many transfers occur in batches based on scheduled operations. This can cause delays at every stage, resulting in cumulative delays throughout the chain.
Translation data loss	Each participant receives, manages, and passes along their own core set of data. Even with decades-old standards, such as Electronic Data Interchange (EDI), some data items may not be passed along from one participant to another, resulting in granular data loss along the supply chain. Also, any data that must be re-keyed because it isn't passed along is subject to human error.
Nonstandard/ unavailable status tracking	Because each participant generally manages their own data, status updates may not be available at each stage. Some participants may either decline to provide status updates or provide them in a manner that is incompatible with status updates from other participants. In the latter case, the status update requestor is required to assimilate status updates in various formats and harmonize them into meaningful output.

The items in Table 6-1 represent just some of the obstacles in supply chain implementations in production today. These problems tend to be more pronounced as the complexity of a supply chain increases. But as many markets mature and become more global, supply chains nearly always become more diverse and complex. Pursuing solutions to these obstacles is important to global commerce.

Examining How Blockchain Can Help Resolve Supply Chain Problems

Blockchain technology can help address many supply chain obstacles. While no single solution is a perfect fit for any situation, blockchain, and Ethereum in particular, can help resolve the majority of the shortcomings in today's supply chain implementations. Table 6-2 lists the obstacles from the previous section and how Ethereum can help resolve each one.

TABLE 6-2   **Ethereum Solutions to Supply Chain Obstacles**

Obstacle	Description
Lack of transparency	Blockchain technology does not have a central authority, and so all transactions are published to the shared blockchain. As a result, any participating node can view transactions and verify their authenticity.
Lack of traceability	Because all nodes have access to all transactions on the blockchain, linking transactions is almost trivial. Any node can easily construct a complete chain of transactions between the original producer and the final consumer.
Transfer time lags	Smart contracts provide the capability to assess the current blockchain state and make decisions on demand. Legacy solutions often require human interaction, which depends on set working hours. Blockchain introduces the opportunity for smart contracts, not humans, to make certain decisions immediately. This benefit can remove the need for human intervention in some types of decisions.
Translation data loss	Ethereum smart contracts define data needed for each transaction and ensure that all participants provide the same input. In short, every node uses the same rules — the rules don't change from participant to participant as you move along the supply chain.
Non-standard/ unavailable status tracking	Instead of each participant responding individually to status update requests, all necessary information is in blocks on the blockchain. Anyone who can access the blockchain can determine the current status of any digital asset.

Ethereum provides a level playing field for many uses, including supply chains. In an environment that includes participants who do not fully trust one another, or are even competitors, Ethereum makes it possible to conduct business in a fair manner. Supply chain implementations can be far more comprehensive than just tracking how products move to the consumer. Participants along the supply chain can also add their own value.

For example, an elaborate supply chain can operate like a distributed manufacturing or assembly line. High-end corporate aircraft often undergo customizations after the aircraft leaves the manufacturer but before delivery to the customer. For example, the aircraft might go to several other companies for interior fitting, painting, and even aftermarket performance upgrades. Each step likely includes additional services and products that add to the original aircraft — for a fee.

Ethereum makes it possible to track and control products through multiple steps, and provides a secure way to provide transparency and traceability for all products to all parties.

Implementing a Blockchain Supply Chain Solution

You now know what an Ethereum supply chain solution can do, but you still need to see how it will operate before you start writing code. For the rest of this mini-book, we show you how to implement a simple supply chain solution in Solidity. This solution provides the absolute basic actions you need to track and manage products and payments from initial production to the final consumer.

Your supply chain solution will consist of two smart contracts: one smart contract to handle payments and the other to handle the asset tracking and management. Because you're focusing on smart contracts, your solution won't implement every imaginable supply chain function. But when you're done, you'll appreciate how powerful Ethereum is and, we hope, be motivated to write your own smart contracts to solve your own problems.

Paying for supply chain services

Each link in a supply chain provides a service. A supply chain participant may ship goods from one place to another, store goods in a warehouse, add value to products, or even place goods on shelves at retail locations. Unless your organization is a nonprofit, the main goal for participating in a supply chain is to make money. That means you have to pay every time a product moves from one participant to another.

Although you could use traditional payment processing, you're going to see how to do it using Ethereum! The easiest way to send and receive funds in Ethereum is by using a token. An *Ethereum token* is a type of cryptocurrency for a particular dApp. You'll be creating a supply chain token based on the popular ERC-20 Ethereum token standard.

TECHNICAL STUFF

Although several Ethereum token standards are available, ERC-20 is by far the most popular. You can see how many tokens exist by navigating to `https://etherscan.io` and clicking or tapping Tokens — ERC-20 Top Tokens. At the time of this writing, more than 450,470 different ERC-20 tokens exist.

You can think of a token as a college student ID with money in a special account. To avoid carrying around cash or multiple cards, many college students pay for things on campus using their IDs. The "college cash" attached to their ID is good only on campus, but it's convenient and makes it easy for on-campus vendors to identify students and offer special pricing.

Your token smart contract will contain all the rules to manage your balance of cryptocurrency. You'll write the code to check your balance, transfer funds to another Ethereum address, and receive funds from another Ethereum address.

Managing assets on the supply chain

The main smart contract for your supply chain will contain the core functions to manage assets. From a technical sense, Ethereum can't manage physical assets. It can manage only digital assets. Think about tracking your bags when you fly on a commercial airline. Many airlines provide status updates via a mobile app. They tell you when your bag gets loaded on the airplane and where to pick it up when you arrive at your destination. However, the airline isn't tracking your bag — they're tracking the tag on your bag. The tag is a generated version of a digital asset that the airline tracks.

The difference between a physical asset and a digital asset is obvious on one hand but subtle on the other hand. Continuing the airline luggage example, problems can occur at the cyber-physical barrier. If the human or device that attaches the tag to the bag doesn't get it right, nothing works from there on. An example we also give in Chapter 2 of this minibook is the scenario of airline personnel attaching tags to checked bags to ensure that the bags arrive at the same destination as the bags' owners. When baggage tags are inadvertently swapped between travelers' bags, the tags arrive at the "correct" destinations, but they're attached to the wrong travelers' bags.

This example should help point out how important it is to maintain the cyber-physical relationship. Physical goods have to be associated with a digital asset to be managed in any computing environment. In many cases, that means the entry point of the supply chain creates a tag or other method of positively identifying the physical asset. Regardless of the identification option you choose, you need a number or an identifier that corresponds to a single physical asset. Table 6-3 lists a few options for associating physical assets with their digital mirror assets.

TABLE 6-3   **Connecting Physical Assets to Digital Assets**

ID Method	Pros	Cons
Engraving an identifier on each product	Unique to each item and difficult to alter	Expensive and slow
Attaching a printed label to each product	Unique to each item and useful for a wide variety of products	Labels can be damaged or lost
Attaching a printed label to a box of products	Fast for products managed in batches	Difficulty handling opened boxes with missing product
Using a manufacturer-generated identifier	Integrates with manufacturer's data, and fast if identifier can be scanned	Potentially different formats or locations for different manufacturers, and depends on external data provider
Attaching an RFID tag	Fast and easy to scan	More expensive than printed labels, and tags can detach

Your supply chain smart contract assumes that some external device or other entity creates a trusted digital string or number that uniquely identifies a physical asset. After you have a digital asset ID, your smart contract defines functions that carry out the following actions:

>> **Creating a new supply chain participant:** Validates a new participant and authorizes the participant to become part of the supply chain process.

>> **Adding a new product to the supply chain:** Puts a product into the supply chain process.

>> **Transferring ownership of a product to another participant:** Carries out the main action of transferring a product from one supply chain participant to another.

>> **Tracking a product:** Provides status updates of a product and its history on the supply chain.

Your two smart contracts will work together every time a product transfers from one participant to another. At the moment a product's owner changes, the participants making the transfer use the ERC-20 token to exchange funds to pay for the asset. Figure 6-1 shows how your supply chain process will work.

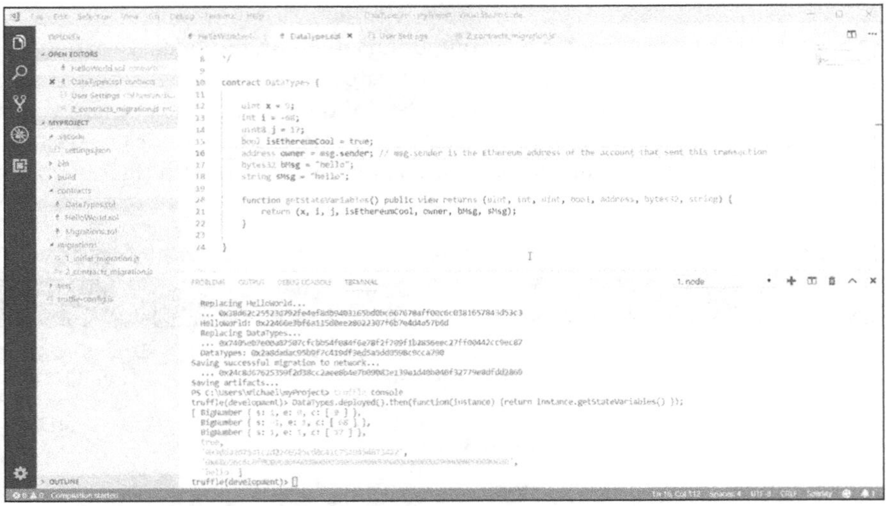

FIGURE 6-1:
Ethereum supply
chain flow.

Digging into Solidity

Solidity is the language you'll use to write smart contracts in the examples in this book. Solidity was proposed by Gavin Wood in August 2014. Although it isn't the only language you can use to write smart contracts, it is the most popular language for writing smart contracts that run in the EVM. It enjoys solid support from the Ethereum community and was developed by the Ethereum project's Solidity team.

Solidity was designed to be similar to JavaScript and was influenced by a few other popular programming languages as well, including C++ and Python. The goal of Solidity is to provide a language that is familiar to web application developers but targeted at smart contract development. Solidity isn't intended as a general-purpose language, but rather to support blockchain-specific operations with code that runs in the EVM.

Before your code can run in the EVM, you have to compile it. That's why one of the components you installed when building your development environment was a Solidity compiler. You first write your Solidity source code in an editor. Then you compile it into bytecode, which consists of the instructions that run in the EVM. After you deploy your smart contract bytecode, it runs on all Ethereum nodes.

Because smart contracts run on all nodes, Solidity must enforce *determinism* — that is, the results must be the same for all nodes running your smart contract code with the same input. If you look at the Solidity documentation, you won't find a `random()` function. That omission is specifically to support Solidity's determinism. Your code gets run first by the node that mines a new block, but then all nodes verify the block and run the code to ensure that they don't get a different result.

In many ways, Solidity is similar to other programming languages. The biggest differences are in how the programs are run and how Solidity deals with data. You find out more about Solidity data handling later in this chapter. But for now, note that Solidity deals with data only in the EVM or the blockchain.

Solidity doesn't interact with the outside world much, but it is possible for it to do so. Solidity supports the concept of an *oracle*, which is a trusted source of information from the outside world. Calling an oracle is easy. However, one problem with an oracle is being able to trust it. Another problem is dealing with an oracle that may return different data each time it's called. Before using any oracles, you must ensure that the data source is trustworthy and consistent. Because of this, it is common for oracles to return data and some proof of authenticity.

TIP

The concept of trust with respect to oracles is just an extension of blockchain trust. Remember that blockchain technology provides a trusted ledger of data in an environment of trustless network nodes. Because trust is such a foundational property of blockchain, it isn't surprising that trusting an oracle is an important concern.

Describing Basic Smart Contract Syntax

You've already seen a little Solidity syntax. Now it's time to build on what you know. When you write Solidity source code, you save that code in a file with the extension .sol. Chapter 5 of this minibook shows you how to store your HelloWorld smart contract in the file `HelloWorld.sol`.

A Solidity program has several main sections, described here:

>> **Pragma:** This tells Solidity what versions of the compiler are valid to compile this file.

>> **Comments:** Developers should use comments for documenting code.

>> **Import:** This defines an external file that contains code that your smart contract needs.

>> **Contract(s):** This section is where the body of your smart contract code resides.

Declaring a valid compiler version

The pragma directive should be the first line of code in a Solidity file. Because the Solidity language is still maturing, it is common for new compiler versions to include changes that would fail to compile older programs. The pragma directive helps avoid compiler failures due to using a newer compiler.

Here is the syntax for the pragma directive:

```
pragma Solidity <<version number>>;
```

Here is a sample pragma directive:

```
pragma Solidity ^0.8.9;
```

All statements in Solidity end with a semicolon.

The version number starts with a 0, followed by a major build number and a minor build number. For example, the version number 0.8.9 refers to major build 8 and minor build 9. The caret symbol (^) before the version number tells Solidity that it can use the latest build in a major version range. In the preceding example, Solidity can use a compiler from any build in the version 8 build range. This is a way to tell readers that your program was written for 0.8.9 but will still compile for subsequent version 8 builds.

Although using the caret in the pragma directive provides flexibility, it is a better practice to drop the caret and tell Solidity exactly what compiler version you expect.

Commenting your code

Adding comments to your code is an extra step that adds a professional look and feel to your code. A well-commented source code file is easier to read and understand and helps other developers quickly understand what your code is supposed to do. Even simple comments can cut down on the time required to fix bugs or add new functionality. Comments can also provide input for utilities to generate documentation for your smart contracts.

You can use single-line or multiline regular comments. Single-line comments start with two forward slashes. Multiline comments start with the /* characters and end with the */ characters. Here is an example of Solidity comments:

```
// Here is a single-line Solidity comment
/* I have a lot more to say with this comment, so I'll
use a multiline comment. The compiler will ignore
```

everything after the opening comment characters, until
it sees the closing comment characters. */

A third type of Solidity comment is called the *Ethereum Natural Specification (NatSpec)* directive. You can use NatSpec to provide information about your code for documentation generators to use to create formatted documentation that describes your smart contracts. NatSpec directives start with three forward slashes and include special tags with data for the documentation. Here is an example of using NatSpec directives:

```
/// @title Greeter smart contract
/// @author Joe Programmer
/// @notice This code takes a person's name and says hello
/// @param name The name of the caller
/// @return greeting The greeting with the caller's name
```

TECHNICAL STUFF

You can find NatSpec documentation and additional information at https://github.com/ethereum/wiki/wiki/Ethereum-Natural-Specification-Format.

Importing external code

The import section is optional but can be powerful. If your smart contract needs to refer to code in other files, you have to import those other files first. Importing files makes it as though you copied the other code into the current file. Using imports helps you avoid actually copying code from one place to another. If you need to access code, just import the Solidity file that contains it.

The syntax for importing other files is simple. You use the import keyword and then provide the filename for the file you want to import. For example, to import the file myToken.sol, use this syntax:

```
Import 'myToken.sol';
```

Defining your smart contracts

In the last main section of Solidity, you define the contents of your smart contract. It starts with the keyword contract and contains all of the functional code in your smart contract. You can have multiple contract sections in Solidity. That means a single .sol file can define multiple contracts. Here is an example contract section (you may recognize this code from Chapter 5 of this minibook):

```
contract HelloWorld {
string private helloMessage = "Hello world";
function getHelloMessage() public view returns (string) {
```

```
return helloMessage;
    }
}
```

Inside the contract section is where you define all of your variables, structures, events, and functions. There's a lot more to the contract section of your code, but for now, you know how to set up a Solidity smart contract. In the next section, you find out more about what goes into the contract section.

Handling Data in Solidity

Solidity is particular about where you can store data. You generally define two types of variables in Solidity: state variables and local variables. You define state variables in the contract section, and those variables are available anywhere in the smart contract. These variables store the state of your smart contract by saving the values in a block on the blockchain. You define local variables inside functions. Local variables don't save their values between function calls. Those values aren't stored on the blockchain and go away when the function ends.

Solidity defines three places for storing data:

>> **Stack:** Where Solidity stores local simple variable values defined in functions.

>> **Memory:** An area of memory on each EVM that Solidity uses to store temporary values. Values stored here are erased between function calls.

>> **Storage:** Where state variables defined in a smart contract reside. These state variables reside in the smart contract data section on the blockchain.

Variable storage location is one of the more confusing aspects of Solidity. This section covers the basics; Chapter 7 of this minibook touches on some finer points. The Solidity language doesn't have a stack keyword but does have memory and storage keywords. Solidity uses its own defaults, depending on where you define variables and how you use them, but you can override some of these defaults and also use the keywords to modify how Solidity treats variables.

Here are a few rules that help keep things straight when storing data in Solidity:

>> State variables are storage by default (values are stored in the blockchain).

>> Local variables in functions are memory by default (values are stored temporarily in memory).

>> Structs are storage by default (values are stored in the blockchain).

Solidity can handle different types of data and provides different types of variables to handle each type. When you define variables, you have to specify the datatype of the variable. The datatype tells Solidity how much space to allocate for the value you will store in the variable and how to treat the data. Table 6-4 lists the data types that Solidity supports.

TABLE 6-4 **Solidity Data Types**

Data Type	Comments	Example	When to Use

uint	32-byte (256-bit) unsigned integer. You can also define smaller uints as uint8, uint16, up to uint256 (which is the same as uint).	uint x = 10;
		
		uint16 x = 44;
			For storing positive integers. Using smaller uints (such as uint8) saves storage space and processing cost.

int	32-byte (256-bit) signed integer. You can also define smaller ints as int8, int16, up to int256 (which is the same as int).	int x = –10; int32 x = 45;	For storing integers with negative and positive values. Using smaller ints (such as int8) saves storage space and processing cost.
byte	A single byte. You can also define arrays of 1–32 bytes using the type bytes2, bytes3, up to bytes32.	byte singleChar = 't'; bytes16 msgHello = 'Hello, world!';	For storing any number of bytes (up to 32). The bytes datatype makes it easy to access and manipulate array contents.
string	32-byte array of characters. This datatype is most often used to store strings of UTF-8 characters.	string myString = "Hello, world!";	For storing character strings. Solidity strings are difficult to manipulate directly. In most cases, using bytes is more convenient.
bool	Boolean, or logical, values (yes/no or true/false).	bool isOK = true;	For storing yes/no, true/false values.
address	20-byte Ethereum address.	address myAddress;	For storing an Ethereum address.
mapping	A dictionary that relates a key to a value. Mappings provide an easy method to look up a value that corresponds to a key.	mapping (address => uint) balances;	For looking up data for a specific key, such as finding the balance of an account.
enum	Enumerated list of options.	enum surveyResult { StronglyDisagree, Disagree, Neutral, Agree, StronglyAgree };	For storing meaningful values from a limited set of choices.

As your smart contracts become more complex, you'll probably need to represent more complex types of data. For example, you may want to define a physical address type that contains several pieces of information, including street address, city, state, and Zip code.

You also may need to store tables or lists of data. Solidity allows you to create your own data structures with the `struct` complex data type. You can also define arrays that store groups of similar data items. Solidity arrays can be groups of simple data types or groups of structs. You use structs and arrays in the smart contracts you write in Chapter 7 of this minibook.

Here is a smart contract that demonstrates some of Solidity's simple data types. In this example, you're using only state variables, which means you're writing to the blockchain. Defining all of your variables as state variables is not a good idea unless you want to store data forever. Data stored to the blockchain requires expensive operations and shouldn't be used unless you need to store your data persistently. For now, you'll use state variables, but in Chapter 7 of this minibook, you find out how to define local variables as well.

Open VS Code for the myProject project.

To open VS Code in the myProject project, open a Windows Command prompt or PowerShell (our favorite) and use the `cd` command to navigate to your project directory (myProject). From here, just type the following command and press Enter:

```
code .
```

Then type the following code:

```
//SPDX-License-Identifier:MIT
pragma solidity 0.8.9;
/*
 * @title Solidity data types
 * @author Michael Solomon
 * @notice A simple smart contract to demonstrate simple data types available in
   Solidity
 *
 */
contract DataTypes {
uint x = 9;
int i = -68;
uint8 j = 17;
bool isEthereumCool = true;
address owner = msg.sender; //Ethereum address of the message sender
bytes32 bMsg = "hello";
```

```
string sMsg = "hello";
function getStateVariables() public view returns (uint, int, uint8, bool,
    address, bytes32, string memory) {
return (x, i, j, isEthereumCool, owner, bMsg, sMsg);
}
}
```

The steps to deploy and test your smart contract are the same as the steps you read about in Chapter 5 of this minibook. Go to that chapter for details.

Before you can deploy and test your new smart contract, you need to add it to the migration JavaScript script. In VS Code, open the 2_contracts_migrations.js file in the Migrations directory. Then add the two lines with comments so your file looks this:

```
var HelloWorld = artifacts.require("HelloWorld");
var DataTypes = artifacts.require("DataTypes");// Add this line
module.exports = function(deployer) {
deployer.deploy(HelloWorld);
deployer.deploy(DataTypes);// Add this line
};
```

Don't forget to save your file after adding the new text!

Here are the steps you can use to deploy and test your new smart contract:

1. **Make sure you have Ganache running.**

2. **In VS Code, click or tap the Terminal tab, type the following, and then press Enter:**

   ```
   truffle deploy --reset
   ```

3. **Type** truffle console **and press Enter.**

4. **At the Truffle console prompt, type the following and press Enter:**

   ```
   DataTypes.deployed().then(function(instance) {return
       instance.getStateVariables() });
   ```

Figure 6-2 shows the values that your new smart contract returns. Truffle displays the return values in an interesting way. Numbers are returned as BigNumber objects. You can call functions in a BigNumber library to convert them, but for now just read the values directly. For the numeric returned values, the first value, s: is the sign of the number, and the third value, c: is the unsigned value the function returned. Also note that the address and bytes32 values are in hexadecimal format.

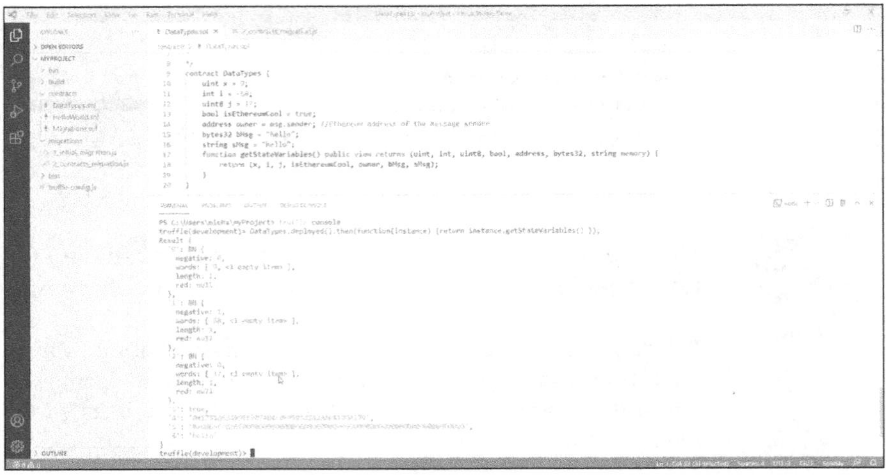

FIGURE 6-2:
Smart contract
return values.

Finding Out about Computation and Gas

One of the difficulties encountered when writing distributed applications is balancing the workload among participating nodes. The way blockchain technology is designed, all nodes do the same amount of work. In fact, all nodes duplicate the same work. This redundancy is necessary to ensure consensus among the nodes.

Workload balance isn't a problem, but node overload is a big problem. Consider what would happen if a malicious user submitted a smart contract that consumed so much computing power that the node running the code couldn't do anything else. That would be a denial of service (DoS) attack. And what's worse, every node would be required to do the same amount of work. If malicious smart contracts were allowed to run, they could render the entire blockchain network unusable.

To avoid DoS attacks and to reduce the overall work network nodes have to carry out, Ethereum introduced the concept of paying for the work required to carry out a transaction. Ethereum also includes a charge for storing data on the blockchain. These requirements encourage smart contract developers to use the blockchain only when necessary, thereby keeping the blockchain from growing unrestrained. Requiring transaction creators to pay for usage is a way of promoting conservative use of shared resources.

Ethereum measures the work required for operations by using *gas*. The amount of work required for each operation is used to calculate the fee to carry out the operations that make up a transaction. According to the Ethereum Yellow Paper (the formal Ethereum definition), every transaction requires a minimum of 21,000 gas units to complete.

TECHNICAL STUFF

The Ethereum Yellow Paper contains the formal definition of Ethereum. You can find the Yellow Paper by opening your browser and navigating to `https://github.com/ethereum/yellowpaper`.

Miners are nodes on an Ethereum network that carry out the intensive mathematical calculations to find a nonce value that satisfies the hash requirements for a block. (You can find out more about mining, hashes, and nonce values in Book 6, Chapter 2.) Paying gas provides an incentive to miners to commit their computing power (and electricity) to the blockchain. Every user that submits a transaction pays a fee in gas, and miners in turn select transactions they think will be profitable and build new blocks with those transactions. The miner that is successful in solving the mathematical puzzle gets the gas fees for the transactions in that block.

So, who pays all these fees to miners? Well, we all do! Every Ethereum transaction requires a small processing fee. Although this might sound like the middlemen that blockchain is supposed to replace, Ethereum fees are tiny compared to existing systems in use today. However, even a relatively tiny Ethereum gas process can grow to be not so tiny during times of heavy network congestion.

Calculating gas fees requires several inputs, including gas price, gas limit, and gas (computation) cost. The user who submits a transaction (that is, initiates some action that invokes a smart contract) sets the highest acceptable gas price and the total limit of gas they will agree to pay. The total fee is the amount of gas used in the transaction multiplied by the gas price the miner charges. All of these values can change from transaction to transaction. Table 6-5 lists the main components of gas charges and how they contribute to transaction fees.

TABLE 6-5   **Ethereum Gas Charges**

Component	Comments
Gas price	The highest price per gas unit a transaction originator is willing to pay. Miners use this limit to determine if the transaction is worth including in a block. If the value is too low, the transaction may not be profitable. If too many transactions are selected with very high gas prices, it may take too long to mine the block and the miner may lose to another node.
Gas limit	The total number of gas units the transaction originator is willing to pay. It must be high enough to allow all operations to complete. If this value is too low, the EVM will terminate the transaction and undo all of its operations. Also, each block has a gas limit, so miners can't just choose the transactions with very high gas limits — they have to choose transactions with gas limits that are cumulatively lower than the block gas limit.
Gas cost	The cost of a single operation. For example, the ADD operation costs 3 gas, and the MUL operation costs 5 gas.
Transaction fee	The total fee for computations in a transaction. The formula is: transaction fee = total gas cost * gas price.
Unused gas	The amount of unused gas returned to the transaction originator if the gas limit for the transaction is greater than the actual gas cost.

If you want to know how much gas will cost, open your browser and navigate to `https://ethgasstation.info`. This webpage shows gas statistics for recent Ethereum transactions. Figure 6-3 shows the recommended gas prices at the time of this writing. Note that a standard gas price is 81 Gwei and the fast gas price is 115 Gwei; and if you want your transaction picked up quickly, you should set your gas price to 126 Gwei. 1 ETH is worth 1 billion (1,000,000,000) Gwei, so 81 Gwei is worth 0.000000081 ETH. At the time of this writing, 1 ETH is worth $2,970.70 USD, so the standard gas price of 81 Gwei (a standard gas price) is worth $ 0.0002406267. If a transaction requires a minimum of 21,000 Gwei, a transaction costs at least 0.0002406267 * 21,000 = $5.0531607, or just over $5.

TECHNICAL STUFF

You can find the gas cost for operations in Ethereum in a spreadsheet located at `https://docs.google.com/spreadsheets/d/1m89CVujrQe5LAFJ8-YAUCcNK950dUzMQPMJBxRtGCqs/edit#gid=0`.

Although the minimum transaction fee doesn't look like it is very expensive, the fees do add up if you waste computation. From a strict cost per computation, it isn't hard to pay for your own node to carry out calculations. But what you're paying for is transparency and validity among a large number of untrusted participants.

Exploring Access Modes and Visibility of Smart Contract Functions and Data

You can restrict who can invoke Solidity functions and who can access variable values. These access keywords are called *visibility modifiers.* You can use four visibility modifiers when you define functions and variables, as shown in Table 6-6.

TECHNICAL STUFF

The Solidity compiler automatically creates a `getter` function for each `public` state variable, which provides an easy way to fetch the value of any variable. The name of the function is the same as the name of the variable. When the `getter` function is called, it returns the value stored in the `state` variable. So if you define a public `state` variable of type `uint` named `myVar`, the function `myVar()` will return a `uint` that is the current value of `myVal`.

TABLE 6-6

Solidity Visibility Modifiers

Visibility	What It Means for Functions	What It Means for Variables
public	Anyone can call this function.	Anyone can access this variable's value.
external	Only external functions can call this function.	This doesn't apply to state variables, and only external functions can access this local variable's value.
internal	Only functions in this contract and any contract deriving from it can call this function.	Only functions in this contract and any contract deriving from it can access this variable's value.
private	Only functions in this contract can call this function.	Only functions in this contract can access this variable's value.

Solidity visibility modifiers make it possible to write functions and define variables that are available only to a specific subset of users. You may want some functions and variables to be available only to other functions in the same contract, say, for internal maintenance. In other cases, you may want other functions or variables to be available to anyone. A getter function (a function that gets the value of some data item and returns it) is often a public function. That makes it available to anyone, while an internal function that manages a contract's date may be a private or internal function.

In addition to providing visibility modifiers, you can specify function access modifiers. *Access modifiers* restrict how functions are allowed to access state variables. Older versions of Solidity used a single access modifier, constant, to indicate that a function did not modify any state variable. Starting with Solidity 0.4.17, two new access modifiers replace the constant modifier: view and pure. A function that exceeds its access modifier will result in a compiler error.

Here are the meanings of each access modifier:

>> **constant:** This access modifier, which was deprecated in Solidity 0.4.17, was used to inform the compiler that the function would not modify any state variables.

>> **view:** This access modifier, introduced in Solidity 0.4.17, is a replacement for constant and informs the compiler that the function will not modify any state variables.

>> **pure:** This access modifier, introduced in Solidity 0.4.17, is more restrictive than view and informs the compiler that the function will not even read any state variables.

Controlling Execution Flow

The simple smart contract code that you've seen so far doesn't do much. It just executes from the top of the code to the bottom. Programs that do something useful have statements in them that alter the flow of execution based on input and calculations. Some statements, called *conditional statements*, enforce conditional expressions and execute only under certain circumstances. Other statements, called *iteration statements* or *loops*, repeat sections of code a certain number of times.

These types of statement are called *flow of execution statements*. Solidity implements many of the flow of execution statements you'll find in JavaScript. Table 6-7 lists the conditional and iteration statements in Solidity.

TABLE 6-7 **Solidity Conditional and Iteration Statements**

Statement	What It Does	Example

if-else	Executes a group of statements if a condition is true, and optionally executes another set of statements if the condition is false (else).	numDonuts = purchasedQty;
		
		if (numDonuts >= 12)
		
		giveDozenPrice = true;
		
		else
		
		giveDozenPrice = false;

While	Executes a group of statements zero or more times until some condition is true (pre-test repetition structure).	numDonuts = 1;
		
		giveDozenPrice = false;
		
		While (numDonuts < purchasedQty) {
		
		numDonuts++;
		
		if (numDonuts >= 12)
		
		giveDozenPrice = true;
		
		break;
		
		}

Statement	What It Does	Example

do-while	Executes a group of statements one or more times until some condition is true (post-test repetition structure). Note that a do-while loop always executes at least once.	numDonuts = 1;
		
		giveDozenPrice = false;
		
		do {
		
		numDonuts++;
		
		if (numDonuts >= 12)
		
		giveDozenPrice = true;
		
		break;
		
		} (while numDonuts < purchasedQty);

for	Executes a group of statements zero or more times until some condition is true (pre-test repetition structure). This differs from a while loop in that the test condition is defined in the statement.	giveDozenPrice = false;
		
		for (numDonuts=1; numDonuts<=purchasedDonuts; numDonuts++) {
		
		if (numDonuts >= 12)
		
		giveDozenPrice = true;
		
		break;
		
		}

Handling Errors and Exceptions

The last topic in your introduction to Solidity smart contract development is knowing how to handle errors and exceptions. By far the best way to handle errors is to avoid them in the first place. A naive and unproductive way to handle errors is to leave this completely up to the user interface. A much better design practice is to anticipate as many errors and exceptions as possible and design your code to handle them. If you can envision an error during the design phase, you can develop code to handle it and even develop a test to ensure that your code handles it properly.

In versions of Solidity before 0.4.10, the only way to handle an error was to throw an exception when something bad happened. For example, pre 0.4.10 code to ensure that a code segment would run only if initiated by the code's owner might look like this:

```
if (msg.sender != owner( { throw(); }))
```

If a smart contract ever encountered a throw() function, all changes to state variables would be undone, the contract would return to the caller passing back an invalid opcode error, and all remaining gas would be used up. In other words, if your code encountered a throw() function, you would never get any gas back. And to make matters worse, you didn't get anything done for that gas.

Starting with Solidity version 0.4.10, you have more options for handling error conditions. Current smart contracts can use the revert(), assert(), and require() functions to proactively handle errors. Table 6-8 lists each of the new guard functions and what each one does.

TABLE 6-8   **Error-Handling Guard Functions**

Function	What It Does	Example
revert()	Undoes all state changes, allows a return value, and refunds remaining gas to the caller. You should use this function to catch expected conditions that indicate that a transaction should be terminated.	if (msg.sender != owner({ revert(); }))
assert()	Undoes all state changes and uses up all remaining gas — that is, like the legacy throw() function, it does not return unused gas. You should never encounter this function in properly functioning code.	assert(msg.sender == owner);
require()	Undoes all state changes, allows a return value, and refunds remaining gas to the caller. You should use this function to proactively execute code when prerequisite conditions have not been met.	require(msg. sender == owner);

Although there is far more to Solidity than what you've seen here, you've grasped enough info to get started writing your own code. Before you know it, you'll be ready to create your own Ethereum dApps.

Chapter **7**

Writing Your Own Smart Contracts with Solidity

You find out the basics of developing Solidity smart contracts for Ethereum in Chapter 6 of this minibook. You also gain an understanding about dif-ficulties encountered with traditional supply chain applications and how Ethereum can help address some of those problems. Developing distributed appli-cations, or dApps, for the Ethereum blockchain may look similar to writing code in other languages, but it does have specific advantages over non-blockchain envi-ronments. However, you have to approach the software development process a little differently when working with blockchain.

Before starting to write a dApp for the Ethereum blockchain, make sure that you understand what your dApp should do and why a blockchain environment is a good fit. Getting these points cleared up in the beginning can help you avoid mistakes that waste time and money. Knowing the tips and tricks of blockchain development before you start writing your own dApps will help you develop better software than just acquiring it as you go.

Ethereum dApps focus on providing some functionality that interacts with data stored in the blockchain environment. Due to the design of blockchain technology, each interaction with the blockchain has an associated cost. Understanding how your dApp will have to pay for blockchain access is critical to getting it right the first time. In this chapter, you find out how to use Solidity to write effective smart contracts for the Ethereum blockchain environment.

Reviewing Supply Chain Design Specification

As you discover in Chapter 6 of this minibook, a *supply chain* is a framework that connects producers to consumers and manages how products and services make their way toward the consumers. In simple cases such as a farmer's market, consumers buy their produce directly from the growers. But in most other cases, at least one intermediary helps get products from producers to consumers. Intermediaries can provide transportation, warehousing, retailing, and other value-added services.

Implementing a supply chain solution in a blockchain environment can reduce the overall cost of providing products and services to consumers and make the entire process more transparent. If you store every step of a product's journey on the blockchain, anyone can track the product along its way.

The first step in developing a supply chain dApp is to look at the data and actions the dApp will need to provide the required functionality. For your supply chain dApp to do its job, you need at least four types of data:

>> **Products:** This data uniquely identifies a specific product that is eventually bought by a consumer.

>> **Participants:** This type of data is a description of all supply chain participants, including manufacturers, suppliers, shippers, and consumers.

>> **Registrations:** This type of data is a snapshot of which participant owns a product at a specific point in time. Registrations track products along the supply chain.

>> **Payment token:** Participants use payment tokens to pay one another for ownership changes of products. For example, a supplier can purchase a product from a manufacturer and use a payment token to pay the manufacturer.

To provide minimal functionality, your supply chain dApp needs to include the following capabilities:

>> **Initialize tokens:** Establish an initial pool of payment tokens.

>> **Transfer tokens:** Move tokens between accounts (that is, pay for products with tokens).

>> **Authorize token payments:** Allow an account to transfer tokens on behalf of another account.

>> **Create products:** Create products and show product details.

>> **Create participants:** Create participants and show participant details.

>> **Move products along the supply chain:** Transfer product ownership to another participant.

>> **Track a product:** Show a product's supply chain history.

The data and functionality your supply chain dApp will support fits nicely into two groups: payment tokens and supply chain. Some of the data and functionality applies to the supply chain, and other data and functionality applies to paying for supply chain activity. You'll separate your data and functionality into two smart contracts.

Payment token smart contract

The *payment token smart contract* handles anything related to payments. Your supply chain participants will buy and sell products by using tokens instead of traditional currency. Although Ethereum includes its own currency, Ether, you will implement your own token for supply chain participants to use. Although you could just have participants pay each other by using Ether, a custom token helps you to manage the entire process.

Defining your own token helps ensure that you limit supply chain participation to only valid supply chain participants; it can also make transfers simpler. Instead of allowing any Ethereum account to interact with your supply chain, only accounts that own your tokens can pay for products. Therefore, the only way a participant can enter the supply chain is to gain the trust of another participant. You have to either sell your products to an existing participant or exchange some other currency for your tokens.

TIP

Many businesses use the token concept. Arcades often set up their games to use physical tokens instead of real coins or paper money. You buy tokens using real currency and then use the tokens to play each game. This approach makes breaking into game consoles less attractive because the games contain only tokens — not real money. The tokens have value only inside the arcade. (Also, any lost or misplaced tokens mean a profit for the house, a nice benefit if you're issuing the tokens.)

Multiple proposed standards for Ethereum tokens in the form of *Ethereum Request for Comments (ERC)* documents exist. Several of these proposals have been accepted to become *Ethereum Improvement Proposals (EIPs)*. ERC-20 (now EIP-20) defines one of the early standards for defining tokens for Ethereum. You'll use the ERC/EIP-20 standard for your tokens.

TECHNICAL STUFF

ERC and EIP are used interchangeably. Technically, *EIP* refers to finalized ERC documents. However, even though a proposal is finalized, such as EIP-20, you will still see it referred to as ERC-20.

Your token smart contract will allow participants to acquire tokens and then transfer them to other participants in exchange for moving products along the supply chain. To complete this process, you need several data items and functions. The data items you'll define are as follows:

>> **totalSupply:** The total number of tokens in circulation

>> **name:** A descriptive name for your token

>> **decimals:** The number of decimals to use when displaying token amounts

>> **symbol:** A short identifier for your token

>> **balances:** The current balance of each participating account, mapped to the account's address

>> **allowed:** A list of the number of tokens authorized for transfer between accounts, mapped to the sender's address

Your token smart contract will define six functions that allow users to manage token transfers. The functions you'll define are as follows:

>> **totalSupply():** Returns the current total number of tokens

>> **balanceOf():** Returns the current balance, in tokens, of a specific account

>> **allowance():** Returns the remaining number of tokens that are allowed to be transferred from a specific source account to a specific target account

>> **transfer():** Transfers tokens from the caller to a specified target account

>> **approve():** Sets a number of tokens that are allowed to be transferred from a specific source account to a specific target account

>> **transferFrom():** Transfers tokens from a specified source account to a specified target account

Supply chain smart contract

Your second smart contract will contain the data and functionality to manage the product, participant, and product transfer data. In other words, it will handle all supply chain activity that isn't related to payment. As you find out how to implement supply chain functionality, you'll probably think of more things that you'd like your dApp to handle. That's okay. The smart contracts you'll develop in this book are just a starting point. You can extend them to handle many more use cases.

To store the supply chain data necessary for managing product migration toward consumers, you'll define the following data items:

» **product structure:** The product structure data item stores data that defines a unique product (model number, part number, serial number, product owner, cost, manufactured time).

» **participant structure:** The participant structure stores data that defines a unique participant (user name, password, participant type, Ethereum address).

» **registration structure:** The registration structure stores data that records a transfer of a product from one owner to another as the product moves toward the consumer (product ID, owner ID, transaction time, product owner Ethereum address).

» **p_id:** The product ID uniquely identifies a product and is mapped to a product structure.

» **u_id:** The participant ID uniquely identifies a participant and is mapped to a participant structure.

» **r_id:** The registration ID uniquely identifies a registration and is mapped to a registration structure.

Now that you know the data and functions you'll need in your smart contracts, the next step is to start writing code in Solidity.

Creating New Smart Contracts

In this section you create the files you need to implement the token and supply chain smart contracts. To get started, use the following steps to create a new project named SupplyChain, initialize it in Truffle, and launch VS Code for your new project.

REMEMBER

You find out how to create projects, initialize them in Truffle, and use VS Code to edit files and code for projects in Chapters 4 and 5 of this minibook. Review those chapters if you need details for each step.

1. **Open a command shell or PowerShell window.**

2. **Type the following to create a new project folder:**

   ```
   mkdir SupplyChain
   ```

3. **Change the current folder to the new project folder:**

```
cd SupplyChain
```

4. **Initialize the new project in Truffle:**

```
truffle init
```

5. **Launch VS Code for the new SupplyChain project:**

```
code .
```

In VS Code, create three new smart contracts as follows. Click or tap SUPPLYCHAIN, then Contracts, and then the New File button next to SUPPLYCHAIN. Type the following filenames to create each new file, making sure your filenames appear under Contracts and look exactly as they do here. (If you download the project files, you don't have to do this.)

>> **erc20Interface.sol**

>> **erc20Token.sol**

>> **SupplyChain.sol**

Now click or tap SUPPLYCHAIN and then Contracts to display your contracts. Your VS Code Explorer view should look like Figure 7-1.

FIGURE 7-1:
Supply chain starting smart contracts in VS Code.

TIP

Don't worry if you mistype a filename. Changing filenames in VS Code is easy. Just click or tap the filename in VS Code Explorer and press F2. You can then type the new filename. If you created your files in the wrong folder, you can fix that in VS Code as well. Just drag them to the right place (under Contracts).

ERC-20 token interface

The first file you'll edit is the interface for the ERC-20 token. An *interface* looks just like a smart contract but doesn't contain any executable code. Developers use interfaces to define minimum functionality for groups of programs. When you define an interface, you define the minimum data items and functions that you want to be common among smart contracts that implement the interface.

TECHNICAL STUFF

ERC-20 tokens aren't the only type of tokens in Ethereum. Another token standard that looks like it may challenge ERC-20's popularity is ERC-777.

In our case, we're going to use the standard ERC-20 (or EIP-20) token interface. Every ERC-20 token that uses this interface is guaranteed to have the same minimum data and functions. That's the purpose of an interface. Your implementation may have more data and functions, but you can count on the fact that it has at least everything defined in the interface. In fact, if you use an interface and forget to define a data item or function, the compiler generates an error and refuses to compile the program.

To make sure that your token complies with the ERC-20 token standard, you use the ERC-20 token interface. Click or tap the erc20Interface.sol tab in VS Code and enter the following code:

```
//SPDX-License-Identifier:MIT
// ----------------------------------------------------------------------
// ERC Token Standard #20 Interface
// https://github.com/ethereum/EIPs/blob/master/EIPS/eip-20.md
// ----------------------------------------------------------------------
pragma solidity ^0.8.9;
abstract contract ERC20Interface {
uint256 public _totalSupply;
function totalSupply() virtual public view returns (uint);
function balanceOf(address tokenOwner) virtual public view returns (uint
    balance);
function allowance(address tokenOwner, address spender) virtual public view
    returns (uint remaining);
function transfer(address to, uint tokens) virtual public returns (bool
    success);
function approve(address spender, uint tokens) virtual public returns (bool
    success);
```

```
function transferFrom(address from, address to, uint tokens) virtual public
    returns (bool success);
event Transfer(address indexed from, address indexed to, uint tokens);
event Approval(address indexed tokenOwner, address indexed spender, uint
    tokens);
}
```

This interface defines the single variable, six functions, and two events that every token contract must implement to support the ERC-20 token standard. You'll find out what each line of code does in the next section, where you implement the interface. At this point, just note that each line of code defines a variable, a function, or an event. There is no code that actually does anything.

ERC-20 token smart contract

After you define the interface, you can implement the code to make your token smart contract work. Click or tap the erc20Token.sol tab in VS Code and enter the following code:

```
//SPDX-License-Identifier:MIT
// -------------------------------------------------------------------------
///Implements EIP20 token standard: https://github.com/ethereum/EIPs/blob/
    master/EIPS/eip-20.md
// -------------------------------------------------------------------------
pragma solidity ^0.8.9;
import "./erc20Interface.sol";
contract ERC20Token is ERC20Interface {
}
```

You can find out about the `pragma` statement in Chapter 5 of this minibook. The `import` statement tells Solidity to open an external file and read it into this file to compile it, just as if you had copied the contents of `erc20Interface.sol` into this file. You can use the `import` statement as your projects grow to help you keep any single source code file from growing too large to manage easily. If any source code file starts to get too big, you can split it into multiple smaller files and import the pieces in the main file.

The last line in the code segment defines the smart contract. You use the `contract` statement to define a smart contract named `ERC20Token`. When you define the contract as `ERC20token is ERC20Interface`, you are telling Solidity that you intend to implement `ERC20Interface` in this file. Therefore, the compiler will check to make sure that every item defined in the interface is implemented in this file.

The first step to make your token work is to add the data items you'll need. Add the following code between the two curly braces (after the contract statement):

```
uint256 constant private MAX_UINT256 = 2**256 - 1;
mapping (address => uint256) public balances;
mapping (address => mapping (address => uint256)) public allowed;
uint256 public totalSupply; // Total number of tokens
string public name; // Descriptive name (i.e. For Dummies Token)
uint8 public decimals; // How many decimals to use to display amounts
string public symbol; // Short identifier for token (i.e. FDT)
```

These lines of source code define the data you'll store on the blockchain for your token. The first data item, MAX_UINT256, is defined as a constant, which means that the value you assign to it can't be changed at runtime. Solidity uses the ** symbol to denote exponentiation, so 3 squared is 3**2 in Solidity. The value of 2 raised to the 256 power minus 1 is stored in the MAX_UINT256 constant. Defining MAX_UINT256 is a convenient way to store the largest possible value in a uint256 variable.

The balances and allowed data items are mappings. They exist to make it easy to look up a balance or a list of token transfer allowances for an Ethereum account address. The remaining data items are state variables that describe attributes of your token.

TECHNICAL STUFF

State variables are stored in the blockchain, and storing data in the blockchain costs gas. So you can conserve gas by minimizing how much and how often you store blockchain data. Don't define more state variables than you need. It is good practice to declare the smallest uint size for the data you'll store, which is why the decimal variable is defined as uint8. When you define more complex data using structs, size matters even more.

Supply chain smart contract

The next step in developing your supply chain dApp is to begin the definition of the supply chain smart contract. Click or tap the SupplyChain.sol tab in VS Code and enter the following code:

```
//SPDX-License-Identifier:MIT
pragma solidity ^0.8.9;
contract supplyChain {
uint32 public p_id = 0; // Product ID
uint32 public u_id = 0; // Participant ID
uint32 public r_id = 0; // Registration ID
}
```

This smart contract starts like the other smart contracts you've seen so far. Inside the contract body, you define three state variables to store the highest ID for products, participants, and registrations. The following sections define the details of each type of supply chain data.

Product structure

The product structure defines the details for each unique product. Type the following code after the state variable definitions in the preceding section:

```
struct product {
string modelNumber;
string partNumber;
string serialNumber;
address productOwner;
uint32 cost;
uint32 mfgTimeStamp;
}
mapping(uint32 => product) public products;
```

In addition to the product structure, the products mapping allows users to look up a product from its product ID (p_id).

Participant structure

The participant structure defines the details for each unique participant. Type the following code after the products mapping in the preceding section:

```
struct participant {
string userName;
string password;
string participantType;
address participantAddress;
}
mapping(uint32 => participant) public participants;
```

In addition to the participant structure, the participants mapping allows users to look up a participant from its participant ID (u_id).

Registration structure

The registration structure defines the details for each unique registration. A *registration* is defined as the point in time when a product's owner changes from one participant to another. Each registration represents a product moving along the supply chain.

Type the following code after the participants mapping in the preceding section:

```
struct registration {
uint32 productId;
uint32 ownerId;
uint32 trxTimeStamp;
address productOwner;
}
mapping(uint32 => registration) public registrations; // Registrations by
    Registration ID (r_id)
mapping(uint32 => uint32[]) public productTrack; // Registrations by Product ID
    (p_id) / Movement track for a product
```

In addition to the product structure, the registrations mapping allows users to look up a registration from its registration ID (r_id). The productTrack mapping returns the supply chain movement history for a specified product (p_id).

Coding Primary Functions

After defining the basic contract structure and data items, the next step in developing your smart contracts is to write the code for each smart contract function. *Functions* provide the actions of your smart contracts and define what your smart contracts can do.

ERC-20 token functions

To define the actions your ERC-20 token smart contract should carry out, you need to define its functions and provide the code for the body of each function. Remember that your ERC-20 token smart contract implements an interface, so you have to at least define the functions required in the interface. Note that you can define more functions than those in the interface.

Click or tap the erc20Token.sol tab in VS Code and enter the code for each of the following functions. (Start entering function source code after the symbol state variable definition.)

ERC-20 token constructor

A *constructor* is a special type of function that runs when the smart contract is deployed to the blockchain. In the constructor, you place initialization steps that are executed only when the contract is first stored in the blockchain. In the case of the ERC-20 token, the constructor initializes the token's attributes and allocates the supply of tokens to the Ethereum address that deploys the smart contract.

Enter the following code to define the smart contract's constructor:

```
constructor(uint256 _initialAmount, string memory _tokenName,
uint8 _decimalUnits, string memory_tokenSymbol) public {
balances[msg.sender] = _initialAmount; // The creator owns all tokens
_totalSupply = _initialAmount; // Update total token supply
name = _tokenName; // Token name
decimals = _decimalUnits; // Number of decimals
symbol = _tokenSymbol; // Token symbol
}
```

TIP

You can use any naming convention for function parameters and variables. Many Solidity developers use the underscore character as the first character for function parameter names. That convention makes it easy to tell whether a data item is a variable or a parameter passed into a function. In this book, parameter names start with the underscore character.

The constructor code for the ERC-20 token is simple. When you deploy the smart contract code to the blockchain, the smart contract assigns the token data items to the provided parameters and assigns all initial tokens to the Ethereum account address that deployed the smart contract.

Defining the `transfer()` function

The `transfer()` function transfers tokens from the calling address to a specified address. Enter the following code after the constructor:

```
function transfer(address _to, uint256 _value) override public returns (bool
    success) {
require(_value >= 0,"Cannot transfer negative amount.");
require(balances[msg.sender] >= _value,"Insufficient funds.");
balances[msg.sender] -= _value;
balances[_to] += _value;
return true;
}
```

The `transfer()` function introduces the Solidity `require()` function, which prevents functions from continuing unless a specific condition is met. If the `require()` condition is not satisfied, it returns a message to the caller and refunds any unused gas. It provides a polite way to stop smart contract execution. In the case of the `transfer()` function, you can transfer tokens only if the sender has a sufficient balance to transfer. The `require()` condition validates that the sender has at least as many tokens as the transfer requires; otherwise, it returns the `"Insufficient funds."` string.

If the sender does have the required funds, you decrease the balance of the sender and increase the balance of the receiver by the amount to transfer, and then return a `true` value that tells the caller that the transfer was completed successfully.

Defining the `transferFrom()` function

The `transferFrom()` function transfers tokens from one specified address to another specified address. Enter the following code after the `transfer()` function:

```
function transferFrom(address _from, address _to, uint256 _value) override
    public returns (bool success) {
uint256 allowance = allowed[_from][msg.sender];
require(balances[_from] >= _value && allowance >= _value,"Insufficient funds.");
balances[_from] -= _value;
balances[_to] += _value;
if (allowance < MAX_UINT256) {
allowed[_from][msg.sender] -= _value;
}
return true;
}
```

The `transferFrom()` function transfers up to a preapproved amount from one address to another. The function looks up the preapproved amount from the `allowed` mapping and stores that value in the `allowance` variable. The function calls the `require()` function to verify that the sender has a sufficient token balance to transfer and then adjusts the balances of the sender and receiver. The last step is to query the `allowance` variable and, if it is set, subtract the amount transferred from the remaining allowance.

Defining the `balanceOf()` function

The `balanceOf()` function returns the number of tokens owned by a specified address. Enter the following code after the `transferFrom()` function:

```
function balanceOf(address _owner) override public view returns (uint256
    balance) {
return balances[_owner];
}
```

Defining the `approve()` function

The `approve()` function grants permission to transfer a specified number of tokens from one address to another specified address. Enter the following code after the `balanceOf()` function:

```
function approve(address _spender, uint256 _value) override public returns (bool
    success) {
allowed[msg.sender][_spender] = _value;
return true;
}
```

Defining the `allowance()` function

Th `allowance()` function returns the remaining number of approved tokens that can be transferred from one address to another specified address. Enter the following code after the `approve()` function:

```
function allowance(address _owner, address _spender) override public view
    returns (uint256 remaining) {
return allowed[_owner][_spender];
}
```

Defining the `totalsupply()` function

The `totalSupply()` function returns the total number of tokens in circulation. Enter the following code after the `allowance()` function:

```
function totalSupply() override public view returns (uint256 totSupp) {
return _totalSupply;
}
```

Supply chain functions

To define the functionality of your supply chain smart contract, you need to define its functions and provide the code for the body of each function.

Click or tap the SupplyChain.sol tab in VS Code and enter the code for each of the following functions. (Start entering function source code after the `productTrack` mapping definition.)

Defining the participant functions

The `createParticipant()` function increments the participant ID (`u_id`), creates a new participant, and sets its attributes to the passed-in parameters. Enter the following code after the `productTrack` mapping:

```
function createParticipant(string memory _name, string memory _pass, address _
    pAdd, string memory _pType) public returns (uint32){
uint32 userId = u_id++;
participants[userId].userName = _name ;
participants[userId].password = _pass;
participants[userId].participantAddress = _pAdd;
participants[userId].participantType = _pType;
return userId;
}
```

The `getParticipantDetails()` function returns the attributes of the specified participant (`p_id`). Enter the following code after the `createParticipant()` function:

```
function getParticipantDetails(uint32 _p_id) public view returns (string
    memory,address,string memory) {
return (participants[_p_id].userName,participants[_p_id].participantAddress,part
    icipants[_p_id].participantType);
}
```

Defining the product functions

The `createProduct()` function increments the product ID (`p_id`), creates a new product, and sets its attributes to the passed-in values. Enter the following code after the `getParticipantDetails()` function:

```
function createProduct(uint32 _ownerId, string memory _modelNumber, string
    memory _partNumber, string memory _serialNumber, uint32 _productCost) public
    returns (uint32) {
if(keccak256(abi.encodePacked(participants[_ownerId].participantType)) ==
    keccak256("Manufacturer")) {
uint32 productId = p_id++;
products[productId].modelNumber = _modelNumber;
products[productId].partNumber = _partNumber;
products[productId].serialNumber = _serialNumber;
products[productId].cost = _productCost;
products[productId].productOwner = participants[_ownerId].participantAddress;
products[productId].mfgTimeStamp = uint32(block.timestamp);
```

```
return productId;
}
return 0;
}
```

TIP

Unlike many other languages, you can't directly compare strings in Solidity. You have to first calculate a hash value of the string and then compare that number to the hash value of another string. If the two hash values are equal, the strings are equal. Solidity includes the keccak256() function to calculate hashes. To calculate a hash value that you can use in a comparison, you have to call the convert to string function by using the api.encodePacked() function, and then call the keccak256() function on the encoded string.

The getProductDetails() function returns the attributes of the specified product (p_id). Enter the following code after the createProduct() function:

```
function getProductDetails(uint32 _productId) public view returns (string
    memory,string memory,string memory,uint32,address,uint32){
return (products[_productId].modelNumber,products[_productId].partNumber,
products[_productId].serialNumber,products[_productId].cost,
products[_productId].productOwner,products[_productId].mfgTimeStamp);
}
```

Defining the supply chain movement functions

The transferToOwner() function records movement along the supply chain. This function transfers the ownership of a specified product from one supply chain participant to another. It creates a new registrations struct, based on r_id, assigns its data items from the passed-in parameters, and pushes the new struct onto the productTrack list. Enter the following code after the getProductDetails() function:

```
function transferToOwner(uint32 _user1Id ,uint32 _user2Id, uint32 _prodId)
    public returns(bool) {
participant memory p1 = participants[_user1Id];
participant memory p2 = participants[_user2Id];
uint32 registration_id = r_id++;
registrations[registration_id].productId = _prodId;
registrations[registration_id].productOwner = p2.participantAddress;
registrations[registration_id].ownerId = _user2Id;
registrations[registration_id].trxTimeStamp = uint32(block.timestamp);
products[_prodId].productOwner = p2.participantAddress;
productTrack[_prodId].push(registration_id);
return (true);
}
```

TIP

You define two local variables, p1 and p2, to temporarily hold the source and target participant data. However, Solidity would create these by default as storage variables because they directly reference storage structs. You have to tell Solidity to make these variable local by using the memory modifier. That reduces the gas cost of your smart contract.

The getProductTrack() function returns the registration history for a specified product. This function shows the path a product has taken along the supply chain from its original producer. This function provides the current status of any product in the supply chain. Enter the following code after the transferToOwner() function:

```
function getProductTrack(uint32 _prodId) external view returns (uint32[]) {
return productTrack[_prodId];
}
```

The getRegistrationDetails() function returns the attributes of the specified registration (r_id). Enter the following code after the getProductTrack() function:

```
function getRegistrationDetails(uint32 _regId) public view returns
    (uint32,uint32,address,uint32) {
registration memory r = registrations[_regId];
return (r.productId,r.ownerId,r.productOwner,r.trxTimeStamp);
}
```

Using Events

Smart contract code runs on each EVM across the Ethereum network. It is essentially server-side code. One of the difficulties you encounter when running server-side code is communicating with the client. Smart contracts don't just run arbitrarily — they have to be called by a client or another smart contract. Communication is pretty easy when a client or smart contract calls another smart contract function. The caller sends input parameters and waits to receive any return values.

TECHNICAL STUFF

One of the more interesting features of Solidity is that its functions can return multiple values. Many languages allow functions to return only a single value, so developers have to figure out ways to pack multiple data items into return strings and unpack them on the client side. Take a look at your getProductDetails() and getParticipantDetails() functions in the SupplyChain.sol file to see how Solidity passes back multiple return values.

Sometimes the caller doesn't want to wait around for a function to finish. Many programs operate under a different flow control model. In an *event-driven* model, one program waits for something to happen and then responds. VS Code operates in an event-driven model. Figure 7-2 shows VS Code as you edit the SupplyChain.sol smart contract.

Your VS Code window should look like the one in Figure 7-2. The program is running, but it isn't doing much right now. In fact, VS Code is waiting on you to do something. After you launch VS Code and open SupplyChain.sol, VS Code just waits for you to tell it what to do. You can type text into the editor, click or tap menu items or buttons, or press function keys or control key combinations.

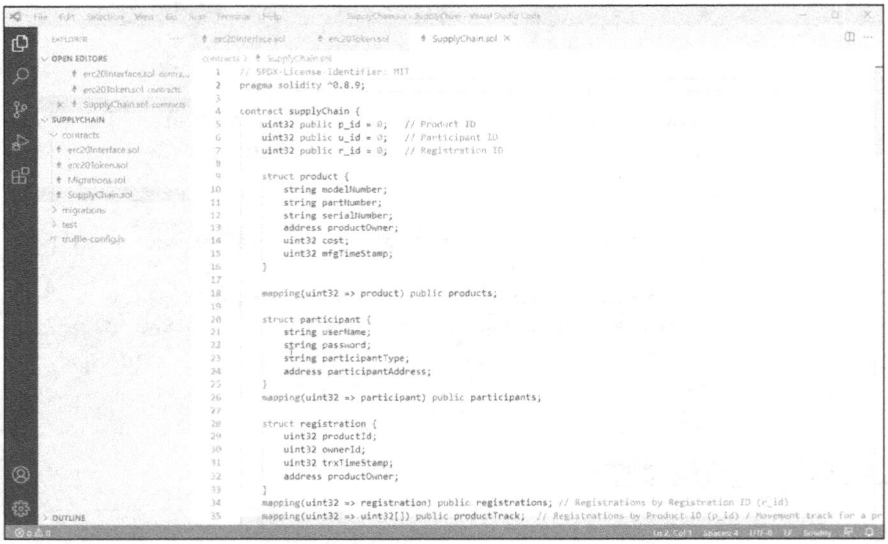

FIGURE 7-2:
Editing
SupplyChain.
sol in VS Code.

You can code event-driven programs in Solidity, too. Solidity allows you to define *events* in your smart contracts and then *trigger* those events whenever you want to. If your calling program is waiting, or listening, for these events, it can respond to the events and carry out some of its own functions. In the case of VS Code, it is listening for many events, including the Ctrl+S keystroke event. When VS Code sees that the Ctrl+S event has occurred, it runs its Save File function. You can code your smart contracts the same way.

TECHNICAL STUFF

Event-driven programming is often described as a *publish-subscribe* approach to program flow. The called programs generate, or publish, events when interesting things happen. The called program doesn't care what programs are listening for the events, if any. Publishing events allows the called programs to communicate *asynchronously* with any listening programs. Programs that want to listen for, and respond to, events must subscribe to those events. It works just like subscribing to a local newspaper. The newspaper publishes a paper every day, but only its subscribers receive the paper.

Follow these three steps to implant events in Solidity:

1. **Define the event.**

   Use the Solidity event statement to define the event, give it a name, and define the data it passes when it triggers.

2. **Trigger the event.**

   Use the Solidity emit statement to trigger a previously defined event and pass data to it.

3. **Receive and respond to the event.**

   You find out how to receive and respond to events in Chapter 8 of this minibook.

Defining events

Your supply chain smart contract uses three events. The ERC-20 token interface requires that you implement two of the events, and you'll define the other one in the main supply chain smart contract.

Click or tap the erc20Interface.sol tab in VS Code to switch to the ERC-20 interface code. Look at the last two lines of code:

```
event Transfer(address indexed from, address indexed to, uint tokens);
event Approval(address indexed tokenOwner, address indexed spender, uint
    tokens);
```

These lines define the Transfer and Approval events. When the Transfer event triggers, it tells any program that is listening for this event that a transfer has just occurred, and that the transfer consisted of sending tokens from one address to another. When the Approval event triggers, it tells any program that is listening for this event that a new approval was just authorized for a token owner to transfer up to some number of tokens to a specific sender. It is up to the listening programs to do something with these events. Your smart contracts need to only define and trigger the events.

Click or tap the SupplyChain.sol tab in VS Code to switch to the supply chain smart contract code. Scroll down to the definitions for the two mappings after the registrations struct. This should be around line 35. Type the following text on a new line:

```
event Transfer(uint32 productId);
```

After you enter this new code, the last few lines of your SupplyChain.sol code should look like Figure 7-3.

FIGURE 7-3:
Defining an event
in VS Code.

```
27      struct registration {
28          uint32 productId;
29          uint32 ownerId;
30          uint32 trxTimeStamp;
31          address productOwner;
32      }
33      mapping(uint32 => registration) public registrations;  // Registrations by Registration ID (r_id)
34      mapping(uint32 => uint32[]) public productTrack;  // Registrations by Product ID (p_id) / Movement track for a product
35
36      event Transfer(uint32 productId);
37
```

You will use your new Transfer event every time you create a new registration. That means you'll use the event to let any listening program know that a product has just been transferred from one supply chain participant to another. The Transfer event sends the transferred product ID to the listening program to tell it what product just moved. The event mechanism makes it easy for external programs to monitor changes that your smart contracts carry out.

Triggering events

After you define the events you'll need in your smart contracts, the next step is to trigger each event at the right time. All you really have to do here is trigger the event in your code when you carry out the action you want to communicate. In other words, you should trigger the Transfer event at the point where your code carries out the transfer action.

In Solidity, you use the emit statement to trigger an event. When you use the emit statement, it is like calling a function. You tell Solidity what event to trigger, and then you provide parameter values, as you do with a function.

Click or tap the erc20Token.sol tab in VS Code to switch to the ERC-20 smart contract code. Update your transfer(), transferFrom(), and approve() functions to include the emit statements shown here (new code is in bold):

```
function transfer(address _to, uint256 _value) override public returns (bool
    success) {
require(balances[msg.sender] >= _value,"Insufficient funds for transfer
    source.");
```

```
balances[msg.sender] -= _value;
balances[_to] += _value;
emit Transfer(msg.sender, _to, _value);
return true;
}
function transferFrom(address _from, address _to, uint256 _value) override
    public returns (bool success) {
uint256 allowance = allowed[_from][msg.sender];
require(balances[_from] >= _value && allowance >= _value,"Insufficient allowed
    funds for transfer source.");
balances[_to] += _value;
balances[_from] -= _value;
if (allowance < MAX_UINT256) {
allowed[_from][msg.sender] -= _value;
}
emit Transfer(_from, _to, _value);
return true;
}
function approve(address _spender, uint256 _value) override public returns (bool
    success) {
allowed[msg.sender][_spender] = _value;
emit Approval(msg.sender, _spender, _value);
return true;
}
```

You can call the emit statement anywhere in your smart contract code. In your ERC-20 token smart contract, you have added the emit statement in three places to signal that some notable action has just occurred.

Click or tap the SupplyChain.sol tab in VS Code to switch to the supply chain smart contract code. Update your transferToOwner() function to include the emit statement shown here (new code is in bold):

```
function transferToOwner(uint32 _user1Id ,uint32 _user2Id, uint32 _prodId)
    onlyOwner(_prodId) public returns(bool) {
participant memory p1 = participants[_user1Id];
participant memory p2 = participants[_user2Id];
uint32 registration_id = r_id++;
registrations[registration_id].productId = _prodId;
registrations[registration_id].productOwner = p2.participantAddress;
registrations[registration_id].ownerId = _user2Id;
registrations[registration_id].trxTimeStamp = uint32(block.timestamp);
products[_prodId].productOwner = p2.participantAddress;
productTrack[_prodId].push(registration_id);
emit Transfer(_prodId);
return (true);
}
```

Introducing Ownership

One of the difficulties you'll encounter when developing blockchain applications is restricting the execution of sensitive functions. Remember that your smart contract code runs on all EVMs. All EVMs have the complete code for your smart contracts, so limiting execution requires careful planning.

Modifiers can make data items and functions unavailable for external entities to access or run. Don't make the mistake of thinking modifiers make smart contracts secure. They can help reduce the availability of these items and functions to external programs, but they don't provide complete security. Remember that data on a public blockchain is there for anyone to see.

Every smart contract invocation has a caller address. Each EVM knows which account carries out each action. In Solidity, you can access the calling account by referencing msg.sender. Open the erc20Token.sol smart contract and look at the first line of the constructor body:

```
constructor(uint256 _initialAmount, string memory _tokenName,
uint8 _decimalUnits, string memory _tokenSymbol) public {
balances[msg.sender] = _initialAmount; // The creator owns all tokens
_totalSupply = _initialAmount; // Update total token supply
name = _tokenName; // Token name
decimals = _decimalUnits; // Number of decimals
symbol = _tokenSymbol; // Token symbol
}
```

The first thing you do when the constructor executes (that is, when you deploy this smart contract) is to assign the total initial number of tokens to the calling address's balance value. Solidity stores the value of the caller's address in the msg.sender value, so you can use that to refer to the sender in your code.

You can also use the msg.sender value to define ownership and enforce access restrictions in your smart contract code. In your supply chain smart contract, you don't want anyone to be able to transfer a product to another participant. Doing so would allow one participant to steal products from others. The transfer process in your supply chain smart contract transfers the ownership of a product as the product moves along the supply chain. It makes sense that only the current owner should be allowed to transfer a product to another owner.

TIP

Ownership is a common concern when buying and selling products. If you sell a car, you have to sign the title over to the new owner. Possession of the car's title proves ownership. As the car's current owner, you must ensure that no one else can transfer the title of your car to another owner.

Solidity provides modifiers to help make the task of enforcing ownership easier. A modifier is like a lightweight function. It has a name, input parameters, and a body, but it doesn't support return values.

Open the SupplyChain.sol smart contract in VS Code and add the following code after the createProduct() function:

```
modifier onlyOwner(uint32 _productId) {
require(msg.sender == products[_productId].productOwner );
_;
}
```

This code defines the onlyOwner modifier. You can use this modifier on any function to allow only a product's current owner to execute that function. The modifier takes a product ID as an input parameter and checks to see if the msg.sender is the same address as the product's current owner address. If the two values match, the modifier is satisfied and the function proceeds. If the two address values do not match, msg.sender is not allowed to run the function and control returns to the caller.

TIP

When you write modifiers, don't forget to add the _; line as the last line in the modifier body. This tells Solidity to proceed to the function that you have modified. You'll only get to that line if the modifier body is satisfied (that is, the condition in the body is true).

You invoke modifiers by adding them to existing functions. Scroll to the transferToOwner() function in the supply chain smart contract code and add the onlyOwner(_prodId) modifier to the function header. Your modified function header should look like this:

```
function transferToOwner(uint32 _user1Id ,uint32 _user2Id, uint32 _prodId)
   onlyOwner(_prodId) public returns(bool) {
```

This modifier tells Solidity that before you execute the transferToOwner() function, it must execute the onlyOwner() modifier. The modifier determines whether the function caller (msg.sender) is the owner of product prodId. If msg.sender is the product owner, the transferToOwner() function proceeds. If not, it just returns without transferring the product.

You can use modifiers to carry out any validation steps that should occur before you run code in a function. Validating ownership is one of the more common uses of modifiers.

Designing for Security

Solidity smart contract code can be as insecure as any other software. Just because your code runs in a blockchain environment doesn't mean that it's secure. You have to keep security in mind throughout the entire software development process. Although you need to consider many things when developing secure software in any environment, developing blockchain dApps requires that you pay special attention to the distributed nature of the blockchain.

TIP

For a great online resource for Ethereum Smart Contract Security Best Practices, go to `https://consensys.github.io/smart-contract-best-practices`. Read through the explanations and recommendations in this resource for a more complete understanding of security issues in Ethereum application development.

When you're developing Ethereum dApps, you'll have to avoid many security weaknesses. Table 7-1 lists a few of the most common security mistakes new Ethereum developers tend to make.

TABLE 7-1 **Common Ethereum Security Mistakes**

Security Mistake	Description	How to Avoid
Lack of randomness	Because smart contract code runs on every EVM, generating random numbers can cause code to run differently on different EVMs.	Use only random numbers that do not affect stored data or smart contract execution flow.
Allowing re-entrancy	The call function forwards all the received gas to the called function. If your code allows a function to run multiple times before changing state data, that code could allow multiple changes, such as multiple withdrawals.	Always update state data before transferring control to another function.
Not checking for overflow and underflow	Incrementing an integer larger than its maximum value or decrementing an integer smaller than the minimum value causes an error that reverts a smart contract.	Always check to make sure that increment and decrement operations do not overflow or underflow.
Permitting delegatecall with visible functions	Delegatecall allows a smart contract to execute a function from another contract, running it using the calling contract's address. Public or external functions that modify state may be able to do so without being detected.	Limit the use of public and external functions that modify state data.

Implementing Minimal Functionality

If you've followed the discussion throughout this chapter, your ERC-20 and supply chain smart contracts should be complete and clean. That is, they should compile with no errors. In VS Code, press the F5 key to start the Solidity compiler. Figure 7-4 shows the results of the Solidity compiler.

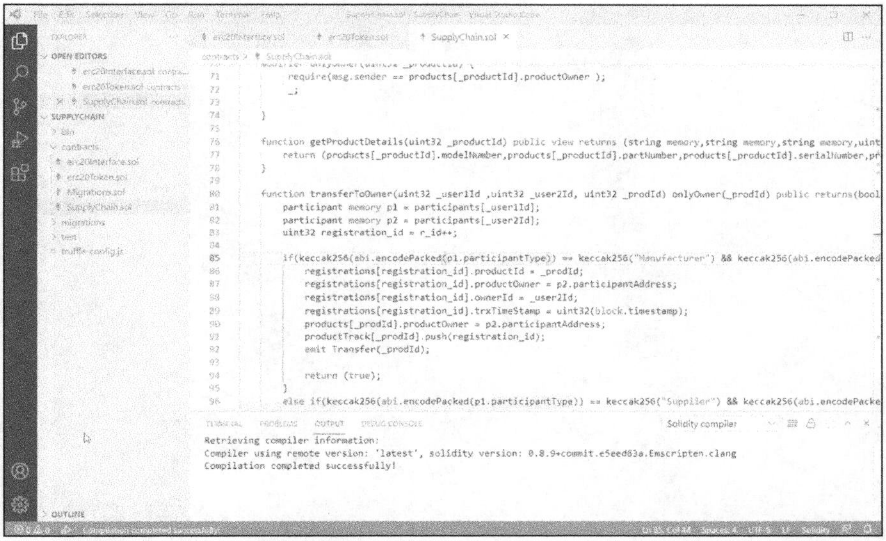

Writing Your Own Smart Contracts with Solidity

FIGURE 7-4:
Compiler output.

If your smart contracts don't compile cleanly, review the code to make sure that what you entered is exactly what you see in the book. Pay attention to capitalization — it matters. Another common problem is copying code and pasting it into an editor. Make sure that you copied just what you expected, and look closely at copied quotes. In many cases, copied and pasted quotes result in a quote that won't compile. If you suspect that problem, just backspace over any pasted quotes and type them directly.

Because it is so easy to introduce minor errors that can stop code from compiling, you should keep your code as simple as possible As you develop your own smart contracts, implement only minimal functionality first. You can always add more features after you get the simple code working.

Chapter **8**

Testing Ethereum Apps

C hapter 7 of this minibook covers writing smart contract software in Solidity. Although writing source code is the most visible phase in the software development life cycle, it is only one part of the complete process. Of course, before you write any code, you should spend time planning and designing your application. Those phases should leave you with a clear specification document that contains the requirements your software must satisfy. After you have an application that compiles, you're ready to test it to see whether it does what it's supposed to do.

Testing software is more than just seeing whether it runs without obvious errors. Testing software ensures that it does what it is supposed to do, doesn't do what it isn't supposed to do, and fulfills the requirements set for the software in the first place.

All too often, a customer agrees to pay for software that does tasks A, B, and C but ends up getting a different program that carries out tasks C, D, and E. It may be somewhat similar to what was intended, but software developers have a tendency to augment customer requests or to at least interpret their needs differently. Software testing doesn't alter or control the scope of a software project, but it does help validate that the software meets its design goals. Meeting design goals ensures that all stakeholders in the software development process are satisfied with the result of the development process. Testing is the only way to see if your software really does what it's supposed to do. In this chapter you find out how to test your smart contracts in a blockchain environment.

Understanding Ethereum dApp Testing

Testing software that runs in a blockchain environment is a little different from testing traditional software applications. Because smart contract code runs in the EVM, you must have an EVM running first. Then you compile your smart contracts and deploy them to your blockchain. After that, you create transactions that call your smart contracts and cause them to carry out tasks. With careful planning, your tests should be able to simulate how your smart contracts will operate in a production environment.

Writing tests from the beginning

The smart contract testing process must start even before you write any software. Waiting to develop tests until after you write the code will take longer and leave more potential gaps in your test coverage. The best time to design tests for your software is when you define the requirements for your software because it makes you think through the code execution and boundaries, which results in better code design. For example, if you know you'll be testing to see if you can overflow a variable, you're more likely to write code up front that doesn't overflow.

Choosing the right test blockchain

You have several blockchain options for testing your smart contracts, and each one has advantages and disadvantages. Table 8-1 lists the smart contract test blockchain options and the pros and cons of each one.

TABLE 8-1   Smart Contract Test Blockchain Options

Type of Blockchain	Pros	Cons
Live, public	The environment is live — no simulations	Slow transactions; costly
Test, public (for example, Ropsten)	Similar to a live environment, but far less costly	Somewhat slow transactions; little or no mining activity
Local, private (for example, Ganache)	Fast, free transactions; easy to reset to a new blockchain	No mining activity; difficult to simulate the effect of many network nodes

Most smart contract developers test their software first using a local private network and then using a public test network. Then they finally deploy to the live blockchain. Using this graduated approach makes it possible to find and fix many of the bugs found in smart contracts before deploying the code to networks, where many users can see it and you have to pay for transactions.

Walking through the steps in the testing life cycle

The process of testing smart contracts is the same, regardless of the type of network you choose. You'll follow these steps over and over again to test your smart contracts running on the Ethereum blockchain:

1. Write smart contract code and test cases.
2. Compile code.
3. Deploy code to a blockchain.
4. Run test cases.
5. Identify failure causes and propose changes to address failures.
6. Go to Step 1.

Although most software developers think that the code they write the first time is correct, testing often finds bugs. These bugs can be the result of sloppy programming, a lack of understanding of what was requested, or simply oversights. Regardless of the cause, bugs allow software to operate in ways that do not meet its design goals.

Testing should be thorough enough to execute software in a manner that validates how it operates in a variety of situations. These situations should simulate the activities of both benevolent and malicious users. For every bug encountered, you must try to determine the cause of the flaw, and then return as much information as possible to developers so that they can change the application to remove all flaws found in testing. This process often iterates multiple times, until all tests complete successfully, at which point your software is ready for production.

Testing for software quality

Test cases can be simple commands to check how well functions work or elaborate sets of programs and scripts that run automatically to exercise your smart contract functions. Either way, the point is to run your software in a way that lets you validate that it works as intended and helps you identify any gaps in functionality.

Don't skimp on testing your smart contract code. Any code that you deploy to the live blockchain is immutable — and so are any bugs. The only way to mitigate bugs in smart contract code is to just stop using that code.

If you do deploy smart contracts with bugs, you'll have to tell your clients to stop using the bad code and use the new, fixed code that you deployed to a new address. You'll need to do this in a way that ensures that all old data written to the blockchain (before you fixed your bug) is still valid and accessible, and that the old, buggy smart contract code is never used again. In short, it is much easier to find all bugs in testing before you deploy to a live blockchain.

Deploying a dApp to a Test Ethereum Blockchain

Before you can test your smart contracts, you must deploy them to the blockchain. In the previous section, you found out that you can use multiple blockchains to test your smart contracts. In Chapter 4 of this minibook, you downloaded and installed the Ganache personal blockchain. You'll use that blockchain for your initial smart contract tests. Ganache makes it easy to set up and launch your own personal blockchain, which works well as a live blockchain simulator.

Telling Truffle to use the Ganache blockchain

The first step in setting up tests on a private local blockchain is to let Truffle know how to connect to the blockchain network. In Chapter 5 of this minibook, you set up a new project and modified the `truffle-config.js` file to tell Truffle to use the Ganache blockchain. You'll need to edit the `truffle-config.js` file for each project you use to write smart contract code, including the supplyChain project that you used in Chapter 7 of this minibook and will continue to use in this chapter.

Follow these steps to hook up Truffle and Ganache:

1. **Get the blockchain address from the Ganache settings window.**

   Launch Ganache, and then click or tap the gear (Settings) icon, in the upper-right corner of the Ganache window. Note the host name, port number, and network ID values. Figure 8-1 shows the Ganache settings window with default values. You can also get the host name and port number from the main window. The RPC SERVER value displays the host name and port number separated by a colon.

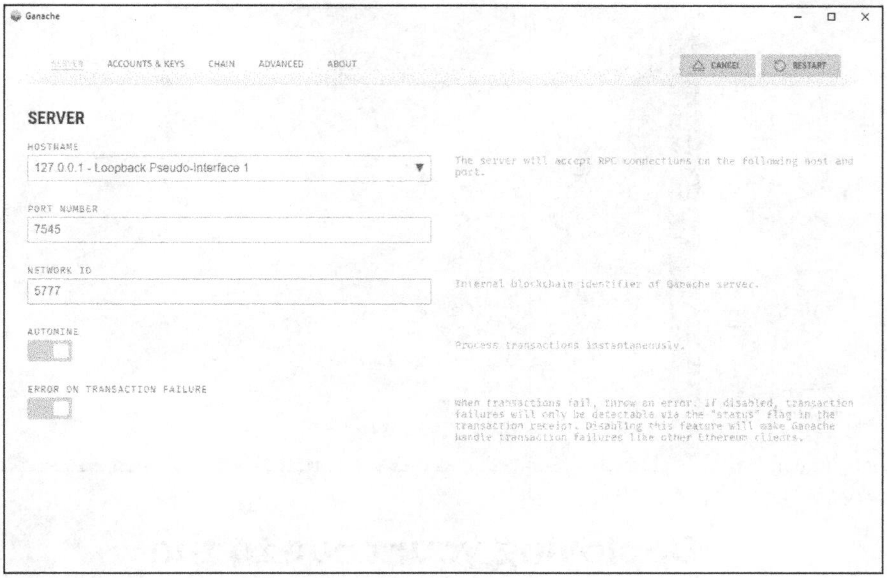

FIGURE 8-1:
The Ganache
settings window.

2. **Launch Visual Studio Code (VS Code) for your project (SupplyChain).**

   Open a Windows Command prompt or PowerShell (our favorite) and navigate to your project directory (SupplyChain). From here, just enter the following command:

   ```
   code .
   ```

   The code command launches VS Code, and the period tells VS Code to use the current directory as the current project.

3. **Modify your Truffle project configuration file to reference the Ganache blockchain.**

   Click or tap truffle-config.js on the left side of your VS Code window to open the file. Add the sections shown in Figure 8-2. Then save the file (choose File ⇨ Save or press Ctrl+S).

When you finish editing the truffle.js file, the uncommented lines (lines that don't start with /*, *, or */) should look like this:

```
module.exports = {
networks: {
development: {
host: "127.0.0.1",
port: 7545,
network_id: "*" // Match any network id
}
}
};
```

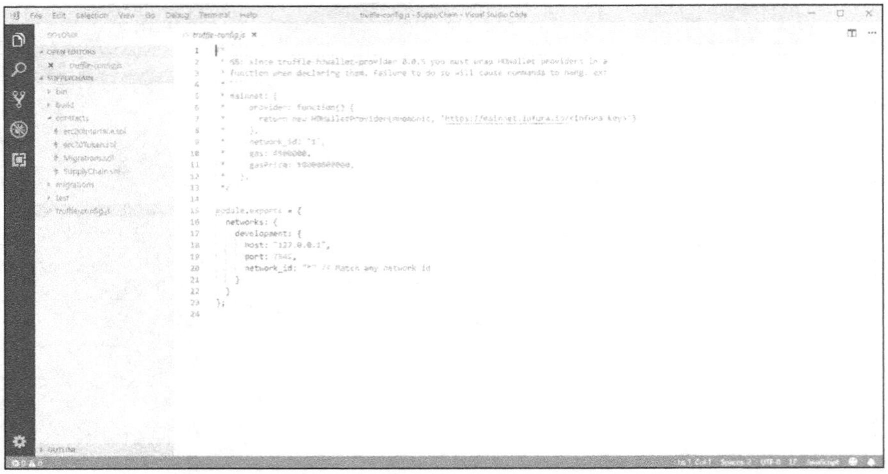

FIGURE 8-2:
Modified
Truffle project
configuration file.

Deploying your code to the Ganache blockchain

After Truffle knows to use the Ganache blockchain, you can deploy your smart contract code to the Ganache test blockchain. Truffle will deploy your smart contracts based on JavaScript instruction files you place in the migrations folder.

Make sure that you have a file in your migrations folder named 2_contracts_migrations.js with the following contents:

```
var erc20Token = artifacts.require("./erc20Token.sol");
var SupplyChain = artifacts.require("./SupplyChain.sol");
module.exports = function(deployer) {
deployer.deploy(erc20Token, 10000, "MGS Token", 18, "MGS");
deployer.deploy(SupplyChain);
};
```

Although you can enter the following commands from any Windows command prompt or PowerShell, you can also use the Terminal tab in VS Code (which gives you access to Windows PowerShell from within VS Code). All three options let you type operating system commands. (Make sure that your SupplyChain project folder is your current folder.)

If you don't see a terminal tab at the bottom of your VS Code window, choose Terminal⇨ New Terminal from the menu bar.

TIP

At the command prompt, type the following to compile your code and deploy it to the Ganache blockchain:

```
truffle deploy --reset
```

This command returns the addresses of each newly deployed smart contract. The --reset option tells Truffle to replace your smart contracts if they have already been deployed. After you deploy each of your smart contracts, you're ready to start testing them.

Writing Tests for Ethereum dApps

You have three common options for writing tests for Solidity smart contracts:

>> Command line interaction

>> Solidity smart contracts

>> JavaScript

To define tests, command line interaction and Solidity smart contracts use the Solidity language, and the third option uses the JavaScript language. In this section, you find out how to write tests using Solidity at the command line and JavaScript. The main advantage of using Solidity is that you'll be using the same language for testing that you used to develop your code.

JavaScript is also a popular option for writing tests. The JavaScript approach provides many more options for writing complex test cases.

Testing using the command line

If you need to carry out a simple test of a smart contract, command line testing may be sufficient. It's quick and flexible but not easily repeatable. You should be writing formal test cases for each smart contract as you develop the smart contract. You'll find out how to do that in the next section. However, you will generally need to create a quick test to see if some aspect of your smart contract is doing what it should be doing. Command line testing may be the easiest way to create a simple, one-time test.

The first step in creating a command line test is to get the smart contract's address. You need that address to access any of the smart contract's public data or functions. Take a look at the output you saw when you deployed your smart contracts. Figure 8-3 shows the output from deploying the SupplyChain contracts.

FIGURE 8-3:
Deployment
output.

Note the two *Saving artifacts* messages. Those messages tell you that Truffle saved the addresses and other descriptive information related to each deployed smart contract. If you want to find the address of any deployed contract, you only have to ask Truffle for it.

You can interact with your smart contracts from the Truffle console. From your operating system command prompt, type the following command to start the Truffle console:

```
truffle console
```

From here, you'll enter your commands to test smart contracts.

REMEMBER

You can enter commands at the Windows command prompt, at the Windows PowerShell, or by using the Terminal tab in VS Code. As long as your current folder is your project folder, you can enter commands in any of these three shells.

At a truffle console prompt, enter the following command:

```
supplyChain.deployed().then(function(instance) {return instance })
```

This command tells Truffle to search the artifacts for deployed smart contracts and return the address of the smart contract named supplyChain in the variable named `instance`. After you know the address of your smart contract, you can access its data and functions.

The next step is to access your smart contract's data and functions to see if your code is operating properly. In general, you want to write tests that ensure that your code is doing what it should be doing and doesn't do anything it shouldn't do. The second goal is much harder to accomplish. You need to think of all the things users could try that could cause your code to do things it shouldn't do.

Here is a brief list of things you should test for with each smart contract:

>> **Overflows and underflows:** Make sure that your code doesn't allow numbers to become larger than the largest valid value or smaller than the smallest valid value. Either situation will cause an error.

>> **Valid return values:** Ensure that each function returns values that are valid for the caller. In some cases the return value is calculated. Your tests should ensure that any calculated return values are always valid.

>> **Boundary conditions:** Always test that your code handles data that meets or exceeds expected limits.

>> **Iteration limits:** Test each looping structure to ensure that it doesn't iterate more times than you intend and burn up all your gas.

>> **Input and output data formats:** Test your code to make sure that it handles data provided or returned in unexpected formats.

>> **Input and output data validation:** Ensure that your code either sanitizes or rejects invalid characters or sequences of characters.

After you know the objectives for testing your code, you can invoke your smart contract's functions and examine the return values. If you need to provide different Ethereum account addresses, remember that Ganache provides you with ten addresses by default. Figure 8-4 shows the main Ganache window with the first seven accounts listed.

TECHNICAL STUFF

Note in Figure 8-4 that the balance of the first account is lower than the rest. You used the first account by default to deploy your smart contracts. The cost of deploying those smart contracts was deducted from that account's ETH balance.

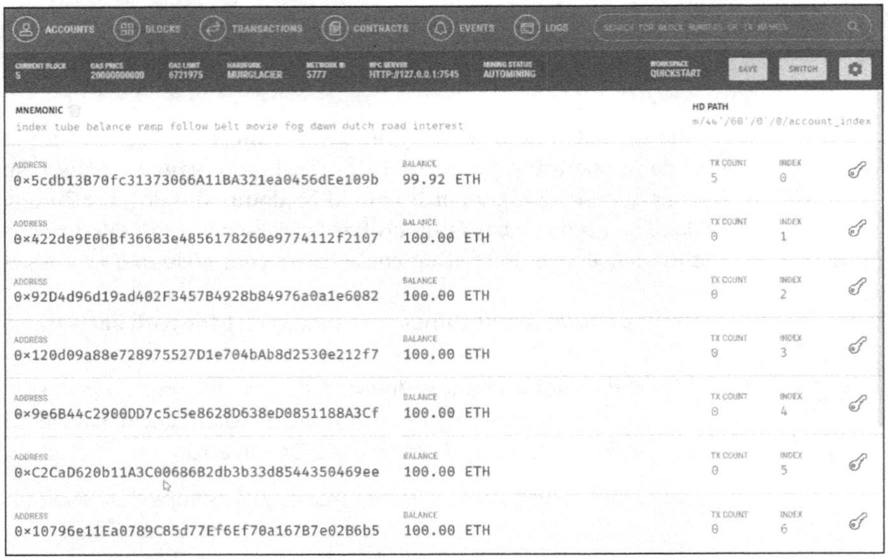

FIGURE 8-4:
Ganache
accounts list.

You'll use the account addresses from Ganache to define supplyChain participants. Enter the following three commands at the Truffle console prompt to create
three supplyChain participants:

```
supplyChain.deployed().then(function(instance) {return
    instance.createParticipant("A","passA","0x5cdb13B70fc31373066A11BA32
    1ea0456dEe109b", "Manufacturer") });
supplyChain.deployed().then(function(instance) {return
    instance.createParticipant("B","passB","0x422de9E06Bf36683e4856178260e97
    74112f2107", "Supplier") });
supplyChain.deployed().then(function(instance) {return
    instance.createParticipant("C","passC","0x92D4d96d19ad402F3457B4928b849
    76a0a1e6082", "Consumer") });
```

You can look at the details returned from each of these commands to see what
happens, but you don't need to read through everything at this point. The easiest
way to see if your functions work as planned is to ask your smart contract to tell
you. You wrote a function to return to you the details of a participant, so you can
use that function to see if your data is stored. Type these commands to get the
participant details for the three participants you just created:

```
supplyChain.deployed().then(function(instance) {return instance.
    getParticipantDetails(0)});
supplyChain.deployed().then(function(instance) {return instance.
    getParticipantDetails(1)});
supplyChain.deployed().then(function(instance) {return instance.
    getParticipantDetails(2)});
```

Figure 8-5 shows the output from these three commands. The output isn't pretty, but you can see that the three participants you created are all there.

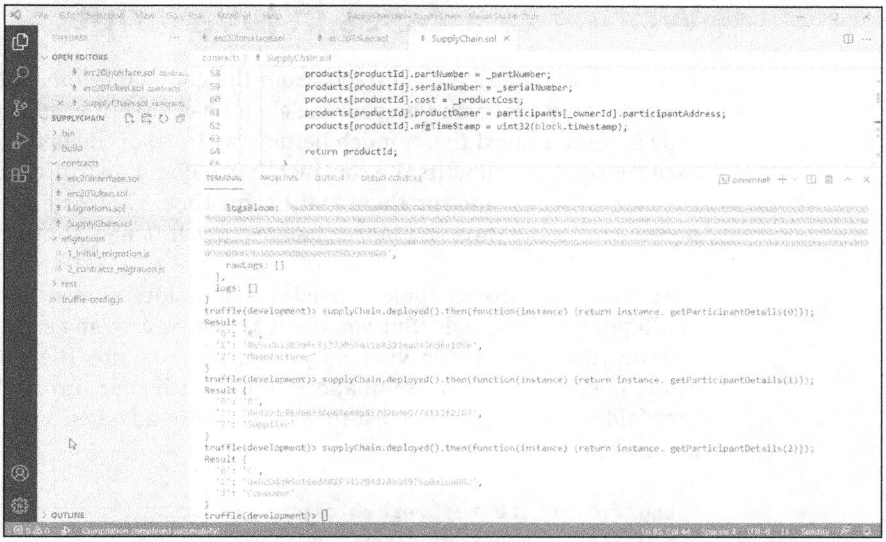

FIGURE 8-5:
Results of
get
Participant
Details().

You can use the syntax of these commands to write your own simple tests to see how your smart contracts function. Before you dive into more complex tests, you need to know one important feature of command line testing. Enter these commands to add a product, and then transfer that product to participant B (the supplier):

```
supplyChain.deployed().then(function(instance) {return instance.createProduct(0,
    "prodABC", "100", "123", 11) });
supplyChain.deployed().then(function(instance) {return instance.transferToOwner
    (0, 1, 0) });
```

Now you want to transfer product 0 from the supplier (participant 1) to the consumer (participant 2). But the transferToOwner() function allows only the product's owner to transfer ownership to another owner. By default, all commands you enter at the Truffle console run as the first Ganache account. If you want to run a test command as another account (and you do), you have to tell Truffle. Enter the following command to transfer product 0 from the supplier (participant 1) to the consumer (participant 2):

```
supplyChain.deployed().then(function(instance) {return
    instance.transferToOwner (1, 2, 0, {from:
    "0x422de9E06Bf36683e4856178260e9774112f2107" }) });
```

Adding the `from:` clause allows you to use a different address as the transaction's sender.

Writing test cases in JavaScript

You can test your smart contracts from the command line, but your options are limited. Every time you test your code, you have to either type each command or copy it from a saved file. A much better way to test code is to write test cases for each contract as you write the contract. If you do this, Truffle will help you organize your test cases and run them at the same time. That way, you can run comprehensive tests any time you make changes to your smart contracts.

Note that your project folder includes a subfolder named test, which is where you'll put your test code. But you don't have to create any script files to test your code on your own. Truffle will help you get started. Enter the following commands at the operating system command prompt (with your project folder as the current folder) to create initial test files for the ERC-20 token and supplyChain smart contracts:

```
truffle create test erc20token
truffle create test supplyChain
```

Click or tap the test folder in VS Code Explorer. You should see two new files, erc-20token.js and supply_chain.js. These two new files are the starting JavaScript test cases that Truffle created for you. You enter your test case statements into each of these files to test your smart contracts. Open each of these JavaScript files in VS Code. The default files don't do much. They just fetch the deployed address of the smart contract and then return. You can add code in these files to run functions, access blockchain data, and run your smart contracts through their paces.

The first step in making these test cases functional is to import the smart contract you're testing. Open the supply_chain.js file and add the following line of code to the top:

```
var SupplyChain = artifacts.require('./SupplyChain');
```

This line of code fetches the address of the deployed smart contract and stores it in the SupplyChain variable. After the test case has the smart contract address, you can automate many of the tests you ran at the command line. Replace the remaining lines in the supply_chain.js file with the following lines of code to carry out the same tests from the previous section:

```
var SupplyChain=artifacts.require('./SupplyChain');
contract('SupplyChain', async accounts => {
it("should create a Participant", async () => {
let instance = await SupplyChain.deployed();
let participantId = await
    instance.createParticipant("A","passA","0x5cdb13B70fc31373066A11BA321ea0
    456dEe109b","Manufacturer");
let participant = await instance.participants(0);
assert.equal(participant[0], "A");
assert.equal(participant[2], "Manufacturer");
participantId = await
    instance.createParticipant("B","passB","0x422de9E06Bf36683e4856178260e977411
    2f2107","Supplier");
participant = await instance.participants(1);
assert.equal(participant[0], "B");
assert.equal(participant[2], "Supplier");
participantId = await
    instance.createParticipant("C","passC","0x92D4d96d19ad402F3457B4928b84976a0a
    1e6082","Consumer");
participant = await instance.participants(2);
assert.equal(participant[0], "C");
assert.equal(participant[2], "Consumer");
});
it("should return Participant details", async () => {
let instance = await SupplyChain.deployed();
let participantDetails = await instance.getParticipantDetails(0);
assert.equal(participantDetails[0], "A");
instance = await SupplyChain.deployed();
participantDetails = await instance.getParticipantDetails(1);
assert.equal(participantDetails[0], "B");
instance = await SupplyChain.deployed();
participantDetails = await instance.getParticipantDetails(2);
assert.equal(participantDetails[0], "C");
})
});
```

One of the advantages of using JavaScript over command line tests is that you not only can run functions and access blockchain data but also test data to see if it matches expected values. That's what the assert()function does. You can see that both the participant mapping and the getParticipantDetails()function return structures of data. JavaScript can access individual data items as if they were in an array. That's why participant[2] refers to the *participantType* from the participant data structure.

You can carry out many more complex types of tests using JavaScript. This brief introduction just scratches the surface.

After you have written your test cases using JavaScript, Truffle will run them all with one command. Enter the `truffle test` command at the operating system command prompt to run all your test cases. Figure 8-6 shows the output of a successful run of the tests just listed.

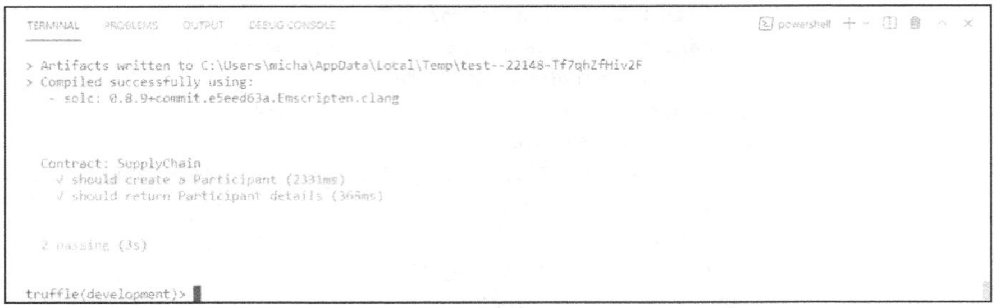

FIGURE 8-6:
Truffle test
results.

Each time you change a smart contract, you can run your test cases to ensure that your application meets its design goals and runs without errors. If your tests do encounter errors, you'll see which test failed, along with information that helps you determine why it failed and what you need to do to fix the problem.

Logging and Handling Errors

Unlike many other languages, Solidity doesn't provide a direct way to output messages to a log file that you can use to test your code and follow along with its execution. Most languages let you at least output messages to a console or local file, but not in an Ethereum environment.

If Solidity allowed you to write to a local file, you could write to the filesystems of every EVM — outside the blockchain. Writing to every EVM's local filesystem would increase the workload and decrease the security of participating nodes, which would make running a blockchain node less desirable. Because you can't just write messages to local files, you have to carefully design your smart contracts to report errors and status to clients in other ways.

Handling errors in Solidity

Client software can determine if any return data was sent back from the EVM and what the return code was. If a smart contract returns as a result of a `revert()` or a failed `require()`, the EVM can send a string, but your smart contract code has to send something that makes sense and the client UI has to use it to determine what happened. The following is an example of a simple smart contract and test code that uses a `try/catch` block to handle errors.

Here is the code for the `basicMath` smart contract, which is stored in the contracts/BasicMath.sol file:

```
//SPDX-License-Identifier:MIT
pragma solidity ^0.8.9;
contract basicMath {
uint256 constant private MAX_UINT256 = 2**256 - 1;
function add(uint256 _numberA, uint256 _numberB) public pure returns(uint256) {
return _numberA + _numberB;
}
}
```

Here is the code for the JavaScript test case code to test the `basicMath` smart contract, which is stored in the test/basic_math.sol file:

```
var BasicMath=artifacts.require('./BasicMath');
contract('BasicMath', function(accounts) {
it('the sum should not overflow', async () => {
try {
// Try to add 2^256 and 5 (should overflow and throw an exception)
const addResult = contractInstance.add((2**256 - 1), 5)
assert.ok(false, 'Threw an exception instead of overflowing.')
} catch(error) {
assert.ok(true, 'Caught the exception.')
}
})
});
```

In the preceding example, the `try/catch` structure can catch errors from the EVM and determine what to do with them. It is important that client software handle errors, but it is even more important that your smart contracts handle as much as possible without resorting to generic error conditions. As much as possible, your code should use the `revert()` and `require()` functions, which means your code is anticipating problems and handling them in a way that you have thought through and included in your application design. That's why writing test cases while you write smart contracts makes sense. The more you plan for errors, the better your smart contracts will be in handling those errors.

Logging activity in smart contracts

Although Ethereum does not have a traditional logging facility, the event feature comes pretty close. In fact, some careful planning can give you good execution information without having to pay full price for storage access. Every time you emit an event, that event and its parameters are stored in a blockchain block. You can query the blockchain for events and even get a list of all events in an address range. You can use that information as a lightweight application logging feature.

Recall that you created a single event for your supplyChain smart contract. That event triggers every time you transfer a product from one participant in the blockchain to another. You could write the following JavaScript code to do that:

```
var transferEvent = SupplyChain.Transfer({_prodId});
transferEvent.watch(function(err, result) {
if (err) {
console.log(err)
return;
}
// return result.args to UI
})
```

This code responds only to transfers that occur after the code runs. But if you want to see any prior transfers for a product, you can use the event indexing feature of Ethereum. You first have to change your event definition. In the SupplyChain.sol file, change the Transfer event definition to this:

```
event Transfer(uint32 indexed productId);
```

Adding the indexed keyword tells Ethereum that this event should be stored in a way that is easy to find. You can index up to three arguments for each event. Your JavaScript code can use the indexed arguments to fetch ranges of event data. Just change the first line of your event watcher code to the following to fetch all prior Transfer events:

```
var depositEvent = cryptoExContract.Deposit({_prodId,
    {fromBlock: 0, toBlock: 'latest'});});
```

Adding the fromBlock and toBlock modifiers tells the EVM to search multiple blocks for Transfer events and returns the details of each event. Using events this way can provide valuable runtime logging. And, as an added feature, event data is far less costly than storage.

Fixing Bugs in a dApp

You test your code so you can identify flaws in it. Software flaws, or bugs, are any bits of code that do not function the way they are supposed to. Bugs that cause errors are generally easy to spot, but silent bugs — those that do not cause compiler or runtime errors — can be much harder to find.

The first step in removing bugs from your smart contracts is to get all of your smart contracts to compile. That step should fix *syntax errors,* which are errors in the way you write statements in the language itself that the compiler can find and report. A syntax error could be a mistyped line of code or a missing parenthesis. The Solidity compiler will find obvious errors as well as code that may cause a future error. For example, if you define a variable but never use it, the compiler will generate a warning. You could ignore the warning, but it is poor practice or a mistake to define a variable that is not used. The best approach is to modify your code to remove all compiler warnings.

The other type of bug is a *semantics error*, in which a line of code is syntactically correct and does not generate compiler warnings, but the code doesn't generate the result you expect. Many times, this type of error shows up only under certain conditions. Successfully finding semantic errors is the main reason testing is crucial to the development process. You don't want bad code to make it to production, especially in a blockchain environment. Testing should be as extensive as possible to find as many of the bugs in your code as possible before you deploy that code to a live blockchain. The quality of your smart contracts is directly related to the quality of your testing.

Chapter 9

Deploying Ethereum Apps

I n Chapter 8 of this minibook, you find out how to test your dApp. You also find out how to deploy your smart contracts to a test blockchain and then interact with them. You see how smart contracts respond to different types of data and how to call smart contract functions. Your tests are an important part of the software development life cycle. You should test your smart contracts thoroughly before you allow them to be deployed to a production environment.

After you complete thorough testing, you're ready to make the transition to production. It's time to deploy your code to a live blockchain, called *mainnet*. Your live environment may be the main live Ethereum blockchain, another public Ethereum blockchain, or perhaps your own organization's private blockchain. Each blockchain has its own characteristics and provides a different operating ecosystem. You must understand the target environment for your dApp when you design its functionality.

Test Blockchain Options versus Live Blockchains

In Chapter 8 of this minibook, you test your smart contracts by using the Ganache test blockchain. This blockchain is a common choice for the initial testing of Ethereum blockchain code because you can control the testing environment and can easily clean up to start testing again without having leftover data from previous tests. Although one of the basic features of blockchain technology is that blocks are immutable, sometimes it's necessary in testing to just remove everything you've done and start over. Although a clean redo isn't possible on a live blockchain, you can do it pretty easily if you're using a local blockchain that you control, such as Ganache.

TECHNICAL STUFF

You may have noticed that every time you quit Ganache, you lose all blocks on your test blockchain. By default, Ganache starts with a new blockchain every time it starts. Although this behavior makes it easy to start over for testing, sometimes you may want to save your blockchain between Ganache sessions. To do so, use `ganache-cli --db /path/to/db` to specify a location for Ganache to save the blockchain state. When you start Ganache again, it will initialize its new blockchain from the previously saved state, instead of creating a new blockchain.

Testing with the Ganache blockchain

Ganache does a great job of simulating how your smart contract code will execute. In fact, it provides the local blockchain and the EVM that executes the code. Although the pieces are good at simulating a live blockchain, it can't realistically simulate the effect of other nodes on the blockchain network. Real blockchain networks have miners and other nodes that communicate and share information around the network. Transactions almost always take longer to complete on a live network than on a test network because a live network has more participants and more work to do.

When you start Ganache, you automatically get the same 10 accounts by default, and each account starts with a balance of 100 ETH. Ganache sets up these defaults to make it fast and easy to start testing your code. You can easily change these defaults in the Ganache settings page if you need more or different accounts, or if your accounts need more ETH.

Ganache also defaults to automining mode, which means that the Ganache EVM processes each transaction as soon as it is received. Although testing your smart contracts without having to wait for each test is helpful, it isn't realistic. When running on a live blockchain, transactions aren't processed until a miner adds them to a new block and then satisfies the consensus requirement. Remember that Ethereum uses the proof-of-work (PoW) consensus protocol, so miners compete to find a nonce value that, when hashed with the previous block's header, results in a hash value that satisfies the current complexity requirements.

Ethereum adjusts the difficulty of the hashing process with each block to ensure that new blocks are added to the Ethereum blockchain every 10 to 19 seconds. If blocks are added faster than every 10 seconds, the difficulty is increased, and if blocks take 20 seconds or longer, the difficulty is reduced. As miners join or drop off the network, the relative available mining computing power changes and can affect how quickly miners can mine new blocks. Advances in hardware and software techniques can also affect mining capabilities. Regardless of the available computing power, the Ethereum blockchain automatically reacts to keep the mining rate within 10 to 19 seconds per block.

Your Ganache test blockchain can either automine or provide a simulated delay. If you turn off Ganache's Automine option in the settings window, you can enter the number of seconds for Ganache to wait between mining new blocks. This wait time helps to simulate the delay your code will encounter on a live blockchain. Figure 9-1 shows the Ganache settings window with Automine turned off and a delay of 14 seconds between block creations.

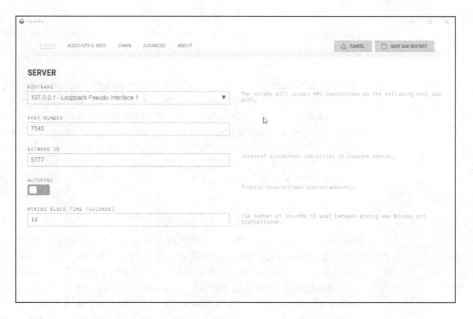

FIGURE 9-1: Ganache settings window with Automine disabled.

Deploying your code to other test blockchains

Although Ganache can help simulate block mining delays, the artificial delays are constant and don't reflect what you'll encounter in a live blockchain environment. Also, it's difficult to share your code with other developers or testers when you use only a local test blockchain. Therefore, the next step in testing your smart contracts for a live environment is to use one of the several public test blockchains. Most blockchain software developers choose a public test blockchain after testing code locally using Ganache or some other blockchain simulator. A public test blockchain allows more people to get involved in the development and testing process.

Public test blockchains are closer to a true live blockchain but still don't give you the exact experience. Public test blockchains do consist of multiple nodes, as you'll find on the live blockchain, but the mining process is simulated. Additionally, different test blockchains use different consensus protocols. The following are the most popular public test blockchains you'll encounter:

>> **Ropsten:** A test blockchain similar to the live Ethereum blockchain

>> **Rinkeby:** An alternative test blockchain that uses a different consensus algorithm and steady block generation time

>> **Kovan:** A test blockchain similar to Rinkeby but with a faster block generation time

Test blockchains give you the ability to deploy and run your code in environments that are close to live environments. You can pay for your code to execute with cheap or free money. The ability to generate Ether, or request as much of it as you want for free, makes it possible to run as many tests as you need but can also lull you into a false sense of wellness. It's easy to ignore the effect of gas cost when you don't have to pay for it. Test networks are great at evaluating code functionality but don't require the same gas conservation skills that live networks do.

Ropsten

The *Ropsten test blockchain* is one of the most popular test blockchains. It uses a PoW consensus algorithm similar to the one that the public live Ethereum blockchain uses. Miners can earn a small amount of ETH for mining new blocks, and new blocks are added to the Ropsten blockchain approximately every 30 seconds. Geth and Parity Ethereum blockchain clients support Ropsten, and it is a good choice if you want to observe the effect of mining on your smart contracts.

Rinkeby

The *Rinkeby test blockchain* uses a different consensus algorithm than the live public Ethereum and Ropsten blockchains. Rinkeby uses a proof-of-authority (PoA) consensus algorithm and adds new blocks to its blockchain every 15 seconds. Before you can get Ether, PoA requires that you prove your existence. All Ether is pre-mined and you simply withdraw the amount you need from a faucet after proving your existence, generally by posting to a social media outlet and providing the evidence of the post. (A *faucet* is simply a mechanism that dispenses free Ether.) Geth supports Rinkeby but not Parity.

Kovan

If you've decided to use the Parity client, you can choose the *Kovan test blockchain*. Kovan supports Parity but not Geth. It uses the same PoA algorithm as Rinkeby, but adds new blocks at a faster rate of every 4 seconds.

Anticipating Differences in Live Environments

Regardless of which test blockchain you choose, it will only be a simulation of a live blockchain. In a live blockchain environment, miners compete for the reward to add new blocks. You will likely encounter many more miners and more node diversity in a live blockchain environment. This diversity can lead to unexpected delays and even an unexpected transaction order. A transaction that pays a higher reward because it uses more gas could be selected by miners before an earlier transaction that doesn't pay as well.

These are just some of the considerations you need to take into account when transitioning from a test environment to a live environment. Thorough testing will identify most of your software's flaws, but there will always be a leftover that you won't find until you deploy to a production blockchain. That's why maintaining your software after you deploy it is still important.

The biggest difference between test networks and mainnet, the live network, is that mainnet uses real money. All of the Ether you use for testing on test networks is essentially worthless. You can get more by changing your configuration for local blockchain, or by requesting it from a test network faucet. Before you deploy anything to mainnet, however, the account you use must own real Ether. You can purchase Ether through any exchange, such as coinbase.com, but it has to be in your account before you try to deploy your dApp.

The other primary difference with mainnet (or public test networks) is that all changes you make to the blockchain are immutable and persist forever. If you deploy a smart contract with a bug, you'll never be able to change it. The best you can do is to deploy a new version of your smart contract with the bug removed, and then ensure that no one uses the smart contract at the old address. And in the case of mainnet, you'll have to pay real money to deploy a new version of your code, which is another good reason to invest in thorough testing before you deploy your code.

Preparing Your Configuration for Deploying to Different Networks

You already know how to set up Truffle to deploy to the Ganache blockchain. Before you can deploy to a public test network or mainnet, you have to extend the Truffle configuration to support more networks. To make most of the changes, you edit the contents of your `truffle-config.js` file. You need to tell Truffle how to connect to each of the networks you'll use to deploy your code.

One of the pieces of information that Truffle needs is the account to use when accessing the network. You've already seen how to use Ethereum addresses to determine ownership. When you use Ganache, Truffle records the Ganache accounts in an array named `eth.accounts[]`. If you don't provide an account, Truffle assumes that you're using the first account from Ganache, which is stored in `eth.accounts[0]`. This approach keeps you from having to manage accounts during development and initial testing.

REMEMBER

When you want to use a public test network or mainnet, you have to use a valid address on each network. The good news is that Ethereum addresses are generic and valid on any network. However, remember that any crypto-assets you own are network-specific. If you own 100 ETH on Ropsten, that doesn't mean you own 100 ETH on mainnet. You can use the same account for multiple networks, but crypto-assets owned by that account are not shared across networks.

One easy way to manage access to multiple networks without having to set up full nodes for each one yourself is to sign up for an Infura account. Infura maintains their own infrastructure that provides easy access to multiple blockchain networks. Infura accounts allow you to deploy code and interact with mainnet, Ropsten, Rinkeby, and Kovan networks. Your Infura account provides you with unique project keys (API keys) for multiple projects that you create. You use each project key to manage a unique dApp. Navigate to `https://infura.io` to explore Infura's offerings and set up your own account.

Launch VS Code for your SupplyChain project and click or tap the New File button next to SupplyChain in Explorer; then type **secrets.js** and press Enter. A new file is created in the project root directory named secrets.js. You'll use this new file to store sensitive account information.

WARNING

Make sure that you protect this file and don't share it with anyone. If you publish your code to any other location, make sure that you exclude the secrets.js file from any publish operations.

Type the following text in the editor for the secrets.js file:

```
var infuraProjectID = "Project ID from Infura";
var accountPK = "Your Ethereum account private key";
var mainnetPK = accountPK;
var ropstenPK = accountPK;
module.exports = {infuraProjectID: infuraProjectID, mainnetPK:
  mainnetPK, ropstenPK: ropstenPK};
```

Replace "Project ID from Infura" with the project ID that you got for the project you created on the Infura website. Also replace "Your Ethereum account private key" with the private key for the Ethereum account you want to use. In this case, use the same account for the Ropsten and mainnet networks.

The secrets.js file stores the private key (or keys) for blockchain network access, but you need another component to securely use your private key to access crypto-assets. To accomplish that task, you need a wallet provider that Truffle can call. Open a Windows command prompt or a Windows PowerShell window, and type the following command to install the Truffle wallet provider:

```
npm install truffle-hdwallet-provider
```

Next, click or tap truffle-config.js in Explorer to open the truffle-config.js file in the VS Code editor. Replace the contents of the truffle-config.js file with the following text:

```
let secrets = require('./secrets');
const WalletProvider = require("truffle-hdwallet-provider");
const Wallet = require('ethereumjs-wallet');
let mainNetPrivateKey = new Buffer(secrets.mainnetPK, "hex");
let mainNetWallet =
    Wallet.fromPrivateKey(mainNetPrivateKey);
let mainNetProvider = new WalletProvider(mainNetWallet,
  "https://mainnet.infura.io/");
let ropstenPrivateKey = new Buffer(secrets.ropstenPK, "hex");
let ropstenWallet =
    Wallet.fromPrivateKey(ropstenPrivateKey);
```

```
let ropstenProvider = new WalletProvider(ropstenWallet,
    "https://ropsten.infura.io/");
module.exports = {
networks: {
development: { host: "localhost", port: 7545,
network_id: "*", gas: 4465030 },
ropsten: { provider: ropstenProvider,
network_id: "3", gas: 4465030 },
live: { provider: mainNetProvider,
network_id: "1", gas: 7500000 }
}
};
```

Previously, you defined only a network named development. The development network connects to your locally running Ganache blockchain. The new `networks` definition you just added now supports Ganache, Ropsten, and mainnet. The code before the `networks` section uses the Truffle wallet provider to instantiate objects that provide access to the Ropsten and mainnet blockchain networks. After you set up your Truffle configuration file, Truffle handles the rest.

TECHNICAL STUFF

For more information on configuring Truffle for other networks, navigate to `https://www.trufflesuite.com/tutorial`.

Deploying a dApp

After you decide on a test network or are ready to deploy to mainnet, you need to complete just three steps to get your code deployed to the blockchain:

1. **Get some Ether.**

   You must have enough Ether to at least pay for the transaction to save your smart contracts to the blockchain.

2. **Compile your code.**

   Ensure that all your code cleanly compiles into bytecode.

3. **Deploy your code.**

   Submit your smart contract code to your chosen blockchain.

Getting enough Ether

You get Ether in your account to pay for deployments and any other blockchain use in two ways: just ask for Ether or buy it. If you're deploying to mainnet, you'll have to buy Ether. You can buy Ether from any exchange that supports Ethereum (such as Coinbase, Gemini, or CEX.IO), and then you can use your wallet to manage access to your Ether. (See Book 1, Chapter 3 for more on wallets and Book 5, Chapter 3 for more about cryptocurrency exchanges.)

TIP

If you're not sure where to buy Ether, check out the Coin Central resource on buying Ether and how to select an exchange. Navigate to `https://coincentral.com/how-to-buy-ethereum-and-best-exchange-ratings` to find this resource.

If you're deploying to a test network, you can just ask that network for some free Ether. Because there isn't any value associated with Ether on a test network, getting what you need for free is easy. The common technique for getting Ether for a test network is to request it from that network's faucet. Each test network has its own method for getting Ether from its faucet.

Getting Ether for the Ropsten network

The Ropsten network Ether faucet is the most straightforward. You simply navigate to `https://faucet.ropsten.be`, enter your account address, and click or tap Send Me Test Ether. In a matter of minutes, your account balance shows that you now own Ropsten Ether. Figure 9-2 shows the Ropsten Ethereum faucet.

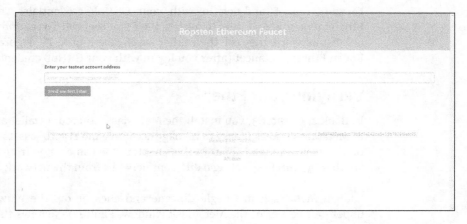

FIGURE 9-2:
Ropsten network Ethereum faucet.

Getting Ether for the Rinkeby network

Getting Ether for the Rinkeby network from its faucet requires a few more steps. Rinkeby attempts to discourage malicious users by requiring simple authentication for Ether requests. You can't simply enter your Ethereum address. Instead, to satisfy the authentication requirements, you initiate Ether requests from a social media account by sending a tweet or publishing a public post on Google+ or Facebook that includes your account. Navigate to `https://www.rinkeby.io/#faucet` to read the full Rinkeby faucet instructions or to provide a social media URL with your Ethereum address. Figure 9-3 shows the Rinkeby Ethereum faucet.

FIGURE 9-3:
Rinkeby network
Ethereum faucet.

Getting Ether for the Kovan network

The Kovan network requires that you have a valid GitHub account before you can request Ether for their network. Navigate to `https://gitter.im/kovan-testnet/faucet` and log in with your GitHub credentials. Then enter your Ethereum account address to initiate the Ether request. To remind you that Kovan is a test network, they call their Ether *Kovan Ethere,* or *KETH.* Figure 9-4 shows the Kovan Ethereum faucet (after you log in with your GitHub credentials).

Verifying your Ether

In Book 2, Chapter 3, you install the MetaMask Ethereum wallet and add Ether to it. MetaMask makes it easy to manage accounts and crypto-assets from any of the networks you've read about in this chapter. You can change from one network to another by simply selecting a different network from the network drop-down list.

Launch MetaMask in Google Chrome and click or tap the network list in the upper-left corner of the MetaMask window. Figure 9-5 shows the networks you can choose in MetaMask.

FIGURE 9-4:
Kovan network
Ethereum faucet.

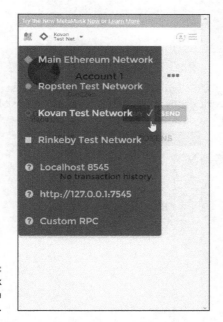

FIGURE 9-5:
MetaMask
Ethereum
network choices.

If you have a GitHub account, you can log in to the Kovan faucet and request Ether. If you don't know your account address, MetaMask will copy it to your clipboard for you. From the network drop-down list, select Kovan Test Network. You should see your current account balance. Click or tap the menu icon (three dots on the right side of the window) and then click or tap Copy Address to Clipboard (see Figure 9-6). You can then paste your address into the appropriate input field in the Kovan faucet web page.

FIGURE 9-6:
MetaMask Copy
Address to
Clipboard option.

After a few minutes, 1.000 ETH will appear in your Kovan Test Net account in MetaMask. From the network drop-down list, select Kovan Test Network to see your updated account balance, as shown in Figure 9-7.

FIGURE 9-7:
Kovan account
balance in
MetaMask.

Compiling your code

Although the deployment process will ensure that all of your code is compiled, it's always a good idea to make sure that everything compiles before trying to deploy. Truffle makes compiling easy. Simply type the following command at a Windows command prompt or Windows PowerShell in the desired project root folder:

```
truffle compile
```

This command compiles all contracts in the current project that have changed since the last compile. If you want to compile all contracts, even if they haven't changed, type the following command:

```
truffle compile --all
```

You can also specify the target network when you compile. Truffle saves compile artifacts to the specified network. You should always include the target network option after you define multiple networks in `truffle-config.js`. Type the following command to compile all contracts and store compile artifacts to the development network:

```
truffle compile --all --network development
```

After you're ready to compile for the live network, type the following command to compile all contracts and store compile artifacts to the live network:

```
truffle compile --all --network live
```

All of your code must compile cleanly (and be thoroughly tested) before you move to the next step of deployment.

Deploying your code

Truffle makes the process of deploying your contracts to a network easy. You've already accomplished the hard work of setting up your account, acquiring Ether, and configuring Truffle to interact with your desired networks. Now all you have to do is tell Truffle what network you want to use when you deploy your code.

In Truffle, the process of creating a transaction to write your contract to the blockchain is called both *migration* and *deployment*. That's why the `migrate` and `deploy` commands do the same thing. You can use either one. Regardless of the keyword you use, Truffle looks in the migrations folder under your project's root folder to find out what contracts to deploy (or migrate) to the network. Truffle runs the JavaScript files it finds in the migrations folder in alphabetical order.

When you're ready to deploy your contracts, type one of the following commands to deploy your code to the development network (your Ganache local blockchain):

```
truffle migrate --network development
```

or

```
truffle deploy --network development
```

Figure 9-8 shows the output from deploying the SupplyChain project contracts to the local development network.

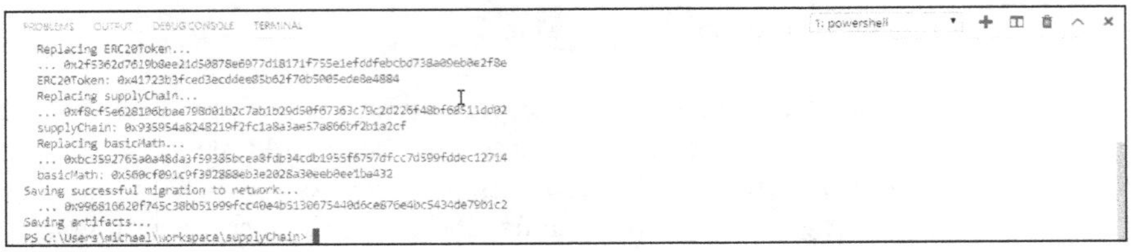

FIGURE 9-8:
The result of the
Truffle deploy
command.

Note that Truffle found existing versions of each contract, replaced each one, and reported the new address for each contract. The last line of output tells you that Truffle is saving the artifacts of the deployment operation on the blockchain. You've already seen how you can query the artifacts and find the current addresses of smart contracts. That's how blockchain users find the contracts they want to interact with.

After you have successfully deployed your fully tested smart contracts, your application is available to anyone else to examine and run. Your blockchain app is now part of Ethereum blockchain history.

5
Cryptocurrency Investing

Contents at a Glance

Chapter **1**

Why Invest in Cryptocurrencies?

Whether you're a seasoned investor who has been exposed only to investment assets other than cryptos or you're just starting to invest (in anything!) for the first time, you're probably wondering why you should consider including cryptocurrencies in your portfolio. Book 1, Chapter 4 provides an overview of the types of cryptocurrencies, what they're made of, and what their purpose is. Books 3 and 4 go into more depth on Bitcoin and Ethereum, respectively. This chapter offers a general overview of the market as a whole to help you decide whether the cryptocurrency industry is the right route for you to grow your wealth.

Cryptocurrency investing may make sense for many investors, for a growing number of reasons — from things as simple as diversification to more exciting stuff like joining the revolutionary movement toward the future of how we perceive money. This chapter shows you some exciting features of this new investment kid on the block.

TIP

Although you can read this book in any order, we encourage you to read Chapter 2 of this minibook right after this one. It explains the other side of the coin: the risks surrounding cryptocurrencies.

Diversifying from Traditional Investments

Diversification is the good ol' "don't put all your eggs in one basket" approach. You can apply this advice to literally anything in life. If you're traveling, don't put all your underwear in your checked-in luggage. Put an emergency pair in your carry-on, in case your luggage gets lost. If you're grocery shopping, don't buy only apples. Even though they say "an apple a day keeps the doctor away," you still need the nutrition in other kinds of vegetables and fruit.

You can go about investment diversification in so many ways. You can diversify with different financial assets, like stocks, bonds, foreign exchange (forex), and so on. You can diversify based on industry, like technology, healthcare, and entertainment. You can allocate your investment by having multiple investment time frames, both short-term and long-term (see Chapters 11 and 12 of this minibook for details). Adding cryptocurrencies to your investment portfolio is essentially one way of balancing that portfolio. Because the cryptocurrency industry is vastly different from traditional ones, this diversification may increase the potential for maximizing your portfolio's growth. One of the main reasons for this higher potential is that the cryptocurrency market may react differently to various global and financial events.

The following sections give you a brief look into some of the traditional markets and explore their differences from the cryptocurrency market. (Find out more about diversification in Chapter 5 of this minibook.)

Stocks

The stock market gives you the opportunity to take a bite of the profits a company makes. By buying stocks of that company, you become a part-owner of that firm. The more stocks you buy, the bigger your slice of the cake — and, of course, the higher the risk you face if the whole cake is thrown into the garbage.

The stock market is perhaps one of the most appealing investment assets. Novice investors may pick up a stock or two just because they like the company. For most investors, the charm of stock investing is the possibility that the prices will increase over time and generate significant capital gains. Some stocks even provide you with a periodic income stream through something called *dividends.* (We explain more about capital gains and dividend income in Chapter 2 of this minibook.) Regardless, for most stocks, the dividends paid within a year are nothing compared to the increase of the stock's value, especially when the economic environment is upbeat.

REMEMBER

This is precisely what stocks and cryptocurrencies have in common: When their respective markets are strong, you can generally expect to benefit from price appreciation.

Make no mistake, though, both markets have their bad days and sometimes even bad years. The stock market has a longer history that can guide investors through navigating the future. For example, even though it may not always seem like it, bad days happen less often than good ones. Figure 1-1 shows that for the 70 years between 1947 and 2017, the Dow, one of the main stock market indexes, ended the year at a lower price only 28.6 percent of the time (20 years). The other 71.4 percent (50 years), it went up.

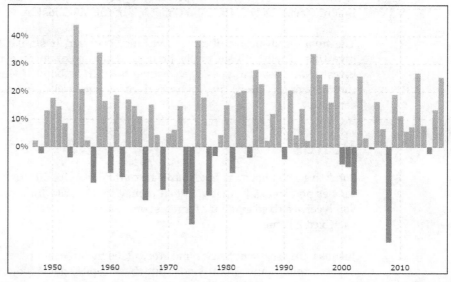

FIGURE 1-1:
Dow Jones
70-year historical
chart by year.

Source: Macrotrends.net

However, stock investing naturally has some disadvantages. For example,

>> **Stocks face different types of risks.** Even the most awesome stocks have risks that you can't easily eliminate, such as the following (see Chapter 2 of this minibook for details):

- Business and financial risk

- Purchasing power risk

- Market risk

- Event risk

- Government control and regulations

- Foreign competition

- The general state of the economy

>> **The stock selection process can be a pain in the neck.** You have literally thousands of stocks to choose from. Predicting how a company will perform tomorrow can also be very difficult. After all, the price today only reflects the current state of the company or what the market participants perceive it to be.

TIP

By investing in the cryptocurrency market, you may be able to balance out some of the preceding risks. The cryptocurrency selection process is also different from that of stocks, as we explain in Chapter 4 of this minibook.

The final disadvantage of stock investing, however, is similar to that of crypto investing. They both generally produce less current income than some other investments. Several types of investments, such as bonds (which we discuss in the following section), pay more current income and do so with much greater certainty.

Bonds

Bonds are also known as *fixed-income securities.* They're different from cryptocurrencies and stocks in that you loan money to an entity for a period of time, and you receive a fixed amount of interest on a periodic basis. Hence its categorization as "fixed income."

Just as with cryptocurrencies and stocks (see the preceding section), you can also expect capital gains from bonds. But these capital gains work a bit differently. Because the companies issuing bonds promise to repay a fixed amount when the bonds mature, bond prices don't typically rise in correlation with the firm's profits. The bond prices rise and fall as market interest rates change.

Another similarity among bonds, cryptocurrencies, and stocks is that they're all issued by a wide range of companies. Additionally, many governmental bodies issue bonds. So if you're looking to diversify only within the bonds market, you can still choose from a range of relatively safe to highly speculative ones.

Compared to cryptocurrencies and stocks, bonds are generally less risky and provide higher current income. But they are still subject to a variety of risks. Some of the risks involved with bond investing are similar to those of cryptocurrencies and stocks — namely, purchasing power risk, business and financial risk, and liquidity risk. Bonds have an additional type of risk known as the *call risk* or *prepayment risk.* Call risk is the risk that a bond will be *called,* or retired, long before its maturity date. If the bond issuer calls its bonds, you'll have to find another place for your funds.

REMEMBER

The potential for very high returns on bonds is much lower compared to cryptocurrencies and stocks. But the risk involved with bonds is also comparatively lower. You can find out more about cryptocurrency risks in Chapter 2 of this minibook.

Forex

Here's an alternative investment that may be even riskier than cryptocurrencies. *Forex* is the geek term for the foreign exchange market. It's the first thing Kiana ever invested in. (Check out Kiana's books about it: *Invest Diva's Guide to Making Money in Forex* [McGraw-Hill Education] and *Ichimoku Secrets* [CreateSpace Independent Publishing Platform].) In fact, her company's original name was Forex Diva, which then switched to Invest Diva, literally to emphasize the importance of diversification.

By participating in the forex market, you buy and sell currencies. Not cryptocurrencies, but fiat currencies such as the U.S. dollar, the euro, the British pound, the Australian dollar, or any other currency any government issues. A *fiat currency* is a country's legal tender that's issued by the government.

Before Bitcoin became the celebrity of financial assets in 2017, most people associated cryptocurrencies such as Bitcoin with the traditional forex market because "cryptocurrency" includes the word "currency," and crypto owners hoped to use their assets to make payments. However, as we mention earlier in this chapter, cryptocurrencies also have a lot in common with stocks.

When you participate in the forex market, you don't necessarily invest for long-term capital gains. Even the most popular currencies such as the U.S. dollar are subject to a ton of volatility throughout the year. A good U.S. economy doesn't always translate into a stronger U.S. dollar.

**TECHNICAL
STUFF**

Heck, sometimes some countries, such as Japan, prefer to have a weaker currency because they rely heavily on exports. If their currencies are stronger than the currency of the country they're trying to sell stuff to, they get a lower rate to sell the same product abroad than domestically.

Participating in the forex market as an investor mainly consists of short-to-medium-term trading activity between different currency pairs. You can buy the euro versus the U.S. dollar (the EUR/USD pair), for example. If the euro's value appreciates relative to the U.S. dollar's, you make money. However, if the U.S. dollar's value goes higher than the euro's, you lose money.

Analyzing the forex market requires a very different approach when compared to stock and cryptocurrency analysis. When looking at the forex markets, you need to focus on the issuing country's economic state, its upcoming economic figures such as its *gross domestic product* (GDP, or the value of the goods produced inside the country), unemployment rate, inflation rate, interest rate, and so on, as well as its political environment.

However, just like the cryptocurrency market, you need to trade forex in pairs. Kiana's online forex education course, the *Forex Coffee Break,* compares these pairs to dancing couples — international couples who push each other back and forth. Traders can make money by speculating on which direction the couple will move next. Figure 1-2 illustrates this metaphor: the Australian dollar (AUD, or Mr. Aussie) is dancing against the U.S. dollar (USD, or Ms. USA).

Source: InvestDiva.com

FIGURE 1-2:
Forex metaphor — the Australian dollar dancing against the U.S. dollar.

You can apply a similar concept to the cryptocurrency market. For example, you can pair Bitcoin (BTC) and Ethereum (ETH) against each other. You can even pair a cryptocurrency such as Bitcoin against a fiat currency such as the U.S. dollar and speculate their value against each other. However, in these cases, you need to analyze each currency, crypto or fiat, separately. Then you need to measure their relative value against each other and predict which currency will win the couple's battle in the future.

TIP

You can also consider cryptocurrencies as a cross between stocks and forex. Although many investors invest in cryptocurrencies for capital gain purposes, you can also trade different cryptocurrencies against each other, the way you can in the forex market. See Chapter 5 of this minibook for more about cross-cryptocurrency trading.

Precious metals

Time to compare one of the most recent man-made means to buy stuff (crypto-currencies) to one of the most ancient ones! No, we're not going back all the way to *bartering*, where people exchanged their goods and services to fulfill their needs. In the following sections, we talk about the stuff with a bling. Before the advent of paper money, precious metals such as gold and silver were long used to make coins and to buy stuff.

REMEMBER

The precious metals comparison is actually the best argument when someone tells you cryptocurrencies are worthless because they don't have any intrinsic value.

Getting a little background

Back in the days of bartering, people would exchange stuff that provided real value to their human needs: chickens, clothes, or farming services. Supposedly, people in the ancient civilization of Lydia were among the first to use coins made of gold and silver in exchange for goods and services. Imagine the first shopper who tried to convince the seller to accept a gold coin instead of three chickens that could feed a family for a week. This change was followed by leather money, paper money, credit cards, and now cryptocurrencies.

Some may argue that precious metals like gold have intrinsic value, too. They're durable. They conduct both heat and electricity and therefore have some industrial application. To be honest, most people don't invest in precious metals because they're trying to conduct electricity. They primarily buy them to use as jewelry or currency. Today, market sentiment mainly determines the value of gold and silver.

**TECHNICAL
STUFF**

Silver has more uses as an industrial metal than gold does. Silver is used in bat-teries, electrical appliances, medical products, and other industrial items. How-ever, despite the additional demand, silver is valued lower than gold. For example, at the time of this writing, silver is priced at $22 per ounce, while gold is traded above $1,800 per ounce.

Keep in mind that England didn't establish gold as its standard of value until 1816. (*Standard of value* means tying the value of the currency to its value in gold.) In 1913, the United States finally jumped on board through its Federal Reserve sys-tem. It backed its notes by gold and aimed to ensure that notes and checks would be honored and could be redeemed for gold.

Even though precious metals don't have an arguable intrinsic value, they have long been a favorite investment tool among market participants. One of the main reasons is their historical association with wealth. Often, when investments such as bonds, real estate, and the stock market go down or the political environment is uncertain, people flock to precious metals. People prefer to own precious metals at these times because they can actually physically touch metals and keep them in their homes right next to their beds.

Comparing precious metals to cryptocurrencies

Besides the fact that you need to mine in order to get your hands on precious metals and some cryptocurrencies, one key similarity between precious metals and cryptocurrencies is that both categories have unregulated characteristics. Gold has been an unregulated currency at various times and in various places. Unregulated currencies become more valuable when investors don't trust the official currency, and cryptocurrencies just seem to be another example of this trend. (You can find out more about cryptocurrency mining in Book 6.)

REMEMBER

Investing in precious metals comes with a number of risk factors you need to keep in mind. For example, if you're buying physical precious metals as an investment, you must consider their portability risk. Transferring precious metals can be expensive given their weight, high import taxes, and the need for a high level of security. In contrast, you don't need to make a physical transfer with cryptocurrencies, besides the hardware crypto wallets that we introduce in Book 1, Chapter 3. But moving cryptocurrencies is much faster and less expensive, even with a hardware wallet, than transferring precious metals.

On the other hand, cryptocurrency prices have been more volatile in the short time they've been available on the markets than all precious metals combined. The 2017 volatility in particular was due to the hype in the market, as we explain in Chapter 2 of this minibook. As cryptocurrency investing becomes more mainstream and more people use it for everyday transactions, crypto prices may become more predictable.

Gaining Capital Appreciation

Capital appreciation refers to the increase in the price or value of cryptocurrencies. And it's one of the reasons many investors (and noninvestors, for that matter) look to jump on the cryptocurrency train. Initial Bitcoin owners waited years before they saw any sort of capital appreciation. Many investors were skeptical and didn't start investing in cryptocurrencies until the price of Bitcoin had surged significantly. More affordable cryptocurrencies were available — although you had to research to find them — and were expected to have similar capital appreciation.

The following sections look at the history of capital appreciation for cryptocurrencies and discuss their growth potential — a big reason to consider investing in them.

REMEMBER

With great expectations of capital appreciation and huge growth potential come great expectations of capital losses. That's why we strongly recommend reading Chapter 2 of this minibook before you start any trading activity in the cryptocurrency market.

Historical returns

Most of the gains in the cryptocurrency market up to 2017 were a result of market hype. In 2013, for example, many people bought Bitcoin as its price approached $1,000 for the first time. Shortly after, as shown in Figure 1-3, its price crashed to around $300, where it stayed for the following two years. The next big wave of growth came in January 2017, when Bitcoin's price broke above the $1,000 level.

FIGURE 1-3:
Bitcoin price between 2013 and January 2017.

Source: tradingview.com

If you had bought one Bitcoin at $311 at the end of 2015, by January 2017 you would've had almost $700 worth of capital appreciation (when the price hit $1,000). But of course, the gains didn't stop there. After the break above $1,000, shown in Figure 1-4, Bitcoin's price eventually went up to $64,863 in April 2021 (and then came crashing down to around $30,000 in July of that year).

For people who had bought (or mined) Bitcoin when it was valued at around $300 and held on to it throughout the 2021 volatility, the crash from $64,863 to $30,000 wasn't that big of a deal. For every Bitcoin they'd bought at $300, they had around $29,700 worth of capital appreciation even if they didn't cash their Bitcoins in when the value reached above $60,000.

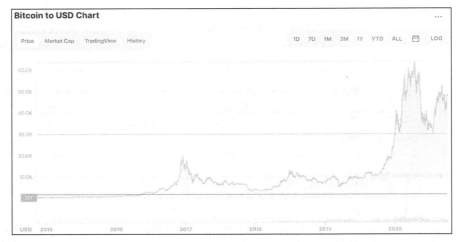

FIGURE 1-4:
Bitcoin price between 2016 and October 2021.

Source: coinmarketcap.com

People who bought Bitcoin at around $1,000 and cashed it out at around $64,000 at its 2021 peak would've made about $63,000 for every Bitcoin they owned. Of course, those who bought Bitcoin at $64,000 had to sit on their hands and eat their losses after the crash.

Many market participants compare Bitcoin and other cryptocurrencies' appreciation to the dot-com bubble from the mid-1990s and early 2000s. According to *Fortune* magazine, from its creation in 2009 until March 2018, Bitcoin saw four bear (falling) waves, where prices dropped 45 to 50 percent, typically rebounding an average of 47 percent afterward. During the dot-com bubble, the Nasdaq composite index had five of those waves, averaging 44 percent declines followed by 40 percent rebounds. Trading volume patterns are also eerily similar.

Nasdaq has clearly rallied nicely from its low in February 2009. Although history and past performance aren't indicative of future behavior, crypto enthusiasts have reasons to believe that growth potential for cryptocurrencies may be similar to the Nasdaq rebound, if not better.

Huge growth potential

Bitcoin and cryptocurrencies were the biggest investment story of 2017. Stories appeared daily on CNBC, and in the *Wall Street Journal* and *New York Times*, about people becoming millionaires practically overnight.

However, after January 2018, the price of Bitcoin fell 63 percent. The media followed suit appropriately, saying the opportunity had passed — that the cryptocurrency bull market was over and the bubble had burst.

This tune was interesting, especially because many billionaires became crypto investors at this point. For example, JPMorgan Chase CEO Jamie Dimon (who had called Bitcoin a fraud and said any JPMorgan traders caught trading Bitcoin would be fired) became one of the most active buyers of a fund that tracks the price of Bitcoin. The price of Bitcoin fell as much as 24 percent in the few days that followed Dimon's statement, and sure enough, right in that period, JPMorgan and Morgan Stanley started buying for their clients at low prices.

This story isn't alone in the crypto market. For example, after slamming Bitcoin at the World Economic Forum in Davos, Switzerland, in January 2018, calling it a "bubble," hedge fund titan George Soros gave the green light to his $26 billion family office to begin buying cryptocurrencies just eight weeks later.

TECHNICAL STUFF

Interestingly, Soros attributes part of his success to his understanding of what he calls "reflexivity." In simple terms, this theory states that investors base their decisions not on reality but on their perception of reality. Soros once said, "The degree of distortion may vary from time to time. Sometimes it's quite insignificant, at other times it is quite pronounced. . . . Every bubble has two components: an underlying trend that prevails in reality and a misconception relating to that trend."

The problem is that most people have no clue what's really going on in the cryptocurrency market. And most have no idea where the price is about to go next. The majority of those interested in the market are taking their cues from market noise, making it way easier for the prices to fall when the big movers downplay for their own benefit.

"Going against the crowd" is one of the key pillars in Kiana's *Invest Diva Diamond Analysis (IDDA)* in Chapter 4 of this minibook, as well as in the *Make Your Money Work for You PowerCourse* at `https://learn.investdiva.com/free-webinar-3-secrets-to-making-your-money-work-for-you`. When the majority of the market panics about the drops in the value of an asset, it is often the best time to stack up on it. You can say the same about the cryptocurrency market. For the cryptocurrencies with strong blockchain technology behind them, once their price bottoms out, their value has nowhere to go but up. See Book 2 to find out more about the basics of blockchain technology.

Increasing Income Potential

Although gaining capital appreciation is one of the most attractive features of cryptocurrency investing (as we explain earlier in this chapter), you can also take advantage of some cryptocurrencies that pay something similar to dividends in the stock market.

A bit about traditional dividends

By definition, a *dividend* is a sum of money public companies pay their shareholders on a regular basis. U.S. corporations pay billions of dollars' worth of dividends every year. Yet in spite of these numbers, many investors (especially young ones) don't pay much attention to dividends. They prefer capital gains because the rewards can be realized more quickly and can far exceed any amount of dividend payment.

TECHNICAL STUFF

In the traditional stock market, companies typically pay dividends on a quarterly basis. A firm's board of directors decides how much to pay shareholders in dividends or whether to pay dividends at all. Sometimes, the directors decide to pay dividends because the stock value isn't doing so well. So they select a higher dividend rate to keep investors interested in buying the stocks.

REMEMBER

Investors with lower risk tolerance may prefer dividend payments to capital gains because dividend payments don't fluctuate as much as the value of stocks do. Furthermore, if the markets crash like they did in 2008, dividends can provide nice protection. The best way to accumulate dividends is to hold onto your assets long-term.

The basics on crypto dividends

During the crypto mania of 2017, many cryptocurrency platforms were quick to realize the importance of regular payments to keep investors happy. But these payments can be a bit different than traditional stock dividends. You can generate regular, passive income in the crypto market in several ways. Here are the two most popular ones:

>> **HODLing:** No, this term is not a typo for "holding," although it has a similar meaning. It stands for "Hold On for Dear Life." It is the closest payment to traditional dividends. Some cryptocurrencies pay out the HODLers, who simply purchase and carry the digital coins in their wallets.

>> **Proof of stake (PoS):** This is a lighter version of proof of work in cryptocurrency mining. When you "stake" a coin, it means you put it aside so it can't be used in the blockchain network. If you have a ton of stakes, you have a higher chance of getting paid at a random selection by the network. Annual returns for staking vary between 1 percent and 5 percent, depending on the coin. See Book 6, Chapter 2 for more about how proof of work and proof of stake work in cryptocurrency mining.

Some of the most popular dividend-paying cryptos in 2021 are NEO, VET, and exchange cryptocurrencies like KuCoin.

REMEMBER While receiving cash (or digital coins) just for holding onto your assets is pretty cool, sometimes it makes more sense to cash out and reinvest your holdings to get a better return.

Fueling Ideological Empowerment

Just as oil is the lubricant that allows a machine to operate, blockchain technology is the lubricant that enables the cryptocurrency market. *Blockchain* is the underlying technology for cryptocurrencies, not to mention one of those breakthrough developments that has the potential to revolutionize nearly every industry in the world completely. (To read more about blockchain technology, see Book 2.)

Blockchain can offer so much more as it's aiming to resolve many economic and financial problems in the world today, from dealing with the flaws of the sharing economy to banking the unbanked and underbanked. Here are some of the kinds of social good that come through cryptocurrencies and blockchain technology.

The economy of the future

We live in an era where the *sharing economy* is exploding. The sharing economy allows people to rent out their own property for use by others. Internet giants such as Google, Facebook, and Twitter rely on the contributions of users as a means to generate value within their own platforms. If you've ever taken an Uber or Lyft rather than a taxi or rented a room on Airbnb instead of a hotel, you're a part of the sharing economy crowd.

The traditional sharing economy has its issues, such as the following:

>> **Requiring high fees for using the platforms.**

>> **Hurting individual users but benefitting the underlying corporation.** In most cases, the value produced by the crowd isn't equally redistributed among all who have contributed to the value production. All the profits are captured by the large intermediaries who operate the platforms.

>> **Playing fast and loose with consumer info.** Some companies have abused their power by getting access to private data without customers knowing.

As the sharing economy expands in the future, its problems will likely become more complicated.

To combat these issues, several companies are developing blockchain-based sharing economy platforms. These platforms are much more affordable to use and provide much-needed transparency. They limit, and sometimes completely cut out, the need for a centralized middleman. This shift allows true peer-to-peer interactions, eliminating the 20-to-30-percent transaction fees that come with centralized platforms. Because all transactions are logged on blockchains, all users can audit the network's operations.

This approach is possible because of the decentralized nature of blockchain technology, which is ultimately a means for individuals to coordinate common activities, to interact directly with one another, and to govern themselves in a more trustworthy and decentralized manner.

WARNING

Some cryptocurrency transactions aren't entirely free. In many cases, every time there is a transaction on a blockchain, you have to pay the "network fees," which are funds payable to the blockchain network members who are mining your coins and transactions.

Blockchain remains the fuel behind the economy of the future, and cryptocurrencies are a byproduct to pave the way by distributing the global economy.

Freedom from government control of currency

The rise of Bitcoin and other cryptocurrencies as a trillion-dollar asset class was spurred without the oversight of a central bank or monetary authority guaranteeing trust or market conduct. Unlike fiat currencies such as the U.S. dollar and the euro, most cryptocurrencies will never be subject to money printing (officially called *quantitative easing*) by central banks. Most cryptocurrencies operate under controlled supply, which means no printing of money. In fact, networks limit the supply of tokens even in cases where the demand is high. For example, Bitcoin's supply will decrease in time and will reach its final number somewhere around the year 2140. All cryptocurrencies control the supply of the tokens by a schedule written in the code. Translation: The money supply of a cryptocurrency in every given moment in the future can roughly be calculated today.

The lack of government control over cryptocurrencies can also help to lower the risk of inflation. History has shown over and over again that when a particular government applies bad policies, becomes corrupt, or faces a crisis, the country's individual currency suffers. This fluctuation in the currency value can lead to the printing of more money. Inflation is the reason why your parents paid less than a dollar for a gallon of milk while you have to pay at least three dollars.

How awesome will it be if cryptocurrencies can get rid of government-controlled inflation so that your grandchildren don't have to pay more for stuff than you do?

Help for the unbanked and underbanked

One of the most noble problems cryptocurrencies can solve is banking the *unbanked*. According to Cointelegraph, "2 billion people in the world still don't have a bank account. Most of them live in low- and middle-income emerging markets, but even in high-income countries, large numbers of people are unable to use banks to meet their day-to-day financial needs. This means they don't have access to the convenience, security, and interest that banks provide."

Moreover, many people are *underbanked;* they have access to a bank account but don't have adequate access to the financial services that banks can provide. Even in the United States, for example, approximately 63 million adults were unbanked or underbanked, according to a 2019 report by the Federal Reserve. Without access to savings and credit, these people can't participate in the cycle of economic growth.

TIP

Cryptocurrencies, with the help of blockchain technology, have the potential to help the unbanked and underbanked by letting them create their own financial alternatives efficiently and transparently. All someone needs to start using cryptocurrencies such as Bitcoin and to send and receive money is a smartphone or laptop and an Internet connection. (Flip to Chapter 3 of this minibook for an introduction on how to buy cryptocurrencies.)

Chapter 2

Recognizing the Risks of Cryptocurrencies

So you're excited to jump on the crypto wagon, perhaps because you expect a gigantic *return* (profit) on your investment. That's basically the reward for investing. However, you can't consider return without also looking at risk. *Risk* is the uncertainty surrounding the actual return you generate.

Kiana spends a lot of time speaking about risk in her investment education courses and how everyone should approach risk individually. What may represent high risk for one person may not be as risky for another due to their unique lifestyles and financial circumstances.

Cryptocurrencies have shown their fair share of volatility, which has made some investors millions of dollars while wiping out others' initial investments. This chapter looks at cryptocurrencies' price volatility from 2017 to 2018. It also defines cryptocurrency rewards and risk, describes different types of risk, and gives you pointers on managing risk.

Reviewing Cryptocurrency Returns

Different assets generate different types of returns. For example, one source of return is the change in the investment's value. Another is the amount you make when you invest in the stock market or the forex (foreign exchange) market; in this case, you may generate income in the form of dividends or interest. Investors call these two sources of return *capital gains* (or *capital losses*) and *current income*, respectively.

REMEMBER

Although most people invest in the cryptocurrency market for capital gains, some cryptocurrencies actually offer current income opportunities. You get an introduction to cryptocurrency returns in Chapter 1 of this minibook.

Capital gains (or losses)

The most popular reason for crypto investing is to see gains in the coins' value. Some people associate the coins with precious metals such as gold. Doing so makes sense because, just like gold, a limited amount is available for most cryptocurrencies, and one way to extract many of them is to mine. (Of course, you don't need to gear up with a pickax and headlamp when mining cryptocurrencies; head to Book 6 for details on cryptocurrency mining.)

With that said, many investors consider cryptocurrencies to be assets even though they're technically currencies that can be used in transactions. People buy these currencies in hopes of selling them when the prices rise further. If the value of your cryptocurrency token goes higher from the time you purchase it, you get a capital gain when you sell the token. Congrats! If the price goes lower, you end up with a capital loss.

Income

Income is a lesser-known type of return in the cryptocurrency market. Income is generated from something called *crypto dividends.*

Traditionally, dividends occur when public companies distribute a portion of their earnings to their shareholders. Traditional types of dividends include cash payments, shares of stock, or other property.

Earning dividends in the crypto market can get a bit more complicated. Different currencies have different operating systems and their own rules and regulations. However, the concept still remains the same. Crypto dividend payments are becoming increasingly popular among *altcoins,* which are the alternative cryptocurrencies besides Bitcoin. When choosing a cryptocurrency for your port-folio, you can consider looking into crypto dividends as well as the potential of capital gains (discussed in the preceding section).

Some of the most popular ways to earn crypto dividends are

>> **Staking:** Holding a proof-of-stake coin in a special wallet

>> **Holding:** Buying and holding a crypto in any wallet

See Book 1, Chapter 3 for more about staking and holding.

TIP

At the time of this writing, some dividend-paying cryptocurrencies included NEO, KuCoin, BitMax, Neblio, and Komodo. (Find out more about these currencies in Book 1, Chapter 4.) In addition, besides staking and holding, you can earn regular interest payments by participating in crypto lending. For example, you can earn up to 5 percent interest on your cryptos by allowing companies like Celsius Network to give out loans to the general public against cryptos.

Risk: Flipping the Other Side of the Coin

Investment returns are exciting, but you can't consider return without also look-ing at risk. The sad truth about any type of investment is that the greater the expected return, the greater the risk. Because cryptocurrencies are considered riskier than some other assets, they may also provide higher returns. The rela-tionship between risk and return is called the *risk-return tradeoff.*

WARNING

Cryptocurrency investing isn't a get-rich-quick scheme. You shouldn't invest in cryptocurrencies by using your life savings or taking out a loan. You must consider your risk tolerance, understand the different sources of cryptocurrency risks, and then develop an investment strategy that's suitable for you — just you, not any-one else — because you're unique, and so is your financial situation.

Also keep in mind that early Bitcoin investors waited years to see any returns. If you don't have the patience required to see meaningful returns on your invest-ment, you may need to forget about investing altogether. .

That being said, a healthy amount of risk appetite is essential not only when investing but also in life. Don't get so paranoid about risk that you just never leave the house for fear of getting into an accident!

Glimpsing Cryptocurrencies' Reward versus Risk

One of the main reasons cryptocurrency investing became such a hot topic in 2017 was the crazy surge in the value of major cryptocurrencies such as Bitcoin.

Although you may have heard of Bitcoin the most, it wasn't even among the ten best-performing crypto assets of 2017. Bitcoin's value grew by more than 1,000 percent, but other, lesser-known cryptocurrencies such as Ripple and NEM were among the biggest winners, with a whopping 36,018 percent and 29,842 percent growth, respectively.

Where did Bitcoin stand on the performance list? Fourteenth!

These returns made investors and noninvestors alike super-excited about the cryptocurrency market. By the beginning of 2018, almost everyone you knew — your doctor, your rideshare driver, perhaps even your grandmother — was probably talking about Bitcoin, whether or not the person had any experience in any sort of investing.

However, as is true of any type of investment, what goes up must come down, including the cryptocurrency market. Because the cryptocurrency prices had gone up so much, so quickly, the crash was equally hard and speedy. For example, by February 2018, Bitcoin had dropped to a three-month low of $6,000 from highs of nearly $20,000.

The cryptocurrency then started to consolidate above the $6,000 support level, forming lowering highs, as shown in Figure 2-1. *Support level* refers to a price that the market has had difficulty going lower than in the past. In this case, the price had difficulty breaking below $6,000 in November 2017. *Lower highs* are those mountain-like peaks on the chart. Every peak (high) was lower than the previous one, which indicated a decrease in popularity among market participants. See Chapter 10 of this minibook for more about support (and its cousin, resistance).

Many analysts considered the great appreciation of major cryptocurrencies' value to be a bubble. This fluctuation is a heck of a roller-coaster ride in such a short period of time! The returns were great for those who invested early and took profit at the highs. But just imagine investing in the market when the prices were up and watching the value of your investment going lower and lower. That's one of the major risk factors in any type of investing.

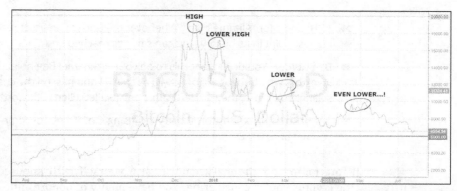

Source: tradingview.com

FIGURE 2-1:
Bitcoin's price action versus the U.S. dollar from 2017 to 2018.

Digging into Different Kinds of Risk

Getting educated about risk puts you right on top of your game. Knowing your risk tolerance, you can create a strategy that protects you and your wealth. The risks associated with cryptocurrencies come from many different sources. Here are the various types of crypto risks.

Crypto hype risk

Although getting hyped up in the thought of buying your dream car is a good thing, the hype surrounding cryptocurrencies isn't always as exciting. The main reason cryptos have a lot of hype is that most people don't know about what they're investing in; they just end up listening to the crowd. The crypto hype in 2017 was one of many drivers of the fast-and-furious market surge. After people started to figure out what they'd invested in, the prices crashed. This type of behavior became so popular that crypto geeks created their very own lingo around it. Here are a few terms:

>> **FOMO:** This crypto-geek term stands for "Fear of Missing Out." This happens when you see a massive surge in a crypto you don't own and you hurry in to get your hands on it as the price goes up. *Hint:* Don't do it! What goes up must come down, so you may be better off waiting for the hype to calm down and buying at lower prices.

>> **FUD:** This is short for "Fear, uncertainty, and doubt." You can use this in a Reddit post when you hear one of those Doctor Doomsdays talking down the market. JPMorgan Chase's CEO, Jamie Dimon, spread one of the biggest FUDs in September 2017 by calling Bitcoin a fraud. In January 2018, he said he regretted saying that.

>> **ATH:** Short for "All-time high." Whenever the price of an asset reaches the highest point in its history, you can say, "It's reached an ATH."

>> **Bag holder:** You don't want this to be your nickname! Bag holders are those investors who bought out of FOMO at an ATH and missed the chance of selling. Therefore, they are left with a bag (wallet) filled with worthless coins.

>> **BTFD:** This one stands for "Buy the f@#&ing dip!" To not become a bag holder, you've got to BTFD.

REMEMBER

Before falling for the market noise, arm yourself with knowledge on the specific cryptos you're considering. You have plenty of opportunities to make lots of money in the crypto market. Be patient and acquire the right knowledge instead of betting on the current hype. An investor who trades on the hype probably doesn't even have an investment strategy — unless you call gambling a strategy! You can find different methods of strategy development in Chapters 4, 5, 11, 12, and 13 of this minibook.

Security risk

Scams. Hacking. Theft. These issues have been a common theme in the cryptocurrency market since Bitcoin's inception in 2009. And with each scandal, the cryptocurrencies' values are compromised as well, although temporarily. Your cryptocurrency can be compromised in three main ways, as outlined in the following sections. You should definitely follow safety precautions in every step of your cryptocurrency investing strategy.

Safety check #1: The cryptocurrency itself

Hundreds of cryptocurrencies are already available for investment, with thousands of new ICOs (initial coin offerings) on the way. When choosing the cryptocurrency to invest in, you must educate yourself on the blockchain's protocol and make sure no bugs (or rumors of bugs) may compromise your investment. The *protocol* is the common set of rules that the blockchain network has agreed upon.

You may be able to find out about the nature of the cryptocurrency's protocol on its white paper on its website. The white paper is an official document that the crypto founders put together before their ICO, laying out everything there is to know about the cryptocurrency. But companies are unlikely to share their shortcomings in their white papers. That's why reading reviews on savvy websites like Reddit and Kiana's site, InvestDiva.com, can often be your best bet.

These types of bugs appear even in the major cryptocurrencies. For example, a lot of negative press surrounded EOS's release of the first version of their open-source software before June 2, 2018. A Chinese security firm had found a bug in the EOS code that could theoretically have been used to create tokens out of thin air. However, EOS was able to fix the bug. To further turn the bad press into positive, Block.one, the developer of EOS, invited people to hunt for undiscovered bugs in return for monetary rewards (a process known as a *bug bounty*).

WARNING

Reliable cryptocurrency issuers should take matters into their own hands immediately when a bug is found. But until they do, you're wise to keep your hands off their coins!

Safety check #2: The exchange

Exchanges are where you trade the cryptocurrency tokens (see Chapter 3 of this minibook for an introduction). You need to make sure that your trading host is trustworthy and credible. Countless numbers of security incidents and data breaches have occurred in the crypto community because of the exchanges.

One of the famous initial hacks was that of Japan-based Mt. Gox, the largest Bitcoin exchange, in 2013. At the time, Mt. Gox was handling 70 percent of the world's Bitcoin exchanges. However, it had many issues, such as lack of a testing policy, lack of a version control software, and lack of proper management. As all these problems piled up, in February 2014, the exchange became the victim of a massive hack, where about 850,000 Bitcoins were lost. Although 200,000 Bitcoins were eventually recovered, the remaining 650,000 have never been recovered.

Many exchanges have learned a lesson from this incident and are keeping up with the latest safety measures. However, exchange hacks still happen almost on a monthly basis.

REMEMBER

Centralized exchanges are the most vulnerable to attacks. Flip to Chapter 3 of this minibook for methods to spot red flags in cryptocurrency exchanges.

TIP

We aren't trying to scare you with these stories. As time goes by, the market learns from previous mistakes and works to create a better and safer future. However, you still need to take matters into your own hands as much as possible. Before choosing an exchange, take a look at the security section on their website. Check on whether they participate in any bug bounty programs to encourage safety. And, of course, ask the right people about the exchange. The Invest Diva's Premium Investing Group keeps an eye on the latest developments in the market and keeps members informed about any shady activities. So feel free to stop by https://learn.investdiva.com/join-group!

Safety check #3: Your wallet

The final round of your security check is all in your own hands because what kind of crypto wallet you use is entirely up to you. Although you don't physically carry your crypto coins, you can store them in a secure physical wallet. You actually store the public and private keys, which you can use for making transactions with your altcoins, in these wallets as well. You can take your wallet's security to a higher level by using a backup. Explore wallet safety methods in Book 1, Chapter 3.

Volatility risk

Volatility risk is essentially the risk in unexpected market movements. Although volatility can be a good thing, it can also catch you off guard sometimes. Just like any other market, the cryptocurrency market can suddenly move in the opposite direction from what you expected. If you aren't prepared for the market's volatility, you can lose the money you invested in the market.

The volatility in the cryptocurrency market has resulted from many factors. For one, it's a brand-new technology. The inception of revolutionary technologies — such as the Internet — can create initial periods of volatility. The blockchain technology (see Book 2) and its underpinning cryptocurrencies take a lot of getting used to before they become mainstream.

REMEMBER

The best way to combat the cryptocurrency volatility risk is by looking at the big picture. Volatility matters a lot if you have a short-term investing horizon (see Chapter 11 of this minibook) because it's an indicator of how much money you may make or lose over a short period. But if you have a long-term horizon (see Chapter 12 of this minibook), volatility can turn into an opportunity.

TIP

You can also offset volatility risk by using automated trading algorithms on various exchanges. For example, you can set up an order like "sell 65 percent of coin 1," "sell 100 percent of coin 2," and so on if the price drops by 3 percent. This strategy can minimize the risk of volatility and allow you to sleep well at night.

Liquidity risk

By definition, *liquidity risk* is the risk of not being able to sell (or *liquidate*) an investment quickly at a reasonable price. Liquidity is important for any tradable asset. The forex market is considered the most liquid market in the world. But even in the forex market, lack of liquidity may be a problem. If you trade currencies with very low volume, you may not even be able to close your trade because the prices just won't move!

Cryptocurrencies can also see episodes of illiquidity. Heck, the liquidity problem was one of the factors that led to the high volatility in Bitcoin and other altcoins described earlier in this chapter. When the liquidity is low, the risk of price manipulation also comes into play. One big player can easily move the market in their favor by placing a massive order.

The crypto community refers to these types of big players as *whales*. In the cryptocurrency market, whales often move small altcoins by using their huge capital.

On the bright side, as cryptocurrency investing becomes more available and acceptable, the market may become more liquid. The increase in the number of trusted crypto exchanges will provide opportunity for more people to trade. Crypto ATMs and payment cards are popping up, helping raise the awareness and acceptance of cryptocurrencies in everyday transactions.

Another key factor in cryptocurrency liquidity is the stance of countries on cryptocurrency regulations. If the authorities are able to define issues such as consumer protection and crypto taxes, more people will be comfortable using and trading cryptocurrencies, which will affect their liquidity.

When choosing a cryptocurrency to trade, you must consider its liquidity by analyzing its acceptance, popularity, and the number of exchanges it's been traded on. Lesser-known cryptocurrencies may have a lot of upside potential, but they may put you in trouble because of lack of liquidity. Find out more about different types of cryptocurrencies in Book 1, Chapter 4.

Vanishing risk

No, we aren't talking about disappearing into the ever-magical blockchain industry. Quite the contrary. Thousands of different cryptocurrencies are currently out there. More and more cryptocurrencies are being introduced every day. In ten years' time, many of these altcoins may vanish while others flourish.

A familiar example of vanishing risk is the dot-com bubble. In the late 1990s, many people around the world dreamed up businesses that capitalized on the popularity of the Internet. Some, such as Amazon and eBay, succeeded in conquering the world. Many more crashed and burned. Following the path of history, many of the booming cryptocurrencies popping up left and right are destined to bust.

To minimize vanishing risk, you need to analyze the fundamentals of the cryptocurrencies you choose to invest in. Do their goals make sense to you? Are they solving a problem that will continue in the years to come? Who are their partners? You can't vanish the vanishing risk entirely (pun intended), but you can eliminate your exposure to a sudden bust. Check out Chapters 5 and 10 of this minibook for more on analysis.

Regulation risk

One of the initial attractions of cryptocurrencies was their lack of regulation. In the good old days in cryptoland, crypto enthusiasts didn't have to worry about governments chasing them down. All they had was a white paper and a promise. However, as the demand for cryptocurrencies grows, global regulators are scratching their heads on how to keep up — and not lose their shirts to the new economic reality.

REMEMBER

To date, most digital currencies aren't backed by any central government, meaning each country has different standards.

You can divide the cryptocurrency regulation risk into two components, the regulation event risk and the nature of regulation itself:

>> The *regulation event risk* doesn't necessarily mean that the cryptocurrency market is doing poorly. It just means the market participants reacted to an unexpected announcement. In 2018, every seemingly small regulation announcement drove the price of many major cryptocurrencies and created a ton of volatility.

>> At the time of writing, there are no global cryptocurrency regulators, so existing regulations are all over the board. In some countries, such as Japan and the United States, for example, cryptocurrency exchanges are legal as long as they're registered with the financial authorities. Some countries, such as China, have been banning financial institutions from providing cryptocurrency services, and are aggressively shutting down crypto mining and exchanges.

The future of cryptocurrency regulations seems to be bright at the time of this writing, but these regulations may impact the markets in the future. As the markets grow stronger, though, these impacts may turn into isolated events.

Tax risk

When cryptocurrency investing first got popular, hardly anyone was paying taxes on the gains. A lot of underreporting was going on. However, as the market gets more regulated, the authorities may become stricter on taxation. Since 2014, the U.S. Internal Revenue Service has viewed Bitcoin and other cryptocurrencies as property, despite the fact that they have the word *currencies* in them. Therefore, transactions using altcoins are subject to capital gains tax.

If you live in the United States or are a U.S. citizen, tax risk involves the chance that the authorities may make unfavorable changes in tax laws, such as limitation of deductions, increase in tax rates, and elimination of tax exemptions. In other countries, tax risk can get more complicated. For example, at the time of this writing, the Philippines hasn't clearly established whether the Bureau of Internal Revenue will treat cryptocurrencies as equities, property, or capital gains.

REMEMBER

Although virtually all investments are vulnerable to increases in tax rates, cryptocurrency taxation is a fuzzy area. Most regulators can't even agree on the basic concept of what a token represents!

And of course, different countries, different rules. Some people have been hit hard by taxes when moving from one country to another, or when the U.S. Congress made changes to tax laws. Doing your due diligence on taxation before developing your investment strategy is crucial. Flip to Chapter 15 of this minibook for more details on taxes in relation to cryptocurrencies.

Exploring Risk Management Methods

The only way you can achieve your investment goals is to invest at a risk level consistent with your risk tolerance assessment. That's why it's so important to explore methods that help you calculate your unique risk tolerance. You can measure your risk tolerance by considering objective measures like your investment goals, your time horizon for each goal, your need for liquidity, and so on. You can increase your risk tolerance by setting longer-term goals, adding to your savings by using methods other than online investing, and lowering your need for current liquidity.

These things are certainly easier said than done, especially considering you never know when you're gonna get hit financially. The following sections provide guidance on how to manage risk by building an emergency fund, being patient with your investments, and diversifying.

TIP

Check out this master class on the Invest Diva website. This class explains how you can calculate your personal risk tolerance, and gives you a collection of analysis tools and questionnaires to help make your money work for you: `https://learn.investdiva.com/free-webinar-3-secrets-to-making-your-money-work-for-you`. See the nearby sidebar for more information, too.

MEASURING YOUR OWN RISK TOLERANCE

Risk tolerance has two main components:

- Your willingness to risk
- Your ability to risk

A financial planner is likely to have you fill out a risk tolerance questionnaire that measures your willingness to risk. This questionnaire evaluates your willingness to take on risk by asking about risk issues. It can help you determine whether you are risk averse or risk tolerant. A *risk-averse* investor requires significantly more return in order to consider investing in a higher-risk investment. A *risk-tolerant* investor is more willing to accept risk for a small increase in return.

However, to really get an understanding about the amount you can invest in the markets, you must also find out your ability to risk based on your unique financial situation and living circumstances. To calculate your risk tolerance, you must prepare your financial statements and analyze some ratios such as

- **Your emergency fund ratio:** You can calculate this by dividing your accessible cash by your monthly necessary spending. The result must be greater than 6.
- **Your housing ratio:** Divide your housing costs by your gross pay. If you live in the United States, the result must be below 28 percent.
- **Your debt ratio:** This one calculates your total debt divided by your total assets. The benchmark varies depending on your age and financial goals.
- **Your net worth ratio:** You can calculate this by dividing your net worth (which is all your assets minus your debt) by your total assets.

Using these ratios and comparing them to benchmark numbers, you can then fill out a simple questionnaire to figure out your risk tolerance.

Build your emergency fund first

Kiana tells this story simply to illustrate the importance of having an emergency fund, no matter what you're investing in or what your strategy is:

> My husband and I were exposed to an unpredicted financial burden. After a year of financial success for both of us, we went ahead and upgraded our budget, bought a new house in an awesome neighborhood, and added some luxury expenses we normally wouldn't go after. It was good times!

Then the unexpected tax law change in the United States put us in a higher tax bracket than usual and took away some of our previously sought tax exemptions and deductions. Right after that, our daughter, Jasmine, was born, and our plans to have our parents take care of her for the first six months fell through because of sudden health issues on both sides of the family. As the saying goes, when it rains, it pours — figuratively and literally. Our area got hit by a few storms, which flooded our basement, damaged our trees, and dropped a few branches on our house. We needed an additional budget for the damages.

Thanks to our emergency fund, we were able to overcome this financially challenging time and turn our focus back on raising our little bundle of joy. Of course, we had to rebuild the fund from scratch.

TIP

You can calculate your emergency fund by dividing the value of your total immediately accessible cash by your necessary monthly expenses. That will give you the number of months you can survive with no additional cash flow. The result *must* be greater than six months. But the more the merrier. For more on risk tolerance calculation, visit https://learn.investdiva.com/free-webinar-3-secrets-to-making-your-money-work-for-you.

REMEMBER

You must have an emergency fund before creating an investment portfolio, let alone adding cryptocurrencies to it.

Be patient

The risks involved with cryptocurrencies are slightly different from those of other, more established markets such as equities and precious metals. However, you can use similar methods for managing your portfolio risk regardless of your investments.

The most common reason many traders lose money online is the fantasy of getting rich quick. Kiana can say with confidence (verifiably) that the vast majority of Invest Diva's long-term students made money, and in many cases a lot of money. The key has been patience.

"Patience is a profitable virtue" is the mantra of Kiana's investment group. The majority of their portfolio holdings had been equities and forex, but the same has been true of Bitcoin holders. It took years (nine years, to be exact) for early Bitcoin enthusiasts to make any return on their holdings. And although a bit of a bubble occurred in 2017, nothing is stopping the markets from reaching and surpassing existing all-time-high levels in the coming years.

The patience mantra doesn't help only long-term investors. It also goes for traders and speculators. Very often, that investment or speculative position you took may go down or sideways for what seems like forever. Sooner or later, the market will take note of the sentiment and either erase losses or create new buy opportunities.

In Figure 2-2, you can see the role patience can play in an investor's returns. Of course, you'd love for the markets to just march up to your profit-target (that is, exit) price level straightaway. But more often than not, it just doesn't work that way.

>> The chart on the left shows a fantasy most traders have when they buy an asset. They hope the price will march up toward their profit target within their trading time frame, whether short-term or long-term, and make them money.

>> The chart on the right shows the reality. Traders and investors alike often see a lot of dips in the price before the market reaches their profit target. Some investors panic on the dips and call it quits. But in the end, those who were patient and held their position through the rough times win. This can be true for both short-term and long-term investors, so the chart's time frame doesn't really matter.

FIGURE 2-2:
Demonstrating why patience is a profitable virtue.

Source: InvestDiva.com

Success follows a bumpy road. Your portfolio may even turn into negative territory at times. However, if you've done your due diligence of analyzing your investment, you must make time your friend to see long-term profit. See Chapter 12 of this minibook for full details on long-term investing strategies.

A great example of this idea is the crash of 2008. Almost all markets around the world, including the U.S. stock market, dropped like a hot rock because of economic issues such as the mortgage crisis. Most people panicked and started to get out of their investments with massive losses. Had they given it some (well, a lot of) patience, they would've seen their portfolios in positive territory in around five years. By 2018, they would've more than doubled the returns on the very same investments.

Diversify outside and inside your cryptocurrency portfolio

Chapter 1 of this minibook defines diversification as the "don't put all your eggs in one basket" rule, and this age-old investing advice remains true to the revolutionary cryptocurrency market. Besides diversifying your portfolio by adding different assets such as stocks, bonds, or exchange-traded funds (ETFs), diversification within your cryptocurrency portfolio is also important. (See Chapter 5 of this minibook for some diversification ideas.)

For example, Bitcoin is perhaps the celebrity of all cryptocurrencies, so everyone wants to get hold of it. But Bitcoin is also the oldest cryptocurrency, so it has some unresolvable problems. Every day, younger and better-performing cryptocurrencies make their way into the market and offer exciting opportunities. (We aren't saying younger is better in all facets of life. We're talking about cryptocurrencies here, not people!)

Besides age, you can group cryptocurrencies in several different ways for diversification purposes. Here are some examples (see Book 1, Chapter 4 for full details):

>> **Major cryptocurrencies by market cap:** This category includes the ones in the top ten. At the time of this writing, these options include Bitcoin, Ethereum, Tether, and Binance Coin.

>> **Transactional cryptocurrencies:** This group is the original category for cryptocurrencies. Transactional cryptocurrencies are designed to be used as money and exchanged for goods and services. Bitcoin and Litecoin are examples of well-known cryptos on this list.

>> **Platform cryptocurrencies:** These cryptocurrencies are designed to get rid of middlemen, create markets, and even launch other cryptocurrencies.

Ethereum is one of the biggest cryptos in this category. It provides a backbone for future applications. NEO is another prime example. Such cryptocurrencies are generally considered good long-term investments because they rise in value as more applications are created on their blockchain.

>> **Privacy cryptocurrencies:** These options are similar to transactional cryptocurrencies, but they're heavily focused toward transaction security and anonymity. Examples include Monero, Zcash, and Dash.

>> **Application-specific cryptocurrencies:** One of the trendiest types of cryptos, application-specific cryptocurrencies serve specific functions and solve some of the world's biggest problems. Some examples of such cryptos are Vechain (used for supply chain applications), IOTA (Internet of Things applications), and Cardano (cryptocurrency scalability, privacy optimizations, and so on). Some get super-specific, such as Mobius, also known as Stripe for the blockchain industry, which was seeking to resolve the payment issues in the agriculture industry in 2018. Depending on the specifics of each project, a number of these cryptos may prove highly successful. You can pick the ones that are solving issues closer to your heart; just be sure to analyze their usability, application performance, and project team properly.

REMEMBER

One key problem the cryptocurrency market faces when it comes to diversification is that the whole market appears to be extremely correlated. The majority of cryptocurrencies go up when the market sentiment turns bullish (upward), and vice versa. Despite this tendency, you can diversify away risk in a crypto-only portfolio by adding more crypto assets to your portfolio. By investing in multiple crypto assets, you can spread out the amount of risk you're exposed to instead of having all the volatility of the portfolio come from one or a few assets. Flip to Chapter 5 of this minibook for the full scoop on diversification in cryptocurrencies.

Chapter **3**

Cryptocurrency Exchanges and Brokers

After you've familiarized yourself with cryptocurrencies' risks and rewards (see Chapters 1 and 2 of this minibook) and have decided that cryptocurrency investing is right for you, you're ready to go crypto shopping! As you may guess, most of crypto shopping, investing, and trading occurs online; after all, we're talking about digital assets. You can pay cash to purchase digital currencies, but such transactions are uncommon. If you have a friend who became a crypto millionaire and is looking to sell some crypto assets, for example, you could simply give that person your cash in exchange for the cryptocurrencies.

The most popular way to buy cryptocurrencies, though, is to go directly through an online cryptocurrency exchange. However, depending on your cryptocurrency investing goals, you may need to consider alternative methods. For example, if you're an active crypto trader, you may find a traditional cryptocurrency exchange or a broker easier to use. But if you just want to buy some cryptos and park them in your wallet, a trusted online/local exchange can do the job. This chapter explains different types of exchanges, brokers, and other cryptocurrency providers and shows you how to choose the right ones for your cryptocurrency goals.

REMEMBER

Choosing a method to get your hands on these hot digital assets can be a lengthy process. However, with the changing regulatory stance, increasing adoption and acceptance, and overall market confidence in cryptocurrencies, the hard work may very well pay off. Regardless of the method you use to purchase cryptocurrencies, you must have a cryptocurrency wallet ready to store your digital assets. You find out all you need to know about cryptocurrency wallets in Book 1, Chapter 3.

Distinguishing Crypto Exchanges

A *cryptocurrency exchange* is also called a *digital currency exchange,* or DCE for short. It's a web service that can help people exchange their cash into cryptocurrencies and vice versa. Most exchanges are more focused on providing services to help you exchange a cryptocurrency such as Bitcoin into other digital currencies like Ethereum, Litecoin, and so on.

Most exchanges operate online, but a number of brick-and-mortar businesses do exist. These exchanges provide services to exchange traditional payment methods and cryptocurrencies. Those options are similar to the currency exchange booths at international airports where you exchange your country's money into the currency of the country you're visiting.

REMEMBER

The most distinguished forms of cryptocurrency exchanges are the following:

>> **Centralized cryptocurrency exchange (CEX):** CEXs are similar to traditional stock exchanges.

>> **Decentralized cryptocurrency exchange (DEX):** DEXs aim to stay true to the pure philosophy behind the cryptocurrency industry.

>> **Hybrid cryptocurrency exchange:** Hybrid exchanges are known to be the next-generation crypto trading marketplace. They combine the best of CEXs and DEXs.

The following sections give you the lowdown on CEXs, DEXs, and hybrid exchanges, as well as some guidance on choosing an exchange.

Centralized exchanges

Centralized exchanges are like traditional stock exchanges. The buyers and sellers come together, and the exchange plays the role of a middleman. These exchanges typically charge a commission to facilitate the transactions made between the buyers and the sellers. In the cryptoworld, *centralize* means "to trust somebody else to handle your money."

Here's how a centralized exchange typically works:

1. You give your money to the exchange.

2. The exchange holds it for you (like a bank or a trusted middleman).

3. You watch the prices of the available cryptocurrencies on the exchange.

4. Depending on the exchange, you can trade your *fiat* currency (a traditional currency, like the U.S. dollar) for a cryptocurrency (like Bitcoin). With most exchanges, however, you find better luck exchanging two cryptocurrencies for one another. Find out more about cryptocurrency pairings in Chapter 5 of this minibook.

5. You place your order.

6. The exchange finds a seller to match your buy order. If you're selling, the exchange finds you a buyer.

7. Tada! You just crypto shopped on an exchange.

Most centralized crypto exchanges have crypto/crypto pairings. But not all of them provide fiat/crypto pairings.

>> A *crypto/crypto pairing* involves exchanging one cryptocurrency (like Bitcoin) for another cryptocurrency (like Ethereum).

>> A *fiat/crypto pairing* involves exchanging a traditional currency (like the U.S. dollar) for a cryptocurrency (like Bitcoin).

We dig into the exchanges that offer these pairings in the following sections.

One of the main issues with centralized cryptocurrency exchanges is their vulnerability to hacks. In some past hacking scandals, however, the exchange has paid the customers back out-of-pocket. That's why choosing a centralized exchange wisely, knowing it has the financial ability to combat hackers and pay you in case it gets hacked, is important. Of course, with the popularity of cryptocurrencies, more centralized cryptocurrency exchanges are bound to pop up in the market. Some will succeed, and some may fail. Therefore, you need to pick your crypto shop wisely. Read more about methods for picking the best exchange later in this chapter.

Centralized exchanges offering fiat/crypto pairings

If you're new to crypto investing, starting at an exchange that offers fiat/crypto pairings may make the most sense. That's precisely the reason why exchanges that provide this service are so popular. At the time of this writing, some of the most popular centralized exchanges that offer fiat/crypto pairings include the following:

>> **Coinbase:** This exchange supports Bitcoin (BTC), Bitcoin Cash (BCH), Litecoin (LTC), and Ethereum (ETH). On the fiat currency side, you can use the U.S. dollar (USD), the euro (EUR), and the British pound (GBP), depending on where you're located. Here's Kiana's referral link for you, so that you both get some free Bitcoin as a gift: www.coinbase.com/join/59d39a7610351 d00d40189f0.

>> **Bittrex:** Based in Seattle, this fast-growing exchange supports the U.S. dollar (USD), Bitcoin (BTC), Ethereum (ETH), Tether (USDT), and a variety of other pairings. You can check them out at https://bittrex.com/.

>> **Kraken:** Kraken has a variety of crypto/fiat pairings with more than just the U.S. dollar (USD) and the euro (EUR); you can view the list on the exchange's website. Check them out at https://www.kraken.com/.

>> **Gemini:** Gemini is based in New York with high regulation standards in the United States. It supports Bitcoin (BTC), Ethereum (ETH), Zcash (ZEC), and the U.S. dollar (USD). Check them out at https://gemini.com/.

However, as explained later in this chapter, you need to consider other characteristics of an exchange beyond its fiat/crypto pairings before choosing one.

Centralized exchanges offering crypto/crypto pairings

Some centralized crypto exchanges provide only crypto/crypto pairings. Some of the most popular ones at the time of this writing include the following:

>> **Binance:** Binance has been one of the fastest-growing exchanges and offers a mobile app. Kiana uses it for her crypto investments. Here's her link for you: www.binance.com/?ref=18381915.

>> **KuCoin:** This fast-growing exchange supports a variety of cryptos found on its website at www.kucoin.com/#/. It also offers a mobile app.

Decentralized exchanges

A *decentralized cryptocurrency exchange* (DEX) is an exchange that doesn't rely on a middleman to hold your funds. It's a marketplace where buyers and sellers come together and process the transactions directly between one another. In other words, DEXs facilitate peer-to-peer trades.

TECHNICAL STUFF

On a decentralized exchange, you can buy and sell your crypto assets directly to and from other market participants. You are able to make the deals using smart contracts and atomic swaps. *Smart contracts,* as explained on Investopedia, are "self-executing contracts where the terms of the agreement between buyer and seller are directly written into lines of code." They're the underlying technology for *atomic swaps,* which enable the exchange of one cryptocurrency for another without using centralized exchanges. With the DEX, smart contracts, and atomic swaps, instead of giving your cryptocurrencies to the CEX, you'll give them to an escrow that's centralized by the network running the exchange. Escrow still exists because transactions take as long as five days to clear. As a buyer, you'll have your cash taken out of your account immediately, although the funds aren't moved to the seller's account until the crypto transaction clears.

You may think that a decentralized exchange makes more sense to buy and sell cryptocurrencies on because the whole market is often billed as decentralized. Heck, cryptocurrencies became popular because they allow you to become your own bank and be in charge of your own assets. That's why many DEX fans argue that if you utilize centralized exchanges, you're essentially jeopardizing the whole point behind using cryptocurrencies.

The following sections give you more information on some of the issues facing DEXs, plus a rundown of some noteworthy DEX options.

Potential problems

Although DEXs may replace centralized exchanges completely in the future, at this point decentralized exchanges have their own problems.

WARNING

Decentralized cryptocurrency exchanges are harder to hack. On the flip side, you're more vulnerable to locking yourself out of your money. That means if you forget your login info, you may get your account locked because the system thinks you're a hacker! Other problems with DEXs include low volumes and low liquidity. *Liquidity* refers to how fast you can buy or sell cryptocurrencies on the marketplace. Because DEXs are less popular than centralized exchanges (at least for now), you may face more difficulty finding someone to match your buy/sell orders on a DEX. This issue is a vicious cycle because as long as DEXs are less popular, their liquidity remains low. As long as the liquidity is low, DEXs may remain less popular. That's why, at least for now, centralized exchanges are more popular than DEXs.

Additionally, most DEXs don't offer services to deposit or withdraw fiat currencies such as the U.S. dollar. They can also be expensive and slow. Everything from canceling orders to transferring crypto requires paying a fee and waiting for block confirmations — at least a few minutes, sometimes hours.

Popular decentralized exchanges

Regardless of possible DEX issues, here are some of the most popular decentralized cryptocurrency exchanges as of 2021:

>> **Uniswap:** A decentralized, Ethereum-based exchange that allows users to swap ERC-20 tokens. As of this writing, it has over 5,500 tokens available for trade, and charges a 0.3% fee for swapping tokens. (www.uniswap.org)

>> **SushiSwap:** Initially a copy of Uniswap's open-source code. SushiSwap's native token is called SUSHI, and holders can vote and propose SushiSwap changes. With about 1,400 tokens available for trade, and a trading fee of 0.3%, you might be tempted to use Uniswap for their additional token collection. SushiSwap is a rising star and the value of the SUSHI token is solid. (www.sushi.com)

>> **PancakeSwap:** Also a copy of Uniswap's open-source code. PancakeSwap was altered to operate on the Binance Smart Chain instead of the Ethereum blockchain. You can swap about 300 tokens, and it has a lower trading fee of 0.2% as of this writing. PancakeSwap also has a token, appropriately named CAKE, which allows users to control the platform through a governance-based voting process. (www.pancakeswap.finance)

>> **1inch:** A unique DEX that acts as an aggregator for other decentralized exchanges. Think of how Expedia, FlightHub, and KAYAK scrape the Internet looking for travel deals, and shift that to the world of decentralized exchanges. 1inch will look for the best deals within your desired trading parameters. (www.app.1inch.io)

Such DEXs are the purest form of decentralized exchanges. They're entirely *on-chain*, which means all orders interact with each other directly through the blockchain (see Book 2 for more about this technology). However, as we discuss in the preceding section, these kinds of exchanges have their own sets of problems. Many of those problems don't exist in the centralized cryptocurrency exchanges that we describe earlier.

Hybrid exchanges

The hybrid approach to cryptocurrency exchanges aims to merge benefits from both centralized and decentralized exchanges to give consumers the best of both worlds. More specifically, hybrids seek to provide the functionality and liquidity of a CEX with the privacy and security of a DEX. Many believe such exchanges are the real future of the cryptocurrency trading experience.

TECHNICAL STUFF

Hybrid exchanges look to provide cryptocurrency trading services with the speed, ease, and liquidity that institutional users are used to in traditional exchanges. A hybrid exchange connects its centralized elements to a network of decentralized elements. This approach allows users to access the trading platform as they do in a CEX and then engage in a peer-to-peer trading activity as they do in a DEX. The hybrid then provides confirmation and record transactions on the blockchain.

Hybrids are also called *semi-decentralized exchanges* because they incorporate both on-chain and off-chain components. An *off-chain* transaction moves your cryptocurrency value outside of the blockchain.

The first ever hybrid exchange was Qurrex (`https://qurrex.com`), which launched in 2018. The Qurrex team got together in 2016, consisting of experts who had years of experience working in the forex (foreign exchange) markets, developers of trade terminals, and founders of successfully operating stock and futures exchanges. They all saw the significant potential in applying the best practices of the traditional exchanges to create a new generation of cryptocurrency exchange, providing a harmonious merging of centralized and decentralized elements.

Another hybrid cryptocurrency exchange that's gaining attention is NEXT. exchange (`https://next.exchange/`). If you own its native token, NEXT, you can trade between fiat and crypto pairs such as Bitcoin (BTC) versus the euro (EUR), or Ethereum (ETH) versus the U.S. dollar (USD).

How to choose an exchange

In the preceding sections, you may notice the Internet has no lack of cryptocurrency exchanges. And more variations of exchanges are bound to make their way into the market. Which type of exchange is best for you: CEX, DEX, or hybrid? Even then, which one of the many exchanges in each category should you choose?

Although we can't give you a solid answer for these questions, we can offer ways to cycle through some of the most important characteristics in an exchange to help you make the best decision. The following sections contain a few things to consider when choosing a cryptocurrency exchange.

TIP

First-time traders are better off doing their research on the cryptocurrencies first and then choosing an exchange. But once you become more experienced, you can simply choose cryptos to trade based on the current market conditions.

TIP

Diversification is always a good thing. Because many of these exchanges offer different sets of pros and cons, you may be wise to diversify your cryptocurrency activities across a number of exchanges, just as many people do when they go grocery shopping. You may go to one store for its better-quality meat but get all your pasta from another.

Security

REMEMBER

Security is one of the biggest issues in the cryptocurrency industry. Exchanges are at constant risk of hacks, frauds, and pump-and-dump schemes. A *pump-and-dump scheme* is when someone encourages investors to buy a crypto asset in order to artificially inflate its value (the "pumping" part) and then sells their own assets at a high price (the "dumping" part). That's why one of the most important things to do before choosing your crypto shop (or shops) is to do your research. Word-of-mouth and online reviews on sites like Reddit or news organizations like Forbes are some of the ways that can help you choose a legitimate and secure platform. Some other safety features you must check on the exchange include the following:

>> **Two-factor authentication (2FA).** *Two-factor authentication* is a method of confirming your claimed identity by using a combination of two different factors: something the exchange knows (like your password) and something it has (like a six-digit number it sends to your mobile phone or your email address for the second step of the verification).

>> **Cold storage for the majority of funds.** This term means the exchange stores your funds offline so that risk of online hacking is lower. Find out more about this feature in Book 1, Chapter 3.

>> **Proof of reserve.** This element requires the exchange to be audited to verify that the total amount of funds held by the exchange matches the amount required to cover an anonymized set of customer balances.

Supported currencies (crypto and otherwise)

When you decide which of the thousands of available cryptocurrencies are right for you, you must make sure your exchange carries them. You can read more about various crypto options in Book 1, Chapter 4.

Additionally, if you're looking to purchase cryptocurrencies for the very first time, you probably need an exchange that allows you to deposit your country's fiat currency.

REMEMBER

As we cover earlier in this chapter, some exchanges use only cryptocurrency for purchases, and some allow you to use fiat currencies such as the U.S. dollar, the euro, or your country's currency.

Liquidity

Without sufficient liquidity, the prices and the speeds of your transactions may be compromised. After you decide which cryptocurrencies you want to purchase, make sure your exchange offers sufficient liquidity and trading volume for fast and easy transactions. Liquidity also ensures that you're able to buy and sell without the cryptocurrency's price being significantly affected by big market movers. The more buyers and sellers there are, the more liquidity that exists.

TIP

The best way to measure an exchange's liquidity is to look up its most recent trading volume. Coinmarketcap.com is one of many cryptocurrency information websites that rank exchanges based on their volume and liquidity.

Fees

Exchanges charge their customers in a number of different ways. It would be great if they didn't, but exchanges aren't charities. Charging customers fees is precisely how they make money to stay in business. The most common method is taking a small percentage of the amount you trade. Most exchanges charge a percentage lower than 1 percent; to stay competitive, some exchanges go as low as around 0.2 percent. Often, a sliding scale decreases the fee percentage as the user's monthly trading volume rises.

REMEMBER

Paying less is always attractive, but prioritize security and liquidity over the fees. Your investment will defeat its purpose if you pay next to nothing on transaction fees and then lose all your funds in a hacker's attack.

Ease of use

This one is especially important for newbies. You want your exchange to provide you with an easy-to-use, intuitive, and fast user interface. This factor also depends on what kind of device you want to use for your cryptocurrency investing activities. If you're always on the go, you may want to choose an exchange with great mobile app services.

A good user experience helps you take more informed and more efficient actions on the exchange. Another benefit of exchanges with great interface and mobile support is that they're more likely to grow more quickly and therefore provide more trading volume and liquidity in their markets.

Location

Depending on where you live, you may find a specific exchange that works better for you in your country than another, more popular one on an international level does. Some of the things to keep in mind are issues like which fiat currency exchanges accept and what fees they charge locals compared to international customers.

Additionally, the location of the exchange dictates the laws it has to comply with. At the time of this writing, many countries don't have any specific regulations on cryptocurrencies. However, if and when they start to regulate, any restrictions may significantly affect your ability to participate in the market through the exchanges in those countries.

Method of payment

Look into the methods of payment the exchange accepts. Some exchanges require deposits by bank transfer, some use PayPal, and some accept credit and debit cards. Typically, the easier it is for you to pay, the more fees you're going to have to pay. For example, many services allow you to pay with a credit or debit card, and you will need to pay for this convenience. (Head to the earlier section, "Fees," for more on fee issues; the later section, "PayPal," has info on that option.) One example of such services is xCoins (https://xcoins.io/?r=62hcz9), which accepts credit cards and PayPal to exchange Bitcoins. They call it "lending," but their concept is similar to buying and selling.

Customer support

Poor customer support was precisely the reason why Kiana decided not to go with one of the major exchanges. We always feel more comfortable knowing that the place we're trusting with our funds has a responsive customer support service. You can check this factor either by directly contacting the customer support department and asking any questions that you haven't been able to find on the exchange's FAQ page or by perusing online cryptocurrency forums like BitcoinTalk (https://bitcointalk.org/). You may find complaints about the exchanges in these forums. However, keep in mind that fast-growing exchanges often combat these complaints by improving their customer service, which is always a good thing.

TIP

Another point you may be able to find on forums is whether an exchange has spurred complaints about locking people out of their accounts. If it has, you may want to consider other options.

Trading options

Trading options are especially important for active and advanced traders. For example, depending on your risk tolerance and financial goals, you may want to have access to certain order types or margin trading. On these occasions, make sure you understand the risks involved with trading activities before getting yourself in trouble.

Transaction limits

Most exchanges have a daily withdrawal/deposit limit. Unless you're an institutional trader who wants to make millions of transactions per day, these restrictions may not be an issue. But these limits are still something you may need to keep in mind depending on your investing style and goals. You can typically find out about the exchanges' transaction limits on their websites without having to create an account.

Considering Brokers

If you're looking to purchase cryptocurrencies online and invest in them as an asset, then cryptocurrency exchanges are the way to go. You can read about these exchanges earlier in the chapter. However, if you're thinking of simply speculating on the price action of cryptocurrencies, then you may want to consider brokers.

As cryptocurrencies have become more popular, some traditional forex currency brokers have started extending their services to cryptos. But keep in mind that the concept of a "broker" doesn't really exist in pure cryptocurrency investing. You can't purchase cryptocurrencies such as Bitcoin through traditional forex brokers. Even though the brokers may carry them, all they're really providing is streaming of a tradable price on their platform. That way, you may be able to take advantage of the market volatility and make (or lose) money based on your speculated trading orders.

This section covers how traditional forex brokers work, the pros and cons of utilizing them in your crypto trading activities, and finally some tips on choosing one.

How brokers work

Traditional forex brokers are market intermediaries who help traders execute trades on their platforms. They're the middlemen between an individual retail trader and networks of big banks. The forex brokers typically get a price from one or multiple banks for a specific currency. They then offer you the best price they've received from their banks. You can then trade your favorite currencies based on the prices that are streaming on your broker's platform.

TECHNICAL STUFF

Such brokers operate on something called *over-the-counter (OTC)* markets. This means that the currencies are traded via a dealer network as opposed to on a centralized exchange. The brokers unload their trading risk to third-party or internal backend warehouses called *liquidity providers*. When it comes to cryptocurrency services on their platforms, these liquidity providers are often cryptocurrency exchanges, which we talk about earlier in this chapter.

WARNING

Forex brokers mainly make money through commission fees, both transparent and hidden. Some brokers even make money when their customers lose money. That's one reason why the forex industry as a whole started getting a bad reputation; some of these brokers were caught by government regulators. You can find out more about forex brokers and the scams involved with the industry in *Invest Diva's Guide to Making Money in Forex* by Kiana Danial: https://learn.investdiva.com/ebook-new-edition-invest-divas-guide-to-making-money-in-forex-31.

The pros and cons of using a broker

REMEMBER

Forex brokers who provide cryptocurrency services have started using hardcore marketing to advertise speculative crypto trading. Here are some of the advantages and disadvantages of trading through a broker as opposed to using a cryptocurrency exchange.

>> **Pro: You get improved liquidity.** Because the brokers get their quotes from multiple exchanges, they're able to provide increased liquidity to customers. That means you have a higher chance of getting your buy/sell orders fulfilled in a timely manner. You also may be able to get a price closer to your initial buy/sell order because the broker has multiple channels to find a buyer and seller to fulfill your order.

>> **Pro: You can start trading immediately.** If you go through an exchange, you sometimes need to wait for days before your account is confirmed. With most brokers, the account confirmation can be quicker.

>> **Con: You can't invest in cryptos as an asset.** By trading through a broker, you're simply speculating on price volatility of the market. You aren't actually purchasing or investing in the cryptocurrency market. This distinction means you don't own your cryptos even if you buy them on the brokerage account.

>> **Con: You don't have access to wallets.** For the same reason as in the preceding point, no real portfolio or wallet is available for you. This fact also means you can't realize your transfers or cryptocurrency acquisitions.

In addition to the preceding pros and cons, some conditions can be both advantages and disadvantages of trading cryptocurrencies through a broker. Of course, if you go to the brokers' websites, they've featured these characteristics as advantages. However, you must understand the risks beneath the surface. Here are a couple of the most common ones.

Pro or con: You can take advantage of a down market

This tricky advantage is one that many brokers advertise. Because you aren't actually purchasing the currencies (fiat or crypto), you can bet on the markets to go down. If the prices do go down as you predicted, you can make money. This process is called *short-selling*. Short-selling is actually available on exchanges and traditional stock markets as well. However, it involves a lot of risk because you need to borrow money from your broker, exchange, or whoever is providing your trading services.

Pro or con: You can trade on leverage

Trading on leverage means borrowing money from your broker to trade. With some brokers, you can open an account with $100 and then use 50-times leverage (or even more), which means you control a $5,000 account with your mere $100! But unless you're Nostradamus or have a crystal ball, using leverage can be problematic because leverage enlarges the risks of gains and losses by the same magnitude.

Here's how leverage can make or break your account: Say you have a $1,000 account. You place a trade order without using any leverage, and you end up making $50. If you had used a 10-time leverage, you would've made $500 instead. That's awesome!

But (and this is a very big *but*) on the flip side, if the markets go against your speculation when you're trading on that leverage, you lose $500 rather than $50, wiping out half of your account. Newbie traders often wipe out their accounts completely within the first few days. Sometimes, depending on the broker's policy, investors' losses can even exceed their initial deposits, which means they actually owe the broker money!

REMEMBER

Using leverage can be an advantage if you know what you're doing and you have high enough risk tolerance to be prepared for a worst-case scenario, which means losing part or all of your initial investment through the broker.

How to choose a broker

REMEMBER

The steps in choosing a broker can be very similar to those of choosing an exchange (covered earlier in this chapter). Some additional rules you need to keep in mind when choosing a broker include the following:

>> **Make sure it's regulated.** Each country has strict international regulatory authorities that audit brokers on a regular basis to ensure their security. Your best bet is to make sure the broker is regulated by two or more regulatory bodies in your country. You can find regulation information on brokers' websites.

>> **Consider ease of deposit and withdrawals.** Good brokers will allow you to deposit funds and withdraw your earnings without a hassle. Brokers really have no reason to make it hard for you to withdraw your profits because the only reason they hold your funds is to facilitate trading. (This point is part of the Invest Diva's *Forex Coffee Break Course.*)

>> **Beware of promotions.** Some brokers have discovered that people love discount sales! So they use such promotions to attract customers. Nothing is wrong with promotions, but you must be careful because sometimes brokers use these promotions to push new traders into making risky investments or using unreliable products and signals. That's why you need to do your due diligence and know your broker before you take advantage of a promotion.

TIP

One of the major brokers in this field is eToro (http://partners.etoro.com/A75956_TClick.aspx). Another place to help you with your broker hunt is Forest Park FX (https://forestparkfx.com/?id=UU1UckhZSVN3OW1WNnNuNHIxaH1qUT09). They help you find a broker suitable for you in your location.

Looking at Other Methods for Buying Cryptos

We cover some of the most popular methods to purchase or invest in cryptocurrencies earlier in this chapter. However, these options aren't the only ones. Check out the following sections for a few other handy ways to buy cryptos. (Find out more about where to store your cryptocurrencies after you purchase them in Book 1, Chapter 3.)

REMEMBER

This type of information is constantly subject to change due to cryptocurrencies' volatile state. The best way to stay on top of cryptocurrency news is on websites such as www.newsbtc.com/ and www.coindesk.com/.

Funds

Many people seek exposure to the cryptocurrency market but don't want to invest in a specific cryptocurrency such as Bitcoin or Ripple. They may be looking for an equivalent of a *mutual fund* or an *exchange-traded fund* (ETF), which tracks a basket of different assets such as stocks and indexes. (See Chapter 7 of this minibook for more information.)

The upside of a fund is that it's somewhat diversified. That's because you get to invest in a number of popular cryptos in one fund, without the hassle of selecting just a few. The downside of most funds is their costs and restrictions.

TIP

Until very recently, Bitcoin ETFs were not approved in any country. In 2021, Canada's Purpose Bitcoin ETF was launched and has been incredibly successful. Other countries have approved Bitcoin ETFs as well. Americans do have options to buy some of these ETFs, but many will probably wait until a U.S. Bitcoin ETF is finally approved.

Credit card

Financial services like Coinmama allow you to buy cryptocurrencies like Bitcoin (BTC), Ethereum (ETH), Litecoin (LTC), Bitcoin Cash (BCH), Cardano (ADA), Qtum (QTUM), and Ethereum Classic (ETC) using a credit card. But they are not available in all countries yet at the time of this writing. You can check them out at `http://go.coinmama.com/visit/?bta=53881&nci=5360`.

PayPal

Earlier in this chapter, we touch on various methods of payment that cryptocurrency exchanges may offer, including transferring money from your bank account and using your credit or debit card. PayPal is another form of online payment system that supports money transfers and serves as an electronic alternative to traditional money.

PayPal.com allows you to buy cryptocurrencies from within their app or website. You can even buy certain products using the crypto funds that are stored within your PayPal crypto balance. As of this writing, U.S. PayPal users can buy, sell, hold, and pay at checkout using Bitcoin, Ethereum, Bitcoin Cash, and Litecoin. Hopefully, PayPal's crypto services will be extended to other countries in the near future.

Cash

TIP

The process for paying cash to buy cryptocurrencies such as Bitcoin is to find someone who owns cryptocurrencies and is willing to sell them in exchange for cash. Here are a couple of options:

>> You can find buyers and sellers of cryptocurrencies for cash at `https://localbitcoins.com/?ch=w7ct`. On this website, you can sign up for free, enter the amount you're looking to buy or sell, and choose your preferred payment method — in this case, cash — to find a counterpart.

>> Other sites connect buyers and sellers using a method where the seller provides bank details that let the buyer make a cash deposit at the bank. You must keep the receipt to provide proof, and the seller can send you the Bitcoins. Some options in this vein include https://www.bitquick.co/ (part of Athena Bitcoin based in Chicago) and https://paxful.com/ (based in Delaware).

Note: If you do an Internet search on how to buy cryptocurrencies with cash, you may get directed to a mobile app called Square Cash, which is indeed an app that helps you buy and sell Bitcoin from friends! However, this isn't the type of cash payment we're talking about in this section.

Cryptocurrency ATMs

Cryptocurrency ATMs are becoming more popular. Many individuals are even trying to start their own such machines to make passive income. Bitcoin (and other cryptocurrency) ATMs work like any other ATM. The first step in the process is to find one near you, something you can do via a quick online search or at https://coinatmradar.com/.

Several different brands of ATMs exist, with differing methods of verifying your ID and *cryptocurrency address* (a code in your cryptocurrency wallet). Naturally, you need to do some research to find a secure and trustworthy ATM with a good online reputation. One simple research method is to enter the ATM name on Google or Bing, and check whether it has any negative press.

The process of buying cryptocurrencies at an ATM may vary from machine to machine. However, here are the general steps most ATMs require:

1. **Verify your identity (using an ID card, for example).**

2. **Select the cryptocurrency you want to purchase.**

3. **Provide a cryptocurrency address for deposit.**

   Book 1, Chapter 3 has more on this address.

4. **Select the amount of cryptocurrency you want to purchase.**

5. **Insert cash into the cryptocurrency ATM.**

6. **Confirm the operation.**

REMEMBER

Some cryptocurrency ATMs even provide services to sell as well as buy digital coins. Keep in mind that these types of cryptocurrency machines aren't ATMs, which help you connect with your bank account, in the traditional sense. Instead, they're machines that are connected to the Internet and direct you to a cryptocurrency exchange to provide you with your cryptocurrency.

Chapter **4**

Identifying Top-Performing Cryptocurrencies

Book 1, Chapter 4 is a huge window to all the different categories of cryptocurrencies because this whole industry isn't just about Bitcoin or a few other famous cryptos you may have already heard of. Having so many options to choose from is exciting! But just like dating in the digital age, having too many options can be tricky; you're always keeping an eye open for the next big thing.

The good news is that you can have multiple "right" cryptocurrencies for you. But swiping through so many cryptocurrencies can become challenging, especially if you don't know exactly what you're looking for.

This chapter guides you through finding your best crypto matches by introducing you to Kiana's golden strategy development method, the Invest Diva Diamond Analysis (IDDA).

Introducing the Invest Diva Diamond Analysis

Most individual traders use one or two methods for analyzing the markets before pulling the trigger and actually executing an investment strategy. For example, most newbie investors rely on things like technical analysis and their favorite economic news anchors on TV. Unfortunately, depending on only one type of analysis can be incredibly dangerous.

Enter the Invest Diva Diamond Analysis. The IDDA suggests analyzing the markets from five different points, as shown in Figure 4-1:

1. Fundamental analysis

2. Sentimental (market sentiment) analysis

3. Technical analysis

4. Capital analysis (personal risk management)

5. Overall analysis

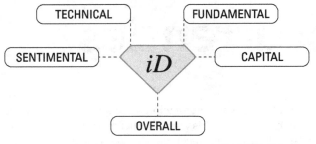

FIGURE 4-1:
Five points
of the Invest
Diva Diamond
Analysis.

© John Wiley & Sons, Inc.

Flip to Chapter 2 of this minibook to read about risk management (part of the capital analysis point); for overall analysis and the latest strategies in the market, visit https://learn.investdiva.com/services. In the rest of this chapter, we discuss fundamentals and market sentiment analysis and introduce technical analysis to help you pick the right cryptocurrencies for your portfolio. Here's a brief overview of these concepts:

>> **Fundamental analysis:** As a fundamental analyst, you look at data from facts to rumors to decide whether that coin is worth buying.

>> **Sentimental analysis:** *Market sentiment* gauges the emotions and attitudes of traders in the market about a specific security. Using sentimental analysis, even non-animal-lovers in the investing world compare market expectations to bulls and bears.

REMEMBER

If traders expect upward price movement of a specific security, the sentiment is said to be *bullish.* On the contrary, if the market sentiment is *bearish,* most traders expect downward price movement.

>> **Technical analysis:** As a technical analyst, you look at how a cryptocurrency's price has been performing, and then you make an investment decision that's right for you. More specifically, you analyze the price action of your favorite cryptocurrency to see the best time to jump into a relationship and a good time to call it quits. You can see the history of the crypto price actions on something called *charts* that are available on your cryptocurrency exchange. (Head to Chapter 10 of this minibook to discover all the dirty secrets about technical analysis methods.)

TECHNICAL STUFF

Kiana introduced the Invest Diva Diamond Analysis investment strategy development method in *Invest Diva's Guide to Making Money in Forex* (McGraw-Hill Education). It then became the key strategy for all their clients and students, from investing.com and Nasdaq to their educational products for universities in New York and at the Invest Diva website (`https://learn.investdiva.com/free-webinar-3-secrets-to-making-your-money-work-for-you`).

Using Fundamental Analysis to Pick Cryptocurrencies

Fundamental analysis is the art of using all the gossip, stories, and facts about a cryptocurrency, its financial situation, and upcoming risk events that may move the market. Going back to the earlier dating metaphor, finding the right crypto category is like picking your type in a significant other — except in this case, you should most certainly think with your brain. And maybe a little bit with your gut feeling. But nothing more than that. Here are some methods you can use to cherry-pick the best cryptos for you.

Go with what you know

Going with what you know is a golden yet simple method also used in the stock market. If you've already been exposed to certain types of cryptocurrencies or, better yet, used them in real life and have liked their performance, consider adding them to your portfolio. In the stock market, for example, many newbie investors make several profitable investments by simply observing their own buying habits. If they prefer to buy from healthier fast-food services like Chipotle (CMG on the New York Stock Exchange, or NYSE) rather than McDonald's (NYSE: MCD), they may consider adding CMG to their portfolio.

Similarly, say you notice that your favorite online store has already added a cryptocurrency payment option to its checkout page and you place an order with it smoothly. That success may be an indication that the trading volume for that cryptocurrency will increase in the future, and the crypto may become a valuable asset for your portfolio.

Choose the right categories

Book 1, Chapter 4 covers crypto categories and where you can find them. Certain categories perform better at certain times in the overall market, not just the crypto market. So, for example, if you notice that the financial technology (fintech) sector is heading higher in equities and that everyone is talking about artificial intelligence (AI), you may want to consider browsing through the AI category and finding cryptocurrencies that are involved with it.

Another way to pick the best categories for medium-term investments is to choose from categories that are already outperforming the overall market. We're not talking about a category that did well just today but rather something that either has been doing well for a few months or even years or is showing signs of picking up. You can pick the hottest category as your top pick and then add on the second and third ones for diversification purposes. For more about diversification, see Chapter 5 of this minibook.

For more-up-to-date information on the hottest cryptocurrency categories, consider joining the Premium Investment Group at `https://learn.investdiva.com/join-group`.

REMEMBER

The cryptocurrency categories may not always follow the rest of the market. Because cryptocurrency is a very new industry to begin with, you may find opportunities in it that you may not necessarily find in the more traditional equities market. Heck, the crypto industry may turn into your safety net if the stock market crashes.

TIP

Exchange-traded funds (ETFs) normally consist of a basket of a number of assets in the same category. They're super-popular in the equities market because they make the selection process much easier. They're also cheaper to purchase than their big, fancy hedge-fund equivalents, mutual funds. Cryptocurrency ETFs became available to the public in 2021, and you can view and compare their charts to identify the best-performing crypto categories. You can find out more about ETFs in Chapter 7 of this minibook and at https://www.investdiva.com/investing-guide/category/etf-trading/.

Check out cryptos' websites

Whether you have a number of cryptocurrencies in mind based on your own experience or you've picked a category and now want to choose the best crypto within that sector, you must now start a more detailed analysis on your finalists.

If you've ever watched *The Bachelor* or *The Bachelorette* on TV (guilty as charged), you're probably already familiar with the process. You start out with around 30 potential matches for your portfolio. By the time you're down to the three or four finalists, you're ready to see what their worlds are all about. In the cryptocurrency world, the company's website is the equivalent of the TV contestant's hometown dates. Here are a few ideas to consider when you're picking your crypto sweethearts that don't involve visiting their high schools and getting a grilling from their families.

Flip through their white papers

A *white paper* is something like a business proposal for new cryptocurrencies. It includes everything potential investors need to know about the crypto, such as technology, purpose, financial details, and so on. More-established cryptocurrencies may already have a page that breaks down all this critical information into easy-to-understand video clips and cool infographics on tabs titled "About" or "How It Works." For others, you may just need to find the white paper on the website and try to digest the information by reading. The good news is that white papers are often written in a language that people who aren't experts in the field can understand.

Identify their teams

No one really knows who created Bitcoin, but the rest of the cryptocurrencies out there normally have a team behind them who guide the company and its blockchain technology (see Book 2). The team behind the crypto is important even if its platform is completely open source, which means anyone can access and modify it.

When you invest in anything, whether it's stocks, a new start-up, or a hot date, understanding the background and how it came to life can play a major role. Here are some things to look for in the management:

>> Bios

>> Resumes

>> Experience in the field

In addition to the core management, also check the backgrounds of the members of the board of advisors if the company has one. You normally can find this information on the company's website, under tabs with labels like "About Us" or "Our Team."

When you invest in a cryptocurrency, you're essentially investing in a start-up company and an entrepreneur. Sometimes these entrepreneurs are young with no qualifying resume, just like Facebook's Mark Zuckerberg or Ethereum founder Vitalik Buterin. That's when the creator's personality can become a factor in your decision making. As Mark Cuban (*Shark Tank* investor and Dallas Mavericks owner) told CNBC, "When you invest in an entrepreneur, you get the personality. And if that's not appropriate or you don't think it's right, buy another stock" (or in this case, crypto).

Browse their partnerships

If you're not willing to take a lot of risk, seeing who in the industry has put their trust in the hands of the cryptocurrency you're considering buying is very important. More established cryptocurrencies have been able to team up with traditional giants like IBM and Microsoft and banks like Goldman Sachs. These companies have expert analytic teams perform due diligence before jumping on board with new investments and partnerships. Having reputable partners can be a sign that the company is solid and on the right track to get ahead of the competition.

Another good thing about having partners in the traditional world is that the cryptocurrency may have a higher chance of getting accepted by the masses. If a cryptocurrency has established partnerships with other companies, they are normally listed under a tab named "Our Partners" or "About Us."

Familiarize yourself with their technology

Many cryptocurrencies are tokens from blockchain companies with multiple products. Well-developed websites walk you through their technology and their products in a not-so-intimidating way. The more you get to know the products and the technology behind the cryptocurrency, the more easily you can make your decision about the finalists on your cryptocurrency list. Book 1, Chapter 2 can be your go-to "cryptionary" along the way.

Check out their contribution to society

What problems are your shortlist cryptocurrencies trying to solve? Does it matter to you? Are they just here to get rich quick, or do they have a long-term plan for the betterment of society? Finding an answer to these questions can also help you narrow down your list of finalists. Companies like Ripple describe their social contributions under a subtab called "Ripple for Good." Other companies often use a similar format or simply put their core social contributions first thing on their home page.

Analyze their road maps

Many companies behind cryptocurrencies have sections on their websites dedicated to their road maps: where they come from, what they've achieved, and what they're planning to accomplish in the future. If available, road maps are a great way to discover a ton of fundamental information about the crypto in a few minutes.

Get involved

Here's your lucky seven! Just like dating, the more you get involved, the more you get to know about the dirty secrets. The majority of cryptocurrency platforms love to increase their followings and encourage people to get involved right there on their websites. Depending on the cryptocurrency, getting involved can mean anything from mining (see Book 6) to joining its social forums or even starting a new cryptocurrency project on its blockchain platform (like Ethereum)! Of course, getting involved also means investing more of your time, so you need to find a balance there.

Choosing Cryptos with Sentimental Analysis

After you've done the essential background check on your prospective cryptocurrencies, you can move on to the second point of IDDA, sentimental analysis. *Sentimental analysis* is the study of the love-hate relationship with cryptocurrencies and traders.

Key sentimental elements

Without getting too sentimental, here are some essential elements to check before setting your heart on your favorite cryptocurrencies.

The crypto community

The company behind the cryptocurrency can play a role in the direction the crypto goes, but the network that participates in the currency's blockchain technology (see Book 2) is an important key to its success. Many cryptocurrencies directly depend on the participation of their communities, like miners and developers. Most of the crypto communities have their own forums on places such as the following:

>> Reddit (www.reddit.com/)

>> Bitcointalk (https://bitcointalk.org/)

>> Steemit (https://steemit.com/)

These forums are great not only because they give you a sense of what type of people are involved in the cryptocurrency but also because you can find out more about the cryptocurrency itself.

TIP

More and more cryptocurrencies use their Telegram channel as a way to communicate with their userbase. To join, you must download the Telegram app on your mobile phone (see https://telegram.org/ for more information).

Exchanges that carry the crypto

REMEMBER

As we discuss in Chapter 3 of this minibook, cryptocurrency exchanges are a big part of the whole ecosystem. You want to make sure that your cryptocurrency exchange carries your cryptos of choice, but choosing cryptos that are listed on many different exchanges is also a good idea. Exchanges choose the cryptocurrencies they carry carefully. Finding your finalists on many different exchanges may be a sign that many exchanges have found those cryptos to be valuable enough to carry. Therefore, the demand for them may be higher, and you may be able to do more with your investment. You can discover which exchanges carry your crypto of choice on websites such as coinmarketcap.com.

For example, say you want to know which exchanges carry Ripple's XRP. After selecting Ripple's XRP on coinmarketcap.com, go the tab labeled "Market," which is located to the right of the Overview tab. There you can view the full list of exchanges that carry XRP.

Volume

TIP

Volume means how much cryptocurrency got traded in a specific time frame. It's important because it tells you how easily you can buy or sell that cryptocurrency. The higher the volume, the more easily you can trade it off. You can check and compare cryptocurrency volume on websites such as `www.cryptocompare.com` and `coinmarketcap.com`, where they show the number of coins that have been traded in the last 24 hours. You can also examine which exchanges had what volume. Generally, the biggest and most popular coins are traded the most. But if you're trying to choose a cryptocurrency within a specific category (and not simply going for the celebrity cryptos), trading volume can be a very important indicator in making your decision.

Coin market capitalization

One of the fastest ways to navigate through cryptocurrencies is to check out their ranking based on their *market capitalization*, or *market cap*. A bigger market cap shows a higher value of all units of a specific cryptocurrency that are for sale right now. This metric can again come in handy when you're trying to select "the one" within a specific category of cryptos. For more on market capitalization analysis, flip to Book 1, Chapter 4.

Circulating supply

Circulating supply (CS) is the number of coins or tokens that people have mined or that companies have generated. The key is that the circulating supply number shows you how many of these coins are currently in the market and that the general public has access to.

You can look at the importance of the CS in a couple of different ways:

>> Some crypto investors believe less is more in terms of the CS. That's if you look at it as an oversupply issue. Any market generally moves based on a principle called *supply and demand*. For example, when stores have a lot of apples and not enough people to buy them, they drop their apple prices because they want to get rid of their stock before it goes bad. The same theory can apply to cryptocurrencies. Although most coins don't have an expiration date (unless the company goes bankrupt, that is), a smaller CS may be more attractive if you're looking to invest short-term to medium-term. Fewer coins available and a higher demand may signal that the prices may go higher in the future.

Identifying Top-Performing Cryptocurrencies

>> On the other hand, a lower CS number may indicate a lack of popularity. Fewer people have put in the effort to mine the coin, which may impact the long-term forecast of the cryptocurrency.

>> In some cases, the CS may not even matter. For example, Ripple's XRP has a circulation supply of almost 40 billion, while Dash has a CS of only 8 million. Meanwhile, they both gained around 3,000 percent in 2017!

You can find out about cryptocurrencies' circulating supply on websites such as coinmarketcap.com.

Total supply

TECHNICAL STUFF

When you add the newly mined cryptocurrencies to the circulating supply (see the preceding section), you get the *total supply* number. In other words, total supply is the total number of coins currently in existence, not just those circulating. For several reasons, some coins are reserved or locked and aren't sold in the public market. Total supply doesn't really impact a coin's price and isn't more important than the circulating supply. We wanted to cover it here in case you come across it on a website and wonder what it is.

Stuff to check in the news

The news has the power to make someone or something incredibly popular. Take reality stars, that whole Yanny/Laurel thing, or the floss dance that became popular thanks to the Instagram sensation @thebackpackkid.

The same thing goes for cryptocurrencies. The media was behind the whole cryptocurrency hype and bullish market sentiment of 2017. Just like you may do a quick cyber check on your potential date before agreeing to meet, you may want to consider looking into the following about your finalist coins.

Recent coverage

TIP

Has your finalist been in the news a lot lately? Is it a hot topic? If the answer is yes, find out whether the news coverage is organic or paid. Of course, crypto companies are aware of the impact of the media, so they pay a ton of money to popular search engines to bring them right up on top of the search results ranking system. Some trustworthy crypto news providers include NewsBTC (www.newsbtc.com), Nasdaq (https://www.nasdaq.com/topic/cryptocurrency), CoinDesk (www.coindesk.com), and of course, Invest Diva (www.investdiva.com/investing-guide/category/cryptocurrencies/).

Another way you can approach this task is to simply go to the "News" tab on your search engine. When you search a topic on Google, for example, you're automatically directed to the "All" tab, which includes everything, from advertisements to news and general information. Find the "News" tab, and you'll get the relevant news coverage that's less likely to be paid ads.

Upcoming events

TIP

You can look for upcoming events in the early stages of finding your crypto soul mate or right at the very end:

>> For the first method, you can check out websites such as `https://coinmarketcal.com/` and `www.newsbtc.com`, and see which cryptos have a busy lineup of announcements and events that may impact the crypto in a positive way. Then take the other approaches we talk about earlier in this chapter to see whether that crypto is right for your portfolio.

>> For the second method, compile your list of finalists, and then either check the cryptocurrencies' websites to see whether they have a blog where they share their upcoming events or check out the third-party crypto calendars for additional information.

Of course, you can also combine both approaches.

Negative press

Public Relations 101 says any press is good press. The reason for that is because people tend to enjoy reading about negative stuff more. Then they get passionate about it and are more likely to remember the entity associated with the bad press in the future — but not necessarily in a bad way anymore. That certainly is the mentality of some celebrities, who believe any coverage of them, good or bad, will bring them positive outcomes in the long run.

And it certainly can be true in cryptocurrency investing as well. During the period when the negative press is a hot topic, the prices are likely to plummet. However, contrary to what you may think, that exact period may be a good time to purchase because everyone is likely dumping the asset. Catch them when they're down, and go to the top with them. A perfect romantic fairy tale, eh?

WARNING

Buying during negative press works *only if* all the other IDDA analysis points indicate the cryptocurrency is worthwhile long-term. If the negative press consists of something ultra-damaging that the crypto is unlikely to recover from, then go ahead and pass.

Trying Technical Analysis to Select Cryptos

When you've got your heart set on a few cryptocurrencies to add to your portfolio, you're ready to decide the best time to buy them. The golden rule to any type of investment comes down to four important words:

"Buy low, sell high."

REMEMBER

But how can you decide when the price is at its lowest point to buy? That's where technical analysis, the third point of IDDA, comes in. *Technical analysis* is the art of using history to predict the future. Read on here for a brief introduction to price action and the best price analysis methods:

>> **Technical analysis basics:** So many fabulous tools and gadgets can help you understand the historical movements and patterns of a cryptocurrency's price. By discovering how each pattern and indicator works, you can have a higher accuracy in predicting future price actions. Flip to Chapter 10 of this minibook to explore some of the most important chart patterns and indicators that can help you develop your winning investment strategy for your favorite cryptocurrency.

>> **Recent price action:** Although the current price of one coin isn't a very good indicator of a cryptocurrency's overall value, analyzing the price action becomes *very* important when you're trying to figure out when to buy and sell. You can check the most recent price action of your selected cryptocurrency on websites such as coinmarketcap.com to see how much the price has dropped or surged in the past day, week, or even months. Analyzing recent price action is more important for short-term traders who are looking to get in and out of the market more rapidly, say, within a day or a week. Chapter 11 of this minibook has more on short-term trading strategies.

>> **Big picture:** If you're a long-term investor, you may find looking at the big picture more useful in your technical analysis. Many cryptocurrencies are too young to have a well-developed price history, but you still can use similar techniques by comparing older cryptocurrencies in the same category and applying big-picture analysis to the new ones. In Chapter 12 of this minibook, we discuss technical analysis methods for long-term investors.

Chapter **5**

Diversification in Cryptocurrencies

This book covers diversification in a few chapters, specifically Chapters 2 and 4, and also Book 1, Chapter 4. This chapter gets to the bottom of what diversification means for your crypto portfolio, why it's important, and how you can manage your portfolio's risk by properly diversifying your assets.

Breaking Down Some Basics on Diversification

Small investors regularly hear about the topic of diversification for their personal stock portfolio. One of the first things a financial expert tells you when you want to get started with investing is "don't forget to diversify!" You don't want to put all your eggs in one basket, regardless of whether that basket is stocks or cryptos. The following sections dig into what that really means, especially for cryptocurrency investing.

What is traditional diversification?

When you're building your personal stock portfolio, *diversification* often means having more than one or two stocks. The most conventional diversification method in a personal stock portfolio is to have around 15 to 20 stocks that are spread across different industries.

REMEMBER

When you diversify among industries, assets, or investment instruments that aren't correlated, you're less likely to see major drops in your portfolio when one of the categories is doing poorly. Diversification doesn't guarantee you have no risk of losses, though. It just reduces that risk if done correctly.

TIP

Websites such as Benzinga (https://pro.benzinga.com/?afmc=2f) can help keep you in the know about the most recent developments across different industries so that you can make better diversification decisions.

How does diversification reduce risk?

You encounter two types of risk in a stock portfolio: unsystematic and systematic. *Unsystematic risk* is the type of risk that you can mitigate by combining multiple industries into one portfolio. Unsystematic risk includes the following:

>> **Business risk:** This risk is associated with a company's earnings and its ability to meet its financial obligations. This risk is also tied to the company's industry, as sometimes all the businesses within a category are exposed to a similar degree of uncertainty.

>> **Country risk:** This is the risk of political and economic instability in the country where the company does business.

>> **Default risk:** This is the risk that a company isn't able to repay its debt and therefore is subject to default.

>> **Executive risk:** This risk is associated with the moral character of the executives who run the company. If they get into legal or ethical trouble, the company's stock may suffer both short term and long term.

>> **Financial risk:** This risk is associated with the amount of leverage (a measure of the amount of debt) a company uses in its financial structure. The more debt the company has, the more leverage it's using, and therefore the higher the risk.

>> **Government/regulation risk:** This is the risk that a country may pass a new law or regulation that negatively impacts the industry that a company is in.

Systematic risk is risk that you can't get rid of simply by diversifying across various industries. This risk category includes the following:

>> **Market risk:** The risk that the market moves against your position due to various reasons, such as political reasons, social reasons, or general change in market sentiment.

>> **Exchange rate risk:** The risk that the exchange rate goes higher or its movements negatively impact your investments.

>> **Interest rate risk:** The chance that changes in interest rates adversely affect the asset's value.

>> **Political instability risk:** The risk that political uncertainties or changes negatively impact the market.

>> **Reinvestment risk:** The chance that you won't be able to reinvest your funds at a favorable rate of return.

>> **Event risk:** The chance of something unpredictable (like bankruptcy and hacker attacks) happening to the company/exchange/broker/wallet that holds your asset, therefore contributing to negative market fluctuation.

Traditional diversification in a stock portfolio helps reduce unsystematic risk. This is when things get interesting. You can't diversify away systematic risk within your stock portfolio, but how about diversifying across other markets? This approach is actually how Kiana got into investing in the first place during the crash of 2008. (You can read about the details in the nearby sidebar, "Kiana's foray into forex.")

REMEMBER

As we get closer to the next inevitable stock market crash, adding unconventional investment instruments such as cryptocurrencies to your portfolio is more important than ever. Here's why: At the time of this writing, the cryptocurrency market is quite different from the traditional markets. It's relatively new. It's largely unregulated, and therefore, traditional systematic risks such as political instability or interest rate risks don't really apply to it. In fact, investors may well see cryptocurrencies as a safety net for when things go south in other markets during a major economic crisis.

Using Cryptocurrencies in Long-Term Diversification

When it comes to adding cryptocurrencies to your portfolio, keep the following two types of long-term diversification in mind:

>> Diversifying with non-cryptocurrencies

>> Diversifying among cryptocurrencies

Here's a bit more about these two types of crypto diversification. (For more about diversification from traditional markets such as stocks, bonds, and forex, see Chapter 1 of this minibook.)

TIP

For more information on many of the topics in this section, check out these Invest Diva resources:

>> The *Forex Coffee Break* education course at `https://education.investdiva.com/forex-coffee-break-with-invest-diva-education-course`

>> The book, *Invest Diva's Guide to Making Money in Forex,* by Kiana Danial (McGraw-Hill Education)

>> Other service listings at `https://learn.investdiva.com/services`

Diversifying with non-cryptocurrencies

You have so many financial instruments to choose from when you consider diversifying your portfolio across the board. Stocks, forex, precious metals, and bonds are just a few examples. As Chapter 1 of this minibook explains, each of these assets has its unique traits. Some assets' inherited risks can offset the risks of the other ones through long-term market ups and downs. The following sections provide guidance on how to use cryptos and non-cryptos together in the long term.

REMEMBER

No single golden diversification rule works for all investors. Diversification percentages and the overall mix greatly depend on the individual investor and their unique risk tolerance, as we discuss in the sidebar in Chapter 2 of this minibook and on the Invest Diva website (`https://learn.investdiva.com/free-webinar-3-secrets-to-making-your-money-work-for-you`).

TIP

The more risk you're willing to take, the higher the chances of a bigger return on investment, and vice versa. If you're just starting out and have a lower risk tolerance, you may consider allocating a bigger portion of your portfolio to bonds and then systematically adding stocks, precious metals, and cryptocurrencies. For tips on calculating your unique risk tolerance, check out the sidebar in Chapter 2 of this minibook.

Some background on trading fiat currencies

Fiat currencies are the traditional money that different countries' authorities declare legal. For example, the U.S. dollar is the official currency of the United States. The euro is the official currency of the European Union and its territories. The Japanese yen is backed by Japan. You get the idea.

The *foreign exchange market,* or *forex,* is a huge market where traders trade these fiat currencies against one another. Having a bit of a background in forex can help you better understand the cryptocurrency market and how you can trade the different types of currencies against one another. We compare this market to a big international party where all the couples are made up of partners from different regions. So if one is the Japanese yen (JPY), their partner may be the euro (EUR). We call them Ms. Japan and Mr. Euro. If one is the U.S. dollar (Ms. USA), their partner can be British, Portuguese, or Japanese.

In the forex market, these international pairs get together and start "dancing." But oftentimes, the paired-up partners aren't compatible, and their moves aren't correlated. For example, every time Ms. USA makes a good move, their partner screws up. Every time the partner picks up the rhythm, Ms. USA is stuck in a previous move. These incompatibilities gain some attention, and a bunch of people who are watching the dancers start betting on which of the partners is going to screw up next. Those folks are the forex traders. You can watch this forex metaphor in action here: https://www.youtube.com/watch?v=abQuHfjaGug&list=PLt3BW8jrlMZvmObHLMjpVySPmex987wyC&index=1

REMEMBER

The point is that when trading currencies — fiat or crypto — you can only trade them in pairs. For example, you can trade the U.S. dollar (USD) versus the Japanese yen (JPY); this is the USD/JPY pair. You can trade the Australian dollar (AUD) versus the Canadian dollar (CAD); that's the AUD/CAD pair.

Quote currency versus base currency

When trading currency pairs, the *base currency* is listed first, and the *quote currency* is listed second. Which currency in a given pair is the base currency and which is the quote currency is normally fixed across the trading markets. For example, when talking about trading the U.S. dollar versus the Japanese yen, the currency of the United States always comes first, followed by the currency of Japan (USD/JPY). In the EUR/USD pair, the euro always comes first, followed by the U.S. dollar.

REMEMBER

These set patterns have nothing to do with whether a certain currency's country is more important or whether one currency in a pair is more popular than the other. It's just how the trading crowd set things up. The system doesn't change, which means everyone is on the same page, and navigating through the pairs is easier.

As the base and quote come together, the currency pair shows how much of the quote currency is needed to purchase one unit of the base currency. For example, when USD/JPY is trading at 100, that means 1 U.S. dollar is valued at 100 Japanese yen. In other words, you need 100 Japanese yen (the quote currency) to buy 1 U.S. dollar (the base currency).

The same concept applies to cryptocurrency pairs. Many cryptocurrency exchanges offer a select number of quote currencies, mainly popular ones such as a fiat like the USD and cryptos such as Bitcoin, Ethereum, and their own exchange cryptos. Then they offer trading opportunities versus all the hundreds of other cryptocurrencies they may carry versus these quote currencies.

Trading cryptos versus fiat currencies

Similar to the forex market, you can trade cryptocurrencies versus other currencies. The most common approach at the time of this writing is trading them versus a fiat currency, typically the one backed by the country you live in. For example, in the United States, most people trade Bitcoin versus the USD. They don't really think of it as trading these currencies in pairs because it feels a lot like buying a stock. But the fact is that when you buy Bitcoin using the U.S. dollar in hopes of capital gain, you're essentially betting that the value of Bitcoin will move higher against the U.S. dollar in the future. That's why if the U.S. dollar decreases in value (not only against Bitcoin but also against other currencies) at the same time that Bitcoin increases in value, you're likely to make more return on your investment.

This is where diversification can help you reduce your trading risk. As explained in the later section, "Diversifying among cryptocurrencies," most cryptos are correlated to Bitcoin in shorter time frames. That's why you can diversify your portfolio with the fiat currencies you trade them against. For example, if you think that at the time you're trading, the U.S. dollar and the Japanese yen aren't correlated, you can open up two Bitcoin trades: one versus the U.S. dollar and one versus the Japanese yen. Of course, in order to do so, you should make sure that your exchange or broker carries these different fiat currencies and offers such trading opportunities.

WARNING

Speculating the markets and short-term trading carry a lot of risk. It may not be suitable for all investors, and you may end up losing all your investment. Before deciding to trade such assets, you should carefully consider your investment objectives, level of experience, risk tolerance, and risk appetite. Also, you should *not* invest money that you can't afford to lose. (If you're still curious, you can read more about short-term trades later in this chapter and in Chapter 11 of this minibook.)

Diversifying among cryptocurrencies

The majority of cryptocurrency exchanges offer a wider selection of cross-crypto pairs than they do fiat/crypto pairs. In fact, some exchanges don't even accept any type of fiat currencies at all.

As you can imagine, the thousands of different cryptocurrencies available to trade mean the mixes and matches can be endless. Many cryptocurrency exchanges have categorized these mixes by creating different "rooms" where you can trade the majority of the cryptos they carry versus a number of more popular cryptos. For example, as shown in Figure 5-1, the Binance exchange has created four rooms or categories for the main cross-cryptos: Bitcoin (BTC), Ethereum (ETH), Binance Coin (BNB), and Tether (USDT). By clicking on each of these categories, you can trade other cryptos versus the selected quote currency, as we talk about earlier in this chapter.

	BTC	ETH	BNB	USDT
★ Favorites				
Q Search		Change		Volume
Pair ▲	Price			Change
★ ADA/BTC	0.00001490			-5.10%
★ ADX/BTC	0.00002809			-1.89%
★ AE/BTC	0.0001597			-6.99%
★ AGI/BTC	0.00000659			-9.23%
★ AION/BTC	0.0000731			-9.98%
★ AMB/BTC	0.00001947			-8.07%
★ APPC/BTC	0.00001257			-6.26%
★ ARDR/BTC	0.00001675			-4.07%
★ ARK/BTC	0.0001045			-2.06%
★ ARN/BTC	0.00004063			-5.31%
★ AST/BTC	0.00001255			-3.83%
★ BAT/BTC	0.00003133			-7.09%
★ BCC/BTC	0.082501			-6.40%
★ BCD/BTC	0.001515			-4.06%

FIGURE 5-1:
Binance exchange cryptocurrency pairing options.

Source: Binance.com

When trading currency pairs, fiat or crypto, the best bet is always to pair a strong base currency versus a weak quote currency and vice versa. This way, you maximize the chances of that pair moving strongly in the direction you're aiming for.

As we cover earlier in this chapter, the reason you diversify your portfolio is to reduce its exposure to risk by including assets that aren't fully correlated. The big problem about diversifying within your cryptocurrency portfolio is that, at least at the time of this writing, most cryptocurrencies are heavily correlated to Bitcoin. In most situations where Bitcoin was having a bad day in 2017 and 2018, the majority of other cryptocurrencies were, too. Figure 5-2, for example, shows a snapshot of the top 12 cryptocurrencies on August 18, 2018. All are in red. In fact, 94 out of the top 100 cryptocurrencies by market cap were plummeting that day. (*Market cap* shows the value of all units of a crypto that are for sale right now; head to Book 1, Chapter 4 for more on this topic.) In the crypto market, this type of short-term market correlation has become the norm.

August 19, the very next day, Bitcoin turned green, and so did the majority of the cryptos in the top 100, as shown in Figure 5-3. In this snapshot of the top 17 cryptocurrencies, all tokens besides Tether (USDT) surged about the same amount that Bitcoin did, around 1.72 percent.

Cryptocurrencies ▾ Exchanges ▾ Watchlist — USD ▾ Next 100 → View All

#	Name	Market Cap	Price	Volume (24h)	Circulating Supply	Change (24h)	Price Graph (7d)
1	Bitcoin	$110,649,855,082	$6,426.55	$4,110,086,955	17,217,625 BTC	-1.73%	
2	Ethereum	$30,275,263,926	$298.55	$1,815,655,842	101,409,291 ETH	-3.57%	
3	XRP	$13,067,008,532	$0.331882	$500,290,020	39,372,399,467 XRP *	-6.18%	
4	Bitcoin Cash	$9,727,259,913	$562.26	$438,690,267	17,300,163 BCH	-1.91%	
5	EOS	$4,681,414,609	$5.17	$864,785,525	906,245,118 EOS *	-4.09%	
6	Stellar	$4,271,146,076	$0.227530	$79,898,204	18,771,755,700 XLM *	-2.51%	
7	Litecoin	$3,313,730,889	$57.23	$253,969,516	57,903,334 LTC	-4.81%	
8	Tether	$2,719,405,730	$0.998995	$3,359,590,344	2,722,140,336 USDT *	-0.10%	
9	Cardano	$2,631,037,998	$0.101478	$107,934,610	25,927,070,538 ADA *	-5.37%	
10	Monero	$1,596,232,879	$97.75	$33,423,127	16,329,214 XMR	-0.48%	
11	TRON	$1,439,869,868	$0.021900	$146,361,621	65,748,111,645 TRX *	-3.83%	
12	Ethereum Classic	$1,393,191,044	$13.41	$298,225,866	103,884,149 ETC	-6.22%	

FIGURE 5-2: Correlation between the top 12 cryptocurrencies and Bitcoin as BTC drops.

Source: CoinMarketCap.com

Cryptocurrencies ▾ Exchanges ▾ Watchlist — USD ▾ ← Back to Top 100

#	Name	Symbol	Market Cap	Price	Circulating Supply	Volume (24h)	% 1h	% 24h	% 7d	
1	Bitcoin	BTC	$112,236,198,598	$6,517.98	17,219,487	$3,313,453,845	1.71%	1.72%	2.66%	···
2	Ethereum	ETH	$30,646,261,019	$302.14	101,429,296	$1,454,877,279	1.35%	2.93%	-8.14%	···
3	XRP	XRP	$13,731,051,598	$0.348748	39,372,399,467 *	$332,539,987	2.20%	7.12%	15.86%	···
4	Bitcoin Cash	BCH	$9,845,137,274	$569.02	17,301,888	$371,039,772	1.61%	2.55%	-0.85%	···
5	EOS	EOS	$4,829,548,557	$5.33	906,245,118 *	$626,183,474	2.51%	5.35%	5.44%	···
6	Stellar	XLM	$4,333,386,117	$0.230846	18,771,755,850 *	$61,335,714	3.03%	2.41%	3.77%	···
7	Litecoin	LTC	$3,372,794,706	$58.23	57,917,023	$205,830,556	1.90%	2.64%	-2.25%	···
8	Tether	USDT	$2,715,888,857	$0.997703	2,722,140,336 *	$2,817,530,199	-0.32%	-0.54%	-0.41%	···
9	Cardano	ADA	$2,675,764,469	$0.103204	25,927,070,538 *	$53,269,411	2.25%	2.96%	-6.70%	···
10	Monero	XMR	$1,604,253,760	$98.23	16,331,966	$17,505,936	1.52%	1.36%	4.94%	···
11	IOTA	MIOTA	$1,539,626,433	$0.553916	2,779,530,283 *	$47,593,558	2.56%	13.79%	2.30%	···
12	TRON	TRX	$1,465,481,398	$0.022289	65,748,111,645 *	$98,160,709	2.05%	4.41%	-1.85%	···
13	Ethereum Classic	ETC	$1,403,395,647	$13.51	103,907,893	$195,425,979	1.28%	2.42%	1.44%	···
14	Dash	DASH	$1,289,364,836	$155.97	8,266,740	$245,592,938	0.20%	3.75%	-7.19%	···
15	NEO	NEO	$1,271,796,082	$19.57	65,000,000 *	$72,961,066	1.94%	6.25%	4.94%	···
16	NEM	XEM	$974,044,126	$0.108227	8,999,999,999 *	$10,775,110	1.77%	2.41%	-0.05%	···
17	Binance Coin	BNB	$968,626,021	$10.14	95,512,523 *	$20,230,165	1.72%	2.91%	13.33%	···

FIGURE 5-3: Correlation between the top 17 cryptocurrencies and Bitcoin as BTC surges.

Source: CoinMarketCap.com

On the other hand, if you look at the bigger picture, say the seven-day price change, you notice that the market correlation to Bitcoin is more mixed, as shown in Figure 5-4. For example, while Bitcoin gained 1.25 percent in the seven days before August 18, Ripple's XRP gained 8.51 percent, and Dash lost 9.79 percent.

#	Name	Symbol	Market Cap	Price	Circulating Supply	Volume (24h)	% 1h	% 24h	% 7d	
1	Bitcoin	BTC	$110,736,482,332	$6,431.58	17,217,625	$4,111,810,815	0.53%	-1.69%	1.25%	...
2	Ethereum	ETH	$30,312,762,760	$298.92	101,409,291	$1,818,755,064	2.74%	-3.45%	-7.42%	...
3	XRP	XRP	$13,058,424,828	$0.331864	39,372,399,467 *	$469,677,279	1.02%	-5.41%	8.51%	...
4	Bitcoin Cash	BCH	$9,739,156,000	$562.95	17,300,163	$438,840,288	2.07%	-1.79%	-1.33%	...
5	EOS	EOS	$4,668,751,666	$5.15	906,245,118 *	$663,755,873	2.42%	-4.46%	0.53%	...
6	Stellar	XLM	$4,268,885,433	$0.227410	18,771,755,700 *	$79,814,088	1.26%	-2.05%	3.35%	...
7	Litecoin	LTC	$3,313,808,803	$57.23	57,903,334	$283,654,509	1.45%	-4.90%	-2.59%	...
8	Tether	USDT	$2,724,937,528	$1.00	2,722,140,336 *	$3,355,187,045	-0.15%	0.32%	-0.20%	...
9	Cardano	ADA	$2,630,299,721	$0.101450	25,927,070,538	$107,974,564	0.86%	-5.51%	-10.62%	...
10	Monero	XMR	$1,596,412,015	$97.76	16,329,214	$33,408,729	1.45%	-0.52%	1.43%	...
11	TRON	TRX	$1,438,597,367	$0.021880	65,748,111,645 *	$146,225,110	3.17%	-3.91%	-5.39%	...
12	Ethereum Classic	ETC	$1,391,586,196	$13.40	103,864,149	$297,763,972	2.54%	-6.39%	0.20%	...
13	IOTA	MIOTA	$1,381,908,847	$0.497174	2,779,530,283 *	$47,610,739	2.09%	-8.27%	-7.14%	...
14	Dash	DASH	$1,249,230,719	$151.15	8,264,930	$184,713,102	1.36%	-6.96%	-9.79%	...
15	NEO	NEO	$1,245,268,169	$19.16	65,000,000 *	$89,026,728	5.62%	-4.25%	1.32%	...
16	NEM	XEM	$959,252,944	$0.106584	8,999,999,999 *	$17,941,269	1.65%	-6.91%	-1.33%	...
17	Binance Coin	BNB	$961,601,420	$9.96	95,512,523 *	$30,765,189	1.14%	-5.42%	-15.00%	...

Source: CoinMarketCap.com

FIGURE 5-4:
The top 17 cryptocurrencies are less correlated in the seven-day time frame.

REMEMBER

This correlation is one key reason short-term trading cryptocurrencies is riskier than many other financial instruments. Considering long-term investments when adding cryptocurrencies to your portfolio may be best. That way, you can reduce your investment risk by diversifying within different crypto categories.

On the bright side, as the cryptocurrency market continues to develop, the diversification methods can also improve, and the whole market may become less correlated to Bitcoin.

Tackling Diversification in Short-Term Trades

If you've calculated your risk tolerance based on the information in Chapter 2 of this minibook and the results are pretty aggressive, you may want to consider trading cryptocurrencies in shorter time frames. To read more about developing short-term strategies, flip to Chapter 11 of this minibook. Here are some suggestions to keep in mind:

WARNING

>> **Beware of commissions.** Cryptocurrency trading exchanges generally require lower commissions and transaction fees than do brokers who offer forex or stocks. But you shouldn't completely ignore the commission cost to your wallet. When day trading, you may end up paying more in commissions than what you're actually making if you trade way too often, getting in and out of trades way too fast without calculating your returns! Also, as we talk about in Chapter 3 of this minibook, cheaper isn't always the best option when choosing an exchange. You always get what you pay for.

TIP

>> **Keep expanding your portfolio.** Some people invest a lump sum in their investment portfolios and then either wipe it out in dangerous day-trading actions or get stuck in a strategy that's working but isn't maximizing their returns. A healthy portfolio requires nourishment. Consider leaving a monthly investment fund aside out of your paycheck in order to expand your portfolio and make your money work for you.

>> **Observe the rule of three.** You have a ton of options when trading currencies. You can mix and match crypto/crypto and fiat/crypto pairs like there's no tomorrow if your account size lets you. However, the key in having a healthy diversified portfolio is to avoid double-dipping the same quote currency in your trades. Try to limit your open short-term positions against each quote currency to three. For example, trade one crypto versus Bitcoin, another versus Ethereum, and a third versus your exchange's cryptocurrency. This approach also helps you keep your portfolio at a reasonable size so it's not too big to monitor.

Chapter **6**

Getting Ahead of the Crowd: Investing in ICOs

CO is short for initial coin offering. In an age where ICOs aren't subject to many regulations, some would call them the easiest path to scams. And though a ton (and we mean a *ton!*) of ICO scams are out there, if you do your homework, you may be able to catch a few diamonds in the rough as well. In this chapter, we explain ICO basics and show how you can get involved.

Understanding the Basics of Initial Coin Offerings

Initial coin offerings are something like fundraising for a new start-up, except that your new idea revolves around a new cryptocurrency rather than a business idea or product. You're trying to raise "money" in the form of other, already established cryptocurrencies such as Bitcoin and Ethereum. In other words, an ICO is crowdfunding, using other cryptocurrencies, for a new cryptocurrency that's (hopefully) connected to an awesome product. The following sections provide the basics on ICOs.

How an ICO works and how to start one

Simply put, an ICO works exactly how start-up fundraising works. You come up with a cool idea for a cryptocurrency. The cryptocurrency may be used for an existing product, or perhaps you have an idea for a product that can work well with a brand-new crypto.

As an example, say a fashion website in New York City showcases display windows in real time. (Okay, this is actually Kiana's friend Jon Harari's website, WindowsWear — check out www.windowswear.com. Jon unfortunately doesn't really understand how the ICO plan can work for his business.) But for the sake of argument, say that Jon decides he wants to change his business strategy, make his website available to the masses, and let people shop on his app using WindowsWear's very own digital currency. Call this brand-new crypto WEAR Coin. But unless Jon is a millionaire who wants to spend all his money on this idea, he needs to raise money to make this new cryptocurrency a reality. He can go to a venture capitalist, a bank, or angel investors and ask for money. The problem with that approach is that he'll most likely have to give up part of his ownership of his company. So instead, he can listen to his friend and go for an ICO.

Here are the general steps to take to initiate an ICO (see the later section, "So You Want to Start an ICO: Launching an ICO Yourself," for more information):

1. **Create a white paper.**

   A *white paper* is a detailed document explaining a business model and the reason a particular coin may really take off. The more use cases Jon has in his white paper for WEAR Coin to show it can actually become a popular and high-volume coin, the better.

2. **Add a tab to your website dedicated to ICO funding.**

   In this example, Jon puts a tab on his WindowsWear site dedicated to WEAR Coin ICO funding.

3. **Spread the word to your connections and ask for funding.**

4. **Sell a quantity of your crowdfunded coin in the form of *tokens,* which means digital assets.**

   Normally ICOs ask for Bitcoin or Ethereum in exchange for the tokens. But you can also accept *fiat* (traditional government-backed) currencies such as the U.S. dollar.

5. **Send the investors coin tokens.**

   In this example, Jon sends his investors WEAR Coin tokens.

If WEAR Coin really hits, starts getting used a lot, and is listed on a ton of crypto exchanges, the early investors can see a significant return on their investments.

WARNING

People who invest in ICOs normally don't have any guarantee that the new cryptocurrency will increase in value in the future. Some ICO investments have been incredibly profitable in the past, but future ICOs may not be. Unless you really trust the management, the company's dedication to success, and its knowledge of the business model and the industry, investing in an ICO is very much comparable to gambling. Flip to the later section, "Investing in an ICO," for more details.

ICOs versus IPOs

A lot of people experience a bit of confusion about the difference between initial coin offerings (ICOs) and *initial public offerings* (IPOs, which is the first time a company sells its stocks to the public). These concepts sound similar, and in many ways, they are similar. Here are the main differences:

>> **In theory, anyone can do an ICO.** At the time of this writing, ICOs aren't regulated in many countries. That means literally anyone can launch an ICO. All you need is a white paper, a pretty website, and a ton of rich connections who are willing to give you money. By contrast, only established private companies that have been operating for a while are allowed to carry out IPOs. (See the nearby sidebar, "Watching ICOs in the United States," for more information.)

>> **You don't even need to have a product to launch an ICO.** Most of the companies that are doing ICOs don't have anything concrete to present to the public; some of them have *proof of concept* (which demonstrates the idea is workable), and others have proof of stake. Starting an ICO is even easier than starting a crowdfunding for a proper start-up. For start-ups to get funded, they normally need something called *minimum viable product* (MVP), which is a product with enough features to satisfy the early investors and to generate feedback for future developments. In the ICO process, you can reduce the MVP to documents like white papers, partnerships, and media relations.

>> **ICOs are easier to invest in — until they're not.** The only thing you need to start investing in ICOs is access to the Internet. You don't need brokers to carry out your investment. At the time of this writing, you can buy any tokens of any company in most countries. However, the list of countries that started adding regulations or banning ICOs altogether started to increase in 2018. In the United States, it's even more complicated because the ICO rules vary from state to state.

WARNING

Many ICOs block investments from their country of residence because regulatory bodies consider ICO tokens to be securities. These strict regulations limit the ICO participation only to accredited investors and severely limit the investor pool, making it difficult to participate in ICOs. That being said, people have been found to use a virtual private network (VPN) to bypass the geo-blocking (geographical blocks), thus making it look like they're coming from an authorized country so they can invest anyway and creating a lot of legal issues.

TIP

You can view ICO regulations by country at www.bitcoinmarketjournal.com/ico-regulations/.

>> **ICOs don't grant you ownership of the project.** When you invest in an IPO, you technically become a partial owner of that company. That's why they call the investors shareholders. This designation doesn't really matter if all you're looking for is to sell the stock as its value rises. ICO investors may benefit in many ways in the future, but they have nothing to do with the company itself. All they're getting are a bunch of digital coins (tokens) that may or may not rise in value in the future.

WATCHING ICOs IN THE UNITED STATES

The Securities and Exchange Commission (SEC) is watching the ICO space in the United States very closely, and it shuts down most of the ICOs that it thinks pose a huge risk to the investing public. The presale option of the ICO can *only* be open to accredited investors (thus not the general public). The ICO for the public can be problematic if the token is considered a security by the SEC as opposed to a platform token (it's absolutely needed to run the platform). Most ICOs launching new cryptos of Ethereum, for example, can't make the case for a platform token (as there is no new platform that requires its own token), so they fall into the securities category.

Also, for U.S.-based companies launching ICOs, there is a lockout period for investors buying in the presale stages, usually 12 months, in which they can't trade the new crypto they invested in. This is done to prevent a pump-and-dump operation, and it's watched very closely by the SEC.

Companies launching ICOs also have to comply with the U.S. federal KYC and AML regulations, which include not accepting or sending cryptos to a large list of wallet addresses that are on the Financial Crimes Enforcement Network's blacklist as either money laundering operators or terrorism financing.

Investing in an ICO

REMEMBER

ICO investing involves a lot of risk. You shouldn't invest money you can't afford to lose in an ICO. If your risk tolerance is low, you can consider many alternative investment assets, as we overview in Chapter 2 of this minibook.

Note also that some ICOs aren't even meant to be investments. They're a tool you can use for a specific product. In the real estate sector, you can use the Propy token to buy properties internationally. Unikrn's CEO Rahul Sood noted in 2017 that "buying a token is buying a product that we're selling that can be used on the Unikrn platform. People should not be looking at this as an investment. If they are looking at this as an investment, they're making a mistake. Tokens are not investments."

But this is an investing chapter in an investing book, and perhaps you've decided to give it a try. Here are some tips on how you can go about it.

Finding ICO listings

You may find out about upcoming ICOs through word of mouth, at a financial event, or through an online ad. If you don't have any specific ICO in mind and just want to search for one from scratch, you can get help from ICO listing websites. But finding the right ICO listing website can also be a challenge because more than 100 of them are already out there, and more are popping up every day.

Here are some tips to keep in mind when searching for an ICO listing website:

>> Start out by comparing two or three ICO listing websites at a time. Are they all featuring the same ICOs on top? This strategy can help you figure out which website is giving you the verified ICO listing.

>> Make sure a site has features such as an ICO calendar, ICO rating, and ICO description.

>> Offering market statistics about the ICO, filters, and scam warning features is a plus.

TIP

At the end of the day, using your everyday search engine may be your best bet to find an ICO listing website. You can consider search terms like "ICO listings," "top ICOs 2022," or "best ICO listing websites."

Analyzing an ICO listing

After you pick your ICO listing website, you're now ready to evaluate and choose the upcoming ICOs you're interested in investing in. With hundreds of ICOs popping up every month, this step can be lengthy, but it's a crucial process. The steps to take when researching an ICO can be similar to those in Chapter 4 of this minibook for selecting cryptocurrencies. The following sections give you some research points to keep in mind.

Who's behind the ICO?

The team of developers and management behind the ICO is the most important thing you need to find out about. Who are they? What are their credentials? The ICO website should give you background on the team; otherwise, move on to the next ICO listing that provides such crucial information readily on its website. Try to find the team members on LinkedIn to verify their backgrounds (or even existence). In addition, try finding ICOs' boards of advisors and financial backers. Are these people you can trust your money with? Are they dedicated to take their idea to the next step?

WARNING

If you go to an ICO pitching conference where the team keeps name-dropping — things like "the prince of Dubai is investing millions in us" or other unverifiable blabs — we recommend running, not walking, and never looking back.

What's the cryptocurrency for?

You want to familiarize yourself with the idea behind the crypto as much as possible. Sure, anyone can start a cryptocurrency and list an ICO. The question is why these people have chosen to do so. What specific value does their token have that other cryptocurrencies already in existence don't offer? Who's their competition? How are they better than the competition? What type of technology are they using? Who is their target market, and how large is it?

WARNING

The idea behind the cryptocurrency is important, but you need to be wary of unrealistic promises. Scam projects often make bold claims about their products but have nothing new or disruptive in their technology. If someone claims a new cryptocurrency will replace Bitcoin, end world poverty within a year, fix global warming, or increase in value by 10,000 percent, you can add that project to your scam list.

Does the team have a prototype or a code?

WARNING

As mentioned in the earlier section, "ICOs versus IPOs," you don't necessarily have to have a prototype to launch an ICO. But those with a minimum viable product can show you that the team is serious about the idea and is able to hit future milestones. If a project has no working code whatsoever prior to an ICO, that's a major red flag.

Does the team have a blockchain?

The majority of ICOs don't have a blockchain (flip to Book 2, Chapter 1 for an introduction to blockchain technology). The founders simply pitch the idea for the utility their tokens can provide. We prefer to search among those that are based on solid blockchain technology that solves a solid problem rather than those that are glorified apps that can be built without creating a brand-new cryptocurrency.

What's the plan to drive prices higher after the ICO?

The main reason you invest in an ICO is in speculation that its price will go higher in the future. That's why the team behind the ICO should provide you with a road map on how it's planning to do so. This part of the analysis can be similar to that of any already-trading cryptocurrency covered in Book 1, Chapter 4. Here are some key features to watch out for:

>> The crypto has a high enough network volume.

>> The crypto is better than the competition.

>> The ICO gives investors an incentive to hold rather than quickly spend the tokens.

>> The new tokens will have sufficient liquidity.

>> The team is proactive in getting the token listed in multiple exchanges.

WARNING

Many teams seek to create their own exchanges to generate the liquidity and volume needed to take off. But that isn't necessarily sufficient evidence for the token's future success. Getting listed on various exchanges can be tough, which is why it's an important indicator of the token's success down the road.

Does the team have a wide, supportive community?

You don't want to be a sheep who simply follows others, but reaching out to the ICO community can give you a sense about the token. How many supporters does a given ICO have on sources like Reddit, Twitter, and Facebook? Do the supporters appear to be robots, or are they real people and crypto enthusiasts? Beware of paid "community members" whose job is to say positive things about the ICO on social media. Also look for proper media coverage, press releases, and the team's presence on social media.

Outlining the ICO investment process

When you find your unicorn ICO, you normally need to have a legit cryptocurrency to invest in it, although sometimes ICOs accept fiat currencies as well. Most importantly, you also need to have a cryptocurrency wallet. Flip to Book 1, Chapter 3 to identify different types of wallets that can work for you.

TIP

Most ICOs are built on the Ethereum blockchain. That's why in many cases you specifically need Ethereum cryptocurrency and an Ethereum wallet to invest in an ICO. Book 4 has more details about this crypto.

REMEMBER

Not all ICOs are created the same. Therefore, we can't show you the exact steps to take when buying into an ICO. Regardless, here are some general guidelines:

1. Make sure that you check the official page of the ICO.

2. If the ICO requires you to pay by another crypto, such as Ethereum or Bitcoin, you must first acquire those coins on an exchange (see Chapter 3 of this minibook) and store them in your crypto wallet (see Book 1, Chapter 3).

3. After completing your due diligence on the ICO's nature (see the earlier section, "Analyzing an ICO listing"), register for the ICO based on its website's instructions.

4. Wait for the launch date and follow the instructions. This step normally consists of transferring your cryptocurrency assets from your crypto wallet to the ICO's public address. This step may also cost a transaction fee.

5. After the ICO is launched, the team sends the new tokens to your crypto wallet.

TIP

Because of the risky nature of ICOs and the difficulty in selecting the best ones, you may consider skipping the ICO and waiting until the token/cryptocurrency is launched before buying it. Although many ICOs see an immediate and rapid surge right after launch, more often than not they come crashing down shortly after. The crash doesn't necessarily mean that the token isn't worthy of holding. Historically, these types of price changes happen in the tech industry quite often, providing an excellent post-launch buying opportunity. When things settle down and more people have analyzed the new token, its price can move back up slowly, giving you an opportunity to invest at your own pace. An ICO is rarely too good to pass up (although it does happen).

Holding your tokens after your purchase

The method you choose to monitor your ICO purchase highly depends on the reasons you bought in the first place. Although not all ICOs are investment vehicles, most teams behind ICOs prefer that you don't buy and dump their tokens after the ICO, so they do whatever it takes to convince you to hold onto the tokens. And doing so may just pay off in the long run.

REMEMBER

If you invested in the ICO for capital gain purposes only, be prepared to hold onto your investment for a while. At first, your investment may turn negative with a loss, or it may consolidate at the same price with no real returns for a while. Often these periods of losses and consolidation are followed by a massive surge, which may give you the opportunity to take profit. Keep in mind that sometimes the big surges are the beginning of an uptrend (or more gains) in the market, so by selling too rapidly you may miss out on more profit. Other times, the surge can be a simple pump-and-dump. Therefore, you need to continuously monitor and conduct the Invest Diva Diamond Analysis (IDDA; see Chapter 4 of this minibook) to create the best exit strategy.

REMEMBER

If you make money on your ICO investment, you have to report it as capital gains. See Chapter 15 of this minibook for more on taxes.

So You Want to Start an ICO: Launching an ICO Yourself

In 2017, everyone seemed to be launching an ICO. But after a number of scams, failed ICOs, and a general buzzkill in the cryptocurrency world, the hype around ICOs cooled down somewhat. By February 2018, 46 percent of the 2017 ICOs had failed, despite the fact that they had raised over $104 million. People realized that in order to be taken seriously and have long-term success, they must give it their all. At the end of the day, integrity wins.

One key debate is whether ICOs will replace the traditional start-up fundraising process. After all, over 50 percent of start-ups also fail within the first five years, so the statistics aren't that far off when comparing ICOs to venture capital.

The following sections give you a few things to keep in mind before deciding to go the ICO route.

Understanding the challenges

Anyone can start an ICO (see the earlier section, "How an ICO works and how to start one," for specifics), but launching a *successful* ICO is a different story. Here are a few things you need right off the bat:

>> A minimum of $60,000 to launch an initial campaign

>> Six months to one year of a pre-public engagement phase

>> A "dream team" to join your project

>> A product that uses your token

>> A meaningful reason to integrate the digital token into your product

Taking a few steps before the launch

If you're A-OK with the challenges in the previous section and want to become the next ICO success story, here are some steps to get you started. Just a heads-up: These steps are overly simplified.

Create a product that needs an ICO

The only thing that can increase the demand for your token is having a real utility. If a decentralized token doesn't really impact the value of your product, then forget about it. People are becoming increasingly smart about ICO investments. To become one of the success stories in the field, you need to have a thorough understanding of your market and your target audience. Most importantly, you must know what people will be willing to give you their money for. You can run a survey on a site like SurveyMonkey or BitcoinTalk Forum (check out `https://bitcointalk.org/`) to see the market reaction to your idea. Make sure that you also find out about your competition in the space.

Get legal advice

Are ICOs legal in your country? Are you legally covered if things go wrong? ICOs are becoming more regulated. That's why you must do your due diligence to comply with all relevant laws and regulations in the field. You can find attorneys who are experienced with ICOs using your search engine or LinkedIn; search for terms like "ICO lawyers near me" or "ICO lawyers [enter your country]."

Create a token

This step is actually the easiest step of the process, especially if you're not planning on creating a blockchain from scratch. You can simply use platforms such as Ethereum and Waves. If you follow their instructions, it can literally take less than 20 minutes to issue your own token on Ethereum. Book 4, Chapter 4 shows you how to create a token on the Ethereum blockchain.

Write a white paper

As explained earlier in this chapter, white papers are essential for analyzing an ICO or a cryptocurrency. So you can imagine that your investors are likely to demand a thorough, clear one before they give you their money. Search for white paper templates online, and make sure you're up-to-date with what investors are looking for.

Create a launch buzz

This step is also very similar to launching any new product or start-up. Kiana is a start-up owner and has been studying launching techniques throughout her entrepreneurial journey — and she's still learning. Launching an ICO has other additional marketing requirements unique to its nature, including the following:

>> Getting listed on hot ICO listing websites

>> Reaching out to ICO journalists and bloggers

>> Creating your own Reddit, Twitter, Facebook, and LinkedIn pages

>> Considering doing an *airdrop,* which means distributing your token for free to the masses to gain attention and media buzz

>> Considering a global road show and participating in well-attended blockchain events/conferences or partnering with an influencer

TIP

Creating a successful marketing campaign around your ICO is well beyond the scope of this book. So if you're not a natural marketer, make sure that you hire the right marketing team to help you along the way! Hiring a great marketing team is yet another challenge that is well beyond the scope of this book, but you can start by searching on your favorite search engine, looking on LinkedIn, or attending local networking events you may find on www.eventbrite.com.

Get your token listed on exchanges

Creating your own exchange can certainly help boost your token's liquidity and volume, but you must be proactive in getting your token listed on as many exchanges as possible. Exchanges are potentially the main place people will buy and sell your token, so getting it accepted on the strongest and most established ones is critical — and something that requires a heck of a lot of hustling, networking, and proving your coin is worth it. See Chapter 3 of this minibook for more about exchanges. If you do want to create your own exchange, companies such as Shift Markets (www.shiftmarkets.com/) can help with that sort of thing.

Chapter **7**

Stocks and Exchange-Traded Funds with Cryptocurrency Exposure

E ven if you're a hard-core fan of cryptocurrency investing, getting some indirect exposure to the industry rather than diving directly headfirst into the market is always a good idea. In this chapter, we overview some methods to find stocks and exchange-traded funds (ETFs) that can get you just the right amount of exposure to the crypto market while diversifying your portfolio in other fields as well.

REMEMBER

Stocks, ETFs, and all other investment assets carry a certain amount of risk. To create an investment portfolio that is unique to your financial situation and goals, make sure you calculate your risk tolerance by checking out Chapter 2 of this minibook and attending Kiana's *Make Your Money Work for You PowerCourse:* https://learn.investdiva.com/free-webinar-3-secrets-to-making-your-money-work-for-you. If you're looking for one-on-one consultations, Kiana recommends a dear friend and author of multiple *For Dummies* books, Paul Mladjenovic.

TIP

To buy stocks and ETFs, you will probably need to open an account with a broker in your area, which is different from your cryptocurrency exchange or broker. While some brokers, like Robinhood (`http://share.robinhood.com/kianad1`), offer cryptocurrencies as well as stocks and ETFs, at the time of this writing, the number of such brokers is limited in the United States. See Chapter 3 of this minibook for more information on brokers and exchanges.

Looking for Stocks with Exposure to Cryptos

When you start the process of strategy development for any asset, we recommend checking all the points of the Invest Diva Diamond Analysis (IDDA), as explained in Chapter 4 of this minibook. That includes analyzing the markets from fundamental, sentimental, and technical points of view and then adding your risk tolerance and portfolio diversity to the mix to achieve a perfect, personalized strategy that works for you. The same works for picking stocks. But if you're looking specifically for stocks with exposure to the cryptocurrency/blockchain industry, you need to do the analysis on both ends — the stock itself and its crypto side. The following sections cover how you can conduct the analysis on your own.

TIP

If you're interested in getting Kiana's up-to-date stock picks and the latest investment strategies, consider joining Invest Diva's Premium Investing Group at `https://learn.investdiva.com/join-group`.

Fundamentals

Blockchain and cryptocurrencies are related, but not all companies that are investing in blockchain technology have direct exposure to the cryptocurrency market. And even though the cryptocurrency market took a hit in 2021, for example, major public companies continued their rapid investments in blockchain technology. In fact, Blockdata.tech states that 81 of the top 100 public companies use blockchain technology. That's an impressive level of support!

As discussed in Book 2, Chapter 1, blockchain is the underlying technology for cryptocurrencies such as Bitcoin and Ethereum. In 2018, companies that were reorganizing their structure to incorporate blockchain included IBM, Accenture, Deloitte, JPMorgan, and HSBC, to name a few. Since then, many more big names have jumped on the blockchain wagon!

Okay, enough about companies that are investing in blockchain. How about cryptocurrencies? How can you get indirect exposure to this byproduct of blockchain technology? You need to think outside the box. The following sections give you some points to search for before you select stocks with crypto exposure. (For more information on fundamental analysis, check out Chapter 4 of this minibook. You can also visit `https://learn.investdiva.com/free-webinar-3-secrets-to-making-your-money-work-for-you`.)

TIP

Companies can get involved with the cryptocurrency market in so many ways. Make sure to stay on top of the news on websites such as `https://cryptobriefing.com/` and `https://pro.benzinga.com/?afmc=2f/` to be in the know.

Crypto payment exposure

Another way to get indirect exposure to the cryptocurrency market through public companies is to go after those that accept altcoins as a payment method for their services. Some pioneers in this area include Overstock.com (stock symbol: OSTK) and Microsoft (stock symbol: MSFT) in 2017 and 2018. You can find out which companies accept cryptos as payment through news sources such as Mashable (`https://mashable.com/`), NewsBTC (`http://newsbtc.com`), and MarketWatch (`www.marketwatch.com/`).

WARNING

If crypto payment exposure is the *only* reason you're investing in these types of stocks, you must remember that their price volatility can be directly correlated to the cryptocurrency market itself and therefore may not give you the diversification you're looking for. For example, Overstock's OSTK shares saw massive gains after it started to accept Bitcoin at the end of 2017 and throughout the beginning of 2018. However, as the Bitcoin price crashed, so did OSTK's share price, as shown in Figure 7-1.

Stocks and Exchange-Traded Funds with Cryptocurrency Exposure

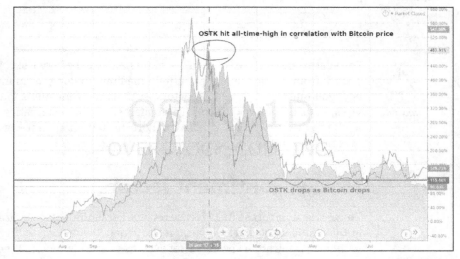

FIGURE 7-1: OSTK share prices throughout 2018 show correlation to Bitcoin prices.

Source: tradingview.com

Crypto trading exposure

While government authorities were trying to figure out regulations around cryptocurrencies, many public trading companies, brokers, and traditional exchanges got ahead of the crowd to offer cryptocurrency trading opportunities for the masses. For example, when Interactive Brokers Group (stock symbol: IBKR) announced on December 13, 2017, that it would allow its customers to *short* Bitcoin (sell it in speculation that its value would drop), its stock price actually dropped. The reason for that may have been that at the time, Bitcoin's price was at its peak, and most people didn't like the idea of shorting Bitcoin. Of course, Bitcoin prices ended up falling a few months later, and IBKR saw a boost in its stock price value, as shown in Figure 7-2. It then dropped again due to factors other than its Bitcoin exposure.

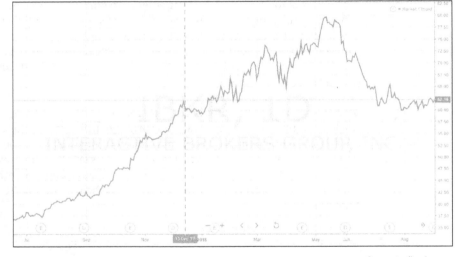

FIGURE 7-2: The stock price of Interactive Brokers (IBKR) dropped on December 13 following the announcement of a Bitcoin speculation service.

Source: tradingview.com

WARNING Speculative trading based on rumors and news can be very risky. When analyzing a stock from a fundamental point for a medium-to-long-term investment strategy, you must consider other factors, such as the company's management, services, industry outlook, financial statements, and financial ratios. See Chapters 11 and 12 in this minibook for more on short-term trading strategies and long-term investing strategies, respectively.

Market sentiment factors

The second point of the IDDA focuses on market sentiment. As indicated in Chapter 4 of this minibook, *market sentiment* is the general behavior and "feeling" of market participants toward a specific asset such as cryptos or stocks. When searching for stocks with crypto exposure, you must measure the market sentiment not only toward that stock but also toward the cryptocurrency industry. This approach gives you an idea about the direction you can take with your investment.

For a very simplified example, say all other IDDA points, including fundamental and technical analyses, are showing that you can expect the price of a given stock to go lower in the future. (The technical term for this move is a *bearish reversal* in a stock price.) But if you want to complete your IDDA analysis, you must also measure the market sentiment, using shorter time frames and indicators such as Ichimoku Kinko Hyo, which is discussed in Chapter 14 of this minibook.

TIP

Other market sentiment indicators include the following:

>> Moving average convergence divergence (MACD) (www.investdiva.com/investing-guide/macd/)

>> Relative strength index (RSI) (www.investdiva.com/investing-guide/relative-strength-index-rsi/)

>> Bollinger Bands (BOL) (www.investdiva.com/investing-guide/bollinger-bands-bol/)

Other considerations

At the end of the day, if you're looking to create a well-diversified portfolio by getting indirect exposure to cryptocurrencies, you may want to avoid *double dipping* (investing in the same category/industry twice). Stocks with exposure to cryptos should only be a proportionate piece of your overall portfolio, as categorized by industry. If you're looking to get an idea of how much you'll make on your investment with the amount of risk you're taking, and how much you should value the company's stock price, you must analyze the industry properly from all points of the IDDA. Then you can focus on picking the best stock in that category.

REMEMBER

Here are some questions to ask before picking the top crypto-related stocks for your portfolio:

>> Is the company working on any new developments in its technology?

>> What impact are potential breakthroughs likely to have?

>> Is the demand for the crypto-related services related to key economic variables? If so, which ones?

>> How much is the company planning to spend on crypto-related services? How is it planning to fund that spending?

>> Is the company rapidly employing and opening new crypto/blockchain-related jobs?

You can find the answers to these questions by researching the company's press releases and public reports. Your broker may also help you get your hands on the most recent developments. Of course, at Invest Diva, they also try to stay on top of all the developments, so make sure you subscribe free to updates at `https://learn.investdiva.com/start`. Then you can move on to the next IDDA points, such as technical analysis (see Chapters 4 and 10 of this minibook) and risk management (as we explain in Chapter 2 of this minibook).

Considering Cryptocurrency and Blockchain ETFs

If you're having a hard time picking the right stock, then you may want to consider another option. One of the easiest ways to get exposure to a specific industry without having to pick the top assets in that category is trading an exchange-traded fund, or ETF.

An ETF is similar to a mutual fund in that they're both "baskets" of assets in the same category. But ETFs are becoming more popular for reasons such as the following:

>> They're more tax efficient than mutual funds.

>> They have lower trading expenses compared to those of mutual funds.

>> They're simpler/more flexible than mutual funds.

>> They're more accessible than mutual funds to an average investor.

The following sections introduce you to ETFs and other indexes that provide exposure to cryptocurrencies and blockchain technology.

Getting an overview of blockchain ETFs

In 2018, a handful of blockchain-related ETFs were accessible to individual investors. However, Bitcoin ETFs or cryptocurrency ETFs didn't have much luck getting regulated, even though many of them were in line to get approval from the Securities and Exchange Commission (SEC). That's why investors who really wanted exposure to the crypto industry through an ETF had to look for the next-best thing, which was a blockchain ETF.

The first blockchain ETFs to hit the markets were BLOK and BLCN, both of which launched on January 17, 2018 (right at the time when Bitcoin was taking a hit). On January 29, 2018, another blockchain ETF, KOIN, showed its face in the competition. Here's a brief introduction to these three ETFs:

>> BLOK's full name is the Amplify Transformational Data Shearing ETF. Its basket holds 52 assets, including Digital Garage, Inc. (stock symbol: DLGEF), GMO Internet, Inc. (stock symbol: GMOYF), and Square, Inc. (stock symbol: SQ). You can find the most recent updates to this ETF at www.marketwatch.com/investing/fund/blok.

>> BLCN's full name is the Reality Shares Nasdaq NexGen Economy ETF. Its top holdings have more attractive stocks with blockchain exposure, including Advanced Micro Devices, Inc. (stock symbol: AMD), Intel Corporation (stock symbol: INTC), Microsoft Corporation (stock symbol: MSFT), and SBI Holdings, Inc. (stock symbol: SBHGF). You can find the most recent developments in this ETF at https://finance.yahoo.com/quote/BLCN/holdings/.

>> KOIN's full name is Innovation Shares NextGen Protocol ETF. This one didn't get as much love as the other two ETFs at the beginning. Its top holdings include Taiwan Semiconductor Manufacturing Co. Ltd. ADR (stock symbol: TSM), Amazon (stock symbol: AMZN), Nvidia (stock symbol: NVDA), Microsoft, and Cisco Systems (stock symbol: CSCO).

This option looks like a pretty good selection because of its focus on artificial intelligence. But perhaps the reason investors weren't as lovey-dovey with this ETF at the beginning was that it appears to have the least amount of direct exposure to the blockchain industry when compared to the other two. However, as shown in Figure 7-3, its returns surpassed those of BLOK and BLCN by September 2018. You can find out about the most recent developments in KOIN at www.morningstar.com/etfs/ARCX/KOIN/quote.html.

Disclaimer: Kiana has personally owned AMD, INTC, NVDA, AMZN, and MSFT in her portfolio since 2018. She also owns Bitcoin, Etherum, and Cardano, among other cryptocurrencies.

REMEMBER

These three ETFs had the early-arrival advantage for some time, but that doesn't necessarily mean they're the best in the game.

REMEMBER

Investing in ETFs makes the stock-analysis process a bit easier, but you still need a general understanding of the ETF's holding companies in order to be able to pick the one that best suits your portfolio. If various ETFs' holdings are widely different even in the same industry, you may want to consider investing in multiple ETFs, as long as their prices aren't correlated.

Source: tradingview.com

Keeping an eye on other indexes

TIP

While cryptocurrency ETFs take their time to get regulatory approval in the U.S., you can look for other indexes in the industry that can give you exposure to the crypto market. For example, in March 2018, Coinbase — one of the largest crypto exchanges in the United States — announced that it was planning to launch its own index fund. The index aims to follow the digital assets listed on Coinbase's exchange, Coinbase Pro (formerly called GDAX), which includes Bitcoin, Litecoin, Ethereum, Bitcoin Cash, plus all the other major cryptocurrencies. Stay ahead of these types of announcements by subscribing to the Invest Diva mailing list (`https://learn.investdiva.com/start`). Here are some other cryptocurrency news sources in alphabetical order:

>> `https://www.cnbc.com/`

>> `https://www.coindesk.com/`

>> `https://www.forbes.com/crypto-blockchain/`

>> `https://www.investing.com/news/cryptocurrency-news`

>> `https://www.nasdaq.com/topic/cryptocurrency`

>> `https://www.newsbtc.com/`

FIGURE 7-3: BLOK, BLCN, and KOIN ETF comparison in 2018.

Chapter **8**

Cryptocurrency Futures and Options

F utures and options are two forms of a general financial instrument called *derivatives.* They derive their value from the price action of something else — traditionally, from financial assets like stocks, commodities, *fiat* (government-backed) currencies, and other market indexes. As the cryptocurrency market becomes more popular, different cryptocurrency derivatives have been popping up and are accessible to individual traders.

In this chapter, you get an overview of the basics of futures and options trading, and then explore how they work in the crypto market.

TIP

At the time of this writing, many regulations exist around such assets, so you can invest in them through a handful of brokers and exchanges around the world. In the United States, Bitcoin futures trading is available through a handful of brokers and exchanges such as these:

>> **CME Group:** www.cmegroup.com/trading/bitcoin-futures.html

>> **E*Trade:** https://us.etrade.com/what-we-offer/investment-choices/futures#tab2_8

>> **Interactive Brokers:** www.interactivebrokers.com/en/home.php

>> **TD Ameritrade:** www.tdameritrade.com/investment-products/
futures-trading/bitcoin-futures.page

TIP
In countries such as the United Kingdom, Japan, and Korea, you may be able to trade cryptocurrency options and futures on Deribit: www.deribit.com/. However, at the time of this writing, the company doesn't offer their services in the United States.

Focusing on the Fundamentals of Futures

Here's a hint: Futures have something to do with the future! For example, when you buy a sack of coffee from your local supermarket, you pay for it right then and there at the market price. But what if you think the price of coffee will go down in the future? You can't buy coffee now at its "future" price in your local market, but you sure can in the futures market. If you think the price of coffee per pound is going down from $5 to $4 by June of next year, you can create a futures contract to buy a certain amount of coffee at $4 next June.

The following sections explain the features of commodity futures (the most common type) and other types of financial futures.

Futures' features

Traditionally, futures are most popular among commodities like grains, coffee, metals, wood, and meat. When you buy coffee in the futures market, you don't receive your coffee until a date in the future that you've agreed on with the seller. That's why your transaction isn't complete for some time. During this time, you own a highly liquid *futures contract* that you can hold or trade in the futures market. No matter what you do with the contract, as long as it's outstanding, the seller has a legally binding obligation to deliver your coffee on that specified date in the future. You have a similar obligation to take the coffee delivery. No return policy!

Two of the most important futures trading features are *hedging* and *speculating*. In fact, the futures market can't exist and operate efficiently without either one. Another characteristic of futures is *margin trading*. Here's how they work:

>> **Futures hedging:** Traditionally, the hedgers are businesses that either produce a commodity or use it as an input to their production process. As an investor, you can use hedging as a type of risk management to prevent losses

and not necessarily to make capital gains. You can hedge one investment by making another investment to offset the risk of the first investment — it's something like investing in an insurance policy to offset the risk of something happening to you in the future.

>> **Futures speculating:** The speculators are quite the opposite of the hedgers. They trade futures simply to earn a profit on expected price swings. They have no inherent interest in the commodity or its financial future other than its price action. For example, if you think the price of a commodity will increase in the future, you may be able to make a profit by purchasing the asset in a futures contract and selling it at a higher price later on. Regardless, the futures market depends on them because their trades help make the market more liquid.

>> **Margin trading:** You can take advantage of something called *leverage* when trading futures, just like in the foreign exchange or forex market (covered in Chapter 9 of this minibook). The difference is that *all* futures contracts are traded on a margin basis. You can't opt out of this feature. When you buy a futures contract *on margin,* it means you need to put only a fraction of the total price in cash. When trading futures contracts, you usually need a margin of about 2 percent to 10 percent of the contract value. The good news is that you don't have to borrow money to finance the balance of the contract, which makes it less risky than how margin trading works in forex.

The margin deposit is simply a security or a guarantee to cover any losses that may occur. It is *not* a partial payment for your purchase.

Financial futures

Although commodities make up for a big segment of the futures market, financial futures are another popular dimension of it. *Financial futures* use a different type of underlying asset than commodities do, and they offer a speculating vehicle for many markets such as forex, interest rates, and stock indexes. They have similar advantages to commodity future trading and have become a major hedging tool for institutions and individual traders alike. One key difference is the way the price of each type of financial futures contract is quoted:

>> Currency futures in the United States are quoted in U.S. dollars per unit of the underlying foreign currency — for example, U.S. dollar per Canadian dollar or U.S. dollar per Japanese yen.

>> Interest rate futures contracts are priced as a percentage of the *par value* (face value) of the underlying debt instrument. For example, the par value of most Treasury-based interest rate futures are $100,000, and therefore each contract trades in whole-dollar bids of $1,000.

>> Stock index futures are quoted in terms of the actual underlying index. Such indexes include the S&P 500 and Nasdaq.

Just like commodities, financial futures can expose you to a ton of profit and loss. But you must thoroughly understand your investments as well as the risks involved in order to be a successful futures trader.

WARNING

Speculating each type of futures can be a very specialized task. If you don't know much about each industry, you may as well be gambling in Las Vegas.

Introducing the Basics of Options

Options help you enter a contract with someone else to buy or sell something of value. If you're the option buyer, you have the right to buy an underlying asset (like coffee) within a given period of time at a price that was agreed upon at the time of the contract. If you're the seller, you must be ready to sell that underlying asset within the contract's instructions.

The following sections compare options to futures, describe types of options, and explain the risks.

Futures versus options

REMEMBER

Futures and options are very similar. They both involve the future delivery of something at a specific price. The big difference between a futures contract and an options contract comes down to the date of buying and selling. Here are some important points to keep in mind:

>> When trading a futures contract, you must buy/sell on or before an agreed-upon date.

>> With options, you can buy/sell over a specified period of time.

>> Put and call options (see the next section) specify the price at which you can buy or sell.

>> Futures prices aren't spelled out on the contract. Instead, the price on a futures contract is established through the trades among traders on the exchange. This means the delivery price is set at whatever price the contract sells for.

Puts and calls

The two basic kinds of options are called puts and calls, which are basically a version of selling and buying:

>> With a *put,* you can sell an underlying security at a specific price over a period of time.

>> With a *call,* you get the right to buy that security at the agreed price within a certain period of time.

Why don't they just call it buying and selling and save trouble? One key benefit of using a different name is that you're forced to remember that with puts and calls, you get no ownership privileges and gain no interest or dividend income. All you get are gains and losses from the price movements of the underlying assets. Just like futures, you can take advantage of the leverage puts and calls offer.

TIP

Paul Mladjenovic, author of a number of *For Dummies* investing books, has a great education course on options investing. You can check it out at www. ravingcapitalist.com/home/ultra-investing-with-options/.

Risks

WARNING

Options trading comes with a couple of notable risks:

>> One of the major risks with options puts and calls trading is that you can't make time your friend. Puts and calls have limited lives; the market may not have enough time to move favorably in your direction before the option expires, and you may end up losing money right before the prices move to your advantage.

>> Another major risk is that you can lose 100 percent of your initial investment if the markets move a tiny bit in an unfavorable direction at a wrong time. Though with normal investing you can wait it out, puts and calls options are totally worthless when they expire.

Cryptocurrency Futures and Options

Understanding Cryptocurrency Derivatives Trading

The ability to access cryptocurrency derivative exchanges was hit and miss prior to 2017, but from 2017 onward more and more exchanges, such as Binance, OKEx, and Bybit, started to offer derivative trading:

>> In May 2021, Goldman Sachs executed its first cryptocurrency trades, which were two types of Bitcoin-linked derivatives.

>> In May 2020, ErisX made history by pioneering the first U.S.-based Ether futures contracts.

At the time of this writing, crypto derivatives trading, including options and futures, is still fairly new. However, with many leading investment organizations already jumping in, you can expect such trading services to be accessible to the masses in no time, perhaps even by the time you have this book in your hands. The following sections give you the scoop.

The advantages of crypto derivatives trading

With crypto derivatives trading, you're betting on the price of specific coins (like Bitcoin or Ethereum) either on a future date or within a certain range of time. Derivatives trading may be more complex than simply buying and selling cryptocurrencies on an exchange, but a quick advantage is that you don't have to worry about storage security. If you're concerned about the risk of losing your crypto wallet or assets in a hacking attack, crypto derivatives have you covered. Because you don't actually own coins when trading options and futures, you don't have to worry about things like a crypto wallet, storage, and security (see Book 1, Chapter 3 for an introduction to wallets).

The advantages of crypto derivatives for the industry

Even if you choose not to trade crypto derivatives, the existence of such trading options may be good for the crypto industry as a whole. Why?

» Crypto derivatives may be able to boost the liquidity and trading volume across digital assets other than Bitcoin, which makes them easier to trade. Higher liquidity helps traders buy and sell more quickly and avoid risk of sudden, massive movements in the price at the time they're placing their trading orders.

» More people may become interested in the cryptocurrency market and put pressure on regulators to advance their views on the industry.

Trading resources

To stay up to date with the latest advancements in the crypto derivatives market, consider checking in regularly with financial news and cryptocurrency update providers such as those in the following list:

» Benzinga Pro (https://pro.benzinga.com/?afmc=2f)

» CCN (www.ccn.com/)

» CoinDesk (www.coindesk.com/)

» Cointelegraph (https://cointelegraph.com/)

» Crypto Briefing (https://cryptobriefing.com)

» Cryptonews.com (https://cryptonews.com/)

» Medium (https://medium.com/topic/cryptocurrency)

» NewsBTC (https://newsbtc.com)

If you like to browse your Facebook stream for news, consider "liking" these news providers. In that case, make sure that you change the setting of the news pages you follow to see them first on your feed. Otherwise, the news updates will get lost among the thousands of baby picture updates you get from your friends.

» Understanding major world currencies

» Exploring the forex market versus the cryptocurrency market

Chapter 9

Dealing with the Dollar and Other Fiat Currencies

C urrency trading, also known as the *foreign exchange market (forex)*, is the art of predicting the future value of fiat currencies against one another. Technically, a *fiat* currency is a legal tender that your local government supports through the central bank. The advent of cryptocurrencies has worried some fiat currency issuers (that is, central banks). Some believe that the cryptocurrencies may replace fiat currencies in the future. But for now, one of the ways to get your hands on cryptocurrencies is to exchange your fiat currencies for them. That's why understanding the basic movements in the world's fiat currencies may come in handy in your cryptocurrency investing endeavors.

This chapter looks at the U.S. dollar (USD) as the world's reserve currency along with other major currencies and their relationships with the cryptocurrency market. (Trading cryptocurrencies versus fiat currencies is introduced in Chapter 5 of this minibook.)

Considering the World's Reserve Currency: The U.S. Dollar

If you live in the United States, your first cryptocurrency investment is likely to be an exchange between the U.S. dollar and a digital asset like Bitcoin. Bitcoin prices can be incredibly volatile, but you also must consider the fluctuations of the U.S. dollar, which may lead to a better or worse trading deal for you. For example, if the U.S. dollar is incredibly strong, you can buy more bits of Bitcoin with it. This section explores some key factors that affect the value of the U.S. dollar.

Focusing on factors that affect the U.S. dollar

The U.S. dollar (USD) is one of the most popular currencies globally. If you travel to any country in the world, that country likely accepts the U.S. dollar in return for its local currency. This clout gives the United States a great privilege. Many people simply pile up on U.S. dollars in their savings account. Often, when the demand for USD goes higher, the dollar becomes even stronger. But when the U.S. economy takes a hit, or when the *Federal Reserve* (the United States's central bank, also called the *Fed*) makes pessimistic remarks about the future of the U.S. economy, the U.S. dollar is normally one of the first financial assets to go down.

Uncle Sam has been on watch because China is ramping up to become a threat to the USD as the world's reserve currency. And now, Bitcoin enthusiasts think the USD and Chinese yuan won't stand a chance against cryptocurrencies in the future.

TIP

If you're buying cryptocurrencies by using the U.S. dollar, you get a better deal if the USD is strong. You can buy more units of a digital coin if its value is low against the USD.

REMEMBER

Many factors affect USD price action. You could study the U.S. dollar's market movements for over a decade and still be unable to say for sure where its price is headed next. However, by conducting the Invest Diva Diamond Analysis (IDDA; see Chapter 4 of this minibook), you can stack the odds in your favor. Market sentiment, crowd psychology, and supply and demand can all contribute to the strength and weakness of the U.S. dollar the same way they impact other financial assets. The fundamental points can be different, though. Some of the fundamental factors that impact the U.S. dollar value include the following:

>> **Interest rates:** The *interest rate* is the price those who borrow money pay. It refers to the percentage of the borrowed amount of money that the borrower pays to the lender. When the U.S. Federal Reserve increases interest rates or is expected to do so, the U.S. dollar often gets stronger versus other fiat currencies and cryptos alike. While all economic calendars on websites such as Bloomberg (www.bloomberg.com) or Yahoo! Finance (https://finance.yahoo.com/) track upcoming and previous interest rate decisions, you can also keep track of the changes directly on the U.S. Federal Reserve website, at www.federalreserve.gov/monetarypolicy/fomccalendars.htm.

>> **Inflation:** *Inflation* is the reason why your grandmother paid less for a dozen eggs than you do. It refers to the general increase in the prices of goods and supplies. When inflation gets high, the Fed tries to control it by raising interest rates. Because of the way inflation affects interest rates, an increase in inflation usually has a positive impact on the USD. Inflation data is measured by something called the Consumer Price Index (CPI), which is also tracked on most economic calendars. In the United States, you can also track inflation on the Bureau of Labor Statistics website at www.bls.gov/schedule/news_release/cpi.htm.

>> **Gross domestic product (GDP):** *Gross domestic product* reflects a country's yearly production and revenue. The U.S. dollar grows stronger when the GDP is high. To get direct access to GDP data, you can check out the Bureau of Economic Analysis website at www.bea.gov.

>> **Unemployment rate:** The U.S. unemployment rate in particular is a huge forex gossip topic. A decline in the unemployment rate means that the economy is doing well and more jobs have been created, which results in a stronger dollar in the United States. You can find the unemployment rate announcement schedules for the United States at www.bls.gov/schedule/news_release/empsit.htm.

>> **Nonfarm payrolls (NFP):** The *nonfarm payrolls* figure shows the total number of paid U.S. workers in every business, excluding employees of places like farms, private households, and general government. An expanding nonfarm payroll is a good indication that the economy is growing and therefore can lead to a stronger USD. You can find the event schedule and data at www.bls.gov/schedule/news_release/empsit.htm.

Looking at Bitcoin versus the U.S. dollar

REMEMBER

Even the biggest Bitcoin enthusiasts don't believe Bitcoin can replace the U.S. dollar anytime soon, if ever. Bitcoin must overcome way too many hurdles before it can claim to be the world's reserve currency. Plus, even though Bitcoin is the celebrity of all cryptocurrencies, other, "better" versions of Bitcoin may climb up the digital currency ladder and replace Bitcoin even before it can replace the USD. A few more reasons why Bitcoin likely won't ever replace the USD include the following:

>> Unknown miners all over the world pose a major security threat. We don't know where some of those massive mining farms are located and how they are planning to spend their Bitcoins.

>> In cryptocurrencies like Bitcoin that can be mined, a group of miners hypothetically can get together to control over 50 percent of the network, preventing the normal transaction process and possibly leading to security issues and hacking.

>> A very limited supply of coins can ever be created (21 million coins).

>> Forty percent of the world's Bitcoins are held by 1,000 people, so the financial inequality has already begun, putting the power in the hands of a small portion of the world's population. This doesn't sit well with one of the main reasons for blockchain technology (see Chapter 4) and the idea of cryptocurrencies, which is to fix the financial inequality issue around the globe.

>> A lack of security exists, as discussed in Chapter 2 of this minibook and in Book 1, Chapter 3.

One of the main differences between Bitcoin and the U.S. dollar is in price fluctuations. As shown in Figure 9-1, even when Bitcoin (BTC) was considered to have calmed down in the period between June and September 2018, its price action was way crazier than that of the U.S. Dollar Index, DXY. The DXY measures the value of the USD relative to a basket of foreign currencies. This relative stability gives the USD an edge in terms of security.

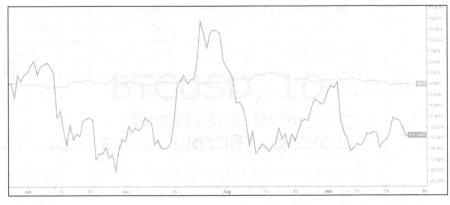

FIGURE 9-1:
U.S. Dollar Index (DXY) price action compared to BTC/USD.

Source: tradingview.com

Even though the forex market is known for its price volatility and unpredictable nature, Bitcoin certainly beats the USD at its own game.

REMEMBER

While the mainstream media usually follows only Bitcoin, other cryptocurrencies such as Ethereum (ETH), Litecoin (LTC), and Bitcoin Cash (BCH) can also be traded versus the U.S. dollar on cryptocurrency exchanges such as Coinbase (www.coinbase.com/join/59d39a7610351d00d40189f0). If you're only speculating on cryptocurrency price actions, you may be able to track other cryptocurrencies' values versus the U.S. dollar on websites like the following:

>> **AVATrade:** www.avatrade.com/?tag=87597&tag2=~profile_default

>> **eToro:** http://partners.etoro.com/A75956_TClick.aspx

Examining the Euro and Other Major Currencies

REMEMBER

You can technically trade any country's currency in the forex market, but seven specific currencies are the most popular. Investors call these currencies the *majors.* They're popular not only because they're more accessible worldwide but also because their movements are more predictable. Moreover, their countries' economies are considered more stable (although this can be debatable). And importantly, transaction fees for trading them are lower compared with other, less popular currencies. Here's the list of majors:

>> European Union euro (EUR)

>> British pound (GBP)

>> Swiss franc (CHF)

>> Japanese yen (JPY)

>> Canadian dollar (CAD; also known as the loonie)

>> Australian dollar (AUD; also known as the Aussie dollar)

>> New Zealand dollar (NZD; also known as the Kiwi dollar)

TECHNICAL STUFF

When you trade the majors against the U.S. dollar, they're called the *major currency pairs.*

The following sections explain a bit more about each currency. A comparison of the general forex market versus the cryptocurrency market appears later in this chapter.

The euro and the British pound

The euro is a shared currency among 19 out of the 28 members of the European Union. If the U.S. dollar is the king of the forex market, the euro is queen; it's the second-most traded currency in the world after the USD.

The British pound is that black sheep in the family that didn't get on with the euro after the United Kingdom became a member of the eurozone. The British pound was more valuable than the euro, and the U.K. government didn't want to give it up. Other countries had to give up their national currencies in favor of the more powerful euro. But having a stand-alone currency may be considered a lucky move because when the United Kingdom voted in 2016 to leave the eurozone (in an act called *Brexit*), the separation became a tad less complicated because the currencies were already separate.

TIP

Although the long-term view of the EUR and GBP remains unclear, some of Kiana's medium-term strategies — using a combination of technical analysis, fundamental analysis, and sentimental analysis to develop these trading strategies based on IDDA (see Chapter 4 of this minibook) — have worked out in making her and her students richer. For example, Kiana traded the GBP/JPY pair (the British pound versus the Japanese yen) multiple times, as shown in Figure 9-2. See more of Kiana's trading strategies in the Premium Investing Group (https://learn.investdiva.com/join-group) and on the Invest Diva blog, for example, in this entry: www.investdiva.com/investing-guide/eurjpy-ichimoku-cloud/.

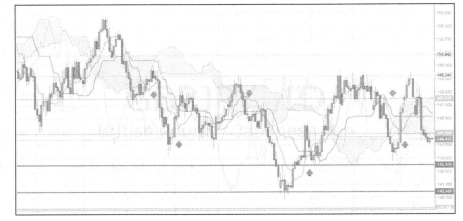

FIGURE 9-2:
Trading GBP/
JPY between
key support and
resistance levels
of 144.85 and
147.50.

Source: tradingview.com

Safe havens: The Swiss franc and the Japanese yen

The Swiss franc and Japanese yen are some forex traders' go-to currencies when the U.S. dollar and euro are doing poorly and getting weaker in value. That's why they're often called *safe havens*. Kiana saw this effect firsthand in 2008 when the USD's value was dropping and JPY became one of the biggest winners, allowing her to double her first-ever forex trade within a month (check out the sidebar in this chapter for details). The Japanese yen is considered more of a safety zone than the Swiss franc, especially because of a sudden move by the Swiss National Bank (SNB) in 2015 that shocked the financial markets and therefore created a ton of volatility in the CHF on January 15, 2015.

TECHNICAL STUFF

January 15, 2015, was a dark day in the forex community. Many traders, including Kiana, had parked their bets on the Swiss franc, thinking the Swiss are too neutral to do anything sudden and outrageous to endanger their investments. Boy, were they wrong! On that day, out of nowhere the Swiss National Bank made a change in its currency valuation policy that resulted in a sudden 30 percent increase in the franc's value against the euro. That also meant that Kiana's bullish position on the USD/CHF ran into trouble. Many companies actually went bankrupt because of this! You can read about the Swiss franc's history and the day that's now remembered as Black Thursday at www.investdiva.com/investing-guide/swiss-franc-trading-history-future/.

Regardless, both the JPY and the CHF remain safe havens for traders because many investors expect them to keep their value in times of global financial crisis.

The Aussie, Kiwi, and Loonie dollars

Forex traders consider the Australian dollar, New Zealand dollar, and Canadian dollar *commodity currencies.* The reason is that they're highly correlated to commodity price fluctuations, among other things. For example, Australia has a lot of natural resources like iron, gold, and aluminum. It also has large farms and a ton of cows that produce milk and other dairy products. Australia's economy depends on these commodities, and that's why the Australian currency, the AUD, often takes cues from commodity prices and the state of imports and exports in the country.

Comparing the Forex Market and the Crypto Market

People rarely view Bitcoin and other cryptocurrencies as currencies when they invest in them. Most investors and market participants alike treat cryptos like securities such as common stocks. But the fact is that to buy any cryptocurrency, you have to trade it versus another currency — fiat or crypto — as explained in Chapter 5 of this minibook. Because of this requirement, many forex brokers have started offering cryptocurrency services to their forex trading crowd. (Flip to Chapter 3 of this minibook to explore how you can trade cryptos by using a forex broker.) The following sections spell out some similarities and differences between the forex and the crypto markets.

REMEMBER

Despite a few similarities, comparing forex with cryptocurrencies is like comparing apples and oranges. They're two different financial instruments and require a different type of approach when you're developing investment strategies around them.

The similarities

One of the key similarities between forex and cryptocurrency trading is that they both carry a huge amount of risk. If you choose to trade cryptocurrencies on a short-term basis versus other digital or fiat currencies, you may need to study their price actions by using the technical analysis methods introduced in Chapter 10 of this minibook. However, as the cryptocurrency market becomes more mainstream, you can expect its movement to become more predictable.

The crazy amount of day-to-day volatility can also be viewed as a similarity. Day traders may benefit from the price fluctuations in both markets. In most cases, liquidity is high enough for major cryptocurrencies and forex pairs to make it easy for trading orders to go through pretty easily.

The differences

Now this point is a lot easier to write about! Here are some of the main differences between the forex and cryptocurrency markets:

>> **Size:** The forex market is by far the largest market in the world, and no crypto, no matter how large its market cap is, comes even close to forex. To give you an idea, the forex market has a daily trading volume of around $6 trillion

USD. The global cryptocurrency market, on the other hand, has a daily volume of about $1.8 trillion USD as of August 10, 2021. It's not bad, but forex is the clear winner. (Book 1, Chapter 4 has more on cryptos and market cap.)

WARNING

The fact that the forex market is ultra large doesn't mean you can make more profit in it. If anything, the daily fluctuations make it riskier and harder to predict.

>> **Variety:** You can choose from a ton of cryptocurrencies, but only seven major fiat currencies are actively traded. This range makes the *choosing* part easier for forex traders, while you have to analyze hundreds of cryptos to find yourself a catch. Head to the earlier section, "Examining the Euro and Other Major Currencies," for more on the seven most popular fiat options.

>> **Purpose:** Forex is more suitable for day traders. Although short-term trading isn't exactly our cup of tea, most forex traders get in and out of positions a lot more quickly than any other types of investors. By contrast, most crypto investors hold on to their assets for longer periods of times.

>> **Money supply:** Money supply is perhaps the key difference between forex and crypto. A country's central bank plays a massive role in determining its major currency's future. But Bitcoin and other cryptocurrencies are products of the blockchain industry; they aren't regulated by a central bank. So the fundamental analysis covered in Chapter 4 of this minibook is entirely different for forex and cryptocurrencies.

Resources for forex trading

Here are some quick tips to get you started in forex trading if you're planning to mix things up a little bit with the crypto world:

>> **Forex brokers:** Finding a forex broker that suits your needs is no easy task. You must make sure that the broker is safe to carry your investments, complies with your local financial guidelines, has enough money supply and liquidity to execute your trading orders quickly, and has reasonable fees for its services, among other things. Invest Diva's education courses cover forex brokers and the steps you need to take in choosing one, but here's a place you may be able to find the right one for you: https://forestparkfx. com/?id=UU1Uck hZSVN3OW1WNnNuNHIxaH1qUT09.

WARNING

>> **Your forex account:** Although many brokers offer you an option to start with as little as $50, keep in mind that in order for you to really make a profit in the forex market, you must have at least $10,000 of disposable money in your account, as well as superior knowledge about how the market works.

Otherwise, you're just gambling and likely to lose your initial investment within months, if not days.

» **Economic calendar:** To know what's going on in the forex market, you must follow the economic calendars of the countries whose currencies you're about to trade. Many websites offer the forex economic calendar for free, such as the following:

- www.forexfactory.com/
- www.investing.com/economic-calendar/
- www.fxstreet.com/economic-calendar

» **Forex news:** Besides the economic data, other factors — such as geopolitical tensions, supply and demand of commodities like oil and gold, and speeches by important political figures in a country — influence currency fluctuations. You can find out about these news items on websites such as these:

- www.dailyfx.com/
- www.fxstreet.com/

WARNING

Forex news outlets often create false hype around the market, which leads to emotional trading decisions. Make sure you don't fall into the trap of clickbait headlines like "The Number One Currency You Should Be Trading Right Now."

» **Education:** Kiana's *Forex Coffee Break* course has won a bunch of awards and is known as one of the easiest and most fun ways to find out all about forex. Check it out at https://education.investdiva.com/forex-coffee-break-with-invest-diva-education-course.

» **Strategies:** Kiana invests in the forex market on a medium-term basis, using the IDDA technique introduced in Chapter 4 of this minibook. If you're not a day trader, then you may find the Premium Investing Group helpful (https://learn.investdiva.com/join-group); it offers not only forex strategies but also cryptocurrency and stock investing signals as well.

Chapter **10**

Using Technical Analysis

S ome people believe that the financial markets, crypto or otherwise, are just another form of legalized gambling. They believe that the markets move randomly and have no connection to market psychology or to the fundamentals, such as the state of the economy or the people behind a blockchain technology.

However, over years of observing and investing in many different markets, many investors have come to see history repeating itself in the markets over and over again. The markets move as a result of a combination of the three top points of the Invest Diva Diamond Analysis (IDDA), which is introduced in Chapter 4 of this minibook:

» Fundamental analysis

» Market sentiment analysis

» Technical analysis

Flip to that chapter for the basics of fundamental and market sentiment analysis in the cryptocurrency market. This chapter shows you how technical analysis can help you identify the best buy and sell price levels, whether you're a long-term investor or an active trader.

TIP

Many cryptocurrency exchanges and brokers offer charting services to make it easier for you to trade directly from their platform. Some of these charts are sophisticated, and some aren't. We recommend using TradingView (`www.tradingview.com/`) for technical analysis, from foreign exchange (forex) to stocks and cryptocurrencies. You can use its free service for almost all assets, or you can choose to upgrade to its paid services to access charts without ads and to get other perks.

Beginning with the Basics of Technical Analysis

In short, *technical analysis* is the art of studying the history of an asset's price action to predict its future. The reason it often works is the result of a bunch of factors, including the following:

>> **Investor behavior:** Research in behavioral finance shows that investors make decisions based on a number of psychological biases that repeat themselves.

>> **Crowd psychology:** Many market participants use the same technical analysis methods, therefore strengthening the key price levels.

When the price movement patterns repeat themselves, investors who spot them early can get an edge in their strategy development and get better-than-average returns. Even though the cryptocurrency market is relatively new, the patterns are already forming in short- and medium-term time frames. The following sections give you the basics on chart types, time frames, and psychological factors.

WARNING

Past performance doesn't guarantee future results. Technical analysis only helps to stack the odds in your favor and doesn't guarantee profits. Therefore, you must conduct proper risk management, as we discuss in Chapter 2 of this minibook.

TIP

Find out more about technical analysis in Invest Diva's *Make Your Money Work for You PowerCourse* at `https://learn.investdiva.com/free-webinar-3-secrets-to-making-your-money-work-for-you`.

The chart art

So you want to get down and dirty with the historical price movements of your favorite cryptocurrency. As technical as this type of analysis sounds, you often find yourself using the creative side of your brain when you do it; the chart is your canvas. You can use different types of charts to plot the behavior of any cryptocurrency's price against other currencies, *fiat* (government backed) or not. Technical analysts love charts because they can visually track an otherwise number-oriented activity. Charts have evolved over the past decades as an increasing number of investors have used them to develop their strategies across different markets, including the stock, foreign exchange (forex), and cryptocurrency markets.

Some charts are simple and track only the price at the end of a session. Other charts are more complex and track every price movement during the session. Some of the most popular charts include the following:

>> **Line charts:** Line charts display only the closing prices of the market. That means that for any given time period, you can know only what the crypto's price is at the *end* of that time period and not what adventures and movements it had *during* that time period. A line is drawn from one closing price to the next closing price, and you can see the general movement of a currency pair over a period of time. Figure 10-1 shows an example featuring Bitcoin versus the U.S. dollar (BTC/USD) over a one-day time frame.

>> **Bar charts:** No, this option isn't a list of the local drinking establishments. At any given time frame, a *bar chart* shows you the opening market price, the price action during that time frame, and the closing price, as shown in Figure 10-2. The little horizontal line to the *left* shows the price at which the market opened. The little horizontal line to the *right* is the closing point of the time period. Find out more about bar charts in this fun video: https://www.youtube.com/watch?v=RghwgzNgZ64.

>> **Candlestick charts:** *Candlestick charts* (see Figure 10-3 for an example) look like bar charts, but the area between the open and close prices is colored to show you the general movement of the market during that time period. If the market generally moved up during the time period (known as *bullish* market sentiment), the area is normally colored green. If the market goes down (*bearish* market sentiment), the area is normally colored red. Of course, you can choose any colors you like; Kiana normally uses green for a bullish market movement and purple for a bearish market movement. A candlestick chart also shows the low and high price of the asset during the time period.

FIGURE 10-1: Line chart of BTC/USD over one day.

Source: *tradingview.com*

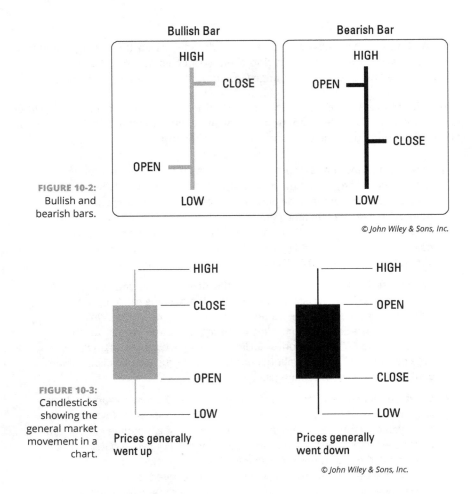

FIGURE 10-2: Bullish and bearish bars.

© John Wiley & Sons, Inc.

FIGURE 10-3: Candlesticks showing the general market movement in a chart.

Prices generally went up

Prices generally went down

© John Wiley & Sons, Inc.

The time factor

Depending on the type of investor you are, you can choose different time frames to conduct technical analysis. For example, if you're a day trader and want to take advantage of the crypto markets' fluctuations, you can study the market prices in the past 30 minutes, hour, or four hours. On the other hand, if you're a long-term investor and want to let the markets find their way toward your buy/sell limit orders, then you can analyze the price actions in the past days or months to find repetitive patterns and key psychological price levels.

All types of charts can be used in different time frames. A one-hour line chart shows you the closing price at the end of every hour. A daily candlestick chart shows you the open, close, low, and high prices during one-day periods as well as the general market movement over a longer time frame, as shown in Figure 10-4. That figure shows Ethereum's price action versus the U.S. dollar (ETH/USD) plotted on a daily candlestick chart.

Source: tradingview.com

FIGURE 10-4:
Daily candlestick
chart of ETH/USD.

The psychology factor: Trends

As you study market movements, you may start finding patterns and prices that keep showing their faces on the chart. A lot of this repetition has to do with market psychology and the crowd's general feeling about the cryptocurrency.

One of the most eye-catching formations on a chart is a trend. A trend on a chart has nothing to do with trends on Twitter or in the fashion world, but the idea behind it is similar. When you notice that a cryptocurrency's price keeps going up on a chart, that movement means the market participants are feeling good about the crypto. They keep buying it and therefore pushing its price higher. You may even say that the crypto is trending.

REMEMBER

You may have heard the famous investing phrase "the trend is your friend." If you spot the trend early enough, you may be able to take advantage of the rising prices and make some money. The same goes for when the crypto's price is moving down, or is on a *downtrend.* If you spot a downtrend early enough, you may be able to either sell your cryptocurrency or set a limit order (see Chapters 11 and 12 of this minibook) to buy more at a lower price.

Spotting the Key Levels

The whole point of technical analysis is to identify the best prices at which to buy and sell. Ideally you want to buy at the lowest price the cryptocurrency can drop to in the foreseeable future. And you want to hold on to it and sell at the highest price it can reach within your preferred time frame. In well-established markets with a ton of historical data, you can identify these prices by spotting key price levels that have created some sort of restriction for the market movements in the past. The following sections break down some of these important levels.

Support levels

REMEMBER

A *support level* is a barrier that prevents the prices from going lower. It's always below the current market price on your chart. Market participants who spot the support generally wait at that level to buy the cryptocurrency. One of the popular ways to spot a support level is to study the cryptocurrency's past performance on the chart. If a price level keeps "supporting" the cryptocurrency's value from dropping lower, you can mark it as a support level.

As shown in Figure 10-5, one of Bitcoin's key support levels was around $30,000 for most of 2021, up until October. Bitcoin's price tested around this psychological level a few times in mid-2021. But each time, the support level prevented Bitcoin from dropping lower.

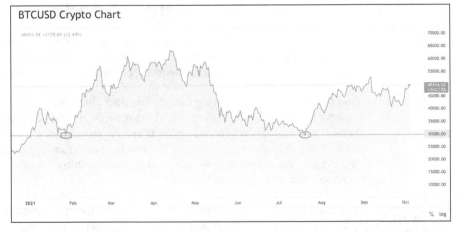

FIGURE 10-5: Bitcoin's key support level at around $30,000 for the first three quarters of 2021.

Source: tradingview.com

REMEMBER

Notice we say "around." Support levels aren't always a concrete number. Even though most news outlets say things like "Bitcoin dropped below the $30,000 psychological level," key supports are often a zone rather than a round number.

TIP

The support level becomes stronger the more it's tested. But after strong support is broken, the market sentiment runs a good chance of shifting to bearish and starting to drop lower toward the next support levels.

Resistance levels

REMEMBER

Resistance is a barrier that prevents the prices from going higher. It must be above the current price on your chart, and you can use it as a point to sell your crypto assets. You can identify a resistance level with your naked eye by looking for *peaks* on the chart. Every peak can be considered a resistance level as long as it's above the current market value.

Check out Figure 10-6 for some of Bitcoin's key resistance levels when it was trading around $49,414 in early October 2021.

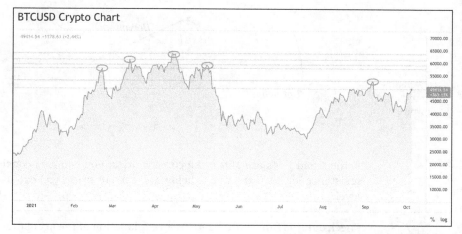

FIGURE 10-6:
Bitcoin's key resistance levels in October 2021.

Source: tradingview.com

TIP

You can use Fibonacci retracement levels to identify support and resistance levels. By applying Fibonacci to a past trend, you can immediately see a number of support and resistance levels without having to apply them one by one on your own. Of course, Fibonacci levels aren't always completely accurate, and you may need to play around with your application a bit to get it right. Check out Chapter 14 of this minibook to see how.

Trends and channels

Earlier in this chapter, we explain how trends can be formed based on market psychology. Some trends are very easy to spot. For example, the period between October 2020 and April 2021 was a period of an extreme *uptrend* in Bitcoin and many other cryptocurrencies when the prices just kept going up. Of course, this strong uptrend caught the attention of many people, both investors and non-investors, which led to the crypto bubble that came crashing down in May 2021. But spotting trends isn't always as easy.

Drawing trend lines is an art. And just as with any other type of art, everyone has a unique opinion on them. Here are two basic methods for drawing an uptrend and a downtrend:

» To draw an uptrend line, when you've casually identified a bullish momentum on the chart, simply click on the trend line instrument on your trading platform and connect two or more major valleys (bottoms), as shown in Figure 10-7.

» To draw a downtrend, connect two or more major peaks (tops).

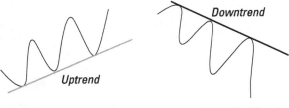

FIGURE 10-7: How to draw uptrends and downtrends.

If the trend lines are above the current price, you can also consider them *angled resistance* levels. If the line is below the current price, you can use it as a support level.

TIP

Check out this fun, short video for an explanation of the art of drawing trend lines: `https://www.youtube.com/watch?v=aHOnBcnDumQ&t=1s`.

Now what if the market is moving between two parallel support and resistance levels? Technical chartists call this formation a *channel.* You can use lengthy channels for short-term trading strategies, as discussed in Chapter 11 of this minibook. For example, a common strategy is buying at the lower band of the channel and selling at the upper band. Figure 10-8 shows basic channels you can identify on your chart.

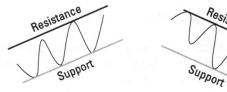
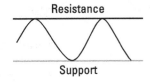

FIGURE 10-8: Basic forms of channels.

When the trend is no longer your friend

Unfortunately, trends don't continue forever. All good things must come to an end. What goes up must come down. And many other clichés. Identifying the exact time a trend ends is one of the hardest jobs of technical analysts. Oftentimes, the market just teases the crowd with a sudden but short-lived change of direction. Many investors panic. But then the price gets back on track with the long-term trend.

TIP

Although key support and resistance levels can help you predict when a trend may end, you must back up your discoveries with fundamental and market sentiment analysis, as explored in Chapter 4 of this minibook.

Picking Out Patterns on a Chart

Technical analysts are constantly looking for ways to identify key support and resistance levels. This is no easy task, but chart formations can help you with your observations. Becoming an expert technical chartist can take time, and many analysts go through years of studying for degrees such as the Charted Market Technician (CMT). But for now, here's the gist of some important chart patterns.

TIP

Check out the award-winning education course, *Forex Coffee Break*, which makes technical analysis as easy and as fun as possible, even for newbies: https://education.investdiva.com/forex-coffee-break-with-invest-diva-education-course.

Bullish reversal patterns

When a *bullish reversal* formation is confirmed, it normally indicates that the trend of the market price will reverse from a downtrend into an uptrend. It reverses the market into a bullish position. Some well-known bullish reversal chart patterns (shown in Figure 10-9) include the *double bottom* (when the price tests a key support level twice, creating two valley shapes at the support level), *the head and shoulders bottom* (when the price tests approximately the same support level three times), and the *saucer bottom* (when the price gradually reaches a key support level and gradually moves up, forming the shape of a bowl).

TIP

A popular trading strategy that uses bullish reversal patterns is to buy when you identify the pattern at its so-called *neckline* (which is a key resistance level) and sell at the next key resistance level.

FIGURE 10-9:
Examples of bullish reversal chart patterns.

Double Bottom **Head and Shoulders Bottom** **Saucer Bottom**

© John Wiley & Sons, Inc.

Bearish reversal patterns

As its name suggests, a *bearish reversal* formation is the exact opposite of a bullish one (see the preceding section). With a bearish reversal, the prices normally hit a resistance during an uptrend and can't go any higher. Therefore, they're forced to reverse into a bear market. Some famous bearish reversal patterns (shown in Figure 10-10) include the *double top* (a formation of two mountain-like shapes on the chart as the price tests a key resistance level), the *head and shoulders* (when the price tests approximately the same resistance level three times, but the second time it goes a bit higher, making it look like a peaking head), and the *saucer top* (when the price gradually reaches a key resistance level and then gradually moves back down).

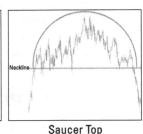

FIGURE 10-10:
Examples of bearish reversal chart patterns.

Double Top **Head and Shoulders** **Saucer Top**

© John Wiley & Sons, Inc.

TIP

Some typical strategies using bearish reversals include the following:

>> Take profit of assets you've been holding after you identify the pattern.

>> Short-sell at the neckline and take profit at the next support levels.

Smoothing Charts Out with Moving Averages

If you find price charts and all the information they contain too complicated, you're not alone! Like-minded investors and chartists often turn to tools categorized as moving averages (MAs) to identify those trends more easily.

By definition, a *moving average* is a mathematical procedure that records the average value of a series of prices over time. You have a ton of ways to calculate moving averages and use them based on your trading needs. Some are basic, and some are more sophisticated. Kiana likes to mix and match MAs with technical chart patterns and, of course, Fibonacci retracement levels. The following sections have more on MAs; flip to Chapter 14 of this minibook for details on Fibonacci retracement levels.

WARNING

You may have gotten used to the idea that trading signals and indicators are often just full of it. The cryptocurrency market often acts in an arbitrary fashion, ignoring all the supposed rules. That's why you should never rely on only one method of analysis and should *always* confirm your decisions with other tools and points of the Invest Diva Diamond Analysis (IDDA) in Chapter 4 of this minibook. Additionally, never invest money you can't afford to lose.

Basic moving averages

On your trading chart, you can find basic moving averages (MAs) that smooth out the prices, ranging from 10 to 200 time periods. For example, if you look at a daily chart, you can select a short-term moving average that calculates a series of 15 data points. This figure is called a *15-day moving average,* or a *fast MA.* If you want to see a longer-term average movement, you can use a longer period, such as as 200 days, and call it a *slow MA.*

REMEMBER

Longer-term moving averages do a better job at picking up the major trends. On the other hand, shorter-term MAs are more sensitive to recent price actions. Technical analysts often use a combination of MAs and study their positioning versus one another.

Sophisticated moving averages

Geeky technical analysts like me often take their MA practice to the next level, using more complex combinations of moving averages to understand the market sentiment better. Here are some of the most widely used sophisticated MAs:

>> **Moving average convergence divergence (MACD):** MACD is an indicator that shows the difference between a short-term moving average and a long-term moving average. Click here for more information: www. investdiva.com/investing–guide/macd/.

>> **Bollinger Bands (BOL):** Created by John Bollinger in the 1980s, this indicator includes two bands above and below the market price. Click here for more information: www. investdiva.com/investing–guide/bollinger–bands–bol/.

>> **Relative strength index (RSI):** RSI is a momentum indicator, or oscillator, that measures the relative internal strength of the cryptocurrency's price against itself. Click here for more information: www. investdiva.com/investing–guide/relative–strength–index–rsi/.

>> **Ichimoku Kinko Hyo:** This option consists of five different MAs all on top of each other. It gives you all you need to know all at once (hence its name, which means "a glance at the chart in balance"). Head to Chapter 14 of this minibook for more details.

Chapter **11**

Short-Term Trading Strategies

Some traders thrive on the thrill of short-term trading adventures, or *speculative trading.* Others sweat on speculations. If you prefer to sit back, relax, have nights of peaceful sleep, and let the markets do their thing, you may want to focus on investing long term. (You can discover some long-term investing strategies in Chapter 12 of this minibook.)

That being said, this chapter walks you through some methods you can use to develop short-term strategies that have worked for Kiana's students. Although the basics of short-term trading are similar across different assets, crypto trading requires you to consider some additional steps to stack the odds in your favor.

Distinguishing Three Short-Term Time Frames

Short-term trading can also be called aggressive trading because you're taking more risk in the hope of making more profit. As discussed in Chapter 2 of this minibook, investment of any kind requires a constant balancing and trade-off between risk and return. To earn more return, you must take more risk. When aiming to make money in the short term, you must be prepared to lose your investment (and maybe even more!) in that time frame as well, especially in a volatile market like cryptocurrencies.

Short-term trading can be divided into different categories within itself based on how quickly you realize the profits — hours, days, or weeks. Generally speaking, the shorter the trading time frame, the higher the risk involved with that trade. The following sections spell out the three most common short-term trading time frames for cryptocurrencies.

Profiting within hours

If you've ever wondered what a day trader does, this is it! *Day trading* is one form of aggressive short-term trading. You aim to buy and sell cryptos within a day and take profit before you go to bed. In traditional markets like the stock market, a trading day often ends at 4:30 p.m. local time. But the cryptocurrency market runs 24/7, so you can define your day-trading hours to fit your schedule. Pretty neat, right? With this great power comes great responsibility, though. You don't want to lose your shirt and get your partner angry at you.

Here are a few questions to ask yourself to determine whether day trading is indeed the right crypto route for you:

>> Do you have the time to dedicate to day trading? If you have a full-time job and can't stick to your screen all day, day trading probably isn't right for you. Make sure that you don't use your company time for trading! Not only could you get fired, but you also won't be able to dedicate the required time and energy to trading either. Double the trouble.

>> Do you have sufficient risk tolerance for day trading? Check out Chapter 2 of this minibook for more on risk management, and attend this webinar to calculate your risk tolerance: https://learn.investdiva.com/free-webinar-3-secrets-to-making-your-money-work-for-you.

>> Even if you can financially afford to lose money day trading, are you willing to do so? Do you have the stomach to see your portfolio go up and down on a daily basis? If not, perhaps day trading isn't right for you.

If you've made up your mind that day trading is the right crypto route for you, the following sections share some tips to keep in mind before getting started.

Defining crypto trading sessions

Because cryptocurrencies are traded internationally without borders, one way you can define a trading day is to go by the trading sessions in financial capitals of the world like New York, Tokyo, the *eurozone* (made up of the European countries whose official currency is the euro), and Australia. Figure 11-1 shows these sessions. This method follows similar trading sessions as in the foreign exchange (forex) market.

FIGURE 11-1: Cryptocurrency trading sessions based on international time zones.

Sydney Market Open	Tokyo Market Open	London Market Open	New York Market Open
Trading Day 5 PM (EST) ↓ Next Day 2 AM (EST)	Trading Day 7 PM (EST) ↓ Next Day 4 AM (EST)	3 AM (EST) ↓ 12 PM (EST)	8 AM (EST) ↓ 5 PM (EST)

TIP

Some sessions may provide better trading opportunities if the cryptocurrency you're planning to trade has higher volume or volatility in that time frame.

Know that day trading cryptos is different from day trading other assets

When day trading traditional financial assets such as stocks or forex, you can follow already-established fundamental market-movers such as a company's upcoming earnings report or a country's interest rate decision. The cryptocurrency market, for the most part, doesn't have a developed risk-event calendar. That's why conducting fundamental analysis (see Chapter 4 of this minibook) to develop a day-trading strategy is way harder for cryptos.

Set a time aside

REMEMBER

Depending on your personal schedule, you may want to consider scheduling a specific time of the day to focus on your trades. The idea of being able to trade around the clock is pretty cool in theory. You can just get on your trading app during a sleepless night and start trading. But this flexibility can backfire when you start losing sleep over it. Remaining alert during day trading, or night trading for that matter, is very important because you need to develop strategies, identify trading opportunities, and manage your risk multiple times throughout the trading session. For many people, having a concrete disciplined plan pays off.

Start small

Day trading involves a lot of risk. So until you get the hang of it, start with a small amount and gradually increase your capital as you gain experience. Some brokers even let you start trading with a minimum of $50.

WARNING

If you start trading small, make sure that you aren't using margin or leverage to increase your trading power. Leverage is one of those incredibly risky tools that's projected as an opportunity. It lets you manage a bigger account with a small initial investment by borrowing the rest from your broker. If you're trying to test the waters by starting small, using leverage will defeat that purpose.

Don't take on too much risk

According to Investopedia, most successful day traders don't stake much of their account — 2 percent of it, max — with each trade. If you have a $10,000 trading account and are willing to risk 1 percent of your capital on each trade, your maximum loss per trade is $100 ($0.01 \times $10,000$). So you must make sure you have that money set aside for potential losses, and that you aren't taking more risk than you can afford.

Secure your crypto wallet

One major challenge with day trading cryptocurrencies is securing your crypto wallet. The least secure cryptocurrency wallets are online wallets; see Book 1, Chapter 3 for more about crypto wallets. Because you're going to need your capital handy throughout the trading day, you may have no choice but to leave your assets on your exchange's online wallet, which can expose you to the risk of hacking.

TIP

One way to enhance your security here is to not actually buy and sell cryptocurrencies but rather to speculate the price action and crypto market movements by using brokers who facilitate such services, as discussed in Chapter 3 of this minibook.

Stay away from scalping

WARNING

Some individual traders choose *scalping*, which is the shortest-term trading strategy. It basically means jumping in and out of trades frequently, sometimes in a matter of seconds. If you're paying commission fees for every trade, not only are you exposing yourself to a ton of market risk when scalping, but you can also get burned out by the fees before you make any profit. Individual traders rarely make any profit scalping. Now, if you're part of an enterprise that has access to discount commission fees and huge trading accounts, the story may be different.

Profiting within days

If you want to trade short term but don't want to stick to your computer all the time, this time frame may be the right one for you. In traditional trading, traders who hold their positions overnight are categorized as *swing traders*. The most common trading strategy for swing traders is *range trading*, where instead of riding up a trend, you look for a crypto whose price has been bouncing up and down within two prices. The idea is to buy at the bottom of the range and sell at the top, as shown in Figure 11-2. If you're using a broker who facilitates short-selling services, you can also go in the other direction.

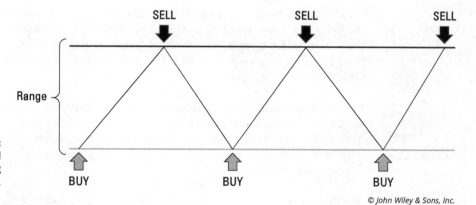

FIGURE 11-2:
A simplified range-trading strategy.

© John Wiley & Sons, Inc.

Of course, in real life the ranges aren't as neat and pretty as in the example shown in Figure 11-2. To identify a range, you must be proficient in technical analysis. A number of technical chart patterns (see Chapter 10 of this minibook) and indicators can help you identify a range. For more on technical analysis, check out the trading courses at https://learn.investdiva.com/services.

REMEMBER

If you choose swing trading rather than day trading, one downside is that you may not be able to get an optimized tax rate that's created for day traders in some countries. In fact, swing trading is in the gray area for taxation because if you hold your positions for more than a year (long-term investing; see Chapter 12 of this minibook), you also get an optimized tax rate. For more on tax optimizations, flip to Chapter 15 of this minibook.

TIP

If you're trading the cryptocurrency market movements without actually buying them, make sure you that aren't paying a ton of commission fees for holding your positions overnight. Consult with your broker before developing your swing-trading strategy, or check out `https://forestparkfx.com/?id=UU1UckhZSVN3OW 1WNnNuNHIxaH1qUT09` to select a broker that suits your strategy.

Profiting within weeks

This time frame falls into the category of *position trading* in traditional markets. Still shorter than a long-term investing strategy but longer than day trading, position trading can be considered the least risky form of short-term trading. But it's still risky. (Flip to Chapter 2 of this minibook to read more about risks involved in trading cryptocurrencies.)

For this type of trade, you can identify a market trend and ride it up or down until the price hits a resistance or a support. As explained in Chapter 10 of this mini-book, a *resistance* level is a psychological market barrier that prevents the price from going higher. A *support* level is the opposite: a price at which the market has difficulty "breaking below."

WARNING

To hold your positions for weeks, you need to keep your crypto assets in your exchange's online wallet, which may expose you to additional security risk (see Book 1, Chapter 3). You may be better off utilizing a broker that provides price-speculation services for this type of trading strategy so you don't have to own the cryptocurrencies.

One popular position-trading strategy involves the following steps, also shown in Figure 11-3:

1. Identify a trend (using technical analysis).
2. Wait for a pullback.
3. Buy at the pullback within the uptrend.
4. Take profit (sell) at a resistance.

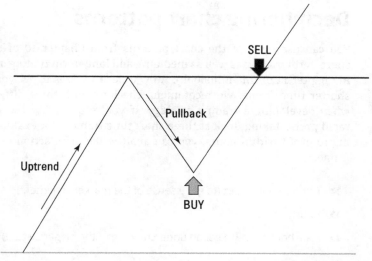

SELL

Pullback

Uptrend

FIGURE 11-3:
Buying at the
pullback in an
uptrend market,
and taking profit
at resistance.

BUY

TIP

The Invest Diva Premium Investing Group often provides position-trading strategies to its members by using the Ichimoku Kinko Hyo + Fibonacci combo technique. See Chapter 14 of this minibook for more about this technique, and visit here to join the group: `https://learn.investdiva.com/join-group`.

Trying Short-Term Analysis Methods

You can't become a successful short-term trader just by reading the news. Short-term trading is an art that combines active risk management with a great understanding of crowd psychology and price actions that goes beyond the scope of this book. Also, the cryptocurrency market isn't as established as other markets, so trading the lesser-known cryptos on a short-term basis can be even riskier. You can compare that to trading penny stocks or gambling, which are almost sure ways to lose money. Regardless, the following sections present some analysis methods that professional traders with large accounts and a high risk tolerance can use.

WARNING

According to Medium (`https://medium.com`), day trading the cryptocurrency market has brought some investors profits between 1 and 2 percent, while on other values they *lose* money. For most, day trading the crypto market has been a zero-sum game.

Deciphering chart patterns

You can use most of the chart patterns from Chapter 10 of this minibook for short-term trading as well as medium- and long-term trading strategies (covered in Chapter 12 of this minibook). All you need to do is to set your chart view to a shorter time frame. We recommend checking with three different time frames when developing a trading strategy. If you're analyzing the markets for more rapid profit-taking, look at three short time frames. For example, if you're looking to profit within hours, you can analyze the price action on these three time frames:

>> Thirty-minute chart (to get a sense of the market sentiment)

>> Hourly chart

>> Four-hour chart (to get an understanding of the bigger picture)

If you see different forms of bullish reversal chart patterns (see Chapter 10 of this minibook) across all three time frames, you may have a higher probability of a new uptrend starting, which can lead you to a successful bullish trading strategy. The following sections show an example of the Bitcoin/U.S. dollar (BTC/USD) crypto/fiat pair on September 5, 2018.

TIP

TradingView (https://tradingview.go2cloud.org/aff_c?offer_id=2&aff_ id=13497) is a great choice for charting, as they provide many technical analysis tools and customizable charts.

A 30-minute chart

You're looking at the 30-minute chart, and at 9:30 a.m., you suddenly see a massive drop that brings Bitcoin's price down from approximately $7,380 to $7,111, as shown in Figure 11-4. This formation is called a *bearish engulfing candlestick pattern* among technical analysts. Is this the beginning of a new downtrend?

An hourly chart

By switching from the 30-minute chart (see the preceding section) to the hourly chart, you notice the same drop (shown in Figure 11-5). But because you can now see the bigger picture, you discover that this drop was after a period of uptrend in the market, which may be a signal of a pullback during an uptrend. But how low can the pair go?

Source: tradingview.com

FIGURE 11-4:
BTC/USD
30-minute chart
on September 5,
2018.

Source: tradingview.com

FIGURE 11-5:
BTC/USD
hourly chart on
September 5,
2018.

A four-hour chart

By switching from the hourly chart (see the preceding section) to the four-hour chart, you notice that the bearish engulfing pattern is formed in a much longer uptrend that has been moving up since the middle of August. By observing the four-hour chart, you can pinpoint the key support levels, shown at $6,890 and $6,720, that the price can pull back toward within this newly established bearish market sentiment. The results in Figure 11-6 are from using the Fibonacci retracement levels to identify the key price levels with higher accuracy. Flip to Chapter 14 of this minibook for more on Fibonacci.

Source: tradingview.com

FIGURE 11-6:
BTC/USD
four-hour chart
on September 5,
2018.

Following the technical analysis guidelines, you can expect a bit of a correction after this sudden drop, followed by more drops to key support levels on the four-hour chart. With this, a potential trading idea may be to sell at correction or at market price and then to take profit at one or two support levels.

After sudden drops in the markets, sometimes the market corrects itself before dropping more. Often, it corrects itself to key *pivot levels* (a level that's considered trend-changing if the price breaks below or above it), which in this case is the 23 percent Fibonacci retracement level at $7,090. The reward for waiting for a correction is that you may be able to take more profit short-selling at a higher price. The risk with it is that the market may not correct itself, and you may miss out. One option, if the market is really going to shift into a bearish sentiment, is to sell some at market price and set a sell *limit order* at the key pivot level just in case the market corrects itself before further drops. This way, you can distribute your risk. A sell limit order is a type of trading order you can set on your broker's platform, which enables you to sell your assets at a specific price in the future.

For a short-term profit-taking, consider setting buy limit orders at both key support levels at 38 percent and 50 percent Fibonacci retracement levels. This example shows aiming to take partial profit at around $6,890, and then exiting the trade completely at $6,720. Again, this approach may limit the gains if the market continues to drop, but it also limits the risk if the price doesn't fall as low as the second key support, so it provides a proportionate risk-reward ratio. Figure 11-7 shows how the market actually performed.

FIGURE 11-7:
BTC/USD
four-hour
chart strategy
performance.

Source: tradingview.com

The BTC/USD price did correct a little bit, but it didn't go as high as the 23 percent Fibonacci retracement level. So if you had only waited for a correction to sell, you would've missed out on the trading opportunity. The market did drop to both key support levels at 38 percent and 50 percent Fibonacci retracement levels. So if you had sold at market price, you would've taken profit at both key support levels. On the other hand, the price continued to drop beyond the 50 percent Fibonacci retracement level, so that may represent a missed opportunity to maximize your returns.

REMEMBER

However, it's always better to be safe than sorry. Strive to avoid being greedy when it comes to strategy developments.

Using indicators

Another popular technical analysis method is to use indicators such as the relative strength index (RSI), Bollinger Bands (BOL), and Ichimoku Kinko Hyo (ICH). These indicators are like elements of a makeup kit. By adding them to your chart, you make it more beautiful and accent the important features just as you would by putting makeup on your face!

Indicators are mathematical tools, developed over the years by technical analysts, that can help you predict the future price actions in the market. You can use these indicators in addition to chart patterns to get a higher analysis accuracy. But in short-term trading, some traders use only one or two indicators without paying attention to chart patterns. In fact, you can create a whole trading strategy by using only one indicator in short-term trading. Flip to Chapter 10 of this minibook for more on indicators. To find out more about using the Ichimoku-Fibonacci combo strategy, check out Chapter 14 and *Ichimoku Secrets* by Kiana Danial (CreateSpace Independent Publishing Platform): `https://learn.investdiva.com/ichimoku-secrets-trading-strategy-ebook`.

Avoiding illegal pump-and-dump stuff

As a cryptocurrency trader, you need to be aware of what can happen among illegal group activities that manipulate the markets, take profit, and leave others shirtless. A *pump-and-dump* scheme happens when a group of people or an influential individual manipulates the market prices in their own favor. For example, a highly influential person named Joe goes on TV and says, "I think Bitcoin is going to reach $70,000 tomorrow," while he already has an established buy-and-sell strategy to trade a ton of Bitcoin. The moment his speculation hits the news, everyone else who's watching TV gets excited and starts buying Bitcoin based on this suggestion. The hype helps Bitcoin's price go up and Joe's strategy to go through. But before the rest of the market can catch up, Joe sells (dumps) his Bitcoins, taking a ton of profit but sending Bitcoin's price crashing down.

REMEMBER

Pump-and-dump schemes can happen in any market. But at least with traditional markets like equities, the Securities and Exchange Commission (SEC) actively tries to go after the bad guys. In the cryptocurrency market, the regulations have yet to be fully established. According to a study published by the *Wall Street Journal*, dozens of trading groups manipulated cryptocurrency prices on some of the largest online exchanges, generating at least $825 million between February and August of 2018.

Managing Short-Term Trading Risk

Managing your risk when short-term trading can be quite different from that of medium- and long-term investing. To avoid a major account meltdown trading short term, you must balance your risk and return more actively. Using a stop-loss order is one method to consider.

A *stop-loss* order is a price at which you tell your broker to "stop your losses" and get you out of your position. For example, say you think Bitcoin is going to go up from $50,000 to $50,100 in the next hour, so you enter a buy position. But instead, Bitcoin starts dropping below $50,000, putting you in a losing position. To avoid losing too much money, you can set a stop-loss order at $49,950. You can set a risk-reward ratio at any number that makes sense to your risk tolerance.

Kiana famously doesn't use stop-losses when investing long term. (Find out more in the free master class at https://learn.investdiva.com/free-webinar-3-secrets-to-making-your-money-work-for-you. Find out about long-term strategies in Chapter 12 of this minibook.) When trading short term, some traders argue that not using a stop-loss can result in an account getting completely wiped out.

WARNING

In medium- to long-term trading, using a stop-loss can be riskier than not using it, especially if you're not a full-time trader. Make sure you have a complete understanding of your trading objectives and risk tolerance before using a stop-loss in crypto trading.

TIP

One easy way to calculate your risk-reward ratio is to divide your estimated net profit (the reward) by the price of the maximum risk you're willing to take. For example, if you want to have a 1:2 risk-reward ratio, that means you're willing to make double the amount of what you're willing to risk. But before you understand how much risk you can take, you must calculate your risk tolerance; see Chapter 2 of this minibook.

Chapter **12**

Long-Term Investing Strategies

D o you know how long the first Bitcoin investors waited to see any type of return? Around seven years. Some Bitcoin miners and early investors actually forgot about their crypto assets and had to go on a treasure hunt to find their Bitcoin wallets during the 2017 bubble.

The point is that just like many other markets, time and patience can be your best friends. But you still need to have a plan based on your risk tolerance and financial goals in order to profit long term. This chapter covers the basics of long-term investing in cryptocurrencies.

Time Is on Your Side: Getting Started with Long-Term Investing

When we talk about long-term investment strategies, we're basically treating cryptocurrencies as assets. And just like any other type of financial investment, you need to create a portfolio that goes along with your risk tolerance and financial goals. To do so, you can begin by examining the criteria for constructing your crypto portfolio (such as risk management, discussed in Chapter 2 of this minibook) and then use these criteria to develop a plan for allocating different types of crypto assets in the various categories explored in Book 1, Chapter 4. The following sections dig into a couple of things to keep in mind when getting started with your portfolio management.

Your personal goals and current situation

REMEMBER

You should consider a wide variety of issues when managing your portfolio long term. Factors like risk and return are some of the obvious ones covered in Chapter 2 of this minibook. But when it comes to long-term investment in risky assets like cryptocurrencies, you need to take it a step further. Here are some questions you should answer:

>> What's your income size now, and where can it go in the future?

>> Are you likely to change your job in the future? Is your current job secure?

>> What's your marital status now? Do you have any children? Where do you see yourself on this front in five years?

>> What's your investment experience?

>> Do you have any other investments in assets such as equities or real estate? How diversified is your overall portfolio?

These questions may sound cliché, and you may already have the answers in your head. But investing long term is a logical process, and actually writing down the most basic elements of your personal goals and characteristics always pays off. When you've assessed your own financial situation and goals, you can have a better understanding of how to move forward with your crypto portfolio. Your needs may even determine the avenue you choose.

For example, if you're retired and your income depends on your portfolio, long-term cryptocurrency investing may not be suitable for you. You may want to consider a lower-risk, current-income-oriented approach. If you're young and willing to take the risk in the hope of getting high returns, you may even consider the short-term trading strategies covered in Chapter 11 of this minibook. For example, as a married person with a secure job and one little baby (Jasmine), Kiana allocated 15 percent of her portfolio to cryptocurrencies in 2017 and gradually increased this percentage as the markets fell. For her parents, she chose a different approach. They're retired and need current income to survive. That's why she recommended that they allocate only 5 percent of their savings to cryptocurrencies in 2018 with the goal of capital gains in the next few years.

To sum it up, build your portfolio around your needs depending on the following variables:

>> Your current income

>> Your age

>> The size of your family

>> Your risk preferences

For more on risk management and calculating your risk tolerance, check out Chapter 2 of this minibook and this free master class: https://learn.investdiva.com/free-webinar-3-secrets-to-making-your-money-work-for-you.

Your portfolio's objectives

Assessing your personal goals and life situation brings you one step closer to creating your own portfolio (see the preceding section). When creating a long-term portfolio, you generally want to consider these objectives:

>> **Generating current income:** These investments can generate a regular payment, which can be at odds with high capital appreciations.

>> **Preserving capital:** This low-risk, conservative investment strategy generates moderate returns.

>> **Growing capital:** Focusing on capital growth requires you to increase your risk tolerance and reduce your need for a current-income-based investment strategy.

>> **Reducing taxes:** If you're in a high tax bracket, you may consider a portfolio that generates capital gains. If you're in a lower tax bracket, you have lower incentive to defer taxes and earn high investment returns, so a portfolio with higher-current-income assets may be suitable for you.

>> **Managing risk:** You should always consider the risk-return trade-off in all investment decisions.

These objectives get tied together with your personal goals and other investments. For example, current income and capital preservation are good objectives for someone with a low risk tolerance who has a conservative personality. If you have medium risk tolerance and don't need to depend on your investment for current income as much, you can select capital growth as your portfolio objective. In many countries, including the United States, taxes also play a major role in your investment goals. For example, if you're in a high tax bracket, focusing on capital gains may be a better option for you because you can defer taxes, as explained in Chapter 15 of this minibook. Last but not least, you should consider your risk-return trade-off in all your investment decisions, whether long term or not.

Creating Long-Term Strategies

Any type of investment can be summed up in four words: Buy low, sell high. But, of course, no one can get it perfectly right every time. With cryptocurrencies in particular, the market is still testing new psychological levels, so predicting the highs and lows can be that much more difficult. The following sections introduce some methods you can use to expand your long-term cryptocurrency portfolio.

Observing psychological levels

The crypto market still isn't mature enough to enable thorough long-term technical analysis. Besides Bitcoin, many cryptocurrencies are so new that they haven't even formed a full cycle on the trading charts. But as time goes by, key psychological support and resistance levels have started to develop. Fibonacci retracement levels (see Chapter 14 of this minibook) are very helpful in identifying key levels even in the newer cryptocurrencies.

The reason psychological levels are already appearing in the crypto market may be that many crypto investors are using traditional technical analysis methods (see Chapter 10 of this minibook) for their cryptocurrency investment strategies. With that, you can expect the crypto crowd psychology to form similar chart patterns to those of other markets, such as equities and the foreign exchange market (forex), in longer time frames like weekly and monthly charts. Crowd psychology is the constant battle between the sellers (the bears) and the buyers (the bulls) in the market that leads to price movements in an asset. Psychological levels are those that the prices have difficulty breaking, due to the strength or weakness of the bears and bulls in the market.

TIP

You can find out a great deal about investing crowd psychology in plain (and funny) videos in the Invest Diva *Forex Coffee Break* education course at `https://learn.investdiva.com/forex-coffee-break-with-invest-diva-education-course`.

After you identify the psychological levels, you can use them to develop different types of strategies based on your current portfolio, your risk tolerance, and your financial goals. Here are some examples:

>> Buy at a key support level and sell at a key resistance level.

>> Buy at current market price and sell at a key resistance level.

>> Wait for a pullback when the price reaches a key resistance level and buy lower. Then sell at the next key resistance level.

>> Buy at a key support level and hold long term.

Selling when you reach your goal

A cryptocurrency's price may continue going higher after it reaches a key resistance level. But how long do you wait? Which resistance level do you choose? Does using resistance levels even make sense for your financial goals? One realistic way to approach your investment strategy is to sell when you've reached your investment goal. (You can use a sell limit order, which is discussed later in this chapter, to do this.) The key here is that you shouldn't look back and regret your decision after you've made the sale, even if the price continues going up after you sell.

REMEMBER

Markets may continue to go up after you sell. Don't let your emotions take over your logical decision to sell. If you need the money and have already achieved your investment goal, you have no reason to regret an early sale. If anything, you can always get back in the market with a brand-new investment strategy.

Keeping tax consequences in mind

TIP

Tax laws change all the time, and they vary in different countries. However, in most cases taxes affect nearly all investment actions. As of 2022, in the United States a maximum of $3,000 of capital losses in excess of capital gains can be written off against other income in any one year. If you have a loss position in an investment and have concluded that selling it is wise, the best time to sell is when you have a capital gain against which you can apply the loss.

Before starting to invest, you must understand the basics of taxes in your country. Flip to Chapter 15 of this minibook for an overview of how you should consider taxes before making investment decisions.

Considering Limit and Stop-Loss Orders

Cryptocurrency exchanges and brokers alike allow you to use various types of orders to buy and sell altcoins. Most active traders use *market orders* to buy or sell at the best available price, but long-term investors can use other types of orders such as limit orders and stop-loss orders.

TIP

Long-term investors can also use market orders in abnormal circumstances if they need to make a quick investment decision. Market orders are normally filled quickly at a price close to the current market price.

WARNING

Using market orders can sometimes involve risks, especially in volatile markets such as cryptocurrencies. Sometimes the price of cryptocurrencies drops or skyrockets in a matter of seconds. If you happen to use a market order on those occasions, you may get blindsided by the actual price at which your order is executed. That's why using a limit order is always safer than using market orders.

Limit orders

A *limit order* is a type of transaction order that allows you to buy or sell at your preferred price. For example, if the current Bitcoin market price is at $56,434, you can set a *buy limit order* to buy at $56,000 or even below that level if you think the price has the potential to drop.

Then you can set a *sell limit order* to take profit when you reach your investment goal, say at $57,000. Limit orders allow you to go about your life without worrying about prices too much while the markets do their usual movements.

REMEMBER

Always double-check your limit orders before putting them through. Make sure your buy limit order isn't above the current market price and your sell limit order isn't below the current market price. Traditional brokers often send you a warning if you make a mistake in setting limit orders, but a lot of crypto exchanges don't offer such courtesies. Unfortunately, Kiana has been the victim of setting a careless buy limit order that was way above the current market price, and it immediately went through without a warning from the exchange.

Just like in other markets, cryptocurrency limit orders have different options for how long they stay in effect. The most common types are good til canceled and fill-or-kill:

>> A *good til canceled* (GTC) order normally stays in effect for six months. If it's not executed within that time frame, your broker or exchange may cancel it. If you still want to keep the position in effect, you may need to renew it after six months.

>> A *fill-or-kill* order is canceled if it's not immediately executed. Therefore, it may be a better fit for short-term trading strategies (like those in Chapter 11 of this minibook).

Other types of limit orders offered by your trading platform may include *good til time* (your order stays in effect until a specific time that you select) and *immediate or cancel* (your order is canceled if it's not immediately fulfilled by your broker). You can set more than one limit order for your cryptocurrencies. You can also choose to buy fractions of a cryptocurrency, especially when, like Bitcoin, it is very expensive. For example, in one account a number of years ago, Kiana set a buy limit order for Bitcoin versus U.S. dollar (BTC/USD) to purchase 0.4 Bitcoin when the price reached $6,000. On the order form, she also added a good til canceled buy limit order to buy 0.2 Bitcoin at $5,851. Having multiple limit orders eliminates the risk of missing out and avoids going all in at one price.

Stop-loss orders

You can use *stop-loss orders* to limit the downside loss exposure of your crypto investment. Stop-losses are basically a form of limit orders (see the preceding section), where you ask your broker to close your position and take losses at a specific price. Not everyone is a big fan of stop-losses, but for some investors cutting the losses short in case of a rapid decline in the market may make sense. Just like limit orders, stop-loss orders have different types like good til canceled.

Long-Term Investing Strategies

WARNING

Volatile markets such as cryptocurrencies normally bounce back up from the lows as rapidly as they fall. That's why by using a stop-loss order, you may end up getting out of your position prematurely and miss out on potential gains. If you're looking to use a stop-loss order, you must analyze the market carefully and choose an appropriate level for your stop-loss. To get the latest cryptocurrency investment strategies and buy/sell limit order ideas, consider joining Invest Diva's Premium Investing Group at https://learn.investdiva.com/join-group.

Chapter **13**

Minimizing Losses and Maximizing Gains

Depending on whether you're a short-term trader or long-term investor, you can manage your portfolio either actively or passively. If you're a long-term investor (see Chapter 12 of this minibook), you may find yourself managing your portfolio passively by buying and holding a well-diversified portfolio over a set amount of time. If you're a short-term trader, you can use the tools in Chapter 11 to manage and obtain your desired objectives in a more active way.

If you're a big fan of long-term investing, that doesn't mean you shouldn't practice active portfolio management. You can get better returns, whether they're long term or short term, by actively managing your portfolio. *Active* doesn't mean you have to stick to your screen all the time and covertly check your investment apps throughout the day during conversations and meetings. This chapter explains some management strategies that can help you find a sweet balance to do it all and still maintain an outside life.

Keeping the Losses Down

A phenomenon called *loss aversion* occurs in behavioral finance when investors keep the losing assets in their portfolios while actively selling the "winners." This tendency is why going against the crowd is one way to curtail your losses. The following sections explain some techniques you can use to keep your crypto investing losses down.

Measuring returns

Managing your cryptocurrency investments can be challenging because your assets may be scattered over different exchanges and cryptocurrency wallets. Additionally, you may have purchased some altcoins by using Bitcoin, some others by using the U.S. dollar (USD), and more by using cryptos such as Ethereum or Litecoin. Keeping a log of your investments is a good idea, including any changes you make to your portfolio. Here are the three steps in determining your portfolio returns:

1. Measuring the amount you've invested

2. Measuring capital gains, which is the profit you make through buying and selling cryptos

3. Measuring income, which is the payment you get by holding some cryptos (if applicable)

To calculate the amount invested, you can create a list similar to the one in Figure 13-1. The table shows numbers of coins, buying date, cost (both total and per coin), and current value.

My Crypto Portfolio as of September 1, 2018

Coin	Full name	Number of coins	Date bought	Total cost (including commission) (USD)	Cost per coin (USD)	Current price per coin (USD)
BTC	Bitcoin	0.5	6/29/2018	2,965	5,900	7,155
ETH	Ethereum	8	8/14/2018	2,250	275	293
XLM	Stellar Lumens	200	8/07/2018	44	0.200	0.2257
EOS	EOS	50	8/16/2018	225	4.45	6.55

FIGURE 13-1: An example of a cryptocurrency investment log.

© John Wiley & Sons, Inc.

TIP

Now, because you may be purchasing different coins by using either *fiat* (government-backed) currencies, such as the U.S. dollar, or other cryptocurrencies, you may need to convert your investment value to one type of currency to keep it simple and easier to track. In Figure 13-1, all the purchasing value was converted to the U.S. dollar (USD). Another way to track your investments is to create separate logs depending on how you purchased your altcoins. For example, you can have a separate log for your investments with BTC and another one for those you purchased with USD.

You can create these logs on a monthly, quarterly, or annual basis depending on your investing time frame. For example, if you're a short-term trader, you may need a monthly log. If you're a medium-to-long-term investor, you can use quarterly and annual logs. You can normally find the return on your investment calculated by your brokerage or exchange services (see Chapter 3 of this minibook for more on brokerages and exchanges).

WARNING

Many crypto enthusiasts have given up measuring returns against fiat currencies like the USD altogether. If you believe Bitcoin is king and Ethereum is queen, you may end up buying most of your altcoins by using the king and queen anyway. Converting your crypto purchase to its USD value can be time-consuming. USD, Bitcoin, and Ethereum all have fluctuations of their own versus other currencies, so a conversion may give you a false impression of gain or loss. By converting to USD, it may look like you've gained profit on your initial investment, while in reality you may be in a losing position versus Bitcoin.

TIP

If you purchased your coins on an exchange by using another cryptocurrency such as Bitcoin, you can find the relevant USD value by searching your coin and the date you purchased it on websites like `https://tradingview.go2cloud.org/aff_c?offer_id=2&aff_id=13497`.

To measure your capital gains and income, you can simply check your account information with your broker and exchange. With cryptocurrency exchanges, your capital gain information is normally under tabs labeled "Wallet" or "Funds." Most exchanges provide the estimated value of your whole account either in Bitcoin or USD. If you have more than one account, you can add up these estimated numbers in your investment log and monitor them on a regular basis.

Monitoring exchange fees

To buy and sell cryptocurrencies, you need services like crypto exchanges and brokers. These companies mainly make money through transaction fees, as discussed in Chapter 3 of this minibook. We don't recommend choosing an exchange based only on low fees, but sometimes fees can become an important decision-making factor, especially for active traders. The fees can get even larger if you're looking to convert a fiat currency to a cryptocurrency like Bitcoin and then send it to another exchange to buy another cryptocurrency by using Bitcoin, and so on. Fees can be the biggest downside to short-term trading strategies for cryptocurrencies.

Here are some tips for keeping your exchange fees minimal while keeping your investment secure:

>> Buy your lump-sum major cryptos on more secure exchanges, which may have higher transaction fees. For example, when you need Bitcoin and Ethereum to trade other cryptocurrencies, you could buy a large amount of both on an exchange with higher fees that allows using the U.S. dollar.

>> For active trading, choose exchanges that offer lower rates for your specific cryptocurrency pair, but make sure to periodically store your profit on a hardware wallet (see Book 1, Chapter 3 for more on wallets).

>> Consider active trading with the exchange's native cryptocurrency; it may have a lower transaction fee than trading other cross-cryptos. For example, the Binance exchange offers cheaper trading options for its cryptocurrency, Binance Coin (BNB).

>> Always include the transaction fee when calculating your profit to be on top of your game. For example, if you buy 0.06 Ethereum coin for $200 but you pay $1.50 in transaction fees, you have spent $201.50 for your investment. While this amount doesn't make a great impact for long-term investments, active traders can feel the accumulative fees over time.

Understanding the art of getting out

Staying true to two of Warren Buffett's most famous investing rules is a smart idea:

1. Never lose money.

2. Never forget rule number one.

But no matter how thoroughly you conduct your analysis, at times you may find that getting out of a bad investment is better than holding onto it. The following sections give a few general strategies when it comes to getting out of an investment. Check out Chapter 4 of this minibook for information on the Invest Diva Diamond Analysis (IDDA) system.

Don't be greedy

REMEMBER

If you're using one of the technical chart patterns presented in Chapters 10 and 14 of this minibook, always set your profit-taking limit order at the price level that's consistent with the technique. You may get a feeling that the market will continue going up after your profit target (PT) is triggered, and you may be tempted to readjust your PT prematurely. Sometimes the market will continue to rise. Sometimes it won't. If you prefer to be safe rather than sorry, refrain from readjusting the PT orders way too often (unless you have a valid fundamental reason to do so besides just your gut feeling).

Take partial profits

Kiana loves this rule and swears by it!

> You can call me a hoarder, but I can never let go of all my coins (or any other assets, for that matter) all at once. I set up strategic, partial profit-taking prices depending on my (or my students') investment goals and let the markets handle the rest.
>
> For example, if I buy one Ethereum coin (ETH) at $3,000 and I'm looking to take partial profit at key levels, I may sell 0.2 of my Ethereum coin at $700, sell 0.2 more at $850, and keep the rest long term. This way, I gain some profit along the way but don't let go of all my coins, so I still feel happy when the Ethereum price continues going up after I sell. Of course, calculating those key levels needs thorough analysis.

TIP

To view more information on partial profit-taking strategies, join the Invest Diva Premium Investing Group at https://learn.investdiva.com/join-group.

Let go of bad investments

Every once in a while, you find yourself holding onto a coin that's just not worth it. With worthy long-term investments, buying more coins as the price drops may be a good idea; however, sometimes the cryptocurrency, its community, and its management simply don't have a future. This is the point when reexamining your fundamental analysis (see Chapter 4 of this minibook) becomes important. When it becomes evident that this coin just ain't gonna bounce back, you may as well just bite the bullet and get out before your losses get bigger. If you're too scared to do so, you can always take losses in parts, using the partial profit method discussed in the preceding section.

REMEMBER

By letting go of your bad investments and taking losses, you may receive tax credits you can use to offset the taxes you must pay on your capital gains. Flip to Chapter 15 of this minibook for more on taxes.

Letting the Profits Rise

What you need to keep reminding yourself is that emotions rarely lead to maximizing profit. You don't want to regret not buying more when the prices were down. And you don't want to give in to the temptation to sell and take profit before reaching your carefully analyzed profit target limit order. At the end of the day, discipline is what enables you to make bank. The following sections detail some tricks to help you avoid emotional investing.

Buying at the bottom

Being able to purchase at the lowest price every time you invest is highly unlikely. But studying the market psychology and historical price patterns can help you get close. A fantastic technical analysis tool that you can use to identify the bottom is the Ichimoku-Fibonacci combo.

As explained in Chapter 14 of this minibook and in the book *Ichimoku Secrets* by Kiana Danial (CreateSpace Independent Publishing Platform), you can use the Ichimoku-Fibonacci combination to gauge crowd psychology and identify key support and resistance levels. (*Support* is a price level where the market has difficulty breaking below; *resistance* is a price level where the market has difficulty breaking above.) For longer-term investing, we generally recommend using the daily chart for Ichimoku analysis. As shown in Figure 13-2, after the price of Ripple's XRP dropped below $0.70 on May 15, 2018, it then broke below the daily Ichimoku cloud. Following the Ichimoku Kinko Hyo's guidelines, there was an indication that the price of XRP may drop further toward key Fibonacci retracement and support levels at $0.57 and $0.47. By conducting this analysis, Kiana was able to set a buy limit order at these levels ahead of time and aim to purchase at lower prices instead of buying immediately. This way, you can maximize your profit and lower your net purchasing price.

TIP

Because the cryptocurrency market doesn't have enough historical data to rely on, sometimes the price continues to drop below the all-time-low levels, creating new lows. If you're confident enough in the fundamentals of the cryptocurrency, the new lows can give you an opportunity to buy more at lower prices. You can use Fibonacci's extended levels to identify new lows. To use these levels, you must first identify a trend where the price went either up or down for an extended period of time recently. Then drag the Fibonacci tool on your charting platform from the top to the bottom of the trend (if it's a downtrend) and from bottom to the top (if it's an uptrend). By doing so, the Fibonacci levels magically appear on your chart. Check out Invest Diva's Premium Investing Group where Ichimoku-Fibonacci strategies are routinely discussed: https://learn.investdiva.com/join-group.

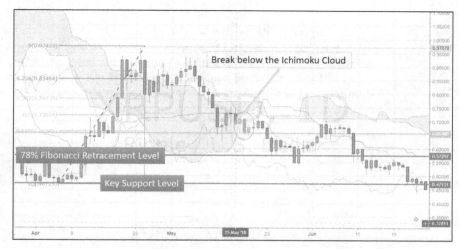

FIGURE 13-2:
Using the Ichimoku-Fibonacci combo to identify bottoms.

Source: tradingview.com

Knowing that patience is a profitable virtue

"Patience is a profitable virtue" is Kiana's main mantra in all the education courses at Invest Diva:

> My students say repeating this mantra has changed the way they invest and has increased their profit returns by a fair bit. Whenever I feel the adrenaline rushing through my head from looking at a chart, I take a step back. I change the time frame and look at the big picture. I do more fundamental research. If all five points of the IDDA (see Chapter 4 of this minibook) aren't aligned, I simply log off my trading account and go about my day.

REMEMBER

Getting nervous is very easy when the markets take a dip and you've invested a bunch of money in an asset. Being patient can often be the ultimate path to making tangible returns.

Identifying the peaks

"Buy low and sell high" is the name of the game! Again, you've got to be either Nostradamus or Lucky Luke to take profit at the highest price every time you invest. But if you use historical data and technical chart patterns, you can stack the odds in your favor. For active trading and medium-term investing in the cryptocurrency market, the Ichimoku-Fibonacci combo is pretty useful, as explained in Chapter 14 of this minibook. Other tools include technical chart patterns and key psychological resistance levels.

Using Ripple's XRP as an example, in September 2018, Kiana identified a double bottom chart pattern in the process of formation on the daily chart, as shown in Figure 13-3. A *double bottom* is a popular formation on charts, where the price has difficulty breaking below a support level twice, forming two valley-shaped bottoms. When confirmed, it can be interpreted as a bullish reversal pattern, meaning that the prices may start going up.

Source: tradingview.com

FIGURE 13-3: A double bottom chart pattern forming on an XRP/USD daily chart.

Following the double bottom chart pattern guidelines (see Chapter 10 of this minibook), medium-term investors can expect the market to take profit when the price has moved up from the neckline ($0.3666 in Figure 13-3) the same distance from the bottom to the neckline, or the next available Fibonacci retracement levels ($0.4273 and $0.5314). To be safe, take partial profits at each level to distribute risk.

As shown in Figure 13-4, on September 21, 2018, XRP reached both levels and then some before dropping back down. A medium-term investor would've taken profit at these levels, while a long-term investor would've stayed in their position.

For long-term investors, timing the profit taking can be a bit more challenging. The crypto market is an exciting new investment opportunity that a majority of people are just discovering. Just like with the dot-com bubble, the hype can lead to extreme volatility. You saw the results of the hype in 2017 when Bitcoin's price surged over 1,000 percent and Ripple's XRP gained a whopping 36,018 percent. Some investors who sold right at the peak became millionaires, and others who bought at the peak had to sit on their losses until the next surge of 2021. In this case, most investors who were able to sell at the peak are those who went against the hype and against the majority of the crowd.

FIGURE 13-4:
A double bottom chart pattern confirms, and XRP reaches profit target levels.

WARNING

Technical chart patterns such as double bottoms, indicators such as Ichimoku, and going against the crowd don't guarantee optimal results. These items are simply tools that increase the probability of identifying the best price to buy and sell. At the end of the day, you must conduct a thorough risk management assessment that applies to your personal financial goals and risk tolerance, as discussed in Chapter 2 of this minibook.

Finding peaks and bottoms with a few trading tools

TIP

Here are cheat sheets of trading tools that we recommend using to identify peaks and bottoms:

>> **Bearish reversal chart patterns:** These patterns form on the chart during a period of surging prices and indicate that the market sentiment and price action may turn bearish and start dropping. Find out more at www.investdiva.com/investing-guide/bearish-reversal-patterns-list1/.

>> **Bullish reversal chart patterns:** These patterns form during a downtrend and indicate the prices may start to turn bullish and rise. Check out www.investdiva.com/investing-guide/bullish-reversal-patterns-list/.

>> **Ichimoku Kinko Hyo:** This Japanese indicator consists of five different moving averages, helping you get a better view of the current market sentiment and predict the future price action. See www.investdiva.com/investing-guide/ichimoku-kinko-hyo-explained/.

Chapter **14**

Using Ichimoku and Fibonacci Techniques

hapter 10 of this minibook covers using technical analysis to develop cryptocurrency trading strategies. Although a ton of moving averages and chart patterns can help you with your strategy, a great technique to use is combining Ichimoku Kinko Hyo and Fibonacci retracement levels. This chapter overviews the basics of these two technical indicators and shows you how you can use them for trades.

TIP

Advanced Ichimoku-Fibonacci methods are beyond the scope of this publication; you can discover more about them in *Ichimoku Secrets* by Kiana Danial (CreateSpace Independent Publishing Platform) at https://learn.investdiva. com/ichimoku-secrets-trading-strategy-ebook.

Getting a Handle on Ichimoku Kinko Hyo

Its name may sound intimidating, but Ichimoku Kinko Hyo is here to make your technical analysis easier, not harder! It's a Japanese phrase that roughly translates to "one-piece balanced table." In cryptocurrency investing, Ichimoku Kinko Hyo allows you to find out everything you need to know about the price action in "one glance": Ichimoku.

The components of Ichimoku Kinko Hyo

REMEMBER

This indicator consists of several different moving averages (MAs). Each of these MAs serves a specific purpose, and their positioning versus each other and the price can help you understand the current market sentiment and predict its future direction. Here are some of the components you see when you add Ichimoku Kinko Hyo (ICH) to your chart:

>> The Ichimoku cloud (Japanese name: Kumo)

>> The base line (Japanese name: Kijun)

>> The turn line (Japanese name: Tenkan)

>> The delay span (Japanese name: Chiko)

Your charting provider may use different colors for each of the components shown in Figure 14-1. The Ichimoku cloud is actually the space between two other moving averages, Senkou (leading) span A and B. Depending on the direction of the cloud, this space is normally colored green for bullish and red for bearish market sentiment. (A *bullish* market sentiment means the price is expected to rise. A *bearish* market sentiment is when the prices drop.)

Name	Kumo	Kijun	Tenkan	Chiko
Meaning	Cloud	Base	Turn	Delayed
Image				

FIGURE 14-1:
Ichimoku Kinko
Hyo components.

© *John Wiley & Sons, Inc.*

TIP

If you're looking for an easy charting service that helps you with technical analysis including Ichimoku and Fibonacci, check out TradingView (`www.tradingview.com/`). You can use this charting service for almost any asset, including cryptocurrencies, foreign exchange (forex), and stocks.

Figure 14-2 shows the Ichimoku Kinko Hyo components in action on a chart that displays the price action of Ripple (XRP) versus Bitcoin (BTC) on a four-hour (or 240-minute) basis. That means each of the candlesticks (see Chapter 10 of this minibook) shows the price movements of XRP versus BTC in four hours. The Ichimoku components dance around the prices, crossing above and below the price action depending on the calculations. You can take these movements as indications about the future price direction.

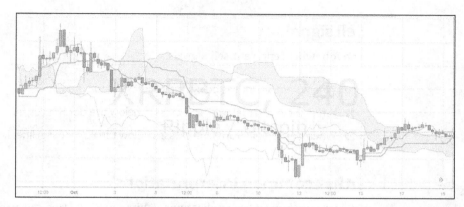

FIGURE 14-2:
Ichimoku Kinko
Hyo applied to
the XRP/BTC
four-hour chart.

Source: tradingview.com

Ichimoku interpretations

You can use the positioning of the Ichimoku components against each other as well as against the price to predict where the price may go next. The following sections present some basic interpretations of Ichimoku Kinko Hyo.

REMEMBER

Past performance is never an indication of future results. Therefore, all these indications are merely an addition to your thorough research on your investments; you shouldn't treat them as guaranteed strategies. For technical analysis, you must study other chart patterns (see Chapter 10 of this minibook) to further strengthen your Ichimoku strategy. Additionally, always conduct all points of the Invest Diva Diamond Analysis (IDDA; see Chapter 4 of this minibook) before making a final investment decision.

Buy signals

If you identify one or more of the following signals on a chart, chances are that the price may continue higher and therefore it's a good time to buy:

>> If the price is moving above the Ichimoku cloud, this movement may indicate a bullish momentum in the market and is therefore a buy signal.

>> When the Chiko (delayed) line moves above the cloud, it can be considered a buy signal.

>> When the Tenkan (turn) line crosses above the Kijun (base) line, that crossing may indicate a shift in the market sentiment from bearish to bullish and therefore be a buy signal.

Sell signals

The following represent sell signals:

» When the price moves below the Ichimoku cloud

» When the Chiko (delayed) line crosses below the cloud

» When the Tenkan (turn) line crosses below the Kijun (base) line

Other common interpretations

Besides pure buy and sell indications, Ichimoku Kinko Hyo can also help you identify support and resistance layers as well as provide a general understanding of market conditions. Here are some of the interpretations:

» As long as the five lines are parallel, the trend will continue in that direction.

» When the prices are inside the Ichimoku cloud, that means that the market is in the process of consolidating, which isn't a good time to buy or sell.

» You can use the lower band of the prevailing cloud as a layer of support, which is a level that the price has difficulty breaking below.

» You can use the upper band of the prevailing cloud as a layer of resistance, which is a price that the market has difficulty breaking above.

TIP

You can use Ichimoku as an entry level for both buy and sell positions. You can also combine two or more of the interpretations to adjust your strategy based on your risk tolerance.

Introducing Fibonacci Retracement Levels

Using Ichimoku Kinko Hyo all by itself gives you just a partial view of the markets and doesn't help you with an exit strategy. (Head to the earlier section, "Getting a Handle on Ichimoku Kinko Hyo," for more on that indicator.) The next step is to identify key support and resistance levels that the market may have difficulty moving below (in case of a support level) and above (in case of a resistance level). You can search for support and resistance levels in many ways. We recommend using Fibonacci retracement levels.

Some background on Fibonacci

Fibonacci is the nickname for Italian mathematician Leonardo Pisano Bigollo, who some refer to as "the most talented Western mathematician of the Middle Ages." Some of his most famous contributions to science include introducing the positional decimal numeral system, also known as the Hindu-Arabic numeral system, to the Western world and popularizing the Fibonacci sequence.

Mathematically, the *Fibonacci sequence* is the series of numbers where each number in the sequence is sum of the two numbers before it. So if you add the numbers 0 and 1, the result is 1, and you add that digit to the sequence. Then add up 1 and 1 and add the result, 2, to the sequence. Now add 1 and 2 — you get the idea. You can continue this way forever: 0, 1, 1, 2, 3, 5, 8, 13, 21, 34, 55, 89, 144. . .

REMEMBER

The Fibonacci sequence has applications in technical analysis, but the sequence itself isn't exactly what you use. The *Fibonacci retracement levels* you use in technical analysis are a result of calculating the alternate ratio between the numbers in the sequence. By applying the ratios to an uptrend or a downtrend, you can identify support and resistance levels easily.

TECHNICAL STUFF

Here's how the ratios are calculated: After the first few numbers, if you divide any of the numbers by the succeeding number, you get approximately 0.618. For example, 34 divided by 55 rounds to 0.618. If you calculate the ratio between alternate numbers, you get 0.382. The ratio between every third succeeding number is 0.235. The sequence used in technical analysis consists of these ratios: 0.78, 0.618, 0.5, 0.382, and 0.236.

How to insert Fibonacci retracement levels into your chart

The good news is that you don't have to do any math calculations at all! All you have to do is to find the Fibonacci tool on your charting service and apply it to the price action. Here are the specific steps you need to take:

1. **Find a trend in the prices.**

   It can be an uptrend or a downtrend. Flip to Chapter 10 of this minibook for an introduction to trends.

2. **Find the Fibonacci retracement tool on your cart and click it.**

3. **Click to apply the Fibonacci tool to the bottom of the trend (if it's an uptrend) or to the top of the trend (if it's a downtrend).**

4. **Drag the Fibonacci tool to the other end of the trend and then click again to drop the Fibonacci retracement levels on the chart.**

   The Fibonacci retracement levels appear. Figure 14-3 shows an example.

FIGURE 14-3:
Fibonacci
retracement
levels applied
to an uptrend
on the
XLM/BTC chart.

Source: tradingview.com

Figure 14-3 shows the price action of Stellar Lumens (XLM) versus Bitcoin (BTC) in a four-hour chart. The bottom of the trend for the XLM/BTC pair is at 0.00003309, and the top of the trend is at 0.00003901. By dragging the Fibonacci tool from the bottom to the top, you can see the Fibonacci retracement levels marked as 0.78, 0.618, 0.5, 0.382, and 0.236.

Combining Ichimoku and Fibonacci Techniques

When you've got your eyes used to having Ichimoku and Fibonacci indicators on your charts separately (see the preceding sections), you can apply both of them to the chart and let the fun begin. Seeing so many lines on the chart may give you a headache at the beginning, but after a while you may even think that a chart without Ichimoku and Fibonacci is totally naked.

REMEMBER

Sometimes you have so many options to choose from when selecting a trend (up or down) for Fibonacci. More often than not, most trends give you the same Fibonacci retracement levels. The key Fibonacci resistance and support levels also often coincide with Ichimoku layers of support and resistance because Fibonacci is working to show you the key psychological levels that remain true across the board. This specifically is the beauty and magic of Fibonacci.

REMEMBER

You can use Ichimoku and Fibonacci in a number of ways to assist you with your technical analysis. It's recommended that you use other technical analysis methods and chart patterns (see Chapter 10 of this minibook) as well to confirm your analysis. For example, you can use Ichimoku to spot a buy or sell signal, and then use Fibonacci levels to determine the price at which you can take profit.

Here's an example: You discover a double bottom bullish reversal chart pattern on a daily chart. (A *double bottom* pattern is a bullish reversal chart pattern that consists of two valleys at a key support level on the chart; turn to Chapter 10 of this minibook to see examples.) You apply Ichimoku to the chart and notice an Ichimoku buy signal (as described earlier in this chapter). This discovery is a perfect opportunity to identify an entry point based on the double bottom chart pattern and the Ichimoku signal.

But where do you go from there, and where do you take profit? This point is when you can use Fibonacci. Depending on your risk tolerance (see Chapter 2 of this minibook), you can select a Fibonacci retracement level as your profit target and create a limit order through your broker account to sell at that level. (A *limit order* is a direction you put through your broker to buy or sell an asset at a specific price.)

Figure 14-4 shows a case study on the XLM/BTC four-hour chart that identifies an Ichimoku-based bearish signal after the price broke below the Ichimoku cloud at 0.00003579.

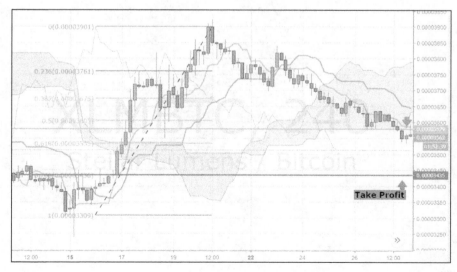

FIGURE 14-4:
Using Ichimoku and Fibonacci to create a bearish trading strategy.

Source: tradingview.com

Based on the Ichimoku strategy, you can create a *sell* limit order either at the lower band of the Ichimoku cloud (0.00003579) or a bit higher at the 0.5 Fibonacci retracement level of 0.00003605.

For profit taking, you can consider the 0.786 Fibonacci level at 0.00003435. For traders who like using stop-losses, you can use the 0.382 Fibonacci level or higher, depending on your risk tolerance. (For simplicity, I'm not mentioning other bearish signals that you can find on this chart.) A *stop-loss* is an order you can put through your broker to get you out of a losing trade before the losses get out of hand; flip to Chapter 11 of this minibook for more info.

WARNING

The preceding case study is conducted on the four-hour chart, which is considered medium-term and thus carries a high level of risk. If you're looking for more conservative investment strategies, consider using the daily and monthly time frames. See Chapter 10 of this minibook for more about the various time frames.

TIP

You can always visit Invest Diva's Premium Investing Group (`https://learn.investdiva.com/join-group`), where Kiana uses Ichimoku and Fibonacci combos left and right to develop investment strategies.

Chapter **15**

Taxes and Cryptocurrencies

Before the 2017 crypto hype, many people who got into cryptocurrencies (whether through mining or investing) probably didn't even think about their tax implications. But as cryptocurrency investing becomes more mainstream, its taxation guidelines have taken center stage. This chapter reviews the basics of cryptocurrency taxation.

REMEMBER

Keep in mind that these guidelines are based on the U.S. tax laws as of 2021. Depending on your crypto investment time frame, type of profit, and personal financial situation, you may need to consult with an accountant to get ready for tax day.

Distinguishing Three Types of Crypto Taxes

The tax setup for cryptos is complicated, to the point that U.S. lawmakers submitted an open letter to the Internal Revenue Service (IRS) in September 2018 asking it to make cryptocurrency taxations simpler. (You can see the letter at `https://waysandmeansforms.house.gov/uploadedfiles/letter_irs_virtual_currencies.pdf`.)

In most cases, you treat your cryptocurrency assets as property rather than currency. That means you pay capital gain taxes on your cryptocurrency investments. In this case, you don't have any tax obligations until you sell your coins for a profit. But what if you got your coins by mining? Or what if your employer pays you in cryptocurrencies? To make it simple, crypto taxation obligations are divided into three likely scenarios in the following sections.

Income taxes

If you've invested in expensive mining equipment (see Book 6, Chapters 5 and 6) and are getting crypto mining rewards as a result, then you may be considered a crypto business owner. You're technically getting paid in cryptos for your business operation, and therefore you're subject to income tax by the IRS. Needless to say, you're also subject to income tax if you work for a company that pays you in cryptocurrencies.

If you receive mining or income rewards in crypto worth over $400 in one year, you must report it to the IRS. If you've set up a mining operation at your home, you can report your mining income as self-employment income on Schedule C of your tax return. Kiana has set up mining activity through Invest Diva, which garners a more generous tax policy when her net income is high. Minimizing your crypto income tax is covered later in this chapter.

REMEMBER

Always make sure to keep a record of your mining activity and financial statements in case you get audited by the IRS. Also, if you're filing as a business entity, make sure to consult with a tax professional to discover the best options for your particular scenario. Don't worry — you can even claim the accountant fees on your business!

REMEMBER

Even as a crypto miner and a business owner, you must understand the basics of cryptocurrency investing. If you sell or trade your cryptocurrencies for other altcoins or any products, then you must pay capital gain taxes as discussed in the next two sections (depending on whether they're long term or short term). Your mining activity profits often rely on the market value of the cryptocurrency as well as the amount of tax you'll be paying on them. To identify the best cryptocurrencies to mine, actively conduct the Invest Diva Diamond Analysis (IDDA) technique introduced in Chapter 4 of this minibook, and swap to better cryptocurrencies if your mining strategy isn't making sense anymore. One point of IDDA is capital analysis, which includes your tax considerations.

Long-term capital gain taxes

Chapter 1 of this minibook points to capital gains as one of the main reasons people invest in cryptocurrencies. That's how the IRS categorizes cryptocurrencies as well. Just like owning stocks and real estate, you must pay capital gain taxes after you sell your crypto assets for a profit. If you take a loss, you can lower your tax bill. Now, if you hold your crypto assets for over a year, you often get a better tax rate. This rate is called a *long-term capital gain tax.*

TIP

You can calculate your capital gains by doing simple math on the amount you gained or lost after you purchased your cryptos. For example, if you buy one quarter of a Bitcoin (0.25) for $10,000 and sell it for $20,000, then you've made $10,000 in capital gains minus the amount you pay for transaction fees.

Short-term capital gain taxes

A *short-term capital gain tax* is very similar to the mining and crypto income tax mentioned earlier in this chapter. If you sell or trade your cryptos regularly and hold them less than a year, then your profit or losses may be categorized as income, which often has less favorable tax implications. Even if you don't officially cash out your cryptos, you may still be subject to short-term taxes if you use the cryptocurrency to purchase stuff, whether it's tangible products or other cryptocurrencies.

INTRODUCING SOME CRYPTO TAX EXPERTS

The crypto investing market is a fairly new industry, and therefore many traditional tax folks may not have the necessary knowledge to help you make the best crypto tax decisions. Searching within her LinkedIn connections, Kiana found a few U.S.-based crypto tax experts who may be able to help you out.

- **Camuso CPA:** This is a CPA firm that works with investors, businesses, and individuals nationwide, and is a market-leading cryptocurrency tax advisor. In fact, Camuso CPA is the first CPA firm in the country to accept cryptocurrency payments in return for professional services. The firm caters to clients from Camuso CPA's network of investors, miners, and small businesses along with taxpayers who need help dealing with Bitcoin and other cryptocurrencies. Kiana's point of contact is the firm's founder, Patrick Camuso. You can reach him through the firm's website at www. CamusoCPA.com.

- **JAG Argueta:** Kiana's point of contact is Shehan Chandrasekera, a certified public accountant in the states of Texas and New Jersey. He has broad tax knowledge of various industries including real estate, start-ups, blockchain, construction, e-commerce, healthcare, cannabis, and manufacturing and distribution. You can check him out through the company's website at https://jagargueta.com.

Active traders who make a few trades every now and then are subject to different tax laws than day traders who trade cryptos for a living. Find out about the difference in the later section, "Reducing your trading tax."

Minimizing Your Crypto Taxes

Whether you've earned your crypto as income or have seen capital gains on your assets, the following sections show you some ways to cut the amount you owe the IRS.

Lowering your mining income tax

In the United States, you may get a better tax rate if you create a company or a business entity around your mining activities instead of mining as a self-employed individual. By doing so, you can take advantage of the tax breaks business owners get for paying for business-related stuff and get a better tax rate than individuals. Got that high-end computer to mine Bitcoin? Claim it on your business and lower your taxable income. Got your computer set up with mining equipment like that discussed in Book 6, Chapter 5? Paying a ton for electricity when mining? Congrats, you can get a tax break on the rewards you got paid through mining.

That is, of course, if your coins are actually worth something. Even at a personal level, your mining operation can be very profitable, but it also can cost you a ton — way more than its rewards, especially if the crypto market isn't doing very well at the time. At the time of this writing, if your overall net income is more than $60,000, filing as an S corporation, or an LLC that's taxed like an S corporation, may help you. Consult a tax professional for guidance.

You can claim your expenses on your business only if the LLC, C corporation, or S corporation was created prior to earning the income from mining. Anything earned prior to the company formation won't be able to be included under the company for tax purposes.

Reducing your trading tax

Do you consider yourself a day trader? Then you may be eligible to pay way less in taxes than occasional traders. But first you must pass the IRS day-trading test by being able to answer "yes" to these three questions:

>> Do you aim to make profit from the daily price changes in the crypto market instead of holding your positions long term or even overnight?

>> Do you spend most of your day trading instead of having a full-time day job?

>> Do you have a substantial and regular trading pattern and make a ton of trades on a daily basis?

If you do qualify as a day trader, you may be able to claim your rewards as a self-employed individual. This designation means you can deduct all your trading-related expenses on Schedule C like any other sole proprietor.

TIP

According to finance.zacks.com, your corporation will be taxed based on your profits and losses whether or not it's a one-owner corporation. You can also use the money you make from day trading to pay for your insurance, healthcare, and employee benefits, if you have any.

WARNING

Tracking your short-term crypto trading activities can be incredibly confusing. The industry has a ton of volatility and market fluctuation, and an exploding number of tradable cryptos are available to you 24/7. These situations make monitoring your resources manually almost impossible. Some tracking resources you can use for your trading activities are introduced later in this chapter.

Bringing down your capital gain taxes

If you can't qualify as a day trader (see the preceding section), your best bet to reduce your crypto capital gain taxes is to be a long-term investor. That means holding your assets for over a year. Don't sell, trade, or buy anything with your cryptocurrencies within a year of your purchase.

As mentioned earlier in this chapter, capital gain taxes on investments held for more than one year (long term) can be much lower than capital gain taxes on investments held for less than one year (short term). In 2021, long-term capital gains are taxed at 0 percent, 15 percent, or 20 percent, depending on your tax bracket. If you're in the high-income tax bracket, for example, your capital gains tax rate may be 20 percent. You can find out more about tax brackets at https://www.investopedia.com/articles/personal-finance/101515/comparing-longterm-vs-shortterm-capital-gain-tax-rates.asp.

REMEMBER

Trading one cryptocurrency for another may put you at risk of paying more taxes. To purchase certain cryptocurrencies at specific crypto exchanges, you have no choice but to convert your cryptos for one another in a shorter time frame, but if you make a huge profit on the initial crypto, you no longer fall into the category of long-term investor. Talk to a tax professional to ensure that you're paying the correct rate.

Checking the rate of your state

In the United States, different states have different state tax laws, and some states have better rates than others for specific groups of people or certain industries. Some states, like Florida, are considered a "retirement haven" because you don't have to pay individual income and death tax, and you also get a ton of asset protection and property tax benefits. When it comes to cryptocurrency investors, certain states, like Wyoming, have great tax incentives for crypto companies and investors because cryptocurrencies are exempted from property taxation altogether. In 2018, Wyoming became the first state to define cryptocurrencies as an entirely new asset class. Wyoming officials called this legislation the "utility token bill" and passed it into law in March 2018; it was designed to exempt specific cryptocurrencies from state money transmission laws.

TIP

As cryptocurrencies become more popular, you can expect more states to create such laws to incentivize businesses and individuals to bring their crypto talents and money there. That's why it's important that you're in the know with the latest developments in the industry. Websites like `https://pro.benzinga.com?afmc=2f` can help you get such information in a timely manner.

Evaluating Taxable Income from Crypto Transactions

REMEMBER

At the end of the day, reporting your crypto income and capital gains is on you. You must keep track of all your taxable events, which means every time you sell or trade your crypto assets for other stuff. At the time of this writing, the IRS doesn't require third-party reporting for cryptocurrencies (meaning the entities you buy the cryptos from don't have to report the sales), which makes the tracking and reporting more complicated. Here are some tips and points to keep in mind when you're evaluating your crypto activities.

Tracking your crypto activity

TIP

The crypto market is expanding, and more monitoring resources are becoming available for traders, investors, and miners alike. Here are a few resources you can check out:

>> **CoinTracker** (`https://www.cointracker.io/?i=eALc60xcyXpD`): CoinTracker automatically syncs your crypto transactions with a growing list of exchanges such as Coinbase, Kraken, KuCoin, and more to generate tax forms. It also has an online support team.

>> **CoinTracking** (`https://cointracking.info?ref=I248132`): CoinTracking analyzes your investment activity and generates a tax report based on your profit and losses.

>> **CryptoTrader.Tax** (`http://cryptotrader.tax?fp_ref=behp6`): This website connects you to a growing list of exchanges such as Coinbase, Binance, Bittrex, and more, and helps you calculate your crypto taxes in a few minutes. It has great online customer support that answers your questions immediately.

Handling crypto forks

Book 1, Chapter 2 talks about how you can get free coins when a cryptocurrency is *forked* (where a portion of a crypto's community decides to create its own version of the currency). Of course, nothing is completely free, and you're likely required to pay taxes on the additional cryptos you receive through the fork. For example, if you own Ethereum and it undergoes a hard fork that pays you an equal amount of the new cryptocurrency in addition to your original Ethereum assets, you must pay ordinary taxes on the new free coins as opposed to long-term capital gain tax. You pay these taxes based on the U.S. dollar value of the new cryptocurrency the day you receive it.

REMEMBER

The IRS still offers little guidance regarding hard forks and taxation. Make sure you consult with a tax professional and stay ahead of the game by tracking all your crypto records using professional websites such as `http://cryptotrader.tax?fp_ref=behp6`.

Reporting international crypto investments

The cryptocurrency market and its rules are constantly evolving. That's why you must remain up to date about all your crypto transactions. But even if you invest in cryptocurrencies outside the United States, you must report the activity to the IRS.

REMEMBER

At the time of this writing, an FBAR (Foreign Bank Account Report) may be required in the U.S. if you held $10,000 or more crypto on foreign exchanges. Make sure you keep up to date with the IRS crypto regulations because they're subject to change every year; consult a tax professional. Also keep in mind that not having to report your cryptos on your FBAR doesn't mean you can hide your foreign cryptocurrency activities from the IRS.

WARNING

It bears repeating: You're responsible for knowing the tax ramifications of your crypto activity. The IRS has been going after cryptocurrency investments inside and outside the United States. It even forced Coinbase to turn over its customer records in 2017. So people who simply didn't know about the crypto tax implications got into trouble alongside those who were trying to hide their crypto investments.

6 Cryptocurrency Mining

Contents at a Glance

Chapter **1**

Understanding Cryptocurrency Mining

Although not all cryptocurrencies require mining, Bitcoin and other mineable cryptocurrencies rely on miners to maintain their network. By solving computationally difficult puzzles and providing consent on the validity of transactions, miners support the blockchain network, which would otherwise collapse. For their service to the network, miners are rewarded with newly created cryptocurrencies (such as Bitcoin) and transaction fees.

When a miner sends a transaction message across the cryptocurrency network, another miner's computer picks it up and adds the transaction to the pool of transactions waiting to be placed into a block and the blockchain ledger. (You can find the details about cryptocurrency and blockchain ledgers in Book 2.) In this chapter, we explore how cryptocurrencies use mining to create trust and make the cryptocurrency usable, stable, and viable.

Understanding Decentralized Currencies

Cryptocurrencies are *decentralized* — that is, no central bank, no central database, and no single, central authority manages the currency network. Conversely, the United States has the Federal Reserve in Washington, D.C., the organization that manages the U.S. dollar, the European Central Bank in Frankfurt manages the euro, and all other fiat currencies also have centralized oversight bodies. (A *fiat* currency is legal tender supported by governments via a central bank. See Book 5, Chapter 9 for more about fiat currencies.)

However, cryptocurrencies don't have a central authority; rather, the cryptocurrency community and, in particular, cryptocurrency miners and network nodes manage them. For this reason, cryptocurrencies are often referred to as *trustless*. Because no single party or entity controls how a cryptocurrency is issued, spent, or balanced, you don't have to put your trust in a single authority.

REMEMBER

Trustless is a bit of a misnomer. Trust is baked into the system. You don't have to trust a single authority, but your trust in the system and fully auditable codebase is still essential. In fact, no form of currency can work without some form of trust or belief. (If nobody trusts the currency, then nobody will accept it or work to maintain it!)

SO WHY IS THE PROCESS CALLED MINING?

When you compare cryptocurrency mining to gold mining, why the process is referred to as mining becomes clear. In both forms of mining, the miners put in work and are rewarded with an uncirculated asset. In gold mining, naturally occurring gold that was outside the economy is dug up and becomes part of the gold circulating within the economy. In cryptocurrency mining, work is performed, and the process ends with new cryptocurrency being created and added to the blockchain ledger. In both cases, miners, after receiving their reward — the mined gold or the newly created cryptocurrency — usually sell it to the public to recoup their operating costs and get their profit, placing the new currency into circulation.

The cryptocurrency miner's work is different from that of a gold miner, of course, but the result is much the same: Both bring a new money supply to the market. For cryptocurrency mining, all of the work happens on a mining computer or *rig* connected to the cryptocurrency network — no burro riding or gap-toothed gold panners required!

In the trustless cryptocurrency world, you can still trust the cryptocurrency community and its mechanisms to ensure that the blockchain contains an accurate and *immutable* — unchangeable — record of cryptocurrency transactions. Cryptocurrencies are established using a set of software rules that ensure that the system can be trusted, and the mining process is part of this system that allows everyone to trust the blockchain.

Cryptocurrencies have no central bank printing new money. Instead, miners dig up new currency according to a preset coin-issue schedule and release it into circulation in a process called *mining.*

Exploring the Role of the Crypto Miner

Cryptocurrency miners add transactions to the blockchain, but different cryptocurrencies use different mining methods, if the cryptocurrency uses mining at all. Different mining and consensus methods are used to determine who creates new blocks of data and how exactly the blocks are added to the blockchain.

REMEMBER

How you mine a particular cryptocurrency varies slightly depending on the type of cryptocurrency being mined, but the basics are still the same: Mining creates a system to build trust between parties without needing a single authority and ensures that everyone's cryptocurrency balances are up to date and correct in the blockchain ledger.

The work performed by miners consists of a few main actions:

>> Verifying and validating new transactions

>> Collecting those transactions and ordering them into a new block

>> Adding the block to the ledger's chain of blocks (the blockchain)

>> Broadcasting the new block to the cryptocurrency node network

The preceding mining process is essential work, necessary for the continued propagation of the blockchain and its associated transactions. Without it, the blockchain won't function. But why would someone do this work? What are the incentives for the miner?

The Bitcoin miner actually has a couple of incentives (other cryptocurrencies may work in a different manner).

>> **Transaction fees:** A small fee is paid by each person spending the cryptocurrency to have the transaction added to the new block; the miner adding the block gets the transaction fees.

>> **Block subsidy:** Newly created cryptocurrency, known as the block subsidy, is paid to the miner who successfully adds a block to the ledger.

Combined, the fees and subsidy are known as the *block reward*. In Bitcoin, the block subsidy began at 50 BTC. (BTC is the ticker symbol for Bitcoin.) The block subsidy at the time of this writing is currently 6.25 BTC. The block subsidy is halved every 210,000 blocks, or roughly every four years; sometime around spring 2024, it will halve again to 3.125 BTC per block.

Figure 1-1, from the BlockChain.com blockchain explorer (https://www.blockchain.com/explorer), shows a transaction with the block subsidy being paid to an address owned by the miner who added the block to the blockchain. A reward of 12.5 BTC is being paid as the subsidy because this transaction was before the most recent reward halving in 2020; the actual sum received by the miner (the full reward, 13.24251028 BTC) is larger, because it also includes the transaction fees for all the transactions in the block.

Making Cryptocurrency Trustworthy

For a cryptocurrency to function, several conditions must be met by the protocol. We like Jan Lanksy's six-factor list (Jan is a cryptocurrency academic, teaching at a university in the Czech Republic). Mining (in the mineable cryptocurrencies; non-mineable currencies have different mechanisms) is an integral part of making sure these conditions are met:

>> **The system doesn't require a central authority and is maintained through distributed consensus.** That is, everyone agrees on the balances

associated with addresses in the blockchain ledger. Mining is an integral part of adding transactions to the blockchain and maintaining consensus.

>> **The system keeps track of cryptocurrency units and their ownership.** Balances can be proven at any point in time. Mining adds transactions to the blockchain in a way that becomes immutable — the blockchain can't be changed. If the blockchain shows your balance is five Bitcoin, then you absolutely do own five Bitcoin!

>> **The system defines whether new cryptocurrency units can be created, and, if so, the system defines the circumstances of their origin and how to determine the ownership of these new units.** A fixed issuance or inflation rate is predefined. Mining provides a way to release new cryptocurrency into circulation at a predetermined, controlled rate, with ownership being assigned to the miner.

>> **Ownership of cryptocurrency units is proved through cryptography.** The three conditions of authenticity, nonrepudiation, and immutability are met, through the use of cryptography. Miners, using cryptography, verify that transaction requests are valid before adding them to a new block. The miner verifies that the transaction request is for a sum that is available to the owner of the crypto, that the owner has correctly signed the request with their private key to prove ownership, and that the receiving address is valid and able to accept the transfer.

>> **The system allows transactions to be performed in which ownership of the cryptographic units is changed.** Transactions can be submitted only by senders who can prove ownership of the cryptocurrency being transferred. Cryptocurrency owners prove ownership by signing transactions using the addresses associated with a private key. Mining is the process through which transactions are accomplished, and miners verify ownership before adding the transaction to the blockchain.

>> **If two different instructions for changing the ownership of the same cryptographic units are simultaneously entered, the system performs at most one of them.** Double-spending the same unit is not possible. The problem of double-spending was one that weakened earlier digital currencies. But with modern cryptocurrencies, miners vet transactions, searching the blockchain record of transactions to determine whether the owner actually has sufficient balance at that moment. If a sufficient balance isn't accounted for within the spend address (the Input address) in the transaction request, the transaction will be rejected by the node software and never mined onto the blockchain. Also, if the same sender has two or more pending transaction requests, but doesn't own enough cryptocurrency to cover them all, miners can decide which of the requests is valid. Additional transactions will be discarded to avoid *double-spending* the same currency.

If even one of these six conditions isn't met, a cryptocurrency will fail because it can't build enough trust for people to reliably use it. The process of mining solidifies and satisfies every single one of these conditions.

Reaching Agreement through Consensus Algorithms

A mind exercise known as the *Byzantine Generals' Problem* (or the *Byzantine Fault*, the *error avalanche*, and by various other names) illustrates the problem that cryptocurrency consensus algorithms seek to solve.

The overall problem? You're trying to reach consensus; in cryptocurrency, you're trying to reach agreement over the history of currency transactions. But in a cryptocurrency network, a distributed computer system of equals, you have many separate computers (nodes); the Bitcoin network, at times, has 50,000 to 200,000 nodes connected. Out of those thousands of systems, some are going to have technical problems: hardware faults, misconfiguration, out-of-date software, malfunctioning routers, and so on. Others are going to be untrustworthy; they're going to be seeking to exploit weaknesses for the financial gain of the people running the node (they are run by "traitors"). The problem is that for various reasons, some nodes may send conflicting and faulty information.

So to deal with this problem, a sort of parable or metaphor was devised, called the Byzantine Generals' Problem. (Three guys — Leslie Lamport, Robert Shostak, and Marshall Pease — first told this story in 1980, in a paper related to general issues of reliability in distributed computer systems.) Originally named the *Albanian Generals' Problem*, it was renamed after a long-defunct empire so as not to offend people from Albania! (Although in this interconnected world of constant social media offense, there must be at least some offended residents of Istanbul.) Apparently, distributed-computing academics like to sit around and devise these little metaphors. You may have heard of the *dining philosopher's problem*, the *reader's/writer's problem*, and so on. In fact, the *Byzantine Generals' Problem* was derived from the *Chinese Generals' Problem*.

Anyway, here is the idea, as described in their original paper:

We imagine that several divisions of the Byzantine army are camped outside an enemy city, each division commanded by its own general. The generals can communicate with one another only by messenger. After observing the enemy, they must decide upon a common plan of action. However, some of the generals may be traitors, trying to prevent the loyal generals from reaching agreement. The generals must have an algorithm to guarantee that A. All loyal generals decide upon the same plan of action [and] B. A small number of traitors cannot cause the loyal generals to adopt a bad plan.

(Search online for *byzantine generals' problem leslie lamport robert shostak marshall pease* if you're interested in seeing the original paper.)

That's the problem that cryptocurrency *consensus algorithms*, as they're known, are trying to solve: how the generals (the computer nodes) come up with consensus (all agree on the same plan of action — or transaction ledger), and avoid being led astray by a small number of traitors (faulty equipment and hackers).

Looking at the Cryptocurrency Miner

To have a chance at the mining reward, miners must set up their mining rigs (the computer equipment) and run that cryptocurrency's associated mining software. Depending on how many resources the miner is committing, they will have a proportional chance of being the lucky miner who gets to create and chain the latest block; the more resources employed, the higher the chance of winning the reward. Each block has a predetermined amount of payment, which is rewarded to the victorious miner for their hard work to spend as they wish.

So how is the winning miner chosen? That depends. In most cases, one of two basic methods is used (see Chapter 2 of this minibook for more about these and other methods).

>> **Proof of work:** Under this method, the miner has to carry out a task, and the first miner to complete the task adds the latest block to the blockchain and wins the block reward, the block subsidy, and transaction fees. Bitcoin and other cryptocurrencies, such as Ether (for now; it plans to switch to proof of stake at some point), Bitcoin Cash, Litecoin, and Dogecoin, use proof of work.

>> **Proof of stake:** In this system, the software is going to choose one of the cryptocurrency nodes to add the latest block; to be in the running, nodes must have a stake, generally meaning that they must own a certain amount of the cryptocurrency. The cryptocurrency network chooses the miner who will add the next block to the chain based on a combination of random choice and amount of stake — for example, with some cryptocurrencies, the more cryptocurrency owned and the longer it has been owned, the more likely the miner is to be chosen. (It's like owning lottery tickets: the more you own, the more likely you are to win.) With other cryptocurrencies, the choice is made sequentially, one by one, from a queue of preselected miners.

When Bitcoin first started, anyone with a simple desktop computer was able to mine. The would-be miner simply downloaded the Bitcoin mining software, installed it, and let the BTC roll in! As time went on, though, competition increased. Faster and more powerful computers were built and used for mining. Eventually, specialized processing chips called Application Specific Integrated Circuits (ASICs) were developed. An ASIC, as the name implies, is a computer chip designed for a specific purpose, such as displaying high-resolution graphics quickly, running a smartphone, or carrying out a particular form of computation. Specific ASICs have been designed to be highly efficient at the forms of computation required for cryptocurrency mining — for example, for Bitcoin mining. Such a chip can be 1,000 times more efficient at Bitcoin mining than the chip in your PC, so in today's Bitcoin mining environment, it's go ASIC or go home!

For high-difficulty cryptocurrencies, such as Bitcoin, the ideal mining environment requires the following conditions.

>> **Low hardware costs:** Those mining rigs aren't free.

>> **Low temperatures:** Lower temperatures make cooling your mining rigs easier.

>> **Low electricity costs:** Mining rigs can use a lot of power.

>> **Fast, reliable Internet connections:** You need to be communicating with the cryptocurrency network rapidly with minimal downtime because you're in competition with other miners.

Fear not, though! With many different copies and mimicry of Bitcoin running rampant, Bitcoin is no longer the only game in town, and you can find lots of alternative mining choices, with varying levels of required computing power. Today, some of the most profitable cryptocurrencies to mine are less known and can be mined using off-the-shelf computer hardware due to less stringent difficulty levels that are associated with lower popularity and adoption.

ASIC SCHMASIC

An ASIC is, technically speaking, an *application specific integrated circuit*: an incredibly specialized computer chip that is good at doing one operation very efficiently. However, you'll likely hear cryptocurrency people refer to the specialized mining box they've purchased as an ASIC, or an *ASIC box*. An ASIC is only good for a specific mining algorithm. For example, if you've got an ASIC built to mine Bitcoin, which uses the SHA-256 algorithm, you're not going to be mining Litecoin with it because that would require an ASIC built for the Scrypt algorithm.

TECHNICAL STUFF

Historically, during the years 2013 to 2020, a large portion of global cryptocurrency mining was claimed to take place in China, at perhaps three times the rate of the next-closest nation (the United States). A combination of cheap electricity and easy access to cheap computer components for building mining rigs gave China an edge that Chinese miners have leveraged and maintained, even with their government's apparent disapproval of cryptocurrencies. Recently, China has gone as far as to outright ban the trading and mining of Bitcoin and other cryptocurrencies, but the fact that the network hardly noticed a disruption during this debacle is a testament to how resilient and difficult to shut down distributed cryptocurrency systems such as Bitcoin are.

Making the Crypto World Go 'Round

A cryptocurrency has value because a large number of people collectively believe that it does. But why do they believe cryptocurrency has value? The answer is trust. (For more on trust, see the earlier section, "Making Cryptocurrency Trustworthy.") A holder of Bitcoin can trust that their Bitcoin will be in their wallet a day from now or 10 years from now. If they want to research how the system works, they can audit the code base to understand the system on a deeper level to see how trust is maintained. However, if they do not have the skillset or the computer science knowledge to audit code, they can choose to trust that other people, more knowledgeable than them, understand and monitor the system; they can trust the overall blockchain community that is managing the particular cryptocurrency.

Without the mining functionality underpinning the distributed peer-to-peer cryptocurrency system, this collective trust (based on the proof of collective work towards the chain) would not exist. (How the pre-mined cryptocurrencies or other weak-consensus mechanisms manage to exist is another story that we're not discussing in this book; we're focusing on mined cryptocurrencies, of course.)

REMEMBER

Mining makes sure that your balances won't change without your authorization. It incentivizes everyone to behave correctly and punishes those who don't. It creates a digital form of value transfer that can be trusted by each individual user as an equal peer in the network because every part of the system is aligned for one purpose: to provide a secure way to create, verify, and transfer ownership of digitally scarce cryptographic units.

» Finding out why proof of work is the most trusted form

» Surveying cryptocurrencies using proof of work

» Working with proof of stake and proof of work together

Chapter **2**

Exploring the Different Forms of Mining

I n this chapter, you find out about the different consensus algorithms used in cryptocurrency. Blockchain technology distributes data across hundreds or even thousands of computers. The challenge is to ensure that each copy of the data, on all those different computers, is correct. Different mathematical algorithms can be used to create consensus — to ensure that everyone working with any particular cryptocurrency agrees on what data should be included in the blockchain and what version of the blockchain is correct.

We explain various aspects of different consensus systems: proof of work, proof of stake, hybrid proof of stake/proof of work, and others.

Proof-of-Work Algorithms

Consensus is the process of ensuring that everyone's copy of the transaction data matches — that every copy of the blockchain contains the same data. Different consensus methods can be used, but at the time of this writing, the primary method is known as *proof of work* (PoW). However, this method has less secure and trustworthy alternatives, and we touch on some of those methods in this chapter.

As the cryptocurrency and blockchain space grows (it's rapidly expanding all the time), it is possible that a different system may end up becoming the "one who rules them all."

The most secure, trusted, yet energy-intensive of all the consensus systems, proof of work undeniably has the best track record. Having existed since the birth of Bitcoin, PoW has been instrumental in maintaining an unbroken chain of transactions since January 2009!

Proof of work predates cryptocurrency blockchains, though. Proof of work was originally developed as an idea for a process to counter junk mail.

The essential concept of proof of work is that in order to use a particular service — to send an email for example, or to add transactions to a blockchain — one has to show that some form of work has been carried out. The goal is to inflict a modest cost (in terms of the computing power required to run the proof-of-work algorithm) on the person wanting to use the service once but to make it very expensive for someone to use the service thousands or millions of times. This makes it cost-prohibitive to attack or disrupt proof-of-work systems.

The concept of using PoW as a countermeasure dates back to around 1993, and since then, quite a few different ideas for ways to use PoW have emerged. In the context of cryptocurrencies, proof of work prevents malicious miners from clogging up the network by submitting new blocks that can never be verified. If no work was required to submit a new block, anyone could repeatedly spam fake transactions inside new blocks and potentially grind the cryptocurrency network to a halt.

By the way, proof of work has a parallel in real-world currencies. For something to work as money, it has to be in limited supply, so either it's something that there simply isn't much of — gold, for example — or it has to be created through a process that takes significant effort.

How about sea shells, then? Sea shells have been used by various cultures as money. Consider wampum, sea shell money used by Native Americans in the eastern part of the continent well into the 18th century. "Shells," you say, "How much work does it take to pick up shells off the seashore?" Ah, but there was more to it than that. Wampum was made from very specific shells (the Channeled whelk and the quahog or poquahock clam shells), found in a very specific area (along Long Island Sound and Narragansett Bay). Furthermore, you couldn't just grab a whelk and buy dinner with it. You had to work the shells. The shells were cut down; for example, it was the inner spiral, the columella, of the Channeled whelk that was used. Then the craftswomen (it was mostly women making wampum) drilled holes through the shells using wooden drills, and the shells were then polished on a grinding stone until they were smooth. They were finally strung together using deer hide or various other materials. This work ensured that time and effort had to be put into the "currency" so that it could acquire value.

Another way to look at this concept is not that the money is "acquiring" value, but that it can't be created without a significant input of work, so the market can't be flooded with new, low-cost versions of the money, thus devaluing it.

Even the early European colonists used wampum. It wasn't until they began using more advanced manufacturing techniques to create wampum, lowering the cost of the creation of this currency and destroying its scarcity, that the value crashed, and wampum was no longer viable as a store of value and currency.

As co-author Peter relates:

> I had trouble fully getting the idea of proof of work and how it fits in when I first got involved in cryptocurrency. In case any readers are still trying to understand the purpose of PoW, I'll put it another way. The whole point of the work that the miners do (competing with each other to win the proof-of-work contest) is to ensure that adding a block to the blockchain isn't easy. If it's too easy, the blockchain is vulnerable. Bad actors could continually attack the blockchain by flooding the system with bad blocks. The idea of proof of work is to make adding a block difficult, rather like the whole idea of laboriously hand-working shells into wampum was to ensure that the wampum economy couldn't be flooded with cheap wampum.

Proof-of-work applications

A proof-of-work algorithm forces the miner to do some work — to use computational power — before submitting a block to the blockchain. The algorithm acts as security for a cryptocurrency by making unwanted actions costly and ensuring that the intended outcome (the addition of only genuine, valid transactions to the blockchain) always occurs.

So what work must be performed? Essentially, the miner is required to solve a mathematical puzzle of some kind. The puzzle needs to be complicated enough to take some computational power but not so complicated that it will take too long to validate and slow down the addition of transactions.

For example, the work being performed in Bitcoin's proof of work is just hashing the previous block of a transaction's header (along with a random number, the *nonce*) in the hope of finding a new hash that meets the required difficulty threshold.

There's a flip side to proof of work. Finding the answer to the puzzle has to be difficult, but checking and verifying the work has to be easy. That is, once the puzzle has been solved, it must be easy for other miners to check that indeed the puzzle has been solved correctly. In the case of Bitcoin, once a miner has solved the puzzle, the new hash is added to the header, and the block is sent to other miners and nodes to confirm. While it's hard to initially pick a nonce that will provide a good outcome — a hash number below the target level — once the nonce has been found, it is very quick and easy for other miners to run the same hashing calculation to confirm that indeed the puzzle has been solved. The work is done, and then everyone can quickly check the winning miner's block and sign off on it.

Note, by the way, that cryptocurrencies using proof of work are usually the only ones that require more efficient, specialized mining equipment. In proof of stake, described later in this chapter, almost any computer can act as a creator, verifier, and chainer of new blocks, as long as it has a significant stake in the underlying currency.

Proof-of-work examples

The use of proof of work is widely adopted in the cryptocurrency world. The largest and most successful cryptocurrency of them all, Bitcoin, uses it along with a host of other popular cryptocurrencies. You may need different mining equipment for these cryptocurrencies, as each of them has a slightly different hashing algorithm, even though they all use proof of work. Here are a few examples of the more common PoW cryptocurrencies:

>> **Bitcoin** is currently the king of cryptocurrency in terms of network *hash rate* (that is, the number of hashes being processed every second), market liquidity, and overall adoption. Bitcoin has never not been the top cryptocurrency. Bitcoin pioneered proof of work and has been going strong for more than ten years on the back of this consensus system. Many other cryptocurrencies have copied the code of Bitcoin as a starting point and then modified it slightly for their own use. Most of them kept the proof-of-work component, although they may use a different hashing algorithm requiring a different mining rig setup than the one for Bitcoin.

Most capital in the cryptocurrency mining world is directed to Bitcoin, and the mining rigs used are specialized in performing the SHA-256 hashing algorithm native to Bitcoin consensus. Bitcoin-specific ASICs (Application Specific Integrated Circuits) now make up a large percentage of the system, and many are based in China, with the United States and Russia closely competing for second place.

» **Ether (on the Ethereum network)** is the second-most popular cryptocurrency, sometimes the third, depending on the day. Ethereum uses its own hashing algorithm for proof of work called *Ethash*. Don't worry too much about what Ethash is, though, as the Ethereum development team has divisive plans to leave proof of work behind and use proof of stake in the future, akin to rebuilding the aircraft engine midflight! In fact, they have a difficulty "bomb" baked into the Ethereum code. As time goes on, it becomes harder and harder to mine Ethereum via proof of work, meaning miners earn less and less. (Despite this bomb, when the price of ETH was at all-time highs, mining Ether was still very lucrative.)

» **Litecoin** is generally considered the silver to Bitcoin's status as "digital gold." Litecoin focuses on fast payments (meaning quicker block times) and low transaction fees. It uses a different hashing algorithm from Bitcoin, referred to as *scrypt mining,* so no *crossover mining* (using the same mining rig for multiple cryptocurrencies) is possible between the two. Other than that, though, in general, the way Litecoin works is very comparable to Bitcoin, as it was essentially a copy of the code. Just like Bitcoin, ASICs have been designed to specifically mine Litecoin, providing the most profitable approach.

» **Monero**, one of the more private (anonymous) cryptocurrencies, was built to allow CPU or GPU mining. That is, you don't need specialized equipment; the Monero community makes a point to keep ASICs out, updating the mining algorithm slightly every few months so manufacturers can't produce ASICs. Building an ASIC designed to process a particular algorithm more efficiently is always possible; outrunning the changes is also possible. Still, designing, producing, and selling a new ASIC takes time. By switching to a different PoW algorithm every so often, Monero has effectively outrun chip manufacturers. This allows CPUs and GPUs to remain effective on that blockchain. Monero uses a very complex cryptographic mechanism called *ring signatures* to hide transaction amounts associated with addresses, making it very hard to analyze the transactions. This sets it apart from the other cryptocurrencies in this list, which have easily searchable public transaction records on the blockchain.

» **Zcash** is also a more private (anonymous) cryptocurrency. It was built using a trusted setup ceremony, as Zcash calls it, with public cryptographic parameters split between various trusted parties. (This is complicated stuff, but if you want to read more, check out the Zcash site at https://z.cash/technology/paramgen/). The Zcash blockchain allows for the use of shielded cryptographic transactions (called zk-SNARKs) that are nearly impossible to track. However, these shielded transactions are computationally expensive, and many Zcash wallets available today do not fully support this feature, instead relying on publicly auditable transactions very similar to Bitcoin.

The Zcash proof-of-work mechanism is referred to as *Equihash.* However, unlike Bitcoin, in which the entire block reward goes to the winning miner, Zcash shares the block reward; there's a miner's reward, but also a founder's reward and a developer's reward, to compensate the team that created and maintains the Zcash codebase and blockchain.

Upsides

The main upside to proof of work is that it works! No other system for reaching and maintaining consensus has as long and impeccable a record as proof of work. The game theory behind proof of work ensures that if all participants are rational and acting in their own economic interests, the system will function as intended, and so far, that has been the case.

Proof of work also prevents spamming of the network from malicious miners. The energy and equipment expenses required to carry out this specialized work makes attacks cost-prohibitive and unsustainable.

Another great benefit to proof of work is the balancing of power. Power is spread over a wide range of miners, potentially a million individuals in the case of Bitcoin. The amount of cryptocurrency owned by a particular miner is irrelevant; the computing power is what counts. Conversely, with proof-of-stake systems, miners *stake* currency — the more they own, the more power they have — so power over the system can become concentrated into the hands of a small number of stakers; this is especially the case for coins' initial coin offerings, also known as *premined distributions.*

This is another advantage that most proof-of-work cryptocurrencies have: fair distribution. To have found a block and gained the subsequent block reward, a miner must have provided adequate work and supported the network according to the ruleset. This, according to *cryptocurrency game theory,* provides an important incentive. Proof-of-work mechanisms, under this theory, ensure that it is much more economically beneficial to work toward consensus than against it.

TECHNICAL STUFF

Game theory is a branch of study involving mathematical models that describe likely decision-making by rational decision-makers in some kind of relationship. Decisions made by these decision-makers, or actors, affect the decisions and actions of others. Thus, within cryptocurrency, the goal is to incentivize all actors to make decisions that result in a stable, trusted network.

Downsides

A big downside to proof of work is the resources required to perform the work. It's not just a single miner using the proof-of-work algorithm and attempting to solve the hashing puzzle. Rather, it's all the miners in the world competing to solve the puzzle first! So, rather than one computer consuming electricity (and adding carbon to the atmosphere), it's thousands of computers doing it at the same time, despite the fact that only one miner gets the right to add a block!

The Bitcoin network, which has the largest number of miners, is estimated to use around 100 TWh (terawatt-hours) per year. This is roughly equivalent to the annual energy needs of a country the size of Malaysia or Sweden.

Another downside is that over time, the mining under proof of work can also become centralized. The setup cost for a mining operation is not insignificant. Miners who already have a data center and ongoing mining operations are in a much better position to add rigs. With a lower cost per mining rig, over time, those who were first movers outcompete later entrants, and centralization can occur.

Related to this centralization is the potential for *51 percent attacks*, a major concern for anyone who mines a proof-of-work cryptocurrency. A 51 percent attack can occur when a single entity gains control over 51 percent (or more) of the total active hashing power. In this scenario, it becomes possible for this majority hash controller to modify a cryptocurrency's blockchain record, destroying the trust that is fundamental to its existence. It is for this reason that decentralization of miners is promoted and encouraged in the cryptocurrency realm.

A final downside to proof of work is the wasted calculations that all the proof of work requires! While the possibility of denial-of-service attacks making a cryptocurrency unusable is very real — thus making the proof-of-work mechanism an effective protection for the blockchain — the search for a nonce provides no economic, social, or scientific benefits to anyone outside of the cryptocurrency's ecosystem. In other words, once the thousands of miners have played the game and one has solved the puzzle and added a block to the chain, all that computing power has no residual value; one may argue that the power has been wasted on a pointless game.

The short story made long is that proof of work is the most proven way we have of keeping a peer-to-peer cryptocurrency system operational. While indeed, some areas need efficiency improvements, no other solution can provide the same security benefits without different economic, consensus, and computer engineering tradeoffs, and as a result, proof of work will remain widely utilized.

Proof-of-Stake Algorithms

In the early days of cryptocurrency, PoW was the only game in town, and new cryptocurrencies primarily copied Bitcoin as the model and a starting point for their slightly different ideas and implementations.

Over time, however, some involved in cryptocurrency recognized the downsides to PoW and set out to find a better way of securing a cryptocurrency, soon settling on PoS — *proof of stake*.

The idea is to make miners stake their cryptocurrency as an entry ticket for adding blocks to the blockchain and earning transaction fees. The penalty for adding invalid transactions to the blockchain ledger would be loss of the coins staked. This was first proposed in 2011 by a user of the Bitcointalk.org forum. In 2012, the white paper for *Peercoin*, which expounded and solidified this idea, was published, describing a new system for securing and reaching blockchain consensus that was much less resource-intensive than pure proof of work. (While Peercoin is technically a hybrid of proof of stake/proof of work, this marked the first real-world implementation involving proof of stake.)

Today, proof of stake, along with its hybrid use (hybrid proof of stake/proof of work), helps secure and maintain trust for a few somewhat successful cryptocurrencies. While still considered the more unproven of the two main consensus systems, proof of stake has some benefits over proof of work. Proof of stake should be understood by any cryptocurrency miner worth their salt. (And you can potentially profit it from it, too!)

Proof of stake explained

Proof of stake is similar to proof of work — it's used to maintain consensus and keep the cryptocurrency ledger secure — but with one major difference: There's way less *work*! Instead of using a specialized mining rig to calculate a targeted hash, a miner who wants to create a new block chooses to stake an amount of the cryptocurrency they want to mine. Staking can be thought of as making a refundable deposit, and the purpose behind its requirement is to prove that you have a vested interest in the welfare of whatever cryptocurrency you're mining. In other words, before you can mine the cryptocurrency, you must prove that you own some of it, and you must stake it during the mining process; that is, you can't just show you own it, sell it, and continue mining. The stake is locked during the mining process.

A miner has to be selected to add transactions to the blockchain; one miner wins the contest. Different cryptocurrencies use different methods for making that selection, but whatever method is used, that selection is made, and the lucky miner is chosen to create and chain a new block of transactions, collecting all of the transaction fees from this new block. The nice thing is, the block being chained can be less computationally expensive and thus created by any computer capable of running that cryptocurrency's node software, if an adequate amount of cryptocurrency is staked. This, in effect, makes most computers capable of functioning as proof-of-stake miners. The catch is that blocks are rewarded proportionally to the amount of coins staked, making for a less even coin distribution among miners in comparison with proof of work–based systems.

MINERS AND VALIDATORS

For simplicity, we mostly use the terms *miners* and *mining*, though you'll also hear the terms *validators* and *validating*. What's the difference? Let's use the Bitcoin blockchain as an example of the difference in a proof-of-work system (where each blockchain is different, and there are many permutations). *Validation* means checking blocks and transactions to ensure that they are *valid* (that they follow all the network's rules). All full nodes validate — by definition, in fact, a full node is one that fully validates transactions and blocks. But only some full nodes are miners, or mining nodes. Miners validate transactions, but they also do the extra work of gathering together blocks of transactions and taking part in the proof-of-work contest to try to win the right to add the block to the blockchain. But the winning miner's work still has to be validated by all the other non-mining full nodes. Mining nodes make up a small subset of the approximately 50,000 to 200,000 full nodes, so the majority of full nodes are keeping an eye on the minority miners — and each other — while checking the miners' work.

As cryptocurrency guru Andreas Antonopolous has said, "Nodes serve the most important purpose. [Each acts] as an authoritative verifier of every single transaction and block. [N]odes decide what the rules are, not miners. Miners get the transactions that nodes decided were valid, and they give back blocks at the pleasure of the nodes that will decide whether they are worthy of being propagated because they are valid. The validity of the consensus rules is not determined by miners; they sequence transactions into a block. The validity of the consensus rules is determined by nodes, because they will not propagate [invalid] blocks." Thus, although mining nodes both validate and mine, mining and validation are separate processes.

In cryptocurrencies that aren't, strictly speaking, *mined* — in which the currency was pre-mined, so no new currency is being provided as a block subsidy — people are still making money by validating transactions. They do this by checking that the transactions are valid, adding them to blocks, and then adding the blocks to the blockchain. These validators earn money from transaction fees.

It's important to note that fewer block rewards are to be won in proof-of-stake cryptocurrencies, as the vast majority of coins issued are generally pre-mined up front prior to the currency's genesis block.

The lack of work required to mine a proof-of-stake crypto, along with minimum mining rewards besides the transaction fees, has given rise to the terms *minting* or *forging* being used to describe this process rather than mining. At the end of the day, though, proof of work and proof of stake attempt to serve the same purpose: ensuring that everyone in the network agrees that new transactions in the latest block are valid, and properly chaining them to a cryptocurrency's blockchain record.

Proof-of-stake selections

In proof-of-stake systems, you have to prove that you own a certain amount of the currency you are mining; you have to put up a stake to play the game. Different currencies have different PoS mechanisms, of course, but the basic concepts are as follows.

First, before you can play the game and have a chance of becoming the miner who adds a block to the blockchain, you need a stake. You have to have some of the cryptocurrency in your wallet, and, with some currencies, it has to have been there for a certain amount of time. Peercoin, for example, requires that the currency has been sitting in the wallet for at least 30 days. Other currencies, though, don't have this limitation. Note, however, that in some systems, while staking your currency, you can't use it; it's locked up in your wallet and may be locked up for a specified minimum time. In fact, if you attack the system in some way, you stand to lose the stake. In other systems, this isn't the case; merely having currency in your wallet is enough to count as a stake.

A second concept used by PoS systems is that of *coin age.* That is, you multiply the number of coins in the wallet by the time they have been in the wallet. A miner who holds 10 coins that are 60 days old (10×60 = a coin age of 600) will have a better chance of being selected than one who holds 5 coins that are 90 days old (5×90 = a coin age of 450). There may be minimum and maximum lengths of time for the coins. In Peercoin, the coins must have been in the wallet for at least 30 days; at the same time, coins that have been there more than 90 days are not counted. (This is to ensure that the blockchain is not dominated by very old or large collections of coins.) Also, the miner who wins has the clock on their staked coins restarted; those coins can't be used for another 30 days. Blackcoin has a simpler concept: Your stake is simply the amount of the cryptocurrency in your wallet that you have assigned as your stake.

But the stake is not enough. If miner selection were based purely on the coin age of the stake, the richest person would always win and would add the block to the blockchain every time.

So a third concept used by PoS systems is that they must have some element of random selection. The staked coins, or the coin age of your stake, determine how many tickets you buy in the lottery, but the winning ticket still has to be selected through some kind of random selection, and different PoS cryptocurrencies use different methods. The more tickets owned (a higher coin or coin-age stake) means your chance of winning is greater, but through chance, even someone with a fraction of your stake may win.) As Blackcoin says (Blackcoin.org), "Staking is a kind of lottery. Some days you'll get more than usual, some days less." Blackcoin uses a randomization method that is a combination of a hash-value contest and the coin stake; miners combine the amount of stake and the staking wallet address, and the miner with the most zeros in front of their hash wins.

The richest and longest-owning cryptocurrency miners typically have an advantage for winning the right to create new coins and chain blocks into a PoS blockchain. In fact, as Blackcoin explains, "if you stake with more coins, you get more blocks and you are more likely to find a reward. Someone staking 24 hours a day, 365 days a year would get more (~24x) than someone staking the same amount of coins an hour a day." Over time, stakers earn Blackcoin in proportion to the amount of money they stake and how long they stake it, and in general that's true of all simple PoS systems.

PoS example cryptocurrencies

There have not been many successful examples of cryptocurrencies deployed that use pure proof of stake; most deploy a hybridized approach, as discussed later in this chapter. However, a couple of noteworthy blockchains have used this technology for a consensus mechanism:

>> **NXT** was created in 2013 and deployed using a pure proof-of-stake implementation. Today, it is not widely used but is still in existence.

>> **Blackcoin** is a cryptocurrency that was released in early 2014 and also functions on a pure proof-of-stake consensus mechanism. Again, it's a relatively small cryptocurrency by value and not widely used.

Upsides

The most obvious upside to proof of stake is its reduced energy consumption when compared to proof of work. Rather than consuming the same amount of electricity as a small country, under proof of stake, the blockchain can be managed with significantly less energy.

The scalability under proof of stake is also greatly increased. While Bitcoin and similar proof-of-work cryptocurrencies struggle to get double-digit transactions per second on the main chain (Bitcoin is around 8), by utilizing proof of stake, they increase their transaction capability into the thousands or even hundreds of thousands per second, depending on the number of validating nodes being utilized (generally, the fewer, the faster).

With the reduction in cost to those who want to validate a proof-of-stake cryptocurrency, the transaction fees are also correspondingly lower. Miners don't have to purchase expensive mining rigs, so creating blocks can be accomplished at a lower energy and equipment price.

While this does impact overall revenues for miners in proof of stake, the relative ease to start mining and low overhead cost still make mining proof-of-stake cryptos a viable option for those who want to experiment. And don't forget, more transactions per second also means more fees per second!

Downsides

The stakes are high when it comes to securing a cryptocurrency and maintaining consensus. In a purely proof-of-stake system, two main issues cause concern.

The first is the problem of originally distributing a new PoS cryptocurrency. Some cryptocurrencies have both pre-mined coins and — once the network is running — mined coins. Frequently, most of the cryptocurrency in circulation for many PoS systems is pre-mined, which creates a large barrier to entry for miners who want to get involved later. If you want to mine, you have a huge advantage if you already have large amounts of the cryptocurrency to stake right from the beginning.

And the more centralized ownership is, the less distributed trust the network has due to the ability of large holders to vote selfishly, using their coins to propagate a chain history that most benefits the larger coin-holders. This could result in manipulation of the blockchain ledger to the advantage of the large coin-holders, such as double spends, selfish issuance, and upgrades that go against the best interests of other users.

CHAIN TIP

The term *chain tip* is often used to describe the highest block number on a particular blockchain. The *chain tip* would be the block that has the most accumulated proof of work hashed toward its chain of blocks.

The second problem with pure proof of stake is called "nothing at stake." This theory states that in PoS systems, validators (miners) are not interested in consensus, because it may be in their financial interest to add invalid blocks to the blockchain, leading to forks in the blockchain creating multiple chains. That is, if one validator adds an invalid block, other miners may accept it and build on it, because they will earn transaction fees on whatever chain wins. (And because it's a PoS system, it doesn't take much computational power to do so.) This leaves open the possibility of the blockchain being manipulated by those who hold the largest stake in that system, which is the opposite of the very purpose of cryptocurrency, which was to eliminate the idea of the traditional banking system and its centralized and manipulatable ledger system.

Under proof of work, this issue would be resolved quickly, as the miners are incentivized to quickly resolve which fork of the blockchain to follow so precious mining rig resources are not wasted. The invalid block is *orphaned,* meaning that no new blocks will be built on top of it, and business continues as usual with only a single blockchain. Under proof of stake, however, it is very easy to continue building new blocks on each chain, and in theory, the blockchain could easily fork. There's a negligible cost to validating multiple chains, and if that occurs, the decentralized consensus mechanism has failed. With proof of work, chain reorganizations occur naturally as orphaned blocks, also known as *uncles*; they have their transactions placed back into the mempool, and, regardless of which *chain tip* eventually becomes confirmed, the transactions and blockchain maintain validity.

Hybrid Proof of Stake/Proof of Work

In light of the disadvantages from PoW's energy consumption and PoS's "nothing at stake" problem, savvy crypto-entrepreneurs thought of a different solution: hybrid proof of stake/proof of work. This helps alleviate the issues of distribution and "nothing at stake" while also slightly reducing the cost to validate transactions from proof of work.

So how do you know if a cryptocurrency is a hybrid? Unfortunately, you may see it referred to as proof of stake, hybrid proof of stake, or hybrid proof of work, all of which are confusing. To figure out what a cryptocurrency is actually using, a quick search engine query will find you the answer. For example, "*consensus algorithm for Bitcoin*" will yield an explanation for Bitcoin's proof-of-work consensus system, and a search of "*consensus algorithm for dash*" will show you that DASH uses proof of work and proof of stake.

Because a growing number of cryptocurrency projects are using both proof of stake and proof of work, understanding what this means for mining is a must.

Hybrids explained

Earlier in this chapter, we discuss how proof of work (PoW) and proof of stake (PoS) function; the question now is how these two components work together in a hybrid proof-of-stake/proof-of-work system. A caveat, though: The variations for different hybrid consensus systems are vast, so if you decide to mine or stake a hybrid cryptocurrency, put some effort into researching exactly how that chain's specific approach is applied to determining blockchain consensus.

In a hybrid system, both PoS and PoW are used. A particular node may carry out both PoS and PoW processes, or it may do just PoS or just PoW.

Here's an example flow for a hybrid consensus system. The miner starts by staking an amount of cryptocurrency *to themself* — that's the proof of stake — and then uses the data from this transaction and combines it with the current time (represented as the number of seconds since some fixed date).

The miner then takes this combined information (transaction information and seconds value) and calculates a hash (that's the proof of work). This scenario doesn't have a nonce, but the integer for the current time has the same effect of changing the hash output as additional calculations are computed.

Because this nonce substitute changes once every second, as time elapses, a new hash can be calculated only every second, and thus the resources required to mine are much lower than with a true PoW system, in which modern ASIC miners can calculate trillions of hashes per second. Rather than calculating numerous hashes every second, only *one* hash calculation is made every second per node. This means that most off-the-shelf computers can function as mining rigs. All you need is a computer with a wallet holding the chain's predetermined staking threshold of the hybrid cryptocurrency.

Once the hybrid miner has this hash, it is checked against a target difficulty. There is a major difference, though. This target difficulty is different for every single miner! This is because the difficulty is lowered (easier to meet) or raised (harder to meet) based on the coin age of the cryptocurrency used in the transaction that was sent at the beginning of this process, giving an edge to existing coin holders and adding barriers to entry for new miners. (*Coin age* is simply the sum of the length of time the miner has owned each of their cryptocurrency units.)

For example, if Peter owned three units of Hybridcoin and they had all been in his wallet for five days, the coin age of that transaction would be 15 (5+5+5=15). If one of these three Hybridcoins had been in his wallet for four days, though, the coin age of the transaction would be 14 (5+5+4=14).

The higher the coin age of the transaction, the easier it is to find a hash that meets the target difficulty, meaning that miners with greater coin ages have a greater chance of winning than those with lower coin ages. Despite this, an element of chance still exists; a higher coin age significantly increases a validator's chances but still doesn't guarantee their winning.

The first miner to solve the puzzle — to find a hash that matches the target — wins. That miner can now chain the latest block of transactions and will receive the block reward (the block subsidy and transaction fees) for doing this.

This system enables a miner to try their luck every second. Because they are sending the cryptocurrency to themselves in this process, it cannot be sent to anyone else and is effectively "staked" or locked to their account. Additionally, in most hybrid systems, when the miner finally does win this lottery, their cryptocurrency coin age is reset, reducing the likelihood that they will win the game again the next time.

HYBRID PROOF-OF-STAKE/ PROOF-OF-WORK REWARDS

So if a cryptocurrency uses proof of stake and proof of work, how do the rewards work? For most hybrid cryptocurrencies, the rewards are lumped together as a single sum and then split between the proof-of-stake validators and proof-of-work miners using a preset percentage. For example, say that the block subsidy is 10 Hybridcoin and the transaction fees in the new block equal 2 Hybridcoin, and there's a preset percentage split of 60 percent to the PoW miners and 40 percent to the PoS miners. In this scenario, the PoW miner who is creating and chaining the latest block earns 7.2 Hybridcoin, and the PoS miner who verifies the latest block earns the remaining 4.8 Hybridcoin. (If a node was both staking and mining, it would get the full amount, of course.) It is important to remember that the percentage split between types of miners can vary depending on the specific cryptocurrency, so always do your research!

Hybridized examples

DASH is the most successful hybrid of PoS/PoW. Dash's codebase is the basis for many other hybrid cryptocurrencies. Originally forked from Bitcoin around 2014 under a different name, and then later modified to allow hybrid PoS/PoW *masternodes*, DASH offers returns of around 6 to 8 percent annually. Dash can handle quite a few transactions per second, but the masternode model is fairly centralized and will cost you a significant upfront investment to begin validating. This creates an underlying demand for that cryptocurrency, manipulating the purchase price in favor of existing coin holders.

PIVX is a fork of the DASH cryptocurrency. While it originally used proof of work, it now works on a proof-of-stake/proof-of-work hybrid model. Staking any amount of your PIVX will net you around 8 to 12 percent annually, paid in PIVX directly to your staked wallet.

At the time of this writing, **Ethereum** is still using a PoW system (Ethash), but plans to switch to a hybrid system at some future date. (The Ethereum community has been discussing the switch for quite some time.) The front runner for the beginning of the switchover (it will likely evolve over time) is currently known as Casper FFG, in which a PoS protocol runs alongside the Ethash PoW protocol, with a network of validators running a PoS checkpoint every 50 blocks.

Peercoin, or PPC, was the first PoS cryptocurrency in operation (back in cryptocurrency ancient history, 2012). However, it is not a pure PoS currency; it is a PoS/PoW hybrid. Peercoin has been mimicked and built upon since then. You can still mine its hybrid proof-of-work and proof-of-stake implementation today for about a 1 percent return annually, assuming the coin price stays steady.

Upsides

Hybrid systems take the best of both proof of work and proof of stake. The PoW component provides security, while the higher efficiency of the PoS component allows a higher throughput of transactions and, therefore, lower transaction fees. The result is a secure and fast, albeit more centralized, cryptocurrency.

MASTERNODES

A *masternode* is a staking and validating node that holds a sufficient threshold of coins, often many hundreds or even thousands. This amount of coins allows the node to vote on code proposals as well as validate and propagate blocks to the network. DASH is the best-known blockchain using the masternode concept.

Downsides

Governance is difficult for hybrid cryptocurrencies. Because the reward split can theoretically be voted on and changed, there's a constant disagreement between the users who want more rewards for proof of stake and those who want a higher percentage for proof of work. While the hybrid approach has some of the benefits of each consensus system, it also carries many of the downsides of both proof of stake and proof of work.

Delegated Proof of Stake

Delegated proof of stake (dPoS) works similarly to proof of stake but with a more centralized concentration of *block producers* or *witnesses* in the dPoS ecosystem. Block producers are elected and take sequential turns to add blocks to the block-chain. Generally, the cryptocurrency owners get to vote for the validators in proportion to the amount of the cryptocurrency they own. And there simply aren't many block producers, with the number being generally in the range of 20 to 100. (EOS has 21, for example.)

dPoS systems also have *validators* who validate that the blocks the block producers are adding are indeed valid; anyone can be a validator. (This shows what a confusing world cryptocurrency is, with different people using words in different ways. In some PoS systems, validators also add blocks to the blockchain.)

In dPoS, a voting mechanism allows witnesses (block validators) to vote for or against other witnesses if some become bad actors by corrupting the chain with invalid transactions or other damaging behavior.

The advantages and disadvantages of this system are very similar to typical proof-of-stake systems. However, a number of blockchains have actually been successfully deployed using this technology, the most noteworthy examples being EOS and Steem.

Delegated Byzantine Fault Tolerance

Delegated Byzantine Fault Tolerance (dBFT) is similar to dPoS. Its name refers to the Byzantine Generals' Problem (see Chapter 1 of this minibook), which Bitcoin and other cryptocurrencies sought to solve. Its challenges include how to find consensus, with everyone working together for the good of the network, in a distributed computer network in which some parties may be unreliable, either because of technical faults or intentional malfeasance.

In dBFT, blocks are put forward by speaker nodes and voted on by delegate nodes. Consensus in dBFT is achieved when at least two-thirds of the delegate nodes agree on a proposed block. Any user can run a speaker node, but to be a delegate node requires being voted in by large token holders. The risk is that this may lead to centralization of power and vote manipulation in the future, but so far, dBFT implementations have maintained chain validity.

With dBFT, once a transaction is confirmed and the block recorded into the chain, it achieves total finality and is irreversible. This leads to almost no chance of forking between delegate nodes.

NEO is one of the few dBFT cryptocurrencies. In the *genesis* block (the first block of the NEO blockchain), 100 million NEO were created (pre-mined), with 50 million sold to the public and 50 million locked up, then trickled out to the team working on NEO at a rate of 15 million per year. The stake you earn for running a speaker node is not paid in NEO. Rather, it is paid in GAS, which is a separate token used to fuel contracts on the NEO network. NEO has only seven voting delegate nodes. More may be added, in groups of three, to allow for the two-thirds agreement required. (The total number of delegates, minus one, can be divided by three, so a block is accepted when at least two-thirds of the delegates plus one vote for it.)

Proof of Burn

Proof of burn (PoB) is a consensus mechanism that proves that adequate resources are expended in the creation of a particular coin or token. This can be an expensive method to choose, but it can be effective for kickstarting a new cryptocurrency that utilizes the accumulated proof of work of a more secure chain. A PoB cryptocurrency typically sits on top of another, PoW, cryptocurrency blockchain.

Essentially, a coin that has been created in the proof-of-work blockchain is sent to a verifiably unspendable address (sometimes known as an *eater address*) — that is, to a blockchain address that the community has verified as being unusable. Such an address may have been created randomly, rather than through the usual process of creating a private/public key pair and then hashing the public key. If the address was created randomly, then the private key cannot be known, and thus the address is unspendable. Thus, any cryptocurrency sent to that address can never be used again. (There's no private key that can be used to send the cryptocurrency to another address.) The cryptocurrency has been, in effect, burned!

Thus, launching a PoB cryptocurrency begins with buying PoW coins and sending them to the eater address. In return, the buyer gets the right to mine. For example, that's how the Counterparty (XCP) cryptocurrency began, back in January 2014, when miners sent Bitcoin to an eater address and in return were issued Counterparty coins, which gave them the right to participate in Counterparty mining.

The benefits of this method include the ability to use the burnt coins' PoW as security for the PoB chain, but the downsides include the fact that the PoB network cannot exist independently of the PoW coin and requires the trust and utilization of the underlying cryptocurrency asset that was burnt.

And MORE. . .

There's more, of course. There's *proof of capacity* (PoC), where miners save a database of puzzle solutions to the node's storage, and when a block contest runs, the node accesses the puzzle solutions to find the correct one. There's *proof of elapsed time* (PoET), where nodes are randomly assigned a wait time and then blocks are added, based on the sequence of wait times (the lowest wait time goes first). There's also *proof of activity* (PoA), a particular form of hybrid PoW/PoS, *limited confidence proof of activity* (LCPoA), and so on.

And more models turn up all the time. There is no perfect consensus mechanism, so the evolution goes on, as new ideas arise and new models are tested.

Chapter **3**

Mining Made Simple: Finding a Pool and Preparing an Account

For most small-scale miners, who seek consistent and predictable crypto-currency mining rewards in today's incredibly competitive cryptocurrency mining industry, the best route to secure steady rewards from mining is to utilize a mining pool service for their mining equipment's hashing power. Unless you're wielding an immense amount of hash power — a considerable portion of the estimated network hash rate (anything nearing a single percentage point in this case would be considerable) — solo mining is a very risky venture and should probably be avoided if you are an entry-level novice miner.

We regard mining pools as a great way to get started in cryptocurrency mining, and for many miners, it's the last stage, too. Even if you plan to move on to solo mining, pool mining is a good way to begin, to test the cryptocurrency mining waters and get your feet wet. Pool mining also helps you discover the hash rate of your equipment, which you need when you read Chapters 4 and 5 of this mini-book. In combination with other information in this book, what you find out here can help you decide whether it makes sense to solo mine, and, if you think it does, what it will take and what it will cost to do so. You must learn to walk (pool mine) before you can run (solo mine).

We also look at a related concept in this chapter, cloud mining. In cloud mining, you essentially invest in a mining operation and earn a proportion of the operation's revenues. It's a hands-off situation where you provide money, and they buy and manage the computing equipment.

Understanding How Pool Mining Works

Pool mining involves a group of miners acting as a team to find blocks. The block rewards are proportionally split across all miners who contributed to the pool's hashed proof of work; that is, the more hashing power you provided to the operation during a particular time period *(the pool mining duration* or *mining round)*, the higher the share you receive for block rewards won by the pool during that time period. (More specifically, shares are calculated a number of different ways, as you find out later in this chapter, but in general, you're rewarded according to the proportion of the hash power you provide to the pool.)

Typically, the mining duration or mining round is the period of time between blocks being mined by the pool. That is, a round begins immediately after the pool has won the right to add a block to the blockchain and stops when it adds a block to the blockchain the next time. The round can range anywhere from a few minutes to many hours, depending on the pool size and the pool's luck.

Here's essentially how this all works:

1. **You sign up with a mining pool.**

2. **You download and install the mining pool's software on your computer.**

3. **The software on your computer communicates with the mining pool's servers; in effect, your computer has just become an extension of the mining pool's cryptocurrency node.**

4. **Your computer helps with the mining operations, contributing spare processing power to the pool's proof-of-work (PoW) hashing.**

5. When the pool wins the right to add a block to the blockchain, and earns a block reward — the sum of the block subsidy and transaction fees — you get to share in the earnings based upon your individual contribution.

6. Periodically, the pool transfers cryptocurrency to your wallet address. Either you're paid in the cryptocurrency you helped mine, or that cryptocurrency is converted to another form (typically Bitcoin) and the converted sum is transferred to you.

Regardless of the hardware you plan to mine with or the cryptocurrency you end up choosing, there's a mining pool for you. Whether you have cryptocurrency Application Specific Integrated Circuit (ASIC) hardware, a graphical processing unit (GPU) mining rig, or just a typical desktop computer with both a central processing unit (CPU) and GPU onboard, pool mining is the best method of consistently earning mining rewards for small operators.

REMEMBER

Mining pools provide a way for the small operator to get into the game when their processing power is so low that solo mining simply isn't practical. In Chapter 4 of this minibook, you find out about *mining calculators,* which are webpages into which you enter your hashing power, and from which you get a calculation of how profitable mining a particular cryptocurrency would be, as well as how long it would take to mine your first block. These calculators simply work on a statistical calculation based on various numbers: the *overall network hash rate* (that is, the combined hashing power of all the computers mining that cryptocurrency), your level of hashing power, how often a block is mined, the block reward, and so on. The calculators take all these numbers, and output the answers based on pure statistical probability. They tell you what you're likely to earn over a particular period, but your results can vary. You might mine your first block immediately, or you might mine your first block in twice the predicted time.

For many small operators, these calculators can be a shock. You may discover, for example, that mining Bitcoin using your paltry processor may result, statistically speaking, in your first block being mined ten years from now. In other words, solo mining simply isn't practical for you. In such a case, if you really want to mine Bitcoin, you have to join a pool.

By design, mining pools are very simple for the miner to use, as they take a lot of the technical details and headache out of the mining process. Mining pools provide a service to individual miners, and miners provide hash rate to the pools.

Choosing a Pool

This chapter provides links to a variety of mining pools. Which one you choose to work with depends on a variety of criteria. Here are the Big Three criteria:

>> **Your equipment:** Some mining pools require that you have an ASIC mining rig. Slush Pool, for example, mines only Bitcoin and Zcash, so if you want to work with Slush Pool, you'll need the appropriate ASICs for those currencies. Other mining pools let you provide hash power from your CPU or GPU.

>> **The cryptocurrency you want to mine:** To begin with, you'll probably want to simply jump into a pool that looks easy to work with, just to get your feet wet. At some point, however, you may want to target specific cryptocurrencies. Chapter 4 of this minibook covers choosing a cryptocurrency to mine.

>> **Payouts:** Different pools pay in different ways and charge in different ways. For example, with some you'll share in the block subsidy but not the transaction fees. With others, you'll share in both. Some pools charge a higher fee — keeping a proportion of the mined cryptocurrency — than others, and so on.

Many pools have multiple cryptocurrencies available to mine, while others list only a small number of specific coins that are available for miners to work with. For example, NiceHash (www.NiceHash.com) works with literally dozens of different mining algorithms, for around 80 different cryptocurrencies, while Slush Pool (SlushPool.com) offers only Bitcoin and Zcash mining pools.

Slush Pool was the first cryptocurrency mining pool, way back in 2010, so it has a proven track record. Many other pools have since been created, and pool mining is now the dominant form of cryptocurrency mining. Some are also designed for lower hash rate CPU or GPU mining applications, and others have software suites that are more useful for specialized ASIC hardware. At this point in the evolution of cryptocurrency mining, most proof-of-work blockchains require the use of ASIC hardware; these machines are so efficient that you simply can't compete using a CPU or GPU. However, you can find opportunities to mine with standard off-the-shelf desktop computers or custom-built GPU mining rigs. These other opportunities include special types of pools that mine a variety of obscure cryptocurrencies but pay out rewards to miners in more common cryptocurrencies such as Bitcoin.

Pools that are good starting points

If you are using nonspecialized computing hardware, then here are a couple of popular and easy-to-use pools that are really good starting points:

» **NiceHash** (www.NiceHash.com) allows users to buy and sell hash rate for a wide variety of different cryptocurrencies.

» **Cudo Miner** (www.cudominer.com) allows users to easily mine with their CPU or GPU for Bitcoin.

» **Kryptex** (www.kryptex.org) gives you the ability to mine using your desktop computer on whatever cryptocurrency is most profitable, but they pay out rewards in Satoshi, the smallest denomination of Bitcoin.

These types of pools act as hash rate marketplaces, allowing you to maximize return on your nonspecialized computer as mining hardware. These hash rate marketplaces and mining services allow for easy and quick mining access for beginners, and they can make any desktop or even laptop computer a mining device.

WARNING

You can find many more services like the ones listed in the preceding list, but some are risky, not as reputable, and can result in loss of funds.

TIP

If you already have your heart set on a specific cryptocurrency, your choice can help dictate which set of pools are most appropriate for you to use. Ideally, you want to choose a fairly popular pool that mines blocks frequently, but you may want to avoid the very largest pool to help mitigate centralization issues and prevent a theoretical 51 percent attack. (A *51 percent attack* occurs when a malicious party takes over 51 percent or more of a blockchain's hashing power, giving it the ability to, in effect, disrupt the blockchain.)

A few of the largest pools

The following sections show some of the largest pools that are mining for some of the most popular proof-of-work cryptocurrencies.

REMEMBER

Other factors should also help dictate your choice in mining pools beyond popularity and percentage of network hash rate. These factors include miner incentives and reward types, pool ideology, pool fees, and pool reputation.

Bitcoin (BTC)

The following are some of the largest pools mining for Bitcoin, listed in alphabetical order:

» **AntPool:** www.antpool.com

» **Binance Pool:** https://pool.binance.com

- » **Bitcoin.com:** http://www.bitcoin.com/
- » **Bitfury:** https://bitfury.com
- » **BTC.com:** https://pool.btc.com
- » **F2Pool:** www.f2pool.com
- » **Foundry USD:** https://foundrydigital.com
- » **Huobi Pool:** www.huobipool.com
- » **Poolin:** www.poolin.com
- » **Slush Pool:** https://slushpool.com
- » **ViaBTC:** https://pool.viabtc.com

Litecoin (LTC)

The following are some of the largest pools that are mining for Litecoin, listed in alphabetical order:

- » **AntPool:** www.antpool.com
- » **F2Pool:** www.f2pool.com
- » **Huobi Pool:** www.huobipool.com
- » **LitecoinPool.org:** www.litecoinpool.org
- » **Poolin:** www.poolin.com
- » **ViaBTC:** https://pool.viabtc.com

Ethereum (ETH)

The following are some of the largest pools that are mining for Ethereum, listed in alphabetical order:

- » **Ethermine:** https://ethermine.org
- » **F2Pool:** www.f2pool.com
- » **Minerall Pool:** https://minerall.io
- » **Mining Express:** https://miningexpress.com
- » **Nanopool:** https://eth.nanopool.org

Zcash (ZEC)

The following are some of the largest pools that are mining for Zcash, listed in alphabetical order:

>> **FlyPool:** https://zcash.flypool.org

>> **Nanopool:** https://zec.nanopool.org

>> **Slush Pool:** https://slushpool.com

Monero (XMR)

The following are some of the largest pools that are mining for Monero, listed in alphabetical order:

>> **F2Pool:** www.f2pool.com/#xmr

>> **MineXMR.com:** https://minexmr.com

>> **Nanopool:** https://xmr.nanopool.org

Incentives and rewards

Different pools use different methods for calculating payouts. Each mining pool's website provides information about which payout method it uses and how they specifically implement the method.

The following list shows a few of the most popular payout-calculation methods. The premise of these methods is that miners are paid a proportion of the gains made by the pool over a period of time. That period of time is known as the *mining duration* or *mining round*. For example, https://SlushPool.com/stats/?c=btc shows Slush Pool's mining results. In Figure 3-1, on the right side, you can see how long the current round has been operating and the length of the average mining round (1 hour 39 minutes).

On the left, it shows the average hash rate (5.345 Eh/S) — that is, 5.345 Exa hashes per second, or 5.345 quintillion hashes per second (5,345,000,000,000,000,000 hashes per second). Now, 14,662 miner accounts are providing hash power to the pool (see on the left side; the number of "workers" are individual computers owned by those 14,662 miners), so for Slush Pool, on average, each miner is providing about 0.0068 percent of the pool's hashing power.

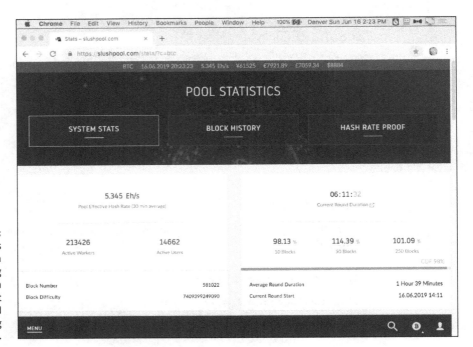

Say that you provide that proportion of the hashing power during the mining round; you'll earn 0.0068 percent of the payout from that mining round (after fees have been taken out by the pool operator). Your hashing power may not have been involved in the actual winning blocks (perhaps your computer was operating at times when the pool did not win the right to add a block, for example), but because you provided hash power during the mining round, you earn your proportional payout.

TIP

Payout calculations are often (as everything in cryptocurrency mining is!) more complicated than a simple proportional payout. The following list describes a few popular methods for calculating mining pool payouts (the term *share* refers to the proportion of the total hashing power during the mining duration that your mining rig contributes to the pool):

>> **Pay-Per-Share (PPS):** With PPS, miners earn a guaranteed income based on the *probability* that the pool mines a block, not the actual performance of the pool. Sometimes the pool will do better than the statistical probability, sometimes worse, but the miner gets paid based on their contribution to the average hash rate required to mine a block.

>> **Full Pay-Per-Share (FPPS):** FPPS is very similar to PPS. However, with FPPS, the pools also include transaction fees as well as the block subsidy in the payout scheme. This usually leads to larger cryptocurrency rewards for pool participants when compared to standard PPS.

- **Pay-Per-Last N Shares (PPLNS):** The PPLNS structure pays out rewards proportionally looking at the last number (N) of shares contributed. It does not consider *all* the shares during the entire mining round but rather considers only the most recent share contributions at the time of block discovery. (How many recent shares? Whatever number is set by N.)

- **Shared Maximum Pay-Per-Share (SMPPS):** SMPPS is a similar reward method to PPS, but it rewards miners based on the actual rewards earned by the pool, and thus never pays out more than the pool earns.

- **Recent Shared Maximum Pay-Per-Share (RSMPPS):** This reward scheme pays out miners in a similar way to SMPPS. Rewards are paid out proportionally to the total number of shares contributed during the mining pool but with more weight on *recent* hash rate shares. That is, shares that were contributed early in the round would be worth a little less compared to shares that were contributed closer to the discovery of a block.

- **Score Based System (SCORE):** This reward system pays you according to your proportion of hash rate provided but gives more weight to more recent hash rate shares than to earlier shares in the mining round. That is, if your hashing was made early in the period and a block was won later in the period, your hash power earns a lower proportion than if it were provided closer to the time of the winning block. So this is similar to RSMPPS, but the scoring hash rate is roughly a rolling average of your mining hash rate. If your mining share is steady and constant, your scoring hash rate is roughly constant as well. But if your mining rig is offline when a block is found by the pool, then you don't earn a reward equivalent to the total hashing you contributed over the block duration; instead, you earn an adjusted rate.

- **Double Geometric Method (DGM):** This reward scheme is a cross between PPLNS and a geometrically calculated reward that equalizes payouts depending on mining round duration. This creates lower mining rewards during short duration rounds and larger reward payouts for longer rounds.

Each of these payout methods was conceived and deployed in an attempt to maintain fairness between pool operators and in pool mining reward distribution to the individual miners contributing to the pool. Some are more successful than others. However, they all have aspects of impartiality that balance the playing field for all the miners participating in the system.

TECHNICAL STUFF

For a more detailed discussion of pool-payment methods and various pools, see `https://en.bitcoin.it/wiki/Comparison_of_mining_pools`.

Pool ideology

An often-overlooked aspect of selecting a pool to contribute your hash rate and mining power to is pool ideology. Ideology can be a tricky concept to nail down, especially when businesses are involved, and that's what mining pool operators are: for-profit businesses. Some are benevolent actors, and some have ulterior motives beyond mining reward and revenue.

Some pools have even historically attempted to undermine the cryptocurrencies they support. This can be seen in pools mining empty blocks in an attempt to game transaction fee rewards, clog transaction throughput, and push alternative systems. Other mining pools have used their hash rate and influence to stall updates to the system or instigate and propagate forks on the blockchain they are mining.

TIP

There's no tried-and-true or easy way to measure mining pool ideology. However, community sentiment and historical actions are often a good barometer to measure if a mining pool is acting in a way that supports the wider ecosystem. The best way to sift through mining pool ideology is to stay up to date on cryptocurrency news, and to peruse online forums, such as BitcoinTalk.org, or social media sites like Twitter or Reddit.

Overall, ideology is a less important factor when you're considering pools compared to mining reward process and pool fees. After all, cryptocurrency is an incentive-based system, and selfishness drives the consensus mechanisms and security of the various blockchains.

Pool reputation

Another important factor in pool selection is pool reputation. Some mining pools propagate scams and steal hash rate or mining rewards from users. These types of pools don't last long, as news travels fast in the cryptocurrency space and switching costs for pool miners are very low, making it easy for users to leave pools that cheat miners. However, despite this, there have been many examples of mining pool and cloud mining service scams. Some of the more noteworthy instances have involved Bitconnect, Power Mining Pool, and MiningMax. The best way to detect a scam may be the old-fashioned mantra, "If it sounds too good to be true, it probably is!" (Strictly speaking, Bitconnect wasn't a mining pool, but it was a service that promised returns on a cryptocurrency investment. A Bitcoin investor could lend Bitcoin to Bitconnect and in return earn somewhere between 0.1 percent and 0.25 percent *per day*. Yep, up to doubling their money each month. Of course, many investors never got their money back from this Ponzi scheme.)

TIP

Other clear hints of mining pool or cloud mining scams include, but aren't limited to, the following:

>> **Guaranteed profits:** Pools or cloud services that offer guaranteed profits are selling more than they can provide. Again, you know the old saying: if it sounds too good to be true . . .

>> **Anonymous perpetrators:** Pools or mining services that are owned and operated by anonymous entities or individuals can sometimes be shady — buyer beware.

>> **Multilevel marketing schemes:** Some mining pools or cloud mining services offer larger rewards for those who recruit others into the scheme. This may not always mean the operation is a scam, but do your research carefully if MLM (also known as a pyramid scheme) is present. (Many online companies pay recruitment bonuses, but MLM takes it to another level.) MiningMax, for example, was a pyramid scheme: Miners would pay to get into the pool and then get paid recruitment bonuses. Reportedly, $250 million went missing.

>> **No publicly auditable infrastructure:** Pools or cloud mining services that aren't *transparent* — that don't publish videos of their mining facilities or publicize hash rate data, for example — may be scams.

>> **No hash rate proof:** Some pools publish provable hash rate data, proof that can't be counterfeited and can be independently verified by any prospective miner. On the other hand, some pools simply publish their hash rate data without any kind of evidence, hoping you'll just trust their claims. (For an example of how hash rate data can be independently verified, see Slush Pool's explanation at `https://slushpool.com/help/hashrate-proof/?c=btc`.)

>> **Unlimited hash power purchases:** If a cloud mining service offers very large, unrealistic amounts of hash power to purchase, then they may just be trying to secure your cryptocurrency for themselves instead of offering any long-term services. Be wary of services that offer sizable packages; it may be more than they can deliver.

In the cryptocurrency mining industry, a good reputation is hard to gain but very easy to lose. For this reason, many of the pool operators functioning today that have acquired large hash rate percentages on the cryptocurrency networks they support aren't scams. If they were in fact scams or illegitimate actors in the space, then enterprising miners would have already switched to a better pool. This doesn't always apply to cloud mining operators (we discuss cloud mining services in more detail later in the chapter) since the switching costs . . . higher. Therefore, this doesn't mean that you can let your guard down. Vigilance and due diligence are a must and highly recommended in this space.

How do you check on a pool's reputation? Visit the mining forums and search on the pool's name to see what people are saying about it.

Pool fees

Pools charge fees in various ways, and these fees are paid by the miners to the pool operator. Most pool fees are in the range of 1 to 4 percent of total pool earnings. These fees are used to maintain the pool infrastructure, host servers for web interfaces, and run full mining nodes and other equipment needed to keep the pool operational — and, of course, to pay a profit to the pool operator.

Don't be fooled by pools that claim they charge no fees. (No fees? How do they stay in business? They're not charities, are they!?) Obviously, the pools have to make money, so somehow you're going to pay.

Pools make money in two ways when they mine a block:

>> Through the block subsidy

>> Through transaction fees from the individual transactions entered into the block

So a pool may take a percentage of the total value — block subsidy and transaction fees — for itself and then share the rest with the miners. Or a pool may share the entire block subsidy among the miners but keep the transaction fees for itself (these pools are most likely claiming to be "zero-fee" pools). Or perhaps they keep the transaction fees and a portion of the block subsidy. But one way or another, you're paying a fee!

Pool percentage of the total network

A pool holds a percentage of the overall network hash rate. How does that affect you? A large pool is going to take a larger proportion of the money being made from mining than a smaller pool. However, over time, this shouldn't affect how much you earn. Here's why. Remember, the network hash rate is the number of hashes contributed, by all miners and all pools, to mining a block. Depending on the cryptocurrency, it may take quintillions of hashes per second, for perhaps ten minutes on average, to mine a block (that pretty much describes Bitcoin mining, for example).

So, you have all these machines, possibly tens of thousands of them, hashing. Who gets to add a block to the blockchain? That's a factor of the amount of hashing power provided, in combination with luck and chance. That means that the miner or pool that gets to mine the *next* block is very hard to determine. It may be the pool that contributes more hashing power than any other pool or miner; but there's chance involved, too, so it could be the miner with the tiniest contribution in the entire network. It probably won't be, but it *could* be. That's the way chance (probability) works.

TIP

Think of it as a lottery. The more tickets you have, the more likely you are to win . . . but you may win if you only have one ticket. Chances are you won't . . . but it could happen.

Over the short term, then, it's impossible to predict who is going to win the hashing contest, or even, over a few mining rounds (or even a few hundred mining rounds), what proportion any pool is likely to win.

However, over the long term, the hashing percentage comes closer to the percentage of wins. So, if your pool contributes 25 percent of all the hashing power, then, over time, the pool is going to mine 25 percent of the blocks.

Here's another analogy: It's like tossing a coin. What proportion of coin tosses are heads, and what proportion are tails? Over the short term, it's hard to tell. Toss twice, and it's entirely possible that it's 100 percent one way or the other. Toss ten times, and it's still unlikely to be 50:50. But toss a thousand times, and you're going to get very close to that 50:50 number (assuming clean tosses of a balanced coin).

So, over time, a pool that represents 25 percent of the network hash rate should mine 25 percent of the network's blocks, and a pool that represents 10 percent of the network hash rate should mine around 10 percent of the blocks.

All right, back to the question: Should you go with a big pool or a small pool? A big pool, over time, will win more blocks than a small pool. But, of course, you're going to get a smaller proportion of the winnings than you would in a smaller pool.

Over time, this means there's no real difference. Whatever the size of the pool you join, *your* hashing power is the same percentage of the overall network's, and thus, over time, you should earn the same percentage.

REMEMBER

There is one difference. The larger the pool, the more frequently you'll earn a cut. That means more frequent earnings than from a smaller pool. Those earnings will be smaller, though; you can't beat the math. You're not going to earn more than your percentage of the earnings represented by your percentage of the hash rate. (Over the long term, that is; over the short term, you may earn considerably more or considerably less, whichever choice you make.)

So you may prefer to go with a larger pool just so you see income more frequently, but don't expect that picking a larger pool will increase your earnings in the long term.

How do you find the relative size of the pools? Many sites provide this information, often in the form of pie charts. (We discuss how to find such information later in this chapter, in the section, "Researching Mining Pools.") For a historic graphical view of network hash rate percentages by pool on the Bitcoin network, see Figure 3-2. You can find this graph at https://data.bitcoinity.org/ bitcoin/hashrate/.

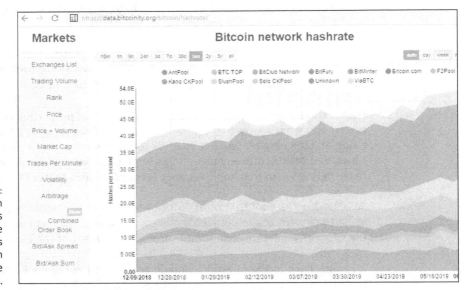

FIGURE 3-2:
A historical graph of each pool's hash rate contributions to the Bitcoin network over the past six months.

Setting Up a Pool Account

For the most part, after you decide which cryptocurrency is right for you (see Chapter 4 of this minibook) and after you select a pool to contribute to that resonates with you, creating and setting up a pool account is fairly simple. The process can be compared to creating an email account or other online web service, such as a social media account. The two requirements you need when setting up a pool account are an email account and a cryptocurrency wallet address. A few oddities and factors to consider during the pool account process include pool server choice, payout threshold, and reward payout addresses.

All mining pools, regardless of the cryptocurrency they happen to be mining, have easy, step-by-step directions to connect your suitable mining equipment (ASIC, GPU, or other) to the pool interface located on their website. You must set up an account, select a server, configure your mining hardware, and register a payout address. Most mining pools also have basic user manuals to help sift through the setup process, helpful FAQs for when you hit a snag, and, in many cases, detailed technical documentation for advanced users.

Server choice

For most mining pools, many different servers are up and running for you to connect your mining hardware to the pool infrastructure. The most important difference in servers is mainly geographical location. The most popular mining pools have servers based in locations across the globe, such as in Asia, Europe, and the Americas.

TIP

To reduce connection latency and avoid connectivity outages, connecting to servers that are in close proximity to your mining hardware is most beneficial for you.

Most ASIC cryptocurrency mining hardware allows you to set three separate servers or mining pools in the mining equipment user interface. Some miners point their equipment to multiple pools to avoid downtime in the event of a pool outage, while others simply point their hardware to different servers of the same pool.

Mining equipment pool settings

Specialized cryptocurrency mining hardware (covered in Chapter 5 of this minibook) is normally equipped with an easy-to-use graphical user interface (GUI). The mining equipment user interface can be accessed via any computer that's connected to the same Local Area Network (LAN) as the mining equipment. Simply open a web browser and type the mining equipment's Internet Protocol (IP) address into the browser to navigate to the user interface.

TIP

If you're unsure of the IP address for your mining rig, you can log into your home router to scan the connected devices on your network. Software such as Angry IP Scanner (AngryIP.org) can also assist you in doing an IP scan to nail down your device's local address if you're unsure how to access your home network modem or router. Your mining hardware user manual or guide should also have information to assist you in setting it up and logging into it.

The following is an example of the settings you'd need to input into your miner for a U.S.-based Bitcoin ASIC running on Slush Pool:

```
URL: stratum+tcp://us-east.stratum.slushpool.com:3333
userID: userName.workerName
password: anything
```

The specific mining pool you choose should provide details on connection settings via their website. For example, instead of requiring you to enter a user account, a mining pool may only need you to input your payout address for the cryptocurrency you're mining. Again, check your pool's documentation for details.

The URL you connect to depends on which location is closest to you. Your username is the same as your mining pool account, and you can get creative with what you decide to name your worker, or mining rig; however, don't duplicate worker names if you're connecting more than one piece of mining gear. (You can have multiple "workers" working within your single mining account, with each worker representing a particular mining rig.) See Chapter 6 of this minibook for more information on setting up your mining rig.

Payout addresses

You can generate a cryptocurrency address to use for mining pool payouts from any cryptocurrency wallet. (See Book 1, Chapter 3 for an overview of cryptocurrency wallets.) In the cryptocurrency space, it is highly recommended that addresses for transactions not be used more than once. This non-reuse of addresses is a best practice to help facilitate more privacy and transaction anonymity.

Actually, setting up a pool account can often be much easier than this if you're using non-ASIC hardware. We show an example earlier in this chapter of setting up a pool account, which took around five minutes from reaching the website to beginning mining.

Payout thresholds

For cryptocurrency mining pools, one of the more finely tuned settings is the *payout threshold*. This is the amount you must earn while mining for the pool before the pool sends a reward to your cryptocurrency address on the blockchain. Most pools allow you to define how frequently you want to receive your earnings. Although some pools allow a manual trigger of mining reward payouts, most require you to set a payout threshold that indirectly determines your payout frequency, depending on your hardware capabilities and pool contribution.

If you select a payout threshold that's too low, you waste a large portion of your reward on transaction fees that may result in dust accumulating in your cryptocurrency wallet. (The term *dust* in the cryptocurrency realm usually refers to small or micro transaction amounts that may be unspendable in the future because the total amount held in the address is less than the transaction fees required to move it. Dust transactions are an occurrence you want to avoid.)

However, if you choose a payout threshold that's too large, you could leave your cryptocurrency rewards in the hands of the mining pool for longer than necessary, which makes them susceptible to theft through hacking or fraud.

TIP

A sweet spot exists — in other words, you can set your payout threshold value to an amount that helps to alleviate both problems. Normally, a good rule is to set your pool account payout threshold to the equivalent mining rewards projected to be earned from your mining equipment over a period of a few weeks to a month, similar to a traditional paycheck. This allows for enough cryptocurrency to be earned to make the transaction worth the effort and also doesn't leave your funds in the control of someone else for too long. Bottom line: You want steady rewards for your work that you contribute (in mining and labor), but hourly payouts for your day job or cryptocurrency mine don't make logical sense with the transaction fees and overhead involved.

Researching Mining Pools

A number of resource sites provide great information about mining pools, in particular for the Bitcoin network. When comparing alternative cryptocurrency pools, the information becomes less trustworthy and more difficult to come by. We recommend searching for the name of the cryptocurrency you're interested in and the term *mining pool* (*dash mining pool*, *litecoin mining pool*, and so on), and visiting public forum sites, such as Reddit, Stack Exchange, and BitcoinTalk, to find more information.

Here are a few Bitcoin resources:

>> https://Coin.Dance/blocks/thisweek

>> https://en.Bitcoin.it/wiki/Comparison_of_mining_pools

>> https://99Bitcoins.com/bitcoin-mining/pools/

>> https://en.BitcoinWiki.org/wiki/Comparison_of_mining_pools

>> www.Blockchain.com/pools

And here are a few for Ethereum and Litecoin:

>> `https://Investoon.com/mining_pools/eth`

>> `www.LitecoinPool.org/pools`

>> `https://Litecoin.info/index.php/Mining_pool_comparison`

Cloud Mining

Another option for aspiring cryptocurrency miners is to work with cloud mining services. Essentially, you fund a portion of a mining operation, and the cloud miners do the rest. You are, in effect, an investor in the operation.

These companies offer hash rate contracts. You buy a certain hash rate, for a certain period of time (see Figure 3-3), and you then benefit proportionally based on the percentage of the overall cloud mining operation that you've funded.

FIGURE 3-3: Genesis Mining sells hash rate packages. Dash starts at 5,000 MH/s for two years, but you can also mine Bitcoin, Ethereum, Litecoin, Monero, or Zcash.

A huge advantage of these services is that it's totally hands-off — no equipment to buy or manage, no space to find for the equipment, no equipment noise, no heat to deal with. Cloud mining services solve those issues for you.

However, cloud mining can also be somewhat risky. Many operations aren't profitable for the durations specified in the contract and can leave purchasers of these services losing money, in some cases, over the long run. Users may be better off simply purchasing the cryptocurrency that their mining contract mines. (That, of course, is often also true of pool and solo mining, but you can find out more about the economics of mining in Chapter 7 of this minibook.)

Other risks include outright scams. A common mantra in cryptocurrency circles is, "Not your keys, not your coin." In the case of cloud mining contracts, one might say, "Not your mining hardware, not your rewards."

We believe the following services rank near the top of trustworthy cloud mining operators. However, *caveat emptor* (buyer beware). For *all* services we talk about in this book, you must do your due diligence, find out what the community is saying about them, and ensure that they are trustworthy and reliable).

>> **Genesis Mining:** www.genesis-mining.com/

>> **ECOS:** https://mining.ecos.am/en/

>> **IQ Mining:** https://iqmining.com/

>> **HashNest:** https://www.hashnest.com

>> **HashGains:** https://www.hashgains.com/

>> **Shamining:** https://shamining.com/en

>> **BitDeer:** www.bitdeer.com/en/

This list is brief because we feel comfortable about only a few cryptocurrency cloud mining providers, as many of the rest aren't trustworthy and don't offer the services they advertise.

However, that doesn't mean the preceding services always provide *profitable* mining contracts. It just means that they do, in fact, deliver on the services that they offer — as far as we know, they provide the hash rates advertised for the period promised. But that doesn't mean profitability at all times.

The profitability of cloud mining contracts varies widely among services. To find out more on how to do a cost/benefit analysis on cloud mining services, pool mining deployments, or anticipated hardware rewards, refer to Chapter 7 of this minibook.

Chapter **4**

Picking a Cryptocurrency to Mine

Chapter 3 of this minibook talks about an easy way to get into mining: using a pool. In this chapter, we discuss preparing to mine for yourself directly, by picking an appropriate cryptocurrency to mine. Of course, getting started is much more complicated than merely picking a target, and, in fact, we recommend that you don't actually begin mining until you finish all the chapters of this minibook, not just this chapter.

This chapter discusses the sort of factors that can help you find a good cryptocurrency to work with — one that is stable enough for you to be successful, for example. But we believe it's a good idea to understand more before you actually get started. This chapter helps you pick an initial target cryptocurrency, but your target may change as you discover more, such as the kind of equipment you'll need to use (see Chapter 5 of this minibook) or the economics of mining (see Chapter 7 of this minibook). In fact, this decision-making process is a bit circular; the cryptocurrency you decide to mine determines the type of hardware you need, and the type of hardware you have (or can obtain) determines the cryptocurrency that makes sense for you to mine.

This chapter helps you to begin figuring out what cryptocurrency makes a good initial target. Book 5 covers cryptocurrency investing. Book 5, Chapter 4 is all about identifying top-performing cryptocurrencies, which may also be particularly helpful to you as you look for a crypto to mine.

Determining Your Goal

Whether you want to be a hobbyist miner or a serious commercial miner, or somewhere in between, you must ask yourself an important question before you go any further down the cryptocurrency mining path. Answering this question will enable you to properly determine which cryptocurrencies to mine and will help you become the most successful crypto miner you can be:

What is your goal for mining cryptocurrency, and how will you reach it?

Let's break down this question and drill deeper into its component parts, by focusing on the following questions:

>> **What do you want to get out of cryptocurrency mining?** Maybe you're looking to gain some insight into this whole cryptocurrency technology, or maybe you're motivated by the possibility of windfall profits. Are you wanting to support your cryptocurrency's ecosystem, or are you more concerned with it supporting you?

>> **How much capital do you plan on using? Are you planning on betting the farm or only wanting to dip your toes in to test the water?** It's always a good idea to start small and ease into the ecosystem, but depending on your financial situation, starting small may mean something completely different for you than for another investor.

>> **How serious is cryptocurrency mining to you, and how much risk are you willing to take?** Markets go up, markets go down, and in cryptocurrency systems they fluctuate more frequently than traditional financial assets. It's your savings on the line, so you should understand the risks. Consider the obligation and the stress to your life, and make sure that you aren't overcommitting before you have enough experience and a feel for the complex systems. It's okay if you just want cryptocurrency mining to be a fun hobby experience, too!

>> **What is the minimum return on investment (ROI) you must meet and in what time frame?** In other words, what's it worth to you to get involved? Are you wanting to get rich quickly, or are you trying to secure some of your value and wealth long term? You should be prepared to try something different if this ROI isn't met, maybe even reduce the footprint of your operation. There's no shame in scaling down or calling it quits, either. Depending on market conditions, simply purchasing a particular cryptocurrency is sometimes cheaper than mining it!

>> **Are you planning to measure your returns in your local fiat currency, or are you measuring your gains in the cryptocurrency asset you plan to mine?** The latter option only makes sense if you have confidence in the future

value of the cryptocurrency, of course. For example, many miners, during Bitcoin's downturns, continue mining due to their strong belief that the price will increase again. As the value of the cryptocurrency drops, and some miners drop out of the business, the other miners' incomes — measured in cryptocurrency — go up, because the block rewards are being shared among fewer miners. At such a time, the remaining miners are increasing their stock of the cryptocurrency, and even though they may be losing money if measured in terms of fiat currency, they're okay with it because they view the cryptocurrency as an investment that will pay off in the future.

To help you answer these questions, we look at some hypothetical cryptocurrency mining stories.

First up is Kenny, an intelligent guy with a background in computers and IT. He knows his way around a data center, and to him, cryptocurrency mining is pretty similar to running a room full of servers. (Kenny is a tad overconfident, as running the mining equipment is only part of the battle when mining cryptocurrency.)

Kenny is looking to profit from cryptocurrency mining and views it as a challenge. With the savings from his tech job, he has set aside around $10,000 for his cryptomining venture, only a fraction of his overall savings. (We said he's smart!) He is very serious about cryptocurrency mining, and he views the undertaking as a challenge of his intellect and skill. The minimum ROI he has decided on is 20 percent annually on every penny he puts into mining, and he plans to adjust his mining strategy every day if he's not on track to meet this goal. Assuming moderate success on his ROI goals, he will do a full reevaluation after one year to decide whether he continues mining.

Our second example is Cathy, a savvy investor who manages her retirement portfolio very successfully. For her, cryptocurrency mining is a way to experience and gain exposure to this new cryptocurrency technology; if it catches on, she doesn't want to miss the boat. She wants to profit but knows that she doesn't fully understand how cryptocurrency works, and she is excited to find out more. She is serious about doing the mining correctly and has initially set aside $500 to put toward cryptocurrency mining. She isn't going to freak out if it ends up not working out, though. She would like to see a 10 percent ROI annually, and after six months, she will decide whether she wants to continue mining. She plans to reevaluate her strategy every two months.

The differences to highlight here are namely the amounts invested and the expectations that both Kenny and Cathy have set for themselves. Cathy is risk-averse in her approach but has taken a lot of pressure off herself if things don't go as planned by starting small with an amount she is willing to lose. She is also reevaluating her strategy every two months, another way to reduce risk and exposure and to also make sure that she won't be too stressed if it doesn't work out.

Kenny has taken a riskier approach, but if he pulls it off, he will stand to profit much more than Cathy. It is important to note that Kenny has some prior experience with running networked computers, giving him a leg up and reducing some of his risk out of the gate. He is also taking a more hands-on approach with his two-week ROI evaluations, which is a good strategy because he's putting more on the line. However, Cathy has also hedged against failure by using less of an initial investment.

Both of these miners went on to reach their goals by the end of their predetermined timelines and ended up happy that they got into cryptocurrency mining. The moral of these stories is that none of your answers to the most important question are inherently wrong, but asking these questions is critical to your success. The questions and answers will play a major role when it comes time to choose the cryptocurrencies you'll mine and how you set up your mining rigs.

Mineable? PoW? PoS?

Many factors contribute to whether a cryptocurrency is a good choice for the aspiring miner. The first decision, of course, is whether it is possible to mine the cryptocurrency. Some cryptocurrencies cannot be mined. This is the case for some of the newest tokens and cryptocurrencies being created and promoted, especially centralized coin offerings and company-based tokens, as these are typically issued prior to release and work on systems more akin to a permissioned database than a decentralized cryptocurrency.

Furthermore, in general, we're going to ignore proof-of-stake (PoS) cryptocurrencies (see Chapter 2 of this minibook). While it is possible to mine PoS cryptocurrencies, PoS mining has some inherent problems that make it less attractive to most miners.

First, you need a stake; in other words, you must invest not only in your mining rig but also in the cryptocurrency you are planning to mine. (Note, however, that the equipment needed for mining PoS cryptocurrencies is generally cheaper than for PoW cryptocurrencies. It can generally be done on regular computers, even an old piece of computer hardware you have lying around.) Before you can start, you'll have to buy some of this cryptocurrency and store it in your wallet. Depending on the particular PoS cryptocurrency you've chosen, this could be a significant investment; the more you stake, the more often you will add a block to the blockchain and earn fees and perhaps block subsidies.

Secondly, the cards are already stacked against you. PoS systems have to have pre-mined currency; after all, if the system requires staking, it can't work unless currency is already available to stake. The founders of the currency will have awarded themselves large amounts of cryptocurrency right from the get-go, so they have a head start and will dominate the process. (Again, the more you have to stake, the more often you will win the right to add a block to the blockchain.)

Thus, PoS mining has this inherent problem for newcomers: You have to invest in equipment, but the ROI will be lower for you than for the cryptocurrency's founders, because they have a much larger stake and so will add more blocks. Hybridized proof-of-work / proof-of-state systems face many of these same issues, but with mining also involved, and so they tend to include many of the downsides of both PoW and PoS systems.

So, most mining is focused on PoW cryptocurrencies, and that's what we focus on here. As far as cryptocurrencies that do in fact have mining implemented and proof of work embedded into their deployed systems, we walk through a few factors that would make some cryptocurrencies better to mine compared to others.

Researching Cryptocurrencies

If you want to go deep and find out more about a cryptocurrency, you're going to need a few information sources. In this section, we look at a number of ways to uncover everything you need to know about a particular cryptocurrency.

Mining profitability comparison sites

So here's the first type of information source, which provides a shortcut around the whole "Is it mineable?" question. Refer to the mining-comparison sites. A number of these sites gather a plethora of data about mineable cryptocurrencies. Here are a few, and more will probably appear over time, so if any of these links break, do a search engine query:

>> www.CoinWarz.com

>> www.WhatToMine.com

>> www.2CryptoCalc.com

>> www.Crypt0.Zone/calculator

>> https://CryptoMining.tools

>> www.Crypto-Coinz.net/crypto-calculator

The first thing these sites do for you is to provide a list of mineable cryptocurrencies; if it's not on this list, it's probably not mineable, or not practical to mine. Some of these sites will have more cryptocurrencies listed than others, but in combination, they will give you a great idea of what's practical to mine right now. (What about the brand-new coin that's coming out tomorrow? Sure, it won't be on those lists, but for a beginning miner, that probably doesn't matter, and in any case, consider the Lindy Effect, explained later in this chapter, in the section, "Longevity of a cryptocurrency.")

Take a look at Figure 4-1, a screenshot of WhatToMine.com. You can see that it lists a variety of cryptocurrencies and compares them to mining Ether on the Ethereum blockchain. There's Metaverse, Callisto, Expanse, DubaiCoin, and so on. At the time of this writing, WhatToMine lists 62 cryptocurrencies that can be mined with GPUs (graphics processing units) and 59 that require ASICs to economically mine. (Look for the GPU and ASIC tabs near the top of the page.) In combination, these sites list around 150 different mineable cryptocurrencies.

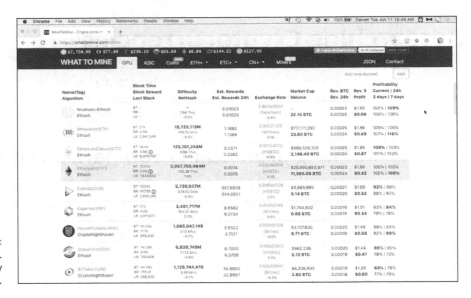

FIGURE 4-1:
The WhatToMine.com profitability comparison site.

In Figure 4-2, you can see CoinWarz.com, another very popular site; CoinWarz compares the various cryptocurrencies to mining Bitcoin, rather than Ethereum. CoinWarz has a much clearer table, allowing you to easily see a few important metrics:

>> Basic information related to the cryptocurrency, including the name, icon, ticker symbol (LTC, BTC, and so on), the overall network hash rate (the

number of tera hashes per second; for more about hash rates, see Chapter 5 of this minibook), the block reward (though strictly speaking, what CoinWarz is showing is the block *subsidy*; the block reward is the subsidy plus the transaction fees), the number of blocks, and the time it takes on average to add a new block to the blockchain.

>> A chart showing the block difficulty and how it's changed over time.

>> An estimate of how many coins you could mine each day based on your mining rig's hash rate and the current block difficulty, and your hash rate and the average difficulty over the past 24 hours.

>> The exchange rate between each cryptocurrency and Bitcoin, and how it's changed over the last two weeks (the numbers are based on the best exchange for that cryptocurrency, which it names, so you can get the best rate when you sell your mined cryptocurrency).

>> The exchange volume over the last 24 hours — that is, how much of the coin has been traded.

>> The daily gross revenue, in U.S. dollars, that you would likely make (again, based on your hash rate), the cost for electricity, and the profit (or loss!) you would make each day.

>> Your daily estimated earnings, denominated in Bitcoin.

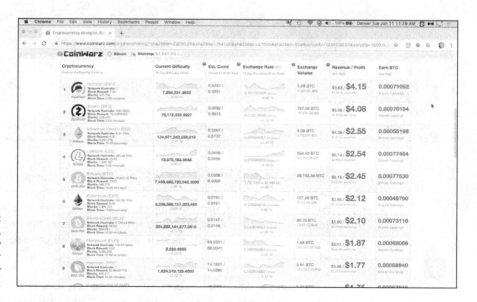

FIGURE 4-2: CoinWarz.com, another very popular profitability comparison site.

Okay, so about your hash rate. As noted, some of these calculations are based on your computer equipment's *hash rate* — that is, the number of PoW hashes it can carry out in a second. That's the basic information these sites need to know to calculate how often you're likely to win the game and add a block to the blockchain. Your hash rate is, essentially, the computational power of your computer.

These sites use default power settings, and the advantage of this approach is that you can at least get an idea of the relative profitability of the different cryptocurrencies, even if you don't know the power of your equipment.

Now, if you *do* know how powerful your equipment is, you can enter that information. In CoinWarz, this information is entered into the top of the page, as shown in Figure 4-3. What are all these boxes? For each mining algorithm (SHA-256, Scrypt, X11, and so on), you see three text boxes. You enter your processor's hash rate in the top box, in (depending on the algorithm) H/s (hashes per second), MH/s (mega hashes per second), or GH/s (giga hashes per second).

FIGURE 4-3:
The top of the CoinWarz.com page, where you enter your hash rate information.

The second box is *watts,* the amount of electrical power your processor is going to use; and the last box is the cost of that electricity, in $/kWh, dollars per kilowatt-hour. Well, that's a complicated subject, one that we get into in Chapter 6 of this minibook. Actually, some of these comparison sites provide data for common processors for you. For example, in Figure 4-4, you can see the calculator at Crypto-Coinz.net.

You can see that the GPU tab has been selected, so this area is showing commonly used GPUs in the cryptocurrency mining arena. These are powerful processors, set up to manage the heat that comes from constant processing. The top box lists a bunch of NVIDIA GPU model numbers; the bottom model numbers are AMD products. Find the models you have and enter the quantity you'll be using into the text boxes, and the site automatically enters the appropriate processing power into the boxes below.

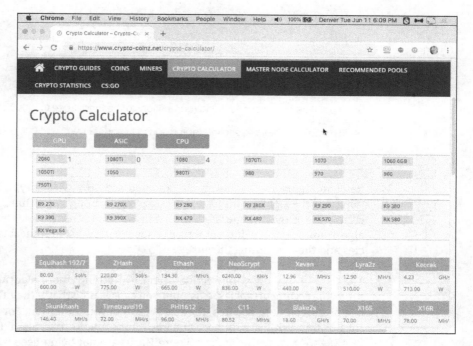

Picking a
Cryptocurrency to Mine

FIGURE 4-4:
Crypto-Coinz.net
actually provides
hashing power
information
for some GPU,
CPU, and ASIC
processors.

TIP

All these sites work differently. We strongly recommend that you try a few, pick one or two that you really like, and then spend an hour or two digging around and figuring out how they function. They provide a huge amount of information, in many different formats, so play a while and really get a handle on them.

Algorithms and cryptocurrencies

When you first start working with these sites, they may seem to be speaking a foreign language. (That's why we suggest you spend a lot of time digging around in these sites, familiarizing yourself with the lingo, and fully understanding what's going on.) It takes time to get used to an arena in which every other word is new to you.

HASH RATE UNITS

In general, hash rates in the Bitcoin ecosystem are measured in tera hashes, but in some cases, you're going to see other units. Here's a quick summary:

- **H/s.** Hashes per second

- **MH/s.** Mega hashes per second (millions of hashes: 1,000,000)

- **GH/s.** Giga hashes per second (billions of hashes: 1,000,000,000)

- **TH/s.** Tera hashes per second (trillions of hashes: 1,000,000,000,000)

- **PH/s.** Peta hashes per second (quadrillions of hashes: 1,000,000,000,000,000)

- **EH/s.** Exa hashes per second (quintillions of hashes: 1,000,000,000,000,000,000)

Refer to Figure 4-3, for example, and you see SHA-256, Scrypt, X11, and so on. What are these? They are the particular PoW mining algorithms. For each algorithm, one or more (generally more) individual cryptocurrencies exist that use the algorithm. The following sections provide a partial list of mineable cryptocurrencies and the algorithms they use.

The lists in the following section aren't everything; more algorithms, and more mineable cryptocurrencies, exist, but you can assume that if they're not on at least one of the comparison sites, they're not worth your attention. For example, at the time of this writing, a number of algorithms (X25, Keccak, SkunkHash, BLAKE2s, BLAKE256, X17, CNHeavy, and EnergiHash) are not being used by cryptocurrencies deemed worthy of these sites.

Notice another thing about the preceding list, something you may want to consider when picking a cryptocurrency that uses an algorithm that requires an ASIC. We have five ASIC algorithms listed, and below each algorithm, we have 7, 13, 8, 7, and 4 cryptocurrencies using each algorithm, respectively. That is, the same ASIC — the same hardware — can be used to mine any of the cryptocurrencies using the algorithm for which the ASIC was designed.

So you could choose to mine, say, CannabisCoin, in which case you would need an X11 ASIC. If CannabisCoin went up in smoke (excuse the pun), you could switch to DASH, IDApay, or Startcoin. But if you bought an ASIC for the Scrypt algorithm, began mining one of the Scrypt cryptocurrencies, and then wanted to switch, you would have not 3 but 12 alternative choices.

Algorithms requiring a specialized ASIC

The following is a partial list of mineable cryptocurrencies and the algorithms they use. The first one, SHA-256, is the most popular algorithm — the one used by Bitcoin and all its derivatives.

>> **SHA-256:**

- Bitcoin (BTC)
- Bitcoin Cash (BCH)
- eMark (DEM)
- Litecoin Cash (LCC)
- Namecoin (NMC)
- Peercoin (PPC)
- Unobtanium (UNO)

>> **Scrypt:**

- Auroracoin (AUR)
- DigiByte (DGB)
- Dogecoin (DOGE)
- Einsteinium (EMC2)
- FlorinCoin (FLO)
- GAME Credits (GAME)
- Gulden (NLG)
- Held Coin (HDLC)
- Litecoin (LTC)
- Novacoin (NVC)
- Verge (XVG)
- Viacoin (VIA)

>> **Equihash:**

- Aion (AION)
- Beam (BEAM)
- Bitcoin Private (BTCP)
- Commercium (CMM)
- Horizen (ZEN)

- Komodo (KMD)
- VoteCoin (VOT)
- Zcash (ZEC)

>> **Lyra2v2:**
- Absolute Coin (ABS)
- Galactrum (ORE)
- Hanacoin (HANA)
- Methuselah (SAP)
- MonaCoin (MONA)
- Straks (STAK)
- Vertcoin (VTC)

>> **X11:**
- CannabisCoin (CANN)
- DASH (DASH)
- IDApay (IDA)
- Petro (PTR)
- Startcoin (START)

Algorithms that may be mined without ASICs

The following algorithms may still effectively be mined without purpose-built, application-specific hardware, or ASICs:

>> **NeoScrypt:**
- Cerberus (CBS)
- Coin2Fly (CTF)
- Desire (DSR)
- Dinero (DIN)
- Feathercoin (FTC)
- GoByte (GBX)
- Guncoin (GUN)

- Innova (INN)
- IQ.cash (IQ)
- LuckyBit (LUCKY)
- Mogwai (MOG)
- Phoenixcoin (PXC)
- Qbic (QBIC)
- Rapture (RAP)
- SecureTag (TAG)
- SimpleBank (SPLB)
- SunCoin (SUN)
- Traid (TRAID)
- TrezarCoin (TZC)
- UFO Coin (UFO)
- Vivo (VIVO)
- Zixx (XZX)

>> **Ethash:**

- Akroma (AKA)
- Atheios (ATH)
- Callisto (CLO)
- DubaiCoin (DBIX)
- Ellaism (ELLA)
- Ether-1 (ETHO)
- Ethereum (ETH)
- Ethereum Classic (ETC)
- Expanse (EXP)
- Metaverse (ETP)
- Musicoin (MUSIC)
- Nilu (NILU)
- Pirl (PIRL)

- Ubiq (UBQ)
- Victorium (VIC)
- WhaleCoin (WHL)

» X16R:

- BitCash (BITC)
- CrowdCoin (CRC)
- GINcoin (GIN)
- GPUnion (GUT)
- Gravium (GRV)
- HelpTheHomeless (HTH)
- Hilux (HLX)
- Motion (XMN)
- Ravencoin (RVN)
- StoneCoin (STONE)
- Xchange (XCG)

» Lyra2z:

- CriptoReal (CRS)
- Gentarium (GTM)
- Glyno (GLYNO)
- Infinex (IFX)
- Mano (MANO)
- Pyro (PYRO)
- Stim (STM)
- Taler (TLR)
- ZCore (ZCR)

» X16S:

- Pigeoncoin (PGN)
- Rabbit (RABBIT)
- Reden (REDN)
- RESQ Chain (RESQ)

- **» Zhash:**
  - BitcoinZ (BTCZ)
  - Bitcoin Gold (BTG)
  - SnowGem (XSG)
  - ZelCash (ZEL)
- **» CryptoNightR:**
  - Monero (XMR)
  - Lethean (LTHN)
  - Sumokoin (SUMO)
- **» Xevan:**
  - BitSend (BST)
  - Elliotcoin (ELLI)
  - Urals Coin (URALS)
- **» PHI2:**
  - Argoneium (AGM)
  - Luxcoin (LUX)
  - Spider (SPDR)
- **» Equihash 192/7:**
  - SafeCoin (SAFE)
  - Zero (ZER)
- **» Tribus:**
  - BZL Coin (BZL)
  - Scriv (SCRIV)
- **» Timetravel10:** Bitcore (BTX)
- **» PHI1612:** Folm (FLM)
- **» C11:** Bithold (BHD)
- **» HEX:** XDNA (XDNA)
- **» ProgPoW:** Bitcoin Interest (BCI)
- **» LBK3:** VERTICAL COIN (VTL)
- **» VerusHash:** Verus (VRSC)

- **Ubqhash:** Ubiq (UBQ)

- **MTP:** Zcoin (XZC)

- **Groestl:** Groestlcoin (GRS)

- **CrypoNightSaber:** BitTube (TUBE)

- **CryptoNightHaven:** HavenProtocol (XHV)

- **CNReverseWaltz:** Graft (GRFT)

- **CryptoNight Conceal:** Conceal (CCX)

- **CryptoNight FastV2:** Masari (MSR)

- **CryptoNight Fast:** Electronero (ETNX)

- **Cuckatoo31:** Grin-CT31 (GRIN)

- **Cuckatoo29:** Grin-CR29 (GRI)

- **Cuckatoo29s:** Swap (XWP)

- **Cuckoo Cycle:** Aeternity (AE)

- **BCD:** Bitcoin Diamond (BCD)

CPU VERSUS GPU VERSUS APU VERSUS ASIC

Do you use a CPU (central processing unit), a GPU (graphics processing unit), an APU (accelerated processing unit), or an ASIC (Application Specific Integrated Circuit)? First, some cryptocurrencies pretty much require an ASIC (see the prior list). You *could* mine using another processor, but there's not much point, because your processing power will be so low in comparison with the ASICs designed for the job that you may have to wait a thousand years to win the right to add a block to the blockchain. (No, we're not kidding, the disparity is on this scale.)

As the preceding list shows, other cryptocurrencies do not require ASICs; they can be mined using a CPU (your computer's main processor), a GPU (a specialized processor designed for managing computer graphics, which tends to be more powerful), or an APU (a processor that combines both the CPU and GPU on the same chip).

In general, CPUs don't make great mining processors, though it can be done. These comparison sites, and the mining calculators we look at later in this chapter, can tell you whether your particular CPU, GPU, or APU can be used. There's a huge range of processing power among processors: some will be useless; some will be viable. You can find out how to figure out the power of your processor in Chapter 5 of this minibook.

>> **YescryptR16:** Yenten (YTN)

>> **YesCrypt:** Koto (KOTO)

The cryptocurrency's details page

Another great place to find information about a particular cryptocurrency is on the currency's details page at the comparison sites. The comparison sites we looked at earlier in this chapter generally link to that page. In fact, refer to the image in Figure 4-1; if you click on a cryptocurrency name, you're taken to a details page that contains additional information about that cryptocurrency. For example, click Callisto (CLO) and you see the page shown in Figure 4-5.

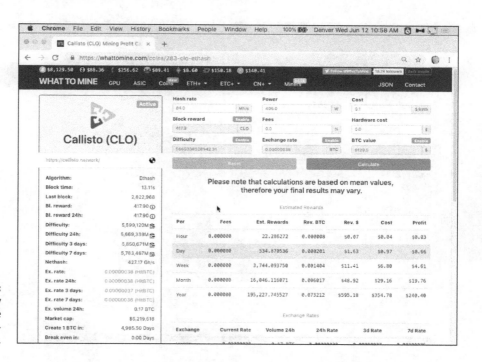

FIGURE 4-5:
A cryptocurrency details page on WhatTo-Mine.com.

This page contains stacks of information about the cryptocurrency, including statistics such as the block time (how often a block is added), the block reward, the difficulty level, and so on. It also lists mining pools that work with this particular currency (see Chapter 3 of this minibook).

Mining-profit calculators

If you want to know what the profit potential is for a particular cryptocurrency, you need to work with a mining-profit calculator. The mining comparison sites generally contain these calculators, though other sites also provide individual calculators without an overall comparison tool. (www.cryptocompare.com/mining/calculator/, for example, provides calculators for Bitcoin, Ethereum, Monero, Zcash, DASH, and Litecoin.)

Refer to Figure 4-5. At the top of the page, you can enter your hardware's hash rate, power consumption, and cost, along with the cost of your electricity, and the calculator will figure out how much you can make (or lose) over an hour, a day, a week, a month, or a year.

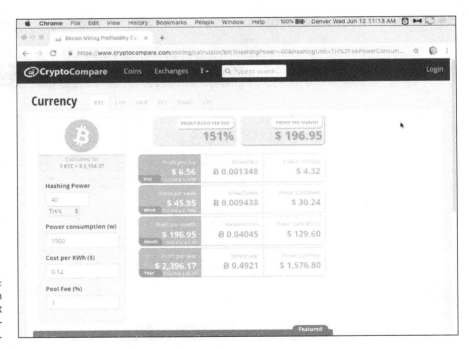

FIGURE 4-6: The Bitcoin calculator at CryptoCompare.com.

Figure 4-6 shows a simpler calculator, from www.cryptocompare.com/mining/calculator/btc, that displays potential revenue and profit from mining Bitcoin. This calculator even allows you to enter a pool fee, to include the costs of mining through a pool (see Chapter 3 of this minibook). This example, even though it shows you making a profit, is actually a losing proposition. (See the nearby sidebar, "Hash power envy? You'd better pool mine.")

HASH POWER ENVY? YOU'D BETTER POOL MINE

In many cases, you're not going to like what you see in these calculators. If your hash power is simply not great enough, the calculators will implicitly — or, in some cases, explicitly — tell you not to even consider mining solo and direct you toward pool mining. For example, in Figure 4-6, you're being told that, using the hash power specified at the left of the page, you'll mine, on average, 0.4921 Bitcoin each year. Well, at present the block subsidy is 12.5 Bitcoin, and you can't get a partial block subsidy; you get all or nothing. Given that 12.5 Bitcoin divided by 0.4921 is 25.4, you're being told that if all things remain the same (which they won't), it would take your hardware 25.4 *years* to win the right to add a block to the blockchain. And that's just the average. Your luck may vary — it may take less time — but it could be 30 years (or more) before you win a block subsidy! (What will change? The block subsidy will be reduced over time, more hashing power may enter the network, and so on.) In other words, you cannot practically mine Bitcoin with only 40 TH/s, so go join a pool if you want to mine Bitcoin (see Chapter 3 of this minibook) or up your game (your mining rig) dramatically (see Chapter 5 of this minibook)!

Some calculators will actually be more explicit. The CoinWarz Bitcoin mining calculator (at www.coinwarz.com/calculators/bitcoin-mining-calculator) would present you with this information:

Bitcoin Mining Calculator Summary

- **Days to generate one block mining solo:** 9,271.5 days (can vary greatly depending on your luck)

- **Days to generate one BTC:** 741.72 days (can vary greatly depending on the current exchange rates)

- **Days to break even:** N/A (can vary greatly depending on the current exchange rates)

The cryptocurrency's home page

Another great place to find information about a cryptocurrency in which you have some interest is, not surprisingly, the cryptocurrency's home page (though, of course, the information you'll find here will be biased toward optimism for the future of the currency). That's easy enough to find. The comparison site's cryptocurrency details pages (refer to Figure 4-5) generally have this information. You can also find this information at other sites, such as coinmarketcap.com.

REMEMBER

Many of these cryptocurrency systems are distributed with the aim of decentralization. This means that for most of these systems, no single party controls them, so many sites may claim to be the home page for that particular peer-to-peer cryptocurrency, with some having more validity to that claim than others. Always do plenty of research and tread lightly.

GitHub

Most cryptocurrencies you're likely to be mining have a GitHub page. GitHub is a software development platform and software repository used by many open-source software projects. Although cryptocurrencies are not open source by definition, most of them are (in fact, any cryptocurrency you're likely to mine is generally open source). You can see an example — the Bitcoin GitHub page — in Figure 4-7.

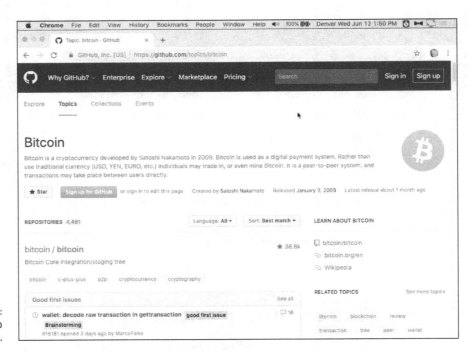

FIGURE 4-7:
Bitcoin's GitHub page.

How do you find the GitHub page? Again, the details page at one of the cryptocurrency sites may hold a link to the currency's GitHub page, or it may not. You may be able to find a link to it in the currency's home page, or you can also search for it within GitHub.com.

At GitHub, you can review the actual source code of the cryptocurrency to see how it functions, if you have the skills to do so, but you can also get an idea of how active the community is, how many people are involved, how often changes are made to the code, and so on. For a deeper dive into the specific mechanisms and intricacies involved with GitHub, refer to *GitHub For Dummies* (John Wiley & Sons, Inc.) by Sarah Guthals and Phil Haack.

The cryptocurrency's Wikipedia page

Many, perhaps most, cryptocurrencies, have Wikipedia pages. These can be useful places to find general background information about a cryptocurrency, often more quickly than using other sources. These pages often provide a little history about the currency, information about the founders and the technology, controversies related to it, and so on. You won't find them for many of the smaller, more obscure cryptocurrencies, though, and the level of detail for the ones that are there ranges from sparse to exhaustive.

You can see an example in Figure 4-8, which shows Dogecoin's Wikipedia page. Notice the info-block on the right side, which provides a quick rundown of important information.

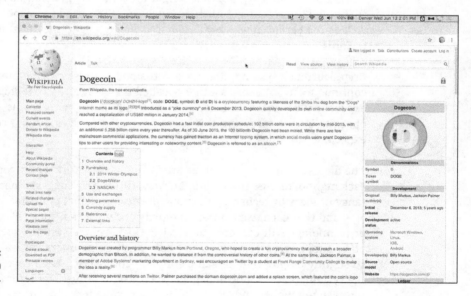

FIGURE 4-8: The Dogecoin Wikipedia page.

Mining forums

Finally, don't forget the cryptocurrency mining forums, of which perhaps the most significant are the Bitcoin (BitcoinTalk.org) forums. You can find forums on numerous subjects here, related to many different Bitcoin and cryptocurrency issues. There's a Bitcoin Mining section, as well as an Alternative Cryptocurrencies section, and within that, a Mining subsection. The Altcoin mining section has more than 800,000 posts in more than 3,000 topic areas, and so a wealth of mining information is there to be digested.

Going Deep

After you know how to find the information on a variety of these cryptocurrency systems — if it's available, that is, because in many cases the information may be hard to find — you may want to consider several other factors.

Longevity of a cryptocurrency

To choose a cryptocurrency that is right for you, it is important to have confidence that it will be around and functioning during the period you choose to mine it, as well as the period in which you plan for the cryptocurrency to store your mining rewards.

Cryptocurrency systems that have withstood the test of time are more likely to continue to do so. There's a theory called the *Lindy Effect* that states that the life expectancy of certain things, such as technology, increases as they age. (The opposite is true for living things, of course; once they reach a certain age, life expectancy declines.)

The theory, by the way, is named after a deli in New York where comedians gather each night to discuss their work. Anyway, this theory suggests that the life expectancy of ideas or technologies (nonbiological systems) is related to their current age, and that each extra duration of existence makes it more likely that the idea or technology will continue to survive. Open-source systems such as Bitcoin or other similar cryptocurrencies are constantly being upgraded and improved ever so slightly by programmers and software enthusiasts. Each code *bug,* or error in the system, that is found and quickly *patched* (a software term for fixed) will leave the system tougher and less prone to error going forward. Software systems such as Bitcoin or similar open-source cryptocurrencies can be considered *antifragile,* with each flaw that is discovered and subsequently fixed leading to a stronger and less fragile technology.

REMEMBER

It is important to choose a cryptocurrency to mine with enough perceived longevity, durability, and endurance to suit your specific risk profile.

Let us summarize with a question: Which cryptocurrency is likely to survive longer? Bitcoin, dating back to January 2009, or JustAnotherCoin, a (hypothetical) new cryptocurrency released to the world yesterday afternoon? *Bitcoin be a better bet*, if you'll excuse the alliteration. There are a couple of thousand cryptocurrencies; most are garbage and can't possibly survive. A new one is likely just one more JunkCoin on the garbage heap.

On the other hand, sometimes apparently stable, long-lasting systems die. Who remembers DEC, WordPerfect, or VisiCalc, for example? (We bet that many readers have no idea what these words even mean!) And sometimes new systems appear in a flash and beat out well-established competitors. (Google, anyone? Facebook?)

But, to continue with the example of technology companies, most newcomers fail; most Internet start-ups in the 1990s Internet bubble went out of business, for example. Most obscure cryptocurrencies will fail, too. So, *in general*, a long-lasting cryptocurrency, such as Bitcoin, Litecoin, or Ether, is a better bet than today's new entry into the cryptocurrency market.

How do you figure out how long the cryptocurrency has been around? It shouldn't be too hard to find. Check the currency's own website, its Wikipedia entry if there is one, and GitHub's history of software commits and releases.

Hash rate and cryptocurrency security

Another important factor involved with the choice of which cryptocurrency to mine is the security encompassing the blockchain being selected to mine. You wouldn't want to put your eggs (mining resources) in a basket (blockchain) with holes in it that cannot support the weight of your precious cargo (value).

This same idea applies to cryptocurrency systems, and security in this sense is relative. A cryptocurrency that has a low level of hash-powered proof of work is less secure than other cryptocurrencies that run on a similar consensus mechanism, as it's more easily hacked or manipulated. This puts the cryptocurrency's chance of surviving at risk and also puts your funds in that blockchain at risk.

TIP

Where do you find the level of hash power being used by the network? One great place to look for this kind of information is BitInfoCharts.com, which will let you select cryptocurrencies to compare against each other. This site provides a huge range of different cryptocurrency metrics, from pricing charts to market cap to lists of the richest blockchain addresses, for a large range of cryptocurrencies.

As shown in Figure 4-9, one thing you can do is select a bunch of cryptocurrencies and create a chart comparing their hash rates; see `https://bitinfocharts.com/comparison/bitcoin-hashrate.html`. You can also find individual hash rates from the comparison sites we look at earlier in this chapter (see the section, "Hash rate and cryptocurrency security").

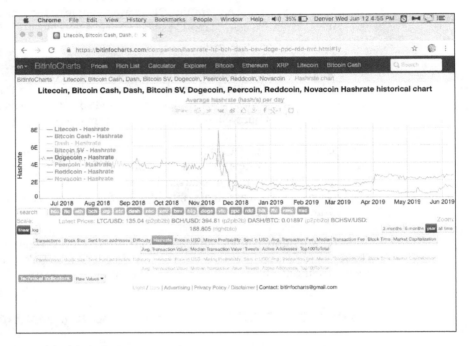

In fact, hash rate is something you'll find on various sites. For example, you can find the hash rate for Bitcoin, Ethereum, and Bitcoin Cash at `www.blockchain.com/explorer`. The pool-mining services provide hash rate statistics for the cryptocurrencies they mine, and statistics sites such as Coin Dance provide some, too (see `https://coin.dance/blocks/hashrate`).

Community support

Another factor to consider and weigh when selecting which cryptocurrency is right for you is community support. Network effects of cryptocurrency systems are important, and wide adoption and utilization are key metrics to look at when choosing which blockchain to mine. Are many people involved in managing and developing the cryptocurrency? (A cryptocurrency with very few people involved is likely to be unstable.) And are many people using the cryptocurrency — that is, is there much trading going on, or are people using it to make purchases?

METCALFE'S LAW

Conceptually, Metcalfe's Law can be applied to any network, such as email networks or telephone systems, but also to cryptocurrency networks, such as Bitcoin. If only two users are on a telephone or email system, then there isn't much value in that network, but if there are four users, the value (along with possible network connections) is exponentially larger. If the system has 12 users, there are dramatically more possible connections, and thus more value (see the figure).

The same logic applies to cryptocurrency networks; each additional user adds a disproportional and exponential amount of potential connections. If the cryptocurrency system you select to mine doesn't have a large user base, there may not be enough possible connections to give that network adequate value for mining long term.

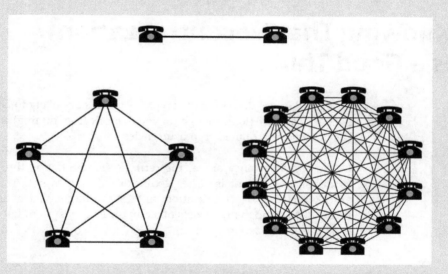

Courtesy of Woody 993 at English Wikipedia.

There's a concept known as *Metcalfe's Law* that explains network effects. The idea, proposed by Robert Metcalfe, one of the inventors of Ethernet, is that a communication system creates value proportional to the square of the number of users of that particular system. Essentially, the more users on a system, the more useful — and more valuable — the network becomes.

Community support is also important in other ways. It can be measured in the form of open-source developers actively contributing to the cryptocurrency's code repository. A healthy and robust cryptocurrency will have a diverse set of many individuals and entities reviewing and auditing the code that fortifies it.

WARNING

Developer support is critical to the longevity and robustness of a cryptocurrency system. Note that many cryptocurrency systems created and issued by companies or consortiums are not open source, not mineable, and do not have a wide range of code auditors outside of the company reviewing and revising their walled-garden systems.

How do you measure community support? The cryptocurrency's GitHub page is a great start; you'll be able to see exactly how active the development process is, and how many people are involved. The currency's web page may give you an idea of activity, too, especially if the site has discussion groups. Another helpful tool to compare support across different networks can be found at `www.coindesk.com/data`, which shows a variety of rankings comparing top cryptocurrencies such as social, market, and developer benchmarks.

Knowing That Decentralization Is a Good Thing

In general, more decentralized cryptocurrencies are likely to be more stable and likelier to survive (long enough for you to profit from mining) than more centralized and less distributed cryptocurrencies.

In the cryptocurrency arena, the term *decentralization* is thrown around as an absolute: The system is either decentralized or it is not. This, however, isn't exactly the case. Decentralization, in fact, can be thought of as a spectrum (see Figure 4-10), and many aspects of a cryptocurrency system fall on different parts of the decentralization spectrum.

FIGURE 4-10:
The spectrum of decentralization.

A major aspect of decentralized peer-to-peer blockchain-based systems is the fact that any user can spin up a node and be an equal participant in the network. Here are a few other factors that can also be used to rank cryptocurrencies on the decentralization spectrum.

>> **Initial coin distribution and coin issuance:** For a proof-of-work cryptocurrency with a predetermined issuance schedule, the distribution of coins can

be considered fairer than a system in which a high percentage of the coin issuance was pre-mined and distributed to a select few insiders. This would place pre-mined cryptocurrencies further toward the centralized spectrum than fairer and more decentralized coin-distribution models. To view a detailed breakdown of the Bitcoin network's coin issuance schedule, see Figure 4-11, which shows the interactive chart being dynamically created at `https://bashco.github.io/Bitcoin_Monetary_Inflation/`. (Go to the website and run your mouse pointer along the lines to see the exact numbers at any time.) The stepping line shows the block subsidy halving every 210,000 blocks, or roughly every four years. The upward curve line shows the amount of Bitcoin in circulation at any time. As for researching other cryptocurrencies, the comparison sites will show how often the currency's coins are issued.

>> **Node count:** The nodes are the gate keepers of valid transaction data and block information for blockchain systems. The more active nodes there are running on the system, the more decentralized the cryptocurrency. Unfortunately, this is a tricky one; it's probably pretty difficult to find this precise information for most cryptocurrencies.

>> **Network hash rate:** The level of the cryptocurrency's hash rate distribution among peers is also an important decentralization measurement for PoW cryptocurrencies. If only a few companies, individuals, or organizations (such as mining pools) are hashing a blockchain to create blocks, the cryptocurrency is relatively centralized. See the earlier section, "Hash rate and cryptocurrency security."

>> **Node client implementations:** Multiple versions of client, or node, software exist for many of the major cryptocurrencies. For example, Bitcoin has Bitcoin Core, BitCore, BCOIN, Bitcoin Knots, BTCD, Libbitcoin, and many other implementations. Ethereum has geth, parity, pyethapp, ewasm, exthereum, and many more. Cryptocurrencies with fewer client versions may be considered more centralized than those with more versions. You can probably find this information at the cryptocurrency's GitHub page and on its website. For an interesting view of the Bitcoin network client versions for nodes on the network, navigate to the following site: `https://luke.dashjr.org/programs/bitcoin/files/charts/branches.html`.

>> **Social consensus:** Social networks of users and the people participating in these cryptocurrencies are also very important in regard to the cryptocurrency decentralization spectrum. The larger the user base and the more diverse technical opinions on the system, the more robust the software and physical hardware are to changes being pushed by major players in the system. If the social consensus of a cryptocurrency is closely following a small set of super users or a foundation, then the cryptocurrency is, in effect, more centralized. More control is in the hands of fewer people, and the system is more likely to experience drastic changes in its rules. An analogy can be seen in sporting

events; the rules (consensus mechanisms) are not changed by the referees (users and nodes) halfway through the competition. The number of active addresses in the cryptocurrency's blockchain provides a good metric indicating social consensus and the network effect. This shows the number of different blockchain addresses with associated balances. This metric isn't perfect, as individual users can have multiple addresses, and sometimes many users have coins associated with a single address (when utilizing an exchange or custodial service that stores all its clients' currency in one address). However, the active addresses metric can still be a helpful gauge to compare cryptocurrencies — more addresses means, in general, more activity and more people involved. A helpful tool to find cryptocurrency active address numbers can be found at `https://coinmetrics.io/charts/`; choose Active Addresses in the drop-down list box on the left, and select the cryptocurrencies to compare using the option buttons at the bottom of the chart (see Figure 4-12). For smaller cryptocurrencies, this information may be hard to find, but the data would be accessible via a cryptocurrency's auditable blockchain.

» **Physical node distribution:** With cryptocurrencies, node count is important, but it is also important that those nodes not be physically located in the same geographical area or on the same hosted servers. Some cryptocurrencies have the majority of their nodes hosted on third-party cloud services that provide blockchain infrastructure, such as Amazon Web Services, Infura (which itself uses Amazon Web Services), DigitalOcean, Microsoft Azure, or Alibaba Cloud. Systems with this type of node centralization may be at risk of being attacked by these trusted third parties. Such systems are more central-ized than purer peer-to-peer networks with large node counts that are also widely geographically distributed. A view of the Bitcoin network node geo-graphical distribution can be found at `https://bitnodes.earn.com/`. For the smaller cryptocurrencies, this information may be harder to find.

» **Software code contributors:** A broad range of code contributors to the client software implementations — and code reviewers — is important for the decentralization of a cryptocurrency; the larger the number of coders, the more distributed and decentralized the cryptocurrency can be considered. With fewer contributors and reviewers, errors in the code can be more prevalent and intentional manipulation more possible. With larger numbers of reviewers and coders, mistakes and malfeasance are more easily caught. The developer count and activity on various cryptocurrency code repositories can be gleaned by exploring their GitHub pages. For Bitcoin's core repository, the link to find out more details is found at `https://github.com/bitcoin/bitcoin/graphs/contributors`. As an example, Ethereum averages just over 200 active repository developers per month, while the Bitcoin network averages just under 100. For most other cryptocurrency networks, that number is much lower. On average, at the time of this writing, about 8,000 developers are currently working on thousands of different cryptocurrency projects each month.

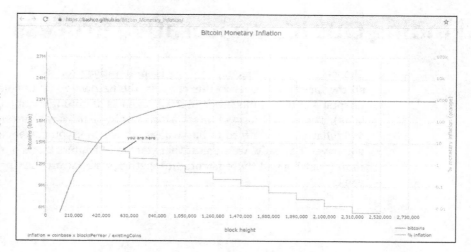

FIGURE 4-11:
Chart from GitHub depicting the coin issuance schedule and inflation rate for Bitcoin. It has served as a model for most proof-of-work distribution schedules.

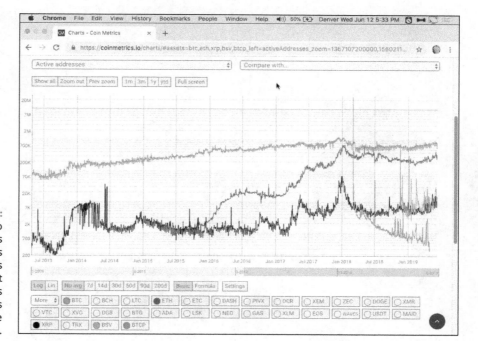

FIGURE 4-12:
Coinmetrics.io compares active-address quantities between different cryptocurrencies (and provides many more statistics).

Finding Out It's an Iterative Process

Choosing a cryptocurrency to mine is an iterative process; it's a combination of all the factors we cover in this chapter, the hardware you're able to obtain (see Chapter 5 of this minibook), and the economics of mining (Chapter 7 of this minibook). The economics will affect which mining hardware you can afford to buy, and what you can afford to buy will affect which cryptocurrency you choose. If you haven't already, we suggest that you read Chapters 8 and 9 of this minibook to find out how all these factors fit together, and put off the final decision until you do.

Chapter **5**

Gathering Your Mining Gear

Mining cryptocurrency is easy; the mining hardware does most of the heavy lifting while you sit back and watch the coin accumulate. However, choosing the right miners, purchasing the gear, and setting up the necessary equipment is the hard part. Selecting the right cryptocurrency, selecting the correct hardware for that specific blockchain, and choosing a suitable location to deploy the mining equipment are early steps that are crucial for any gains and short- or long-term success.

We look at selecting a cryptocurrency in Chapter 4 of this minibook. In this chapter, we dive into the factors you need to consider when choosing mining hardware. (See Chapter 6 of this minibook for additional information about mining hardware.)

Selecting the Correct Computational Mining Hardware

You can mine any cryptocurrency with any computing equipment (CPUs, GPUs, or ASICs), but if ASICs are available for a particular cryptocurrency's algorithm, in most cases using a CPU or GPU puts you at a huge disadvantage — perhaps such a big disadvantage that there's really no point in mining without an up-to-date ASIC.

Thus, the hardware you need varies for the different blockchains and their specific hashing algorithms. For example, the ASIC hardware needed to mine Bitcoin runs the SHA-256 algorithm, and there's no real point mining with a CPU or GPU; the disadvantage is simply too great. Ethereum uses the Ethash algorithm, and although Ethash ASICs are available, some miners still mine it using GPUs. Scrypt ASIC mining rigs are also available that can mine Litecoin or Dogecoin, and ASICs for the DASH and Petro cryptocurrencies use the X11 mining algorithm. (Of course, as we explain in Chapter 4 of this minibook, any American wanting to maintain their freedom should steer clear of the Petro; also see Chapter 4 of this minibook for a list of numerous cryptocurrencies and their algorithms.)

For cryptocurrencies like Monero, however, an off-the-shelf computer with a functioning CPU and GPU (that is, pretty much any computer) can be used to mine it effectively.

REMEMBER

Don't forget the pool-mining services — such as NiceHash, Cudo Miner, and Kryptex — which let you use their software to point your off-the-shelf, common computer cycles toward a pool and cryptocurrency of their choosing, and then reward you for your contribution in a more stable cryptocurrency, such as Bitcoin. These services may be the easiest way to test out mining, by using your existing computational hardware that may very well sit idle most of the day on your desk. For those who want to test the waters before acquiring more expensive equipment, pool-mining services are highly recommended. (See Chapter 3 of this minibook.)

If you want to go further in your mining endeavors, possibly even buying specialized mining equipment — which, by the way, can be used for both pool mining and solo mining — you must consider a few rating factors.

Specified hash rate

The first and foremost factor when selecting mining hardware is the hash rate that the rig is stated to deliver. Normally, companies that provide mining hardware ASICs provide a guaranteed hash-rate value that the mining rig will output on average. Sometimes it may be slightly more, and other times it may be slightly less, but over longer periods of time, it should average out to the guaranteed rate.

For Bitcoin-based SHA-256 mining hardware — the most advanced and efficient equipment — this hash rate is typically specified in tera hashes per second, or TH/s. Figure 5-1 shows the specified hash-rate capabilities for some of the most capable Bitcoin SHA-256 ASIC mining hardware, from 2017 to 2019. As you can see, the equipment varies greatly, from a low of around 5 TH/s to around 80 TH/s.

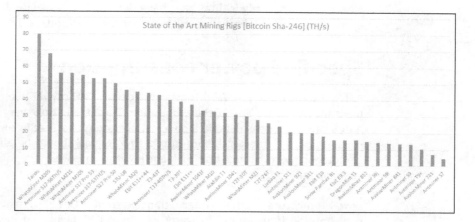

FIGURE 5-1:
A graph showing the highest hash-rate SHA-256 mining equipment being deployed on the Bitcoin network between 2017 and 2019.

Over the past few years, many different manufacturers have jumped into the Bitcoin-mining hardware-production game, increasing competition in the space and creating an ASIC-mining hardware arms race. This space has seen enormous growth, in terms of diversity of suppliers and hash-rate capability, within the last couple of years.

TIP

To stay competitive in the Bitcoin or other cryptocurrency mining realms, you need to use the latest and greatest hardware. Most proof-of-work blockchains have seen ASIC mining rigs developed for their network's algorithm. This is arguably a good thing for those blockchains (though many complaints still exist about it), as it provides greater security for the blockchain and decreases the likelihood of attack by increasing the resources needed to attack the blockchain. Remember, the whole point of proof of work is to make finding a block difficult so that it's not easy to attack the blockchain.

The danger in ASIC mining hardware when it is first released, however, is that the hardware will be quickly made obsolete . . . it will be superseded by new, more efficient products. You may think that in order to stay ahead of the crowd, you should buy the very latest equipment, even preorder equipment before it's ready. However, that strategy comes with its own risks. Some shady manufacturers have sold mining hardware with long lead times and with implied or calculated earnings that will not match the earnings that the equipment will realistically gain once the mining hardware is delivered. As you wait for delivery, the blockchain's block difficulty and hash rate increase, perhaps dramatically, during early-stage ASIC development. The longer you wait, the less competitive the ASIC will be once you get it into action.

Dishonest ASIC sales are not as bad a problem as they were in the past, at least for most mature proof-of-work blockchains because of manufacturer diversification and the fact that, as ASICs mature, ASIC efficiency gains are harder to come by. However, for new algorithms that have not had ASIC-specific hardware developed, there may still be significant risks for early-edition hardware purchasers.

Specified power consumption

ASICs are far more powerful than your regular CPU or GPU, so they are able to hash much faster. That's the whole point, after all. However, nothing's free; ASICs can use a considerable amount of electricity. Each ASIC has a rated power consumption — that is, before purchasing it, you should be able to check the equipment specifications and find out how much power it's going to use when you start mining.

Power is measured with the International System of Units, using *watts*, and energy consumption is measured in watts per hour. Old-fashioned incandescent light bulbs typically consume about 20 to 100 watts — when you buy incandescent light bulbs, you're probably usually buying 60, 75, or 100-watt light bulbs — while today's LED light bulbs may output the same amount of light while using between 4 and 15 watts. Say that you have a 15-watt light bulb and run it for an hour; you've just used 15Wh — 15 watt-hours. What does that cost you? That depends on where you are. For example, in Denver, a watt-hour is about 0.01 cent, so running a 15W light bulb for an hour — consuming 15Wh — costs around 0.15 cent; run it for 100 hours, and it costs you about 15 cents.

A typical desktop computer with a CPU and GPU on board may consume anywhere from 400 to 1,200 watts, perhaps a little more. (The most recent Mac Pro uses around 900 watts.) Laptops generally use much less power; co-author Peter Kent's MacBook Pro has an 85W power supply, for example.

However, state-of-the-art ASICs now being deployed onto the Bitcoin network consume between 1,000 and 6,000 watts (1.0 to 6.0kW — that is, kilowatts; a kW is 1,000 watts). For a comparison of some of the Bitcoin SHA-256 ASICs being used on the network today, see Figure 5-2.

TECHNICAL STUFF

How do you figure out your own power cost? Check your electricity bill, find your most recent paper bill, or log on to your power-company website account. You may have to look at the actual bill or you may find a summary. Figure 5-3 shows an example of the electricity consumption area on a bill.

Notice that the electricity is billed for kilowatt-hours, not watt-hours. Figure 5-3 shows that this utility company has billed a base rate of $0.05461 per kWh (with two different time periods, Non-Summer and Summer Tier 1, although in this case, the rate is the same for both periods). Then the utility has charged additional rates for various special fees: the Trans Cost Adj, the Elec Commodity Adj, and so on . . . whatever these things are (and we really don't care). We just add up the different rates — $0.05461, $0.00203, $0.03081, $0.00159, $0.00401, and $0.00301 — to come up with the kWh charge: $0.09606. That is, this utility charges 9.606 cents per kWh of power consumed.

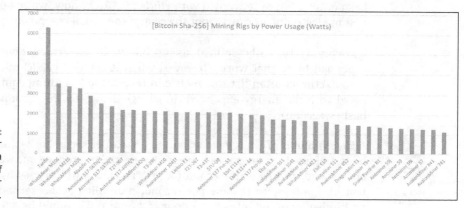

FIGURE 5-2:
Power consumption for a range of SHA-256 ASICs for Bitcoin hashing.

ELECTRICITY CHARGES		RATE: R Residential General	
DESCRIPTION	USAGE UNITS	RATE	CHARGE
Service & Facility			$5.41
Non-Summer	165.82 kWh	$0.054610	$9.06
Summer Tier 1*	176.18 kWh	$0.054610	$9.62
Trans Cost Adj	342 kWh	$0.002030	$0.69
Elec Commodity Adj	342 kWh	$0.030810	$10.54
Demand Side Mgmt Cost	342 kWh	$0.001590	$0.54
Purch Cap Cost Adj	342 kWh	$0.004010	$1.37
CACJA	342 kWh	$0.003010	$1.03
Renew. Energy Std Adj			$0.74
GRSA			- $1.12 Cr
Subtotal			**$37.88**
Franchise Fee		3.00%	$1.14

METER READING INFORMATION

METER 40444910		Read Dates: 05/15/19 - 06/17/19 (33 Days)	
DESCRIPTION	CURRENT READING	PREVIOUS READING	USAGE
Total Energy	70461 Actual	70119 Actual	342 kWh

INVOICE NUMBER: 0787050602

FIGURE 5-3:
You can find your electricity cost from your utility bill.

Power consumption inputs and hash-rate outputs for mining hardware are important factors when considering which mining equipment is right for you. However, both of these metrics are more useful when combined. After all, what we care about is how many hashes we can get for a buck, as it were. What good is an ASIC that consumes almost no energy if it outputs almost no hashes? Or an ASIC that outputs a huge amount of hashes but at twice the cost per hash of other equipment? What counts is how much we're going to have to pay for a particular hash output. We're concerned with *efficiency*. (Right now, we're talking about the cost in electricity, of course, not the cost of the actual equipment.)

Efficiency is typically defined as useful work performed divided by energy expended to do that work. However, when it comes to ASIC mining hardware, manufacturers often list this metric in reverse. ASIC mining equipment is often listed with the energy expended (in *joules*) divided by the work performed (tera hashes/second).

TECHNICAL STUFF

A *joule* is a unit of energy equivalent to a watt per second or 1/3,600th of a watt-hour. Wikipedia defines it as "the work required to produce one watt of power for one second, or one watt-second (W·s)." Thus, a watt-hour (Wh) is the equivalent of 3,600 joules (1 joule per second, multiplied by 60 seconds in a minute, multiplied by 60 minutes in an hour is 3,600; 1kWh would be 3.6 megajoules — 3,600,000 joules).

So ASIC manufacturers often show an 'energy expended per output' value that allows users to easily compare mining hardware efficiency. ASIC specs are often provided in terms of *joules/hash*. For example, look at this excerpt from a review of mining equipment:

"Thanks to the DragonMint 16T's new DM8575 generation of ASIC chips, the 16T has become the most electrically-efficient miner on the market. **Consuming merely 0.075J/GH, or 1,480W** *from the wall, the 16T is 30% more electrically-efficient than the Antminer S9 . . . . When compared to its closest competitor, the Antminer S9, the DragonMint 16T is the clear winner. It hashes at 16 TH/s, as opposed to the S9's 14 TH/s. Moreover, the 16T consumes 0.075J/GH,* **whereas the S9 consumes 0.098J/GH.**"

The review states that this particular miner (the DragonMint 16T) uses 1,480W, so over an hour, it would consume 1.48kWh of electricity. (In Chapter 7 of this minibook, you can see how that affects the cost of running the equipment.) But we're also told that it consumes 0.075J/GH. (That is, .075 joules per giga hash, or .075 joules of energy is consumed every time the device runs a million hashes.) As you can see, this data can be used to directly compare mining equipment; the S9 consumes 0.098J/GH. That is, the S9 consumes around 31 percent more energy for the same number of hashes.

For a ranking of the most recent SHA-256 hardware released to mine on the Bitcoin network, see Figure 5-4. On the left, you see the less efficient equipment. The Antminer S7 requires around 275 joules to output a tera hash per second, while at the other end of the charge, we see equipment that is outputting a tera hash per second while consuming around 40 joules.

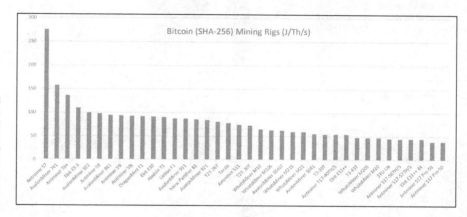

We've provided similar charts for a few other common mining algorithms. Figure 5-5 shows X11 ASIC miners designed to operate on the DASH network, Figure 5-6 displays Scrypt ASIC miners built to hash toward the Litecoin network, Figure 5-7 ranks Equihash ASIC miners that can mine on the Zcash network, and finally, Figure 5-8 plots Ethash ASIC miners by efficiency. Miners on the left of these charts with a lower energy (joules) consumption per output (hash) would be more profitable to operate as electricity cost per work would be less.

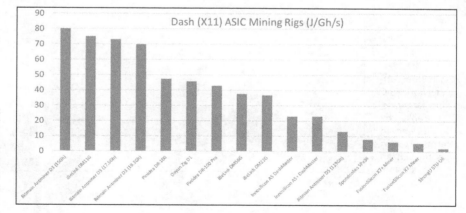

Gathering Your
Mining Gear

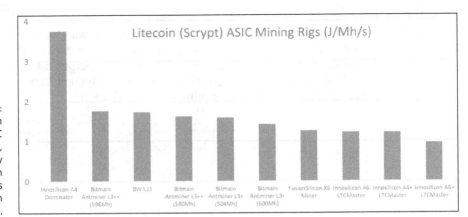

FIGURE 5-6: Scrypt Litecoin network ASIC mining hardware, ranked by efficiency in terms of joules per mega hash per second.

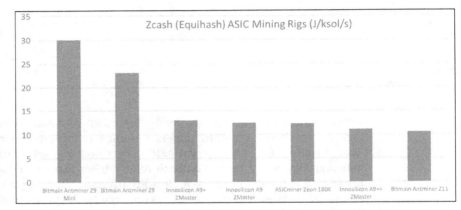

FIGURE 5-7: Equihash Zcash network ASIC mining hardware, ranked by efficiency in terms of joules per kilosolution per second.

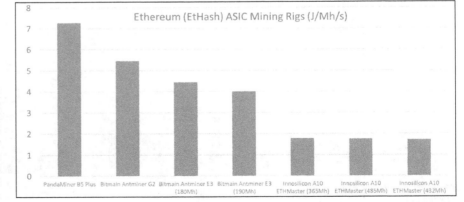

FIGURE 5-8: Ethash Ethereum network ASIC mining hardware, ranked by efficiency in terms of joules per mega hash per second.

REMEMBER

Mining equipment efficiency is a very important factor in deciding what hardware is right for you. The lower the energy usage per work output, the less power will be spent, the lower power bills will be, and the more cost effective the mining hardware will be.

Cost effectiveness is critical to long-term survival in the mining industry, whether you're deploying a commercial mining facility or becoming a home hobbyist miner. Over time, most of the costs will be from operational expenditures, of which the biggest part is the cost of electricity. For more on the economics of mining, refer to Chapter 7 of this minibook.

Equipment cost and other considerations

The cost and affordability of mining hardware fluctuates wildly, similar to the market capitalization of cryptocurrency assets. During some periods, the cost of mining equipment moves surprisingly in tandem with the market. If the price is going up, new and used mining equipment sells at a premium. If the price is down, the hardware sells at a steep discount as large mining firms and manufacturers liquidate equipment stockpiles.

In any market condition, however, the newest, most efficient equipment is always expensive. These high-efficiency mining rigs are in high demand, regardless of the price of the cryptocurrency they mine. At the time of this writing, the state-of-the-art SHA-256 ASIC equipment can range from a few hundred to a few thousand dollars.

TIP

For the best prices on new hardware, the most dependable route is to purchase straight from the manufacturer and avoid the middleman who sells hardware above the manufacturers' listed prices.

On the other hand, some manufacturers simply don't sell small retail quantities. Other manufacturers don't allow purchasers to use local fiat currencies to acquire their products, and sell their hardware only for Bitcoin or the cryptocurrency the hardware specializes in mining. Another thing to really carefully check is the lead time for delivery after purchase. If you're buying the latest and greatest piece of hardware at a premium, your advantage may be minimized if actual delivery is delayed for a long time.

You may also be able to buy used hardware. Check marketplaces, such as eBay, Amazon, Newegg, Alibaba, or Craigslist. However, beware of sellers on most second-hand markets, and remember that some markets are more reliable than others. (For example, on Amazon, you can return the equipment if it turns out to be faulty or oversold in some way.) Always do your research on the equipment specifications, such as hash rate, power consumption, and efficiency, before you buy.

Length of time your hardware will be viable

Another thing to consider is how long the ASIC equipment you're buying is going to be able to keep up and stay profitable. That is, as block difficulty and hash rate requirements increase, how long will it be until your hardware is hopelessly left behind?

A number of factors determine the viability of a cryptocurrency ASIC miner, including the network hash rate and thus block difficulty, market exchange rate for the cryptocurrency you're mining, mining equipment efficiency, and your time preference.

For the most part, network hash rate on any cryptocurrency lags the exchange price. Remember, network hash rate increases as more miners enter the network or existing miners buy more mining equipment, and network hash rate goes down as miners leave. So, if the cryptocurrency price soars for a month, the hash rate for the forthcoming months will most likely go up as more miners jump in, and vice versa; if the exchange rate falls, then in the following months, hash rate may also fall as miners shut down their unprofitable equipment.

During a period in which the cryptocurrency prices rise, you may earn less of the cryptocurrency — as miners bring more equipment online, your percentage of the network hash rate drops, leading to less frequently mined rewards — but you may still be earning more money in terms of dollars (or whatever fiat currency you work with). You mine fewer coins, but those coins are worth more.

The inverse is also true. During times of falling value of the cryptocurrency you're mining, and subsequent falling hash rate, your mining equipment will produce more reward when measured in the mined asset, but those larger quantities of cryptocurrency may be worth less overall when measured in your local fiat currency.

This is where your time preference factor comes in, in combination with your assessment of the future value of the cryptocurrency you are mining. *Time preference* is the value you place on receiving something now, as opposed to the value you would place on receiving it in the future. An individual with high time preference is more concerned with their present well-being and satisfaction when compared to a low time preference individual who would rather put that reward off until a later date when their satisfaction may be increased.

REMEMBER

If you believe in the cryptocurrency you're mining, and you believe that the price will go up in the long term, you may want to continue mining. Even during market downturns, as network hash rate comes down, competition is reduced. Your percentage of the network hash rate goes up, and so it costs you less to mine the same amount of cryptocurrency.

Here's an example. In December 2018, Bitcoin dropped below $3,300 (USD) per coin. For many miners, perhaps most, mining became unprofitable, but mining didn't stop. Why? Because the people who continued mining believed that the price would come back. They were right. A few months later, a coin was worth almost four times that value. So if you're willing to defer present gain for future gain, and if you're sure that there *will be* a future gain, then you'll want to continue mining through the bad times (which, if you're right, will eventually look like the good times!).

Cryptocurrency miners with a low time preference, and faith in the cryptocurrency, may continue to use slightly "unviable" mining equipment during what appear to be unprofitable mining conditions, because they anticipate profits in the future.

As network hash rate increases, and as competing mining equipment gets more efficient — as the newer equipment is able to output more hashes for each kWh of power consumption — your equipment will become less profitable. It will mine fewer coins than before, and each coin will cost more. At some point, it will make economic sense to replace the mining equipment with more efficient equipment.

A typical state-of-the-art Bitcoin or cryptocurrency mining rig today may have a viable life of four or more years. However, going forward, the viable life of an ASIC may increase as hardware efficiency gains of ASICs become slower and more difficult to come by. Refer to Figure 5-4 to see how efficiency gains have trended for mining equipment released over the past four years.

For example, the Bitmain Antminer S7 was released in late 2015 as the most efficient and capable miner on the market at the time. In some situations, if miners have a low time preference and access to abundant or cheap electricity, the S7 is still a profitable miner and is still being operated today roughly four and a half years later. The S7, however, is close to its end of life and is the least efficient Bitcoin ASIC miner listed in Figure 5-4. Compare the S7 (at 275 J/Th/s) with the Antminer S17 Pro-15, which uses around 40 J/Th/s. That is, the former uses around seven times the electricity to do the same work.

REMEMBER

Useful life spans of computer hardware are never guaranteed, especially in the fast-moving cryptocurrency mining industry, but with proper research, due diligence, and knowledge, these risks can be mitigated. Always perform product research prior to purchase and reference profitability projection tools to ensure life cycle profitability. See Chapter 7 of this minibook for more information on calculating mining profitability.

Mining Equipment Manufacturers

Today, many manufacturers produce computer equipment (both ASIC and GPU) that is tailored to hash toward and mine various cryptocurrencies.

ASIC rig producers

Here's a list of some top ASIC producers who make the most capable equipment and the most efficient hardware, designed specifically to hash and mine towards Bitcoin and other cryptocurrencies that utilize the SHA-256 hash algorithm. For a list of other cryptocurrencies that use this algorithm, see Chapter 4 of this minibook.

>> **Whatsminer:** The Whatsminer company makes the M series line of Bitcoin SHA-256 mining hardware (https://whatsminer.net/shop).

>> **Bitfury:** Bitfury is the manufacturer of the Tardis Bitcoin SHA-256 mining hardware (https://bitfury.com/crypto-infrastructure/tardis).

>> **Bitmain:** Bitmain produces the Antminer series of mining hardware and sells ASIC equipment that specializes in SHA-256, Equihash, and other popular mining algorithms (https://shop.bitmain.com).

>> **Innosilicon:** Innosilicon produces mining equipment that specializes in the Equihash, SHA-256, Scrypt, X11, and other popular mining algorithms (https://innosilicon.com/html/miner/index.html).

>> **Canaan:** The Canaan company created and manufactures the Avalon series of SHA-256 Bitcoin miners (https://canaan.io).

>> **Ebang:** Ebang produces the EBIT line of ASIC miners that specialize in the Bitcoin SHA-245 hashing algorithm (http://miner.ebang.com.cn).

WARNING

Beware of new manufacturers selling ASICs with sensational specifications and industry-leading hash rate and efficiency numbers! A number of cases have occurred in the past (and we'll likely see more in the future) where newly created hardware manufacturing companies released a presale on new ASIC hardware with amazing specs. Often, these scams only accepted Bitcoin or other cryptocurrencies as payment for the presale. Of course, the hardware was never created or delivered, and the "manufacturer" was never seen or heard from again. (This is sometimes known as an *exit scam*.)

GPU rig producers

Check out the following list of prebuilt GPU mining hardware providers:

>> The **MiningStore** provides a variety of different services, including mining hosting, mining containers, as well as prebuilt GPU and ASIC mining rigs (https://miningstore.com/).

>> The **Coinmine** is a GPU mining rig with an easy-to-use interface that has the ability to mine a variety of cryptocurrencies, such as Ethereum, Grin, Monero, and Zcash (https://coinmine.com).

>> The **PandaMiner B Pro series** are prebuilt GPU mining rigs that can mine Ethereum, Grin, Monero, and Zcash (www.pandaminer.com/product).

>> **MiningSky** provides the V series of GPU miners with potentially eight onboard GPUs to amplify mining capability (https://miningsky.com/gpu).

>> The **MineShop** has many products for sale, including ASIC miners, large-scale cryptocurrency mining operations built into 20-foot shipping containers, and Ethereum GPU rigs (https://mineshop.eu).

>> The **Mining Store** provides prebuilt GPU mining rigs that can mine a variety of cryptocurrencies with 6, 8, or 12 onboard GPUs to maximize mining returns (https://miningstore.com.au).

This equipment is designed off the shelf to mine a variety of cryptocurrencies and algorithms. Chapter 6 of this minibook covers steps and gear to help you build similar GPU mining rigs.

Finding a Wallet to Store and Protect Your Private Keys

Besides the mining equipment itself, you're also going to need an address in the blockchain to which your mining profits will be sent, and a wallet to store your keys. Wallet security is everything. Lose your private keys, or have them stolen, and your cryptocurrency is gone for good! We cover wallets and private keys in Book 1, Chapter 3, but consider also viewing co-author Peter Kent's video course on cryptocurrency, *Crypto Clear: Blockchain and Cryptocurrency Made Simple*, which you can find at CryptoOfCourse.com.

Where to Mine? Selecting a Viable Location

Once adequate hardware is attained (both mining and key storage equipment), finding and securing a place to run your mining equipment becomes a priority. A few requirements for any cryptocurrency mining location include space, communication connectivity, proper ventilation or air-conditioning, and adequate power supply.

Vet your home for cryptocurrency mining

The easiest and most affordable place to start slowly testing the waters in cryptocurrency mining is at home. You already have the resources that would be required to start a cryptocurrency mine: Internet access, electrical power, and space.

Some homes are more suitable for mining than others. An apartment, for example, may not be the best location due to limited space and the noise of the mining equipment. A single-family house would be a better location when compared to a multifamily dwelling like an apartment; you wouldn't want to keep yourself or your friendly neighbors up at night while your mining equipment hums along.

Mining equipment, ASICs specifically, is typically cooled by an intake and an exhaust fan that run anywhere from 3,600 to 6,200 rotations per minute. (6,200 RPM fans produce 60 to 100 decibels or more!) These high-RPM cooling fans create quite a bit of noise and exhaust and an even greater amount of heat. Some places in a home are better than others. For example, you wouldn't want a 6,200 RPM fan buzzing on your bedside table or in your kitchen.

TIP

The best places to run mining equipment in a residence, if that is the place you select, would be in a garage, an easily vented garden shed, or a cool basement with plenty of airflow for ventilation.

Regardless of whether your residence, an industrial facility, or some other suitable location is the place you select to deploy cryptocurrency mining hardware, there are a few things to consider in the space you choose. Ease of ventilation, cooling in hot months, Internet connectivity, and adequate power supply are all essential. Ventilation becomes easier and more affordable if the climate you're mining in is cool, cold, or mild for large portions of the year.

Communication requirements

Cryptocurrency miners have to connect to a global network of blockchain nodes, so communication connectivity is key. Most importantly, you need a reliable connection to the Internet. This connection can come in many forms, but for mining, you need to be able to send as well as receive information, so both upload and download links are important. A high-bandwidth connection is not absolutely required, but low latency in connectivity is often best as every millisecond (thousandth of a second) in the mining sphere counts.

Bandwidth is the amount of throughput: how much data can be transferred, often measured in megabits per second (Mbps). *Latency* is the time delay that the data takes to make it from A to B, often measured in milliseconds (ms) or thousandths of a second.

Traditional Internet access

The simplest method of connection for cryptocurrency mining is just traditional Internet access. Most broadband speeds today are more than adequate to satisfy the requirements for a cryptocurrency miner. In fact, a fully synced and decently connected Bitcoin node rarely goes above 10 to 50 kbps (kilobits per second) and could, in theory, be run on a 56 kbps dial-up modem from years past. (No, we're not advising this!)

Ideally your mining equipment would connect to your Internet service provider's modem with an Ethernet cable; you may need an additional router or network switch to connect multiple miners. You could, however, use a Wi-Fi connection if the mining hardware is not easily hardwired to your ISP's modem.

Satellite access

Remote areas that are otherwise suitable for mining equipment may not have hardwired Internet infrastructure, but alternatives are available. A few companies provide satellite-based Internet connections to areas otherwise unserved with Internet access. Search for *satellite internet* to find these services.

SATELLITE BLOCKCHAIN?

A free service distributes the Bitcoin blockchain worldwide via satellite, allowing you to set up a full node anywhere in the world. This satellite Bitcoin data is provided by Blockstream, Inc., and you can find the information on the free service at `https://Blockstream.com/satellite/`.

However, as revolutionary as this service may be, it is currently limited to only distributing the blockchain data and does not allow for data uploads. So, it's not useful for Bitcoin mining, which requires that you send the blocks you've mined back to the network. It instead acts as a good backup to keep nodes up to date and fully synced with the blockchain, but perhaps services like this will allow for both upload and download in the near future.

Power source thoughts

The place where you set up your mining equipment must have an adequate power supply for that equipment. If the mining you're planning to do is on a normal desktop computer, a typical 120-volt outlet can feed enough power to your computer's power supply. In the case of dedicated cryptocurrency mining hardware, the equipment consumes thousands of watts of electrical power to produce many trillions of hashes per second.

In addition to the 120-volt circuit that you plug most of your devices into — your TV, hair dryer, lamps, and so on — your home also has 240-volt circuits; that's what your air conditioning and clothes dryer connect to. A 240-volt circuit can feed the higher-voltage ASIC mining equipment you may use.

Still, you need a few pieces of electrical gear to ensure safe and reliable power delivery to any piece of cryptocurrency mining hardware. You need power delivery units (PDUs), properly rated power supply units (PSUs), and upline electrical wiring and breaker panel infrastructure.

Power delivery units

Power delivery units route power from electrical outlets to power supply units. These are typically 240-volt devices in the United States. They deliver power and protect against circuit overload. These PDUs may also be able to connect and feed multiple power supply units, depending on their rating. They typically have an internal 240-volt line-to-line electrical bus that feeds a few breakers providing electrical surge protection to the outlets they are feeding. Figure 5-9 shows a PDU from CyberPower.

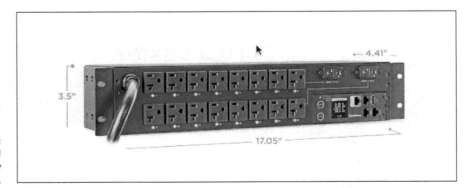

FIGURE 5-9:
A PDU manufactured by CyberPower.

For example, an adequately rated electrical supply line, per the specifications in the National Electrical Code (NEC), feeding a PDU rated at 240 volts and 30 amps, may then feed three separate 240-volt 10-amp breakers in the PDU.

The equation to calculate electrical power (P, measured in watts) from voltage and amperage is fairly simple. We use $P=V*I$, where P is power (the rate of energy flow, in watts), V is voltage, and I represents current, measured in amps.

Using this equation, a 240-volt 10-amp PDU outlet would be able to provide about 2,400 watts (2,400W = 240V * 10 amps), and thus each PDU could power most of the ASICs specified in Figure 5-2 (shown earlier in this chapter) . . . but not all of them. As shown in that figure, a few on the left side are going to require more power than that!

This configuration provides individual electrical overload protection to the three outlets on the PDU and helps isolate any equipment or electrical faults downstream of any of the outlets while maintaining power to the other two outlets.

PDUs are not always necessary, depending on the size and configuration of the mining equipment, but their use can provide additional electrical fault protection and safety to multiple pieces of mining equipment. PDUs are reasonably priced for the electrical connectivity, convenience, and peace of mind they provide and can be purchased from many web-based suppliers.

Power supplies

Power supplies for the cryptocurrency mining space have come in all shapes and sizes, from a typical power supply unit (PSU) that would be found in a desktop computer all the way to dedicated pieces of hardware specially designed for cryptocurrency mining applications. See Figure 5-10 for an example from Bitmain.

FIGURE 5-10:
A PSU sold by Bitmain, a major ASIC manufacturer, for its line of Antminer ASICs.

PSUs are often bundled with ASIC mining hardware in a package purchased directly from the manufacturer with the specific cryptocurrency mining hardware they can support. PSUs can also be found on many online marketplaces. Power supply units can come in 120-volt or 240-volt varieties, and some are able to be dual voltage (connecting to either voltage), depending on the outlet type you have available. If buying a PSU separately, you need to ensure that the PSU's rated wattage is greater than the maximum power consumption of the mining hardware it's going to power.

WARNING

The rated wattage of the power supply should exceed the rated maximum power consumption of the cryptocurrency mining hardware being used. Otherwise, the power supply won't be able to service the electrical load. This underrating could lead to electrical faults, frequent power supply failures, or mining rig failures. All of these outcomes are dangerous and costly, so you really need to use a power supply that's adequately rated for the hardware (the ASIC or GPU mining rigs) you're trying to power. Refer to the manufacturer's mining equipment manual for more specific information.

WARNING

Be really careful with your mining installations! An improperly configured and installed mining operation represents a serious fire risk. Don't think this can't happen to you; it's happened to others. If you're at all unsure of what you're doing, get a professional electrician to help you set up your gear!

Existing electrical infrastructure versus new installations

If you plan to use existing electrical infrastructure to serve your mine, it is important that the outlet, the wire from the panel, and the breaker panel from which you plan to feed your cryptocurrency mining equipment be properly rated for the electrical load. It is also important that the service wire from your utility and the transformer feeding it also be rated for the increase in load from your cryptocurrency mining gear. Consult your local electric utility as well as a local electrician to find out whether your proposed loading requires additional electrical upgrades.

WARNING

The conductor or electrical line and the breaker protecting the circuit in question also need to be adequately rated for the load you plan on feeding. The breaker in the panel feeding the wires may give you an idea of the maximum current, or amperage, that the circuit can carry. However, if you have any questions as to the wire, breaker, or outlet rating, consult a local qualified and licensed electrician to ensure electrical safety and reliability and to avoid electrical faults for your proposed mining hardware.

For larger deployments of dedicated cryptocurrency mining gear, especially with the power consumption involved with state-of-the-art gear, you're almost certainly going to need new circuitry and electrical installations. The typical home electrical service panel is rated around 100 to 200 amps, so the amount of mining hardware that can be installed in a typical residence is limited. Unless you're a qualified electrician, consult the experts and get in touch with a local licensed electrical expert to perform your electrical upgrades or new installations for you. For midsize or larger deployments, you may need to use a commercial data center, a mining hosting facility, or your own entirely new mining facility in a commercial space.

WARNING

Although this won't be a problem for most people, check with your power utility to see whether you're even *allowed* to run mining gear! In some localities, mining is banned in private homes, particularly in rural areas that have relatively little power demand and thus run the risk of being overwhelmed if a few miners set up shop. For example, a few years ago, Chelan County in Washington State, which is mostly national forest and has a population of little more than 70,000 people, required mining permits and at one point, implemented a moratorium on cryptocurrency mining, as they were concerned that the mining operations in the county were a fire risk and also represented a burden on the electricity supply. On the other hand, Hydro-Québec welcomes cryptocurrency miners but still requires that mining operations be registered with the utility.

Data centers and other dedicated commercial locations

Aspiring cryptocurrency miners who want to scale up to a significant mining deployment will find that commercial locations, such as warehouses or dedicated data centers, may be the best route. Large mining operations simply won't fit into your apartment or home.

You have essentially three options:

>> **Build your own data center.** Find some warehouse space, for example, and build from scratch.

>> **Work with a colocation center.** Colocation centers are all over the world and are designed primarily to manage web servers. They come with reliable power, flood, and fire protection, redundant Internet connections, and so on. They charge for the space you take up in their racks and the bandwidth you use.

>> **Work with a mining-service company.** These services charge reasonable fees to host equipment that you own, including space and electrical costs in their tailor-made and ready-to-deploy commercial spaces. They are, in essence, colocation services but designed specifically for cryptocurrency mining. Here are a few popular cryptocurrency mining equipment hosting services:

- Blockstream: `https://blockstream.com/mining/`
- MiningStore: `https://miningstore.com/bitcoin-mining-hosting-service/`
- Compass Mining: `https://compassmining.io/`
- Compute North: `https://www.computenorth.com`
- Citadel 256: `https://www.citadel256.com`
- Upstream Data: `https://www.upstreamdata.ca/products`
- Bitcoin Mined: `https://www.bitcoinmined.net/`
- TeslaWatt: `https://teslawatt.com/`
- MiningSky: `https://miningsky.com/miner-hosting/`
- Mining Colocation: `https://miningcolocation.com`
- LightSpeed Hosting: `https://www.lightspeedhosting.com/`

Upsides

Whichever way you choose — build it yourself, use a colocation service, or work with a mining-service company — these types of bulk commercial deployments allow you to install vast amounts of cryptocurrency mining equipment. The latter two have the advantage of making it easy to get set up quickly. They may already be equipped with bulk access to the power grid and adequate internal electrical infrastructure to service your mining hardware needs. Colocation centers and mining-service companies also have powerful air-conditioning equipment to cool your valuable cryptocurrency mining equipment. (Some warehouse situations may, too.) They have lightning-fast Internet connectivity as well, allowing for lower-latency mining and giving you a slight edge. In other words, some of these locations can provide the entire package, everything required to hit the ground mining in a timely fashion; and in the cryptocurrency space, *time is coin*.

Downsides

The downsides for these types of installations can, in some situations, be significant. They may include cost, length of lease, and lack of direct control or access to your equipment. A warehouse may be cheaper, or not. The colocation and mining-service businesses are sharing the costs between all customers. If you try to build from scratch, the entire cost burden falls on you, and it's going to be expensive.

TIP

In general, building a very large mining operation in a dedicated location is cheaper. For small operations, however, working with a colocation center or service will likely be cheaper.

In hosted facilities, you may not have direct physical control of your equipment. In some cases, it may be at the whim of the service provider. If it is a commercial space or data center of your own deployment, extra costs (above what it would cost to run a cryptocurrency mining rig at your residence) may include Internet connectivity, space rental costs, and insurance fees. These may not seem like much, but if not adequately prepared for, they can add up to significant impediments to profitability in times when hash rate competition increases or when the market exchange rate falls.

Chapter **6**

Setting Up Your Mining Hardware

After selecting a cryptocurrency you intend to mine, acquiring all the needed supplies and hardware, and choosing a suitable location to run your mining equipment, the next step is to bring it all together and set up your mining rig. Whether you plan to use application specific integrated circuit (ASIC) mining hardware, or a custom-built graphical processing unit (GPU) mining rig, we look at how to assemble the mining equipment, hook up all the needed cables, and install and run the correct software.

ASIC Mining Rigs

ASIC mining equipment is manufactured in a prebuilt package that takes care of much of the technical software and physical setup requirements that make GPU cryptocurrency mining somewhat more difficult. ASICs are designed to be virtually plug and play. After all, ASIC mining equipment is specially intended and built for cryptocurrency mining, so it is designed to be easy to use in that very application. Your ASIC should come with an installation manual, of course, with detailed instructions. This chapter is more of an overview to give you a feel for what will be required.

Racks

Computer colocation facilities are full of racks that are a little over 19 inches wide and 40 to 50 inches high. A rack contains different customers' installed mining rigs, with one setup above the other. Each rack is subdivided into vertical units; 1U means a vertical space 1.75 inches high. Thus, computer equipment designed to fit into racks may be 1U or 2U or 3U, and so on. A piece of equipment that is 2U will fit into a 3.5-inch-tall space in the rack, for example.

Well, *some* ASICs are designed to be *rack mountable.* This typically means that the ASIC slots right into a standard 19-inch computer rack and may take up several vertical units. However, this is actually relatively rare. In general, ASICs are not designed to be rack mountable. You can see an example of the typical form factor of an ASIC in Figure 6-1.

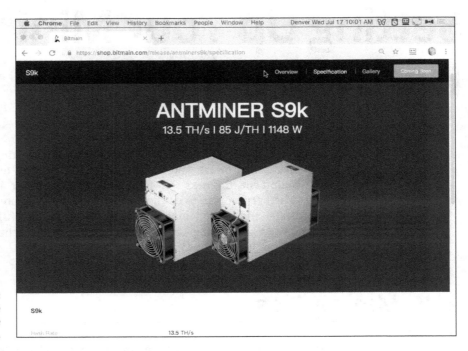

FIGURE 6-1:
A typical ASIC size and shape; the Antminer S9k.

So how do you rack-mount an ASIC that isn't rack-mountable? You use a case. A few companies sell rack-mount shelves designed to hold particular ASICs and mount them in server racks. For example, Figure 6-2 shows an example of a Gray Matter Industries rack designed specifically for the Antminer Bitmain S9 and L3 ASICs (www.miningrigs.net). This rack holds three Bitmain ASICs, and the PSU (power supply unit), too. The case is 7U tall.

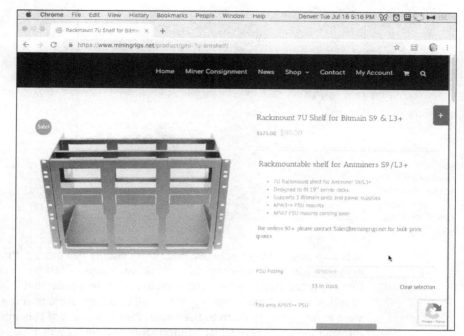

FIGURE 6-2:
A Gray Matter Industries shelf designed to hold, and rack mount, three Bitmain ASICs and a PSU.

These rack-mount shelves are not terribly expensive (usually less than $200), and if you are running a large mining operation, with dozens of ASICs, you'll probably want to use some kind of mounting equipment. However, there's no need to go overboard if you have a small mining operation! There's nothing wrong with sitting a couple of ASICs on a table, or perhaps on utility shelving from your local hardware store or big box outlet. Computer server racks in data centers are typically electrically grounded, and if you are using a metal rack or shelving, it should also be grounded so you and your equipment are safe.

Power supply

Most ASIC mining rigs use external power supplies (PSUs); you can see an example in Figure 6-3. In general, when you buy an ASIC, you'll probably get an appropriate PSU bundled with it — not always, though, so if not, you'll need to carefully select the right PSU and buy it separately.

Power supplies convert the alternating current (AC) supplied from the electrical utility to direct current (DC) electricity used by computer equipment. So, you'll connect your ASICs directly to the appropriate PSUs.

WARNING

It is critical that you ensure that none of your devices are plugged into a wall socket before you begin connecting components. Connect the power supply to the ASIC first and then the power supply to the PDU prior to connecting the PDU to the wall outlet.

It is also important to only use one power supply per mining rig. Trying to connect a single ASIC miner to multiple power supplies can be dangerous and lead to equipment failure or electrical faults. Also, be aware that while some power supplies are equipped with a power switch, others are not and will power on as soon as you connect them to the outlet. (See Chapter 5 of this minibook for more information on the electrical requirements and equipment.)

TECHNICAL STUFF

Power supplies are equipped with PCIe (Peripheral Component Interconnect Express) power cables that allow for easy and quick connection. If you've worked on personal computer hardware, you'll be familiar with these. There are many variations of PCIe cables, but for mining power supplies, the 6-pin version is typically used.

Your ASIC will have multiple PCIe connectors. Each hash board has several PCIe plugs — likely at least 2, maybe 3 or 4 — and each mining rig has about three hash boards (though some may have more) for a rough total of 6 to 12 PCIe ports for hash boards per ASIC. Each ASIC mining rig also has a control board that must be powered, so you'll also see a PCIe connection for that board. In Figure 6-4, you can see a page from the installation manual for the Antminer Z9 ASIC in which power connections are discussed.

PDUs

Power delivery units, or PDUs, are not necessary for running cryptocurrency mining equipment, especially in small installations. However, they are recommended, as PDUs make the connection of multiple mining power supply units (PSUs) easier and safer.

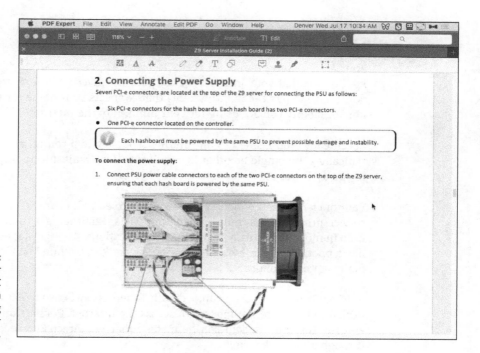

FIGURE 6-4:
The Antminer
Z9 ASIC
documentation
showing
the power
connections.

To install your PDUs, they must be connected to the mining PSUs via cables that are typically provided with the purchase of the PSU. Once that is complete, you can connect the PDUs to the electrical outlets. We discuss electrical infrastructure requirements in more detail in Chapter 5 of this minibook. For a view of a typical PDU, see Figure 6-5.

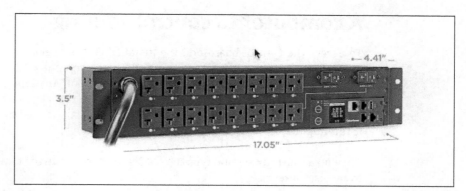

FIGURE 6-5:
A typical PDU.

WARNING

Fire risk is real (see Chapter 5 of this minibook). You must make sure that you're using the right equipment, configured correctly. If you're not sure, you *must* get the assistance of a professional electrician. Keep a fire extinguisher accessible but not too close to your mining rig.

Network and Ethernet connection

Your ASIC mining hardware needs Internet access, of course. You'll need some kind of box that your Internet service provider gives you (or that you buy so you don't have to pay the monthly rent) that connects your home (or whatever other kind of facility you are using for your mining) to the Internet.

Specifically, you need both an Internet modem and a router, and these days you typically get a single box that has both functions built into it. Anyway, that's up to you and your ISP.

Your modem/router, whether you own it yourself or it is provided by your Internet service provider, has multiple Ethernet ports. Ethernet is a connection standard used in most local area network (LAN) applications. An Ethernet port looks a little like a phone line port but is slightly larger and can be found on most desktop and many laptop computers.

ASIC control boards are equipped with Ethernet ports as well and must be connected to your Internet modem to access the Internet. Connections to your miner and the Internet modem can be made either via direct Ethernet connection or through a network switch.

Once your power supply and Ethernet connections are hooked up to your miner, the next step is to power the equipment on. Make sure that everything is properly connected — ASIC PCIe cables are connected to the PSU, and the PSU is connected to the PDU. Then, and only then, should you plug the PDU into the wall socket and turn everything on.

A computer to control your rig

To access the control board and the installed GUI of specialized cryptocurrency mining ASICs, you will need to access it via any computer that is connected to the same local area network as the mining equipment. Any laptop or desktop will work. Even a cellphone can connect as long it is on the same LAN. The computer managing your ASIC doesn't need to be powerful. It's just used to set it up and get it running; the ASIC itself is doing all the work.

Open up a web browser and type the ASIC's IP address into the browser to navigate to the user interface.

Where do you find the IP address? You can use software, such as the free Angry IP Scanner (www.angryip.org), or log on to your network's router and scan. Your ASIC manufacturer may provide a tool to find the IP number. For example, some of the Bitmain Antminer ASICs work with a Windows program called IP Reporter (downloaded from the Bitmain website). You run the software and then press the IP Report button on the ASIC and the ASIC reports its IP number to the software (see Figure 6-6). You can then take that IP number, enter it into a web browser, and connect to the ASIC. Refer to your ASIC's documentation; each ASIC is going to function a little differently.

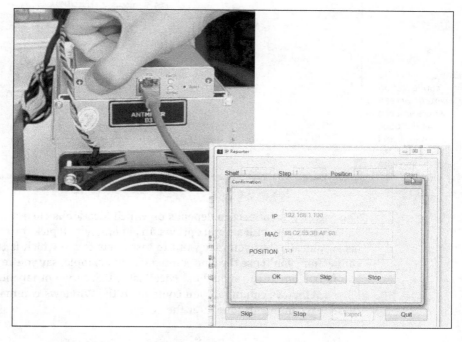

FIGURE 6-6: Bitmain Antminer's IP Report button on the ASIC, which reports the ASIC's IP number to the IP Reporter software.

You'll then use the ASIC software, accessed through your web browser, to point to the pool you're working with. Here's an example of the settings required to input into your miner for a United States–based Bitcoin ASIC running on Slush Pool:

```
URL: stratum+tcp://us-east.stratum.slushpool.com:3333
userID: userName.workerName
password: [yourpoolpassword]
```

In Figure 6-7, you can see the Bitmain Antminer ASIC user interface in the pool configuration screen.

The specific mining pool you choose will also provide details on connection settings. Sometimes, for example, instead of requiring you to enter a user account, a mining pool will need you to input only your blockchain payout address for the cryptocurrency you are mining. Again, check your pool's documentation for details.

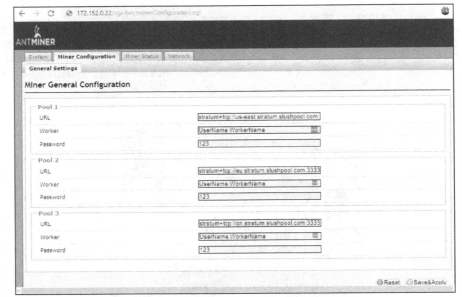

FIGURE 6-7:
The Bitmain ASIC configuration settings screen where you can set the pool, username, and server URL for pool mining with your ASIC rigs.

The server you connect to depends on which location is closest to you; your pool will provide you with several options. In general, you'll pick the one closest to you geographically, but you may want to test a few to see which is really the fastest connection; you'll use the *ping* command. For example, say you're in Australia and you're not sure if you should use NiceHash's U.S. server or Japanese server. If you have a Windows computer, you could open the Windows command line and run these two commands, one after the other:

```
ping -n 50 -l 128 speedtest.usa.nicehash.com
ping -n 50 -l 128 speedtest.jp.nicehash.com
```

On the macOS, you can use the Network Utility app's Ping screen. For each one, you'll get a response something like this:

```
50 packets transmitted, 50 packets received, 0.0% packet loss
round-trip min/avg/max/stddev = 62.156/67.665/83.567/7.214 ms
```

For Linux machines (Ubuntu, Debian, and so on), you'll just need to open the terminal and run these two commands (after 10 to 15 seconds, you'll need to press CTRL+C to obtain a report of the ping test):

```
ping speedtest.usa.nicehash.com
ping speedtest.jp.nicehash.com
```

You can then compare the average ping time to find the fastest connection (the smaller the number, measured in ms, or milliseconds, the faster the connection, of course). That's the server you'll want to use because with cryptocurrency mining every fraction of a second is important.

If you need to enter a username rather than your blockchain address, it will be the same as your mining pool account. You can get creative with what you decide to name your worker, or mining rig, but do not duplicate worker names if you are connecting more than one piece of mining gear. (You may have multiple workers — individual GPU rigs or ASICs — working within your single mining account. See the particular pool's instructions to find out how to provide this information.)

GPU Mining Rigs

If you bought a prebuilt GPU mining rig, setting it up is as simple as setting up an ASIC. Building it yourself requires a lot more work and planning.

Getting your GPU rig online

Some mining-equipment providers sell preconfigured GPU mining rigs (see the list of prebuilt GPU mining rig manufacturers in Chapter 5 of this minibook for some popular equipment providers), but these preassembled mining rigs come at a premium cost when compared to the sum of the cost of the computer parts. These preassembled rigs are easier to set up and get mining, of course, and are similar to ASIC miners — they're essentially plug and play. Figure 6-8 shows you a prebuilt 8-GPU mining rig with slots for eight individual GPUs. You will essentially treat a preassembled GPU like an ASIC, with the exception that a GPU rig is itself a computer and does not need an external computer to manage it. Thus, you will do the following:

1. Place it on a table, in a rack, or on a shelf.

2. Connect it to a PSU.

3. Connect the PSU to a PDU.

4. Connect it to an Ethernet network.

5. Install an operating system (unless it came with one, as some prebuilt rigs do).

6. Connect a mouse, keyboard, and screen (unless it came with a screen).

7. Install mining software on the computer (unless the prebuilt rig came with the software already installed).

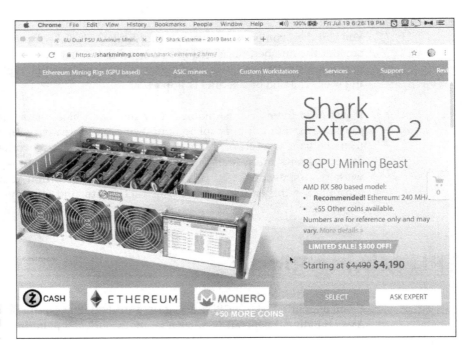

Building your own GPU miner

Prebuilt GPU mining hardware rigs can be expensive, so some aspiring miners acquire the parts needed off websites, such as Newegg and Amazon, or retailers, such as Micro Center or Best Buy, and assemble their rigs themselves. Building your own GPU mining rig comes at quite a discount compared to the prebuilt options. However, this route is also more complex, with some assembly required as well as sometimes fairly complicated software implementations.

A typical desktop computer will have space onboard for only a single GPU or two. Some custom-built computers have space for up to three in standard tower cases, but in general, for GPU mining applications, special mining rig frames and custom-assembled hardware are needed to be able to run 6 to 12 GPUs.

You can buy all these parts separately, or perhaps buy a bundle and put it all together. For example, gpuShack (gpuShack.com) sells bundles that come with a motherboard configured for 5 to 13 GPUs (depending on the bundle), RAM, and a small amount of flash data storage with the ethOS operating system already installed. These range from $189 to $399, but you'll still require riser cards, various cables, a rack, and so on.

WARNING

There are many different possible configurations, so our explanation here is really quite basic and just outlines the essential principles. Before you jump into building your own GPU mining rig, we strongly recommend that you spend some time viewing videos from people who have already done it so that you can get a really good idea of what it entails. You can easily find many examples and detailed guides by typing **build gpu mining rig** into your favorite search engine.

Mining rig frame

Gamers often custom-build their own high-power desktop computers, buying a tower case and all the individual components — motherboard, CPU, graphics cards, power supplies, and so on — that they place into the case. The principle is the same when building a GPU mining rig, except that you can't use a typical tower case because of the size limitations for multiple GPUs. Rather, you need a special mining-rig case or frame.

Simple mining-rig frames are around the same price as regular computer cases, or sometimes cheaper (depending on the type you choose), hold more GPUs, of course, and allow for greater ventilation to remove the heat from the GPUs. The frame allows you to connect a motherboard, a power supply unit, and multiple GPUs in a compact form factor.

However, there's a wide range of what you can get when buying GPU frames, from the very basic (just a metal frame with holes to help you mount components); to more expensive versions that come with a CPU, hard drive, RAM, fans, all the necessary connectors, and even an operating system (essentially everything but the GPU cards); to the full-blown GPU racks with everything ready to go. The Mining-Sky Mining Rig shown in Figure 6-9, for example, is $899, but it comes ready to plug GPU cards into it, making it very simple to work with.

Some frames are also designed to allow for stacking other frames on top, in case you want to deploy multiple mining rigs in a small space. Other frames can be mounted in a computer-server rack, allowing for scalability and easier deployment. Many online retailers sell mining rig cases or frames (Amazon, eBay, Newegg, Walmart, the mining-gear companies we mention in Chapter 5 of this minibook, and so on). The companies that sell preassembled GPU mining rigs generally also sell individual parts, including mining rig frames. (Some miners build their own frames to save on costs, though the extra hassle may not be worth it in many cases.)

Figure 6-10 shows a Rosewill GPU Mining Case, or Frame (see www.Rosewill.com), which takes up to eight GPU cards and is also rack-mountable (6U tall). The diagram shows where the motherboard, GPUs, PSUs, and fans are installed. This case retails for around $100.

FIGURE 6-9:
The MiningSky
V1 GPU Mining
Rig — everything
you need but the
GPU cards.

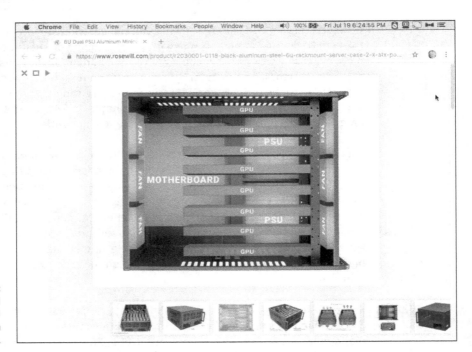

FIGURE 6-10:
The Rosewill
6U Dual PSU
Aluminum
Mining Case.

In Figure 6-11, you can see an open-air design, which is popular with many miners. All you get is the bare frame, with space to mount everything you need, such as the motherboard, fans, GPUs, and so on.

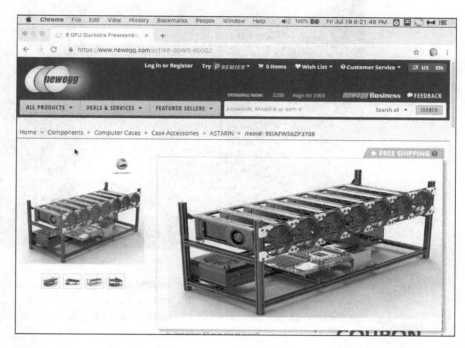

FIGURE 6-11:
An open-air
GPU mining
frame, shown
after all the
equipment has
been mounted (it
comes empty).

Motherboard

The *motherboard* is the piece of computer hardware that ties everything else together. It provides connections on the board for installation of the CPU, the GPUs, and the power supply, as well as the RAM and hard drive.

It would be handy if your motherboard has plenty of slots for GPU cards. However, few motherboards have more than a couple of slots available. If you're using one of the more sophisticated, prebuilt mining-rig frames, that's okay — all the connectors are built in. You'll install your motherboard into the frame and connect it to the frame following the manufacturer's instructions. If you're using a simpler frame, then you'll need to use a riser card to connect your GPUs.

In fact, you may want to purchase a motherboard that is designed for cryptocurrency mining, which will likely have all the connectors you'll need. ASUS, the well-known computer company, manufactures a mining motherboard, the B250 Mining Expert, which you can see in Figure 6-12. This board allows you to connect up to 19 GPUs.

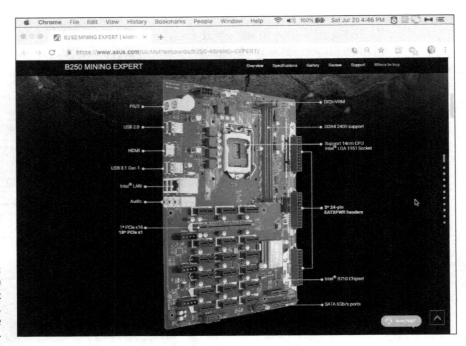

FIGURE 6-12:
The ASUS B250
Mining Expert
motherboard,
which can handle
up to 19 GPUs.

REMEMBER

Make sure to securely mount your motherboard to your case or mining rig frame with the provided screws that come with the motherboard. Ensure that the motherboard that you select is compatible with the CPU model you purchase.

Central processing unit

The *central processing unit* (CPU) is the main computer chip, the brain of your desktop or laptop computer. It serves this same function for GPU mining rigs. The individual GPU cards are the specialized processors, and they still need a CPU to manage them all.

In general, any off-the-shelf CPU is sufficient; it doesn't take much power to manage the GPU cards. However, in some circumstances, you may also use the CPU to mine, depending on the software you're using. Both the GPU cards and the CPU will be hashing. In such a case, you'll want a faster CPU. Faster CPUs will have many different cores (both physical and virtual) that will allow for more mining capability and hash rate from the CPU.

Make sure that the CPU you purchase is compatible with your motherboard. Some motherboards are usable with Intel CPUs, while others work with AMD CPUs. (The difference is in the number of pins for the CPU socket connection. The AMD chips use 938-pin sockets and the Intel chips use 1,366-pin sockets.) The manufacturer of the motherboard will list which CPU it is designed to work with. Figure 6-13 shows a fairly standard AMD CPU from Micro Center that would be able to run a GPU mining rig.

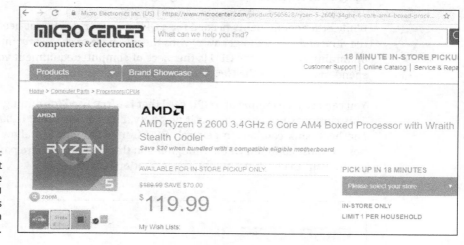

FIGURE 6-13:
An AMD CPU that would be suitable to run a GPU mining rig. This CPU comes with a fan.

Mount the CPU to the motherboard, following the manufacturer's instructions. It is best to also use a CPU fan and heat sink to cool the CPU chip. CPU fans are powered by a four-pin connection to the motherboard, and the fan pin will be labeled 'CPU' on the motherboard. The heat sink and fan should be connected to the CPU via a heat sink bonding compound or paste, known as *thermal grease*, which allows for a proper connection and heat dissipation from the CPU to the heat sink and fan apparatus. Figure 6-14 shows a heat sink that is designed to attach to a motherboard and cool the CPU with an equipped fan.

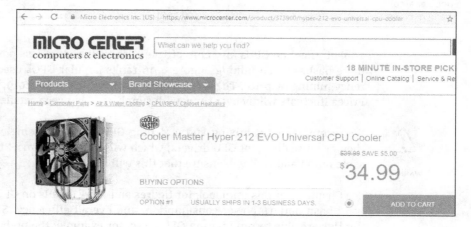

FIGURE 6-14:
A CPU heat sink with built-in fan (from Cooler Master). The pad shown directly under the fan sits directly on top of the CPU chip to pull the heat way from the chip.

Graphical processing units

The *graphical processing units,* or GPUs, are the essential and keystone piece of equipment required for GPU mining rigs.

TIP

While other components needed for a GPU mining rig may not need to be top-of-the-line and you could get away with the purchase of cheaper components to save on mining rig costs, the GPU is the piece of computer equipment you may want to spend more on. It's the GPU that does the hashing, after all.

You can see an example of a GPU card that is often used for mining in Figure 6-15. This card was not cheap when it was new, but it's powerful. It has built-in fans and heat-sink cooling. In general, GPU frames are built to allow for the thickness of most common GPUs, though if you think your GPUs are particularly thick, you'll want to check the frame's specifications carefully.

FIGURE 6-15: GPU cards are popular among certain miners.

Top-of-the-line GPUs are more efficient, so they require less power and output more hashes when mining. Figure 6-16 ranks popular GPUs used in cryptocurrency mining by price. These costs are an average from late 2019, but be warned: Prices fluctuate wildly over time, with supply, and between retailers.

WARNING

We recommend not mixing and matching GPU types on a single mining rig, as they may use different GPU drivers, which will cause problems. Sticking with the same brand and type will ensure that this will not be an issue.

See Chapter 7 of this minibook for figures and more details on GPU mining hardware hash output, power consumption, and overall efficiency. Some GPU mining rigs are able to run up to 12 GPUs (see, for example, the prebuilt mining rigs from `https://miningstore.com.au`). These mining rigs require larger frames, multiple power supplies, and, in some cases, two motherboards to run that many GPUs. Six GPUs is a common deployment and is near the limit that can be safely and easily powered by a single power supply.

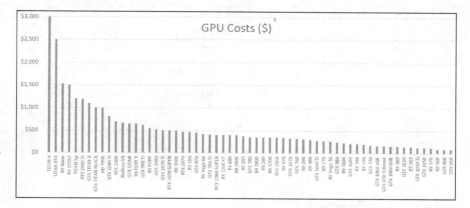

Riser card and cables

A special GPU riser card and cables may be required to connect your GPUs to the motherboard. Most motherboards have only a few onboard PCIe connections for GPUs. Depending on your hardware setup and motherboard, you may be able to plug the GPU directly into the motherboard, but if you have more GPU cards than PCIe connections, you won't be able to.

However, if your motherboard doesn't have enough PCIe connections, you can use GPU riser cards, one for each GPU card you want to use. (They are around $15 to $20 each.) The riser cards are mounted on the frame; they then plug into the motherboard via USB (Universal Serial Bus) connections, of which most motherboards have plenty.

Some GPUs are powered directly from the motherboard connection. However, the most modern and powerful GPUs (the ones best suited for mining) require the GPU to be powered directly from the power supply by a separate PCIe 6-pin cable.

Each GPU is then plugged into a riser card via the PCIe port and physically mounted to the mining case or frame. You can see an example of a riser card being sold on the popular Newegg electronics site in Figure 6-17.

FIGURE 6-17:
A riser card designed to connect a single GPU card to a motherboard.

Memory

Random access memory, or RAM, is needed for any computer as well as for a GPU-based mining rig. RAM is cheap, but mining doesn't actually need very large amounts of memory (unlike the graphics-intensive operations the GPU cards were originally designed for), so you won't need to go overboard. Still, your rig will run better with a decent amount of RAM, and anywhere from 4 to 16GB of RAM is most likely adequate.

RAM sticks or cards can be plugged directly into the motherboard, but be sure to follow your motherboard manufacturer's instructions carefully. For example, you may need to plug two chips into slots 1 and 2 with some motherboards, or slots 1 and 3 with others. Typical modern motherboards are equipped with four slots for expandable RAM, but because GPU-mining rigs do not require much RAM, you generally don't need to use all four slots.

Power supply

You'll need a power supply — maybe several. GPU-rig power supplies, similar to their ASIC counterparts, also come equipped with PCIe 6-pin cables, allowing for easy and quick connection to the various pieces of gear that require power.

REMEMBER

Make sure to properly calculate your mining rig's power supply needs before purchasing your power supplies. GPU manufacturers will list the maximum rated power consumption of their graphics cards. Multiply this number by the number of GPUs you have and install enough power to supply them all. Also account for the CPU, fans, and motherboard power consumption. The power requirements for these additional items should be provided in the manufacturer's documentation but do not normally exceed 200 to 400 watts. Typically, computer power supplies range between 600 and 1,600 watts and can easily power between 3 and 8 GPUs, depending on the GPUs' electricity consumption. Refer to Chapter 7 of this mini-book for a ranking of popular GPUs' power consumption in watts when mining a cryptocurrency such as Ethereum.

Hard drive

The storage mechanism for digital data, the hard disk drive (HDD) is needed for any computer, and a GPU mining rig is essentially a specialized computer. Some solo miners, with their own full cryptocurrency node, use state-of-the-art solid-state drives (SSDs), but in pool mining this type of technology isn't needed. With pool mining, the pool is managing the blockchain itself. All your gear is doing is the hashing, so you don't need a particularly fast or large hard drive. A smallish HDD is fine.

For solo mining, though, it's a different matter. You'll have a full copy of the blockchain on the hard drive. What that means as far as a choice between HDD and SDD is concerned depends on the cryptocurrency you're mining. In the case of many smaller cryptocurrencies, the choice probably isn't terribly important. In some cases, though, in particular if you're mining the Ethereum blockchain using an *archival* blockchain (a copy of the blockchain that includes all historical data), the choice is more important. You'd need a multi-terabyte SSD, because the archival blockchain is huge, and an HDD really wouldn't be fast enough to keep up or sync. (On the other hand, it's possible to solo mine in the Ethereum blockchain using what is known as a *pruned* blockchain, one in which nonessential historical data has been removed, which is much smaller.)

SSD drives are more expensive than HDDs but much faster and can help solo-mining equipment quickly read and write block data into storage. This isn't needed for pool mining, but in solo cryptocurrency mining, every (split) second counts. If you're trying to download, sync, and verify an archival Ethereum block-chain, for example, you cannot even catch up to the real-time blocks being added to the chain without using an SSD, as an HDD is just too slow. (On the other hand, this isn't a problem with most cryptocurrencies.)

Drives are connected to the motherboard, generally using a Serial ATA (SATA) cable, as well as connected to the power supply via a six-pin PCIe power cable.

Fans

Air flow is essential for any mining application, as the computational processes generate quite a bit of heat. The GPUs best suited for cryptocurrency mining have built-in, onboard fans to cool off large heat sinks. You'll also need a CPU fan. The mining-rig frame itself may also be equipped with a place to mount a few external fans to the unit. These can be connected to the motherboard via four-pin fan power connections and will help dissipate heat off the mining rig and keep your equipment running optimally.

Ensure that all these connections are firmly secured and plug in your GPU mining rig. Once online, the next step is to install the software to get your mining rig pointed to your cryptocurrency blockchain or pool of choice.

An operating system, mouse, keyboard, and screen

Unlike working with an ASIC, which requires an external computer to manage the ASIC, your GPU rig is going to be managed by an operating system stored on the HDD or SSD that you installed into the frame. The GPU mining rig itself is a computer. Just like your desktop or laptop PC, it has a motherboard, CPU, RAM, and a disk drive.

If you bought a prebuilt GPU rig, it likely already has an operating system included. The Shark Mining rig we looked at earlier in the section, "GPU Mining Rigs," has something called SharkOS installed, which is a Linux-based operating system with mining software included, and the MiningSky V1 GPU Mining Rig comes with Windows preinstalled on the disk (though not registered). Otherwise, you'll have to install an operating system, probably downloaded to the rig's hard drive through your Internet connection.

Note that some of the software we look at in this chapter is also, like the SharkOS, a combination of operating system and mining software. You install the operating system, and it comes with the mining functions ready to run.

You'll also need to control that GPU rig computer, so you'll need a mouse, keyboard, and display. (A few, like the Shark Mining rig, may have a built-in touch screen.)

CPU Mining

CPU mining was very popular and, in fact, was the only method of mining in the early days of Bitcoin and other cryptocurrencies, pre-ASIC. Since then, specialized mining hardware has evolved to be much more effective and efficient. However, it is still viable to CPU mine on a variety of smaller cryptocurrencies or cryptocurrencies that intentionally discourage the development of ASICs, such as

Monero. These days, almost nobody builds CPU "rigs." Instead, you either use a spare computer that's sitting around or decide that if you have a GPU rig running, you may as well use the CPU in the rig, too. It's there, controlling the GPU cards, so why not use the additional computational power that is sitting idle to mine as well?

Still, the easiest way to mine using a CPU in a spare machine is by using pool software, such as NiceHash, Cudo Miner, and Kryptex. You can also use other programs, such as Easyminer and Hive OS.

If you want to solo mine, you'll generally install the cryptocurrency's core software on the computer holding the CPU you're planning to use, though a few other solo-mining programs are also available to use. We talk more about mining software in the next section.

REMEMBER

With any form of mining, you need to understand the numbers and whether you can mine profitably (see Chapter 7 of this minibook). This is even more important with CPU mining, which is far less likely to be profitable.

Mining Software

After you have your hardware running, you'll need to install the appropriate software. The software you'll use depends on whether you're pool mining or solo mining, your hardware setup (ASIC, GPU, or CPU), and the particular cryptocurrency you plan to mine.

In some cases, the mining software replaces the entire operating system (ethOS and Braiins OS, or Braiins OS+, for example), but in other cases, the software is application software that runs within another operating system, typically Windows, Linux, or macOS (such as MultiMiner, NiceHash, and Cudo Miner).

Pool mining

Pool mining (which we discuss at length in Chapter 3 of this minibook) is a cooperative mining system: Thousands of individual miners work together to mine blocks. They share in the rewards proportional to their individual contributions of hash power.

We recommend pool mining for steady and consistent mining rewards, and later in this section, we discuss some software options for getting your mining rig (CPUs, ASICs, and GPUs) set up and working with a mining pool. Some work with all three, while some only work with one of these systems.

If you bought an ASIC or a prebuilt GPU rig, your rig most likely already has mining software installed on it. ASIC mining rigs generally come equipped with a manufacturer-provided operating system (running on the ASIC's control board), with a simple graphical user interface. You will work with this operating system from another computer connected to your local network; you'll use a web browser to navigate to the unit's IP address on the LAN.

See the manufacturer's documentation to properly set up the mining software. For a view of a typical mining manufacturer's GUI, refer to the snapshot in Figure 6-6 showing the pool-configuration screen in the software that ships with Bitmain's ASICs, and the discussion earlier in this chapter in the section, "A computer to control your rig." If you purchased a prebuilt GPU frame, it most likely comes with an operating system and mining software, too.

However, many of these manufacturer-provided systems are not open-source. Some implementations have been prone to issues, such as backdoors, remote monitoring, and lack of full overclocking or other efficiency limitations, so miners often replace the manufacturer's software. (If you're interested in finding out more about possible efficiency limitations or backdoors, search for *bitmain asic-boost scandal* and *antbleed scandal*.)

A lot of downloadable programs are specifically designed for mining cryptocurrencies. However, many of them are from unreliable sources, and some may include malware or other computer viruses. We have compiled this list of reliable mining software programs designed to mine towards pools:

» **ethOS:** This Linux-based mining operating system for GPU cryptocurrency mining rigs is highly recommended for pool mining GPU applications and is easy to install, set up, and operate (for people who have worked with Linux software!). ethOS currently supports mining Ethereum, Zcash, Monero, and others. ethOS is free software licensed under the General Public License (GNU), but it is highly recommended that you purchase a copy to support the ongoing development of the software. (While free, it is not open source; it is, according to the website, provided under the "'Small Goat with Red Eyes' license. You should buy one ethOS from gpuShack.com per each rig on which you intend to run ethOS. If you don't, a small goat with red eyes will visit you while you sleep.") The software can be directly downloaded, or you can purchase a preloaded flash drive or SSD. Follow the documentation to get your mining rig fully set up and hashing (http://ethosdistro.com).

» **NiceHash:** This is a pool-mining service and mining configuration software (which also allows people to buy and sell hash rate; see Chapter 3 of this minibook) that is used for a wide variety of different cryptocurrencies. It is specifically designed to mine via GPUs, ASICs, and CPUs and runs only on the Windows operating system. So, you could GPU mine by installing it into the

Windows operating system that is installed in your mining rig, and CPU mine by running it on a Windows PC to use that computer's CPU. To ASIC mine, you use its instructions to point your ASIC rig to its server (see Figure 6-18). Follow the documentation to get your mining rig fully set up and hashing (www.nicehash.com).

>> **Honeyminer:** Honeyminer is another pool-mining service that provides its own software for you to work with (Windows and macOS). You can use it on your desktop computer (or GPU mining rig, if Windows is installed) to mine using whatever CPU and GPUs the software finds. It will mine toward whatever cryptocurrency is most profitable but pays out rewards in Satoshi, the smallest denomination of Bitcoin. Follow the documentation to get your mining rig fully set up and hashing. See Chapter 3 of this minibook for a quick example (https://honeyminer.com).

>> **Easyminer:** This free, open-source mining tool allows for the mining of various coins, such as Bitcoin, Dogecoin, Litecoin, and others. It can be configured to mine with CPUs, GPUs, and ASICs and can mine pointed to a pool as well as solo mine. It runs only in Windows (www.easyminer.net).

>> **Hive OS:** Hive OS is a free operating system for up to three mining rigs but requires a monthly fee for larger deployments. It can be configured to mine with CPUs, GPUs, and ASICs and can mine a variety of different hashing algorithms (https://hiveos.farm).

>> **Braiins OS:** Braiins OS is a great alternative to manufacturer-provided web-based GUIs when mining Bitcoin on ASIC rigs. It is an open-source, completely auditable, operating system designed for the Antminer S9 and the DragonMint T1 ASICs (and maybe more by the time you read this). In some hardware configurations, it allows for an increase in hash power with the same electricity expenditures, increasing your efficiency and returns. Follow the documentation and installation guide to flash the operating system software to your mining rig's control board to get set up and hashing toward your chosen pool (https://braiins.com).

>> **Mother of Dragons:** Mother of Dragons is software that runs on your Linux computer (implementations such as Debian, Ubuntu, and CentOS) or other LAN-connected Linux-based device, such as a Raspberry Pi (a tiny, cheap, single-board computer; see www.raspberrypi.org). You enter your settings — pool server, user, password, clock speed, fan speed — and then the software automatically detects ASIC miners (DragonMint/Innosilicon) that are connected to your network and changes their settings. It has a built-in monitoring system and will also update firmware for your ASICs as well as reboot any miners that fall offline. It saves quite a bit of work, but is built for the expert user. Follow the documentation on the following GitHub page for setup instructions: https://github.com/brndnmtthws/mother-of-dragons.

>> **MultiMiner:** MultiMiner is an open-source mining tool designed for Windows, Linux, and macOS. It is designed to work with GPUs, ASICs, and FPGAs (Field Programmable Gate Arrays). MultiMiner actually uses the BFGMiner mining engine (discussed in the later section, "Solo mining") in combination with an easy-to-use interface for simple configuration and monitoring. It can be configured to mine toward pools and, similar to Mother of Dragons, it has monitoring systems and automatic updates (https://github.com/nwoolls/MultiMiner).

FIGURE 6-18:
To ASIC mine with NiceHash, pick an algorithm and server location, and NiceHash tells you how to configure your ASIC.

TECHNICAL STUFF

Although setting up pool-mining software designed for Windows and macOS to run on your laptop or desktop PC is generally pretty simple (as you can see in Chapter 3 of this minibook, for example), working with some of these other systems can be far more complicated.

Setting up, say, ethOS or Braiins OS can be fairly straightforward for an experienced Linux user. However, if you've never left the Windows or macOS operating systems or your idea of dealing with a complicated software installation process is letting your employer's tech guy have the computer for the afternoon, then some of this stuff will be out of your zone of experience! You'll either need to find a friendly geek to help, or understand that you will have to read instructions very carefully and quite likely will expend serious amounts of time finding out how to get the job done.

FPGA?

FPGA (Field Programmable Gate Array) chips are for really advanced, truly expert miners, not for beginners to dabble in as they can be quite difficult to work with. FPGAs are configurable computer chips — blank slates, in effect. Unlike most computer chips that come from the manufacturer already configured and ready to use, FPGAs are designed to be configured by the user.

FPGA chips are sometimes used to mine cryptocurrencies, such as Monero, which discourages the user of ASICs. The Monero community changes the algorithm periodically to make it hard for manufacturers to design, build, and distribute ASICs for Monero. (By the time an ASIC can be brought to market, the algorithm changes again.) Expert miners use FPGAs as a more efficient way to mine Monero than CPU or GPU mining. These miners will reprogram the chips when the algorithm is changed. They are, in effect, homemade ASICs, though generally not as efficient as a true ASIC would be. They may also be used for smaller, unpopular coins that do not have a large enough market to encourage manufacturers to design ASICs for them.

WARNING

Most mining software is designed for ASIC and GPU mining because they are the most efficient systems and the sorts of systems used by most experienced miners. The non-ASIC cryptocurrencies, such as Monero, are an exception, as they are intended to be mined with CPUs and GPUs. (If you can GPU mine, you can CPU mine, too, but GPUs are far more powerful.) Some mining programs do work with CPUs. However, in many cases, miners who are CPU mining Monero or smaller cryptocurrencies simply use the *core software* — the software provided by the cryptocurrency itself — either on the cryptocurrency website or from the cryptocurrency's GitHub account. However, it is difficult to CPU mine profitably. Most Monero miners are GPU mining, though they often also use the CPU in the GPU rig.

It's generally not worth it to CPU mine. If you do intend to mine with your CPU, probably the only software it makes sense to use is NiceHash.

Solo mining

Solo mining is not recommended unless you have very carefully run the numbers (see Chapter 7 of this minibook) and are sure it makes sense. You need to fully understand and accept your odds (which may be low), or you need a significant enough network hash rate to ensure profitability. With that said, quite a few software implementations allow for configurable solo mining.

Most solo mining tools require that you download and sync a full node of the cryptocurrency you intend to mine on a separate computer system on your network, and then point the software running on your ASIC or GPU mining rig to the full node on that computer. Heavily research the documentation for the software you plan on using before firing up your mining equipment.

Check out the following list of solo-mining software:

>> **Core Cryptocurrency Software:** Some cryptocurrencies, such as Monero, have mining functionality built into the GUI of their core full-node software (Bitcoin also did at one point, though it's been removed). Simply download their core node, sync up to the blockchain (this may take a while), and enable mining under the Mining tab. Refer to the cryptocurrency's main site for the software download and documentation. (For example, for Monero, go to `https://web.getmonero.org/get-started/mining`.)

>> **CGMiner:** CGMiner is open-source software created for Bitcoin mining with ASICs or FPGAs and runs on Linux, Windows, and macOS. Its codebase is also open source (`https://en.bitcoin.it/wiki/CGMiner`).

>> **BTCminer:** BTCminer is a Bitcoin-mining software designed for FPGA mining that is open source. It runs on Windows and Linux (`https://en.bitcoin.it/wiki/BTCMiner`).

>> **BFGMiner:** This free and open-source software for Windows, macOS, and Linux can be configured for mining with CPUs, GPUs, FPGAs, and ASICs (`https://en.bitcoin.it/wiki/BFGMiner`).

Chapter **7**

Running the Numbers: Is It Worth It?

The best way to avoid making bad investments in the cryptocurrency mining industry is to do your homework and research before putting any considerable amount of funding into cloud-mining services, personal mining hardware, or hash-rate marketplaces. You really need to understand the numbers so you can see whether you're likely to be able to make money.

In this chapter, we walk through the various aspects of cryptocurrency mining equipment and deployment benchmarks that can help you figure out whether your planned arrangements will lead to mining profitability.

Factors That Determine Mining Profitability

When you're calculating the rate of return on your investment (ROI), consider these factors:

>> Cost of your equipment

>> Hash rate of your equipment

>> Efficiency of your equipment

>> Maintenance costs

>> Facility costs (renting space, cost of cooling the space, and so on)

>> Electricity costs to run your equipment

>> Total network hash rate of the cryptocurrency you're planning to mine

>> If you're mining through a pool (see Chapter 3 of this minibook), the proportion of the total network hash rate provided by the pool and fees charged by the pool

>> Block earnings (block subsidy and transaction fees)

>> Conversion rate of the cryptocurrency into your local fiat currency

In the following sections, we look at these factors one by one and then bring them all together to help you calculate your potential ROI.

Cost of equipment

A significant factor determining mining profitability is the initial cost of your equipment. Equipment costs are often the largest portion of capital expenditures (CapEx) for cryptocurrency mining endeavors. *CapEx* is defined as costs incurred by businesses or organizations to secure equipment, assets, or locations.

New cryptocurrency mining equipment, both capable GPUs and application specific integrated circuit (ASIC) miners, fluctuate wildly in purchase price depending on demand and market sentiment. In 2019, the market prices for some top-of-the-line Bitcoin SHA-256 ASIC mining rigs varied from $10 to $60 USD per TH/s. (See Figure 7-1 for a visualization of this data for each mining rig, and see Figure 7-2 for a normalized cost per TH/s.) This variation in price mostly depends on the age of the equipment and unit efficiency (the amount of electricity consumed per TH/s; see Chapter 5 of this minibook), as well as its popularity and the age of the mining rig. Cost per TH/s is higher for newer, more efficient hardware. Older and less-capable mining equipment is generally sold at lower prices, and the newest and most electrically efficient gear is sold at a premium. In fact, it's sometimes hard to buy new ASIC releases at the manufacturer's intended retail price, as fresh inventory is often low and speculators snap them up and resell them at higher prices, in some cases two or three times the original price.

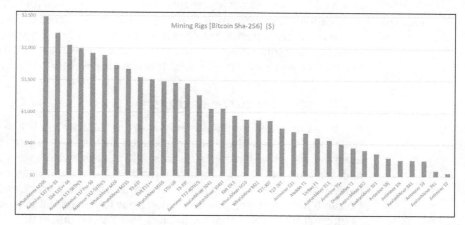

FIGURE 7-1: Purchase cost in U.S. dollars, in 2019, of some of the latest and most capable SHA-256 Bitcoin-mining ASICs.

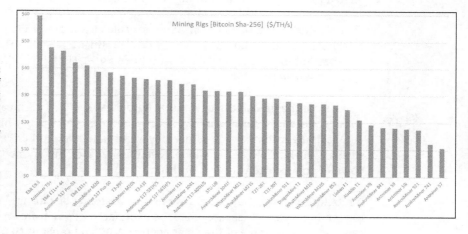

FIGURE 7-2: Purchase cost of SHA-256 mining ASICs, in U.S. dollars per hash rate (TH/s), of some of the latest and most capable Bitcoin-mining equipment at time of this writing.

So there's a balance to be considered here. If ASIC A is cheaper than ASIC B in terms of TH/s, it may be because it is less efficient; that is, it may be costing you more in electricity for each tera hash per second (each trillion hashing operations per second). See Chapter 5 of this minibook for a breakdown of mining gear efficiency for various hash algorithms.

Hash rate of your equipment

You need to know the hash rate of the equipment you own or the equipment you plan to buy. You can figure out the hash rate of equipment in a few ways.

REMEMBER

We want to reiterate that your equipment doesn't have an inherent hash rate. Rather, it has a hash rate specified for a particular mining algorithm. ASICs, of course, are designed for a particular algorithm. But CPUs and GPUs can be used with various cryptocurrencies and their algorithms. Thus, a GPU, for example, can have different hash rates depending on the different cryptocurrencies you're interested in mining. So before you can figure out a CPU or GPU hash rate, you need to know for *which* algorithm you're trying to discover the hardware's hash rate.

ASIC manufacturer ratings

If you've purchased, or plan to purchase, an ASIC, the job is easy; the manufacturer should provide the equipment's rated hash rate. (Refer to Chapter 5 of this minibook for a list of manufacturer-specified hash rates, in tera hashes per second, for some of the most capable Bitcoin SHA-256 mining ASICs on the market today.) As always, though, make sure to do your homework and due diligence. Research manufacturer documentation prior to purchase and study forums, such as BitcoinTalk.org, or social media sites, like Twitter or Reddit, to find discussions related to your prospective mining equipment.

Figure 7-3 shows a selection of ASICs for sale at Amazon. Notice the text in the product description stating the hash rate: AntMiner L3+ ~504MH/s, AntMiner V9 ~4TH/s, AntMiner S9 ~14.0TH/s, AntMiner V9 ~4TH/s (~ is the mathematical symbol for *approximation*).

TECHNICAL STUFF

What about the Innosilicon device that outputs 50Ksol/s? This means 50,000 *solutions* per second, a term you may hear sometimes, particularly in relation to the Equihash algorithm, which is used by Zcash and some other cryptocurrencies, such as Bitcoin Gold and Komodo. (See Chapter 4 of this minibook for a breakdown of cryptocurrencies by algorithm.)

A retailer's website may not always list the hash rate of a device you're considering mining with. In that case, go to the manufacturer's website for the details. You can find a list of some of the most popular ASIC and prebuilt GPU mining equipment manufacturers in Chapter 5 of this minibook.

Processor benchmarking sites

Another way to find your equipment's hash rate is to check out the third-party mining-equipment benchmark sites. These are particularly useful if you're planning to mine using CPUs or GPUs, for which the hash rate is not published by the manufacturers (because they're not designed for cryptocurrency mining!).

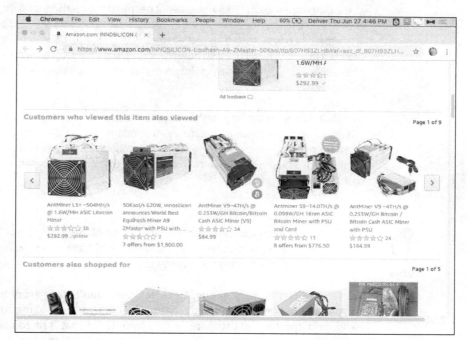

FIGURE 7-3:
A snapshot of an Amazon page showing ratings of various ASIC mining rigs from the fall of 2019.

HASHES VERSUS SOLUTIONS

Unfortunately, there is a lot of confusion in the Equihash community about *solutions* and *hashes* and their relationship. This confusion exists because cryptocurrency algorithms are complicated, and it's possible to mine without understanding them. Miners need to understand how to set up and operate the relevant hardware and software but not the function of the underlying, and highly complex, algorithm. Few miners intimately understand the algorithms they're using.

However, this lack of understanding has caused a little problem: While some equipment may be rated in *solutions per second,* some online mining calculators for Equihash cryptocurrencies require that you enter the *hashes per second* for your equipment. While MinerGate (https://minergate.com/calculator/equihash) uses solutions/second, for example, WhatToMine (https://whattomine.com/coins/166-zec-equihash), CryptoCompare (www.cryptocompare.com/mining/calculator/zec), and Minerstat (https://minerstat.com/coin/ARRR) all use hashes/second.

(continued)

(continued)

Solutions — or *sols*, as they're known in the Equihash community — are solutions to the Equihash proof-of-work challenge. Equihash's puzzle is a variation of what is known as the Birthday Problem (With *x* number of people in the room, what is the likelihood of two people having the same birthday?). Just like with Bitcoin's SHA-256 algorithm, in which every hash is tested against a target, with Equihash, each "solution" is tested against a target. In fact, Equihash doesn't use hashing in the same way SHA-256 does, and hashes per second is really an inappropriate metric; solutions per second is more correct.

Still, you'll sometimes see the hashes/second metric used in relation to Equihash and can usually assume it's being used to mean solutions/second. If you plan to mine an Equihash cryptocurrency, though, you should probably make sure of that when it really counts, such as when making calculations related to profitability based on expressed hashes/second.

REMEMBER

The hash rate depends not only on the power of the equipment but also on the cryptocurrency algorithm being used. A GPU will have a hash rate of *x* on cryptocurrency *A* but of *y* on cryptocurrency *B*.

These sites can be very handy. However, they don't have every processor listed, so you may not be lucky enough to find the data you're looking for. (On the other hand, perhaps you can estimate — find equipment that *is* rated and that is similar to your hardware, based on more general CPU and GPU metrics.)

Check out the following list of benchmarking sites for various devices, including CPUs, GPUs, and ASICs:

>> **CPU Benchmarks**

- Monero Benchmarks (`https://monerobenchmarks.info`)

>> **GPU Benchmarks**

- Bitcoin Wiki Benchmarks (`https://en.bitcoin.it/wiki/Non-specialized_hardware_comparison`)

- WhatToMine GPU specifications (`https://whattomine.com`)

- Miningchamp GPU lists (`https://miningchamp.com`)

>> **ASIC SHA-256 gear**

- Crypto Mining Tools Benchmarks (`https://cryptomining.tools/compare-mining-hardware`)

- Bitcoin Wiki Benchmarks (`https://en.bitcoin.it/wiki/Mining_hardware_comparison`)

You can also find tools that combine information related to the performance of the equipment with an actual profitability calculator. See, for example, `https://whattomine.com/miners`.

Mining pools

Another way to figure out the hashing power of your gear is to use it for mining. Find a reputable mining pool for the cryptocurrency you're interested in, create an account, set up your gear, and let it run for a while. The mining pool software will tell you what your hash rate is for that cryptocurrency. See Chapter 3 of this minibook for more information on mining pools.

Downloadable processor testers

What if the equipment you're attempting to utilize for cryptocurrency mining doesn't have hash-rate specifications listed from the manufacturer and isn't listed on any of the preceding benchmarking sites? If you don't want to bother setting up a pool account, here's another way to discover your hash rate.

Search for *what is my hash rate,* or a similar phrase, and you'll likely find sites that provide programs that run on your system and check your hash rate. They generally do this by actually mining, so the site providing the download is using your processing power to actually mine and earn them cryptocurrency.

WARNING

However, be careful with such sites. They may also come with adware, malware, or worse! We don't advise using these services unless you're absolutely sure they're safe. (We don't feel confident enough in any of them to actually list them here, so definitely research them prior to using them, and download them at your own risk.)

Mining rig efficiency

Behind operational expenditures (which we discuss further in the section, "Cost of electricity") and capital expenditures, the next most important factor in a cost/benefit analysis for your mining operation is your mining equipment efficiency. This number is determined by your mining equipment hash rate (hashes per second) as well as the unit's power consumption, normally measured in watts.

As explained in Chapter 5 of this minibook that these two pieces of data can be combined to form an efficiency metric for each piece of equipment. This mining rig efficiency is typically specified in joules per tera hash per second (or, depending on the equipment, joules per giga hash, or joules per mega hash). As shown in Chapter 5, a joule is a unit of energy, which can be considered equivalent to a watt of power consumption per second. A tera hash is a trillion hashes, a giga hash is a billion hashes, and a mega hash is a million hashes. See Chapter 5 in this mini-book for figures showing mining rig efficiency of popular ASICs running on some of the more common hash algorithms.

Hash-rate capability

Mining rig effectiveness, and thus its profitability, hinges on the hash rate that the equipment can output toward the blockchain proof-of-work algorithm for the cryptocurrency you choose to mine — that is, how many hashes the equipment can process each second. The more hashes your equipment processes every second, the higher your proportion of the network hash rate, which translates to you earning more of the mined cryptocurrency. (As we we explain in Chapters 4 and 5 of this minibook, as we explain in Chapters 4 and 5 of this minibook, that in general and over a long enough period of time, you earn a proportion of the network's mining rewards equal to the proportion of the network hash rate that you provide.)

See Chapter 5 of this minibook for a graph of the hash-rate rankings of a range of popular Bitcoin SHA-256 mining ASICs as well as other common hash algorithms. For a quick summary of estimated GPU mining hash-rate capabilities toward the Ethereum Ethash algorithm, see Figure 7-4. These ratings range anywhere from 5 to 40 mega hashes per second; note that they do not include GPU overclocking and act only as an estimation.

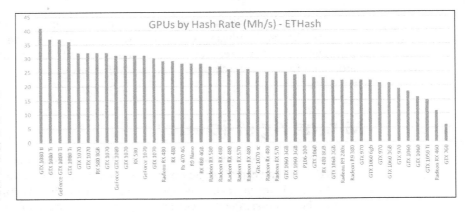

FIGURE 7-4: Hash rates for a range of common GPU cards in 2019, mining Ether using the Ethereum proof-of-work algorithm Ethash.

TECHNICAL STUFF

Overclocking is a term used to describe increasing the output of a computer processor above the standard manufacture rating by increasing its clock rate, or frequency, which can sometimes be done through the BIOS or through manufacturer's software. For example, to overclock a piece of hardware, you could increase the frequency of the equipment in the settings from 600 MHz to 750 MHz. (*MHz* or *megahertz* is a unit of frequency cycle time measuring a million times per second.) Overclocking produces more heat, consumes more electricity, and ultimately produces more hash-rate capabilities in a cryptocurrency-mining application. The practice of overclocking is hard on processing units and can reduce the life of equipment, though miners sometimes do overclock. Miners may overclock a piece of equipment they know is coming to the end of its life, for example, because its hash rate is quickly dropping as a percentage of the network hash rate.

Efficiency

The combination of the mining equipment's hash rate with the mining equipment's power consumption provides you with an important metric to determine your hardware's efficiency. The more efficient your mining equipment is, the more profitable it will be.

As discussed in Chapter 5 of this minibook, efficiency is typically defined as useful work performed divided by energy expended to do that work. However, when it comes to typical mining hardware, manufacturers often list this metric in reverse. Mining equipment efficiency is often listed as the energy expended (joules) divided by the work performed (hashes/second).

For an efficiency comparison of a range of popular Bitcoin network SHA-256 and other common algorithms' ASIC mining hardware, see Chapter 5 of this minibook. In Figure 7-5, you can see an efficiency comparison for a variety of top GPU cards when used to mine Ethereum's Ethash hashing algorithm. The typical unit used to rank these graphics cards by efficiency is joules per mega hash per second or J/MH/s.

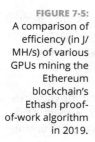

FIGURE 7-5:
A comparison of efficiency (in J/MH/s) of various GPUs mining the Ethereum blockchain's Ethash proof-of-work algorithm in 2019.

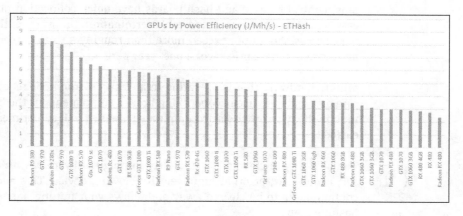

Cost of maintenance

While most of the mining equipment on the market today is highly reliable, failures still occur, and so a maintenance cost is associated with those breakdowns.

The most likely components to fail on cryptocurrency mining hardware, for both ASIC and GPU deployments, are the fans that distribute air to cool the heat syncs. These fans spin at thousands of rotations per minute, and with 24/7 operation, they are likely to fail every once in a while. Luckily, these fans are standardized, very affordable (ranging anywhere from $15 to $25), and can often be found at the manufacturer's website, any electronics store, or your favorite online marketplace.

ASIC mining hardware has a control board that senses fan failure, safely shuts down mining, places the hardware into a failure alert state, and (normally) displays a red LED light. This is to alert the equipment operator of the failure and protect the equipment. For GPUs, the boards will lower their output to what the thermal management system can handle while the fan has failed. Unfortunately, GPU fans are not as standardized or easy to fix and will most likely warrant an entire GPU replacement upon failure.

Another component that sometimes fails is commonly referred to as a *hashing board*. ASIC mining rigs normally have three or so of these hashing boards, and a single board can contain many ASIC chips. The hashing boards connect directly to the ASIC controller. (In general, the controllers do not seem to fail very often, as they're not running the processes that heat up the ASIC mining chips and lead to failure.) However, when the control boards do fail, their replacement price can range anywhere from $150 to $750 (these are commonly sold by the original equipment manufacturer [OEM]).

The hashing boards can be replaced fairly easily, and many manufacturers or online marketplaces have them for sale independently of the mining rigs. The fans, control boards, and hash boards have quick connection plugs to allow for easy and fast replacement and cable termination. On average, the total maintenance costs should not exceed more than roughly 5 to 10 percent of the mining hardware purchase price over a one-year period.

Mining hardware that is operating in a clean environment requires only limited care and maintenance beyond fixing broken components. If the hardware is running in dusty or otherwise contaminated areas, it will sometimes also need to be cleaned.

TIP

The best way to clean dusty and dirty mining hardware is with an air compressor, canned air, or other high-velocity blowing device. This allows most of the contaminants to be cleared away and allows your mining hardware to continue hashing along.

Cost of facilities

If you choose to deploy your mining hardware at home, the majority of your facility costs should already be taken care of in your normal expenses. Some hosting or mining service providers, however, charge anywhere from $100 to $160 USD per month to run your equipment at their facilities, electricity not included. See Chapter 5 of this minibook for popular cryptocurrency mining hosting providers.

A commercial data center may, however, charge a much steeper fee. In any deployment case, how you cool your equipment — whether by exhausting wasted heat, cooling it with an air conditioner, or using the heat to warm the space — also determines your facility's cost. Cooling your equipment and space with an air conditioner would be the most effective but also the most expensive method. If you can find some way to reuse your exhausted heat, you may be able to enjoy significant savings.

Predicting exactly how much cooling you'll need is difficult, but consider this. You can assume that all the electricity that goes into your mining equipment comes out as heat. Thus, if you are running a 1,500W ASIC, it's the equivalent of running a 1,500W room heater (a pretty common spec for a room heater, and in fact, if you visit your local hardware store, you'll probably find that most of the heaters they sell are 1,500W or less). So you can at least get an idea of how much heat you're going to be creating, and perhaps that can help you determine how much cooling you'll need.

Cost of electricity

One of the most important costs that goes into your mining profitability calculations is the cost of electricity. In fact, the cost of electricity for cryptocurrency mining equipment and operations *is* the largest part of your mining operational expenditures.

These operational expenditures, commonly referred to as *OpEx*, are the recurring expenses or costs of running a business, venture, or, in this case, a cryptocurrency mining operation. In fact, electricity costs are so significant in mining that cryptocurrency miners often go out of their way — literally — to seek cheap electricity. Cheap access to energy allows a cryptocurrency mine to remain profitable with even less-than-optimal hardware. This is why you may have heard of people, such as students mining in college dorms, stealing electricity to mine with. You can't get cheaper — and thus more economically efficient — than sourcing electricity for free! (No, we are not recommending this.)

To further reduce energy bills, you could develop your own auxiliary energy sources with no fuel costs, such as renewables, hydroelectricity, wind, or solar. Other mining deployments use resources, such as flared, unmarketable, and otherwise wasted natural gas (methane), and repurpose that energy toward mining cryptocurrencies. A cryptocurrency mining company that has made its mark specializing in this type of deployment is Upstream Data Inc. (www.upstreamdata.ca).

Wherever you're getting your electricity, your operation's cost of electricity depends on two things: how much electricity you're going to use, and how much you're going to be charged for each unit of electricity.

Measuring your power consumption

Similar to manufacturer-specified hash rate, most ASIC mining equipment has a rated power consumption value in watts from the manufacturer. (Refer to Chapter 5 of this minibook to see a list of some of the more popular SHA-256 Bitcoin network mining hardware and its manufacture-rated power consumption ranked in watts.) This data is helpful in planning electrical infrastructure as well as calculating cryptocurrency revenue and ROI.

Finding this data is more of a problem when mining using CPUs or GPUs. In fact, they use different amounts of electricity when mining different cryptocurrencies, as the algorithms require different levels of processing power.

You can estimate power consumption for GPU and CPU hardware by using the manufacturer's maximum power rating associated with these processor devices. However, in many cases, this may overestimate power utilization and won't be a precise number, and so it will affect your ROI calculations. In Figure 7-6, you can see estimated power consumption for some of the more popular GPU cards when they're mining the Ethereum Ethash mining algorithm.

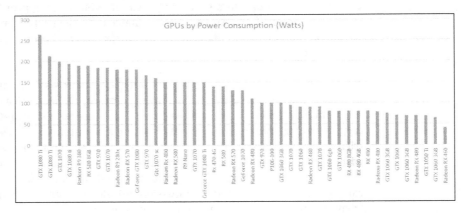

FIGURE 7-6: Estimated power consumption of a variety of popular GPUs on the market in 2019, mining with the Ethereum Ethash mining algorithm.

The best way to figure out your gear's power consumption is to measure it directly. Ideally, of course, you would measure the power consumption while it's actually hashing the particular algorithm used by the cryptocurrency you want to mine, but if you haven't started mining yet, um, you can't do that.

A few devices can measure power consumption, such as a Fluke full watt meter that measures voltage and amperage. However, these devices can be fairly costly and difficult to operate.

TIP

We recommend a simpler device, a basic electricity usage meter (which you can often find for around $30 at your local hardware store or online), such as the Kill A Watt meter. Plug the device into a 120V wall socket and then plug your computer equipment into the socket on the front of the device, and it will show you real-time power consumption.

Finding the cost of electricity

After you determine how much electricity you'll use, you need to figure out the unit cost of the power. Electric utility providers generally bill in total consumed kilowatt-hour (kWh) energy increments over a monthly billing period. To find what your energy charge is per kWh, study your electric bill at the location where you intend to mine, check the utility's website, or call your electric utility provider. (See Chapter 5 of this minibook for more information on finding your electricity cost.)

On average in the United States, electricity ranges from $0.08 to $0.15 per kWh, not including any connection or service charges. For our example calculations here, we will assume $0.10 per kWh.

Estimating monthly energy usage and cost

After you have an estimate or measurement of your mining equipment's instantaneous electrical power consumption, measured in watts, extrapolating that to kWh is a matter of simple arithmetic.

A kWh is 1,000 watts of consumption over a one-hour period. There are 24 hours in a day, as you probably know, and on average, about 30 days in any given month (30 days and 10 hours, if you want to be more precise). This makes for about 720 hours in the average month (okay, 730). This value allows you to multiply your measured or estimated mining hardware power value in watts by 730 hours for a quick estimate of monthly energy consumption as measured in kWh.

So, if you discover that your device is using 1,280W (the consumption level of the Antminer S9 SE, for example), then running the device for an hour uses 1,280Wh (watt-hours), or 1.28kWh. Multiply that by 730 hours in a typical month, and we end up with 934.4kWh.

So now all this information can be combined into a single equation: power (watts) * time (hours) = energy (kWh). This energy value can then be converted into local electrical cost with this equation: energy (kWh) * price ($) per energy (kWh) = total energy cost ($).

So, if your cryptocurrency mining hardware draws an instantaneous electrical power value of 1,280 watts, and your electricity price per kWh is $0.10, this is how you would estimate your monthly electrical bill:

1,280 watts * 730 hours = 934.4kWh

934.4kWh * $0.10 per kWh = $93.44/month in electricity costs

Some electrical utilities also charge a demand fee, capacity charge, or maximum power (kW) consumption charge, ranging from a few dollars to upwards of $15 per kW. The fee is generally charged to particular customer classes, such as commercial and industrial (though if you build a large enough mining operation at home, you may end up changing your class!).

The charge is calculated based on the 15-minute period during the month that had the highest electric power consumption. In other words, you multiply the demand charge by the highest kW level you reach at any point during the month.

Say that you have a mining operation that at some point during the month reaches 5kW, and your utility has an $8 demand charge. In this case, you'd be charged $40. (You may reach this peak for only 15 minutes, or consume that much power over the entire month; regardless, the demand charge is the same.)

Total network hash rate

You're also going to need to know the network hash rate for the cryptocurrency you plan to mine. The always-useful BitInfoCharts site provides hash rates (and much, much more) for many of the most popular cryptocurrency networks (see https://bitinfocharts.com). If you can't find it there, you may find it on the cryptocurrency's own website, at a pool mining site, or through an online search.

Again, your revenues will be in proportion to the amount of the network's hash rate that you provide. Provide 1 percent of the hash rate, and, over time, you're likely to earn 1 percent of the network's mining rewards. (We're using 1 percent as an example, of course; you're unlikely to be able to provide such a large proportion of the hash rate, even for smaller, less popular cryptocurrencies.)

Nothing lasts forever, though. Typically, over the life of a cryptocurrency (assuming it's successful and lasts), the network hash rate steadily increases. More miners enter the market, and the equipment being added becomes more efficient.

Only in a handful of instances over the past decade of the Bitcoin network's existence, for example, has hash rate dropped and block difficulty gone down. (This has happened after the value of Bitcoin has dropped significantly, dragging down market sentiment with it.) So, as the network hash rate goes up, your equipment's proportion of the hash rate goes down, of course (unless you add more equipment). And as your proportion of the hash rate goes down, so, too, does the proportion of the rewards you earn. In other words, a mining rig that provides a constant hash rate toward the network will produce a diminishing return as measured in the asset being mined, as both the network hash rate and mining competition increases.

In terms of your local fiat currency, however, that may still be fine. If the proportion of the cryptocurrency that you earn goes down, while the value of the cryptocurrency, say, doubles, you're still ahead of the game. See Book 5, Chapter 9 for more about fiat currencies.

Information about your pool

If you're working with a pool, you need information about that pool. (In fact, you may want to run the calculations for both pool mining and solo mining.)

You need to know several things: the pool's total hash rate, how often the pool mines a block, and how much reward is paid to the miners each time the pool mines a block (that is, the block subsidies and transaction fees, minus the fees charged by the pool). You can find this information at the pool's website, of course. See Chapter 3 of this minibook for more information on pools and links to various pools.

Block earnings

Our calculations require some information about the blocks you intend to mine. We need to know two things: how often the network adds a block to the blockchain, and what the winning miner earns when the block is added — the block subsidy, if any, and the transaction fees, if the miner earns those. (Different networks pay miners in different ways. See Chapter 3 of this minibook for more information.)

The rate at which each cryptocurrency adds blocks to the blockchain, as well as the amount of the rewards paid for each block, varies by cryptocurrency. This data also varies in time due to transaction-fee and hash-power fluctuations. Fees may vary from block to block and more generally over time, and if hash power has increased since the last block-difficulty adjustment, blocks will be found more frequently. Again, you may be able to find this information on BitInfoCharts (https://bitinfocharts.com) or a similar site, on the cryptocurrency's own website, or through an online search. For the Bitcoin network, you can find the average blocks found by each major pool over a week's time at `https://coin.dance/blocks/thisweek`.

Cryptocurrency conversion rate

Cryptocurrency market values measured in local fiat currencies fluctuate widely in price over any given day, and even more over extended periods. The following sites offer some good resources for checking the exchange rate of the cryptocurrencies you want to mine:

» **CoinMarketCap:** `https://coinmarketcap.com`

» **CoinCap:** `https://coincap.io`

» **Messari:** `https://messari.io/onchainfx`

» **CoinGecko:** `www.coingecko.com/en`

» **BitInfoCharts:** `https://bitinfocharts.com/index_v.html`

» **CryptoCompare:** `www.cryptocompare.com`

» **Coinlib:** `https://coinlib.io`

Calculating Your ROI

After you know the factors that contribute to a mining operation's profitability and return on investment (ROI), you can now run the numbers and see what is likely to happen with your projected mining operation. Will you make money? Or is it a losing proposition?

We end up with two numbers: your absolute gain (or loss), and a percentage ROI number. ROI is typically calculated by the following formula:

Profit divided by Total Investment multiplied by 100 = ROI (%)

If your calculated ROI is a positive percentage, the venture was a net benefit to you. If the percentage is less than zero, you would have been better off staying in bed.

To start, figure out how much cryptocurrency you're going to mine (the value of the block subsidies and transaction fees that you will earn). Oh, and you need to calculate monthly numbers: your income (or loss) and ROI on a monthly basis.

Your block earnings

To estimate your earnings, we begin right at the top, with how much a miner earns each time a block is mined and how often that happens. You'll earn only a fraction of this, but it's our starting point. We begin by calculating under the assumption that you are solo mining — running your equipment directly connected to the cryptocurrency network rather than through a pool. Then we look again at the calculation assuming that you're going to work with a pool.

Calculating for solo mining

We use mining Monero (XMR) in the fall of 2019 as an example. Each time a block is added to the Monero blockchain, the winning miner earns a block subsidy of about 2.6XMR. The miner also earns transaction fees. These fees fluctuate, of course, but at the time of this writing, a good sample average is 0.00277, for a total of 2.60277XMR. At the time of this writing, each Monero coin is worth $104.57, so the total block earnings are around $272.17.

Now, the Monero blockchain adds a block roughly every two minutes (you can find all these Monero stats at `https://bitinfocharts.com/`). So around 720 new blocks are added to the blockchain every day, which comes out to an average of about 21,900 per month.

In 2019, those 21,900 blocks mined each month were therefore worth about 57,000XMR ($5,960,559.33) to the miners (21,900 blocks x 2.60277XMR x $104.57).

Okay, now you need to know how much of that reward you're going to grab. First, we assume that you are solo mining rather than working with a pool. The first thing you need to figure out is what proportion of the blocks you'll mine. You need to divide your hash-rate contribution by the total Monero network hash rate to find the fraction of the network hash rate that you'll provide.

The Monero network has, at the time of this writing, a hash rate of around 325MH/s (mega hashes per second; millions of hashes per second). Assume that you have a fairly nice GPU that will output 1.95 kH/s (kilo hashes per second; thousand hashes per second) — that's how many hashes an AMD RX VEGA 64 GPU will output, for example.

Make sure that you're using the same units, of course. Depending on the cryptocurrency you're working with, your equipment may be rated in GH/s (giga hashes per second, or a billion hashes per second), while the network hash rate may be expressed in, say TH/s (tera hashes per second) or even PH/s (peta hashes per second) 1 trillion hashes per second or 1 quadrillion hashes per second, respectively. Or even EH/s (exa hashes per second; a quintillion hashes per second). So, of course, you'll need to convert one side to match the other before running this calculation.

QUICK CONVERSION

These long numbers get very complex. If you find working with all these zeros confusing, you may want to look for a converter. You may be able to find an actual hash-rate converter (see, for example, https://coinguides.org/hashpower-converter-calculator/), and there are also large-number converters (see, for example, www.endmemo.com/sconvert/billiontrillion.php). Here's a quick tip for converting downward: You can convert downward each level by multiplying by 1,000. Say, for example, your equipment is in GH/s, and the network hash rate is in TH/s. You can convert the network hash rate to GH/s by multiplying the TH/s value by 1,000. Say the network hash rate is 300 TH/s — that's 300,000 GH/s.

You need to divide your mining equipment's hash rate (1.95 kH/s) by the network hash rate (325 MH/s), but you can't simply divide 1.95 by 325, because the first number is stated in thousands and the latter is in millions. The numbers, fully expressed, are

1,950 hashes per second (the equipment hash rate)

325,000,000 hashes per second (the network hash rate)

So you divide 1,950 by 325,000,000 to arrive at 0.000006. That's the fraction of the network hash rate that the equipment will contribute. To see it expressed as a percentage, multiply by 100 (0.0006%).

Okay, so you know that each month during 2019, Monero miners

>> Mined approximately 21,900 blocks

>> Earned approximately 57,000XMR in block subsidies and transaction fees

At that time, this was worth around $5,960,559.33, so

>> 0.0006% of 21,900 was 0.1314 blocks

>> 0.0006% of 57,000XMR was 0.342XMR, or $35.76 at the exchange rate of $104.57.

So, on average, you could expect to earn $93.08 each month with this particular piece of equipment. Of course, you can't mine a fraction of a block, so when the numbers show that you mine, on average, 0.1314 block a month, what this really means is that, on average, you'd mine a block every 7.6 months or so, during 2019. Data today would be slightly different, of course.

Depending on various factors — the popularity of the cryptocurrency you want to mine, the amount of money you're willing to invest in equipment, and so on — you may find that the calculations are telling you that you'll mine a fraction of a block each month. What does that mean? What does it mean, for example, if it tells you that you'll mine 0.01 block each month? It means that, on average, you'll mine a block every 100 months! You may mine and discover a block the very first day, or you may have to wait years before you mine a block!

On average, over time — a hundred years, for example, considering all factors remain stable — you could expect to mine a block every 100 months or so (every 8.33 years). What this is telling you is that your numbers don't work! Your percentage of the hash rate simply isn't enough to mine solo, at least not with the equipment you have or are planning to use. You would need to increase your hash rate — by buying better equipment, or more of it — or you may try pool mining, which provides an effective mechanism for accruing steady mining rewards. (See Chapter 3 of this minibook for more information on working with pools.) See the next section for how to calculate the pool mining numbers.

Calculating for pool mining

If you're mining through a pool, rather than solo mining, you approach the calculation a little differently. You need to know the total hash rate of the pool, how often the pool mines a block on average, and how much all the miners are paid each time a block is mined. From this, you can calculate your earnings.

We use a different example this time. Assume that you are mining Bitcoin with a Bitmain Antminer S9 with a 14 TH/s hash rate. (The Antminer S9 actually comes in a few different batch versions with different hash rates, but we'll use the current highest, 14 TH/s.) You choose to point your mining hardware toward the Slush Pool, which typically mines 10 to 12 blocks per day with a pool hash rate of 5.0 EH/s (5 million TH/s).

We start by calculating your pool contribution percentage. Divide your hash rate by the total pool hash rate, and multiply by 100.

14 / 5,000,000 = 0.0000028

0.0000027 * 100 = 0.00028%

Thus, your hash rate, from your S9, is roughly 0.00028 percent of the Slush Pool's hash rate. So now, to find your estimated earnings for your contribution to the pool, you would take that percentage and multiply it by the average block rewards (the block subsidy and transaction fees).

Now, Slush Pool takes the entire block earnings, both block subsidy and transaction fees, subtracts 2 percent as a pool fee, and pays out the other 98 percent to its miners. At present, the block subsidy for Bitcoin is 6.25 Bitcoin (sometime in 2024, probably in May, this will decrease to 3.125). Transaction fees fluctuate from block to block and day to day, but currently average somewhere around 0.1 to 0.5BTC. Say the average block earns Slush Pool 12.9BTC, of which 98 percent (12.642) is paid out to the miners.

Say that Slush Pool mines 11 blocks a day. That's 139.062BTC being paid out to miners each day. But wait, you're calculating monthly numbers, so multiply that by 30.42 (to get a really average month!); 139.062 x 30.42 is 4,230.26604BTC paid out to miners each month, a considerable sum.

As you saw a moment ago, you are contributing 0.00028 percent of Slush Pool's hash rate; 0.00028 percent of 4,230.26604BTC is 0.01184474491BTC. How much is that in dollars? Well, that depends, of course. At the time of this writing, 1BTC = $11,220.20. (By the time you read this, it could be very different). Thus, 0.01142172BTC is, at the moment, worth $132.90.

So, in this scenario, you would earn $132.90 from a month of mining with an S9 toward the Slush Pool.

TECHNICAL STUFF

In our calculations, we assume a cleanly proportional sharing of the mining rewards. As we point out in Chapter 3 of this minibook, pool rewards are a little more complicated than this. Different pools calculate rewards in different ways, but Slush Pool uses the *scoring hash rate* method (see `https://slushpool.com/help/reward-system`), which can increase or lower your proportion based not only on the total number of hashes you contributed but also on how consistently your equipment was hashing. (Inconsistency may lead to earning a lower proportion. In theory, if you keep your mining equipment running 24/7, you may actually earn a little more than your percentage.)

So, now you know how much money you'll make each month in your local fiat currency (and whether solo or pool mining). Next, you need to know how much it's going to cost to run the mine.

Your expenses

This step's a little simpler. You need to know how much you're spending in order to run your mining operation over a month. Add up these numbers:

>> Maintenance costs per month

>> Facility costs per month

>> Electricity costs per month

You may also amortize your equipment. Consider how long you are likely to use your equipment — how long it will remain viable considering increasing network hash rates and the increasing efficiency of new ASICs. You may, for example, divide the cost of your equipment by 36 and apply the value to your monthly expenses, allowing three years of use. Or perhaps you may allow for four years and divide by 48 months.

Calculating ROI

You're almost there, and the next step is so simple, you may have already jumped ahead. You know how much you'll earn each month *(Earnings)*, and how much it's going to cost to run the operation *(Expenses)*. So now you can calculate the profit and ROI like this:

Earnings – Expenses = Profit/Loss

If, for example, you're mining enough blocks each month to make $1,200 once the cryptocurrency is converted to dollars (or whatever fiat currency you work with), and you're spending $800 to run the operation, then

$1,200 – $800 = $400 profit

As for a percentage ROI, we calculate it like this:

(Profit or Loss/Expenses) * 100 = % ROI

So, with the previous example,

($400/$800) * 100 = 50% ROI

Of course, if you're losing money, the calculation looks a little different. Say that your expenses are still $800, but you're only earning $600 and thus losing $200 a month. Now the calculation looks like this:

(−$200/$800) * 100 = −25% ROI

For example, if you invested $1,000 into cryptocurrency mining over a certain period and your total revenue from the venture was $1,200, your profit would be $200 from a total investment of $1,000. The ROI formula for this exercise would work out to be 20 percent: ($200/$1,000) * 100 = 20%. But if your $1,000 investment only produced $800 in total revenue, your net profit would be −$200. Thus, your ROI calculation would work out to be negative 20 percent, and you should not have made that investment!

(−$200/$1,000) * 100 = −20%

Knowing the unknowns

Many variables exist in the cryptocurrency mining arena, and only some of them are within your control. As Donald Rumsfeld, former U.S. Secretary of Defense, famously stated, "There are known knowns things we know that we know. There are known unknowns things that we now know we don't know. But there are also unknown unknowns things we do not know we don't know."

In this chapter, we help you figure out the known knowns: the cost of equipment and electricity, your hash rate, the network hash rate, and so on.

But you also need to be aware of the known unknowns. We don't know when the overall network hash rate will rise or by how much or whether it may fall. But we do know this is a possibility and that it will affect the profitability of the mining operation. We don't know how much the value of the cryptocurrency we're mining will fluctuate, but we do know this is a possibility, and we know it will affect profitability, both up and down.

Unfortunately, you can't do much about the known unknowns. At least, we can't help you with them. These are things you'll have to guess at, perhaps based on your belief regarding what is likely to happen with the cryptocurrency you're mining, and you'll have to accept the risks that the unknown unknowns pose. That's the miner's life!

WARNING

Our calculations are based on static metrics. Over time, your proportion of the network hash rate may well drop — though at times it could go up.

Projecting cryptocurrency mining returns into the future is a tricky exercise that contains many assumptions and different variables that will greatly skew the results of your projections. Some of these variables include network hash rate, which varies wildly from day to day — though it generally increases over time (at least for a successful cryptocurrency), which would reduce your returns as measured in that cryptocurrency. And there is also the cryptocurrency exchange rate, which also fluctuates frequently and can significantly alter your estimated returns.

As for the unknown unknowns, the things we don't even know are possible? Well, there really aren't that many in this realm, at least we think that's the case, but of course, how would we know that for sure!?

Online profitability calculators

Cryptocurrency mining profitability is a difficult subject to grasp and even harder to accurately project. This chapter explains how you make these calculations. Luckily for us, many sites provide easy-to-use tools in which you input your mining equipment's data and get an estimated value for your cryptocurrency rewards, based on current network conditions and the different fluctuating variables.

These calculators also provide useful information when considering which cryptocurrency mining hardware to buy or use. There are weaknesses, though, because the calculators can't predict the future. (They know neither the known unknowns nor the unknown unknowns.) For example, they may overestimate the amount of cryptocurrency mining returns by basing the calculation on constant network hash rate, rather than allowing for increasing network hash rate and block difficulty. They may also underestimate the fiat-currency value of the mined cryptocurrency by not taking into account future increases in value (or overestimate by not considering drops in value). Still, these tools offer a great way to run the calculations, as long as you're aware of their weaknesses. You can see an example of one of these calculators in Figure 7-7.

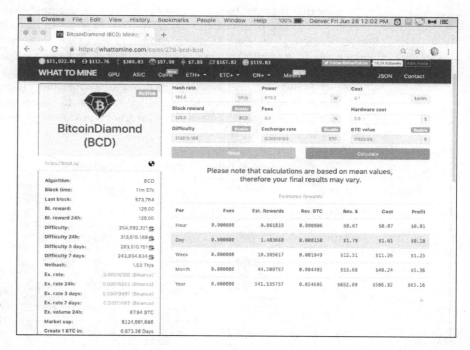

FIGURE 7-7:
A cryptocurrency calculator at WhatToMine.com.

Here is a list of popular web-based cryptocurrency mining projection sites:

>> **CoinWarz:** This site will project cryptocurrency returns on a large variety of cryptocurrencies based on an expansive list of hash algorithms. It also has tools that will allow you to enter the data we looked at in this chapter to estimate and project how your mining hardware's specifications will perform on any given cryptocurrency (www.coinwarz.com/calculators).

>> **WhatToMine:** The WhatToMine site also works with a wide range of crypto-currencies, allowing you to estimate mining rewards for a large swath of hardware as well. They allow GPU, CPU, and ASIC hardware categories so that you can test out many different scenarios and hardware setups to discover what's right for you (https://whattomine.com/calculators).

>> **Crypto Mining Tools:** The Crypto Mining Tools site has a very useful mining reward estimator that specializes in the SHA-256 hashing algorithm specific to the Bitcoin network and a few other blockchains. It also allows you to input estimations of some of the known unknowns (https://cryptomining.tools/bitcoin-mining-calculator).

Historical estimates

You may find it useful to run a real-world model to see how your mining equipment would have performed historically. That is, you use historical data for the cryptocurrency you want to mine, combined with your equipment performance and costs, to see how much you would have earned or lost over a particular period.

You can do this fairly easily using the average network hash rate data from your selected cryptocurrency on a historical basis. You could enter your equipment's hash rate, and the varying hash rates for the cryptocurrency network over time, into a spreadsheet like this:

Date	Network TH/s	My TH/s	My Hash %
7/4/18	35728406.94	14	0.0000391845%
7/5/18	36528296.65	14	0.0000383265%
7/6/18	42660784.4	14	0.0000328170%
7/7/18	41594264.79	14	0.0000336585%
7/8/18	42127524.6	14	0.0000332324%
7/9/18	36261666.74	14	0.0000386083%
7/10/18	39727855.48	14	0.0000352398%
7/11/18	35995036.84	14	0.0000388943%
7/12/18	37594816.26	14	0.0000372392%
7/13/18	38128076.06	14	0.0000367183%
7/14/18	35461777.04	14	0.0000394791%
7/15/18	35461777.04	14	0.0000394791%

Ideally you'll want to find data you can download, of course. For Bitcoin, you can find this information at www.blockchain.com/charts/hash-rate. (Look for the little CSV button within the Export Data drop-down list that lets you download the data for the period you selected on your chart.) You can find the data for many other popular cryptocurrencies at https://bitinfocharts.com, though that service doesn't provide a download at present. Perhaps it will by the time you read this, but if not, it shouldn't take too long to type the values into your spreadsheet for, say, every five or ten days over a year. Or you may be able to find downloadable data for the particular cryptocurrency you are interested in from some other site.

So this spreadsheet takes your mining equipment's average hash rate for that network's hash algorithm (in the *My TH/s* column) and divides by that day's (or week's or whatever period you choose) network hash rate (*Network TH/s*) to show you the rolling percentage of the network hash rate that your equipment would have been mining. Figure 7-8 shows an example of an estimated network hash rate percentage over time for a Bitmain Antminer S9.

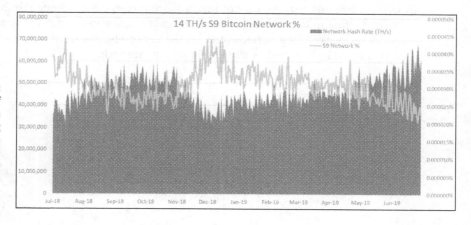

FIGURE 7-8: An example of the Bitcoin network rolling hash rate percentage calculation of an Antminer S9 14 TH/s miner over the previous year.

You can now multiply your rolling percentage value over time by the network mining rewards during that same period to arrive at an estimated value for your equipment's mining rewards. (Again, you can find this information for many cryptocurrencies at https://bitinfocharts.com.) For the Bitcoin network, the block subsidy is 6.25BTC per block, with around 0.08BTC additional earnings in transaction fees (it fluctuates, but we'll use that for a rough average), for a total of 6.33BTC. On average, 144 blocks are mined each day, resulting in roughly 911BTC earned by miners each day.

For example, say that you calculate on any given day that your SHA-256 mining hardware would have been 1 percent of the total Bitcoin network hash rate on that day. (Again, this is just for the sake of an example; 1 percent of network hash rate is a monstrous amount!) Take the mining rewards for that day, which for the Bitcoin network would be valued at around 911 Bitcoins, and multiply your 1 percent mining percentage by the daily network reward to arrive at your estimated earnings for the day, roughly 9.11BTC.

Cryptocurrency mining reward projections and mining rewards as measured in your local fiat currency, even with the handy tools found online, are very fickle and can vary wildly in either the positive or negative directions. If the cryptocurrency you intend to mine becomes more difficult to mine, your projections will be inaccurately high. If the local fiat exchange rate of your chosen cryptocurrency goes up in value, your projections will be inaccurately low.

As Nobel prize-winning physicist Niels Bohr said, "It's very hard to make predictions, especially about the future." There is no way to accurately predict your mining future, and these reward calculators depend on input variables that will inevitably change. Do not invest more into cryptocurrency mining than you are willing to lose! Mining is often one of the best ways to steadily acquire cryptocurrency over long periods of time, but it can also occasionally be a losing venture. Tread lightly, and as always, do your homework.

Chapter **8**

Reducing Negatives and Gaining an Edge

The cryptocurrency mining business has upsides and quite a bit of opportunity for rewards. However, a handful of obstacles and negative aspects are involved with mining as well as plenty of room for error. Some of these difficulties can be overcome and even used to your advantage to maximize your benefits from mining.

The impediments of profitable cryptocurrency mining include electrical costs, thermal heat discharge, an ever-changing cryptocurrency landscape, block difficulty increases, and fierce mining competition. We discuss strategies for tackling and mitigating these obstacles in this chapter, so you can maintain a competitive advantage in the cryptocurrency mining industry.

The cryptocurrency mining space is an incredibly competitive and fast-changing environment that forces miners to craft creative strategies to maximize returns and minimize cost and losses. You can pursue a few routes to help improve — or maintain — your mining, such as upgrading your mining hardware to the latest and greatest equipment, reducing electricity costs, using otherwise wasted heat, and staying up to date on current events. Strategies like this can help fully capitalize on your mining deployments and help maximize your cryptocurrency mining gains.

Profitability through Efficiency

In the cryptocurrency mining arena, every bit counts (pun intended). Profit margins are often slim, especially during market downturns in the exchange rate between the cryptocurrency and your fiat currency (for example, when the value of the cryptocurrency drops). This makes it especially important to squeeze every last benefit from the scarce and expensive cryptocurrency resources you're committing to mining.

Upgrading aging equipment

As block difficulty and total cryptocurrency network hash rate increase steadily over time, your proportion of the mining rewards will diminish, which (depending on the value of the cryptocurrency in your fiat currency) may also mean your overall profitability will drop. In other words, your mining equipment will eventually become unprofitable.

You can help mitigate aging equipment by upgrading your mining gear as it nears its end of life. The average useful life span of modern cryptocurrency-specific ASIC mining hardware is generally between four and five years. By upgrading to newer, more efficient mining hardware, you can maintain your cryptocurrency mining competitive advantage.

Mining different cryptocurrencies

Upgrading equipment often can be expensive and wasteful, however, so another route is to find alternative cryptocurrencies for your ASIC or GPU mining hardware to mine.

We cover the various types of cryptocurrency hashing algorithms and the different cryptocurrencies that use them in Chapter 4 of this minibook. Even if you're mining using an ASIC, the ASIC will work with other cryptocurrencies that use the same algorithm.

If your mining hardware becomes unprofitable mining the cryptocurrency you originally set out to mine, you may find that you can still generate rewards on other proof-of-work blockchains that use the same algorithm. Perhaps a new cryptocurrency has come on the scene since you began, or perhaps a cryptocurrency that you looked at and disregarded earlier has become more profitable. So keep your eyes and ears open and don't think you're stuck with your cryptocurrency mining choice forever.

Using exhaust heat

The intense computational processes involved in mining proof-of-work cryptocurrencies produce quite a bit of typically wasted heat exhaust. This is especially the case for ASICs — algorithm-specific processors — and for large-scale GPU mining rigs, as they are essentially electric space heaters converting electricity into heat while they steadily mine cryptocurrency.

A way to stack value and increase margins when mining cryptocurrency is to not waste this heat exhaust and instead utilize it for your own benefit. According to the U.S. Energy Information Association (EIA), the estimated winter heating bills of the average American household range from around $600 to $1,600, depending on home size, fuel source, and local climate. Figure 8-1 shows the past few winters of EIA data by fuel type as well as an average value from all sources. (The data is from www.eia.gov/todayinenergy/detail.php?id=37232.)

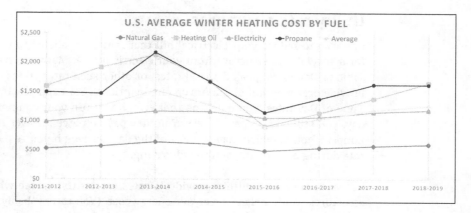

FIGURE 8-1:
EIA data on average winter heating costs from propane, heating oil, electricity, and natural gas.

If you live in a colder climate and are running a mining operation at home, the equipment is going to pump heat out, reducing the level of heating you need for your home, and thus in effect reducing the cost of your mining operation. (Take this into consideration when running your calculations; see Chapter 6 of this minibook.)

CREATIVE USES FOR HEAT DISCHARGE

Crafty cryptocurrency miners have put the heat discharge from mining equipment to good use in other ways. Some have used it to heat greenhouses or other grow facilities during the winter. Other enterprising miners have also created heat exchangers and used their mining heat exhaust to warm bodies of water, such as outdoor pools or hot tubs. Miners have also submerged mining equipment in mineral oil and other engineered fluids, which act as a dielectric, electrically insulating liquid to help dissipate the heat for reuse and to dampen the noise from the mining equipment. Admittedly, some of these more intricate methods of heat management would take quite a bit of skill and planning to properly deploy, but they are possible and have allowed creative miners to put their equipment's excess heat waste to good use.

Reducing electricity bills

As discussed in Chapter 6 of this minibook, electrical expenses for proof-of-work mining equipment make up the largest portion of operational expenditures for cryptocurrency mines. So reducing your electrical bills is obviously a good thing! It may be enough to push you into — or keep you in — profitability. The following sections discuss a few ways to save.

Utility rate structures

One way to reduce your electrical bill that may be available to you is to sign up for a special rate structure from your electric utility. Many electric utilities offer Time of Day rates, peak demand rates, or other such rates (rates that sometimes provide pretty decent discounts on energy prices). For example, if you sign up for Time of Day rates, you may find that even if you run your equipment 24 hours a day, you still end up paying less. You may pay 50 percent lower rates during the nonpeak hours, which may be most of the day, so even if you're paying twice that rate during peak hours, you're still saving.

Research your local utility provider's rates (or tariffs) to see whether any rate structures would help reduce your energy cost. (You can probably find the information you need on their website.) Commercial electrical rate structures normally provide cheaper bulk electric rates, but are not available for homes, a factor to take into consideration when trying to decide whether you need a home-based or industrial mining facility.

You should also shop around, if possible. Some states, such as Texas, have deregulated electrical markets that allow the consumer to choose from a variety of retail electrical providers (REPs). If you're in such an area, you really need to check around and find the best deal; you'll want to know how much electricity you're going to be using before you start shopping, of course.

Another option is to relocate your mining equipment to the service territory of an electrical utility that has more affordable electricity or a variety of rate structures that can benefit you. You may be surprised at how much electricity costs vary around the country. Figure 8-2 shows average electricity prices per kWh throughout the United States (www.eia.gov/electricity/monthly). As you can see, mining profitably in Hawaii is likely to be pretty tough (it's hot, too, so you have additional cooling costs). A state like Wyoming may be good, though. Not only does it have electricity costs near the bottom of the rankings, but it's one of the coolest states, too; one of the coldest states in the summer and in the top ten coldest states in the winter.

FIGURE 8-2:
Average electricity cost per kWh by state compiled from EIA data produced in March 2019.

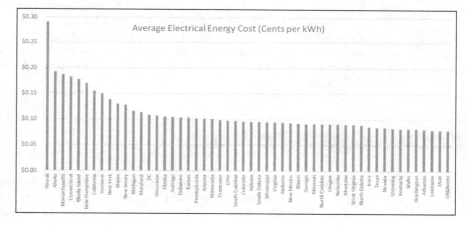

Alternative energy sources

Beyond researching alternative rate structures or transferring to a different retail electrical utility provider, you may have other options for securing more affordable electricity for your cryptocurrency mine. Cryptocurrency miners have sought out sources of excess electrical energy that would otherwise be wasted, such as areas with excess hydroelectricity or flared natural gas.

Perhaps these options are not practical for your mine. However, another option would be to explore alternative energy sources (renewable energy), ideally ones with zero fuel cost. Renewable energy technology is rapidly developing, and costs are dropping dramatically, to the point where, in many contexts, renewable energy is now cheaper than fossil fuel energy.

According to a team of researchers from MIT, solar panels now cost just 1 percent of the 1980 price. ("Solar is cost-competitive with natural gas and coal in most geographies in the United States," the team said. "We've already reached that threshold.") The researchers also expect prices to continue dropping, perhaps 40 percent over the next five years.

Wind and solar can be excellent auxiliary sources to reduce electrical grid consumption and can increase margins on cryptocurrency mining (though, of course, you need to factor in the capital costs; free energy is great, but you'll have the upfront equipment and installation costs).

Installing a wind tower at a residence or commercial facility may not be feasible, perhaps, but solar panels are more affordable and much easier to install, and they can be used in many situations, especially in a home application. Some electric utilities and most solar installation companies offer turnkey solutions that require little effort on the part of the consumer and may not even require upfront investment. If you went this route, you'd also have the benefit of trained, licensed professionals specifying your system and installing it. Solutions like this would allow for increased mining returns and less electrical consumption from the grid to help reduce your electrical bills, and thus increase your mining margins. And even if you stop mining, you will still be getting free energy to use or sell back to the utility.

Knowledge Is Power

TIP

The best method of checking the pulse of the burgeoning cryptocurrency mining industry is to stay up to date using online resources, such as social media and specific online forums covering the topic. Due to the infancy of this space, many news sources in the space can be misleading, downright inaccurate, or even propagate bought-and-paid-for content without a sponsored label. A recent study found that many of the top cryptocurrency news sites were posting sponsored content — essentially ads — under the guise of news.

This kind of misinformation makes it important to stay plugged into the community and various other peer-based resources: don't trust, verify. Check out the following list of resources that we like to pursue to stay up with current events.

>> **BitcoinTalk:** Use BitcoinTalk to inquire into almost any cryptocurrency topic, including (but definitely not limited to) mining. Despite the name, it's not just for Bitcoin anymore. You'll find many different cryptocurrencies being discussed. For example, it is where most popular alternative cryptocurrencies were announced prior to launch (https://bitcointalk.org).

>> **Bitcoin subreddit:** The Bitcoin subreddit provides a great forum for lots of breaking news and current events, and provides a window into the current

sentiment in the community. It's not all serious stuff, though; you'll find plenty of memes, jokes, and other nonmining content, so do surf lightly (www.reddit.com/r/Bitcoin).

» **BitcoinBeginners subreddit:** The BitcoinBeginners subreddit is an even better resource for recent entrants into the ecosystem, providing plenty of great information for newbies (www.reddit.com/r/BitcoinBeginners).

» **CoinDesk:** CoinDesk is a decent news source in an industry riddled with faulty cryptocurrency news outlets. It also provides exchange-rate data from a variety of different cryptocurrencies (www.coindesk.com).

» **CoinJournal:** CoinJournal is also a good source for cryptocurrency-related news; it clearly separates press releases from news articles so users can differentiate public relations from journalism (https://coinjournal.net).

» **Bitcoin Magazine:** *Bitcoin Magazine* has long been a reliable news outlet in the cryptocurrency space. Although print releases of the magazine stopped years ago, it still provides good and consistent news coverage on its website (https://bitcoinmagazine.com).

» **Merkle Report:** The Merkle Report curates a wide variety of relevant content from various news sources in the cryptocurrency space. It offers a good one-stop shop for news across the industry (www.merklereport.com).

» **Messari:** Messari has a ton of cryptocurrency-focused data, research, and news from across the industry. It also offers a periodic daily newsletter to stay up to date on current trends (https://messari.io).

» **Block Digest:** Block Digest is an excellent source of news in the form of a weekly podcast that features various community members discussing and digesting news and headlines from the Bitcoin space (www.youtube.com/c/blockdigest).

» **Stack Exchange:** The Bitcoin Stack Exchange has a large trove of questions answered by other cryptocurrency enthusiasts. Anyone can post a question or an answer. If you are looking for specific insight, chances are someone has already answered the question you may have (https://bitcoin.stackexchange.com).

Why current events are important

Cryptocurrencies and blockchains act as an immutable record of data, indisputable information that is accessible to anyone with the tools and knowledge to look for it. This isn't the case with off-chain data, such as current events and news in the space, which is why it is very important to stay up to date on accurate information from reliable sources if you intend to mine cryptocurrency.

REMEMBER

Current events affect what's going on in the mining space. They can affect the value of the cryptocurrency, and thus, in response to fluctuation in the value, the network hash rate, your percentage of the network hash rate, the number of blocks you'll mine, and ultimately your loss or profit.

There is plethora of news sources in the cryptocurrency mining space, but not all can be trusted. Some peddle misinformation with the intent of misleading you. Staying up to date on the latest and greatest in the mining industry is crucial to your continued success in the space. Reliable content from sources such as those listed in the preceding section is the best defense against spin and distortion from those who would lead you astray. Without information, you may find yourself mining a cryptocurrency without much future value, or on the uneconomical side of a blockchain fork.

The "fork wars"

You may have heard of the concept of *forking* a cryptocurrency. Understanding blockchain forks is critically important to maintaining your mining competitive advantage. Forks can provide a great little bonus — free money! But make the wrong decisions when a fork occurs, and you could end up losing money. If you're not paying attention and pick the wrong side of the cryptocurrency fork, you may find yourself mining the side of a fork that is not economical.

Also, some forks are pitched as upgrades by their participants, but tread lightly: You may find yourself being duped by bad actors and cheap imitations that simply copied the code and branding of the original cryptocurrency blockchain. This is another reason why being up to date on information and news in the cryptocurrency mining space is so vital to the long-term viability of your venture.

TECHNICAL STUFF

The term *fork* is used in the software-development business to describe a situation in which a line of development splits into two lines, and the two different lines proceed independently of each other. Think of it as a fork in a road. You're driving along a road and arrive at a fork; you can take the left fork or the right fork, but whichever you take, you're now on a different road.

Software forks are especially common in the open-source community. Here's an example of a successful open-source fork (most are not successful, by the way): OpenBSD, an open-source operating system, is a fork of NetBSD that forked off from the original NetBSD development in 1995. NetBSD had already been in development for several years before that. After the fork, OpenBSD and NetBSD were two separate software systems, with different features, different software developers working on each one, and so on.

Now, in the cryptocurrency world, the term *fork* has an additional meaning. Certainly the software itself can be forked; a developer takes a copy of existing cryptocurrency software and begins modifying it and running a new cryptocurrency. For example, Ixcoin was an exact copy of the Bitcoin code that was launched in the early days of Bitcoin (in 2011). The founder took a copy of the Bitcoin code, set it up, and created a brand-new blockchain (that ran in exactly the same way as Bitcoin). It's still running, though not much activity occurs in the Ixcoin markets. In other cases, copies of Bitcoin have been downloaded, modified, and then set up as new cryptocurrency networks with new features, even using different algorithms. In fact, this has happened dozens of times.

TIP

However, *forking* can mean something else, something, from our perspective, far more important. Forking in the cryptocurrency space is what occurs when a node or group of nodes in a cryptocurrency system break away from consensus of the original blockchain. *Consensus* is the rule set that the nodes on the network comply with, so they ensure that all copies of the blockchain remain in sync and all agree on the transactions added to the blockchain. When nodes fork and fall out of consensus on the blockchain, an entire new chain of blocks is created; thus two different blockchains, two different networks, move forward from the fork point. They both have the same transaction history — the same blocks up until the fork point. But after the fork, there is no longer only one blockchain, one cryptocurrency, and one network; now, two blockchains, two cryptocurrencies, and two separate networks exist.

Some people in the cryptocurrency field refer to this situation — the hard forking of both the code and the blockchain — as forking, and the other kind of fork — taking the code and starting a brand-new blockchain — as *cloning.* Many of the blockchains in existence today are clones of the Bitcoin code, some with only slight modifications. In the case of Ixcoin, it began as a clone of the Bitcoin blockchain, but later the Ixcoin code and blockchain forked, producing another cryptocurrency named IOCoin. (At one point, an IOCoin was worth as much as $7.26; today, it's worth around 11 cents. It's sometimes suggested that IOCoin's lack of success is partly due to the fact that nobody knows how to spell or pronounce it!) By the way, here's a link to a great chart showing how many different cryptocurrencies have evolved — through forks and clones — from Bitcoin: https://mapofcoins.com/bitcoin/.

Anyway, when we use the term *fork* or *forking* from now on in this discussion, we're referring to the forking of the blockchain, typically in conjunction with modifications to the software. That's the issue you need to understand if you're going to mine.

Here's what happens. A schism occurs in the developer community for a particular blockchain. One group wants to do something to the code that another group doesn't approve of. At some point, the disagreement reaches a point at which some of the developers are so dissatisfied that they break away. (The term *civil war* is sometimes used to describe the level of conflict in the community that leads up to a fork!)

For example, the cryptocurrency's code may be modified in some way, and some of the developers say, in essence, "No, we want the code to remain the way it was!"

That's the situation with Ethereum Classic, by the way. Ethereum was forked in July 2016 (in response to the theft of around $50 million worth of Ether, the blockchain was forked to restore the lost money). Some in the community felt this fork should not have been created, and thus continued using the original Ethereum code and blockchain (read more about this in Book 2, Chapter 5). So then there were two networks, two blockchains, and thus two different cryptocurrencies.

In most cryptocurrency forks, the forked network is given a new name and ticker symbol. The Ethereum fork was a very unusual situation, though; the network that had forked away from the original network *kept the original name and the ticker symbol* (ETH)! The people who wanted to continue with the original blockchain and software, in a minority, were forced to come up with a new name (Ethereum Classic) and ticker symbol (ETC).

Thus Ethereum is a fork of what used to be known as Ethereum, but is now known as Ethereum Classic. The Ethereum fork is also unusual in that it's generally a minority that breaks away — that forks — from the original cryptocurrency. In Ethereum's case, the *majority* forked from the original code and blockchain, while a minority continued running the original software, network, and cryptocurrency.

Here's another example, but of the opposite situation: Bitcoin and Bitcoin Cash. In August 2017, a small group of Bitcoin developers forked the code in order to increase the blockchain's block-size limit. The majority continued developing on, and operating nodes with, the original code, and the minority developed the new, forked code and managed the new network and blockchain. The forked code was renamed Bitcoin Cash (BCH).

Technically, forking is really cheap and easy; remember, most cryptocurrencies are open source, which means anyone can go to the code repository (usually on GitHub; here's the Bitcoin repository, for example: `https://github.com/bitcoin/bitcoin`), download the code, tweak it (change the consensus rules, for example), and relaunch as a new cryptocurrency. Because it's so cheap and easy to do this, hundreds, maybe thousands, of new cryptocurrencies have been created from forks of existing cryptocurrencies, and forks created from forks.

Many of the most popular cryptocurrency networks over the years have had small groups of their users change the rules of consensus and fork off, taking minority portions of their networks (the nodes and miners) with them. At the time of this writing, around 74-plus Bitcoin network forks — including Bitcoin Cash (BCH) and Bitcoin SV (BSV) — now exist as their own coins on separate, active, albeit less secure, cryptocurrency systems.

Other popular blockchains that have been forked many times include Ethereum (Ethereum Classic, Ether Gold, Ethereum Zero), Litecoin (Litecoin Cash, Super

Litecoin), and Monero (Monero Original, Monero Classic, MoneroV). It is relatively inexpensive for developers to fork a cryptocurrency system and easy to mimic a blockchain with slight changes in the codebase and branding, so it's likely we'll continue to see forking into the future, and you need to be aware of that. (Litecoin, by the way, was itself a clone of the Bitcoin code — with significant modifications — though not a fork of the Bitcoin blockchain.)

WARNING

Each of the newly created minority-forked blockchains has a few things in common: a reduced node count, fewer developers, lower hash rate, and reduced blockchain security. We recommend treading lightly when dealing with forked blockchains and, in most cases, avoiding them completely. Some forks may not have *replay protection* enabled, which could lead to a loss of funds, and other forks drastically lose exchange rate value over time as measured in both local fiat currency and the original blockchain's cryptocurrency.

Your forking decisions

If you are mining a cryptocurrency and it forks, you have two primary decisions to make:

>> Which fork do you continue mining?

>> What do you do with your new currency?

Imagine you're mining a coin called DummyCoin. And assume that instead of selling your mined DummyCoin as soon as you receive it, you have been keeping DummyCoin, so you have an address (maybe a few addresses) in the DummyCoin blockchain that is storing your mining revenues.

REPLAY PROTECTION

Replay protection is a technical safeguard that developers can implement prior to or during blockchain forks. Replay protection makes the transaction on the new forked blockchain invalid on the first blockchain, preventing duplicated transactions on both sides of the fork, and thus preventing nodes and users from spending or misspending funds after the fork. This replay protection helps to prevent what is referred to as a replay attack. A *replay attack* is a node mimicking the valid transaction message on one side of the forked blockchain and replaying it onto the second chain. This type of attack could potentially lead to a theft or accidental loss of funds on one side of the fork or the other. Without replay protection, it is also very easy for unsuspecting cryptocurrency users to lose funds accidentally or have them stolen in some other way.

You realize that a fork war is going on in the developer community (because you have been paying attention to the community news and conversations), and one day, in fact, the cryptocurrency splits. Now there are two networks, two blockchains, and two cryptocurrencies (DummyCoin and DummerCoin).

The nice thing is that you now not only have coins in the DummyCoin blockchain, but you have the same number of DummerCoins in the DummerCoin blockchain. Remember, both cryptocurrencies use the same blockchain up until the split point. Thus, the founders of DummerCoin took a copy of the DummyCoin blockchain and began building on that, so all the original transactions from DummyCoin are now in the DummerCoin blockchain, too. The transactions — and your coins — are in *both* blockchains!

Now, this sounds great. You've just doubled your money, right? Well, not quite. First, there are situations in which the forked cryptocurrency fails quickly and badly, and you may not even be able to get to the new coins in DummerCoin. But say that in this case, DummerCoin does enjoy a modicum of success, and you are able to safely manage your DummerCoins in the new blockchain.

What do you mine?

Let's get back to those two decisions you have to make. The first decision is, what are you going to mine: DummyCoin or DummerCoin? The original cryptocurrency or the forked cryptocurrency? In most cases, forked cryptocurrencies don't fare as well as the original cryptocurrency, from the perspective of the coin's market value. But deciding which to mine is a more complicated subject than that.

ANOTHER PROBLEM WITH CUSTODIAL WALLETS

Many people in the cryptocurrency arena disapprove of *custodial wallets* (wallets managed for you by another party). The belief is that you need to control your own private keys. Exchanges, for example, get hacked and have money stolen, and in some cases custodians have ripped off their clients. Well, here's another reason. There have been occasions in which exchanges have decided to not support forks of a cryptocurrency that they have on their platform. So, you have a wallet on an exchange managing DummyCoin. The cryptocurrency forks, so you now own both DummyCoin and DummerCoin. But the exchange does not set up a wallet that will allow you to manage the DummerCoin, so you may own it, but you can't get to it! (There have been lawsuits related to this very issue.) Not your keys, not your DummyCoin or DummerCoin.

You may find that the new cryptocurrency has a lower value but is still worth mining because your equipment's hash rate is a larger percentage of the new network's hash rate than the previous network's hash rate. In other words, you'll be able to win more blocks on the new network than the old. On the other hand, what if the value of the new cryptocurrency declines precipitously? Perhaps, you may decide to mine the new cryptocurrency and sell the coins as soon as you receive them. But whatever you decide — to stick with the original network or move to the new one — it's a tricky decision, and it greatly depends on your values and your assessment of what is likely to happen to the forked cryptocurrency. Which is why you need to be plugged into the cryptocurrency's community, to get a feel for the community sentiment.

TIP

Here's a general rule: The side of the fork that has the most community support, that the most nodes are supporting, and that most of the hashing power is supporting, is the side that is most likely to survive, most likely to remain stable, and most likely to thrive. But these factors can also switch back and forth. As miners see an opportunity — a lower overall network hash rate on one side of the fork — they may switch their hashing power (many, perhaps most, miners are mainly motivated by profit, after all); as miners switch, network hash rate goes up, returns decrease, some miners may leave, and so on. We generated a chart at the wonderful BitInfoCharts site that shows this phenomenon (see `https://bitinfocharts.com/comparison/hashrate-btc-bch.html`). In Figure 8-3, you can see the Bitcoin network hash rate (top line) in comparison with the Bitcoin Cash network hash rate when it first forked. As the Bitcoin Cash hash rate went up, the Bitcoin hash rate went down. Miners switched back and forth, and on a couple of occasions, the fork's network hash rate was actually higher than the original network's hash rate.

Cryptocurrency miners are opportunistic and motivated by profits (of course!). Thus, during times when Bitcoin Cash was slightly more profitable to mine than Bitcoin, portions of the SHA-256 hash rate moved to the Bitcoin Cash network, and vice versa. Bitcoin Cash profitability didn't last, however, and today Bitcoin Cash has around 1 percent of the hash rate that Bitcoin does. See `https://fork.lol` for real-time comparisons on hash rate, value, and miner rewards between these two forks.

There's another twist in the Bitcoin Cash story. Originally, Bitcoin Cash had more pledged support, as far as hash rate goes, than Bitcoin. Large companies that were providing a very significant portion of the network hash rate supported the idea of a fork, but many people did not. The majority of network nodes did not switch to the forked network, and most of the miners' hashing did not ultimately switch either, as you can see from Figure 8-3.

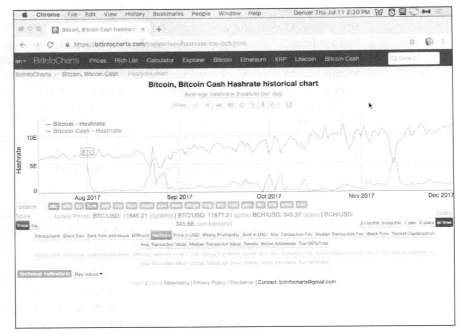

FIGURE 8-3:
A BitInfoCharts.
com chart
showing how
miners switched
their hash rate
back and forth
between the two
sides of the
Bitcoin and
Bitcoin Cash fork
during the Bitcoin
blocksize debate.

What should you do with your new cryptocurrency?

Assuming you can get to your DummerCoin, the cryptocurrency in the new block-chain, what do you do with it? First, consider if (and how) it has value. How can there first be one cryptocurrency with a real-world value, a currency that can be converted into goods or fiat currency, and then, all of a sudden, there are two, and both have value?

Well, it all depends on whether people want to buy the new cryptocurrency. There may well be a futures market before the fork actually occurs, in which the market will set a value for the new coin. Such markets will generally value *both* sides of the upcoming fork, providing some idea of what the market is thinking, and per-haps help you decide which currency is most likely to survive and thrive. The cur-rency with the highest future value is being voted for, in effect, by investors and the cryptocurrency community. But, regardless, once the fork occurs, you then have coins that can be sold if someone out there is willing to buy. Sometimes they are (and sometimes they aren't).

There's no reason to believe, however, that both coins will have the same value. One side of the fork will typically be more successful than the other, and value may slip from one side to another as the market (the multitudes of investors) make their choices. If people really like DummerCoin, then DummerCoin may rise in value while DummyCoin drops a little.

In the case of Ethereum, for example, the forked side became far more valuable than the original side. (Remember, Ethereum Classic was the original software, network, and blockchain, while Ethereum was the fork.) At the time of this writing, Ethereum Classic is worth just 1/50 of Ethereum; so the fork is worth more. On the other hand, Bitcoin Cash, a fork of Bitcoin, is currently worth merely 1/90 of the Bitcoin price; in other words, the fork is worth far less.

WARNING

If one side of the fork is clearly supported by a minority, or thought by the community to be somehow technically inferior, then it's likely that many owners will sell, either dumping their old coin for the newly forked cryptocurrency, or vice versa. One coin will crash while the other will skyrocket.

So there's no clear answer. In general, it does seem likely that the new cryptocurrency will be more valuable in the first few days of its life and drop off as enthusiasm wanes. That seems to have happened frequently, but there's no hard-and-fast rule that says this will happen.

In general, forks die

Forking a cryptocurrency is a risky business. It's likely that most forks will die or at least fade away to insignificance. Clearly, some don't, however. Ethereum is still around, bigger than the original blockchain. Bitcoin Cash may not be worth anywhere near as much as Bitcoin, or as much as it was when it forked, but it is still alive (in fact, it has also forked and is likely to fork again ad infinitum), and on the day we wrote these words, more than one billion U.S. dollars' worth of Bitcoin Cash were bought and sold. It's very hard to predict these things, which is why keeping up with community sentiment is so important as well as understanding the fundamentals.

Here Today, Gone Tomorrow

You need to keep an eye on trends in both the cryptocurrency you are mining and the alternatives. It's a simple fact that cryptocurrencies are very volatile. A hugely productive cryptocurrency today may be worthless tomorrow.

Zcash (ZEC) is a great example. When Zcash launched in 2016, it was very popular, greatly hyped by the community, and the first few hours of trading were crazy. As miners mined blocks and were rewarded with Zcash coins, and those coins came onto the market, they were snapped up. In Figure 8-4, you can see a chart we created at CoinMarketCap.com (see https://coinmarketcap.com/currencies/zcash/), showing the first few days of Zcash's life, priced in both U.S. dollars and Bitcoin.

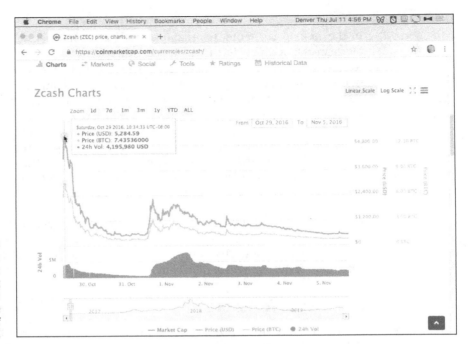

FIGURE 8-4:
A Coin
MarketCap.com
chart showing
Zcash's wild
pricing ride the
first few days of
its life.

Within hours of launch, it was trading at around $5,200 a coin and was worth more than 7 Bitcoin. Six days later, it was worth less than $600 and around three-quarters of a Bitcoin. (Today? Around 0.003BTC!)

Another classic example is Auroracoin (AUR). There was huge hype around this coin; it was, in theory, supposed to be an Icelandic Bitcoin, and even to act as an alternative to the Icelandic króna. Every Icelandic citizen was supposed to receive some (in the end, around 11 or 12 percent of the population did receive Auroracoin). AUR launched on the markets with a value of around $3 USD, reached almost $100 within a week, and then began dropping. Today, it's worth about twenty cents (about $150 worth traded on the world's Auroracoin markets today!)

Cryptocurrencies come and go. What's worth mining today may be a total waste of time tomorrow. So stay informed, monitor the community, and keep your eyes peeled for opportunities.

Evaluating Your Mining Resources

You need to know the value of the equipment, resources, and time you plan to dedicate to cryptocurrency mining. Having a good grasp on this information makes you better prepared to gain and maintain an edge while mining. In Chapter 7 of this minibook, we discuss the various types of mining profitability tools found online, which are great resources to use when estimating your mining income.

However, some aspects of cryptocurrency mining systems may make those predictions slightly inaccurate as you project further into the future. These aspects include block difficulty levels, mining competition, and ultimately, diminishing return of cryptocurrency rewards.

Increasing mining competition

As blockchains become more popular and mining equipment more capable, cryptocurrency mining trends toward a tougher, more competitive environment. As more miners spin up equipment pointed to your chosen cryptocurrency's proof-of-work algorithm, this leads to the same scheduled amount of predetermined coin issuance being split between more miners and hash rate.

Increasing block difficulty

Over time, as more miners and more effective mining equipment connect to a blockchain, the block difficulty will automatically increase to ensure block issuance time-interval stability — that is, that the same amount of cryptocurrency is issued, on the correct schedule, regardless of how much computing power is being used to mine it.

Over the Bitcoin network's history, block difficulty has trended upward. There have only been nine months in the Bitcoin network's decade-long life where the block difficulty finished at a value lower than it started with; in other words, block difficulty reduction is a fairly rare occurrence on the Bitcoin network, and on other successful cryptocurrency networks. The increase in competition will lead to blocks being harder to find. Thus, your mining equipment, with a constant hash rate, will be less effective at finding blocks or contributing to a pool.

Diminishing returns due to halving events

With the increase of competition, hash rate, and block difficulty, your mined cryptocurrency rewards, as measured in the cryptocurrency you are mining, will be reduced.

There is also the block subsidy halving cycle to be aware of. On the Bitcoin network, every 210,000 blocks (or roughly every four years), the amount of Bitcoin issued to miners is cut in half. On May 11, 2020, the Bitcoin block subsidy halved, from 12.5 Bitcoin per block awarded to the winning miner, to 6.25. Sometime in the middle of 2024, the Bitcoin block subsidy will be halved, from the current 6.25 Bitcoin per block awarded to the winning miner, to 3.125. (The miner's reward comprises the block subsidy — the new coins issued — and the transaction fees.)

These issuance halving events will further affect the amount of cryptocurrency your equipment will earn. This trend of diminishing mined cryptocurrency returns is something to be very wary of when considering if mining is right for you. Of course, if the value of the cryptocurrency goes up (when measured in terms of dollars or whatever local fiat currency you are working with), there's still potential for profit. If, for example, the value of Bitcoin triples before the halving event, well, you're still ahead of the game. However, if the value of the cryptocurrency drops *and* the block subsidy halves well, you really are in trouble.

These halving events are not unique to the Bitcoin network. Many other cryptocurrencies reduce the block subsidies periodically, so this concept affects a wide range of cryptocurrencies.

The BitInfoCharts.com website offers a historical perspective on how much reward a miner would have earned with a tera hash per second (TH/s) of SHA-256 mining capability per day as measured in present-day U.S. dollars, using the present-day exchange rate. This graph from `https://bitinfocharts.com/comparison/bitcoin-mining_profitability.html` provides a good perspective on diminishing mining rewards over time (see Figure 8-5). It takes into account the block subsidies and the halving episodes (the BTC icons on the chart show a description of important events when the mouse points at them, including halving events in 2012 and 2016).

Of course, a TH/s was not attainable in a single mining rig until the 2013–2014 time frame. However, the chart still gives a good idea of how computing power has in effect been devalued over time. That is, it takes far more computing power to get the same result. Back at the beginning of 2011, a TH/s mining on the Bitcoin network would have earned you over $21,000 dollars a day. Now it earns less than a dollar a day.

Note, by the way, that this chart is a *logarithmic* chart, so the dramatic reduction appears even less than it actually has been. The effect is even more dramatic when you see the linear chart from `https://bitinfocharts.com/comparison/bitcoin-mining_profitability.html`, as shown in Figure 8-6.

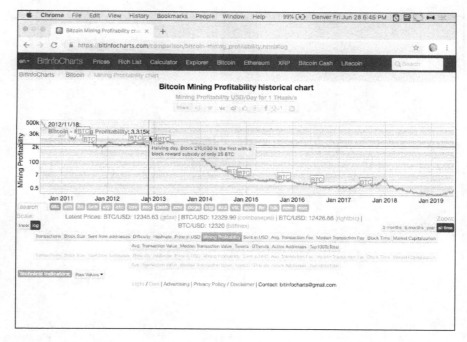

FIGURE 8-5:
A logarithmic chart showing the Bitcoin mining profitability of 1 TH/s, in U.S. dollars per day, from late 2010 to 2019.

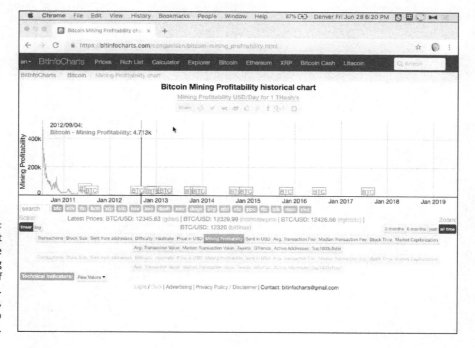

FIGURE 8-6:
The linear chart showing the Bitcoin mining profitability of 1 TH/s, in U.S. dollars per day, from late 2010 to 2019.

Chapter **9**

Running Your Cryptocurrency Business

Once you're in business — you've determined what cryptocurrency to mine, deployed mining equipment, and have collected rewards back to your cryptocurrency wallet — the next issue to deal with is what you're going to do with your cryptocurrency earnings.

In fact, you have a variety of things to consider. You need to watch the market conditions for the cryptocurrency you're mining and others that you may consider switching to. You also need to understand the tax liabilities incurred during your mining adventure — both keeping your cryptocurrency and selling your earnings will have implications. (As Ben Franklin said, nothing's certain but death and taxes!) We also discuss scaling up your mining deployments and upgrading your equipment when it becomes obsolete or unprofitable.

What to Do with Your Mined Cryptocurrency

You can do various things with your mined cryptocurrency. With cryptocurrency being a scarce, electronic, decentralized digital asset that is borderless, sovereign, censorship resistant, and portable, you have many ways to use it.

Convert your cryptocurrency

The most obvious thing, of course, is to sell your mined cryptocurrency, most likely through an exchange, for your local fiat currency. After all, your business has expenses, most notably the cost of the equipment and electricity, and these bills have to be paid somehow. You may also want to recover the initial expense of setting up your cryptocurrency mining operation, and in most cases, you won't be paying bills directly with cryptocurrency.

You can often buy mining equipment with cryptocurrency — most commonly Bitcoin — as we discuss later in this chapter, but few utilities accept cryptocurrency, and if you've just begun mining, you probably bought your equipment with dollars. We discuss how to pay bills with cryptocurrency in the upcoming section, "Buying equipment and paying bills."

You should consider a number of things when converting your cryptocurrency:

>> **Would you be better off holding the cryptocurrency?** That's a subject we come back to in the section, "Hodling your cryptocurrency," later in this chapter.

>> **Are you mining a very volatile cryptocurrency?** If so, you may want to dump it as soon as you mine it, converting it into fiat currency or another cryptocurrency, one that you feel is more likely to increase in value, or at least hold value.

>> **What are the tax liabilities for converting your mined cryptocurrency into fiat currency?** (In fact, you'll encounter tax liabilities if you don't, too!) We cover this subject later in this chapter in the section, "Tax and Your Mining Business."

Buying equipment and paying bills

You may want to just pay bills and make purchases directly using your cryptocurrency. You *can* often buy mining equipment using cryptocurrency. Newegg, for example, one of North America's largest electronics retailers, accepts Bitcoin, and companies that build mining equipment or otherwise cater to the mining or cryptocurrency markets typically also accept cryptocurrency.

However, they typically accept only a small range of cryptocurrencies — generally Bitcoin, though sometimes also a few other popular cryptocurrencies. While gateways exist, such as CoinGate (`www.coingate.com`), that help ecommerce stores integrate far more cryptocurrencies (CoinGate currently accepts around 50), in general, most stores accept only Bitcoin and one or two others.

Here's a short list of places you can spend your Bitcoin (some also accept other cryptocurrencies), but many more are out there.

>> **Overstock:** `www.overstock.com`

>> **Newegg:** `www.newegg.com`

>> **Dish Network:** `www.mydish.com`

>> **Microsoft:** `www.microsoft.com`

>> **AT&T:** `www.att.com`

>> **Virgin Galactic:** `www.virgin.com`

Coinmap (`https://coinmap.org`) can also help you locate many other local retailers where you can spend Bitcoin.

Paying with crypto when you can't pay with crypto

Various services allow you to spend cryptocurrency with retailers and service providers that don't accept cryptocurrency. For example, Amazon doesn't accept cryptocurrency. However, services such as Moon (`https://paywithmoon.com/`) and Purse (`www.purse.io`) let you buy at Amazon using cryptocurrency.

For example, Moon lets you use Bitcoin, Bitcoin Cash, Ether, and Litecoin to make purchases on Amazon. But, of course, all you are doing is converting your cryptocurrency and making a purchase in the same process; Moon acts as an exchange and payment service, taking your cryptocurrency, exchanging it for dollars, and then paying Amazon for you.

Those two companies work specifically with Amazon, but various others have sprung up recently that offer a Bitcoin or cryptocurrency-based bill-pay service in easy-to-use applications. The concept is straightforward: You make a purchase;

the company then pays the retailer using dollars or other local fiat currency; you then pay the company in cryptocurrency. Some of these companies even provide a credit card. Coinbase, for example, perhaps the largest U.S.-based cryptocurrency exchange, provides a Visa card (see Figure 9-1). Use it anywhere you can use a Visa card, and Coinbase pays the bill and deducts the equivalent value of cryptocurrency from your Coinbase account.

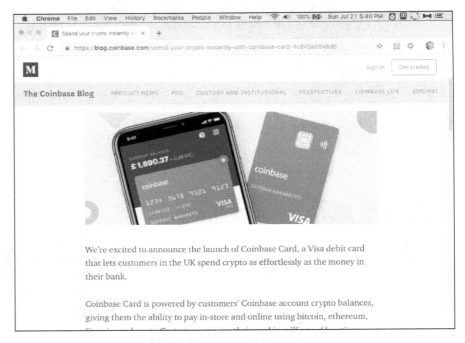

FIGURE 9-1:
Coinbase, a large exchange, lets you spend your cryptocurrency using a credit card; see www.coinbase.com/card.

Here are a few other companies you can check out:

>> **Spend:** Provides you with a Visa card, funded by your cryptocurrency (www.spend.com).

>> **Gyft:** Buy gift cards with Bitcoin (www.gyft.com).

>> **Bitrefill:** Gift cards and mobile-phone refills; 1,650 businesses in 170 countries (www.bitrefill.com).

>> **Bylls:** A Canadian Bitcoin bill-pay company (https://bylls.com).

>> **Piixpay:** An Estonian bill pay company, operating in 120 countries, including the United States (www.piixpay.com).

>> **Living Room of Satoshi:** An Australian company that lets users pay credit cards and BPay online banking bills with Bitcoin (www.livingroomofsatoshi.com).

Expand or upgrade your mining operation

Later in this chapter (see the section, "Scaling Up?"), we discuss the subject of expanding and upgrading your business. Cryptocurrency mining hardware is often sold directly from manufacturers in local fiat currency, but they may accept only Bitcoin or other cryptocurrencies. Some also accept wire transfers, and if you have ever gone through that painstaking process, you will understand why Bitcoin and cryptocurrencies are such an innovation. So, of course, you might also buy your expansion or upgrade equipment directly using cryptocurrency. Again, such purchases are business expenses; you won't be paying tax on the mining income you use to buy more equipment.

But don't forget the tax

Your mine is a business. You spend money with the intention of making money — that is, making more money than you spend. That's what profit is, and it's taxable!

Consider that your purchases are part of your taxation picture. If you use your cryptocurrency to make business purchases — to pay utility bills, buy new mining equipment, pay rent for a mining facility, and so on — those expenses are tax deductible. (Exactly *how* you deduct them is complicated, but we get to that later in this chapter — see the section, "Tax and Your Mining Business.")

However, if you use your cryptocurrency to make personal purchases — groceries, your apartment rent or mortgage, nights on the town, and so on — then those expenses are *not* deductible. That is, they become taxable to you personally. They are regarded as payments to you personally, from your business.

Hodling your cryptocurrency

You can choose to do nothing but keep possession of your mined cryptocurrency rewards as an investment, with the expectation that eventually their value will increase. This is often known within the cryptocurrency community as *hodling*. Why? Because way back when, in the distant cryptocurrency past (that is, 2013), someone in a Bitcoin forum mistyped a message. Intending to say that he was planning to hold on to his Bitcoin, with the solid belief that its price would rise, he instead wrote, "I AM HODLING!" The message poster claimed he was drinking whisky at the time that he posted this message. (You can see it here if you're interested. It is somewhat entertaining, and hey, you're seeing a bit of Bitcoin history live: https://bitcointalk.org/index.php?topic=375643.0.)

LAW-ABIDING TAXPAYER, OR CRYPTO ANARCHIST?

There's a strong crypto anarchist thread running through the cryptocurrency community. What's a *crypto anarchist,* you ask? The term was likely first coined (if you excuse the pun!) by Tim May, in his 1988 *Crypto Anarchist Manifesto.* He explained that cryptography was "on the verge of providing the ability for individuals and groups to communicate and interact with each other in a totally anonymous manner. Interactions over networks will be untraceable. These developments will alter completely the nature of government regulation, the ability to tax and control economic interactions."

Crypto anarchists believe in the use of cryptography to protect personal, economic, and political freedoms. These freedoms have to be protected from the state, crypto anarchists believe. And, quite frankly, many don't believe in paying taxes. We're going to assume in this chapter that that's not you. We're also going to assume that you want to stay on the right side of the state, at least as far as paying taxes goes. For more about cryptocurrency and taxes, see Book 5, Chapter 15.

Anyway, the terms *hodl* and *hodling* have now become part of the cryptocurrency culture. The principle is simple. If you are convinced the cryptocurrency will rise in value, why would you sell? If you're so sure it will go up, then hodl!

In fact, this choice is very popular, and the long-term scarcity of many cryptocurrencies and the community's expectation that the value will go up often makes this a self-fulfilling prophecy. (But not always. Many of the smaller cryptocurrencies have dropped to zero.)

We're not going to tell you whether to hodl or sell. Both choices come with risk. Many people have lost huge sums of money investing in cryptocurrencies. But many multimillionaires have been made, too.

In fact, with the exception of a catastrophic one-year crash, from mid-December 2017 to late December 2018, Bitcoin has been an incredible investment. Had you purchased in August 2017, and held your Bitcoin for four years until the time of this writing (August 2021), your investment would have increased tenfold. Investors who have held since May or June of 2016 have seen the value increase around 100 times (see Figure 9-2). Still, past performance is no guarantee of future results, as they say in the investment business! And Bitcoin is the world's primary cryptocurrency; others are often much less successful in value appreciation. Always do your research on the viability and history of your cryptocurrency before you decide to hodl for any significant amount of time.

FIGURE 9-2:
A graph of
various types of
network value
estimations
for the Bitcoin
network over
the past nine
years (https://
charts.
woobull.com/
bitcoin-
valuations).

So, should you sell, or should you hodl? Keep an eye on the market and make your own decision!

Invest your cryptocurrency

Some ventures can be invested in via Bitcoin or other cryptocurrencies. Many early Bitcoin miners have invested in cryptocurrency-related businesses using their mining profits. For example, Kraken, a major cryptocurrency exchange, was mostly bootstrapped by early Bitcoin investors.

Does this make sense? Perhaps. But also consider that when you invest your cryptocurrency into a stock, real estate, or other business opportunity, you are betting that the return on the investment will be greater than the return on simply hodling that cryptocurrency. That hasn't always been true.

On the other hand, you may consider investing mining profits into other businesses as a form of investment diversification, spreading your overall financial risk by holding different types of investments with different risks and benefits.

Donate your cryptocurrency to charity

Many organizations accept cryptocurrency donations to help support their charitable efforts. There may also be tax benefits associated with donating assets, such as cryptocurrency, to charity. Following are just a few noteworthy efforts you could donate to that accept cryptocurrency donations.

>> **The Internet Archive:** https://archive.org

>> **The Tor Project:** www.torproject.org

>> **The Electronic Frontier Foundation:** www.eff.org

>> **WikiLeaks:** https://wikileaks.org

>> **Wikipedia:** https://wikipedia.org

>> **The Free Software Foundation:** www.fsf.org

>> **The Red Cross:** www.redcross.org

>> **United Way:** www.unitedway.org

>> **Bit Give:** www.bitgivefoundation.org

>> **The Water Project:** https://thewaterproject.org

Gift your cryptocurrency

One use of your freshly mined cryptocurrency that is sure to get friends, family, and other individuals interested in finding out more about blockchains and cryptocurrencies is to have them try it out for themselves. Gifting them some of your cryptocurrency is a great educational tool as it requires them to set up a wallet and to witness a transaction. There is no direct tax benefit to you, the person giving away the cryptocurrency (except that you won't pay tax on any gains you've made by hodling).

But, on the other hand, the person receiving the gift doesn't have to declare it to the Internal Revenue Service or to pay tax on it, so many people use gifts to pass on wealth to their children. There is something known as the *gift tax* — above a certain (truly huge) level, the giver has to pay tax on the money given. But in the United States in 2019, that's anything over $15,000. That is, no tax is due on the first $15,000 gifted during the year. And, in fact, there's an $11.7 million lifetime exclusion in addition to the $15,000 a year.

Talk to your tax advisor if you're making enough mining money to consider this. (But before you do, read *The Millionaire Next Door* [Taylor Trade Publishing]. Author William Danko will probably convince you *not* to give money to your kids; it really hurts them. Sorry, kids!)

Determining When to Sell

Cryptocurrency miners may believe in the longevity of the blockchain system they decide to mine and decide to part ways with their coins only when it's absolutely needed to cover expenses or due to market conditions, such as exchange rate downturns.

On the other hand, miners sometimes take a different approach and sell very frequently to quickly realize any profits generated from mining. They may feel that as long as a profit is there to be taken, it should be taken, because the cryptocurrency price could drop at any moment.

There isn't a right or wrong answer (well, until you look back with hindsight, of course!), and individual miners must make these types of decisions themselves. If or when you do decide to sell, however, a handful of helpful resources can assist you to determine the right timing and the right amount to part with. Important ramifications also come with selling, including tax liabilities and custodial exchange rates and associated fees, which we discuss later in the chapter (see the section, "Tax and Your Mining Business," and also Book 5, Chapter 15 for more about taxes and cryptocurrency).

Cryptocurrency market indicators

Market indicators may help you get a feel for where your cryptocurrency's market is headed. No market metric is a 100 percent predictor, but they are still good resources to use when trying to figure out what's going on in the market cycle. Here are a few examples of metrics related to Bitcoin.

>> **Mayer Multiple:** The Mayer Multiple, created by Trace Mayer, tracks the current price of Bitcoin in U.S. dollars, divided by the 200-day moving average price (a *moving average* is one that filters out short-term fluctuations). For example, if the price today is $12,000, and the price over the previous 200 days has been on average $6,000, then the Mayer Multiple is 2. This indicator gives a good relative signal as to when the market has spiked up in price or, inversely, crashed. Higher multiples are warning signs; lower multiples are suggestions that it may be a good time to buy (https://mayermultiple.info).

>> **NVT ratio:** The *network value to transactions ratio* (NVTr) tracks the dollar value of on-chain cryptocurrency transactions to the relative total network value. It is calculated by dividing the daily average market capitalization (or total market value) in dollars by the amount of daily on-chain transactions in dollars. In other words, it's a measure of how much transaction activity is going on with the cryptocurrency (see Figure 9-3; https://charts.woobull.com/bitcoin-nvt-ratio).

» **NVT signal:** The NVT signal is very similar to the NVT ratio. However, instead of taking the market value and dividing it by the daily on-chain transaction total, it is the 90-day average market value divided by the daily on-chain transaction value (https://charts.woobull.com/bitcoin-nvt-signal).

» **Realized market capitalization:** A popular metric in the cryptocurrency space is the market capitalization, which is calculated by multiplying the current market price of a cryptocurrency by the total amount of the cryptocurrency in circulation. The realized market capitalization, however, is calculated by adding up the market value of each coin at the time it was last spent as a transaction on the blockchain. This page has a great explanation of how the RMT metric works; look for the link to the actual chart lower on the page: https://coinmetrics.io/realized-capitalization.

» **MVRV ratio:** The MVRV ratio, or *Market Value Realized Value ratio,* is calculated by taking the market value or capitalization and dividing it by the realized market value or capitalization. This indicator can help put the market value in perspective to detect over- and undervaluations (https://charts.woobull.com/bitcoin-mvrv-ratio).

TIP

Two of the sites we mention in the preceding list — charts.woobull.com and coinmetrics.io — have really interesting and potentially useful metrics. Dig around a little and see what you find!

The charts we mention are all for Bitcoin. How about other cryptocurrencies, though? You may still be able to find such metrics for other cryptocurrencies. Coinmetrics, for example, provides them for literally dozens of cryptocurrencies. The chart shown in Figure 9-4 shows an NVT measurement for both BTC (Bitcoin) and VTC (vertcoin). Notice the option boxes at the bottom of the screen? You can add (or remove) cryptocurrencies to (or from) the chart by clicking these boxes, and you can find more choices in the More box at the top left of these three rows. (You can't retrieve all metrics for all cryptocurrencies.)

Lots of cryptocurrency data and statistics websites can be very useful, helping you put each cryptocurrency in perspective. Here are a few.

» **Coin Metrics:** https://charts.coinmetrics.io/network-data/

» **BitInfoCharts:** https://bitinfocharts.com/cryptocurrency-charts.html

» **Bitcoinity:** https://data.bitcoinity.org/markets/volume

» **CoinDesk:** www.coindesk.com/data

FIGURE 9-3:
The Woobull
NVT Ratio chart,
an indication of
activity in the
Bitcoin market.

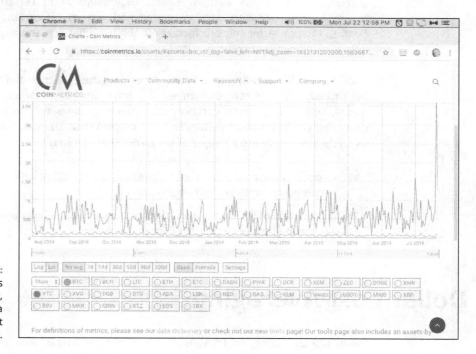

FIGURE 9-4:
A Coinmetrics
NVT chart,
showing data
for two different
cryptocurrencies.

>> **How Many Confs:** `https://howmanyconfs.com`

>> **Crypto51:** `www.crypto51.app`

>> **Bitcoin Visuals:** `https://bitcoinvisuals.com`

>> **Coin Dance:** `https://coin.dance`

Unfortunately, many of the smaller cryptocurrencies are simply not popular enough for folks to do this type of in-depth study or real-time graphical analysis. Still, watching metrics for other cryptocurrencies can at least give you a feel for the overall market sentiment for cryptocurrencies in general, and often cryptocurrencies do move up or down together. See Book 5, Chapter 10 for more information on how to use technical analysis to identify the best buy and sell price levels.

Where to sell: Cryptocurrency exchanges

If you intend to cash out and exchange your cryptocurrency earnings for local fiat, you should consider cryptocurrency marketplaces and exchanges. Some exchanges have a good track record, some exchanges are risky, and others are outright frauds. Some exchanges ban individuals from certain jurisdictions to avoid complying with laws associated with citizens of certain countries. See Book 5, Chapter 3 for more information about exchanges and using a broker to help you sell cryptocurrency.

Exchanges collect trading fees, which depend on the exchange and the trade being performed, and different exchanges also have different market rates. In other words, selling your cryptocurrency on some exchanges will be more profitable (meaning you'll get more dollars for your crypto) than on others. How do you tell which is best? Here are a couple of resources that can help:

>> `https://data.bitcoinity.org/markets/books/USD` provides cool charts comparing ten different exchanges.

>> `https://en.bitcoin.it/wiki/Comparison_of_exchanges` provides a comparison between a couple of dozen exchanges.

Dollar Cost Averaging

Dollar cost averaging, or DCA, is a very common investment strategy that is intended to reduce exposure to volatility that comes from making large, high-cost purchases of an asset. The idea is that you avoid the harm caused by a sudden decline in value of the asset immediately after making a large purchase. Instead, you spread your purchase over a long time period. (Find out more on DCA here: https://www.investopedia.com/terms/d/dollarcostaveraging.asp.)

Many miners like the DCA concept, because in effect, that's what mining is: buying a little of the cryptocurrency each month, rather than buying a large lump sum. For example, you may invest $10,000 in mining gear and then mine month by month, instead of taking that $10,000 and buying your favorite cryptocurrency all at once.

Dollar cost averaging your purchases

Assume that you intend to invest $1,200 into an asset such as Bitcoin this year (or stocks, bonds, whatever). You could make that purchase all at once in an attempt to time the buy at a low price, for a relative discount on your trade. However, if you were to dollar cost average that purchase over the course of a year, you would buy periodically — say, once a month. Thus, instead of spending $1,200 right now, you'd spend $100 per month over the entire year.

In bear markets, with a downtrend in price, this strategy is effective as it does not expose your investment to all of the reductions in price. In fact, each time you buy, you'll be getting the asset at a lower price. However, in bull markets, where the price is trending up, the DCA method would result in lower quantities of the asset being acquired, at overall higher prices.

The best thing to do, of course, is to invest everything at once into the asset at the point at which it's at its lowest price; but how do you do that? That's called market timing, and it's essentially impossible. You may be lucky and pick the market just right, but you won't be able to do that consistently.

So DCA is a way to spread risk. It's also a way for you to avoid FOMO (Fear Of Missing Out) investing. Instead of jumping into a market and grabbing a big stake, because you've seen the price jump up recently — because you're scared you're going to miss a huge opportunity — DCA provides a more disciplined mode of investing, almost set and forget. (Well, you have to remember to make the purchase each month.) On the other hand, some exchanges — such as Coinbase — let you set up automatic periodic purchases.

In fact, it may be argued that what we are really discussing here is known as *automatic investing*, which is similar to DCA but subtly different. We use the term *dollar cost averaging*, because that's the term people commonly use in the cryptocurrency arena (and, actually, in other areas of investing).

DCA works really well in markets that trend down for extended periods and then back up. DCA reduces your losses as the market declines (every time you buy an asset, the asset costs less than the previous time) and increases your profits when the market recovers (because you will have purchased much of the asset at a lower price than an original lump-sum purchase).

Here's an example. Say that you purchased a single Bitcoin on December 9, 2017. You would have spent around $13,680 (depending on the time of day, of course). During the month of July 2019, your Bitcoin would be worth $10,011. You've lost. But say, instead, you dollar cost averaged. Instead of spending $13,680 all at once, you invested $684 on that date and each of the following 19 months. Your Bitcoin would be worth about $18,072.

Of course, the opposite is true during a long period of price appreciation. Each time you buy, you'll get less Bitcoin than the time before. Had you just invested the lump sum, you'd be much better off. But again, how do you time the market? You pretty much can't!

The Dollar Cost Averaging Bitcoin website (at https://dcabtc.com) can show you the effects of DCA in the Bitcoin market. You enter a periodic investment sum, an interval (daily, weekly, biweekly, or monthly), and how many years you want to go back in time for a starting point, and the system calculates how much you would have invested, how much your Bitcoin would now be worth, and the profit you would have made.

What does this have to do with cryptocurrency mining? This minibook is about mining cryptocurrency, not buying it! Well, in effect, cryptocurrency mining is a form of dollar cost averaging cryptocurrency assets (or, as co-author Tyler Bain likes to call it, *electricity cost averaging*). If you are mining toward a pool, the rewards are steady and predictable. You spend money — for equipment, maintenance, and electricity — and every day or week, you gain more cryptocurrency. Your investment grows slowly over time, just like a DCA strategy.

Cost averaging your exits

For miners and hodlers alike who want to sell their cryptocurrency gains, the DCA approach can also be used to methodically time your exits. The same theory applies: If you intend to sell $1,200 worth of Bitcoin or other cryptocurrencies over a one-year period, instead of making this sale all at once, you can plan to sell $100 of cryptocurrency every month to reduce your exposure to volatility.

However, the inverse is true for DCA sales versus purchases: If the market is trending downward, your DCA strategy will result in less local fiat currency acquired, but if the cryptocurrency market is trending upwards, the DCA method will yield more fiat currency gains. This method of timing is very effective if costs from the mining venture need to be covered.

Custodial exchange risk

Over the history of Bitcoin and other cryptocurrencies, there are many examples of exchanges that have been hacked, lost funds, or closed down due to insolvency, theft by management, or other mismanagement issues. Because of this, it is best to exercise extreme caution and due diligence when selecting an exchange to use.

TIP

It is important to not leave funds on exchanges any longer than absolutely necessary, to avoid exchange risk. As cryptographer (and potential Satoshi Nakamoto) Nick Szabo once said, "Trusted third parties are security holes." Remember, there is a rich history of exchange users losing access to their cryptocurrency funds on exchanges. The mantra in the cryptocurrency space is, "Not your keys, not your cryptocurrency." Let someone else manage your private keys for you, and you are risking that the manager (the custodian) steals from you or does not protect the keys properly.

Tax and Your Mining Business

Taxation for cryptocurrency is a complicated subject. At the time of this writing, buying and selling crypto in the United States is taxable because the IRS identifies crypto as property, not currency. (We're discussing this issue from the perspective of taxation in the United States. However, some of the basic ideas we discuss here are likely to be valid in other countries, too.) However, quite a bit of tax relief is available to businesses that is not available to individuals, and for this reason, many miners elect to mine via a business entity.

The tax situation for investing in and mining cryptocurrency is likely to be very different. For information about taxes and cryptocurrency investing, see Book 5, Chapter 15.

But you're mining, not investing

Mining is very different from investing. Here's how we see it (but remember, don't trust us! You need to talk to a tax accountant who understands cryptocurrency and current tax legislation in that area!).

Your mining operation is a business. You put money into it, and out pops cryptocurrency (you hope). The profit you get out is immediately taxable. You'll want to account for everything in dollars. (The IRS doesn't have tax forms or tables that run calculations in cryptocurrency!)

Like any business, you have to track expenses: what you spend to buy your equipment, what you pay for electricity, the cost of rent (if your mining operation is in your home, you can deduct part of the cost of your home proportionate to the amount of space taken up by the equipment), and so on. Anything you spend to run your business is a deductible expense. Some of your expenses — sums spent on the mining equipment that has a multi-year life — may be depreciable. That is, instead of deducting the full price of the equipment in the year you spend the money, you may have to deduct a portion over several years. Again a question for a tax accountant. (The rules are complicated.)

You also have to track your income — that is, the money, valued in dollars, you earn when you receive your cryptocurrency rewards. In other words, for reporting and tax calculation purposes, you have to convert the value of the cryptocurrency, at the time at which you receive it at your blockchain address, into dollars.

Even if you hodl this cryptocurrency, you'll owe tax on it. Think of it this way. Gold is an asset, and if you buy it and hold it, as long as you hold it, you don't owe tax on any appreciation in value. But do some work for someone and get paid with a gold coin, and you've just earned taxable income. It's the same with cryptocurrency. If you earn cryptocurrency from a mining operation, you owe tax on the gain you make after deducting mining expenses. Indeed, the Internal Revenue Service has ruled that mining gains are regarded as "gross income" (see Q-8 in www.irs.gov/pub/irs-drop/n-14-21.pdf).

How do you figure out the gain? You take your total cryptocurrency income for the year, valued in dollars at the time you earned the income, and then you deduct all your business expenses. What's left over is your profit, and your business owes tax on that profit.

What are you living on? Are you taking some of your cryptocurrency gains and converting them to dollars, so you can pay rent and buy groceries? Or even using the cryptocurrency to pay personal (nonbusiness) expenses directly?

Well, depending on your business form (a sole proprietorship, an LLC — limited liability corporation — a C Corporation, or whatever), the money you give yourself or spend on yourself will be regarded as payroll or distribution. It will be a deduction for your business, but taxable to you.

Okay, this can get complicated, and our goal is not to teach Taxation 101. Some forms of business structure — such as the sole proprietorship or LLC — treat you and your business as a single entity for taxation purposes. So if you give yourself money or spend money on yourself, it's not a deduction to your business because your business is you. You simply don't use those expenditures when calculating your deductions.

It gets complicated

Did we mention it gets complicated? Did we say that a lot of this is unclear right now? Perhaps we mentioned you should talk to a crypto-knowledgeable tax accountant?

What happens if you hodl? Say that you mine DummiesCoin, and it's worth, say, $1,000 at the point it's mined. But you don't sell it, you *hodl* it — keep possession of your mined cryptocurrency rewards as an investment, with the expectation that eventually the value will increase, as we discuss earlier in this chapter. (It's essentially a long-term investment strategy, as explained in Book 5, Chapter 12.) So, by the end of the year, the value is $2,000. Do you regard $1,000 as the taxable income, or $2,000?

Well (most likely see what your accountant says!), you'll file your taxes using $1,000 as the income from that block that you mined. But you'll now have an asset on the books with a basis of $1,000. In effect, you have purchased that Dummies-Coin for the $1,000 original price (that you paid tax on). Say that a year later, you sell the coin for $3,000; you'll owe tax on the difference between the $1,000 you "paid" for it, and the $3,000 you sold it for. You'll owe tax on $2,000.

You really need to track your cryptocurrency *basis* — that is, the original cost to you if you purchased it, or, if you mined it, the dollar value at the time it was mined. You also need to track the value when you disposed of the cryptocurrency; this is the amount you received in dollars when converting it to dollars, or the dollar value of the product or service you purchased when you made a purchase with cryptocurrency. All this can get, well complicated. You need help, and we can provide a little for you with the following resources, a selection of systems for tracking the numbers and tax firms that specialize in cryptocurrency accounting:

- » **CryptoFolio Tax:** https://cryptfolio.com/tax
- » **CryptoTrader.Tax:** www.cryptotrader.tax
- » **ZenLedger:** https://zenledger.io
- » **TokenTax:** https://tokentax.co
- » **Crypto Tax Girl:** https://cryptotaxgirl.com
- » **BitcoinTaxes:** https://bitcoin.tax

Scaling Up?

If you're making money in cryptocurrency mining, and if the current rewards and profits are significant, it is very tempting to scale up your mining operation. But think long and hard before you do so. This is a very volatile business, with a boom and bust nature. What may look like good market conditions showing an opportunity to expand may quickly turn around, resulting in a loss of critical funds that could have helped cover your operation's cost when the market turns down. In other words, sometimes it's nice to have a little financial padding to help you through the bumps, rather than investing every penny up to the limit.

We discuss some things to contemplate when considering whether to expand your mining operation.

Do not overextend

WARNING

It is important to not overextend if you plan on scaling up your mine. If you grow your mining operation too quickly, you can evaporate any savings you have in local fiat currency, which would force you to liquidate mining returns to cover mining costs.

When the value of Bitcoin and other cryptocurrencies goes down, there has been speculation on the possibility of a *mining death spiral*. The theory is that as the price drops, and as the Bitcoin and cryptocurrency that miners generate becomes worth less, miners are forced to trade their mining rewards for local currencies at prices that may not be able to cover operating expenses. Cryptocurrency systems themselves are immune to the mining death spiral because of regularly scheduled block difficulty adjustments that ensure block rate production is kept steady over the long term.

Individual miners, however, are still exposed to the mining death spiral. If the exchange market prices of cryptocurrencies fall significantly enough over the short term, your mine may very well lose profitability, forcing you to shut down if you cannot afford your mining expenses. Overextend your mining operation, and you won't be able to continue to hodl your cryptocurrency rewards.

If you do intend to grow your mine, make sure you have plenty of funding to cover normal expenses in the case of a cryptocurrency market downturn. The best financial experts recommend that small businesses keep about three to six months of operating expenses on hand to cover expenditures in case of unforeseen market conditions.

However, in Bitcoin and cryptocurrency markets, the longest downturns have lasted up to 36 months! In extreme cases such as these, even the most profitable mining businesses are forced to rethink their operation and potentially make drastic changes.

Milestones to meet before you reinvest

Successful businesses, including cryptocurrency mining ventures, have set financial goals and long-range plans to make sure they will survive ongoing market conditions. Some miners measure their returns in the underlying cryptocurrency that they are mining, while others measure it in their local fiat currency. There is some confusion in this area among many miners. Many don't like to think in terms of fiat currency. This harks back to the crypto anarchist roots of cryptocurrency, the idea that fiat currency is bad because it comes from the state, and that it will ultimately be replaced by cryptocurrency created and managed by the masses. This is a big mistake!

Any asset only has value *in comparison with something else!* You might say, "I own ten DummyCoin," and we can ask, "Well, what's it worth?" What would you answer? "It's worth ten DummyCoin"? That just doesn't make any sense, any more than asking someone how much an orange is worth and being told it's worth one orange!

"What's it worth?" means "What can you get for it?" How many pizzas could you buy with it, how many oranges could you get, could you buy a car with it? Or, to make things much, much, simpler: How many dollars is it worth?

So nothing has a value in isolation. You can compare it to apples, or oranges, or gold or fiat. But one way or the other, cryptocurrency has some kind of value, which can be measured in units of some other thing, not in terms of itself.

Sure, you could convert your mining rewards into the number of oranges it could buy, but what's the point? Why not just use the most common medium of exchange in your country: your country's fiat currency!

If you measure your results purely in how many coins you mine, you have no real idea whether your mining operation makes sense. Even if your goal is to accumulate a particular cryptocurrency that you just *know* is going to be worth, one day, ten times what it costs you to mine it, you still need to understand the numbers in terms of fiat currency. After all, if you don't, you have no idea if you are spending more money to mine the cryptocurrency than you would spend to buy it.

So the most important metric you are watching should be profit or loss, based on fiat currency. Without knowing whether or not you are making money, it's hard to make any rational decisions about expansion.

On the other hand, perhaps this is just a hobby or cool experiment for you, and your goal is to find out about, and become proficient at, cryptocurrency mining and the cryptocurrency space in general. Or maybe it's an ideological statement; you *are* a crypto anarchist, or crypto libertarian, and want to see cryptocurrency succeed, and thus want to be involved. That's fine. Your goals may be different in that case.

Or maybe you're not so ideological, but you still believe in the future of the currency you mine, and cryptocurrency in general, and want to help support and secure the blockchain (if only because it holds some of your wealth!).

Some miners believe in what the cryptocurrency community is trying to accomplish, and thus are willing to mine at a fiat-loss for a short period, knowing they are supporting the blockchain and still accumulating cryptocurrency (which, they believe, will increase in value).

And, well, let's be honest here. There are also miners who are mining so that the cryptocurrency they earn is anonymous. If you purchase cryptocurrency from an exchange in the United States, the exchange has a record of that transaction and who you are. If you solo mine a cryptocurrency, nobody but you has a record of who you are. (This isn't true of pool mining.)

So there may be other reasons to continue mining, other metrics to consider. But from a *business* standpoint, you must know if you are making money or losing money, and how much either way. If you don't, you can't make a rational decision regarding expansion. (And even if you are mining for some other purpose, you can't fully understand your operation until you look at the numbers in terms of fiat. Or oranges if you prefer, but fiat will be much easier.)

Decide your goals prior to setting out on your mining adventure, and check back on them periodically. How *much* profit is sufficient, in relation to the investment you are making in time and money, for example?

And what would the effect of expansion be? Consider, for example, that doubling a small cryptomine will cost money for the equipment, but won't take much more of your time. You'll have to spend time to set up all the equipment, of course (though that should be much faster the second time), but it won't take much more of your time to watch over your additional equipment and keep it running. So, as far as your time input goes, there is a huge economy of scale in cryptomining. That is, as your mine gets larger, the amount of time contributed to earn each dollar declines dramatically.

Planning your expansion

Mining equipment has improved dramatically over the last decade. Hash rate output per rig has skyrocketed into the many trillions of hashes per second, and hashing efficiency has also increased, drastically reducing power consumption and doing more proof of work for less electrical cost.

This translates into easier deployment of staggering amounts of computational power. If you are planning to expand your cryptocurrency mining operation, you can do it with much less equipment and overhead compared to even a couple of years ago. Also, if your cryptocurrency mine is on the older side — say, two to five years (about the lifespan of an ASIC mining rig) — you may be able to simply replace your aging mining rigs with new state-of-the-art equipment and drastically increase your overall hashing capability.

But all this gear is expensive. "Is it worth expanding?" is a question that can only be answered by very careful calculations. Cryptocurrency mining is, after all, the consummate numbers game. It's all about dollars to buy equipment, the cost of the electricity to run it, the number of hashes the equipment outputs, the number of hashes the entire network outputs, the block time, and on and on. Mining for a while will give you a baseline to work with, but spending hours with a spreadsheet (or online calculations discussed in Chapter 7 of this minibook) is the only way you can predict what an expansion may do for you, and even then, it is only a *prediction*.

But remember, if you'd like to grow your operation from its current hobbyist deployment, you can take various different routes (which we discuss in Chapter 5 of this minibook), such as colocation hosting facilities, hash-rate marketplaces (in which thousands of people with hashing power sell that power to thousands of people who want to mine without the hassle of setting up equipment), or even cloud-mining companies, in which individuals buy hash power from the company itself.

REMEMBER

When expanding, be careful to not overextend, to plan thoughtful objectives and goals, and to maintain adequate cash reserves to cover multiple months of mining expenditures in case of market downturns or times of increased volatility.

Index

About the Authors

Kiana Danial is author of *Cryptocurrency Investing For Dummies.* She is an award-winning, internationally recognized personal investing and wealth management expert. She's a highly sought-after professional speaker, author, and executive coach who delivers workshops and seminars to corporations, universities, and investment groups. She frequently appears as an expert on many TV and radio stations and has reported on the financial markets directly from the floor of the New York Stock Exchange and Nasdaq. Kiana has been featured in the *Wall Street Journal*, *TIME* magazine, *Forbes, TheStreet.com,* and many other publications as well as on CNN. She has won numerous awards, including Best Financial Education Provider at Shanghai Forex Expo in 2014, New York Business Women of Influence Honoree in 2016, and the Personal Investment Expert of the Year award from Wealth & Finance International in 2018.

Born and raised in Iran as a religious minority, she was awarded a scholarship from the Japanese government to study electrical engineering in Japan, where she obtained two degrees in that field and conducted research on quantum physics in classes taught in Japanese. Being the only woman and foreigner in her classes made her decide to dedicate her life to empowering minorities, especially women in male-dominated industries.

Tiana Laurence is the author of *Blockchain For Dummies,* 2nd Edition. She is a blockchain pioneer, investor, and start-up founder. She is a founder of Factom, Inc., a software company that builds innovative technology within the blockchain space. She loves writing about emerging technologies and helping the average person understand them. Her passion is growing great companies, and she loves helping young aspiring entrepreneurs learn about business and technology. Tiana has a BA in business and leadership from Portland State University.

Peter Kent is co-author of *Bitcoin For Dummies,* 2nd Edition and *Cryptocurrency Mining For Dummies.* He has been explaining technology to ordinary people for almost 40 years through his more than 60 books (including *SEO For Dummies* and *Complete Idiot's Guide to the Internet*), corporate consulting, online courses, seminars and workshops,and court testimony (as an expert witness in technology-related litigation). He recently created an 8-hour video course on working with cryptocurrency (*Crypto Clear: Blockchain and Cryptocurrency Made Simple*). See CryptoOfCourse.com.

Tyler Bain is co-author of *Bitcoin For Dummies,* 2nd Edition and *Cryptocurrency Mining For Dummies.* He has been in the cryptocurrency mining trenches gaining experience in the ecosystem for several years. He's a professional engineer registered in the state of Colorado and studied engineering with an electrical specialty at the Colorado School of Mines in Golden, Colorado. He has consulted with cryptocurrency mining firms, currently works as an electrical engineer for a local utility cooperative, and is an avid cryptocurrency and Bitcoin miner. He is also an active member of the Institute of Electrical and Electronics Engineering and the Rocky Mountain Electrical League, and he has advised the Electric Power Research Institute. His passions include financial and transportation electrification, peer-to-peer systems, and the electrical grid.

Michael G. Solomon, PhD, CISSP, PMP, CISM, PenTest+, is author of *Ethereum For Dummies.* He is a security, privacy, blockchain, and data science author, consultant, and speaker who specializes in leading teams in achieving and maintaining secure and effective IT environments. As an IT professional and consultant since 1987, Dr. Solomon has led project teams for many Fortune 500 companies and has authored and contributed to more than 20 books and numerous training courses. From 1998 until 2001, he served as computer science instructor in the Kennesaw State University Computer Science and Information Sciences (CSIS) department. He is a professor of Cyber Security and Global Business with Blockchain Technology at the University of the Cumberlands and holds a PhD in Computer Science and Informatics from Emory University.

Publisher's Acknowledgments

Executive Editor: Steven Hayes

Editorial Project Manager and Development Editor: Christina Guthrie

Compiling Editor: Nicole Sholly

Copy Editor: Marylouise Wiack

Technical Editor: Mark Hemmings

Production Editor: Tamilmani Varadharaj

Cover Image: © Wit Olszewski/Shutterstock